The Cold War

The Postwar World
General Editors: A.J. Nicholls and Martin S. Alexander

As distance puts events into perspective, and as evidence accumulates, it begins to be possible to form an objective historical view of our recent past. *The Postwar World* is an ambitious series providing a scholarly but readable account of the way our world has ben shaped in the crowded years since the Second World War. Some volumes will deal with regions, or even single nations, others with important themes; all will be written by expert historians drawing on the latest scholarship as well as their own research and judgements. The series should be particularly welcome to students, but it is designed also for the general reader with an interest in contemporary history.

The Cold War

The Great Powers and their Allies

SECOND EDITION

J.P.D. Dunbabin

PEARSON
Longman

Harlow, England • London • New York • Boston • San Francisco • Toronto
Sydney • Tokyo • Singapore • Hong Kong • Seoul • Taipei • New Delhi
Cape Town • Madrid • Mexico City • Amsterdam • Munich • Paris • Milan

PEARSON EDUCATION LIMITED

Edinburgh Gate
Harlow CM20 2JE
Tel: +44 (0)1279 623623
Fax: +44 (0)1279 431059
Website: www.pearsoned.co.uk

First edition published 1994
Second edition published in Great Britain in 2008

© Pearson Education Limited 1994, 2008

The right of J.P.D. Dunbabin to be identified as author of this work
has been asserted by him in accordance with the Copyright,
Designs and Patents Act 1988.

ISBN: 978-0-582-42398-5

British Library Cataloguing-in-Publication Data
A catalogue record for this book is available from the British Library

Library of Congress Cataloging-in-Publication Data
A catalog record for this book is available from the Library of Congress

10 9 8 7 6 5 4 3 2 1
12 11

Typeset in 10/13.5pt Sabon by 35
Printed and bound in Great Britain by 4edge Limited, Hockley.

The publisher's policy is to use paper manufactured from sustainable forests.

Contents

PART 3 Europe West and East, and the Sino–Soviet split

PART 4 Conclusion

Abbreviations

ABM	Anti-ballistic missile
ALCM	Air-launched cruise missile
ARVN	South Vietnamese army
ASEAN	Association of South-East Asian Nations
BBC	British Broadcasting Corporation
BJP	Bharatiya Janata Party (India)
CAP	Common Agricultural Policy (European Community)
CCP	Chinese Communist Party
CDU	Christian Democratic Union (West Germany)
CIA	Central Intelligence Agency (USA)
CMEA	Council for Mutual Economic Assistance (Communist countries). Colloquially known as 'Comecon'
CND	Campaign for Nuclear Disarmament (UK)
COSVN	American term for 'Vietcong' headquarters, situated just over the border in Cambodia
CPSU	Communist Party of the Soviet Union
CPT	Communist Party of Thailand
CSCE/OSCE	Conference (later Organisation) on Security and Cooperation in Europe
CWIHP	Cold War International History Project
DC	Christian Democratic Party (Italy)
DDR/GDR	German Democratic Republic (East Germany)
DEFCON	United States Defence Condition – numbered stages of preparedness
DRV	Democratic Republic of Vietnam (North Vietnam)
ECSC	European Coal and Steel Community
ecu	European Currency Unit
EDC	European Defence Community
EEA	European Economic Area

EEC	European Economic Community; EC European Community; EU European Union
EFTA	European Free Trade Association
EMS	European Monetary System
EPU	European Payments Union
ERM	Exchange Rate Mechanism (of the EMS)
Euratom	European Atomic Energy Community
FDP	Free Democratic Party (West Germany)
FLN	National Liberation Front (Algeria)
FNLA	National Front for the Liberation of Angola
FO	Foreign Office (Britain)
FRUS	*Foreign Relations of the United States*
G7	USA, Japan, Germany, France, UK, Italy, Canada. The group of the seven leading OECD members; with the addition of the Russian Federation, later G8
GATT	General Agreement on Tariffs and Trade
GDP	Gross domestic product; GNP Gross National Product
GLCM	Ground-launched cruise missile
HSP	Hungarian Socialist Party (reconstituted in Oct 1989 from the Hungarian Socialist Workers (Communist Party))
IAEA	International Atomic Energy Agency
IATA	International Air Transport Association
ICBM	Inter-continental ballistic missile
IISS	International Institute for Strategic Studies
IMF	International Monetary Fund
INF	Intermediate range nuclear force
IPC	Iraq Petroleum Company
IRBM	Intermediate range ballistic missile
ITT	International Telephone and Telegraph
JCS	Joint Chiefs of Staff (USA)
K-FOR	Nato-led UN force in Kosovo
KGB	State Security Committee – Soviet secret police
KLA	Kosovo Liberation Army
KMT	Kuomintang (Nationalist Party) (China)
KOR	Committee for the Defence of Workers (Poland)
KPD	Communist Party of Germany – merged, in the Soviet zone, with SPD to create the SED
KRDC	(South) Korean Representative Democratic Council
MAD	Mutual Assured Destruction
MBFR	Mutual and Balanced Force Reductions

MIRV	Multiple independently targeted re-entry vehicle
MPLA	Popular Movement for the Liberation of Angola
MRP	Popular Republican Movement (France)
MSI	Italian Social Movement – neo-fascist political party (Italy)
NATO	North Atlantic Treaty Organisation; NAT North Atlantic Treaty (1949)
NLF	National Liberation Front (South Vietnam)
NPT	Nuclear Non-Proliferation Treaty
NSC	National Security Council (USA)
NSF	National Salvation Front (Romania)
OAS	Secret army organisation of settler resistance in Algeria
OAS	Organisation of American States
OAU	Organisation of African Unity
OECD	Organisation for Economic Co-operation and Development
OEEC	Organisation for European Economic Cooperation
OPEC	Organisation of Petroleum Exporting Countries
PCF	French Communist Party
PCI	Italian Communist Party
PDS	Democratic Party of the Left (Italy – the former PCI)
PKI	Communist Party of Indonesia
PLO	Palestine Liberation Organisation
PS	Socialist Party (France). *See also* SFIO
PRO	Public Record Office (Britain)
RIIA	Royal Institute of International Affairs
ROK	Republic of Korea (South Korea)
SAC	Strategic Air Command (USA)
SACEUR	Supreme Allied Commander Europe (NATO)
SAM	Surface to Air Missile
SALT	Strategic Arms Limitation Talks (or Treaty)
SDI	Strategic Defense Initiative (pejoratively known as 'Star Wars')
SEATO	South-East Asia Treaty Organisation
SED	Socialist Unity Party of Germany (East Germany)
SFIO	French Socialist Party, reconstituted in 1969 as the Parti Socialiste (PS)
SIOP	Single Integrated Operations Plan (US)
SIPRI	Stockholm International Peace Research Institute
SLBM	Submarine-launched ballistic missile

SPD	Social Democratic Party of Germany (West Germany)
START	Strategic Arms Reduction Talks (or Treaty)
UAR	United Arab Republic (Egypt and Syria; later just Egypt)
UK	United Kingdom (of Great Britain and Northern Ireland)
UN	United Nations
UNITA	National Union for the Total Independence of Angola
UNRRA	United Nations Relief and Rehabilitation Administration
US or USA	United States of America
USSR	Union of Soviet Socialist Republics
VAT	Value Added Tax
WEU	Western European Union
WTO	Warsaw Treaty Organisation/Warsaw Pact
WTO	World Trade Organisation (Successor to the GATT)

Preface to the Second Edition

Pearson were so kind as to ask me to revise this work in the light of the knowledge and material that has become available since it was originally written. I have done so fairly thoroughly, also taking the opportunity to revise the sequence of the earlier chapters; and I have extended coverage of Europe west of Russia, Belorus, and Ukraine up to, and in some contexts beyond, the great extension of the EU in 2004 to incorporate most of what had once been 'Eastern Europe'. Sadly the additions have meant that, to keep the book a manageable length, there have had to be deletions, notably that of the chapter on 'The Domestic Background in the Soviet Union and the United States'. This *does not* mean that I have become a convert to the *primat der aussenpolitik*; indeed I have been able to add material both on the continuing pressure on Gorbachev from Soviet economic weakness and on the still more important way in which he, and his entourage, so redefined Soviet foreign policy interests as first to make possible, and then to accommodate to, the unravelling of the USSR's previously zealously guarded power position in Eastern Europe, thus bringing the Cold War to a previously generally unexpected conclusion.

Originally this *Cold War* volume was accompanied by a more extra-European one, *The Post-Imperial Age: The Great Powers and the Wider World*. At first the intention was to revise both volumes in parallel; for, to look no further, recent developments in (and writing on) the Middle East would provide ample scope for such revision. But immediate revision fitted neither the economics of book production nor my own wish to complete a monograph on the gentler, but still instructive, subject of the determination (over the course of more than a century) of the line of what is now the US–Canadian border. In this volume, therefore, cross-references to *The Post Imperial Age* are to the original 1994 edition.

Two other points should be noted. Most Chinese names are rendered according to the *pinyin* phonetic system commended by the People's Republic, but for pre-communist, Kuomintang and Taiwanese names the old transliterated spelling is retained: thus Mao Zedong, but Chiang Kai-shek. Secondly, where the seasons of the year are used to give a general idea of date (as in, say, 'the winter of 1948–9'), they refer to the seasons of the northern hemisphere.

Beyond this, I have little to add to my previous Preface. The politics of academic funding have grown even worse. So I repeat that most of the work for this book was done on the basis of salaries and sabbatical leave, and now I should add pension, from my college and university (in that order of financial magnitude); both too must be thanked for their continuing hospitality to me after my retirement. But my greatest debt continues to be to my wife Jean, for more than I can easily record, and to my daughters Bridget and Penny. (My grandchildren Callie and Danny are too young to have yet made any academic contribution to this work.)

March 2007   *St Edmund Hall, Oxford*

Preface to the First Edition

*'I know that it will be said by many, That I might have been
more pleasing to the Reader if I had written the Story of mine
own times . . . To this I answer that whosoever in writing
a modern History shall follow truth too near the heels, it may
haply strike out his teeth.'*

Fortunately the enterprise is no longer so dangerous as in Sir
Walter Raleigh's time. My thanks are due in the first instance
to the series editors for suggesting that I undertake it, and more particularly to Tony Nicholls for many helpful comments and suggestions; also to
Longman both for accepting and producing the book and for important
advice as to its structure and coverage. Responsibility for mistakes, of
course, rests with me.

I am naturally greatly indebted to Oxford libraries and colleagues. Of
the libraries, the Bodleian must have pride of place; but I should like to
take this opportunity of thanking my former pupil, Andrew Peacock, for
gifts that have made my college library far more useful, in this context,
than one would a priori have expected. As for colleagues, it would be
invidious to single out any of the living; but I owe much to both Alastair
Buchan and Hedley Bull. The tragedy of Hedley's early death is of special
relevance to this project. For it was originally hoped that he would accompany my narrative with a companion, and more analytical, volume; it is a
great loss that he was not able to do so.

Beyond Oxford, I have (particularly in the mid-1980s, when British
libraries were going through a bad phase) benefited from hospitality, talks,
seminars, libraries and bookshops, especially in North America. My
thanks are due to: the Canadian Institute of International Affairs; the
libraries of the University of Toronto and of McMaster University; the

Woodrow Wilson Center; the Library of Congress; the Hoover Institution; the libraries of Stanford University and of the University of California, Berkeley; and to Princeton University (at which time my wife was at the Institute of Advanced Study). On two of these journeys I enjoyed support as a British Academy/Leverhulme Foundation Visiting Professor; otherwise the current politics of academic funding compel me to add, work for this book was done on the basis of salaries and sabbatical leave from my college and university (in that order of magnitude).

My greatest debt, though, is to my wife Jean, for more than I can easily record, and to my daughters Bridget and Penny – at least the latter will not be able to say of this, as of my more domestic academic writing, that it is just 'the history of the garden wall'.

St Edmund Hall, Oxford

Editorial Foreword

The aim of this series is to describe and analyse the history of the World since 1945. History, like time, does not stand still. What seemed to many of us only recently to be 'current affairs' or the stuff of political speculation, has now become material for historians. The editors feel that it is time for a series of books which will offer the public judicious and scholarly, but at the same time readable, accounts of the way in which our present-day world has been shaped since the Second World War. The period which began in 1945 has witnessed political events and socio-economic developments of enormous significance for the human race, as important as anything which happened before Hitler's death or the bombing of Hiroshima. Ideologies have waxed and waned, the industrial economies have boomed and bust, empires of various types have collapsed, new nations have emerged and sometimes themselves fallen into decline. While we can be thankful that no major armed conflict occurred between the so-called superpowers, there have been many other wars, and terrorism emerged as an international plague. Although the position of ethnic minorities improved in some countries, it worsened dramatically in others. As communist tyrannies relaxed their grip on many areas of the world, so half-forgotten national conflicts re-emerged. Nearly everywhere the status of women became an issue which politicians were unable to avoid. The same was true of the global environment, apparent threats to which have been a recurrent source of international concern. These are only some of the developments we hope will be illuminated by this series as it unfolds.

The books in the series will not follow any set pattern; they will vary in length according to the needs of the subject. Some will deal with regions, or even single nations, and others with themes. Not all of them will begin in 1945, and the terminal date may vary; as with the length, the time-span chosen will be appropriate to the question under discussion. All the books, however, will be written by expert historians drawing on the latest research, as well as their own expertise and judgement. The series should be particularly welcome to students, but it is designed also for the general reader with an interest in contemporary history. We hope that the books will stimulate scholarly discussion and encourage specialists to look beyond their own particular interests to engage in wider controversies.

History, and especially the history of the recent past, is neither 'bunk' nor an intellectual form of stamp-collecting, but an indispensable part of an educated person's approach to life. If it is not written by historians it will be written by others of a less discriminating and more polemical disposition. The editors are confident that this series will help to ensure the victory of the historical approach, with consequential benefits for its readers.

A.J. Nicholls
Martin S. Alexander

PART 1

Overview

CHAPTER 1

The Cold War: an overview

US–Soviet rivalry dominated post-war international relations, and drew into its orbit many initially unconnected issues (like the Arab–Israeli dispute, in which both countries at first supported Israel) – so much so, indeed, that commentators often spoke rather glibly of a 'bipolar world'. Once firmly established, the system proved deep-rooted and slower to change than observers often hoped. One development that *might* have ended the Cold War would have been the emergence of a new external challenge great enough to give the USSR and USA overriding common interests. Something like this has indeed happened in other contexts: early in the twentieth century the challenge of Imperial Germany did much to end Franco-British rivalry, while Franco-German reconciliation after the Second World War was helped by the perceived Soviet threat. But the emergence of new Powers does not necessarily drive old ones into the arms of their former enemies: both Hitler and Stalin hoped in vain that Britain would so respond to the rise of the United States.

Since 1945 only two Powers have so far emerged with a fraction of this capacity for realignment – Japan and China. By the 1980s Japan had the world's second largest economy, and its trade imbalance with the US sometimes strained relations and led to forecasts of more serious consequences. But the Japanese challenge was purely economic, and Japan still adopted a low profile in international politics. China is the world's most populous country. In the early 1960s its official position was extremely militant, and both superpowers were seriously concerned as to what it might do when it had acquired nuclear weapons. A decade later it was the USSR that worried about China's long-term intentions and its capabilities should the West be foolish enough to help it modernise. One of Kissinger's aides has argued that Brezhnev's detente policy was largely directed at isolating China: hence 'the many overtures . . . attempting to lure us into arrangements whereby we would acquiesce in China's destruction. When it became clear that we would not go along with this . . . Brezhnev's interest in detente may have flagged as well'.[1]

Although no individual Power emerged capable of bringing about a Soviet–American realignment, theoretically a coalition might have done so. The 1950s saw the growth of a 'non-aligned movement' (anxious both to keep out of East–West quarrels and to stop them monopolising the political agenda) and of an overlapping Afro-Asian one. In the 1960s much of Latin America, too, was drawn into the so-called 'Group of 77', which sought reforms of the international economic system. Its high point came in 1974–5 when, encouraged by the 1973 success of the Organisation of Petroleum Exporting Countries (OPEC) in raising the price of oil, it demanded the negotiation of a New International Economic Order. To some commentators 'North–South' issues seemed to have eclipsed 'East–West' ones – one 1976 article was subtitled 'From Non-alignment to International Class War' – and, though the Communist world, economically far less important than the industrialised Western states, managed to stand largely on the sidelines, it did share some interests with the other 'Northern' countries. But the 'South', though not wholly unsuccessful, proved unable to keep its demands at the centre of 'Northern' consciousness; nor, with the occasional exception of OPEC, did it appear to the North as a serious threat. New issues did not render East–West antagonism obsolete; so it worked itself out according to its own intrinsic dynamics.

The causes of the Cold War: rival interpretations

So dominant and so long-lasting a development as the Cold War is unlikely to have had only a single all-purpose explanation; and oceans of ink have in fact been devoted to its interpretation. Some approaches – like the view, shared by Pope John Paul II (a leading player in the East European developments of the 1980s), that it represented in large part the working out of the prophecies of Our Lady of Fatima – demand a particular mindset.[2] But commentators are perhaps most usually grouped,

---

[1] Henry Kissinger *Years of Upheaval* (1982) (hereafter *Memoirs ii*) pp. 1, 173 – paraphrasing W.G. Hyland, *Soviet-American Relations: A New Cold War?* (Santa Monica, 1981) pp. 26–8.

[2] See, for example, Timothy Tindal-Robertson, *Fatima, Russia and Pope John Paul II* (Leominster, 1998 edn) esp. pp. 9–13, 23–5, an 'account of how the end of the former

following an article by John Lewis Gaddis, into 'orthodox', 'revisionists', and 'post-revisionists'.[3]

'Orthodox' 'traditionalists' see Stalin's wartime and post-war policy as expansionist, and his aspirations as extending to a communist takeover, in one form or another, of at least the greater part of Europe. Had the United States, clearly the stronger power, moved at a sufficiently early stage in the war to restrain him, he *might* have accommodated himself to such constraint as he had accepted the status quo for most of the inter-war period. But he was first apparently given a green light by the West so that his power, opportunities and appetite all grew, then, at the end of the war, criticised and interfered with, but for a goodish time not effectively countered. Only gradually did the USA come to see the need to organise a rival coalition – not to contest the gains the Soviet Union had already made, but to 'contain' it by preventing further expansion. That the USSR was expansionist and had to be contained was the official view of the NATO alliance, and was almost unchallenged until the 1960s. Politicians like Churchill and Eden sought in their memoirs to build a record as having perceived the need to contain Soviet expansion fairly early in the war, but as having been thwarted by Roosevelt's naivety and the general American inexperience in foreign affairs. Opportunities were therefore missed and costs unnecessarily incurred, but eventually the Truman Administration came to see the light.

In the 1960s much of this came under 'revisionist' attack. The real expansionist power had been the United States. This was driven by an economic need for markets, and by a 'universalist' ideology that legitimated both their pursuit abroad and the suppresssion of the leftist and communist tendencies at home that had spread in the Roosevelt era to the alarm of big business, the churches and conservatives generally. The US monopolised the occupation of Japan, excluded Russia from influence in Italy, and soon gave up trying to work with her in Germany. But while thus acting unilaterally in its own sphere, it would not accord Stalin the right to do likewise in his. For the USA misperceived as expansionist moves that sought only to secure for the USSR (after its catastrophic experience of

Soviet Union is attributable to the hand of God through the intercession of the Blessed Virgin Mary', showing 'how the events in Eastern Europe are connected to the requests and prophecies Our Lady made at Fatima in 1917'; and John Paul II, *Crossing the Threshold of Hope* (1994) pp. 131, 220–1.

[3] John Lewis Gaddis, 'The Emerging Post-Revisionist Synthesis on the Origins of the Cold War', *Diplomatic History*, vii (1983).

two major wars with Germany) a limited defensive glacis; and America's ideology impelled it to foster in Eastern Europe and elsewhere a political and social system incompatible with Soviet security. One inspiration of such criticism was a European 'Gaullist' recognition that the American 'hegemony', like the Russian, imposed constraints, and that the institutions of the post-war Western world, drawn up at the height of US power, were well adapted to the spread of American business, economic and cultural influence – as, indeed, the Soviets had always maintained.[4] But the principal motor of revisionism was an American domestic disenchantment that became increasingly strident as the Vietnam War turned sour. 'Universalism' and the 'arrogance of power' had led to worldwide involvement, often on behalf of very shady clients and with disastrous consequences both for the local population and for the domestic society of the United States. And all for no good reason, since there either never had been a threat to the USA, or (if there had) it had come about only because the US had first taken the offensive. Such views were basically isolationist, though sometimes cast in a loosely Marxist guise.

Some of the extreme 'traditionalist' and 'revisionist' contentions are untenable: Stalin did not have a '*blueprint* for world revolution'; and the primary purpose of dropping atom bombs on Japan was not the intimidation of the Soviet Union. Equally both the USSR and the USA would seem to have been expansionist, albeit in very different ways. So it is not surprising that a degree of convergence eventually came about between the two historiographical traditions – as Gaddis observed in 1983, that 'is the way history usually gets written'. For what he saw (or advocated) as the new synthesis, Gaddis coined the term 'post-revisionism'. This caught on, to the point where most historians came to describe themselves as 'post-revisionist'. But Gaddis's detailed suggestions as to the content and concerns of the new approach were less influential.[5]

---

[4] The Marshall Plan, Zhdanov explained in 1947, 'amounts in essence to a scheme to create a bloc of states bound by obligations to the United States, and to grant American credits to European countries as a recompense for their renunciation of economic, and then of political, independence' – RIIA, Documents on International Affairs 1947–8, p. 130.

[5] Few have given the centrality Gaddis recommends to the nature of the American 'empire' – though in a later work he himself presents the difference between this and its Soviet counterpart as largely decisive in determining the Cold War's outcome, a fairly 'traditionalist' conclusion: 'in Europe and Japan . . . where possible, the inhabitants resisted the Soviet Union and collaborated with the United States; where impossible,

'Post-revisionism' is accordingly a very broad church. But it inclines to see the Cold War as the natural outcome of a situation where there were now only two first-class Powers, both drawn into the power vacuums created by the defeat of Germany and Japan, the exhaustion of most of Europe and the decline of the British Empire. In terms of international relations jargon, this is to explain the Cold War 'at the level of the international system': in the circumstances of 1945, any two superpowers would have been drawn by their perceived security interests into a contest, through a process of action and reaction, almost regardless of their nature and the personalities of their leaders ('state' and 'sub-state' level factors). Such a view fits squarely into the 'realist' tradition of international relations thinking; and indeed rivalries – like those between Rome and Carthage, Habsburg and Valois, France and Britain, and (despite, it is interesting to note, a good deal of reluctance on both sides) Britain and Germany – have run through much of history. Soviet–American antagonism can be seen as a sequel on a global scale.

An early, and remarkably perceptive, prophecy of the Cold War along these lines was that of Adolf Hitler, in April 1945:

With the defeat of the Reich and pending the emergence of the Asiatic, the African, and perhaps the South American nationalisms, there will remain in the world only two Great Powers capable of confronting each other – the United States and Soviet Russia. The laws of both history and geography will compel these two powers to a trial of strength, either military or in the fields of economics and ideology. These same laws make it inevitable that both Powers should become enemies of Europe. And it is equally certain that both these Powers will sooner or later find it desirable to seek the support of the sole surviving great nation in Europe, the German people.[6]

By the 'laws of geography' Hitler would have understood the view (derived from Mackinder and Haushofer) on which he had himself acted, that control of the area between the Rhine and the Caucasus would, in the long run, carry with it dominance of the world. As he knew to his cost, the United States had twice intervened to prevent the establishment of such control. Already in 1900 Theodore Roosevelt had written privately that 'If England should fail to preserve the European balance of power, the United

most wished passionately that they could have done so' (*We Now Know. Rethinking Cold War History* (Oxford, 1997) p. 286).
[6] A. Hitler, *The Testament of Adolf Hitler* (1961 edn, n. pl.) p. 107.

States would be forced to step in and re-establish it . . .' Franklin Roosevelt deployed similar arguments in public:

At this moment [December 1940], the forces of the states that are leagued against all peoples who live in freedom are being held away from our shores . . . [But] If Great Britain goes down, the Axis powers will control the continents of Europe, Asia, Africa, Australasia, and the high seas – and they will be in a position to bring enormous military and naval resources against this hemisphere.[7]

Should the Soviet Union ever be perceived as mounting another threat beyond the power of Britain to contain, it would be wholly in character for the United States to step in again.

This is the view taken by the eminent historian of the Truman administration, Melvyn Leffler. He accepts that the USA was strongly anti-communist, but does not see this as an important cause of its *international* actions. It had been equally anti-communist between the wars, but had largely ignored the USSR (even during Stalin's murderous rule in the 1930s). For the Soviet Union had then been too weak to constitute a threat. After 1945 it was, if not necessarily correct, at least reasonable to see it as such. Truman reacted to this perception – and not, Leffler insists, either to distaste for Stalin personally or to concern for his violations of human rights – by building a 'preponderance of power', an external coalition sufficient to prevent the United States being left face to face with a communist Eurasia and responding by metamorphosing into a garrison state quite alien to its former liberal traditions. In so doing, Truman harnessed, or at least collaborated with, US anti-communism. More reprehensibly, in Leffler's opinion, Truman's successor, Eisenhower, continued to fight the Cold War in the same fashion, instead of responding to the overtures from Stalin's successors to soften or end it.[8]

Though Leffler's principal focus is on US determination to maintain 'a preponderance of power', it will be seen that his interpretation allows a role for ideology in respect of the repugnance with which US leaders regarded the prospect of a 'garrison state'. Others go further, suggesting that it was only by invoking anti-communism that a domestic consensus

---

[7] George E. Mowry, *The Era of Theodore Roosevelt* (paperback edn, 1962) p. 148; State Department, *Peace and War. United States Foreign Policy 1931–1941* (Washington, 1943) pp. 599–600.

[8] Leffler encapsulates his views in *The Specter of Communism. The United States and the Origins of the Cold War, 1917–1953* (New York, 1994).

could be maintained for foreign involvement. Such invocation was not simply manipulative; by and large, most leaders themselves believed it. *Mutatis mutandis*, this was true also of their Soviet counterparts – as Mastny puts it, 'the thinking of insiders [as it emerges from the archives] conformed substantially to what Moscow was publicly saying . . . There was no double bookkeeping; it was the single Marxist-Leninist one'.[9]

There has therefore recently been an attempt to reinstate ideology as a major component of the Cold War.[10] Unsurprisingly, one would have thought. For the central 'realist' tenet is that states seek security against threats.[11] But these threats must be *perceived*: after 1945 the US had a physical capacity to harm Britain far greater than that of the USSR, but it was not perceived in the same way; nor indeed has the United States ever encountered the coalition of lesser powers to restrain it that classical 'balance of power' theory would predict. Threats may, admittedly, be perceived in the absence of ideological differences – these were, after all, not that great as between (say) Austria and Russia in 1914. But perceptions of friends and enemies often guide beliefs, thus intertwining ideology and security. The process is well exemplified (albeit with special reference to 'Communist China') in a 1965 US memorandum:

China – like Germany in 1917, like Germany in the West and Japan in the East in the late 30s, and like the USSR in 1947 – looms as a major power . . . The long-run US policy [to contain it] is based upon an instinctive understanding . . . that the peoples and resources of Asia could be effectively mobilized against us by China or by a Chinese coalition and that the potential weight of such a coalition could throw us on the defensive and threaten our security. This understanding of a straightforward security threat is interwoven with another perception – namely, that we have our view of the way the US should be moving and of the need of the majority of the world to be moving in the same direction . . . toward economic well-being, toward open societies, and toward cooperation between nations; the role we have inherited and have chosen . . . is to extend our power and influence to thwart ideologies that

---

[9] Vojtech Mastny, *The Cold War and Soviet Insecurity. The Stalin Years* (New York, 1996) p. 9.

[10] See e.g. Nigel Gould-Davies, 'Rethinking the Role of Ideology in International Politics During the Cold War', *Journal of Cold War History*, i (1999).

[11] The alternative 'realist' view, that states invariably seek to maximise their 'power', is disproved by e.g. the behaviour of the US in 1920 and of the USSR in 1989–90.

*are hostile to these aims and to move the world . . . in the direction we
prefer. Our ends cannot be achieved . . . if some powerful and virulent
nation – whether Germany, Japan, Russia or China – is allowed to
organize their part of the world according to a philosophy contrary
to ours.*[12]

Nor did 'ideology' serve only to frame statesmen's perceptions; it also
operated directly on the 'correlation of forces'. In the 1940s there were
many communists in the 'West', and (as their acrobatics over the Nazi-
Soviet pact had shown) they followed Moscow's lead and put its interests
above those of their own countries. It was to such loyalties that the USSR
initially owed most of its foreign spies (and the nuclear information they
communicated). Moreover, communist parties of this nature were a major
force in French and Italian politics, credible challengers for power if
(as many people expected) the capitalist system collapsed into a second
Great Depression. However, they never enjoyed majority support, and
over time their size and their devotion to the USSR both waned, and their
identification with the existing liberal order increased.[13] Communists had
always been a minority in Eastern Europe too – only in Czechoslovakia
did they contemplate an electoral route to power, and even there they
abandoned it in 1948. But over the years their intense enthusiasm ebbed
into a mere administration of the status quo, while around (and to a fair
degree among) them a perhaps naive enthusiasm for 'Western' practices
and prosperity predominated. By 1990–1 this trend was clearly present also
in the Soviet Union, though not to the same degree.

The USSR depicted itself as a Marxist-Leninist state, the 'socialist
motherland', and the director of the world communist movement. In
accordance with Marxist doctrine it represented capitalist states as intrinsically hostile (even if not always immediately dangerous). US ideology
was less systematised than Soviet, but it too was strong. As expressed in,
for instance, the Declaration of Independence or the inscription on the

---

[12] Defense Secretary McNamara to President Johnson 3 November 1965 (*FRUS,
1964–1968*, iii, pp. 514–15).

[13] The Party was strongest in Italy, where the US believed that there was at least a
chance that the PCI–PSI Popular Front would win the 1948 elections – actually it
secured 31% of the vote to the DC's 49%. Over the next decade the Socialists broke
with the USSR and the communists, and in 1963 joined the governing coalition. The
PCI did not move as far; but by the 1970s it too had broken with Moscow, and though
it was not allowed into government, it was prepared when necessary to support this
against threats from the right.

Statue of Liberty, it was not necessarily for export. But a universalist strain had accompanied the USA on to the world scene – Woodrow Wilson's Fourteen Points and the League Covenant sought to set the tone of international politics. Similarly when Roosevelt responded to the Axis challenge he did so in language remarkably like that of the Cold War – 'the Axis not merely admits but proclaims that there can be no ultimate peace between their philosophy of government and our philosophy of government' – and followed up with the Atlantic Charter and the Yalta Declaration on Liberated Europe. He did not mean to quarrel with Stalin, and some say that, had he lived, he could have avoided doing so. But the ideological materials for a quarrel were there; and if a quarrel came, the United States was, on past form, as likely as the Soviet Union to conduct it in an ideological fashion.

This is, of course, not to say that ideology was dominant at every twist and turn of the Cold War. For people readily operated on the maxim that 'the enemy of my enemy is my friend'. Thus the USSR supported Arab nationalist movements and regimes, knowing they were not communist, but perceiving them as weakening Anglo-American imperialism.[14] Likewise Nixon and Kissinger sought to co-opt China into helping contain the USSR, even though they saw China's leaders as 'tough ideologues who totally disagree with us where the world is going'.[15] And if Carter reacted against his predecessors' emphasis on 'geopolitics' by pushing US concepts of 'human rights' (to the annoyance not only of the USSR but also of allies like Brazil), even he made exceptions for really exposed 'Western' countries like South Korea.

But if pragmatism often led to the bending of ideologies, their true importance emerges from the way the Cold War ended. In the 1980s Reagan restored US self-confidence, but did not essentially alter the country. Gorbachev, on the other hand, transformed the USSR both internally (releasing political prisoners, freeing the media, and introducing at least the beginnings of elective pluralist politics) and externally, with the result that its leaders ceased to perceive the West as a threat and vice versa. As part of the process, he left the communist regimes in Eastern Europe to sink or swim on their own, without Soviet military support. In 1989 they mostly sank; and German reunification in October 1990, followed in

---

[14] Even so, progressive leaders like Nasser were exhorted to insitutionalise their break with imperialism by socialising their economic and political systems.

[15] Kissinger to Nixon, 5 February 1972 (William Burr (ed.), *The Kissinger Transcripts. The Top Secret Talks with Beijing and Moscow* (New York, 1998) p. 29).

November by the Charter of Paris (tidying up the military implications and prescribing non-threatening conventional force deployments), make as good a date as any for the Cold War's end. Of course there had been changes before Gorbachev – in the 1940s and 1950s Soviet leaders, and many others, saw communism as the wave of the future, whereas by 1985 the 'socialist commonwealth' seemed in most fields to be falling behind the West. But few doubt that without Gorbachev the international regime of the Cold War would have lasted a good deal longer.

If, however, its passing is to be explained quite largely in individual terms – for effective reform in the USSR certainly started at the top – and also at the level of changes within states rather than at that of 'the international system', so perhaps should be the 1940s slide into Cold War. Such an explanation in fact forms part of many 'revisionist' accounts. Roosevelt, it is held, would have continued to cooperate with Stalin, striking deals as at Yalta; but he omitted to brief Truman, who, in his inexperience of foreign affairs, turned to bureaucrats for advice with the result that the anti-communist 'Riga axioms' soon prevailed over those of Yalta. Not everyone would accept this reading of Roosevelt. But of the importance of the personal element there can be no doubt. For Truman's predecessor as Vice-President, and therefore heir-apparent to the very sick Roosevelt, had been Henry Wallace; and Wallace really did oppose Truman's foreign policy as British-influenced and gratuitously anti-Soviet, to the point of standing against him in the 1948 elections. Wallace had been dropped from the electoral ticket in 1944 as a result of the *domestically* oriented intervention of big-city Democratic bosses; had this not happened, he would have taken over on Roosevelt's death, and his policies would not have been the same as Truman's.[16]

If one can thus argue the importance of personality for the United States, *a fortiori* one can do so for the Soviet Union, a state Stalin had done so much to cast in his own image, and to which he bequeathed inflexible institutions that continued for decades to project his 'operational code'. As Holloway puts it, one can

imagine the Soviet Union pursuing a more cooperative relationship with the United States, along the lines suggested by Litvinov. Such a policy

---

[16] Wallace later said that he had intended, if he became President, to make Lawrence Duggan his Secretary of State and Harry Dexter White Secretary of the Treasury. Both were Soviet agents – Christopher Andrew and Vasili Mitrokhin, *The Sword and the Shield. The Mitrokhin Archive and the Secret History of the KGB* (New York, 1999) p. 109.

might well have prevented ['or at least moderated'] the Cold War . . .
[But] it would have required of Stalin a different concept of international
relations . . .

All attempts to imagine alternative courses of post-war international
relations run up against Stalin himself . . . If ever personality mattered
in politics, it surely did so in the Soviet Union under Stalin. His death
resulted in a significant reduction in tension in the Soviet Union and
abroad, but the patterns that had been set in the early post-war years
remained strong.[17]

Nor indeed were Stalin's policies sound in the long run, even from a
realpolitik security perspective. For his internal planning system, designed
for 'the primary accumulation of capital', proved ill-adapted to a mote
'developed' economy. His 1950s rearmament had by 1953 brought Eastern
Europe to crisis. Far from providing defensive security, his takeover of
Eastern Europe entailed, as competitors like Dulles observed, a conflict
with local nationalisms that was not indefinitely sustainable. His annexation of western Ukraine (around Lvov/Lviv) and of the Baltic states
ensured that this conflict spilt back into the USSR – with the result that this
split apart in 1991, returning Russia almost to the geographical position of
Peter the Great.

Some of the above draws on hindsight, but none of these interpretations depend on material unavailable in 1991. Since then there has been
a partial opening of the Russian (and other ex-communist) archives.
This goes some way towards correcting the besetting sin of much Cold War
historiography – the tendency of many writers to concentrate almost
exclusively on the copious American evidence, and either derive Stalin's
calculations and motives from his actions or impute to him what they
themselves regard as the natural responses to American actions. The new
material has helped resolve some controversies; thus almost (not quite)
everybody now accepts that Stalin authorised and assisted Kim Il Sung
to invade South Korea in 1950. On the whole, most of what has so far
emerged is probably more supportive of a moderately 'traditionalist' than
of any other viewpoint. Gaddis used it to launch 'The New Cold War
History', which seems rather of this nature. But many scholars remain
unpersuaded – one review of his *We Now Know* was entitled 'We Still
Don't Know!'

---

[17] David Holloway, *Stalin and the Bomb. The Soviet Union and Atomic Energy*
1939–1956 (New Haven, 1994) pp. 365–6, 370.

Odd Arne Westad expected that, with the new sources, 'we would be in for a re-writing not just of Soviet history, but of contemporary history as well . . . and create revisions of the somewhat stale interpretations forged during the Cold War era'; but in 1996 he concluded that, despite 'much good work in the field of Soviet foreign policy history, the revisions have been slow in showing up.'[18] This is partly because the release of Soviet documents has been both slow and haphazard; so, especially for the period before 1970, knowledge of the USSR remains less verifiable, and often more anecdotal, than that of (say) the UK or US. Of course even a much greater flood of new material would not resolve all disagreements; though the documents of Nazi Germany have been open for decades, argument continues over such central topics as the nature of Hitler's planning and the scale and timing of his aspirations. But Cold War history is more deeply contested. It would be folly to disregard the Soviet material. But this is still often mobilised in support of pre-existing positions, and has not effected a paradigm shift comparable to that occasioned, for the interwar period, by the release of the British official documents into a field previously studied on the basis of the captured German ones. In this sense, we have perhaps not yet fully reached a 'post post-revisionist' Cold War perspective.

The initial phase of the Cold War

Despite the debate on the Cold War's causes and essence, the sequence of events is fairly clear. During the war there had been three 'summit' conferences of the 'Big Three' (US, USSR, UK) plus mutual visits by Foreign Ministers and the like. At Potsdam in July–August 1945, the expectation was that summits would continue; meanwhile the 'Council of Foreign Ministers' (now joined also by France) would meet regularly to prepare the European peace treaties. The model was of Great Power 'concert' diplomacy. A little earlier the United Nations had held its inaugural meeting in San Francisco; it was not clear quite how the UN would develop, but it too was obviously meant to embody a collective approach to the management of international relations resting on the cooperation (as Permanent Members of the Security Council) of the same four Great Powers plus China. These Powers had conflicting interests and attitudes aplenty, and mutual suspicions and tensions were clearly in evidence (chiefly, though by

[18] *Diplomatic History*, xx (1996) p. 491.

no means exclusively, between Britain and the USSR). But Potsdam had been at least a qualified success, since important agreements were reached. However, the London Foreign Ministers Council meeting that autumn was not, which came as something of a shock, especially to 'Western' public opinion. Later there were indeed further agreements, notably on the Italian and East European peace treaties. But politics became less and less manageable through the Four Power mechanism, until in December 1947 the London Foreign Ministers Council meeting adjourned *sine die* after complete failure to agree on Germany. As for the United Nations, it had become clear in 1946, with the failure of the Baruch Plan, that this could not become, as many had optimistically hoped, the sole keeper of that awesome new weapon, the atom bomb. And though the UN did prove important in peripheral issues (notably, in 1947, Palestine, where, untypically, US and Soviet goals overlapped), the USSR's Security Council veto ensured that this was not so with regard to the increasingly numerous disputes where its interests were at odds with those of the (then) 'Western' majority of members. By late 1947, then, the habits and institutions of East–West diplomatic cooperation had atrophied.

They did so against the background of two crises in 1946. For the USSR reneged on its commitment to remove its troops from Iran (which had been subjected in 1941 to pre-emptive Anglo-Soviet military occupation) six months after the end of the war; it also installed 'autonomous' communist governments in Kurdistan and Azerbaijan. Iran negotiated in Moscow. But in March it also appealed to the UN with US and British backing; the USSR then promptly promised withdrawal, and an Iranian–Soviet agreement was reached in April. The Turkish dispute lasted longer. In 1945 the USSR had denounced its non-aggression treaty with Turkey, and demanded as the price of a new one both territorial concessions and revision of the Montreux Convention governing the use of the Straits out of the Black Sea. Turkey saw this as the prelude to a takeover; and in early 1946 Truman feared unilateral Soviet military action. In August the USSR demanded that the defence of the Straits be assumed by the Black Sea powers jointly (in effect by itself). With 'Western' encouragement Turkey rejected this, and the US signalled its support by conspicuous naval movements. No Soviet action followed, but Soviet demands were not dropped until after Stalin's death.

These crises were not typical. But they broke against a background of increasingly divergent regimes in 'East' and 'West'. Stalin gave priority to the establishment of communist control over Poland, Romania and Bulgaria, with the intention that Hungary should follow, albeit more slowly. He also fully endorsed the communist takeovers in Yugoslavia and Albania. Late 1946 saw a serious communist rebellion in Greece, with Yugoslav support; whether or not it had Stalin's approval (below, p. 154), it was naturally attributed to him. Meanwhile the US refused to permit Soviet participation in the occupation of Japan. In France and Italy the communist parties functioned, with Stalin's blessing, as partners in a 'bourgeois' coalition; they expected this to continue indefinitely, but in both countries they were dropped from government in May 1947. In Germany Potsdam had provided for a mix of collective Four Power control and individual occupation by zones, but on the ground the latter proved the more important. What Stalin really wanted for Germany is still debated. But 1946 saw growing British and US readiness to proceed on their own even if it led to partition; the merger of their two zones in January 1947 clearly created the potential for a West German state; and the Moscow Foreign Ministers Council meeting that April failed to reach any agreement on an all-German peace treaty.

1946 saw the growth not only of alarm in Washington and London, but also of a set of attitudes that would condition their responses. Collectively these have become known as 'containment', the view that the USSR and 'international communism' (seen then, with considerable justice, as two sides of the same coin) were inherently expansive – though, in Churchill's words, Stalin wanted not war 'but the fruits of war'. The best remedy was to eliminate the conditions in which communism flourished, principally through economic reconstruction – for, as Kennan put it, 'World communism is like a malignant parasite that feeds only on diseased tissue'. But this might need to be underpinned. For people might need to feel secure before they could effectively exert themselves to promote recovery. Also 'there is nothing the Russians admire so much as strength, and there is nothing for which they have less respect than for military weakness' (Churchill, at Fulton, Missouri); so if their 'adversary has sufficient force and makes clear his readiness to use it, he rarely has to do so. If situations are properly handled there need be no prestige-engaging showdowns' (Kennan, 'Long Telegram'). In 1946 the US had not yet given up hope of enlisting Soviet cooperation; but if this proved impossible, 'we should be prepared to join with the British and other Western countries in an attempt to build up a world of our own' (Clifford, September 1946 report).

The milestones commonly cited in charting the crystallisation of such attitudes are Kennan's 'Long Telegram' of February, Churchill's 'Iron Curtain' speech at Fulton, Missouri, of March, and Clifford's secret report to Truman of September 1946.[19] But there are others. Nor was there ever a single 'monolithic' line: London and Washington sometimes disagreed, and in neither was there unanimity; also individual policy-makers could change their minds, and could favour different approaches for different parts of the world. But by 1947 there was widespread support for some kind of 'containment'. The US administration drew on it first to gain backing for a relatively small programme to sustain Greece and Turkey (thus generating the 'Truman Doctrine'), and then to launch a huge one for the economic underpinning of Western (and possible attraction of Eastern) Europe – Marshall Aid.

Stalin's vision of international relations is much debated, and will be discussed in Chapter 3. But it would be agreed that he was badly jolted by the advent of the atom bomb, and that this made him more rather than less stubborn: 'using America's monopoly . . . ['Washington and London'] want to force us to accept their plans on questions affecting Europe and the world. Well, that's not going to happen!'[20] But the process of repeatedly saying *nyet* drove the two sides steadily further apart.

Moreover, the economic incentives to cooperation quickly evaporated. 'The United States and England', Maisky had recommended in 1944, 'could be a crucial source of rehabilitation of our national economy'; and Americans like Treasury Secretary Morgenthau believed it could also help the USA maintain full employment during the transition to a peacetime economy and/or gain it a safe supply of raw materials. A post-war loan had been discussed since 1943; and in January 1945 Molotov demanded $6 billion credits, while in Washington Morgenthau proposed $10 billion (as Soviet intelligence presumably learnt from his deputy, Harry Dexter White). Things turned out very differently. Lend-Lease ended abruptly with the war, not a deliberately hostile move but one that was resented in London as well as Moscow. By August the US administration had secured funding for a $1 billion credit and invited a Soviet application, but the State Department then stalled, with the idea of attaching political conditions. Accordingly Stalin decided in December against joining the IMF and World Bank (from which there had been hopes of further aid) – 'as the government of the USA did not offer the USSR a credit, our membership . . . could be read as our weakness, as a forced step taken under the

[19] Kennan, 'Long Telegram', *FRUS* 1946, vi, pp. 707–8; Churchill, Fulton, Missouri, *Keesing's* 7771; Clark Clifford's September 1946 report, printed in Arthur Krock, *Memoirs: Sixty Years in the Firing Line* (New York, 1968) p. 476.
[20] Andrei Gromyko, *Memories* (1990 edn) p. 141.

pressure of the USA.'[21] There remained German reparations. In 1944 Stalin had apparently thought of $5 billion, but was persuaded to double that for negotiating purposes.[22] At Yalta $10 billion was therefore sought, and repeatedly thereafter. At Potsdam it was agreed that each occupying Power should take reparations primarily from its own zone. The USSR was also to receive some from the Western zones; but their amount was never clearly specified, and in May 1946 deliveries from the US zone were suspended (in an attempt to force compliance with other Potsdam provisions). Little, therefore, was to be gained economically from the West, at least in comparison with the USSR's unilateral exploitation of its own zone and of Eastern Europe generally.

But if the two sides thus drifted increasingly apart, the Iran and Turkish crises remained the only confrontations. However, in June 1947 the international scene was transformed by Secretary of State Marshall's offer to assist 'the revival of a working economy in the world so as to permit the emergence of political and social conditions in which free institutions can exist'. Everybody, London and Paris as well as Moscow, had rapidly to improvise a response, and Moscow did so very badly. First it was decided to participate, then that Molotov should walk out; later that the East Europeans should attend the Paris conference called to draft a concrete plan, though only to cause trouble; then fears arose that they might find the offers too tempting, and they were abruptly bullied into reversing their acceptances.[23] The eventual Soviet response was a hastily convened conference in September of the East European communist parties plus those of France and Italy. Here Zhdanov and Malenkov laid it down that 'two camps' had been formed in the world, each with the basic aim of eventually eliminating the other; in the meantime East European communists were to accelerate the complete takeover of their countries, the French and Italian ones to abandon 'parliamentary illusions' and seek to make their countries ungovernable by strikes in opposition to Marshall Aid (though not to attempt a direct seizure of power). It took a little time

[21] Vladislav Zubok and Constantine Pleshakov, *Inside the Kremlin's Cold War. From Stalin to Khrushchev* (Cambridge, Mass., 1996) p. 32; Gaddis, *We Now Know*, p. 193; George C. Herring, *Aid to Russia 1941–1946. Strategy, Diplomacy and the Origins of the Cold War* (New York, 1973) esp. Chaps 6, 9. In fact the USSR got nearly $500m in UNRAA and other US aid in 1945–6 – less than France, a little more than the Netherlands.
[22] Zubok and Pleshakov, *Inside the Kremlin's Cold War*, p. 31.
[23] ibid. p. 86; Gaddis, *We Now Know*, pp. 41–2.

for the last pieces of the jigsaw to fall into place – despite Stalin's impatience a communist takeover of Czechoslovakia did not come till February 1948, while Italy's destiny remained in doubt until the DC electoral victory that April. But Marshall Aid, and Stalin's reaction to it, is commonly seen as marking the definitive division of Europe and the inauguration of a new and much colder stage in the Cold War.

It was, however, still unclear quite where this would leave Germany and Austria, which had from 1945 been jointly occupied by the USSR, US, UK and France. In 1948 the latter three moved to create their own West German state, despite the 1948–9 Soviet blockade of West Berlin. This state, and its Eastern counterpart (the DDR), came into existence in 1949. But it was not until 1955 that it became certain that West Germany would be militarily integrated into the Western NATO alliance, to prevent which the USSR *might* have been prepared to accept a united but neutral liberal-democratic Germany. When the USSR failed to gain its point, it withdrew from Austria (which it had previously been holding as a hostage). Thereafter the demarcation between East and West in Europe was not seriously at issue, though from 1958 to 1962 Khrushchev caused major crises by threatening to squeeze West Berlin, chiefly in order to force a Western recognition of the DDR that did not in fact come for another decade.

Stalin's closing years, 1948–53

The closing years of Stalin's life represent the coldest phase of the Cold War. For the first time there was, in the 1948–9 Berlin Blockade, a direct challenge to an established Western position, even if it was handled with caution on both sides. Then conflict spread to East Asia. This had, initially, been treated as marginal, and, despite the universalistic rhetoric of the Truman Doctrine, the USA had remained largely detached from the Chinese civil war – to the surprise of Stalin, who confessed in 1948 that he had not believed 'the Chinese communists could win. I was sure the Americans would do everything to put down an uprising'.[24] In 1949 the USA again looked on while Mao's forces crossed the Yangtse and completed the 'liberation' of mainland China. Stalin was then at pains to give at least verbal encouragement to China's wider aspirations, declaring that 'the center of the revolutionary movement had shifted from the West to the

---

[24] February 1948 – Holloway, *Stalin and the Bomb*, p. 274.

East';[25] and in 1950 he (and Mao) authorised a further challenge – though again a limited one: North Korea's invasion of South Korea (below, pp. 175–6).

This gave an enormous push to the militarisation of the Cold War, since it destroyed Western confidence that the USSR would not seek to expand by force. Things were, of course, already running in that direction. In both the US and USSR military numbers (heavily cut after the war) had started to rise again in 1948; 1949 saw the creation of NATO, at the time a largely symbolic organisation but one that (in marked contrast to the interwar period) embodied a US–British guarantee of Western Europe; and following the (unexpectedly early) Soviet nuclear test that August, there was heavy lobbying (NSC-68) for American rearmament. The Korean War removed all resistance to this latter, and also contributed towards NATO's military transformation and its 1951 extension to include Greece and Turkey; 1950–1 also saw Stalin set on military build-up – that winter East European leaders were summoned to Moscow and directed to participate, despite their warnings that this would wreck their economies.[26]

East and Southeast Asia

The initial crises of the Cold War had concerned Turkey and Iran, but Eastern Asia had at first been largely uninvolved. However, 1948–9 saw great changes. In China Mao's communists drove out Chiang Kai-shek (who then regrouped on Taiwan); Mao then decided to 'lean to one side' (the Soviet side) in the world conflict. Over the same period the US occupation of Japan shifted from eradication of what were seen as the roots of pre-war aggressiveness to economic and political reconstruction on an anti-communist basis; and in the 1949 elections Yoshida's Liberals secured an absolute majority in the Diet, inaugurating a political ascendancy that was to outlast the Cold War.

East Asia was then shaken by the Korean War. Occupation of Korea, as of Germany, had by 1948 hardened into the creation of a communist and a non-communist state. In June 1950 the former sought to conquer the latter. US and 'United Nations' forces intervened, and had by November

---

[25] To Liu Shaoqi, July 1949 – Gaddis, *We Now Know*, p. 159; General Ivan Kovalev, interviewed by S.N. Goncharov, *Journal of Northeast Asian Studies*, x (Winter 1991) pp. 59, 61.
[26] Teresa Toranska, *Oni: Stalin's Polish Puppets* (1987) pp. 46–7, 298. See also below, pp. 195–6.

overrun most of North Korea. But they were driven out by China, which itself sought to push south but was held roughly along the pre-war demarcation line. Fighting stopped in 1953, but the border has remained ever since both tense and rigidly sealed. The war also brought the USA and its Asian allies into confrontation with China in two further ways. For it led the US to 'interpose' its fleet between Taiwan and mainland China, thus providing Chiang Kai-shek with the breathing space (and, later, aid) that enabled him to consolidate a viable regime on the island. To Beijing, this constituted sustained and hostile US intervention in internal Chinese affairs. Secondly, supplying the Korean war gave a massive boost to the Japanese economy, inaugurating two decades of growth that transformed the country and, arguably, the world. The war also created an international context in which the occupation could be ended, and Japan launched into independence in 1952 within a US security treaty and an alignment (for two decades) with Chiang's regime on Taiwan, not Mao's on the mainland.

Even before the Korean War, however, the US started to involve itself in Southeast Asia. For though it had remained largely aloof from the 1946–9 Chinese civil war, it decided in 1949 to try to stop communism spreading down into French Indochina. It failed; by 1954 Chinese aid had enabled communist insurgents to defeat the French in a 'war of national liberation'. The Geneva Conference then partitioned Vietnam between communist North and non-communist South; after a brief intermission local, but Northern-assisted and controlled, insurrection broke out in the South, and would have overthrown it had not US combat troops intervened in 1965. The Vietnam War, like the Korean, was, in the first instance, a civil one. But the USA had, since 1949, expected the fall to communism of one Southeast Asian country to lead to the destabilisation and collapse of its neighbours, like a row of dominoes; hence US intervention (with the support of South Korean, Australian and New Zealand, but *not* West European, troops). In the event North Vietnam (which came to receive war material and economic assistance from both the USSR and China) outlasted the USA and in 1975 overran South Vietnam. This triumph was accompanied by communist takeovers in Laos and Cambodia (which had been sucked into the Vietnam War), but *not* in any other putative 'domino'. Korea and Vietnam had seen the only actual 'East–West' fighting. But the containment of China also gave rise to two of the most alarming post-war crises, those of 1954–5 and 1958 over offshore islands still held by Chiang Kai-shek; at least in the first, there was a measurable chance of the USA using atomic weapons. It can, therefore, be argued that the Cold War was considerably more intense in Eastern Asia than in Europe.

Khrushchev

Stalin's final years had been gloomy ones for the Soviet Union; and, as he had been warned, his rearmament damaged Eastern European economies, and led in 1953 to serious anti-communist riots in at least three countries. Stalin's successors backtracked and sought an East–West detente. Accordingly the ensuing years saw useful agreements (the Korean armistice, the Geneva Conference on Indochina, and Austrian independence) culminating in the largely atmospheric 1955 Geneva summit conference. But if Soviet leaders, and notably Khrushchev, were determined to avoid nuclear war and genuinely anxious for some improvement in East–West relations, they still expected to out-compete the West. Here Khrushchev looked partly to what he hoped would prove the manifest attractiveness of the communist system, and partly to the influencing of the newly emergent 'Third World' states away from the 'imperialist camp', whether by economic and military aid or by support for 'wars of national liberation'. Indeed the summer of 1955 saw not only the summit conference (with its 'spirit of Geneva') but also the Egyptian arms deal whereby the USSR first gained an *entrée* into the Arab world; and from 1956 to 1958 struggle for influence in that world was very much at the centre of the East–West stage (even though, confusingly, both the US and the USSR condemned the 'Suez' November 1956 British–French–Israeli attack on Egypt).

The autumn of 1958 saw the winding down of a crisis in, and the temporary stabilisation of, the Middle East. It also brought a US–British–Soviet moratorium on nuclear testing. But in November Khrushchev again raised the diplomatic temperature with an apparent 'ultimatum' on Berlin. As he later explained, 'The American foot in Europe had a sore blister on it . . . Anytime we wanted to step on the Americans' foot and make them feel the pain, all we had to do was obstruct Western communications with the city'.[27] Unlike Stalin, Khrushchev never seriously obstructed Western access, but he invoked the possibility. He allowed the tension to subside in 1959, but revived it in 1960 when he responded to American U-2 espionage overflights by breaking up a Four Power summit in Paris. Next year brought the failure of the US–Soviet summit held in Vienna to resolve the crisis. Then, in August, East Berlin was sealed off by what developed into the Berlin Wall. The action was probably a necessary condition for the stabilisation of East Germany, but in the short run it occasioned the quite

---

[27] N.S. Khrushchev, *Khrushchev Remembers*, ii, *The Last Testament* (1974) p. 501.

serious 'Checkpoint Charlie' crisis; and it was followed in September by the resumption of atmospheric nuclear testing to demonstrate Soviet resolve.

Finally in 1962 Khrushchev attempted the secret installation in Cuba of nuclear missiles. America's discovery of these weapons, and her apparent willingness to risk war to force their withdrawal, triggered the most direct US–Soviet crisis of the post-war period, the time when the world is conventionally regarded as having come closest to nuclear war. Of course Khrushchev had his reasons for action; nor was he, when the chips were down, irresponsible – indeed he took a good deal of flak from the Chinese for his 'capitulationism'. But the succession of challenges he mounted in 1958 and in 1960–62 constitute a second peak in the Cold War. Then, on the rebound, Moscow and Washington moved into a new detente whose most visible features, the Test Ban treaty of 1963 and the teleprinter 'hot-line' between the two capitals, symbolised acceptance of a certain joint responsibility (or 'adversary partnership') in controlling world affairs to prevent the ultimate disaster of nuclear war.

There had, of course, been earlier detentes: from Stalin's death to the 1956 repression of the Hungarian uprising; and the 1959–60 'spirit of Camp David' that accompanied Khrushchev's tours of the US and of France, only to dissolve into new tensions over the U-2 incident and Berlin. The 'post-Cuba' detente was to inaugurate similar cycles of rapprochement (and limited collaboration) followed by renewed antagonism. Nevertheless, it has been persuasively argued that it constituted a watershed, and that there were 'two distinct phases of the Cold War: first, bipolar brinkmanship; and second, multilateral permanent truce'. Of course, as the USSR continuously protested, truce (or 'peaceful coexistence') did not 'in the least abolish . . . the laws of class struggle', nor was it incompatible with support for 'the national liberation movement' and intense, though indirect, competition in the Third World. But it did ameliorate crises – without it, as Brezhnev once said, 'the confrontation in the Middle East could become far more dangerous' (see pp. 370, 382, 389 below). Also, as Gaddis observes, after 1962 'Neither side would ever again initiate direct challenges to the other's sphere of influence'.[28]

Among the explanations that have been advanced for this change in the conduct of the Cold War are the advent, during the 1960s, of a dependable 'Mutual Assured Destruction' deterrent as between the superpowers, and the increasing multipolarity of the international system as China and to a

---

[28] Zubok and Pleshakov, *Inside the Kremlin's Cold War*, esp. pp. 7–8, 273–4, 281–2; Gaddis, *We Now Know*, p. 279.

much lesser extent France and West Germany came to act with growing independence. But even before these applied, the US had shown itself, over the East German rising of 1953 and the Hungarian one of 1956, unprepared directly to challenge the Soviet sphere.[29] As regards the USSR, the most important factor was probably the change in its leaders. Stalin and (at a much lower level) Khrushchev were men of the Revolution, and both ruled in a highly personalised 'voluntarist' way, resolving problems by 'campaigns' (or, as Khrushchev's successors termed his, 'hare-brained schemes'). Brezhnev's defining memories were of the 1941–5 War, which he did not wish to repeat; and (despite his involvement in the coups against Beria and Khrushchev) his political style was one of administration and the avoidance of trouble – 'the stability of cadres'. For him the USSR was a superpower, and he looked for its eventual ascent to preponderance primarily to a steady expansion of its military resources; in the meantime he was even keener than his predecessors to be co-opted as an equal by the previously pre-eminent United States, and markedly less attracted by short cuts.

Johnson and Nixon

The post-Cuba detente did not exactly end: nuclear negotiations continued, culminating in 1968 in joint US–Soviet sponsorship of a Nuclear Non-proliferation Treaty; and President Johnson seems to have been anxious for continued good relations with the USSR. But Khrushchev's successors thought he had been altogether too soft, thereby jeopardising Soviet influence in North Korea and North Vietnam. They also saw the escalation of the Vietnam War as an arrogant use of the USA's power, and (though ready to negotiate over it) were distinctly cool towards Johnson personally. By 1968, however, they had decided to negotiate over anti-ballistic missiles (ABMs); their intervention in Czechoslovakia made them all the more eager, so as to direct attention elsewhere.

Nixon was less keen – initially he judged the USSR by its (un)readiness to pressure North Vietnam into winding down the Indochina War. But in 1970 he decided seriously to pursue a summit. Several threads here came together. One was domestic, the constraints placed on his ability to

---

[29] It can be argued that it did very seriously consider such a challenge to China in 1953–5; and though restrained in its response to the 1958 Offshore Islands crisis, it at least contemplated direct action against the Chinese nuclear programme in 1963–4.

act in the foreign and defence fields by mounting American rejection of 'Vietnam' and the policies that had led to it. Another was Chinese. In the 1950s Sino-American hostility may have worked against detente; for the Chinese thought Khrushchev should be taking a much tougher line, and this *may* have been a factor in his 1960 decision to do so. After the Cuban missile crisis, the USSR as well as the USA worried over China; and Kennedy at least hoped this might lead to joint action. Khrushchev's fall put paid to such ideas; but, after a brief interlude, Sino-Soviet relations continued to worsen, and by 1968–9 China was so alarmed as to welcome US overtures. Under Nixon, these were forthcoming. One motive for Brezhnev's pursuit of detente was to preclude the emergence of a hostile American–Chinese alignment and instead draw the USA into joint mangement of the Chinese problem. Another thread was *Ost-politik*. The 1960s had seen first France then West Germany seek openings in Eastern Europe. In 1969–70 the USSR and West Germany managed to improve their hitherto very antagonistic relations, and West Germany agreed both to accept Germany's 1945 borders and to recognise the DDR. The USA was suspicious; but it could not risk alienating Bonn by opposing this process, and was able to integrate it into its own dealings with Moscow by negotiating a definitive settlement of the Berlin question. Lastly both the USA and the USSR had good reason to seek an ABM agreement.

The upshot was the conclusion, at the 1972 Moscow summit, of a Strategic Arms Limitation Treaty (SALT I), flanked by a wide range of commercial and cultural agreements. This was, from Washington's viewpoint, by far the most ambitious detente to date, for, instead of directly containing the Soviet Union, the USA sought to provide it with a place and stake in the existing international system such that it would not risk losing these advantages by hostile or adventurous behaviour. But whereas the accompanying US–Chinese and *Ost-politik* detentes had lasting results, the 'Moscow' US–Soviet detente progressively came unstuck as neither country achieved from it what it had hoped. What remained was a continuing nuclear arms race (only mildly curbed by the SALT I and II treaties) and Soviet conventional arms build-up, and a Soviet readiness to take up opportunities for the spread of communism in the Third World (which seemed the more alarming since the USSR now had, for the first time, a global military reach). That several such opportunities emerged from 1975 onwards may, of course, have been fortuitous; equally the 'Moscow' detente might never have transpired had takeover plots by the Soviet-oriented Egyptian security apparatus or the communist coup in the Sudan succeeded in 1971.

Carter and Reagan

Be that as it may, East–West relations worsened dramatically in 1979–81. President Carter was shocked by the Soviet invasion of Afghanistan and declared himself ready to fight for US interests in the Gulf. His successor, Reagan, saw the Marxist Sandinista takeover in Nicaragua as part of a Soviet–Cuban challenge in Central America, a whole new area of the Cold War. He also imposed sanctions on the USSR and Poland in response to Poland's December 1981 repression of the non-communist trades union movement, Solidarity; and he denounced the USSR as the 'evil empire' with such vigour that people were soon talking about a 'new Cold War'.

How cold it was is debateable. Low-level functional cooperation continued; delegations travelled abroad from communist countries, and Westerners were readily allowed through the 'iron curtain'. During the original Cold War East–West relations had largely dried up, and the border resembled that between the two Koreas. Now it did not, and it is tempting to argue that, though there had certainly been ups and downs in East–West relations, these had only been cycles in an improving trend line. But this would be wrong. At least some Western circles feared that the USSR might capitalise on its perceived military superiority to secure real gains in Western Europe.[30] Far more seriously, as Dobrynin recalls, Andropov believed 'the Reagan administration was actively preparing for war and he was joined in this belief by Ustinov, the defense minister'. As early as May 1981 Andropov launched operation RYAN (or VRYAN, 'surprise nuclear missile attack'), the collection of intelligence on supposed Western plans for a first strike; for 'Not since the end of the Second World War has the international situation been as explosive as it now is'. Many Soviet experts were sceptical. But for the next three years Soviet intelligence was repeatedly ordered to watch for specific pointers to the launching of a surprise nuclear attack. During a November 1983 NATO exercise fears were expressed that US preparations for one might actually have started, apparently prompting a Soviet nuclear alert.[31]

---

[30] *The Changing Western Analysis of the Soviet Threat*, ed. C-C. Schweitzer (1990) esp. Chaps 5, 16.

[31] Anatoly Dobrynin, *In Confidence. Moscow's Ambassador to America's Six Cold War Presidents* (New York, 1995) pp. 522–3; cf. also Markus Wolf (with Anne McElvoy), *Man without a Face. The Autobiography of Communism's Greatest Spymaster* (1997) pp. 221–3 (which suggests that Andropov's suspicions stemmed from the Carter era, though no doubt intensified by Reagan's further defence increases); and, more

These fears gradually subsided in 1984, a process helped by deliberately reassuring signals from Washington and London, and by Andropov's death. Another factor will have been the failure of Soviet hopes that NATO moves to deploy Cruise and Pershing missiles would produce a revulsion of feeling in Western Europe. The proposed deployment did indeed generate 'peace' movements and accusations that the US meant to fight a nuclear war in Europe; left-wing sentiment rose in the British Labour and German Social Democrat parties, and both (in opposition) broke with the NATO defence consensus that they had upheld when in office. In both countries, however, elections in 1983 returned conservative governments, and later that year deployment of missiles went ahead. The immediate Soviet reaction was to pull out of nuclear arms limitation talks. But in 1984 both sides moderated their language, Gromyko held discussions with the US leadership, and (following Reagan's re-election) steps were taken to resume negotiations.

Gorbachev and the end of the Cold War

There are many explanations for the subsequent transformation in international relations. But the most obvious relate to the changes effected in the Soviet Union, both domestically and in its foreign policies, by General Secretary (later also President) Gorbachev between 1985 and 1991. Such 'great men' explanations are no longer fashionable in academe. Yet the world of business (and now also of university administration) devotes both effort and money to head-hunting entrepreneurial leaders in the belief that their skills are crucial to the fortunes of their institutions. Sometimes this is certainly the case. The great British engineering conglomerate GEC was put together by Sir Arnold (later Lord) Weinstock; in his later years much of its original dynamism evaporated, but it remained solid and possessed of a huge cash mountain. After 1996 Weinstock's successor, Lord Simpson, rebranded the concern as the telecoms and technological company Marconi, selling off GEC's other divisions and splashing out on ill-advised purchases. Marconi collapsed in 2001, when the dotcom bubble burst; 2002 saw it in the hands of its creditors, and new mangement installed. But despite improvements, Marconi proved impossible to

generally, Peter V. Pry, *War Scare. Russia and America on the Nuclear Brink* (Westport, Conn., 1999) Part 1; and Andrew and Mitrokhin, *The Sword and the Shield* pp. 213–14, 392–3, 433, 457. RYAN continued until at least November 1991, when Primakov announced its cancellation.

rehabilitate; and in 2005 the brand and most of the businesses were sold.[32] Of course the history of the USSR/Russian Federation since 1985 differs from that of GEC (especially in its eventual outcome under Putin); but there are parallels.

Things began slowly. In December 1984 Gorbachev visited London, partly to enlist Mrs Thatcher's advocacy with President Reagan; next July (shortly after his accession to the Soviet leadership) he and Reagan met in Geneva. The summit proved a striking success and opened up the prospect of a new detente. But there was, at this stage, no sign of anything more – relations were again strained for much of 1986, and a hastily called summit in Reykjavik that October broke up in disagreement. Though Gorbachev was an impressively flexible bargainer, Soviet tactics still seemed largely aimed at putting the United States in the wrong on the issue of ABM research ('Star Wars'). At home important changes were clearly afoot, but the jamming of BBC broadcasts did not stop till January 1987, that of Deutsche Welle not till December 1988. So in mid-1987 Defense Secretary Weinberger could still maintain that

much as the new Soviet leadership would like to convince the world otherwise the Soviet Union is not just another member of the community of nations: it is a tightly-controlled, totalitarian state whose values are alien to free societies, whose military might is a constant threat to our survival, and whose goal is still to conquer all who do not support its communist policies.[33]

However, in 1987–8 Gorbachev proceeded to tangible concessions. He shelved his opposition to 'Star Wars' and in December 1987 visited Washington to sign an INF Treaty based on the 'zero option' Reagan had always wanted (below, p. 70); a year later he announced unilateral cuts in, and suggested serious negotiations on, conventional forces in Europe; in April 1988 it had been agreed that Soviet troops should leave Afghanistan, and in December the USSR helped broker a deal that ended the Cuban presence in Angola in return for South African withdrawal from Namibia.

Such moves, together with Gorbachev's striking visit to the UN in December 1988, helped still Western suspicions. But the pace at which these faded varied considerably. Public opinion probably took the lead –

[32] *The Times*, 26 October 2005 p. 62.

[33] *Keesing's*, 35012, 37094; Schweitzer, *Changing Analysis of the Soviet Threat* pp. 46, 91. Also, as Helmut Schmidt warned in 1988, there was always the possibility that Gorbachev might fail and the USSR revert to an 'aggressive and expansionist' strategy.

by 1988 Gorbachev was at least as well regarded in Western Europe as Reagan, while polls in early 1989 showed that 80 per cent of West Germans felt no threat from the East and that few Soviet citizens feared Western intentions (though 90 per cent believed themselves threatened by their own *nomenklatura*). Some Western politicians (notably the German Foreign Minister Genscher) were more attuned to the new mood than others. But by June 1988 Reagan was himself speculating that 'Quite possibly we are beginning to break down the barriers of the post-war era, entering a new era of history, a time of lasting change in the Soviet Union'. The Moscow summit from which he was returning had been a success; but his 1987 call to 'tear down the Berlin Wall' still seemed unrealistic and pro-pagandistic. Next year the Wall did come down, and Communist rule in Eastern Europe collapsed. The Soviet Union took all this in its stride, and in 1990 showed itself ready to accept German reunification and to agree a phased withdrawal of its troops. The year concluded with a treaty reducing conventional armed forces in Europe to equal ceilings for East and West, thus on paper abolishing any special Soviet threat, and with a joint declaration affirming that its signatories 'are no longer adversaries'.[34] Meanwhile the US, UK and France had removed substantial forces from Europe for use against Iraq in a UN operation that enjoyed (slightly uneasy) Soviet support. The world was indeed changed. But not com-pletely: for the USSR sought to evade the Conventional Forces in Europe Treaty by relabelling its excess tanks as naval units, while in 1991 its Prime Minister 'revealed' a Western plan to flood it with banknotes, thus creating hyperinflation and so bringing to power the 'advocates of swift privatisation' at fire-sale prices.[35] Such attitudes underline the extent to which the Cold War's ending was dependent on the internal transforma-tion of the USSR, a process that resumed at breakneck speed after the collapse in August 1991 of a reactionary coup.

[34] Schweitzer, *Changing Analysis*, pp. 262, 284; *Keesing's*, 36060, 37838.
[35] *The Independent*, 19 January 1991 p. 13 and 11 February p. 8 (also 24 October 1989 p. 1 – admitted Soviet breach of ABM treaty – and 25 July 1991 p. 1 – East European claims of breach of INF treaty); *Keesing's*, 38012.

CHAPTER 2

The strategic dimension of East–West competition

Military competition represented an important dimension of East–West rivalry, and, especially in the 1970s and 1980s, it came to form the staple of US–Soviet negotiations. In part this was because there were few other subjects in high politics that could profitably be discussed. It came too from the fact that leaders on both sides were not only sobered by the knowledge that they had the capacity to bring unimaginable catastrophe on the world, but also imbued by the feeling that this set them apart from other statesmen. In this respect, as Kissinger's aide Sonnenfeldt put it, 'Americans and Soviets do have certain concerns not shared by other nations ... because we have looked into the abyss together.'[1] Given these perspectives, and since the subject is rather technical, it will be convenient to abstract the strategic dimension (as far as possible) from our general account of East–West relations and attempt to survey it here.

The likely consequences of war probably go far towards explaining why both the Soviet Union and the United States were far more cautious than earlier Great Powers had been. They avoided mutual hostilities; indeed, except around 1950–1 and conceivably during the 1961–2 Berlin and Cuba crises and the 1981–4 Andropov era in the USSR, nobody really expected these to break out.[2] So when US and British troops were actually preparing to fight Iraq in 1990, they were given a level of training,

---

[1] L. Sloss and M. Scott Davies (eds), *A Game for High Stakes* (Cambridge, Mass., 1986) p. 26.

[2] For Andropov's fears, see pp. 402–4; for more general official attitudes in the 1950s and 1980s, C-C. Schweitzer, *The Changing Western Analysis of the Soviet Threat* (1990) *passim*.

spare parts and ammunition far higher than had been thought adequate when they were only passively confronting the forces of the Warsaw Pact in Germany. But if hostilities were not expected, East–West relations were antagonistic; both sides felt that, if they let their guard really drop, they would certainly suffer politically and might encourage their opponent to take cruder advantage of the changed military position. This meant that considerable military and intellectual interests were devoted to the maintenance of a credible defence posture, and much thought was given to developing, and securing political backing for, strategies for conflicts that fortunately never occurred.

Writing about them is necessarily a theoretical exercise, and the more so since we are not comparing like with like. This is the case even in the nuclear field, and it is even more true of the conventional balance in Europe. As one scholar remarked, NATO and Warsaw Pact military doctrines

are quite different . . . the Pact prefers large numbers of major weapons and formations (. . . 'tooth') over training . . . logistics, and the command and control functions . . . (. . . often referred to as 'tail') . . .

. . . Pact doctrine tends to extol the advantages of the offense . . . NATO . . . a more balanced view of the relative advantages of defensive and offensive tactics . . .

The net result . . . is that the Warsaw Pact generates military forces that, at first glance, look substantially more formidable than those of NATO . . . the tendency in both official and unofficial balance assessments has been to highlight Pact advantages in tanks, guns, planes or divisions. The possibility that NATO's higher spending [$360 billion as against $320 billion in 1982, according to a US Defense Department estimate] might be generating less visible, but equally important . . . military capability seldom receives much consideration.[3]

The defence of Western Europe

Stalin's Russia was a formidable military force, but its capacity to project power to distant parts of the globe was much inferior to Britain's, let alone

---

[3] Barry Posen, 'Measuring the European Conventional Balance', *International Security*, ix (1984–5) pp. 51–2. Another reason for NATO's poor showing was its refusal to standardise on US (as the Pact did on Soviet) equipment; this raised costs and hampered cooperation between units of different nationalities.

the USA's. So any military interaction with the West would be primarily in Europe. After Stalin's death, the USSR acquired a 'strategic' capability to hit the USA with rocket-borne nuclear weapons, and by the 1970s was thus broadly on a par with the United States. In the 'conventional' field it developed ocean-going navies and an airlift capable of ferrying significant numbers of Cuban troops to Angola and Ethiopia. But outside Europe its presence (and in most areas[4] its potential power) remained inferior to that of the West. So the most important conventional military confrontation was that in Central Europe.

After the destruction of Germany, potential Soviet preponderance in Europe was arguably as much a function of geography as the even more marked US preponderance in the Pacific that followed the defeat of Japan. It seemed more important since Europe had been, until recently, the centre of the world; and Western European resources were such that a state dominating Europe from the Atlantic to the Urals might well come to dominate the world. In 1917 and 1941 the USA had intervened to prevent this, and during the Cold War it did so again. Initially the perceived threat was one of economic collapse, subversion, intimidation and political takeover rather than of open conventional invasion. But in 1950 NATO came, not necessarily wrongly, to fear the latter. The response was, as we have seen, the despatch of US troops to Germany and the decision to build up the alliance's conventional forces. In February 1952 the Lisbon NATO Council meeting set a target of 96 divisions (including reserves) in Western Europe – to counter what was then estimated at 175 rather smaller Soviet divisions that could be considerably increased on mobilisation. Initial Western rearmament was considerable – US defence expenditure in 1953 was nearly four times, British nearly double, that of 1950.[5] But neither country was prepared to continue at these levels. Even during the 1952 Lisbon NATO Council Eden was also grappling with a British cabinet crisis over economic policy, which led him to favour substantial cuts in the rearmament programme. In a defence review that summer the British Chiefs of Staff were no longer, as in 1950, apprehensive of an imminent Russian attack but instead expected a prolonged Cold War. In

---

[4] The USSR perhaps possessed, but did not exercise, the capacity to intervene massively in the Persian Gulf.

[5] Such spending perhaps accounted for nearly 14% of GNP in the USA, over 10.5% in Britain (nearly 2% more than in the rearmament year of 1938) – J.L. Gaddis, *Strategies of Containment* (paperback edn, 1982) p. 359; A. Seldon, *Churchill's Indian Summer* (1981) pp. 499–500.

December British lobbying contributed to a modification of NATO's Lisbon targets.[6]

The USA's conversion came with the change of President in 1953. Eisenhower rejected the idea of preparing for a year of 'maximum danger' (1954), and held that 'If you are going on the defensive, you have got to get a level of preparation you can sustain over the years'. So he aimed at a 25 per cent reduction in military manpower, rather more in costs, by 1957–8. This would involve bringing home substantial numbers of foreign-based troops; the United States could not afford to maintain 'a sort of Roman wall to protect the world'. But this 'New Look' did not involve any abandonment of commitments. Instead primary (though not exclusive) responsibility for local ground defence should rest on America's allies. They would be backed as necessary by US nuclear power – 'In the event of hostilities', declared the new policy directive NSC 162/2, 'the United States will consider nuclear weapons to be as available for use as any other munitions'. These weapons would be not only strategic but also, especially in Europe, 'tactical', that is intended for battlefield use. Deployment of tactical nuclear weapons began in 1954, and seemed admirably suited to remedy NATO's shortfall in conventional troops. As General Gruenther (Supreme Allied Commander Europe – SACEUR) explained, NATO forces constituted a 'shield' that would compel 'an enemy to concentrate prior to attacking. In doing so, the concentrating force would be extremely vulnerable to losses from atomic weapon attacks'.[7] In line with this thinking NATO authorised its commanders, in December 1954, to base their planning on the use of nuclear weapons. But strangely little effort was devoted to reducing the radioactive contamination that would flow from the tactical use of such weapons.

The strategy of the shield did not, in theory, involve any reduction of NATO forces in being, though it did restrict the length of time for which they might be expected to have to fight (and hence the importance of reserves). Thus in 1957 NATO adopted a target of 30 combat-ready divisions for the central front (as against the 25 envisaged at Lisbon), while reducing the alliance grand total (including reserves) from 96 to some 70–75. But countries that no longer feared an imminent Soviet attack

---

[6] Other countries too cut defence spending for financial reasons – Seldon, *Churchill's Indian Summer*, p. 332; M. Gowing, *Independence and Deterrence. Britain and Atomic Energy. 1945–1952*, i (1974) pp. 440–1; Lord [H.L.] Ismay, *NATO. The First Five Years* (no pl., 1955) pp. 47, 104, 106, 107, 111.

[7] Ismay, *NATO* p. 108.

found appealing the idea that, with tactical nuclear weapons, troop numbers were less important. In 1954 France began withdrawing divisions (ultimately 4) for use in Algeria; in 1956 West Germany responded to the domestic unpopularity of conscription by reducing its target force from 500,000 to 350,000; in 1957 Britain withdrew two divisions, and in 1959 it abandoned conscription, thus considerably reducing its trained reserves. Eisenhower also withdrew some troops as he had always intended; but his options were severely restricted by the outcry that – especially in Germany – followed the leaking in 1956 of the 'Radford memorandum' that proposed reducing US forces in Europe to token levels. The corollary of all this was that there came to be available for the central front not 30 but only some 16–18 combat-ready divisions, and that these relied on the early use of nuclear weapons: their adoption by the *Bundeswehr* in 1958 (albeit with continued US control over the warheads) was wildly unpopular in West Germany, though the political storm soon subsided (perhaps because of renewed Soviet pressure on Berlin).[8]

By the end of the 1950s, therefore, NATO's more ambitious targets were clearly not going to be met. Its conventional forces constituted something between a 'shield' – capable, if not of indefinite resistance, at least of compelling a major and deliberate concentration of Soviet forces that would be vulnerable to nuclear attack – and a 'tripwire' that would set off nuclear weapons in the event of any sizeable incursion. The 1960s saw attempts to modify this stance, for the Kennedy administration distrusted overreliance on nuclear weapons. Acheson toured Europe in 1961 to urge a massive increase in conventional forces, and in 1962 McNamara secured NATO acceptance of 'Guidelines' that envisaged the possibility of a 'limited' conventional engagement with a non-nuclear Soviet attack. Neither West Germany nor Britain liked this. In 1963 German ministers were briefed to tell President Kennedy that 'for the Federal Republic a conventional war [inevitably on its territory] is just as deadly as a nuclear one'. Meanwhile the British had, since 1961, been pushing the idea of using nuclear weapons, but on a limited scale against East German military targets not important enough to prompt major Soviet retaliation; this might make the enemy 'pause long enough to realise that he had miscalculated Western determination to resist, and confront him with the choice of withdrawing accordingly or precipitating all-out war'. Since the British were

---

[8] R.E. Osgood, *NATO. The Entangling Alliance* (Chicago, 1962) esp. pp. 117–21; R. Hilsman in K. Knorr (ed.), *NATO and American Security* (Princeton, N.J., 1959) pp. 30–1.

by now more afraid of Soviet probes and miscalculation than of all-out aggression, they hoped withdrawal would result. McNamara was sceptical: it might work, but he doubted it, and felt it was more likely to 'radically transform' the previous battlefield encounter.[9]

The upshot was a general NATO strategic review, with American ideas particularly strongly opposed by France. After French withdrawal from NATO, the pace of discussion picked up, and was marked by increasing Anglo-German cooperation. The British Defence Minister, Denis Healey, claims to have acted 'as a bridge between McNamara, who . . . really wanted NATO to abandon the first use of nuclear weapons altogether, and the Germans, who really wanted to go back to the strategy of massive nuclear retaliation, triggered by a tripwire on their Eastern frontier'. In 1967 NATO agreed on a compromise, generally known as 'flexible response'. This was sharpened in 1969 by the adoption of an Anglo-German recommendation of options for the 'Initial Defensive Tactical Use of Nuclear Weapons' primarily against targets in the DDR, Poland and Czechoslovakia, with a view (Healey said next year) to restoring 'the credibility of the overall deterrent in a situation in which a large-scale conventional attack shows that . . . credibility has disappeared'. Should this not work, 'follow on' strikes might ensue, and thought switched in the early 1970s to options for these.[10]

'Flexible response' remained NATO's official policy for the rest of the Cold War, but its details were further refined. Two contradictory tendencies emerged. The advent, in the 1980s, of high-tech US weaponry and the 'Follow-on-Forces-Attack' concept of disabling the enemy's second echelon forces increased the chances of non-nuclear defence. At the same time, however, West Germany's constant pressure for an early use of nuclear weapons secured agreement that commanders might request this when they feared a defensive collapse, i.e. *before* German territory was actually overrun. Also the combination of better satellite intelligence and

[9] However, US actions were not consonant with their professions: while McNamara was Defense Secretary tactical nuclear weapons in Europe increased from 2,500 to over 7,000; and though US troops there were reinforced during the Berlin crisis, they later fell from 434,000 in 1962 to 300,000 in 1979, partly for economic reasons, partly because of Vietnam – Beatrice Heuser, *NATO, Britain, France and the FRG. Nuclear Strategies and Forces for Europe 1949–2000* (Basingstoke, 1997) pp. 44, 50–1, 193n; Denis Healey, *The Time of My Life* (paperback edn) p. 310.

[10] Heuser, *NATO, Britain, France and the FRG*, pp. 52–6; Healey, *The Time of My Life*, p. 310.

longer-range and more accurate missiles, especially after the advent of Pershing II and Cruise, made more feasible strikes further east (away from both Germanies) and against precise targets with fewer civilian casualties. In particular, to show that there could be no 'sanctuaries', strikes were scheduled against Soviet as well as East European territory, despite some US reluctance. Heuser's surprising conclusion is that it was

the British-European version of deterrence . . . with a greater emphasis on nuclear weapons than on conventional forces . . . [that] prevailed in NATO thinking. The emphasis of this concept was on the threat of escalation through a selective, discriminating, and relatively early use of nuclear weapons launched from European soil, while American preferences would have been to limit any war to Europe and, where possible, to avoid any nuclear use.[11]

Soviet policy towards Western Europe: NATO and Warsaw Pact military doctrines, and WTO exercises

Soviet policy appears more straightforward. Stalin had no direct defence against a US nuclear monopoly. One response was to give maximum priority to the development of nuclear weapons. But, though they were tested in his lifetime (an 'atomic' explosion in 1949 and a small 'hydrogen'-type one in mid-1953), the USSR is believed to have had no bomb operationally deployed in January 1953, at which time the USA had 1,600.[12] Instead, NATO believed, Stalin planned to overrun a largely undefended Western Europe with his conventional forces. These were apparently built up from 2.9 million in 1948 to a peak of 5.4 million in 1953, supplemented by about 1.5 million East Europeans. Khrushchev, however, like Eisenhower, believed in cutting conventional defence spending to the benefit of rockets and nuclear bombs. By 1956 Soviet forces had been reduced by a million, with a further 1.5 million following by 1959. Then in January 1960 Khrushchev announced a further 1.2 million cut. This was very much a

---

[11] Heuser, *NATO, Britain, France and the FRG*, pp. 56, 60–1, 144. She adds that were US decision-makers 'to delay first use longer than their European allies thought bearable . . . the British component of NATO's deterrent' could compel it. In the March 1989 command exercise, German players favoured and US opposed a strike on Soviet territory, and it was assigned to a British Tornado. How realistic this was, no one can tell.

[12] Ambrose, *Eisenhower the President*, p. 93.

personal initiative, analogous to several others his successors were to call 'hare-brained schemes'. He had told the Praesidium that Soviet security was guaranteed by its – actually still unachieved – plethora of nuclear missiles. The cut would play well abroad, promoting 'our Marxist-Leninist ideas, our teaching, our struggle for peace'. It would be economically beneficial; and 'if our enemies do not follow our example', so much the better 'in the light of struggle between communism and capitalism' – their armies 'would devour their budgets, reduce . . . [their] economic development . . . thereby contributing to the increasing advantages of our system'. However, the cut (with its harsh redundancies among career officers) encountered massive military opposition, and was suspended with the onset of the 1961 Berlin crisis. After Khrushchev's fall defence expenditure again built up – perhaps by 4–5 per cent per annum before 1976, 2 per cent p.a. in 1976–82 and 3–5 per cent p.a. in 1982–5.[13] These rates were initially in line with the growth of the Soviet economy, but by the 1980s defence was outpacing such growth and becoming a significant burden.

Of course not all Soviet power was targeted on Western Europe: Khrushchev recalls, sceptically, a map exercise in which the Black Sea fleet broke through into the Mediterranean and landed in the Middle East;[14] and in later years extra-European missions certainly grew. But the great bulk of Soviet forces were stationed in the west of the USSR and in Eastern Europe. The usual view is that they had, from about 1948, been

postured to repel an initial attack and then move over to the offensive. The concept . . . reflected . . . Soviet military theory and the conviction that victory could only be achieved through offensive operations. Both beliefs had been reinforced by the successful campaign against Germany.

The offensive also meant that war would be waged on enemy territory . . . [which] would make [East European] defections less likely. The capability for offensive operations into [Western] Europe had the

[13] T. Wolfe, *Soviet Power and Europe, 1945–70* (Baltimore, 1970) esp. pp. 10n, 42–3, 165; Matthew Evangelista, *'Why keep such an Army?': Khrushchev's Troop Reductions* (CWIHP Working Paper 19, December 1997) pp. 4–6, 40, 42; Vladislav Zubok, 'Khrushchev's 1960 Troop Cut: New Russian Evidence', CWIHP *Bulletin* 8–9 (1996–7) pp. 416–20; IISS, *The Military Balance 1986–7* pp. 32, 34–5; D. Holloway, *The Soviet Union and the Arms Race* (1984 edn) pp. 114–17; Roy and Zhores Medvedev, *Khrushchev. The Years in Power* (Oxford, 1977) p. 150n.

[14] *Khrushchev Remembers*, ii, p. 29.

ancillary advantage of posing a counterthreat that might deter the United States from exploiting its atomic monopoly . . .[15]

This seems very natural; the alternative would have been to sit and be destroyed by Western air-power.[16]

There were, therefore, in the 1950s similarities between Eastern and Western concepts of major war. Both envisaged this as starting with an offensive by the other side; this they would absorb, and sooner or (in NATO's case) later assume the offensive on the ground, with a view to achieving (at least in Europe) complete victory as in the Second World War. For Moscow it was axiomatic that in any final conflict socialism would prevail over capitalism. For Washington, the 1949 DROPSHOT plan envisaged 'Establishment of control [over the USSR] and enforcement of military surrender terms', listing the points that would need to be occupied to compel a change of regime.

The late 1950s and early 1960s, however, brought a radical divergence in military planning. After Stalin's death, NATO came to see war as arising (if at all) not from all-out Soviet invasion but from either miscalculation or a limited probe; so NATO directives were, by 1957, no longer talking of 'ultimate victory', but of 'a rapid conclusion' to fighting that would 'maintain or, if necessary . . . restore the integrity and security of the NATO area'. There was to be much debate in the 1960s as to whether this would be best achieved through conventional warfare alone, or by an early, but deliberately limited, warning use of nuclear weapons. The aim, however, remained consciously defensive; in the mid-1980s West Germany even insisted on modifying the US AirLand Battle strategy so that NATO troops would not cross into Warsaw Pact territory.[17]

---

[15] Michael McGwire, *Military Objectives in Soviet Foreign Policy* (Washington, 1987) p. 71.

[16] Mastny, however, refers to 'the essentially defensive strategy [before 1961] inherited from the Stalin era', citing Czech evidence (Vojtech Mastny and Malcolm Byrne), *A Cardboard Castle? An Inside History of the Warsaw Pact, 1955–1991* (Budapest, 2005) pp. 15, 18, 118, 139, 209. I am not sure this really supports his contention. Moreover in 1952 exercises Czech forces were first to rebuff an enemy attack and then reach the Alps 17 days later; by 1954–5 'the CSLA prepared itself almost exclusively for offensive operations'; 1950s exercises ended around the tenth day with fighting on the Nuremberg–Ingolstadt line, but in 1960 the CSLA 'was supposed to operate on the Stuttgart–Dachau line by the 4th day of conflict' – Petr Lunak, 'Planning for Nuclear War: the Czechoslovak War Plan of 1964', CWIHP *Bulletin* 12/13 (2001) pp. 290–1, 279n.

[17] Beatrice Heuser, 'Victory in a Nuclear War? A Comparison of NATO and WTO War Aims and Strategies', *Contemporary European History*, 7 (1998) esp. pp. 314–20.

However, 1961 saw a growing ambition on the part of Soviet military planners, perhaps in response to the renewed Berlin crisis. In May Defence Minister Malinovsky told commanders that whereas the army used to be tasked to advance at 40 to 50 kilometres a day, now tank advances of 100 kilometres a day could be planned, with double the previous penetration beyond enemy lines.[18] That autumn a huge Warsaw Pact command exercise was mounted, with the ominous scenario of war breaking out after the signature of a Soviet–East German peace treaty.[19] The 'East' immediately seized the initiative, and after three days had crossed the Rhine and also occupied Munich. There were mishaps – nobody could find Luxembourg on the map. But with nuclear weapons clearing the path, fighting extended well into France, and the enemy sued for peace. There followed toasts all round, 'for the brave commanders, for friendship among nations, and of course – for peace.'[20]

Succeeding decades saw a profusion of such exercises, many, like the 1979 'Seven Days to the Rhine', involving heavy use of nuclear weapons, but (by the 1980s) some that did not. Some also, like 'Seven Days to the Rhine', stopped there, leaving the nuclear powers Britain and France unharmed. Others, like SOYUZ-83, envisaged the occupation of Denmark, West Germany, the Netherlands, Belgium and France 'by day thirty or thirty-five', or simply spoke (as in 1988–9) of 'the transition' after reaching the Rhine 'to a general attack with the aim of taking the European NATO states out of the war'. Though scenarios started with a NATO attack, 'Except for a few exercises in the late 1980s, defense against [such an] . . . attack was not practiced because such an attack was obviously considered implausible'. Rather there was good reason to seek such early territorial gains in the four or five days that, Soviet analysts estimated in 1967, it would take NATO to decide on a nuclear response.[21] Until 'the mid-1980s . . . military doctrine . . . was frankly described as "offensive" in Soviet publications, such as an officers' manual of 1971'; and the

[18] Mastny, *Cardboard Castle?* pp. 120–1.
[19] Following its failed attempt to break a blockade of West Berlin, NATO launched a nuclear attack, to which the WTO managed to reply within five minutes.
[20] Mastny, *Cardboard Castle?* pp. 131–6.
[21] February 1992 German Defence Ministry report, CWIHP *Bulletin* 2 (1992) p. 14; Beatrice Heuser, 'Warsaw Pact Military Doctrines in the 1970s and 1980s: Findings in the East German Archives', *Comparative Strategy*, 12 (1993) p. 441. DDR espionage kept the WTO well informed as to NATO's real plans.

'available exercise plans . . . until about 1988 indicate that the occupation of territory was always the ultimate aim of Pact forces'.[22]

How seriously all this should be taken is unclear. These were only exercises, and we do not have access to the real war plans designed and held in Moscow. But planning went some way beyond military training: a 1971 scenario followed the surrender of Hannover with the installation there of a KPD–SPD municipal government; military currency was printed to pay East German, Polish and Czech troops on 'the adversary's territory'; and on German reunification, 8,000 'Blucher' medals for bravery during the offensive were found in the former DDR Defence Ministry.[23] True expectations may have been somewhat lower, especially in the 1980s as concern mounted as to NATO's lead in high-tech conventional weaponry[24] and the 1986 Chernobyl disaster had so dramatically demonstrated the dangers of nuclear contamination.[25] But the machine would not have trained for operations radically different from those it intended to mount, if ever it had to. At the same time there is no indication that leaders like Brezhnev ever seriously thought of unleashing war in Europe. In this sense, the analogy lies with the early Schlieffen Plan, which, before 1911, German leaders had no intention of putting into effect (though it seriously constrained their options when they later moved to the brink of war), rather than with Hitler's Red and Green plans against Czechoslovakia and France, which he had every intention of implementing as soon as he judged it safe.

[22] David Rennie, 'World War III seen through Soviet eyes', Telegraph.co.uk (26 November 2005, describing documents just released by Poland); German Defence Ministry report, CWIHP *Bulletin* 2 (1992) pp. 14–15; Heuser, 'Warsaw Pact Doctrines' pp. 441–2, 446.

[23] Mastny, *Cardboard Castle?* pp. 380–1; Heuser, 'Warsaw Pact Doctrines' p. 451; *Sunday Times*, 28 March 1993, p. 1.24.

[24] General Wojciech Jaruzelski writes that to compare WTO and NATO tanks was to compare a DC-3 with a Boeing 747 (*Mein Leben für Polen. Erinnerungen* (Munich, 1993) pp. 199–200, 205–6); also Mastny, *Cardboard Castle?* pp. 47, 49–50.

[25] The Warsaw Pact formally discarded its offensive strategy for 'defensive sufficiency' in May 1987, but in reworking the doctrine the military 'tried to preserve as many offensive elements as possible'. This became difficult once the USSR began in 1989 to implement the unilateral cuts Gorbachev had announced the previous December at the UN, and acceded to Hungarian (and later Czech) pressure to withdraw troops. In 1990 the USSR adopted a doctrine very similar to NATO's, the 'repulse' of aggression, 'the defence of the . . . integrity of the state . . . the creation of conditions to stop the war as quickly as possible and the reestablishment of a just and solid peace' – Mastny, *Cardboard Castle?* pp. 61–2, 64; Heuser, 'Warsaw Pact Military Doctrines', pp. 448–50.

Conventional strength in Europe was one aspect of Soviet defence policy, nuclear weaponry another. Initially this too was directed against Western Europe for the simple reason that the USA could not be reached, a position that lasted in essence into the 1960s. So, in 1961, West European vulnerability was pointedly stressed; *Izvestia* declared

Khrushchev believes absolutely that when it comes to a showdown, Britain, France and Italy would refuse to join the United States in a war over Berlin for fear of their absolute destruction. Quite blandly he asserts that these countries are, figuratively speaking, hostages to the USSR and a guarantee against war.[26]

In the 1960s the USSR did acquire an intercontinental (ICBM) capability against the USA. But it did not scrap its intermediate range (IRBM) missiles targeted on Western Europe (unlike the USA, which for various reasons did dismantle the IRBMs it had from 1957 onwards deployed in Europe). Instead, in the 1970s the USSR modernised them, substituting mobile SS-20s for the fixed base SS-4s and SS-5s. The overall number of delivery systems was in fact reduced, but their capacity greatly increased since the SS-20 had three independently targetable warheads. Dobrynin asserts that the deployment was made on purely military grounds, with little thought for its political consequences; the secrecy with which it was conducted, and the disingenuous attempts to minimise its dimensions, aroused considerable Western suspicion, and in 1979 NATO prepared to counter it with new US missiles. At this point, Dobrynin says, Chancellor Schmidt offered a compromise: the European members of NATO would refuse to accept these US missiles *if* the USSR restricted the number of SS-20 warheads to those on the rockets these were displacing. Kosygin was attracted by the overture, but Ustinov's opposition killed it: he would not reveal, still less reduce, the number of SS-20s the USSR proposed to deploy.[27]

[26] Holloway, *The Soviet Union and the Arms Race* pp. 66–7; *Khrushchev Remembers*, ii, pp. 47–8. Targeting Western Europe also served to catch US bombers/missiles on the ground and so reduce damage to the USSR. In the later 1970s and 1980s the capability was also sought to achieve this 'conventionally' through air drops and the use of special units.

[27] Anatoly Dobrynin, *In Confidence. Moscow's Ambassador to America's Six Cold War Presidents (1962–1986)* (New York, 1995) pp. 432, 542–3.

Reactions to Soviet build-up: NATO's 1979 response

Taken with the build-up of Soviet conventional forces and ICBMs, the SS-20 deployment seemed to the West to presage Soviet escalation dominance: an offensive conventional superiority; nuclear superiority within Europe; at least 'strategic' parity with the USA, which might inhibit the covering of Western Europe with the American 'strategic umbrella'. Questions had been raised for some time as to this umbrella. As early as 1959 Secretary of State Herter had doubted whether any President would engage 'in all-out war unless we were in danger of all-out devastation ourselves.' Such doubts, fed by the 1960s American stress on conventional options, served as an explicit rationale for the development of the French nuclear deterrent, and a less openly stated one for Anglo-German advocacy of a Europe-based nuclear element in NATO's 'flexible response' strategy. And the nearer the USSR approached to parity with the US in 'strategic weapons', the louder became what Kissinger subsequently termed the repeated European demands for 'additional reassurances of an undiminished American commitment', and the stronger the pressure for an improvement in the European theatre nuclear balance. The need for some such reassurance was enhanced by President Carter's apparent indecision, evident in (for instance) his 1978 abandonment of his own proposal for the deployment of 'neutron' anti-personnel bombs, *after* European governments had incurred political costs by accepting it.[28] Hence the 1979 NATO decision to deploy 576 US 'cruise' and Pershing intermediate-range missiles. These were intended to enhance NATO's 'flexible response' by improving its capacity to mount strikes in Eastern Europe and western Russia that would at once 'display resolution' and weaken Soviet capacity to control and reinforce its original offensive, thus inducing second thoughts. Were, however, the USSR to continue, or to attack the missiles themselves, enough might be discharged to destroy Soviet command posts and inflict such damage that the unharmed US 'strategic' force would become dominant. Soviet recognition of this danger should keep West European defence 'coupled' to US-based nuclear forces and preserve extended deterrence. NATO's decision to deploy was to prove central to the politics of the 1980s.[29]

---

[28] Cf. the Herblock cartoon on 'Carter Policy Turns' captioned 'It's the Cartron bomb – it knocks down supporters without damaging opponents'.

[29] Henry Kissinger, *Diplomacy* (1995) p. 776 – Kissinger in fact sees the decision as more political than strategic.

US nuclear superiority in the 1950s and 1960s

The most important dimension of Soviet nuclear policy was, however, that targeted directly against the United States. In the 1950s Soviet capacities were very limited, and the decision to concentrate on rockets rather than aircraft as delivery systems prolonged the period of this weakness. The USSR covered this with bluff. In 1955 US observers were misled by repeated bomber overflights at parades into a gross overestimate of their numbers. Then in 1957 the USSR put the world's first satellite into space. Khrushchev played this success for all it was worth, boasting that he could send rockets anywhere on earth with such accuracy as to hit a fly. This led many Americans to fear that a 'missile gap' had opened up. But Eisenhower knew – partly from U-2 reconnaissance overflights conducted since 1956 – that it had not, and was thus emboldened to resist Congressional pressure for a massive increase in the American missile programme.

Khrushchev's expectations were the opposite – that given American superiority, overflights and other intelligence would make it 'easier for them to determine the most expedient moment to start a war'.[30] The cure, of course, was the acquisition of equality. An opportunity to achieve this through a quick fix came when Cuba turned to the USSR in 1961 for protection after a CIA attempt to topple Castro's leadership through an emigré invasion. Agreement was secured for the installation of 42 medium-range missile launchers, a great adjunct to Soviet strength given that the USSR then had only about 20 ICBMs, which (Kissinger says) took longer to fuel than it would have taken US forward-based bombers to reach them.[31] The deployment was, however, detected while still incomplete, and Kennedy forced the missiles' withdrawal (see pp. 267–73). A Soviet diplomat negotiating this withdrawal remarked, 'You Americans will never be able to do this to us again';[32] and some historians claim (though others deny) that, while humiliation over Cuba improved the climate of East–West relations in the short run, it also spurred the subsequent Soviet defence build-up.

In the early 1960s, however, it was the US build-up that was more in evidence. During his 1960 election campaign Kennedy had promised to close the 'missile gap'; and by the time he discovered it was really an

---

[30] *Khrushchev Remembers*, ii, pp. 410–11.
[31] *New York Times*, 29 January 1989, pp. 1, 10; H.A. Kissinger, 'NATO: The Next Thirty Years', *Survival*, xxi (1979) p. 265.
[32] Kissinger, *Memoirs*, i, p. 197.

inverse gap in the USA's favour, it was too late to alter course. Eisenhower had developed high-quality missiles – 'Minuteman' ICBM's, which appeared to be invulnerable in their hardened underground silos, and Polaris submarine-launched missiles (SLBMs) that were also invulnerable though less accurate. These programmes were rapidly carried forward, until in 1967 the US had 1,054 ICBMs and 656 SLBMs. That, Defense Secretary McNamara decided, was enough; in future the USA would rely not on more rockets but on multiplying the number of warheads carried.

'Healey's theorem'

The question – 'Enough for what?' – raises the whole area of atomic strategy. This has generated a vast literature, necessarily theoretical. One reaction is that of Kennedy's security adviser, McGeorge Bundy:

There is an enormous gulf between what political leaders really think about nuclear weapons and what is assumed . . . in simulated strategic warfare. Think Tank analysts can set levels of 'acceptable' damage well up in the tens of millions of lives. They can assume that the loss of dozens of great cities is somehow a real choice . . . In the real world of real political leaders – whether here or in the Soviet Union – a decision that would bring even one hydrogen bomb on one city of one's own country would be recognized in advance as a catastrophic blunder; ten bombs on ten cities would be a disaster beyond history; and a hundred bombs on a hundred cities are unthinkable.[33]

It is likely that most Western, and especially West European, governments worked chiefly on this basis. What they saw as important was the preservation of ambiguity. Any serious conventional invasion might meet a nuclear response; once the fire-break between conventional and nuclear (even tactical nuclear) weapons was crossed, there might well be escalation to major nuclear war. But, according to what has been termed 'Healey's theorem',[34] 'if there is one chance in a hundred of nuclear weapons being

[33] Quoted by L. Freedman, 'The First Two Generations of Nuclear Strategists', in P. Paret (ed.), *Makers of Modern Strategy from Machiavelli to the Nuclear Age* (Oxford, 1986) p. 769. It has, however, been observed that Stalin did inflict comparable casualties on his people in the 1930s in the general pursuit of Soviet power.

[34] Named after the British Defence Minister, 1964–70. Bundy professed belief in this theorem in his defence of conventional strategic doctrine against Kissinger's recantation and criticisms – 'The Future of Strategic Deterrence', *Survival*, xxi (1979) pp. 271–2.

used, the odds would be enough to deter an aggressor'. And, added the Gaullist advocates of the French deterrent in the 1960s, the existence of a number of independent centres of nuclear decision-making must complicate the potential aggressor's calculations of the likelihood of nuclear response and hence add to deterrence. This doctrine cannot be regarded as intellectually rigorous. But it must derive some support from the fact that neither the Cold War nor the possibly even more acute Sino-Soviet antagonism led to serious hostilities between the major powers – unlike many earlier Great Power rivalries and a number of contemporary confrontations between non-nuclear powers in the Middle East and South Asia.

Evolution of US strategic doctrine: 'Mutual Assured Destruction'

'Healey's theorem' also had much support in the United States. But it does not explain the evolution of the American nuclear arsenal into what is very much more than a minimum deterrent. Initially things were fairly simple. The 1940s, and still more the 1950s, saw an enormous build-up in the manned bomber force under Strategic Air Command (SAC). This would initially have dropped such few atom bombs as were available on industrial complexes in Soviet cities, the only targets it could be confident of finding. Even if all 133 bombs went off perfectly, it was reported in 1949 that this would not 'bring about capitulation' or even halt an invasion of Western Europe. As more bombs became available, as intelligence improved, and as the USSR itself started to acquire nuclear weapons, SAC added more targets (reaching 3,261 by early 1957) – to retard the Red Army's conventional advance and to destroy Soviet command, air and nuclear bases. SAC's priorities were challenged in the later 1950s by the US Navy, which advocated limiting deterrence to an invulnerable force (presumably its own Polaris SLBMs then under development) capable of destroying 200 Soviet cities. The result was a study that predictably came out for an 'optimum mix' of 'high priority military, industrial and governmental control targets', and the construction of a Single Integrated Operations Plan (SIOP) to eliminate inter-service targeting duplication in achieving this. Were the Plan ever to have been implemented, all these targets would have been struck at the outset, leaving nothing in reserve. Nor was there any provision for targeting the USSR that did not also involve attacking China and Eastern Europe. The incoming Kennedy administration was shocked by this all-or-nothing approach. By 1962

McNamara had had the SIOP reworked to allow choice both of which countries to strike and as between different 'tasks' within each country. The emphasis was now on Soviet forces and their infrastructure/communications, while 'holding in protected reserve forces capable of destroying urban society'.[35]

Although McNamara began by publicising the new idea of sparing Soviet cities (while retaining the capacity to destroy them) in the hope that this would lead the enemy to reciprocate,[36] his *speeches* soon changed – to stress the importance of being seen to possess the capacity to absorb any conceivable Russian strike and still be able to destroy Soviet society. This had admittedly always been McNamara's bottom line. But he discovered that the more he emphasised 'counter-force' and 'options', the more weapons the military demanded to make this possible. So though McNamara left his SIOP's largely counter-force targeting intact, at the *declaratory* level he came to focus almost entirely on 'Assured Destruction'.

However, 'Assured Destruction' was more than just a device for bureaucratic in-fighting; it was also central to the doctrine of 'arms control' as it emerged in the 1960s.

As long as the USA possessed under all circumstances the capability of destroying about a quarter of Soviet population and half Soviet industry, it was held, 'deterrence' was assured, since there could be no conceivable Soviet incentive to push the USA to such retaliation. From this perspective, all that mattered was the survivability of the US deterrent, which seemed assured by its continued development as a 'triad' along lines that were probably in any case inescapably determined by service interests: ICBMs in their 'hardened' silos; SLBMs fired from submarines an enemy would

---

[35] A.L. Friedberg, 'The Evolution of US Strategic Doctrine, 1945–1980', in S.P. Huntington (ed.), *The Strategic Imperative: New Policies for American Security* (Cambridge, Mass., 1982); and D.A. Rosenberg, 'The Origins of Overkill. Nuclear Weapons and American Security, 1945–1960', *International Security*, vii (1963); Scott D. Sagan, 'SIOP-62: The Nuclear War Plan Briefing to President Kennedy', *International Security*, xii (1987–8) esp. pp. 38–9; Desmond Ball, 'The Development of the SIOP, 1960–1983' in Ball and Jeffrey Richelson (eds), *Strategic Nuclear Targeting* (Ithaca, NY, 1986) esp. pp. 62–70, 82.

[36] Eisenhower had regarded counter-force second strikes as unfeasible. If the worst came to the worst, 'We are not going to be searching out mobile bases for ICBMs, we are going to be hitting the big industrial and control complexes' (Rosenberg, 'The Origins of Overkill', p. 62).

find hard to locate; and manned bombers that could escape attack by leaving the ground in an emergency.[37]

Logically, what went for the United States went also for the Soviet Union. McNamara accepted this; as early as 1961 he had told the President that a capability to destroy all Soviet nuclear weapons was not only 'almost certainly unfeasible' but also undesirable since it 'would put the Soviets in a position which they would be likely to consider intolerable'.[38] He came to see Soviet acquisition of an 'assured destruction' capability as not only inevitable but also stabilising, since once they had attained it (by the later 1960s) they would no longer feel the need to get their blow in first.

Accordingly 'Mutual Assured Destruction' (MAD) became widely valued in Washington. It was thought that there was an objective mutual US–Soviet interest in preserving this condition, by negotiated arms control, in as stable and cheap a form as possible. Perhaps the Soviets did not yet fully recognise this. If so, educating them would be a subsidiary function of strategic arms limitation talks.

Nuclear Test Ban Treaty 1963

Arms control theory was not the only source of the SALT process. Others were the long-established habit of nuclear conversations, Soviet needs, and the defence problems of the Nixon administration. Nuclear conversations had begun as a result of the growing concern in the 1950s as to the consequences of atomic testing in the atmosphere, a subject initially brought to international notice in 1954 when unexpected winds carried fall-out from a US test to contaminate some Pacific islanders and, more deeply, the crew of the Japanese fisherman the *Lucky Dragon*. The Indian Prime Minister, Nehru, invoked Asian sentiment and called for immediate test suspension and the working out of a comprehensive disarmament agreement. This soon led to the appointment of a UN disarmament subcommittee and the tabling of proposals by both East and West. At least initially these should be seen as propaganda, but it is significant that it

---

[37] Democratic administrations would happily not have replaced these when they became obsolete. But, at least in the 1960s, they had massive Congressional support, and scrapping them was never an option. Besides they had non-nuclear uses (in Vietnam); in the 1980s their strategic significance was revived by the advent of air-launched cruise missiles.

[38] Rosenberg, 'The Origins of Overkill', p. 68.

was felt necessary to appeal to, and reassure, public opinion both internationally and in the USA and Britain. Still tests continued to multiply.

A breakthrough came in 1958, when, on the completion of a major Soviet series, Khrushchev announced a moratorium. Eisenhower (who had for some time been worried by fall-out) responded by suggesting a technical meeting of Soviet and American scientists to examine the possibility of monitoring a test ban. This Geneva meeting went well, and the world was impressed by the apparent ability of the scientific community to talk across the East–West divide. Eisenhower, having completed his series, then proposed negotiations for a general test ban treaty and announced a suspension of explosions as from 31 October to facilitate these. There followed a positive orgy as the US, UK and USSR sought to squeeze in last-minute tests, then a lull until the first French test in 1960. The negotiations for a complete ban failed: Eisenhower's scientific advisers had been too sanguine, and had to concede (to their pro-testing compatriots) the possibility of concealing underground tests of up to 20 kilotons, barring an inspection system far more elaborate than that envisaged by the 1958 Geneva meeting and quite unacceptable to the USSR. Still the three nuclear powers continued to observe the moratorium until, in September 1961, the USSR resumed massive tests in the atmosphere as part of Khrushchev's general challenge to the West. The USA promptly followed, initially underground but in 1962 also in the atmosphere. However, when tensions again subsided after the Cuban missiles crisis, agreement was fairly readily reached: the vexed issue of inspection was bypassed by permitting underground tests, but the US, USSR, UK, and (by adhesion to the 1963 Test Ban Treaty) most other countries foreswore atmospheric testing.[39]

This was arguably the most significant post-war arms agreement reached (at least until 1987) in that it removed a source of radioactive fall-out that was killing people and that threatened, if tests continued to multiply, to cause appreciable contamination. (It also greatly worsened Sino-Soviet relations – see pp. 552–3). But the Treaty did not halt the arms race. Some say the United States, by not moving decisively to end testing in

[39] R.A. Divine, *Blowing in the Wind. The Nuclear Test Ban Debate 1956–60* (New York, 1978). A US–USSR Treaty banning underground tests of over 150 kilotons was signed in 1974, but not ratified until 1990 (owing to concern over verification). A 'Comprehensive Test Ban Treaty' was negotiated in 1996, but had not come into force by 2006 as too few states had ratified it; among those not ratifying is the USA.

the early 1950s, missed an opportunity to halt the nuclear race while it was ahead. This seems unlikely. Both France and China went forward with atmospheric testing despite the 1963 Treaty (to which they did not adhere), until they felt their weapons technology sufficiently developed. Had there been earlier attempts at a ban, the USSR and Britain would presumably have done the same. Just possibly, though, the conclusion in the later 1950s of a complete test ban treaty, even if inadequately monitored, might have inhibited the subsequent arms build-up by preventing the testing of small warheads for multiple-tipped missiles. The chief immediate obstacle to such a treaty was the USSR's unreadiness to permit more than a very limited number of inspections on its territory of doubtful occurrences (like earthquakes) that resembled tests. Other countries, too, were probably less tolerant of inspection than they portrayed themselves; but Soviet hostility to the idea from Stalin to Chernenko, though it had some reasonable basis,[40] verged on paranoia. Without inspection a ban looked uninviting. Admittedly most (perhaps even all) underground tests have been detected by foreign satellites and seismic stations. But the possibility of cheating did not seem negligible (especially given the recent bypassing of the Korean armistice provisions for monitoring communist troop movements); and there have in fact been some unexplained occurrences.[41]

The Nuclear Non-Proliferation Treaty 1968 (NPT)

Be that as it may, one of the features of the Test Ban Treaty was that it gave status to the three chief nuclear powers, a status they had a common interest in maintaining. This distaste for further nuclear proliferation severely strained US–French relations in the 1960s and had far graver consequences for the Soviet–Chinese alliance. But it also led on naturally to the next stage in the US–Soviet nuclear relationship, the pursuit of a treaty to keep these terrible weapons in safe (i.e. existing) hands. Negotiating this was more complicated since it required measures to ensure that other countries

[40] Since Western society was more open, the USSR had in its ability to exclude foreigners a comparative espionage advantage that it did not want to jeopardise. Khrushchev also feared that the USA would be dangerously encouraged were it to discover just how weak Russia was.

[41] Experts are still divided as to whether a 1979 occurrence off South Africa was purely natural or, more probably, an Israeli/South African test (Carey Sublette, *Report on the 1979 Vela Incident* (1 September 2001 – http://nuclearweaponarchive.org).

did not divert nuclear fuel and turn it into bombs. As atomic electricity-generation then looked economically promising, these countries (even if willing to forego nuclear weapons) did not wish to be disadvantaged by constraints on their peaceful use of nuclear technology that did not apply to the atomic weapons powers. But a treaty was presented to, and blessed by, the UN in 1968, and had, by 1970, secured enough ratifications to come into force. By it the nuclear states[42] undertook not to transfer nuclear weapons or weapons technology to non-nuclear countries, and also gave a vague undertaking to negotiate on an 'early cessation of the nuclear arms race', on 'nuclear disarmament, and on a treaty of general and complete disarmament under strict and effective nuclear control.'[43] They also provided assurances, outside the treaty, that they would seek immediate UN Security Council assistance to any non-nuclear state that was the subject of nuclear threats or aggression. As they all had Security Council vetoes, this was not perhaps very meaningful; but it later crystallised into promises not to use nuclear weapons against any non-nuclear signatory except 'in the event of an attack on themselves or their allies' by (in the US format) 'a state allied to a nuclear weapon state or associated with . . . one in carrying out . . . the attack'.[44] For their part, non-nuclear signatories undertook not to acquire nuclear weapons, and to allow the inspection of their nuclear energy and research facilities by an International Atomic Energy Agency (IAEA) based in Vienna. Controls to deter the diversion of fissile material were further reinforced by collective agreements of the 'Nuclear Suppliers Group' (comprising industrialised countries of both West and East), and by the unilateral requirements of individual supplying countries.

Attempts to secure nuclear weapons

Before the Treaty's conclusion a number of developed countries had contemplated the acquisition of nuclear weapons. Most attention was attracted by the case of West Germany. On independence, this had under-

---

[42] Initially the UK, USA, and USSR. France so disliked the UN that it would not sign, but it undertook to behave 'exactly as the [nuclear] states adhering to the Treaty'; it finally signed in 1992, as did China.

[43] Article 6. Subsequent SALT talks limited, and the INF and START I treaties largely ended 'the nuclear arms race'; the number of nuclear weapons has also been greatly reduced, but only at Reykjavik in 1986 was their complete elimination considered. Non-nuclear states regularly raise the subject at the NPT's five-yearly review conferences, though largely *pro forma*.

[44] http://dosfan.lib.uic.edu/acda/treaties/npt1.htm.

taken not to manufacture them on its own territory. In 1957–8, however, alarmed by the apparent weakening of US protection as Soviet power grew, it concluded agreements to support Franco-Italian manufacture and share its products. But these were vetoed by de Gaulle when he came into office. Thereafter West Germany made no further attempt to secure direct acquistion, though it continued to advocate either a 'European' deterrent or a Europe-based NATO one not subject to US veto. But one of the purposes of the 'Multi-lateral Nuclear Force' advocated by the Kennedy administration was to head off West Germany's anticipated demands for nuclear weapons of its own. Wartime memories were still strong enough for many to find this prospect neuralgic: de Gaulle once said it 'would be the last *casus belli* existing in the world . . . War could break out over that alone';[45] and the USSR felt quite as strongly. Ratifying the NPT enabled Brandt to set that question at rest.

The two heavily armed neutrals, Sweden and Switzerland, came a good deal closer. Switzerland apparently began serious nuclear studies in 1957, and in 1963 produced detailed proposals for weapons acquisition; money, however, was never made available, and Switzerland signed the NPT in 1969. Sweden began preparations in 1952, and could supposedly have commenced manufacture in the 1960s; the establishment was divided on its desirability; preliminary tests continued until 1972, but in 1974 all plutonium facilities were dismantled. Australia had been intimately involved in the UK nuclear programme; against the background of instability and war in Southeast Asia, some politicians (notably Prime Minister Gorton, 1967–71) came to feel it needed weapons of its own. So, though Australia signed the NPT in 1970, it did not immediately ratify. In 1972 the incoming Labor premier, Gough Whitlam, felt very differently, and ratification came in 1973.[46]

But if, in the 1960s and early 1970s, many countries embraced the idea of nuclear non-proliferation, others did not. Israel was surrounded by enemies, and in 1958 began building extraction facilities at Dimona; over the next decade it apparently received assistance from France, the US, Britain and Norway, and also itself clandestinely acquired nuclear materials. It did not sign the NPT, but staged no nuclear tests, declaring that it would

---

[45] Heuser, *NATO, Britain, France and the FRG*, pp. 125–6, 149–51, 153.
[46] 'States Formerly Possessing or Pursuing Nuclear Weapons', http://nuclearweaponar-chive.org; On Line Newshour (Jim Lehrer), 2 May 2005; 'Australian Nuclear Weapons: the story so far', Nautilus Institute at RMIT, July 2006 (Internet); also Wayne Reynolds, *Australia's Bid for the Atomic Bomb* (Melbourne, 2000).

not be the first to introduce nuclear weapons into the Middle East, and generally preserving a policy of 'ambiguity'. But it is widely believed to have acquired nuclear weapons by 1973, and may even have readied them when apparently facing disaster early in that war. In 1986 a whistle-blower published revelations about Israel's nuclear weaponry, and its capabilities are usually believed to be considerable.[47]

Other significant countries, too, did not sign the NPT. India developed nuclear weapons in the context of its rivalries with both Pakistan and a China that had gone nuclear in 1964. Its first test was in 1974, but there-after so little was heard about its programme that commentators often overlooked it. The 1990s, however, was a decade of increasing national-ism; and in 1998 the new BJP government showed off its deterrent in well-publicised tests (that no doubt helped also with the design of missile warheads and hydrogen bombs). Where India led, Pakistan was sure to follow; but the immediate stimulus appears to have been defeat by India in 1971 and the loss of East Pakistan (Bangla Desh). The programme began with A.Q. Khan's stealing of blue-prints for the Dutch civilian uranium centrifuges; it appears to have had assistance from China with nuclear design, and from North Korea with missile technology. Khan was to claim in 1987 that Pakistan had achieved the bomb, but the government prud-ently denied this. Under US pressure it supposedly froze its programme in 1991, but clearly not for long. When India went public with its nuclear tests in 1998, Pakistan followed suit. This incurred US sanctions, but they were lifted in 2001 when Pakistan's assistance was needed for the 'War on Terror' overthrow of the Taliban in Afghanistan.[48]

Two other states are known to have acquired nuclear weapons. South Africa was concerned in the 1970s by the growth of Soviet power in Africa and the takeover of (parts of) Mozambique and Angola by communist liberation movements. With Israel's help, it developed fairly crude atom bombs (six by 1990, with one more under construction) as a lever to com-pel Western aid *in extremis*, by threatening to use them if it were witheld. Communism's collapse in 1989 reduced white South Africans' perception of threat, and President de Klerk decided in 1990 to release Nelson Mandela

---

[47] 'Israel's Nuclear Weapon Capability: an Overview', Wisconsin Project on Nuclear Arms Control, *The Risk Report*, ii, no. 4 (July–August 1996) (www.wisconsinproject.org/countries/Israel/nuke/html); Stephen Green, *Living by the Sword: America and Israel in the Middle East 1968–87* (Brattleboro, Vt., 1988) pp. 89–91. Britain had deployed the first nuclear bombs in the Middle East (in Cyprus, in support of CENTO).
[48] Wikipedia, *Pakistan and Weapons of Mass Destruction, Abdul Qadeer Khan, List of States with Nuclear Weapons.*

and negotiate a transition to majority rule. He also decommissioned the bombs, and in 1991–3 acceded to the NPT, calling on the IAEA to verify this. Until then the world generally had been unaware of the South African programme, though the superpowers must have been better informed since they cooperated to head off a projected test in 1977.[49]

Probably no border has been more tense than the Korean ceasefire line. Both Koreas signed the NPT (South Korea in 1975, North in 1985), but neither took it very seriously. South Korea has admitted extracting plutonium in 1982, and enriching uranium to near-weapons grade in 2000. By 1989 North Korea was suspected of building separation facilities at Yongbyon, and soon even of having a 'rudimentary' weapon. In 1991 the two Koreas agreed that the peninsula should be a nuclear-weapons-free area; but a senior civil servant said, three years later, that South Korea had planned to develop weapons if the North did not stop. It continued; and 1993–4 saw a major crisis with the USA threatening strikes on Northern facilities. But 1994 apparently brought a resolution: North Korea agreed to freeze its plutonium extraction (and in 1997 allowed the IAEA to install monitoring equipment at Yongbyon); the USA, South Korea and Japan were to deliver fuel oil for conventional power stations and build light-water nuclear power plants that could not easily be diverted to military purposes (though these were soon behind schedule). In 2002, however, North Korea apparently admitted it had continued with uranium extraction; the USA halted oil deliveries under the 1994 agreement; and North Korea told the IAEA to remove its monitors from Yongbyon. In 2003 it withdrew from the NPT, started to claim that it already had nuclear weapons, and staged rocket tests that alarmed Japan. It also declared that it was about to be attacked, and threatened pre-emptively to engulf South Korea (to whose capital, nuclear weapons or not, it poses a very credible threat). Tension later eased, leading to several rounds of talks in Beijing between North Korea, its neighbours, and the USA, and North Korean hints that it might be prepared to strike a deal in direct negotiations with the United States. Meanwhile North Korea continued with its rocket and nuclear programmes, and in 2006 staged a small nuclear test that drew general condemnation. Perhaps as a result of Chinese pressure, agreement was reached next February for the synchronised resumption of oil deliveries and an IAEA-inspected closure of Yongbyon. Implementation dragged, enabling North Korea, cynics said, to extract enough plutonium for several bombs; but Yongbyon was shut down in July 2007.

[49] 'States Formerly Possessing . . . Nuclear Weapons'; Wikipedia, *South Africa and Weapons of Mass Destruction*.

But if North Korea now has nuclear weapons, it is, in contrast to the original nuclear powers, a very weak state, dependent on foreign aid to mitigate famine in the 1990s and grave food shortages since, and vulnerable to the cut off of foreign power supplies. In the context of President George W. Bush's ouster of Saddam Hussein and designation of North Korea as the other end of the 'axis of evil', its Leader could see the possession (though not the use) of nuclear weapons as a safeguard for his regime. But the programmes clearly started far earlier, when there was no particular external threat, and are probably better explained as the product of paranoia and/or as a prestige project.[50]

The readiness of the great majority of states (188 by late 2006) to sign the NPT shows that international norms are adverse to nuclear proliferation. But North Korea's history demonstrates that even NPT adherence does not always preclude attempts to acquire nuclear weapons; and several states, some signatories, some not, have in fact had clandestine programmes.[51] Of these the most prominent was perhaps Iraq. This adhered to the NPT and allowed inspections that satisfied the IAEA. But Israel had better information, and in 1981 bombed Iraq's research reactor. Iraq had in fact been actively seeking to develop a bomb since 1974. It was not deterred by Israel's action, and resumed its search. In 1991 it was ejected from Kuwait by UN forces. The ceasefire agreement provided for inspectors to track down all Iraqi nuclear facilities; their reports suggested that Iraq had been within eighteen months of developing a weapon. In 1991–3 nuclear plants were destroyed, and enriched material transported to Russia for treatment; but Saddam's general reluctance to cooperate with UN inspectors left the impression that he hoped to resume his programmes once UN sanctions were lifted.[52]

---

[50] Wikipedia, *North Korea and Weapons of Mass Destruction*; *The Times*, 19 July 2007 p. 31; Jack Kim in the *Boston Globe*, 11 July 2007 (internet).

[51] Besides those cited in the text the following are claimed to have had serious programmes: Argentina (1978 until the restoration of civilian rule in 1983), Brazil (1978 until the 1990s), Egypt (1954–67), Poland, Taiwan (1964–1980, when it was discontinued under US pressure), Romania (under Ceausescu), Yugoslavia (from the 1950s until after Milosevic's fall, when the enriched uranium was returned to Russia). Also the USSR's collapse left Belarus, Khazakhstan and Ukraine with quantities of nuclear arms and material on their territory; by 1996 all had been returned to Russia, though not without some earlier Russo-Ukraine friction – 'States Formerly . . . Pursuing Nuclear Weapons'; *List of States with Nuclear Weapons*.

[52] *Keesing's*, 38648, 38698, 39577, 1993 R138; 'States Formerly . . . Pursuing Nuclear Weapons'.

Like Iraq, Colonel Ghadaffi's Libya sought the bomb. In the 1970s, it tried in vain to buy one from China; then, despite its 1975 ratification of the NPT, it embarked on a lengthy attempt to build one, partly to counter Israel, but perhaps chiefly as a function of Ghadaffi's personal ambition. The process was slowed when Libya's 1988–9 terrorist mid-air-explosion of US and French airliners led to UN and other sanctions; but the lifting of UN sanctions in 1999 again improved the programme's prospects. In 2003, however, shortly after Saddam Hussein's overthrow (for supposedly retaining 'weapons of mass destruction'), Libya approached the UK to broker an accommodation with Washington. The final consideration was perhaps the subsequent US interception of a clandestine consignment of centrifuge parts; and in December 2003 Ghadaffi agreed to destroy chemical, biological and nuclear weapons and open Libya's facilities to inspection. It had, apparently, progressed further than many had believed, but the IAEA judged that it was still three to seven years from producing a weapon.[53]

If Libya ended its nuclear programme in 2003, Iran seemed to be moving the other way. It had been an early NPT signatory. But the Shah planned to build twenty nuclear power stations, no doubt as part of his vision of modernity; it would not have been out of character had this vision extended also to the acquisition of nuclear weapons. The programme was disrupted by revolution, war, and Iraqi bombing. In the 1990s it was revived, despite Iran's copious supplies of cheap oil; and the USA was unable to persuade Russia to forego lucrative nuclear contracts. For such a programme, Iran claims that it requires the capacity to refine uranium, which it is, in international law, perfectly entitled to do. It also protests that it has no intention of using this to build weapons, and indeed cites a 2005 fatwa of its Supreme Leader, Ayatollah Khamenei, to the effect that to build or use such weapons would be un-Islamic. However, in 2003–5 the IAEA reported that Iran had breached its NPT obligations, concealed facilities, and admitted to separating out small quantities of plutonium. In 1987 it had acquired 'from a foreign intermediary' the Dutch separation plant designs on which the Pakistan programme was based. In 2004 A.Q. Khan confessed to having supplied nuclear technology to Iran, Libya and North Korea. Though the Pakistan government denied complicity, he is said to have told investigators the transfers had been authorised

[53] M. Heikal, *The Road to Ramadan* (paperback edn, 1976) pp. 74–5; GlobalSecurity.org, 'Weapons of Mass Destruction – Libyan Nuclear Weapons' (28 April 2005); CNN News, 29 December 2003.

by the Chief of Staff, General Beg; Beg himself said in 2006 that Iran had in 1990 sought to buy a Pakistani bomb, and that (according to Prime Minister Bhutto, 1988–90, 1993–6) it had offered over $4 billion for the technology.

Many countries therefore see Iran's programme as directed more towards weapons than energy, and, given Iran's geopolitical position, find this alarming. It is the patron of Shia Muslims, whose position has been much enhanced by the overthrow of Saddam's Iraq and by the rise of Hezbollah in Lebanon; and some feel that if it achieves nuclear weapons, Saudi Arabia (and perhaps Egypt) will seek to follow. It is vehemently opposed to Israel, which lies within the range of Iranian rockets, and for whose obliteration President Ahmadinejad has called. Fears have also been expressed that it might make nuclear materials available to Hezbollah, or other extremist Muslim groups that, with a mystique of martyrdom, would have less to lose than a conventional state, and be correspondingly harder to deter. (On the other hand, though it has supplied Hezbollah with modern weapons, Iran seems, at least so far (2006), to have itself retained control of the longer-range rockets stationed in Hezbollah territory.)

Given such fears, the USA has declined to rule out air strikes on Iran's nuclear facilities; and Israel has suggested that, if no other country acts, it will do so itself. This, however, is easier said than done – the facilities in question are deliberately dispersed, and may not all be known. Moreover Iran has, and in 2006 staged manoeuvres to demonstrate, a formidable capacity to retaliate, by closing the Straits of Hormuz to oil tankers, by striking Israel both directly and from Lebanon, by destabilising Iraq and the Gulf, and by unleashing martyrdom attacks within Western states. Instead the EU, as represented chiefly by Britain, France and Germany, has (with US approval) engaged Iran in dialogue, to facilitate which Iran 'froze' nuclear enrichment at Natanz; and Russia offered to construct on its own territory a joint facility that would be subject to inspection but would supply Iran with a dedicated source of fuel. However, talks failed. In January 2006 Iran resumed work at Natanz, announcing in April that it had enriched uranium and 'joined the group of countries which have nuclear technology'. In July the UN Security Council threatened sanctions if Iran did not stop; its bluff was called, leaving it to mull over sanctions that (Russia insisted in the light of the Iraq experience) should not in any way authorise the use of force in the event of further Iranian defiance.[54]

---

[54] Wikipedia, *Iran and Weapons of Mass Destruction* (Nov. 2006), *Abdul Qadeer Khan*; FAS, 'Weapons of Mass Destruction around the World, Iran' (www.fas.org/nuke/guide/iran/nuke – June 2006).

Strategic Arms Limitation Talks: ABM and SALT I Treaties 1972

If the Non-Proliferation treaty had only incomplete success, it did continue the habit of East–West nuclear discussion that had begun in the 1950s, and paved the way for the opening of Strategic Arms Limitation Treaty (SALT) negotiations on more controversial aspects of the power relationship. The chief reason for these talks must have been that both sides hoped to gain from them, and from the subsequent political detente (for which, see Chapter 9). But a major catalyst was the – leisurely – Soviet deployment, from 1963, of the 'Galosh' anti-ballistic missile (ABM) system to protect Moscow, and the inauguration of anti-aircraft defences that the Americans initially saw as another ABM line from the Baltic to Archangel. These deployments led to considerable Congressional concern, hence to a 1967 decision to deploy US ABMs. The Johnson administration dragged its feet, preferring on the one hand to improve its missiles' penetrating power by developing multiple independently-targeted warheads (MIRVs) and, on the other, to seek negotiations with the USSR that would ban ABMs and so conserve Mutual Assured Destruction.[55] Nixon, too, wished to negotiate, but he also decided to go ahead with a modified ABM system, 'Safeguard'. Sentiment in Congress had by now swung round; in August 1969 Safeguard was only kept alive by the Vice-President's casting vote, and the administration was eventually reduced to lobbying for it as a bargaining chip in arms control negotiations. It is, however, unlikely that the Soviet politburo, which lacked experience of independent parliaments, appreciated this major weakness in the US negotiating position.

Publicly, at least, Kosygin showed no acceptance of the desirability of a Mutual Assured Destruction posture. Defensive systems, he observed, were not 'a cause of the arms race but designed instead to prevent the death of people'; nor, at the June 1967 Glassboro summit, would he contemplate negotiations to ban ABMs. But in 1968 the USSR decided to open talks, perhaps to encourage other countries to accede to the Nuclear Non-Proliferation Treaty, but probably chiefly from fear that an effective US ABM system would shut off the recently acquired Soviet capability to inflict major damage on the continental United States. Galosh, after all, did

---

[55] The USA started developing MIRVs to make possible the coverage of a greatly expanded Soviet target list (Seymour Hersh, *The Price of Power. Kissinger in the White House* (New York, 1983) p. 150). But the advent of an ABM threat to the US deterrent soon provided an extra rationale for SALT talks.

not work very well, and its US counterpart would probably be more sophisticated. Before talks actually opened the Warsaw Pact invasion of Czechoslovakia supervened, but this only made the USSR the more anxious to hold them to divert attention; nor did the Johnson administration want more than a symbolic delay. This delay was stretched by the change of US administration, but SALT talks formally began in November 1969.

Nixon certainly hoped they would encourage the Soviet Union to help end the Vietnam War. He also needed to cash the bargaining chip of his Safeguard ABM system before Congress axed it. But his chief strategic worry was the unexpectedly rapid growth in the numbers of Soviet ICBMs which the USA was then ill-placed to match – partly because it had stopped deploying additional missile launchers in 1967 and partly because of the extensive hostility to new defence programmes. So, despite occasional wavering, the White House made an ABM agreement conditional on one restricting ICBM numbers. As Kissinger later put it, 'We traded the defensive for the offensive limitations'.[56] The actual negotiations had their ridiculous side. Soviet military men were furious when Americans discussed the performance of Soviet weapons in the hearing of representatives of the Soviet Foreign Office, who had no clearance for such secret information. On the US side, Kissinger insulated himself from Washington pressures and leaks by confining serious negotiation to the 'back-channel' between himself and Soviet ambassador Dobrynin; the official US SALT delegation sometimes only learnt what was going on by courtesy of their better briefed Soviet counterparts. Still, 1972 saw the conclusion and signature at the Moscow summit of an ABM Treaty and an 'Interim Agreement on . . . the Limitation of Strategic Offensive Arms'.[57]

MIRVs: vulnerability of US ICBMs and implications for 'extended deterrence'

The ABM Treaty sought to prevent 'defensive' technologies upsetting 'strategic stability', but offensive innovation might have the same effect.

---

[56] Kissinger, *Memoirs*, i, p. 1245; cf. also Nixon's June 1972 statement that the absence of arms limitation would have been disadvantageous 'since we have no current building programmes for the categories of weapons which have been frozen, and since no new building programme could have produced any new weapons in those categories during the period of the freeze' (*Keesing's*, 25136).

[57] For texts, see *Keesing's*, 25310 ff. and W. Stützle, B. Jasani and R. Cowen (eds), *The ABM Treaty* (Oxford, 1987) Appendix.

The first SALT talks may have missed a chance to foreclose this by banning multiple warheads. Instead they concentrated on reaching an Interim Agreement, to which we shall return, limiting the numbers of nuclear missiles. Yet, in conditions of approximate parity, single-headed missiles do not offer much scope for a disarming first strike; for, given the certainty of errors and malfunctions, it will need more than one of your own missiles to kill one of your opponent's. However, if each of your missiles carries several independently targetable warheads, at least a theoretical possibility opens up of a disarming strike that still leaves you plenty of rockets in reserve. Recognising this, the Johnson and Nixon administrations made some moves to limit the threat to Soviet silos.[58] However, neither was prepared to forego MIRV, which were tested in 1968–9, deployed from 1969. Kissinger was warned that, if MIRVs were not banned and the Soviets also acquired them, US land-based ICBMs would become vulnerable. He nevertheless went ahead, regarding much of the opposition as the standard resistance to all new American programmes, and advising Nixon that a freeze on MIRVs 'might create pressures to halt the Minuteman III and Poseidon programs [that were to carry them] . . . thus further unravelling the US strategic program'. An additional consideration was the then widespread underestimate of the time it would take Russia to acquire workable MIRVs.[59]

Given that the USA already had a deployable MIRV system by the time SALT talks started (which would not have been the case had they opened, as originally intended, in 1968), it would have been hard to negotiate an arrangement that did not *either* freeze Soviet inferiority (by banning tests) or neutralise the current US advantage by banning deployment while leaving Soviet development free to catch up.[60] Proposals along these lines were made in 1970, but there was no serious negotiation and probably neither side wished it.[61] According to his later account, Kissinger had always doubted whether a MIRV ban was acceptable either to the Pentagon or to the Soviets and manoeuvred accordingly. But by 1974 he was already

[58] T. Greenwood, *Making the MIRV: A Study of Defense Decision Making* (Cambridge, Mass., 1975) pp. 70–1.

[59] Kissinger, *Memoirs*, i, pp. 210–12; Hersh, *The Price of Power*, chaps 12, 13.

[60] This advantage came to seem increasingly important as the USSR overhauled the USA in numbers of missiles and explosive megatonnage.

[61] Garthoff's contacts on the Soviet delegation encouraged him to believe that it might have been receptive to further exploration; but that delegation's head, Semenov, suggested that the MIRV issue would only impede agreement on other matters.

openly wishing that he had in 1969–70 thought through the implications of a MIRVed world more thoroughly.[62]

Their importance was magnified by the fact that the USA came in the 1970s to place more reliance than ever before on its now potentially vulnerable ICBMs.[63] This arose partly out of a concern for the continuing deficiencies in SIOP (even as reworked by McNamara), and partly from a need to be able to reassure Western Europe that it was still effectively covered by extended American deterrence even in an era of approximate US–Soviet strategic parity. The reworked SIOP had given an US President a choice between options; but as late as 1974 the smallest apparently involved the use of 2,500 strategic weapons plus, probably, 1,000 NATO strikes from Europe.[64] So there was more point that is sometimes allowed to Nixon's 1970 rhetorical question, 'Should a President, in the event of a nuclear attack, be left with the single option of ordering the mass destruction of enemy civilians, in the face of the certainty that it would be followed by the mass slaughter of Americans?[65] Accordingly SIOP was reworked 'to provide the President with a wider set of much more selective targeting options', and the result was announced in 1974 as the Schlesinger Doctrine. Asked to suggest a 'real' example when a limited number of nuclear weapons might be used, Defense Secretary Schlesinger replied that the only one he could think of was

the overrunning of Western Europe . . . I don't know what we would do under these circumstances in terms of the strategic forces, but I believe that it is necessary for our strategic forces to continue to be locked into the defence of Europe in the minds of Europeans and of the Soviet Union.[66]

[62] Kissinger, *Memoirs*, i, pp. 541–8; R.L. Garthoff, *Détente and Confrontation. American–Soviet Relations from Nixon to Reagan* (Washington, 1985) pp. 133–41; Gerard Smith, *Doubletalk* (Garden City, N.Y., 1980) chap. 4 and pp. 471–2.

[63] The first Soviet tests of true MIRVs came in 1973, with significant deployment from 1975. The USSR may not have achieved a reliable capacity to destroy the bulk of US silos until 1983–4 (W.T. Lee and R.F. Staar, *Soviet Military Policy since World War II* (Stanford, 1986) pp. 160–1); but the perception that this would come was already influential by the mid-1970s.

[64] A.H. Cordesman, *Deterrence in the 1980s: Part 1. American Forces and Extended Deterrence* (IISS, Adelphi Paper no. 175) p. 13.

[65] Friedberg, 'Evolution of US Strategic Doctrine 1945–80' pp. 61, 75 – Nixon was questioning the doctrine of 'assured destruction'.

[66] Lynn Etheridge Davis, *Limited Nuclear Options: Deterrence and the New American Doctrine*, 1975–6 (Adelphi Paper no. 121, p. 5).

In its turn, the incoming Carter administration further reworked targeting, instructing the Pentagon to develop yet more options, and to maintain a 'safe reserve' of strategic nuclear forces and command systems for use if nuclear war became extended; they should be capable not merely of executing pre-planned missions but of being redirected to find and destroy new targets during the course of hostilities. The upshot, in 1980, was PD-59, whose emphasis on 'intra-war deterrence' and the need for strategic forces to continue to function even after initial exchanges struck European critics as indicating an ominous propensity to fight a nuclear war. PD-59 was then developed into a new SIOP with a yet more extensive range of packages and options that took effect in 1983.[67]

However, the greater the emphasis on precise strikes and on wartime control and retargeting, the more important became the United States' land-based ICBMs, the part of the triad best suited to these missions.[68] Unfortunately this was the most vulnerable part of the US strategic triad.

During 1975–8 it steadily became clear that the USSR would create a major counterforce capability against the Minuteman force by the early 1980s. Virtually every three months . . . the US discovered yet another significant improvement in Soviet ICBM design . . . accuracy . . . reliability and fractionation capability'.[69]

Fear of ICBM vulnerability led in three directions: a vain search for an invulnerable basing mode for US ICBMs; acquisition of some countervailing capability against Soviet ICBMs; and criticism of an allegedly complacent liberal establishment that had exposed the USA to such vulnerability. The Ford administration bequeathed to its successor the decision to deploy a far more accurate, hence powerful, warhead (Mark 12A) cum guidance system on some of the Minuteman III missiles, and this was promptly endorsed. Official estimates of the implications vary considerably. But an Arms Control Impact Statement of March 1979 suggested that, were

---

[67] These options are discussed by Ball, 'Development of the SIOP' pp. 80–3. It was also decided not to attack population centres *per se*, while retaining as a deterrent the ability to do so later, and to avoid the 'enemy's national command/control'. This was intended to facilitate intra-war bargaining so as to stop short of old-fashioned Mutual Assured Destruction.

[68] Bombers might not get through. Communications difficulties with submarines inhibit continuous, hence detailed, command and control; and their missiles are both less easily retargetable and less accurate.

[69] Cordesman, *Deterrence in the 1980s*, p. 19.

Mark 12A to be fitted to all 550 Minuteman IIIs (in fact it was fitted only to 300), Soviet ICBMs would by 1982 become distinctly vulnerable.[70] The Russians will have found such vulnerability the more alarming since ICBMs accounted for a far greater proportion of Soviet than of American warheads. As early as the 1974 summit, Brezhnev had briefed Nixon on what he claimed was the US first strike potential; and in 1981–4 Andropov apparently feared that the West was planning for offensive nuclear war.

US interpretations of Soviet intentions

The Americans too were wondering precisely what the Russians were up to. Originally it had been assumed that the ABM treaty and SALT dialogue indicated their acceptance of US ideas of strategic stability through Mutually Assured Destruction;[71] it was easy to quote Soviet leaders to the effect that nuclear war would be a disaster for all concerned. Now a rival school came to feel that the USSR was seeking a superiority that would enable it to fight and win a nuclear war. As is often the case, the parties to the debate directed their gaze in different directions. Optimists ('doves') focused on the statements of the Soviet political leadership (which from 1977 onwards explicitly denied seeking military superiority); pessimists ('hawks') regarded these as soft soap, emphasising aspirations to just such superiority and claims of 'the objective possibility of achieving victory' in Soviet military writing (notably the classified internal journal *Military Thought*). Doves noted that the USSR was well behind in overall numbers of warheads: they held that part of the trouble lay in the lag between the formal concession in the first SALT talks of Soviet strategic equality and its real acquisition; so what hawks saw as a bid for superiority was really just the actualisation of this parity. Hawks looked rather at Soviet conventional build-up (at a time when US defence spending was falling), at the emphasis on chemical weapons (whose production the US unilaterally suspended in 1969), and at the numbers and power of Soviet ICBMs rather than the comparison with the US triad as a whole.[72]

[70] Garthoff, *Détente and Confrontation*, pp. 791, 798; John Prados, *The Soviet Estimate. US Intelligence Analysis and Russian Military Strength* (New York, 1982) pp. 289–90.

[71] Both adherents and assailants of MAD often underestimated the extent to which US nuclear targeting diverged from it.

[72] See e.g. J. Baylis and G. Segal (eds) *Soviet Strategy* (1981) esp. Chap. 1, and J. Van Oudenaren, *Deterrence, War Fighting and Soviet Military Doctrine* (1986 – Adelphi Paper no. 210); also the tables in Cordesman, *Deterrence in the 1980s*, pp. 47–9.

Within the USA, the hawks gained the upper hand in the later 1970s. To some extent this simply reflected the souring of detente. But an important development was the 1976 competition (over the National Intelligence Estimate) between the CIA – which had overreacted to its earlier mistaken apprehensions of a bomber and missile gap, and was in any case suspect of tailoring estimates to meet political pressures – and a 'B team' chosen to oppose its 'arms control bias'. The B team claimed victory. It also played some role in turning the CIA around; in 1976 the latter doubled its estimate of the cost of defence to the Soviet economy, and subsequently acquiesced in worried estimates of Soviet arms levels. All this was probably not without effect on the Carter administration, in which hawks like Brzezinski became increasingly influential. It came to note Soviet military literature and to sponsor significant rearmament.[73] Moreover the B team, and a distinguished array of sympathetic past and present political figures, went public after the 1976 election under the guise of the 'Committee on the Present Danger'. Its propaganda contributed to growing Congressional qualms about SALT, but its real importance came in 1980. Just as the Democrats had used feelings of a 'missile gap' in 1960, so Reagan now rode the new mood; after the election his transition team cited twelve 'intelligence failures', notably 'the general and continuing failure to predict the actual size and scope of the Soviet military effort' and 'the consistent gross misstatement of Soviet global objectives'.[74] Much of Reagan's first term has to be seen against this background.

SALT II negotiations 1972–9

All this was what 'arms controllers' aim to prevent. They seek a stable balance that cannot easily be upset, confidence that neither side wishes to upset it, and some system of verification to show that neither is upsetting it. From this perspective the Strategic Arms Limitation Agreements of the 1970s left much to be desired. SALT I (in 1972) represented an exchange

[73] In 1980 Defense Secretary Brown told the Senate that, while the new Presidential Directive 'does *not* assume that a nuclear war will necessarily be prolonged . . . [it] *does* take into account Soviet literature which considers such a scenario to be a real possibility' (Friedberg, 'Evolution of US Strategic Doctrine 1945–80' p. 83) This represented a certain East–West convergence, but on the basis of Soviet military doctrine, not American MAD.

[74] Prados, *The Soviet Estimate*, pp. 248–57, 279; John Ranelagh, *The Agency. The Rise and Decline of the CIA* (1986) pp. 663–4; IISS, *The Military Balance, 1987–8* p. 31.

of defensive for offensive limitations. The USSR may have felt itself the chief defensive gainer; in return it accepted limits on offensive missile numbers that impinged slightly on its own building programmes and not at all on those of the United States (which had no immediate deployment plans anyway). But the USA made no bones about its intention to continue developing new strategic systems, while Brezhnev was overheard to confirm that the agreement on silo dimensions would not impede Russia's new rockets.[75] Much therefore hung on the extent to which subsequent negotiations could convert the 1972 'Interim Agreement' into a more comprehensive settlement.

The problem was largely one of asymmetries. To offset apparent Soviet conventional force supremacy in Europe, the USA 'needed' to 'extend' deterrence (which made demands on its nuclear forces beyond the requirements of an insular Power). 'Forward-based' systems in Europe could hit the USSR,[76] whereas their Soviet counterparts (though, to West European eyes, more considerable) could not reach the United States. Even within the 'strategic' systems to which the talks were confined, after 1972 the USSR led in overall rocket numbers, throw-weight, etc., the USA in numbers of warheads.

One of the greatest contributions to stability would have been for the Warsaw pact to switch to a *defensive* conventional military posture and strategy. Negotiations did not directly address such topics. In the 1950s there had been proposals (chiefly Polish) for a degree of military disengagement in Central Europe. Eden was quite interested. But the West saw them (not necessarily wrongly) as tending to freeze Germany into a special status, impede West German rearmament, and remove US troops from Europe.[77] Discussion flagged in the 1960s, but detente led to new negotiations. NATO was fortunate that it did so. For in May 1971 the US Administration was shaken by Senator Mansfield's amendment

---

[75] For Brezhnev, Hersh, *The Price of Power*, p. 547; Defense Secretary Laird told the House that 'Just as the Moscow agreements were made possible by our successful action in such programs as Safeguard, Poseidon and Minuteman III, these future negotiations in which we are pledged can only succeed if we are equally successful in implementing such programs as the Trident system, the B-1 bomber' etc. etc. (Smith, *Doubletalk*, p. 340).

[76] As could the Chinese, French and British deterrents (though arguably the complex 1972 deal on Soviet SLBMs made informal allowance for the latter two).

[77] Had both US and Soviet troops gone home, the Americans would, for geographical reasons, have found it harder to return in a crisis.

seeking a mandatory unilateral 50 per cent cut in US forces in Europe. This was eventually defeated, but only after Acheson's mobilisation against it of virtually the entire former foreign and defence policy establishment – and by a helpful speech of Brezhnev's offering negotiations on mutual reductions.[78]

Brezhnev's motives can only be guessed. Presumably he did not wish the controversy to endanger the current negotiations over Berlin or SALT; he also conditioned the force reduction negotiations on his pet plan for a European Security Conference that he saw as ratifying the USSR's major gain from the Second World War, the post-1945 East European order. But the Vienna Conference on the Mutual Reduction of Forces (MBFR) in Central Europe, which opened in 1973, dragged on without any outcome. Kissinger says, 'We succeeded in keeping the issue of mutual force reductions alive to block unilateral American withdrawals by the Congress; at the same time we succeeded in prolonging the negotiation without disadvantageous result'. This assessment may do the USA a certain injustice – in December 1975 it did suggest trading off some of its 'forward-based' nuclear systems (on which the USSR always focussed attention) against Soviet tanks (the chief Western bugbear).[79] However, negotiations were always confined to Vienna, not taken up on a direct back-channel basis between the superpowers; and they got thoroughly bogged down over an inability even to agree on the size of the forces in question.

So the burden of ensuring military stability rested on negotiations over nuclear rather than conventional arms. 1972 saw the limitation of strategic missile numbers. The parties then proceeded to discuss a more comprehensive settlement; but as they were both deploying improved weapons, the longer they took, the worse the problem of ICBM 'vulnerability' would become. 1973 was largely taken up with advancing maximum negotiating positions on both sides, and by internal fighting in Washington. Senator Jackson, a would-be Democratic presidential candidate in 1976, had accepted SALT I even though it allowed the USSR more missiles than the USA;[80] but he carried against the Administration a call for a future treaty

---

[78] Kissinger, *Memoirs*, i, pp. 938–47; Garthoff, *Detente and Confrontation*, pp. 115–16.

[79] Kissinger, *Memoirs*, i, pp. 947–9; R.F. Staar, *USSR Foreign Policies after Detente* (Stanford, 1987 edn) p. 185.

[80] US: 1054 ICBMs + 656 SLBMs = 1710. USSR: 1408 to 1618 ICBMs + 740 to 950 SLBMs = 2358 (*The Military Balance, 1972–3*, pp. 3, 83–5).

'which would not limit the United States to levels of intercontinental strategic forces inferior to the limits provided for the Soviet Union'.[81] The language was vague; but it strengthened reluctance in Washington to accept any formal deal involving a visible US inferiority, i.e. any deal not based on (at least) 'equal aggregates'. Kissinger, on the other hand, conscious that Congress would not support extra defence spending, preferred to trade acceptance of the existing Soviet numerical superiority against limits on its MIRVed rockets that would lessen the prospective threat to US ICBMs. In March 1974, after some difficult meetings, Kissinger did secure Brezhnev's acceptance of the idea of such an exchange. At the ensuing summit Brezhnev seemed ready to bargain, but not on the basis of what Kissinger felt able to offer. So it was agreed merely to pursue the matter further, either on the basis of 'counterbalancing asymmetries' or on that of 'equal aggregates.'[82]

Nixon resigned in August 1974. Kissinger was soon back in Moscow, where the outlines of a deal on either basis were struck and a summit arranged for Vladivostok in November. To avoid trouble with Defense Secretary Schlesinger, President Ford chose to go for equal aggregates. So at Vladivostok he and Brezhnev settled that, by 1985, the two countries would converge on the basis of 2,400 intercontinental launchers (including heavy bombers as well as missiles), of which no more than 1320 should be MIRVed. This achieved formal equality, though the Soviets saw the disregarding of US 'forward-based systems' as a considerable concession. But the levels of MIRVed launchers were higher than those talked of earlier in the year; warhead numbers were free to grow; and the prospect of ICBM vulnerability was not reduced.[83]

It was hoped that the various points left open at Vladivostok would soon be resolved and a treaty signed, but again the early stages of negotiation dragged, and 1975 saw little progress. Kissinger's January 1976 Moscow visit achieved, if not complete agreement, at least substantial progress. The Pentagon, however, was hostile. So, after trying unsuccessfully for an interim agreement, Ford decided that further SALT negotiations would have to wait till after the 1976 election (which he lost).[84] The new Carter administration did not want simply to pick up where the

---

[81] *Keesing's*, 25585.

[82] Kissinger, *Memoirs*, ii, pp. 1006–28, 1153–72; Garthoff, *Detente and Confrontation*, pp. 418–30.

[83] ibid. pp. 442–6; *Keesing's*, 26869.

[84] Garthoff, *Detente and Confrontation*, pp. 446–52, 540–4.

Republicans had stopped. It hoped to unite Kissinger's critics, both conservative and liberal, behind a search for much deeper cuts. So Carter disregarded clear Soviet warnings that any deal would have to be based on both Vladivostok and the formula agreed with Kissinger in January 1976. The new US proposals were turned down flat, and the inexperienced Secretary of State, Cyrus Vance, then gave details in a press conference, thus breaching the convention that negotiating positions were confidential. This angered the Russians. It also provided a benchmark against which SALT critics could test later agreements and find them wanting. However, the negotiating climate improved surprisingly quickly, and by September 1977 the numerical limits under consideration were very close to those ultimately agreed.

That further negotiations took so long was due not only to the worsening international climate, but also to the introduction of important new issues over verification, maximum numbers of warheads per missile, and the testing and deployment of new missile types. In these respects the treaty, finally signed at the June 1979 Vienna summit, represented a distinct improvement on both Vladivostok and the tentative January 1976 agreement. Furthermore, there were to be new negotiations for 'significant and substantial reductions', which might also address the question of forward-based systems. But the deployment of ground-launched cruise missiles, and of mobile ICBMs, was only delayed until 1982. The Carter administration was now lobbying for the NATO decision, finally reached in December 1979, to deploy mobile cruise and Pershing II missiles, albeit subject to the offer of prior negotiations. It also decided to shuttle the new mobile MX missile between multiple protective shelters, although at Vienna the Soviet Defence Minister had (with some justice) declared this mode of deployment to be unverifiable and so incompatible with the treaty.[85]

SALT II can, therefore, be seen only as a limited arms control success. It immediately ran into trouble in the US Senate – the Foreign Relations Committee only narrowly commended it, while Armed Services called nem. con. for 'major changes'. So its chances did not look good in January 1980, when Carter temporarily withdrew it in response to the Soviet invasion of Afghanistan. Thereafter it remained in limbo. Ostensibly both countries continued to observe it. But, in the American perspective, the USSR did not reduce its missile launchers from its current 2,500 to the

[85] Keesing's, 30119 ff.; Garthoff, Detente and Confrontation, pp. 732–5, 741–5, Chap. 23; Brzezinski, Power and Principle, pp. 156–7, Chap. 9.

limits envisaged in the treaty,[86] deployed more than the one permitted new type of missile, and impeded verification by encryption and jamming. In May 1986 Reagan warned that, failing action to remedy 'direct Soviet non-compliance', the USA would no longer adhere to treaty limits – by suppressing old submarines to leave room for bombers carrying air-launched cruise missiles – and after the failed Reykjavik summit, he deliberately exceeded them, though not by much.[87]

Cruise and Pershing missiles in Europe

Arms control was thus at a discount when Reagan took office, but it was nevertheless to occupy a central place in East–West relations for most of the 1980s. Initially the limelight was taken by intermediate range (INF) missiles. The 1979 NATO decision to deploy ground-launched cruise (GLCMs) and Pershing missiles in 1983 had reflected differing and to some extent incompatible concerns. The military wanted actual deployment to enhance its capacity for 'flexible response' to Soviet conventional aggression. But deployment was generally represented as a small counter to the steady build-up of Soviet SS-20 missiles; many governments hoped that if these could be bargained away it would not prove necessary. So NATO also called for US–Soviet negotiations on INF missiles. Brezhnev professed a readiness to talk. Washington was in no great hurry, and both the Carter and Reagan administrations came under pressure from West Germany to move faster.[88] Talks began in November 1981, but the omens were not good. The international climate was promptly soured by the suppression of Solidarity in Poland; and in any case the US and Soviet negotiating positions were poles apart. The US sought the 'zero option' of complete abolition of INF missiles, whereas the Soviets said there was already a rough East–West INF parity that NATO deployment would upset. From this basis they made offers to halt further SS-20 deployment (or even cut existing numbers) provided the USA did not deploy, which the US always rejected as tending only to perpetuate the existing Soviet INF superiority. In July 1982 the negotiators at Geneva jointly formulated a solution, the reduction of SS-20s to 75, to be counterbalanced by 75 US GLCMs

---

[86] 2400 (reducing to 2250 in 1981), of which only 59% could be for MIRVed 'strategic' missiles/ALCM-carrying heavy bombers.

[87] *The Economist*, 18 May 1985 pp. 16–17, 15 June p. 18; Staar, *USSR Foreign Policies after Detente*, pp. 267, 269; *Keesing's*, 34972–4.

[88] *Keesing's*, 30159–60, 31099–31100.

but by none of the more feared Pershings. But neither Moscow nor Washington wished to pursue this.[89]

Moscow indeed had little incentive to do so as long as there was a chance that the huge protest movements would make deployment in Western Europe impossible. There was the encouraging precedent of the neutron bomb. The early 1980s saw in Britain the revival of the Campaign for Nuclear Disarmament (CND, last significant twenty years before) and the opposition Labour Party's conversion to full unilateralism.[90] In 1979 one house of the Dutch parliament had voted against deployment, and in 1980 Belgian political divisions led to the postponement of any decision as to whether to allow it. Anti-nuclear sentiment also grew steadily in the German SPD, though it did not capture the party until 1983 after this had lost office.[91] This upsurge of feeling stemmed chiefly from fear that the NATO deployment might be followed by an arms race spiralling into nuclear war. It also reflected distrust of Reagan, who was believed to take cowboy attitudes and to be ready to countenance a nuclear war that the advent of INF missiles would enable him to confine to Europe.[92] Some observers thought that, in rearming to counter swelling Soviet military power, NATO might have undercut the domestic consensus that sustained Western Europe's Atlantic orientation. Against this background the Soviet and American governments turned increasingly to abuse, and to appealing to Western public opinion with lurid pictures of their opponent's defence programmes and capabilities.

Negotiations deadlocked, the chief new development being the Soviet attempt (from late 1982) to draw the British and French deterrents into the INF talks – which Britain, France and the US all rejected out of hand. But

[89] *Keesing's*, 31979–85, 32461; Garthoff, *Detente and Confrontation*, pp. 1024–5.

[90] The salience of nuclear issues was further enhanced by the British government's decision to start replacing its elderly Polaris SLBMs with the more powerful Trident.

[91] Anti-nuclear sentiment was even stronger in Denmark (though this was not scheduled to accept GLCMs), less marked in Italy (which was), and only slight in France (which was not directly involved but which strongly supported the decision to deploy).

[92] People were alarmed by the new Pentagon policy, formulated in 1980 and 1983, of seeking (as a deterrent) the capability to 'prevail' in a limited but protracted nuclear war. They fastened on to Reagan's 1981 answer to the question of whether a nuclear exchange could be limited, 'I don't honestly know . . . [but] the only defence is, well, you shoot yours and we'll shoot ours . . . And if you had that kind of stalemate, I could see where you could have the exchange of weapons against troops in the field without it bringing either one of the powers to pushing the button' (*Keesing's*, 31430, 31977, 31983).

the course of their domestic politics in 1982–3 made it clear that both Britain and West Germany would continue to be led by governments committed to INF deployment; the installation of missiles began there (and in Italy) in November 1983. The immediate Soviet response was to break off both the INF negotiations and those for a 'Strategic Arms Reduction Treaty' (START), which had begun in mid-1982. But early 1984 saw both the death of Andropov and the softening of US rhetoric; also it was clear that Reagan would be re-elected. So in September Gromyko returned to Washington. Once the election was over it was announced that he and Secretary Shultz would discuss resuming arms control negotiations that should now also extend to space weapons.[93] 'Nuclear and Space' talks restarted in Geneva in March 1985. That month Gorbachev became General Secretary; and a summit with Reagan in Geneva was soon arranged for November 1985.

The 'Strategic Defense Initiative' (SDI), the 1985 Geneva and 1986 Reykjavik summits, and the 1987 INF treaty

Neither leader had much use for arms control as understood in the 1960s and 1970s, the limiting of 'the composition and . . . characteristics of strategic forces to reduce the incentive for surprise attacks to a minimum'. Reagan would, if necessary, have been prepared to conclude a deal on the basis of equal numbers of INF missiles, but much preferred his own 'zero–zero' option. He deplored the idea of basing policy on the idea of 'Mutual Assured Destruction', feeling that the world could not go on indefinitely 'with this kind of weapon [the MX ICBM] on both sides poised at each other without someday some fool or some maniac or some accident triggering the kind of war that is the end of the line for all of us'.[94] So in 1983 he launched the 'Strategic Defense Initiative' (SDI) – research to determine the feasibility of 'rendering the ballistic missile threat impotent and obsolete' – in the hope that it would 'result in real negotiations leading to the total elimination of nuclear weapons'.[95]

---

[93] *Keesing's*, 33347–50.

[94] Henry Kissinger, *Diplomacy* (1995 edn) pp. 714–16, 781.

[95] David Baker, 'The Making of Star Wars', *New Scientist*, 9 July 1987, pp. 36–40; Kiron Skinner, Annelise Anderson, Martin Anderson (eds) *Reagan. A Life in Letters* (New York, 2003) p. 424 – see also Chap. 10.

For their part, the Soviets, in the run-up to the Geneva summit, hinted at a previously unthinkable 50 per cent cut in nuclear weapons. At the conference, Gorbachev confirmed this, but contended that SDI was the chief obstacle to achieving it. On SDI there was no meeting of minds; but the final communiqué endorsed 'the principle of 50 per cent reductions in the nuclear arms of the US and USSR'. In January 1986, the USSR followed up with a 'peace offensive', a 'step-by-step programme for moving towards a nuclear-free world' by the year 2000.[96] However, the two superpowers remained at odds over SDI, which Gorbachev, ignoring considerable past Soviet efforts in the same direction,[97] had represented as aimed 'at achieving a [US] first strike capability by having an anti-missile shield' that would 'defend against a *retaliatory* [Soviet second] strike'.[98]

Relations floundered in 1986, until Gorbachev suddenly invited Reagan to an October summit in Reykjavik, with the aim of bouncing him into dropping SDI. At this Gorbachev began by saying 'the mutual ultimate aim was the total elimination of nuclear weapons . . . This stemmed from what had been agreed upon in Geneva, i.e. that a nuclear war must never be fought.' Agreement was reached in principle on 50 per cent cuts over five years in strategic delivery vehicles (to equal aggregates, which implied slightly greater Soviet reductions), with the intention of eliminating the remainder in a further five.[99] The USSR also dropped its earlier attempts to draw the British and French deterrents into the INF negotiations; and a 'zero–zero' option was settled on for Europe, leaving 100 Soviet missiles in the Far East (facing China and Japan), to be balanced by 100 US ones in Alaska. But Gorbachev made it clear that all this depended on agreement to confine SDI research to the laboratory for ten years, and the talks broke up when Reagan held out for freedom to test (though not to deploy) elements of the system in space. Kissinger suggests that a wiser 'tactic for Gorbachev would have been to propose publishing . . . the [agreed]

[96] Richard Reeves, *President Reagan. The Triumph of the Imagination* (New York, 2005) pp. 281–2, 294; Mikhail Gorbachev, *Memoirs* (1996) pp. 406, 408, 411.

[97] *Keesing's*, 35553; cf. also Stützle, Jasani and Cohen, *The ABM Treaty*, Paper 4 and pp. 192, 198–9, and US administration estimates that the USSR would spend $26bn on *its* SDI in 1985–9 (*Keesing's*, 33915).

[98] Reeves, *Reagan* pp. 286–7 – certainly an anti-missile programme was more likely to protect against limited retaliation after a disarming first strike than against a full initial attack.

[99] For the second period the US formulation was 'offensive ballistic *missiles*', narrower than the Soviet 'strategic offensive *arms*'; but this was not the issue on which talks collapsed.

abolition of missile forces . . . and to refer the issue of SDI testing to the arms control negotiators in Geneva. This would have frozen what had already been agreed, and would surely have produced a major crisis, in both NATO and US–Chinese relations.[100]

To Thatcher, the news of how near the USA had come to agreeing the complete abolition of strategic ballistic missiles came as 'an earthquake . . . The whole system of nuclear deterrence which had kept the peace for forty years was close to being abandoned . . . Somehow I had to get the Americans back onto the firm ground of a credible policy of nuclear deterrence.' She and Mitterrand issued a statement asserting the centrality of such deterrence to Western defence, and she invited herself to Washington in November. Reagan received her at Camp David, going off in a golf cart for private talks, and then approved the communiqué she had brought. This accorded priority to an INF agreement, a 50 per cent cut over five years in US and Soviet 'strategic offensive weapons', and a ban on chemical weapons; it also endorsed the current 'SDI research programme'. But it emphasised 'that NATO's strategy of forward defence [on the inner-German border] and flexible response would continue to require effective nuclear deterrence', and that the proposed INF and other nuclear cuts increased 'the importance of eliminating . . . disparities' in conventional forces. (It also committed the US to continue the SLBM Trident programme and the arrangements to make it available 'to modernize Britain's independent nuclear deterrent'.)[101]

Developments over the next four years followed this blueprint fairly closely. At Reykjavik Gorbachev had in fact been authorised to 'untie' the issues of missile cuts and of SDI, but had chosen not to. In March 1997 he relented, though he still blamed Thatcher 'for frustrating the moves towards the elimination of nuclear weapons which had been discussed at Reykjavik'.[102] In September the US and Soviet Foreign Ministers announced agreement in principle on the INF 'zero option' and on seeking

[100] George P. Shultz, *Turmoil and Triumph. My Years as Secretary of State* (New York, 1993) Chap. 36; Reeves, *Reagan*, Chap. 16; Kissinger, *Diplomacy*, p. 783. Shultz attributed Soviet concessions to SDI, and believed that confining it to the laboratory would have killed the programme, leaving the US 'no leverage to propel the Soviets to continue moving our way'.

[101] Margaret Thatcher, *The Downing Street Years* (1993) pp. 471–3; Paul Sharp, *Thatcher's Diplomacy. The Revival of British Foreign Policy* (Basingstoke, 1997) p. 134.

[102] Gorbachev, *Memoirs*, pp. 349–40; Thatcher, *Downing Street Years*, p. 482 – as a result, much of her March 1987 visit to Moscow was taken up with arguments over nuclear deterrence in the context of Soviet conventional superiority in Europe.

a 50 per cent cut in strategic weapons. Gorbachev still tried to bring in SDI, but desisted when the US refused. Details were tied up at a December summit in Washington, and an INF treaty signed that provided for the verified destruction of all ground-launched missiles with a range of 500–5,500 kilometres (including those in the Far East).[103]

The world hailed it as the most important disarmament treaty ever signed, and it was indeed the first since the 1922/30 Washington and London Naval Treaties to provide for any significant destruction of weapons systems. But it did pose problems for NATO: SACEUR was distinctly unhappy, and both the Pentagon and the West German government had, at various stages, been worried by the disappearance of shorter-range missiles. For this might lead on to a denuclearised Western Europe vulnerable to political pressure stemming from Soviet conventional superiority. The need to replace NATO's ageing short-range Lance missiles brought up the question in a concrete form, and led in 1989 to sharp exchanges between the British and West German governments – the former seeing it as essential for the preservation of flexible response (as opposed to the less credible automatic massive retaliation), whereas the latter had been brought by public opinion to resist it as likely to concentrate the danger of nuclear explosions exclusively on German territory (East and West).

Gorbachev's defence cuts and the Paris Charter 1990: START I and II

Events soon made such disputes obsolete by reducing Soviet conventional superiority. Until 1987 Gorbachev had let defence spending go on rising; he then froze it, and turned actively towards shifting the military away from its traditional offensive orientation towards his new concept of 'reasonable sufficiency'. In 1988 he proposed a pan-European disarmament summit, and in December announced significant unilateral cuts. NATO responded by suggesting East–West reductions to a common ceiling (thus eliminating the Warsaw Pact superiority that it put at 3 to 1 in tanks). In early 1989 the useless MBFR talks were replaced by geographically less restricted ones, and in May the Warsaw Pact agreed to common ceilings in central Europe. Later that year communist rule in Eastern Europe collapsed. Hungary and Czechoslovakia pressed strongly for the withdrawal of Soviet forces, and the USSR chose to make a graceful exit, agreeing to

---

[103] *Keesing's*, 35485, 25601 ff.

leave both countries in a little over a year. Nor did it long stand in the way of German reunion or seek to prevent reunited Germany remaining in NATO (see pp. 427–31). Instead it struck a deal permitting its forces to stay in eastern Germany until 1994. Moreover, so far from increasing its armed forces as a result of taking over the DDR, Germany undertook to cut them from half a million to 370,000 – a level the USSR could have no cause to fear.

Chancellor Kohl had been unhappy with the idea of Germany being singled out for defence constraints. But by mid-1990 it had become clear that a general European system was close to being worked out. US–Soviet negotiations proceeded to set limits for the conventional forces NATO and the Warsaw Pact could deploy in Europe, with sub-limits for the maximum number of tanks allowed to any one country (i.e. the USSR), though with the safety valve that Soviet forces in Asia (to which the USSR was relocating equipment) were not covered. The settlement – incorporated in the November 1990 Charter of Paris – presumed the continued existence of the two alliance systems (albeit 'no longer adversaries'), but there were signs that the Warsaw Pact was falling apart, and its military functions were in fact dissolved in March, its political in July 1991.[104]

The Paris Charter was followed in July 1991 by a Strategic Arms Reduction Treaty (START I) cutting such weapons by about a third.[105] This had been under negotiation ever since the INF treaty, and Reagan had originally hoped to sign it before leaving office; but such was the turmoil in the USSR that the media now saw START rather as a relic from a bygone era of bipolar Soviet–American power parity. Once Yeltsin had replaced Gorbachev, he declared a wish for deep further cuts in nuclear weapons. Bush responded by himself making far-reaching proposals. 1992 proved

---

[104] *Keesing's*, 37267, 37552, 37796–7, 37838, 37979, 1992 R160. In view of the Warsaw Pact's disappearance, the Conventional Forces in Europe Treaty/'Paris Charter' was revised in 1999 on a country-by-country basis. However, NATO states declined to ratify the new treaty until Russia withdrew the troops it maintained in Georgia and Moldova; and in 2007 President Putin threatened to end Russian compliance in protest against the expansion of NATO bases 'near our borders' and, in particular, the proposed siting of elements of a US anti-missile system in the former Pact territory of Poland and the Czech Republic. Putin also questioned the anachronism of restrictions on Russian domestic troop deployment when no such constraints applied within the USA (*The Times*, 27 April 2007, p. 43).

[105] To 1600 launchers and 6000 warheads apiece; there was also tacit agreement to limit to 880 missiles launched from surface ships – *The Independent*, 8 June 1991, p. 10; *The Times*, 30 July, p. 8.

something of an *annus mirabilis* for arms control;[106] and January 1993 saw the signature of the START II treaty under which the number of US and Russian warheads would again be halved, and MIRVs banned. However, it never came into force, since the Duma delayed ratification by way of protest against US policies on Iraq, Kosovo, and NATO expansion. In 2000 the Duma conditioned ratification on US declarations on the ABM treaty which the Congress found unacceptable. Finally in 2002 the US formally withdrew from ABM with a view to deploying a limited system to ward off missiles from 'rogue states' (like North Korea), and Russia denounced SALT.[107] Bush and Putin, who were then on good personal terms, fixed up a replacement (SORT), but the whole subject had by now been eclipsed by US concern over 'weapons of mass destruction' in the hands of 'rogue states' and international terrorists.[108]

[106] Ceilings were agreed in the CSCE for national land forces in Europe. A system of inspections was set in place to verify observance of the 1972 treaty banning biological weapons. And there were to be talks on US–Russian cooperation over a joint anti-missile 'Global Defence System' – *Keesing's*, 39121; *The Independent*, 30 December 1992, pp. 1, 7.
[107] Neither Russia nor, still more, China (with, supposedly, only 130 warheads in 2006), were comfortable with even a limited US ABM programme.
[108] Deployed strategic warheads were to be cut to 1700 by 2012; but they might still be stockpiled, and there were no verification provisions (Wikipedia, SALT II and SORT).

PART 2

East–West relations 1945–1991

CHAPTER 3

The start of the Cold War

Stalin's Popular Front policy

In 1939–40 the Nazi–Soviet Pact had enabled the USSR to take over the Baltic States and eastern parts of Poland and Romania. The 'sovietisation' of captured areas had been assumed in Army writings of the inter-war period,[1] and it was implemented with extreme violence. The German invasion supervened in 1941, but it was always likely that the process would resume in the event of a Soviet victory. Stalin felt deeply the distinctiveness of the socialist and capitalist worlds – 'They will never accept the idea that so great a space [as the USSR] should be red, never, never' (1944); and in 1945 he declared that 'This war is not as in the past; whoever occupies a territory also imposes on it his own social system. Everyone imposes his own system as far as his army has power to do so. It cannot be otherwise.'[2] There were, admittedly, uncertainties and exceptions at the margin, but Stalin's forecast proved substantially accurate.

However, his technique changed. In 1941 foreign communists had been told to reverse course and resume working with other political parties in broad 'anti-fascist' Popular Fronts. From 1943 more detailed instructions went out as to a new strategy for gaining power indirectly. Thus in July 1944 the Polish Central Committee was told to work for a communist-controlled 'government supported by a majority of the people'. This could be achieved 'if there is a sustained and consistent national front policy, if the working class led by our party plays the leading role in the national

[1] P. H. Vigor, *The Soviet View of War, Peace and Neutrality* (1975) pp. 115–16.
[2] Andrei Gromyko, *Memories* (paperback edn, 1989) pp. 126–7; Milovan Djilas, *Conversations with Stalin* (paperback edn) pp. 62, 90.

liberation war, if the reactionary forces can be made to fall apart.'
Excessive radicalism was dangerous, both externally – it would 'make
Poland a bone of contention between the Teheran powers' (UK, US, USSR),
and internally – as entailing 'abandonment on our part of efforts to win
over the majority of the people. It would give rise to a powerful reactionary underground on a wide social base. Our aim, on the contrary, is
to create a situation in which our own forces would be sufficient to
overwhelm the reactionaries.' So the 'correct policy for a national front
requires a series of concessions and compromises which will split our
opponents without fundamentally altering our aim: satisfying the major
demands of the masses and creating a situation favorable to our long-term
plans.'

All this was compatible with the use of force. In March 1945, immediately after Soviet troops had installed a Left coalition government in
Romania, the well-briefed Romanian leaders spoke privately not only of
the operation of this 'National Democratic Front' but also of the need for
'purging, not letting people onto the street who will become active enemies, but possibly sending them into camps': for 'we must not forget that
we also have active enemies whom we must now fell with the state apparatus'. They should not, though, 'begin to talk about our final purpose',
but rather of 'the role of the party in resolving problems in the context of
bourgeois democracy'. Or, as Stalin himself put it to the Bulgarians as late
as September 1946, they should unite 'the working class with the other
toiling masses on the basis of a minimalist programme'; such a party
'would be Communist, but you would have a broader mask for the present
period. This would help you to achieve Socialism in a different way –
without the dictatorship of the proletariat.'[3]

So far our examples have been East European. But the July 1944
instructions for Poland noted that 'these ideas are [also] the basis of the
national fronts in France, Czechoslovakia, Italy, Yugoslavia, etc.' The
March 1944 programme of the Italian Communist Party was framed, in
discussion with Dimitrov,[4] along very similar lines: the PCI should assume
'the character of a mass popular organization, consistently struggling

---

[3] Eduard Mark, *Revolution by Degrees: Stalin's National Front Strategy for Europe,
1941–1947* (Cold War International History Project Working Paper no. 31, esp.
pp. 21–2, 25–30, 33).
[4] Formally the Soviet-controlled Comintern had been dissolved in 1943 (to mislead
Western public opinion), but Georgi Dimitrov continued to send out Moscow's
instructions.

for the freedom and independence of the Italian people, for the genuine interests and hopes of the working class, the peasant masses, the working intellectuals for the rebirth of Italy as a progressive democratic country', pushing for 'Broad agrarian reform . . . and curbing monopolistic trusts', seeking the confiscation of the property of traitors and fascists, but defending 'small and middling properties from ruin and absorbtion by the calamity of speculation'. 'The resemblance,' Mark comments, 'to the program for winning popular support mapped out at the Romanian Communist Party's meeting on 7 March 1945, could hardly be greater – or less coincidental!' And in November 1944 Stalin himself urged conciliatory policies on the French Party, which had been too confrontational towards the Socialists. Without allies, it risked being 'strangled'; so it should seek a front of parties of the Left, workers, intellectuals, and peasants.[5]

There was, though, one inevitable difference. In the East there were few qualms about using force to help the process along, should the communists prove less popular than they had expected[6] – 'Do not take offence, gentlemen,' Gomulka told the non-communist 'London' Poles, 'that we offer you only as many places in government as we think possible . . . We desire an understanding . . . But do not think it is a condition of our existence. Once we have attained power we shall never give it up.'[7]

In Western Europe this was impossible; communists could not go beyond demanding the punishment of fascists and collaborators. The March 1944 PCI programme had stressed support for the Anglo-American-backed Sforza coalition government. Khrushchev tells us that 'Stalin restrained Togliatti. He warned that an insurrection would be crushed by American forces that were occupying Italy and France, much as the English crushed

[5] Mark, *Revolution by Degrees*, pp. 33–5.

[6] East European communists seem greatly to have overestimated their potential support (Mark, *Revolution by Degrees*, pp. 22, 26, 30). Only in Czechoslovakia did they perform well in competitive elections, securing 38% of the national vote, well above any other party (Joseph Rothschild, *Return to Diversity. A Political History of East Central Europe since World War II* (New York, 1993 edn) pp. 89–92. (Communists may also have been popular in parts of Yugoslavia, but Tito eschewed competitive elections.)

[7] June 1945 – Nicholas Bethell, *Gomulka. His Poland and His Communism* (paperback edn, 1972) p. 99. Even in Czechoslovakia the leading pre-war parties were banned as collaborationist; and the communists responded to electoral defeat in Slovakia by securing legislation to curb that country's autonomy.

the [December 1944] Greek insurrection.' Togliatti, indeed, probably needed little restraint. But in September 1946 it seems still to have been felt necessary to repeat the advice to Thorez:

Because the Soviet Union is in the position of having to avoid during a relatively long period participation in a major war, it follows that the French Communist Party should not advance too rapidly and above all must not endeavor to seize power by force since to do so would probably precipitate an international conflict from which the Soviet Union could hardly emerge victorious. The eyes of the United States and England are directed towards France and should the French communists become too openly aggressive, they would bring about a major crisis which might too deeply involve the Soviet Union.[8]

Things, therefore, should move slowly in Western Europe. But still there was a degree of anticipation in Moscow. Khrushchev claims that in late 1944 Stalin had been excited about the prospects once Thorez returned to France; he 'had hopes that the Communists would lead and that a new government headed by the Communists would come to power.'[9] In April 1945 Stalin agreed with Tito 'that socialism was now being achieved in ways different from those of the past'; it 'is possible even under an English king'. Next year he elaborated the idea to the British Labour politician Harold Laski, deftly combining it with his other theme of Anglo-American competition: Europe's future, he suggested, was socialist; Soviet communism and British socialism could collaborate 'in the realisation in all Europe of socialism', albeit not necessarily by the past Soviet route; he hoped for much improved relations with Britain and 'political unity against American imperialism and the international warmongers'.[10]

This, of course, was only aspiration. The 'national front' strategy was designed to lead to it, but no one could say precisely how. Two developments, though, might help the process on. One was early US military withdrawal from Europe. This was quite often forecast by Roosevelt, and seems to have been assumed by Soviet Foreign Ministry planners. In

---

[8] *FRUS*, 1946, v, pp. 472–3.

[9] Jerrold Schechter with Vyacheslav Luchkov (eds), *Khrushchev Remembers. The Glasnost Tapes* (Boston, 1990) [subsequently, *Khrushchev Remembers*, iii] p. 100; the PCF was indeed usually the largest single party during the Fourth Republic.

[10] Djilas, *Conversations with Stalin*, p. 90; Karel Kaplan, 'Il piano di Stalin', *Panorama* (Milan), 26 April 1977 pp. 174–7.

January 1944 Maisky had envisaged a Europe with 'only one great land power – the USSR, and only one great sea power – England', and looked forward to the advent throughout most of continental Europe of governments 'based on the principles of broad democracy in the spirit of the ideas of the Popular Front', some arising naturally, some installed by the Big Three in a cooperation that he thought 'possible, if not always easy'. In such an environment, the USSR might in ten years recover from its war damage and become 'so powerful as not to be threatened by any aggression in Europe or Asia'. Then 'in thirty [years] minimum, fifty maximum', continental Europe, at least, would 'become Socialist, thereby excluding the very possibility of a war in that part of the globe'.[11]

Another route to this distant but ideologically promised land was economic. For it was always assumed both that socialist central planning was intrinsically superior and that, sooner or later, the capitalist world would encounter not merely recessions ('crises of overproduction') but also a 'crisis of the capitalist system of the world economy' analogous to the 1930s Slump.[12] Khrushchev recalls that:

We still had our hopes. Just as Russia came out of World War I, and made the revolution, and established Soviet power, so after the catastrophe of World War II, Europe too might become Soviet. Everyone would take the path from capitalism to socialism.

However, after Potsdam . . . [t]he powerful economy of the United States prevented the devastated economies of the European countries from reaching the point of a revolutionary explosion. Things did not happen the way we expected and predicted in accordance with Marxist-Leninist theory. Unfortunately all these countries stayed capitalist, and we were disappointed.[13]

---

[11] Vladimir Pechatnov, *The Big Three after World War II: New Documents on Soviet Thinking about Post-War Relations with The United States and Great Britain* (CWIHP Working Paper no. 13, 1995) esp. pp. 2–10; Vladislav Zubok and Constantine Pleshakov, *Inside the Kremlin's Cold War. From Stalin to Khrushchev* (Cambridge, Mass., 1996) pp. 28–9.

[12] William Curti Wohlforth, *The Elusive Balance. Power and Perceptions during the Cold War* (Ithaca, NY, 1993) esp. pp. 111–13, 116–18; William Taubman, *Stalin's American Policy. From Entente to Detente to Cold War* (New York, 1982) esp. pp. 135–9 holds that in 1946–7 Stalin displayed considerable personal curiosity as to Western economic conditions and prospects.

[13] *Khrushchev Remembers*, iii, p. 100.

Stalin's wartime move into Eastern Europe

In 1939 Stalin had not only joined Hitler in destroying Poland, but had also murdered most of the Polish officers he then took prisoner. The discovery of mass graves at Katyn in 1943 led to the breaking of relations between the USSR and the Polish government-in-exile in London. But a meeting of minds had never been very likely. The exiled 'government' was understandably anti-Soviet, and in this representative of the majority of Poles; even under heavy British pressure in 1943–4, it was not prepared (at least before the restoration of the Polish state) to concede Stalin's (not unreasonable)[14] border demands. This convinced Stalin – or, more probably, confirmed him in his conviction – that only a communist-dominated Poland would be friendly; and in 1944–5 he moved inexorably to obtain one by installing his own government, the 'Lublin Committee'. As he said at Yalta, while he took Churchill's point 'that for Great Britain the Polish question was [by reason of the 1939 Anglo-Polish treaty] one of honor . . . for the Russians it was a question of both honor and security . . . one of life and death.'[15]

Roosevelt had previously provided little support for Churchill's attempts to broker a deal between the London Poles and Stalin, and had indeed given Stalin the impression that his chief concern lay rather with the ethnic Polish vote in the 1944 US Presidential elections. At Yalta he tried for a genuine coalition government, but settled for a limited expansion of the Lublin Committee whose support rested almost entirely on the Red Army. The new 'Provisional Government of National Unity' thus created should hold 'free and unfettered elections as soon as possible'; but Stalin was allowed to rebuff any proposals for their external supervision.

Already by October 1944 Stalin had been confident enough to assure Polish communists that 'the [Grand] Alliance will not break up over Poland'. Yalta proved him right. Privately Roosevelt accepted it was 'so elastic that the Russians can stretch it all the way from Yalta to Washington without technically breaking it'; 'But it's the best I can do for Poland at this time.'[16] However, if neither Roosevelt nor (later) Truman,

[14] Basically the 1939 border, which was closer to the ethnographic 'Curzon' line (recommended by the Allies in 1919) than had been the border Poland had imposed in 1921.
[15] FRUS, The Conferences at Malta and Yalta 1945, p. 669.
[16] R. Dallek, Franklin D. Roosevelt and American Foreign Policy 1932–1945 (New York, 1979) pp. 507–8, 513–16; Vojtech Mastny, The Cold War and Soviet Insecurity. The Stalin Years (New York, 1996) p. 20.

nor therefore the British, were prepared to contest Russian doings in Poland, the Cold War cannot be understood without remembering that some of these left a very nasty taste – notably the hampering of Western assistance to the anti-German Warsaw rising of 1944,[17] and the arrest in 1945 of leading Polish Home Army figures who had gone to Moscow to discuss the broadening of the Provisional Government. Hitler had been less perturbed by the, in fact even more violent, way in which Stalin had consolidated his sphere of influence in 1939–40.

Poland was not the only country Stalin was determined to secure. When the Red Army reached Bulgaria in 1944, the USSR promptly declared war so as to control its reordering.[18] As for Romania, immediately after the Yalta conference Soviet troops occupied government buildings to force the Prime Minister's dismissal and the establishment of a fellow-travelling government. It would appear that Poland, Romania and Bulgaria consti- tuted a non-negotiable inner ring. They were joined by Yugoslavia when the Red Army's sweep up the Danube installed Tito in Belgrade; but by then his partisans had already secured a clear ascendancy over other local forces, and were, once the Germans had been removed, in a position to realise Tito's stated intention 'to seize power, and to seize it in such a way that the bourgeoisie would never regain it'.[19]

Beyond these countries the position was less clear. For although the Red Army also overran Hungary, communists there were told to hold back in what was apparently known at the top of the Party as the 'Polish trade- off'. The immediate need, it was explained in 1945, was the sovietisation of Poland, so the Hungarians should 'not scare the Anglo-Americans' for the time being. However, the party leader Rakosi soon elaborated, 'if the situation changes – and in years the situation will change – then the line will change too', Stalin's expectation apparently being that a communist takeover would occur, but in 'no less than 10 to 15 years'. Meanwhile, there as elsewhere the Red Army transferred control of the police directly to the communists. A takeover, then, was purposed. But Hungary was less important to the USSR than Poland (or Romania–Bulgaria), and it is *just*

[17] The rising was admittedly anti-communist in seeking to present the advancing Red Army with the *fait accompli* of 'London' Polish control of the capital. But the Soviet reaction – to leave the Germans to crush it – was of a piece with their response to both the Slovak national rising of 1944 and the Prague one of 1945.

[18] Bulgaria had previously been at war with Britain, but not Russia.

[19] Rothschild, *Return to Diversity*, pp. 54–8.

possible that a resolute display of Western interest might have kept it from going the same way.[20]

Much the same can be said of Czechoslovakia. In 1943 President-in-exile Beneš had concluded a friendship treaty that Stalin may have seen as a model not only for Eastern Europe but for countries like France and Italy.[21] In 1945 Beneš returned to Prague with a coalition government within which communists were well represented but not dominant. Again the communists retained control of the police, and also of the resettlement of the lands vacated by the exiled Sudeten Germans. They naturally aspired to power, but initially seem to have hoped, especially after their strong performance in the May 1946 elections, to gain it through the ballot box.

A 'sphere of influence' in Eastern Europe?

In 1939 Stalin and Hitler had reached an explicit spheres of influence agreement. By June 1941 this had broken down. Such agreements, therefore, do not necessarily ensure peace, or even an absence of dispute over their margins.[22] But throughout the Cold War it was accepted in the West that the USSR had, at least *de facto*, a special position in Eastern Europe; and it is often suggested that the Cold War itself could have been avoided, or at least moderated, by an early and formal recognition of the fact.

Neither Churchill nor Roosevelt had any doubt that the USSR was entitled to friendly regimes on its borders – in contrast to Eastern Europe's inter-war anti-Soviet 'cordon sanitaire'. Both were voluble in reassuring Stalin to this effect – though from Stalin's perspective their reassurances were undercut by their promotion of free elections, which he did not trust to produce that result. Also, while both Churchill and (more sporadically)

---

[20] Charles Gati in Melvyn Leffler and David Painter (eds), *Origins of the Cold War. An International History* (1994) esp pp. 179, 197; Taubman, *Stalin's American Policy* p. 78; M. Charlton, *The Eagle and the Small Birds. Crisis in the Soviet Empire from Yalta to Solidarity* (1984) p. 67.

[21] Mastny, *Cold War and Soviet Insecurity*, p. 22.

[22] Hitler worried Stalin by sending troops to Finland (in the Soviet sphere) to safeguard his nickel and iron-ore supplies; Stalin irritated Hitler by going beyond the recovery of ex-Russian Bessarabia to annexations in Bukovina (uncomfortably close to the Romanian oil Germany desperately needed) and, finally, by insistence on the inclusion of Bulgaria within the Soviet security zone and on a base commanding the Black Sea outlets.

Roosevelt were anxious to limit the spread of the USSR's control beyond its borders, both accepted that there were wide areas where it could not be challenged.

Churchill was the more active, both in proposing to limit these areas by pushing Anglo-American troops up through the Balkans (1943) or at least up from the head of the Adriatic, and in seeking to mediate a settlement between Stalin and the Polish government-in-exile. Roosevelt offered little support: the US was less drawn than Churchill to the military strategy of 'indirect approach', preferring to concentrate on landings in France; and from 1943 Roosevelt was anxious to strike up a personal relationship with Stalin, if necessary sidelining Churchill in the process.

Against this background, Churchill decided to reach a deal with Stalin over the Balkans (which, in military terms, fell within the British rather than the US orbit). In the celebrated 'percentages' deal of October 1944 he informally traded Soviet dominance in Romania and Bulgaria for British in Greece; and in December–January he used force to secure the major Greek cities against a communist revolt occasioned by attempts to disarm their resistance movement ELAS. This was clear-cut. Further north, however, the deal did little to avert possible future clashes: it set the Anglo-Soviet balance in Yugoslavia (where Britain had been Tito's chief military supplier) at the unstable figure of 50:50, though Churchill privately accepted that the country was likely to be communist-dominated; and while Stalin initially accepted equal influence over Hungary, Molotov then haggled successfully for a preponderant voice. Nor could the deal address the Polish problems then dominating Allied diplomacy since that country lay exclusively within the Soviet military orbit.

American public rhetoric had been strongly opposed to geopolitical deals, and in clearing with Roosevelt his wish to strike one over Greece and Romania, Churchill was at pains to assure him that it would apply 'only to war conditions' and not 'carve up the Balkans into sheres of influence'. It was on this basis that Roosevelt reluctantly accepted it.[23] Next year he expounded the Yalta agreements to Congress in strongly 'Wilsonian' terms, as spelling:

the end of the system of unilateral action, the exclusive alliances, the spheres of influence, the balances of power, and all the other expedients that have been tried for centuries – and have always failed. We propose to

[23] May–June 1944 – Winston S. Churchill, *The Second World War*, vi (1954) pp. 64–9.

substitute for all these, a universal organization in which all peace-loving nations will have a chance to join.[24]

But this represented less Roosevelt's true appreciation of the outside world than the domestic politics of securing US membership of his new 'United Nations', which he saw as the key to preventing a post-war return to isolationism.

Privately Roosevelt could use very different language, even telling Cardinal Spellman in September 1943 that he was 'better fitted to come to an understanding with Stalin' than was Churchill, since he, like Stalin, was 'a realist', whereas 'Churchill is too idealistic'. He planned 'to make an agreement among the Big Four. Accordingly the world will be divided into spheres of influence: China gets the Far East; the US the Pacific; Britain and Russia, Europe and Africa.' Hence it was 'probable that Communist Regimes would expand, but what can we do about it'; indeed 'Austria, Hungary and Croatia would fall under some sort of Russian protectorate'.[25] A year later Roosevelt struck his Moscow ambassador, Averell Harriman, as 'having little interest in Eastern European matters except as they affected sentiment in America'.[26] However, he feared that extension of Soviet or British control 'to other than military fields' might lead to quarrels between them and/or to the alienation of US public opinion – he supposedly inspired a newspaper report that the British had been told, after their actions in Greece, 'that the [internationalist] mood can change as mercurially as the English weather if the American people once get the idea that this war . . . [is] just another struggle between rival imperialisms.'[27]

In practice, Roosevelt told Senate leaders, the idea of 'spheres of influence . . . kept coming up because the occupying forces had the power in the areas where their arms were present and each knew that the others could not force things to an issue.' It 'was obviously impossible' to break with the Russians over Eastern Europe, so 'the only practicable course was to use what influence we had to ameliorate the situation'.[28] This he did

[24] Dallek, *Roosevelt and American Foreign Policy*, p. 520.
[25] Robert I. Gannon, *The Cardinal Spellman Story* (New York, 1962) pp. 222–4.
[26] November 1944; Roosevelt also said that, though much concerned with the Pacific, 'he considered the European questions . . . so impossible that he wanted to stay out of them as far as practicable, except for the problems involving Germany' (Dallek, *Roosevelt and American Foreign Policy*, p. 503).
[27] Dallek, *Roosevelt and American Foreign Policy*, p. 505.
[28] 11 January 1945 – Thomas Campbell and George Herring (eds) *The Diaries of Edward Stettinius . . . 1943–1946* (New York, 1975) p. 214.

with the Yalta 'Declaration on Liberated Europe' and its promise of free elections (though its other purpose was to dispel American doubts about their Allies and so help build support for UN membership). Hopefully such actions would stop wartime arrangements hardening into 'exclusive' spheres.

This distinction between open and 'exclusive' spheres was often elaborated in the State Department, and has been seen as underlying much of US diplomacy towards the USSR in the second half of 1945. 'It is important', ran a memorandum much of which Secretary Byrnes incorporated into a speech on 31 October:

to distinguish between a fair and reasonable definition of legitimate influence on the part of a great power . . . and the illegitimate extension of such interest in the direction of domination and absolute control. In this sense we have an excellent precedent in our present relation with the Latin American countries. While we do claim the right of the United States to have a guiding voice in a certain limited sphere of foreign relations . . . we do not attempt . . . to dictate their internal life or to restrict their intercourse with foreign nations except in that limited sphere . . . We would, for example, oppose and even forbid the conclusion of military and political alliances between a Latin American state and a European or Asiatic power. We do not . . . attempt to prevent normal trade, cultural exchange, and other normal international intercourse. With reference to the country [sic] whose geographical location makes them of especial interest to the Soviet Union our policy should be guided by the same considerations . . . we should continue to make plain to the Soviet Union that we do not seek to deny their legitimate interest or influence in these areas . . . [citing] the fact that there was no opposition on the part of the United States to the Soviet-Czech Treaty . . . [and even offering] a commitment that the United States would . . . actively discourage any attempt on the part of those states to . . . join combinations of a political or military nature to which the Soviet Union was not a party.

. . . [But] we should continue to oppose any extensions of this [legitimate] influence into illegitimate fields leading towards the establishment of a rigidly and exclusively Soviet-controlled bloc. The chief difficulty . . . is that from all our indications the Soviet mind is incapable of making the distinction between legitimate and illegitimate influence . . . between influence and domination, or between a friendly government and a puppet government. The only hope of a solution is is the constant

*endeavor to break down these identifications in the mind of the Soviet
Government . . . to demonstrate . . . that they will receive American
cooperation and help to the degree to which they are prepared to limit
their influence to the legitimate sphere, and . . . that such help and
cooperation will not be forthcoming . . . in any attempt to translate
a legitimate influence into domination and exclusion.*[29]

In this perspective, what the United States came to object to was not Soviet
pre-eminence in Eastern Europe, but the ways in which the USSR chose
to exercise this pre-eminence and the possibility these suggested that its
concerns extended beyond mere security.

Stalin and the post-war world

In January 1945 Stalin told Dimitrov that 'The crisis of capitalism revealed
itself in the division of capitalists into two factions – one fascist, the other
democratic . . . Now we side with one . . . and in the future [we will also
turn] against this faction.'[30] He could never be sure that such an approach
would not be reciprocated. Throughout the war he had displayed ideologically ingrained suspicion that Britain and America had plans to join
Germany against the USSR; it burst out again in March–April 1945, when
feelers to arrange a German surrender in Italy led Stalin to protest – to
Roosevelt's fury – against what he saw as a deal to 'open the front and permit the Anglo-American troops to advance to the east' while 'the Germans
continue the war with Russia'.[31] This particular spat passed; and, despite
some tough bargaining, the USSR emerged from the Potsdam Conference
not dissatisfied. But Stalin still sometimes regretted the collapse of his earlier German alignment; 'he was in the habit of repeating, "Ech, together
with the Germans we would have been invincible." '[32] So any Soviet policy
of Big Three cooperation was bound to be fragile, since it sprang not from
conviction but from wildly oscillating calculations of expediency.

[29] The memorandum was written by Byrnes's special assistant on the Secretary's official
notepaper – Eduard Mark, 'Charles E. Bohlen and the Acceptable Limits of Soviet
Hegemony in Eastern Europe: A Memorandum of 18 October 1945', *Diplomatic
History*, iii (1979) esp. pp. 207–11; Mark extends his argument in 'American Policy
toward Eastern Europe and the Origins of the Cold War, 1941–1946: An Alternative
Approach', *Journal of American History*, lxi (1981–2) pp. 313–36.
[30] January 1945 – Zubok and Pleshakov, *Inside the Kremlin's Cold War*, p. 37.
[31] Churchill, *Second World War*, vi, p. 392.
[32] Svetlana Allilueva, *Only One Year* (1969) p. 369.

Nevertheless, it seems that Stalin anticipated continued cooperation on a Three Power basis, for which he had publicly called in November 1944. For, as Molotov put it years later, 'It was to our benefit to stay allied to America.'[33] Only so could Moscow achieve goals that lay beyond the reach of its armed forces, like reparations from western Germany, a mandate for Tripolitania, and any chance of influence in Japan or of the spread of communism in Western Europe.[34]

Moreover, the USSR wanted help with post-war reconstruction. It had convinced itself that this would be forthcoming since it was at least equally in the US interest – Molotov's January 1945 request for $6 billion credits was worded as an act of kindness: 'Having in mind the repeated statements of American public figures concerning the desirability of receiving ... large Soviet orders for the postwar and transition period, the Soviet Government considers it possible to place orders on the basis of long term credits'.[35]

Lastly Moscow looked to the 'inevitable intensification of economic competition ... between the United States and Great Britain'.[36] There might, of course, be temporary Anglo-American capitalist alignments, to which the proper response was firmness. But expectation that such a capitalist alignment could not last was deeply rooted in the Leninist doctrine of imperialism, and predominated in Moscow until 1947. Moves were sometimes made to hasten the Anglo-American breach: in May 1943 ambassador Maisky suggested to London, apparently not for the first time, that the USSR and Britain should regard their alliance as aimed chiefly at the US, an imperialist power dangerous to both. Maisky saw Britain as a country of 'conservative imperialism' challenged by the 'dynamic imperialism'

---

[33] Albert Resis (ed.) *Molotov Remembers. Inside Kremlin Politics. Conversations with Felix Chuev* (Chicago, 1993) p. 51.

[34] Mark argues, indeed, that Stalin 'wanted *both* ['communist revolution in Europe' and 'continued cooperation with his allies'], and the strategy of the national front was the vehicle for temporarily harmonizing goals that were ultimately in conflict. Stalin did not adopt this course merely because he wished to avoid the adverse consequences of an early break with the Western powers. He *needed* the United States and Britain if he was to achieve, in the shorter term, certain important goals of his foreign policy' – *Revolution by Degrees*, pp. 7, 11 ff, 42–6.

[35] *FRUS 1945*, v, p. 942.

[36] This, Litvinov felt, should prompt them both to maintain 'the best possible relations with us in order to preclude our protracted conjunction with one of them against the other' – Pechatnov, *The Big Three after World War II*, p. 11; the passage was underlined, apparently approvingly, by Molotov.

of the US, and in 1944 forecast that eventually 'interests in the struggle for global positions will push Britain to the Soviet side'. As late as December 1946 reports from London claimed that 'a broad, practically national bloc for agreement with the Soviet Union is possible', and that 'Soviet diplomacy has in England practically unlimited possibilities'.[37] Molotov himself apparently inclined in this direction. For in September 1946 he guided his Washington ambassador, Novikov's, analysis of US foreign policy. '[S]triving for world supremacy', America sought 'to impose the will of other countries on the Soviet Union.' Financial and military links with Britain, and close policy coordination at 'recent international conferences' were underpinned by a spheres of influence agreement covering India and points east; but this did *not* extend to the Middle East, where the US was interested in competing with Britain for oil, not in supporting it. Moreover current Anglo-American relations 'are plagued with great internal *contradictions* and cannot be lasting'; 'It is quite possible that the Near East will become *a center of Anglo-American contradictions* that will explode the agreements now reached between the United States and England.'[38] By contrast, though the politically important economist Eugen Varga also highlighted 'the Anglo-American contradiction', he saw Britain as the more immediate adversary, one that would seek to form a 'West European bloc' against *both* the USSR and the US. In his view, the US would content itself with Latin America and the Far East, and the Soviet Union should cultivate good relations with it so as to curb Britain.[39]

In practice, the USSR thought in 1945–7 that it could await developments, unleashing press barrages first against Britain, then, during the 1946–7 winter, switching them on to the USA while extending Britain the offer of a military alliance. But though the 'contradictions' the Russians had perceived were not imaginary, they ran less deep than they had thought. Attempts to exploit them backfired, consolidating in 1946–7 a US readiness to back and underpin British positions in a way that reversed

[37] Mark, *Revolution by Degrees*, p. 13; Zubok and Pleshakov, *Inside the Kremlin's Cold War*, p. 29; Wohlforth, *Elusive Balance*, pp. 70–1, which notes that in December 1946–January 1947 Attlee was indeed arguing for an attempt at an Anglo-Soviet settlement [below, pp. 111–12].

[38] 'The Novikov Telegram', *Diplomatic History*, xv (1991) pp. 527–37 (with Molotov's underlinings), and 'Commentary' by Viktor Mal'kov, pp. 554–8. The contradictions were: British financial dependence; the conditions this created 'for the penetration by American capital of the British Empire'; and the likely reorientation towards the US of the British Dominions and the Arab client states.

[39] Wohlforth, *Elusive Balance*, pp. 68–9.

Roosevelt's policy of not 'ganging up' on Stalin. One result was the 1947 offer of 'Marshall Aid', which prompted a hasty rethink of Soviet policies and the proclamation instead of 'two camps', the 'imperialist and anti-democratic camp headed by the United States, and the anti-imperialist and democratic camp headed by the Soviet Union'. Even so, in 1952 Stalin restated his belief that 'first capitalist Britain, then capitalist France will ultimately be forced [by economic problems] to wrest themselves from the USA's embrace and enter into conflict with the USA.'[40]

Stalin's pursuit of incremental gains

If cooperation between the Big Three was to continue, not only Stalin and Molotov, but also semi-detached advisers like Litvinov, assumed it would rest on acceptance of spheres of influence. So in 1945 Stalin rejected the idea that the Red Army should have extended its westwards advance; and he discountenanced Yugoslav wishes to take parts of Italy and Austria.[41] But he was not always so restrained.

In 1939–41 Stalin had been aligned with Hitler in an explicit spheres of influence deal. He was also, at least from the time of Hitler's defeat of France in mid-1940, fearful that Germany might turn East. But neither explicit understandings nor fear precluded – and the latter may even have prompted – the going beyond the 1939 Pact in search of minor territorial gains in Eastern Europe that threw Romania into the arms of Germany, and that made impossible the alliance Germany *appeared* to be seeking in November 1940. Most of these gains Stalin had secured by 1945, but one remained outstanding – a base commanding the Black Sea straits.

From 1943 Stalin seems again to have followed a policy of seeking to pocket *incremental* gains, especially in the immediate vicinity. As he explained in December 1945 to Chiang Kai-shek's Soviet-educated son, 'it was his intention to strengthen himself everywhere that he could in the domination of his adjacent areas and to attain as many strategic positions as was possible at this time.'[42] Fear-induced demonstrative stubbornness may again have been one reason. But Molotov was later to suggest another:

---

[40] Wohlforth, *Elusive Balance*, pp. 69–71, 85.

[41] Mastny, *Cold War and Soviet Insecurity*, p. 23.

[42] Averell Harriman and E. Abel, *Special Envoy to Churchill and Stalin* (1976) p. 540. The USA, too, was a great collector of strategic positions (see Melvyn Leffler, *A Preponderance of Power. National Security, the Truman Administration, and the Cold War* (Stanford, CA, 1992) pp. 56–9), but in the less sensitive form of bases and islets.

In his last years Stalin got puffed up a bit . . . I had to demand exactly
what Miliukov had demanded – the Dardanelles. Stalin said, 'Go ahead,
press them for joint possession!' Me: 'They won't allow it.' 'Demand it!'

In fact, Stalin should have gathered from the Potsdam Conference that,
though he would have had Western cooperation in revising the Montreux
Convention on passage through the Black Sea straits, territorial and
military demands on Turkey would be resented.[43]

'Of course,' Molotov later observed, 'you had to know when and
where to stop. I believe in this respect Stalin kept well within the limits.' In
one sense, yes: unlike Hitler, who said that the only gambler's call he ever
made was the all-or-nothing 'go bank', Stalin never, after 1945, pushed
to the point of entangling the USSR in war; and there are clear cases of
caution. Thus Bulgaria often pressed for the re-annexation of the disputed
Greek territory that would give access to the Aegean; but 'Raising this
issue would have caused trouble right at the beginning of the peace . . .
[Molotov] consulted with the Central Committee and was told not to
bring it up, that the time was not right . . . It was desirable, but not timely.'
Similarly, while Zhdanov advocated making Finland 'socialist', Molotov
opposed it; 'I believe we acted correctly. If we had crossed a certain line, we
would have gotten mixed up in utter adventurism.'[44]

But if Stalin was careful not to cross this 'line', he was also anxious to
locate it to see how far he could safely push. On Turkey, the Soviet agent
Donald Maclean was asked to find out 'exactly how far the West would go
to defend this part of the world.' Later, over the Berlin blockade (below,
pp. 144–6), Stalin told his subordinates that if the USA tried to push a
relief convoy through overland, the Red Army should resist; but if it
seemed about to mount a general attack, he would himself decide on the
Soviet response. 'That,' Kissinger concludes, 'was the point at which he
would presumably have settled.'[45] Moreover, short of the 'line', Stalin was
readier to probe than is sometimes imagined. He sought to improve the
Soviet position in the Caucasus: pointing to a map of the USSR's new

[43] *Molotov Remembers. Conversations with Felix Chuev*, pp. 73, 74; Miliukov had been
Foreign Minister in Russia's 1917 Provisional Government. For Western concern over
Turkey at Potsdam, see *FRUS, Conference of Berlin (Potsdam) 1945*, pp. 256–8, 302–5,
1439–40.
[44] *Molotov Remembers. Conversations with Felix Chuev*, pp. 59, 65–6; cf. also p. 10.
[45] Yuri Modin, *My Five Cambridge Friends* (paperback edn) p. 145; Henry Kissinger,
Diplomacy (1995 edn) p. 436 (recording a 1989 conversation with Gromyko).

frontiers, he declared himself pleased with those in the north, west and east: '"But I don't like our border right here!" Stalin said and pointed south to the Caucasus.' The result was what proved to be markedly counterproductive pressure on Turkey and Iran in 1945–6. At the same time, he was demanding a UN trusteeship over Libya, an area of British rather than Soviet interest. And in mid-1947, when Zhdanov (presumably following established Kremlin policy) declined to arm the communist insurrection in Greece, Stalin overruled him.[46]

No doubt Stalin was confident that, in all these cases, he could draw back if necessary. But one of his great weaknesses was his insensitivity to the effects his actions were having on other leaders. This had been the case in late 1940 with respect to Hitler. It was still more so after 1945 with regard to the West. Stalin probably assumed that international politics – indeed nearly all politics, for his domestic suspicions were almost as great – was a Hobbesian struggle in which leaders were basically enemies, whether transparent (like Churchill who, he told the Yugoslavs in 1944, 'will pick your pocket of a kopeck if you don't watch him'), or more devious (like Roosevelt, who 'dips in his hand only for bigger coins'). In such an environment, incessant competition was only to be expected – 'They steal our dispatches, we steal theirs.'[47] Accordingly, throughout the wartime alliance, the USSR maintained major intelligence operations against both Britain and the US, and was convinced that they were doing likewise.[48] All this, Stalin probably felt, need be no bar to cooperation as long as there was a congruence of interests; and this was, up to a point, true. But this congruence waned with the ending of hostilities, leaving only the perception of antagonism. On Stalin's side, this had never been deeply submerged – witness his suspicions of Western collusion in the bitter German resistance to the advancing Red Army. And it was to be fully revived by more forceful American policies in 1945, especially against the background of the US nuclear monopoly. Churchill's suspicions, though more deeply buried, also had an ideological basis; and they too revived quickly. This was less obviously true of Roosevelt, Truman, Attlee or even

[46] *Molotov Remembers. Conversations with Felix Chuev*, pp. 8, 74; Zubok and Pleshakov, *Inside the Kremlin's Cold War*, pp. 96–7, 128.

[47] Djilas, *Conversations with Stalin*, pp. 61, 67.

[48] Christopher Andrew and Vasili Mitrokhin, *The Sword and the Shield. The Mitrokhin Archive and the Secret History of the KGB* (New York, 1999) Chaps 7, 8. For disbelief that SIS was not recruiting against the USSR as many agents as against Germany, see ibid. pp. 113, 119–21.

Bevin. But Roosevelt died before the end of the war, and Stalin's tendency to probe did much to alarm Truman and Bevin. For such a degree of competitive pressure lay outside the prevalent style of dealings between major Western states, and seemed more reminiscent of Hitler (who had not known where to stop). Stalin, admittedly, was not quite classed in this light – at least until 1950 he was not expected to seek to move West by force. But by 1946 his probes were not seen as subject to any other self-restraint.

Approaches to Stalin – Churchill, Roosevelt, Truman

By 1943 Churchill had become acutely conscious of the USSR's likely post-war strength. Cromwell, he mused, had established France as a great power by supporting it against a declining Spain: 'Do you think that will be said of me? Germany is finished, though it may take some time to clean up the mess. The real problem now is Russia. I *can't* get the Americans to see it.'[49] Since he could not, he concluded the 1944 'percentages deal' that at least reserved Greece for the British sphere, and, that December, used force to keep the communists there from power.

Stalin took this more calmly than much Western liberal opinion. And after the Yalta Conference, Churchill continued in some moods to project confidence: 'Poor Neville Chamberlain believed he could trust Hitler. He was wrong. But I don't think I am wrong about Stalin.' However, this optimism, never absolute, was soon shaken by subsequent Soviet behaviour; and by late March Churchill was appealing to Stalin 'to come to a good understanding about Poland with the Western Democracies and not to smite down the hands of comradeship and future guidance of the world which we now extend.' Ideally, too, he felt that such appeals should be reinforced by:

a firm blunt [Anglo-American] stand . . . in order that the air may be cleared . . . I believe this is the best chance of saving the future. If they [the Soviets] are ever convinced that we are afraid of them and can be bullied . . . then indeed I shall despair of future relations with them and much else.[50]

---

[49] John W. Wheeler-Bennett and Anthony Nicholls, *The Semblance of Peace. The Political Settlement after the Second World War* (1972) p. 290.

[50] Dalton's diary, 23 February 1945 (cited by Martin Kitchen, 'Winston Churchill and the Soviet Union during the Second World War', *Historical Journal*, xxx (1987) p. 433);

In the spring and summer of 1945 Churchill was looking, albeit not quite consistently, for a bargain with the USSR – struck from a position of Western strength, but a prelude to future friendship rather than confrontation:

We have several powerful bargaining counters on our side, the use of which might make for a peaceful agreement.

First, the Allies ought not to retreat from their present positions until we are satisfied about Poland and also about the temporary character of the Russian occupation of Germany, and the conditions to be established in the . . . Russian-controlled countries in the Danube Valley . . .

Secondly, we may be able to please them about the exits from the Black Sea and the Baltic as part of a general settlement.

All these matters can only be settled before the United States Armies in Europe are weakened. If they are not settled before . . . the Western World folds up its war machines, there are no prospects of a satisfactory solution and very little of preventing a third World War.[51]

At the 1814–15 Vienna Congress a similar, indeed more drastic, confrontation had produced mutual recognition of danger, concessions, and harmony. But then Tsar Alexander had been a man of genuine goodwill; Stalin was not. At most he might have been constrained to greater caution, but also to (yet) greater paranoia. And his choice of response would have depended on how he assessed the credibility of such a Western stance. In 1941, faced with huge German troop concentrations, Stalin appears to have envisaged an ultimatum from Hitler followed by negotiations, then, after the invasion had started, to have contemplated buying it off with major concessions along the lines of the 1918 peace of Brest–Litovsk.[52] On this analogy, a really hard Western line (had such been conceivable) *might* have enforced Soviet withdrawal from Eastern Europe; it could hardly have led to the renewed partnership for which Churchill was still hoping.

Martin Gilbert, *Winston S. Churchill*, vii, *1941–1945* (1986) p. 1280. Churchill also said, on 28 February, that he did not mean to be 'cheated over Poland, not even if we go to the verge of war with Russia' (ibid. p. 238).

[51] To Eden, 4 May 1945 – ibid. p. 1330.

[52] For the Kremlin's expectation of an ultimatum followed by negotiations, not of a simple attack, see Gabriel Gorodetsky, *Grand Delusion. Stalin and the German Invasion of Russia* (1999) esp. pp. 310, 312–13; for overtures for a second Brest–Litovsk, Christopher Andrew and Oleg Gordievsky, *KGB. The Inside Story of its Foreign Operations from Lenin to Gorbachev* (1990) p. 220.

In any case the pressures for which Churchill was arguing in 1945 seem fairly limited. A refusal to withdraw Western troops to their agreed German occupation zones would in the short term have cost the USSR little, a refusal to accept Stalin's interpretation of Poland's western boundary still less. There may, though, have been more substance to Churchill's claim that a Western liberation of Prague, which would have been easy, 'might make the whole difference to the post-war situation in Czechoslovakia and might well influence that in nearby countries'. Certainly Beneš, who had earlier largely given up on the West and sought arrangements with Stalin, was overjoyed when news arrived that US troops had entered the country; 'Judging from the expression in his eyes, he was already largely envisaging the beneficial consequences.'[53]

Whatever its abstract merits, there were two reasons why Churchill's policy of seeking an East–West settlement through showdown was unlikely to be adopted. For Britain to suppress the 1944 communist rising in liberated Greece had been unpopular enough. To turn directly on the USSR would have caused a domestic explosion, since Russia had been built up as a gallant ally that had done most of the war's fighting, while the darker side of Soviet doings in Eastern Europe had been deliberately kept from the Western publics. In any case, as Churchill realised, Britain alone was not strong enough. US action would have been necessary, and it was not forthcoming. One of Roosevelt's chief goals at Yalta had been to ensure that, after Germany's defeat, the USSR would enter the war against Japan. This wish did not change until July 1945; then, with Japan's August decision to surrender, US public opinion turned to demobilisation and getting 'the boys' home, not to new foreign crusades.

Moreover, Churchill's approach cut across those of both Presidents Roosevelt and Truman. Whether from a preference for playing things by ear, or because he was unsure what the US public would then endorse, Roosevelt had always been anxious to avoid addressing post-war questions until after the end of hostilities. He had, too, tried, since 1943, to manage Stalin by personal diplomacy, a precondition of which was that Stalin should not be given the impression that Britain and the USA were 'ganging up' on him. The British, Roosevelt remarked in March 1945, were 'perfectly willing for the United States to have a war with Russia at

---

[53] Churchill to Truman, 30 April 1945 (ibid. p. 1322); Edward Taborsky, *President Edvard Beneš between East and West, 1938–1948* (Stanford, CA., 1981) p. 212, citing his own diary. The US chose not to liberate Prague; but Czechoslovakia did manage, later in 1945, to arrange a simultaneous withdrawal of Soviet and US troops.

any time,' and 'to follow the British programme would be to proceed toward that end.'[54] Whether Roosevelt would have continued with this approach, had he lived, nobody can say. Very possibly not – 'we can't do business with Stalin,' he burst out later that month, 'He has broken every one of the promises he has made at Yalta.' But though deeply angered by Stalin's suspicions, his final message to Churchill still sought 'to minimize the general Soviet problem as much as possible because these problems, in one form or another, seem to arise every day and most of them straighten out . . .' even if it also concluded, 'We must be firm, however, and our course thus far is correct.'[55]

After Roosevelt's death, President Truman took advice both from Roosevelt aides (like Harry Hopkins) who sought to continue to cajole Stalin, and from the Ambassador in Moscow (Harriman) and the State Department, whose views were a good deal closer to Churchill's. What gradually emerged was the (largely correct) view that agreements with the USSR 'had so far been a one way street, and that could not continue'; 'we could not, of course, expect to get 100% of what we wanted but . . . on important matters . . . we should be able to get 85 percent'. The upshot was a policy of adhering to past agreements (as the US understood them) – not, as Churchill recommended, of refusing to do so until the USSR also complied – but also of insisting that the Soviets did likewise: in a celebrated interview, Truman told Molotov 'that what we wanted was that you live up to your Yalta Agreement as to Poland. We will live up strictly to ours . . .' Molotov declared (implausibly for a subordinate of Stalin) that he had never been so talked to in his life, Truman's response being, 'Carry out your agreements and you won't get talked to like that.'[56] From August this was coupled with a policy of seeking to stop the USSR expanding beyond past agreements, at least in the Far East (which Washington tended to view as an American sphere). Accordingly Soviet annexation of southern Sakhalin and the Kuriles was accepted, as agreed at Yalta, but not an occupation zone in northern Japan. In Korea, joint Soviet–US occupation was agreed, but 'with the [dividing] line as far north as possible'. In China

---

[54] Walter Millis (ed.) *The Forrestal Diaries. The Inner History of the Cold War* (1952) p. 53.
[55] *Semblance of Peace*, pp. 297–8; Roosevelt to Churchill, 12 April 1945 (Gilbert, *Churchill*, vii, p. 1289). Roosevelt deeply resented Stalin's charges that the Bern negotiations for the surrender of German forces in Italy represented an anti-Soviet move.
[56] Harry S. Truman, *Year of Decisions 1945* (1955) pp. 79–82, 85; *FRUS 1945*, v, pp. 233, 253.

the USA airlifted government troops, and even committed its own, so as to preclude communist seizure of key cities (ii, pp. 94–5, 152, 195).

The Far East, however, still appeared to be something of a sideshow, and Stalin was, in fact, not unhappy with his gains there (below pp. 156–7). What chiefly mattered in the summer of 1945 was, on the one hand, East-Central Europe, and, on the other, relations between the 'Big Three'. In May Truman had sent the pro-Soviet Hopkins to Moscow to 'straighten things out', hoping that 'by the time he met with the Big Three . . . most of our troubles would be out of the way.' Stalin responded with token concessions on Poland (though not to the point of releasing the Home Army emissaries he had arrested), and broke the deadlock on voting arrangements at the United Nations (something to which the US then attached extreme importance). In this context, a tripartite summit was fixed for Potsdam in July, with Truman declaring that 'the Russians are just as anxious to get along with us as we are with them'.

The Potsdam Conference and the atom bomb

The Potsdam Conference itself was a qualified success. Further arrangements were made for Soviet entry into the war against Japan, though the US was coming to set less store by this. There was to be a Soviet–US–British–French Council of Foreign Ministers to prepare peace treaties, and Four Power arrangements (though they ultimately proved unworkable) for the overall government of Germany. Stalin gave almost no ground in the face of US–British pressure for externally supervised and competitive elections in Eastern Europe. But the chief sticking points related to Poland's western border, and to reparations from Germany. There had been ambiguity as to whether the border should in the south follow the eastern or the western river Neisse. Stalin had unilaterally given the Poles the latter, along with the mouth of the Oder.[57] The British wished to use the issue to force a settlement over Poland's political development. On reparations, Stalin sought acceptance of the $10 billion Soviet demand he had floated at Yalta, with guaranteed deliveries from western Germany and ideally Four Power control of the Ruhr, the former industrial powerhouse in the British zone. Eventually the US Secretary of State, Byrnes, solved these problems by negotiating a package deal with the Russians, then bringing the British on board. Poland would *de facto* retain the western Neisse (the 'Oder–Neisse line'), and the US and UK undertook to

[57] See the map in *Semblance of Peace*, p. 336.

support this at a peace conference. As for reparations, each occupying power would take them chiefly from its own zone; but 25 per cent of plant dismantled in the West should be transferred to the USSR, three-fifths of it in return for food and raw materials from the Soviet zone and Poland.

At one level Stalin was not displeased: 'In general,' he told Dimitrov, 'these decisions are beneficial to us.' He thanked Byrnes warmly for arranging the deal; and the message given that August to East European communists was that Potsdam amounted to a Western acknowledgement of having 'lost eastern Europe and the Balkans'.[58] But if Truman had hoped to convince Stalin 'that we are "on the level" and interested in peace and a decent world, and had no purposes hostile to them', he failed.[59]

The first test of the atom bomb occurred during the conference, and Stalin was then told of the bomb's existence. In theory, of course, he already knew, for the project had been deeply penetrated by Soviet intelligence. The USSR had conducted its own research since 1943, and was, in its capture of Berlin, extremely anxious to seize the uranium stocks and equipment there. But it was probably not until mid-1945 that Stalin realised the full implications; in August he told his scientists, 'Hiroshima has shaken the whole world. The balance has been destroyed. Provide the bomb ["in the shortest possible time"] – it will remove a great danger for us.' Meanwhile, correctly anticipating increased US pressure, he decided to act stubborn: 'using America's monopoly, in fact America's and Britain's, they want us to accept their plans on questions affecting Europe and the world. Well, that's not going to happen.'[60]

Romania: London (September) and Moscow (December 1945) Foreign Ministers Councils

In all this, of course, there was an element of action and reaction. Stalin was alarmed by the detonation of the atom bomb. Equally the US was encouraged: it had, Byrnes remarked, 'given us great power, and . . . in the final analysis, it would control.'[61] In the Far East the US moved quickly

[58] Zubok and Pleshakov, *Inside the Kremlin's Cold War*, p. 37; Mastny, *Cold War and Soviet Insecurity*, p. 22.
[59] Truman to Joseph Davies – cited in Kissinger, *Diplomacy*, p. 433.
[60] David Holloway, *The Soviet Union and the Arms Race* (1984 edn) pp. 17–20; Gromyko, *Memories*, p. 141.
[61] 29 July 1945 (John Lewis Gaddis, *The United States and the Origins of the Cold War 1941–1947* (New York, 1972) p. 264).

to fill the gap left by Japan's sudden surrender. In Europe, Truman had, at Potsdam, refused to recognise the Soviet-installed governments of Romania, Bulgaria and Hungary until American journalists were allowed to observe what was going on there. In August he went further, pronouncing that Bulgaria, Romania and Hungary were not to be in the sphere of interest of any one power; and Byrnes told the US representative in Bucharest to let it be known 'that this Govt. hopes to see established in Rumania, through the efforts of the Rumanians themselves, and if necessary with the assistance of the three Allied Govts as provided in the Crimea Declaration on Liberated Europe, a more representative regime.' Encouraged, the King sought the resignation of the government imposed on him after Yalta, and appealed to the Big Three for help in constituting a more representative one. But the Prime Minister refused to resign; and by 25 August Byrnes drew back: 'We hope no action will be taken which might seem to give ground for Soviet suspicion that crisis was brought about by "Anglo-American intervention" . . . We do not think that any advice or assurances should be given to the King.'[62]

Thereafter Byrnes still talked as if the prestige deriving from possession of the bomb would prove effective at the Foreign Ministers Council meeting in London in September – 'he looks to having the presence of the bomb in his pocket, so to speak, as a great weapon.'[63] But he now sought not to challenge Soviet pre-eminence in Eastern Europe, only to humanise it. Thus he found it 'impossible to believe that a temporary Romanian government could not be formed which would be both friendly to the Soviet Union and also representative of the people'; on still meeting resistance, he suggested that the Polish model (of a government expanded to include one-third non-Communists) 'gave the various parties . . . adequate representation'.[64]

Even so he was to be disappointed. Stalin told Molotov to 'stand firm and make no concessions on Romania', and viewed with equanimity the possibility of deadlock, followed by unilateral peace treaties of the Western 'Allies' with Italy and the USSR with 'our satellites'.[65] Moscow

---

[62] Geir Lundestad, *The American Non-Policy towards Eastern Europe 1943–1947* (Oslo, 1975) pp. 238–42; *FRUS 1945*, v, p. 594.

[63] Gaddis, *United States and the Origins of the Cold War*, p. 264.

[64] Lundestad, *American Non-Policy* pp. 242–3; Taubman, *Stalin's American Policy*, pp. 117–18; *FRUS 1945*, ii, p. 245.

[65] 12 and 13 September 1945 – Vladimir O. Pechatnov, *'The Allies are pressing on you to break your will . . .' Foreign Policy Correspondence between Stalin and Molotov . . . September 1945–December 1946* (CWIHP Working Paper no. 26, 1999) p. 2.

would not tolerate external involvement in its sphere. Instead it sought advances in British and American-dominated areas. Invoking a US promise of support in principle for Soviet acquisition of mandates,[66] Molotov demanded one over the former Italian colony of Libya; such a Soviet presence in the Middle East was quite unacceptable to Bevin. Molotov nevertheless saw these deadlocks as 'normal for the start' of negotiation: 'ahead lies bargaining and an intense search for compromise.' Stalin thought otherwise, and rebuked Molotov fiercely for departing from the Potsdam agreements by allowing France and China to participate in the discussion of peace treaties with countries with which they had not been at war; expansion of the number of countries involved increased the likelihood of the USSR being placed in a minority, a concept that Stalin said had never been applied in Big Three meetings.[67] Molotov's line duly hardened.

Meanwhile Byrnes floated the idea of a long-term alliance to keep Germany demilitarised and prevent any repetition of its revival and Hitlerian aggression. Byrnes saw this as reassurance that this time the United States would not abandon Europe as it had after Versailles. But the State Department also believed that such a treaty 'would go far to weaken British and Soviet justifications for the maintenance of spheres of influence in Western and Eastern Europe respectively'.[68] Molotov was attracted, but not Stalin, who saw the overture as an attempt:

to divert our attention from the Far East, where America assumes a role of tomorrow's friend of Japan . . . second, to receive from the USSR a formal sanction for the US playing the same role in European affairs as the USSR, so that the US may hereafter, in league with England, take the future of Europe into their hands; third, to devalue the treaties of alliance that the USSR has already reached with European states; fourth, to pull out the rug from under any future treaties of alliance between the USSR and Rumania, Finland, etc. Having said this, it would be, of course, difficult to reject an anti-German pact with America. But we should exploit American fear of the growing influence of the USSR in Europe and . . . stipulate that the US-Soviet anti-German pact . . . be conditioned on an anti-Japan pact with the US. Hence our proposal: to conclude, first

---

[66] A *quid pro quo* for Soviet acceptance at San Francisco of UN 'Trusteeships' – *FRUS 1945*, i, pp. 1235–6, 1428–9.

[67] Pechatnov, *Correspondence*, pp. 3–4.

[68] *FRUS, The Conference at Berlin 1945*, i, p. 263 (briefing document for Potsdam), 1945, ii, pp. 267–8, 1946, ii, esp. pp. 62, 166–7, 190–3.

*. . . an anti-Japan pact . . . [and] to indicate to the (American) partner that
without the anti-Japan pact we cannot possibly conclude an anti-German
pact with the US*[69]

Clearly Stalin did not want prolonged US involvement, and therefore
competition, in Europe. But he also worried as to US intentions for Japan,
and so tried to use Byrnes's unwelcome initiative to secure a Soviet entry
there. Independently, too, Molotov was instructed to press hard for the
creation of a Japanese Allied Control Council and the curtailment of the
'one-person rule' of General Douglas MacArthur; US reluctance to do so
should be represented as a screen to cover an Anglo-American deal to seize
the Japanese gold reserve. Byrnes, though, proved no more forthcoming
over Japan than Bevin over Libya.

   Molotov then suggested to Stalin the linking of the Italian peace treaty
to US concessions over the Balkans and Japan. Stalin preferred to hang
tough:

*The Allies are pressing on you to break your will and to force you
into making concessions. It is obvious you should display complete
adamancy . . . It is possible that the session of the [Foreign Ministers']
Council would come to nought . . . But we should not grieve.
A failure of the conference would mean the failure of Byrnes, and
we must not grieve over that.*

When the conference duly failed, Soviet diplomats were told to attribute
this to an Anglo-American 'attack on the foreign policy gains of the Soviet
Union made during the War'.[70] That was not how it generally struck
Western public opinion.

   That autumn US policy appeared more than usually splintered. The
Soviet application for a loan was stalled in an attempt to gain political
leverage; there was no disposition to allow Soviet participation in the
occupation of Japan; mounting concern was felt about Soviet activities in
Manchuria; and public opinion cooled rapidly towards the USSR (though
also towards Britain). On the other hand, in an attempt to mend fences,
Truman sent Ambassador Harriman to Stalin with a personal letter. Stalin
received him graciously, but was more put out than Harriman realised by
the letter's ignoring Japan. He insisted that the USSR should continue to

---

[69] 22 September 1945 – Petchanov, *Correspondence*, p. 5.
[70] Pechatnov, *Correspondence*, pp. 5–7; Zubok and Pleshakov, *Inside the Kremlin's
Cold War*, p. 97.

demand that occupation decisions be taken by unanimity, and, for good measure, humiliated Molotov for having offered to lift Soviet censorship on foreign press correspondents.[71]

The atmosphere in Moscow remained chilly; Litvinov secretly told Harriman that the US could now do nothing to improve relations, and the general party line accused America of nuclear blackmail in the Balkans. Harriman, indeed, agreed that Soviet hardening stemmed partly from the atom bomb's having suddenly revived traditional feelings of insecurity. Perhaps for this reason Byrnes intended to use proposals for sharing scientific nuclear information to secure another package deal. This was to be a centre-piece of the Three Power Foreign Ministers' meeting which he arranged (with minimal consultation of Britain) for December in Moscow. Stalin saw the meeting as proof that, 'thanks to the policy of tenacity', 'we won the struggle' to restrict the number of peace treaty makers: 'It is obvious that in dealing with partners such as the US and Britain we cannot achieve anything serious if we begin to give in to intimidation or betray uncertainty.'[72]

At Moscow agreements were indeed concluded: there should, as the US wished, be a UN Atomic Energy Commission to control nuclear weapons and materials and share knowledge, though, as the USSR insisted, it should report to the Security Council not the veto-proof General Assembly; a consultative Allied Council should be established in Tokyo, but General MacArthur's decisions would be 'controlling'; the Romanian and Bulgarian governments should be recognised after they had taken in two more non-Communists and given assurances of their intention to hold free elections; and the composition and date of a peace conference was fixed. Molotov was pleased – 'we managed to reach decisions on a number of important European and Far Eastern issues and to sustain development of cooperation among the three countries that developed during the war.'[73]

Byrnes too saw the Moscow Conference as a success. Truman did not. He had been lobbied by influential senators, partly as a result of Byrnes's style but largely because they feared that, to secure an agreement, he was giving way on vital nuclear safeguards. Truman was also extremely reluctant to recognise the communist-dominated governments of Romania and Bulgaria. More generally he resented the way in which Byrnes had

---

[71] Harriman, *Special Envoy*, pp. 510–16; Petchanov, *Correspondence*, pp. 10–13.

[72] Pechatnov, *Correspondence*, pp. 13–14.

[73] Pechatnov, *Correspondence*, p. 14.

bypassed instructions and held back information; and he deplored the final communiqué's omission of all reference to 'Iran or any other place where the Soviets were on the march. We had gained only an empty promise of further talks.' Bevin had in fact asked awkward questions about both Iran and Turkey at the conference, but Byrnes had settled over his head.

While Truman fumed over Romania and Bulgaria, 'those two police states', and declared that he would not recognise their 'governments unless they are radically changed',[74] he had already abandoned serious hopes of altering things there. What he worried about was how many more countries would follow. As he had put it in December, the Russians:

confront us with an acknowledged fact and then there is little we can do. 'Now they have 500,000 men in Bulgaria and some day they are going to move down and take the Black Sea straits and that will be an accomplished fact again. There's only one thing they understand.'

'Divisions?' Ross asked.

The President nodded and added that we can't send any divisions over to prevent them moving from Bulgaria. 'I don't know what we're going to do.'[75]

The slide towards Cold War, 1946: Stalin's election speech, Kennan's 'long telegram', Churchill's Fulton speech, Wallace's critique and dismissal

In the next few months, these fears appeared to be confirmed by Soviet behaviour and came increasingly to inform Western policy. Meanwhile, expectations of future Soviet–Western cooperation fell sharply on all sides, though not, as yet, to zero.

When Byrnes returned from the Moscow Conference, and scheduled a radio broadcast without further consulting the President. Truman plucked up courage to tell him off. His actual words were almost certainly gentler; but he spoke from a memorandum that likened Soviet behaviour in Iran to its previous doings in the Baltic states and Poland, and declared that:

[74] In fact, Romanian recognition followed fairly quickly, but Bulgarian not until late 1947, after the entry into force of the peace treaty (and one week after the execution of the leading opposition politician).
[75] G. Herken, *The Winning Weapon: The Atomic Bomb and the Cold War 1945–50* (New York, 1980) p. 354, also p. 79.

Russia intends an invasion of Turkey and the seizure of the Black Sea
Straits . . . Unless Russia is faced with an iron fist and strong language
another war is in the making. Only one language do they understand –
'how many divisions have you?'
  I do not think we should play compromise any longer . . .
  I'm sick of babying the Soviets.[76]

As we shall see, Byrnes did not stop seeking deals with the USSR, nor did
Truman wish him to. But he adapted to this harder line.

In Moscow, February 1946 brought a general election campaign. Its
basic theme was the need to rebuild the Soviet economy by reverting
to 1930s methods, probably the only way of ruling with which Stalin felt
comfortable. There was nothing directly aggressive about this message –
indeed Molotov stressed the need for 'a lengthy period of peace'. But the
whole message was resolutely unilateralist. In an echo of Stalin's March
1939 speech indicating that he was no longer committed to his previous
Western treaty alignment, Malenkov declared that 'We do not want to pull
chestnuts out of the fire for others. If we have chestnuts, let us use them
for the benefit of our own glorious people.' Stalin himself depicted the
Second World War as the inevitable result of 'the capitalist system of
world economy' (and therefore, presumably, as likely to recur); he praised
Soviet performance as validating its communist system, but without any
hint of the Western aid he had earlier acknowledged; and he concluded
that only if pre-war production were tripled could 'we regard our country
as guaranteed against any eventualities. That will require three new Five
Year Plans, perhaps more.'[77] Some historians have seen this timescale as
uncomfortably reminiscent of his emotional claims (in private) the previous April that Germany would revive over that period, and that 'We shall
recover in fifteen or twenty years, and then we'll have another go at it
[war].'[78]

Be that as it may, Stalin did not so fear another German attack as
to embrace the American offer of a long-term alliance to forestall it.
Byrnes had suggested this at the September 1945 London Conference, and
reverted to it in Moscow in December. Outwardly Stalin then 'heartily
approved the idea'; but when a draft treaty was submitted next February,

---

[76] Harry S. Truman, *Year of Decisions 1945* (British edn, 1955) pp. 492–3.
[77] Hugh Thomas, *Armed Truce. The Beginnings of the Cold War 1945–46* (1986)
Chap. 1.
[78] Djilas, *Conversations with Stalin*, pp. 90–1.

the USSR did not even acknowledge it. Byrnes brought the subject up again in April, describing it as a test of 'the exact aim of the Soviet Union – whether it was a search for security or expansionism'. Molotov simply stalled; and his (or more accurately Stalin's) approach was endorsed through wider consultation in May: Litvinov described Byrnes's aim as 'political/propagandistic', to appear to provide 'full security for us from Germany and Japan. If our security is guaranteed then many of our claims and actions that caused disagreements with the Western states would lose their meaning.'[79]

Not everyone shared Navy Secretary Forrestal's reaction to Stalin's 9 February speech, that it 'came close to convincing me . . . there was no way in which capitalism and communism could live together'. But US opinion was steadily hardening. Within a fortnight news broke of arrests of a Soviet atomic spy ring in Canada and London.[80] Then on 22 February there arrived in Washington the celebrated 'long telegram' from its Moscow chargé George Kennan, deriving Soviet behaviour and hostility from internal and ideological causes, and arguing that it responded not to appeals or cajolery but only to external constraint:

It does not take unnecessary risks. Impervious to logic of reason, it is highly sensitive to logic of force. For this reason it can easily withdraw – and usually does – when strong resistance is encountered at any point. Thus, if the adversary has sufficient force and makes clear his readiness to use it, he rarely has to do so.[81]

Circulated by Forrestal throughout official Washington, Kennan's telegram proved an enormous success since it expressed clearly attitudes that many people from the President down were instinctively coming to adopt.

One illustration of this was Truman's escorting of Churchill to Fulton, Missouri, in March, and approval (perhaps by way of a 'trial balloon')

---

[79] Zhukov thought the Americans wanted 'to finish the occupation of Germany as soon as possible and to remove the armed forces of the USSR from Germany, and then to demand a withdrawal of our troops from Poland, and finally from the Balkans' – Pechatnov, *Correspondence*, p. 18; *FRUS* 1945, ii, pp. 267–8, 1946, ii, esp. pp. 62, 166–7, 190–3.

[80] This ring had been revealed by the September 1945 defection in Ottawa of the GRU operative Igor Gruzenko. Then on 6 February Truman learnt of FBI suspicions of the loyalty of Assistant Treasury Secretary Harry Dexter White – Thomas, *Armed Truce*, pp. 69, 481–4.

[81] *FRUS* 1946, vi, pp. 707–9.

of the text of his speech. This noted that 'From Stettin in the Baltic to Trieste in the Adriatic, an iron curtain has descended across the continent. Behind that line . . . all are subject . . . not only to Soviet influence but to a very high and increasing measure of control from Moscow.' Churchill did not think 'Russia desires war':

What they desire is the fruits of war and the indefinite expansion of their power and doctrines . . . Our difficulties and dangers will not be removed by closing our eyes to them . . . nor by a policy of appeasement. What is needed is a settlement, and the longer this is delayed the more difficult it will be . . . From what I have seen of our Russian friends . . . I am convinced that there is nothing they admire so much as strength, and nothing for which they have less respect than for military weakness . . . We cannot afford . . . to work on narrow margins offering temptations to a trial of strength. [But] if the Western democracies stand together in strict adherence to the principles of the United Nations Charter, their influence for the furthering of those principles will be immense and no one is likely to molest them.

This, effectively, had been Churchill's wartime plea, but the US administration had not then been convinced. Now it largely was – though Churchill's call for what looked like an Anglo-American directorate (operating through the UN) still drew opposition and hence a non-committal public stance by the State Department.[82]

Commerce Secretary Wallace was unconvinced by this, and lobbied privately throughout the summer against what he saw as a provocative US policy. In September 1946 he went public:

to make Britain the key to our foreign policy would be . . . the height of folly . . . We must not let British balance-of-power manipulations determine whether and when the USA gets into war. Make no mistake about it – British imperialistic policy in the Near East, combined with Russian retaliation, would lead the USA straight to war unless we have a clearly defined . . . policy of our own . . . To prevent war and ensure our survival in a stable world, it is essential that we look abroad through our own American eyes and not through the eyes of either the British Foreign Office or a pro-British and anti-Russian press.[83]

---

[82] *Keesing's* 7771–2; Gaddis, *United States and the Origins of the Cold War*, pp. 307–9.
[83] *Keesing's*, 8151.

Byrnes saw this speech as undercutting his foreign policy, and, now with Republican support, successfully demanded Wallace's dismissal.

Shortly thereafter the Presidential aide Clark Clifford completed a summer of high-level consultations by submitting a very different report:

. . . If we find it impossible to enlist Soviet cooperation in the solution of world problems, we should be prepared to join with the British and other Western countries in an attempt to build up a world of our own which will pursue its own objectives and will recognise the Soviet orbit with which conflict is not predestined but with which we cannot pursue common aims.

Accordingly the US:

should support and assist all democratic countries which are in any way menaced or endangered by the USSR. Providing military support in case of attack is a last resort; a more effective barrier to communism is strong economic support.

Truman did tell Clifford to lock his report up, since publicity 'could have an exceedingly unfortunate impact on our efforts to try to develop some relationship with the Soviet Union', but he was already in general sympathy with its approach. In the course of 1947, the USA came to act along the lines Clifford had suggested.[84]

The evolution of British policy, 1945–7: Attlee's reservations overcome

Charting the evolution of British policy is more difficult; for, surprisingly, it is unclear where power really lay. Already by 1944 the Chiefs of Staff saw the USSR as the only significant post-war threat, since at worst the US would simply return to isolationism. During the war the Foreign Office sought to damp down such ideas. But it quickly adopted a similar perspective: in 'Stocktaking after VE Day' Sir Orme Sargent, soon to become its civil service head, favoured a British initiative in 'challenging Communist penetration . . . in eastern Europe and in opposing any bid for control

---

[84] Kennan's telegram, *FRUS 1946*, vi, pp. 707–9; Clifford's report, Arthur Krock, *Memoirs. Sixty Years on the Firing Line*, (New York, 1968) esp. pp. 476, 479; Truman's reaction, Daniel Yergin, *Shattered Peace. The Origins of the Cold War* (Harmondsworth, Middlesex, 1990 edn) p. 245.

of Germany, Italy, Greece and Turkey'; and in March 1946 a high level 'Russia Committee' was established to 'think out how to minimise both by measures of defence and counter-offensive the Russian . . . attack against this country'.

How far these attitudes were shared by ministers is less clear. They certainly resonated with Bevin, but he worried about an open breach with the USSR. Pressed in April to abandon the Potsdam arrangements and establish 'a German Government *in our zone*,' he replied that 'this meant a policy of a Western Bloc and that meant war'; moreover (May 1946) the Americans were 'not yet ready for a "western" policy . . . But full American support would be essential.' Even when Washington suggested the merger of the British and US occupation zones (below p. 127), he remained cautious about such 'a complete break with Russia'. So, while preparing the ground in cabinet, he postponed action until the Paris Foreign Ministers Council clarified things. Not until late July did he come round and sell the merger of the two zones to his colleagues.[85]

Elsewhere agreement came less easily. For Attlee diverged fundamentally from both Bevin and the Chiefs of Staff. In January 1946 he had wanted to cut defence expenditure now that 'there is no one to fight', and to look for security rather to the United Nations. In particular he wished to shed commitments in the Middle East, which he saw as expensive, strategically unsound, and provocative: 'it was becoming difficult to justify our staying in the Middle East for any reason other than to be prepared for a war against Russia'. This was, indeed, one of the area's attractions to the Chiefs, who saw 'little or no obstacle in Europe to a Russian advance to the western seaboard', and regarded the capacity to launch air strikes from Middle Eastern bases as a 'valuable deterrent to Russian aggression'. Bevin, for his part, felt that 'If we move out of the Mediterranean, Russia will move in'.[86]

Debate over the proper British posture in the area from Libya to Greece and Turkey rumbled on for eighteen months. In December 1946 Attlee brought it to a head. Britain neither could nor should afford to keep troops

[85] Anne Deighton (ed.) *Britain and the First Cold War* (Basingstoke, 1990) esp. pp. 37, 63, 66, 95; Anthony Adamthwaite, 'Britain and the World, 1945–9: the view from the Foreign Office', *International Affairs*, lxi (1985) p. 226; Alan Bullock, *Ernest Bevin. Foreign Secretary 1945–1951* (1983) esp. pp. 267–8, 271, 309–10.

[86] Raymond Smith and John Zametica, 'The Cold Warrior: Clement Attlee Reconsidered, 1945–7', *International Affairs*, lxi (1985) esp. pp. 245–7; Bullock, *Bevin*, p. 242.

in Greece for a further year, as the Chiefs of Staff were now advocating. Attlee feared provoking the USSR into actions there or in Western Europe that Britain could not resist; and he was 'disturbed by the signs of America trying to make a safety zone around herself while leaving us and Europe in No Man's Land.' The Middle East was 'only an outpost position'; instead Attlee urged pull-back to a line from Nigeria to Kenya: for

I do not think that the countries bordering on Soviet Russia's zone, viz. Greece, Turkey, Iraq and Persia, can be made strong enough to form an effective barrier . . . If it were possible to reach an agreement with Russia . . . that they become a neutral zone, it would be much to our advantage. Of course it is difficult to tell how far Russian policy is dictated by expansionism and how far by fear of attack by the US and ourselves. Fantastic as this is, it may very well be the real grounds of Russian policy . . .

Next month he added that:

Unless we are convinced that USSR is irrevocably committed to a policy of world domination . . . I think that before being committed to this strategy we should seek to come to an agreement with the USSR after consideration with Stalin of all our points of conflict.

To Bevin, this 'would be Munich over again, only on a world scale . . . If I am right about Russian ideology, Russia would certainly fill the gap we leave empty whatever her promises'.

I think we must accept the fact that the present rulers of Russia are committed to the belief that there is a natural conflict between the capitalist and communist worlds. They also believe that they have a mission to work for a communist world . . .
Your proposal would involve leading from weakness . . . When we have consolidated our economy, when the economic revival of Europe has made progress, when it has become finally clear to the Russians that they cannot drive a wedge between the Americans and ourselves, we shall be in a position to negotiate with Stalin from strength.

Essentially Bevin's view prevailed, perhaps as a result of his character or arguments, perhaps (if we can believe Montgomery's later claim) because of a collective resignation threat by the Chiefs of Staff were the Middle East to be abandoned. This did not mean the end of East–West negotiations; they continued for a further year, and even in December 1947 Bevin still had slight hopes of a Soviet about-turn once it became clear that the

Western position was firm.[87] Nor did Attlee drop his search for retrench-
ment – 1947 saw British decisions to pull out of Greece and Palestine, and
the actual transfer of power in India. There was, though, no more talk of
reassuring Stalin's supposed security fears by negotiation and the creation
of a 'neutral zone', but rather of recovering economic strength and of
holding on to 'essential positions', 'with US help as necessary'.

Iran and Turkey

All this, of course, was only talk, but 1946 also saw real confrontations
over Iran and Turkey. In both cases, the USSR seems to have thought it
could safely press since it was faced only by the British, a judgement apparently confirmed when Bevin, but not Byrnes, remonstrated during the
December 1945 Moscow Conference. As such, Soviet behaviour may
have fitted into the pattern of power-political competition between the Big
Three, playing on a presumed Anglo-American rivalry, that had been
advocated in Moscow during the latter part of the war. If so, it represented
a mistake that helped engage the US on a West–East basis.

In 1941 the USSR and Britain had jointly occupied Iran; a smaller US
presence followed, and in 1943 the USA obtained a promise that they
would all withdraw their troops within six months of the end of the war.
But in 1944 Beria had raised the desirability of seeking an oil concession in
northern Iran analogous to that then being pursued by Anglo-American
companies in the south. Iran's refusal to entertain *any* such proposals
while war and foreign occupation continued seemed to Moscow the
product not of nationalism, but of 'Reactionary and pro-English elements';
it led to the idea of using the Soviet position in the north to manage the
elections there and so secure a substantial bloc of support in the Iranian
Majlis (parliament). In mid-1945 orders were given both for the start of
oil prospecting and drilling, and for the establishment of 'national
autonomous' Azerbaijani and Kurdish 'oblasts' 'with broad powers
within the Iranian state', together with preparations for the Majlis elections. Autonomous regimes were duly installed that autumn, under the
protection of Soviet troops. Meanwhile, at the diplomatic level, the USSR

---

[87] Smith and Zametica, 'Attlee Reconsidered', pp. 248–51; Bullock, *Bevin*, pp. 339–40,
349–51, 353–4, 496; Ritchie Ovendale, *The English-Speaking Alliance. Britain, the
United States, the Dominions and the Cold War 1945–51* (1983) pp. 45–53, and the
documents in his *British Defence Policy since 1945* (Manchester, 1994) Chap. 1. Dalton
and Morrison appear to have shared Attlee's doubts.

refused to commit to military withdrawal, invoking the 1921 Soviet–Iranian treaty by way of justification.[88]

When nothing emerged from the Moscow Foreign Ministers Conference, Iran took the issue of withdrawal to the United Nations in January 1946. It was at first shelved, pending direct Iranian–Soviet negotiations. At these Stalin took a tough line with the new Iranian premier, Qavam: 'We don't care what US and Britain think and are not afraid of them.' Come the 2 March 'deadline', the USSR declined to offer more than a limited troop withdrawal; indeed alarmist reports from the young US Consul in Tabriz suggested that it was preparing to move on Teheran. Iran therefore enlisted American diplomatic support, and on 18 March returned the issue to the UN Security Council; this time the USA insisted that it be heard, not shelved.

Truman certainly treated the matter very seriously, worrying (he later claimed) about a 'giant pincers movement' on the Middle East, and telling Harriman 'this may lead to war'. Quite how strong a line he took with Stalin has since been debated; but the USA certainly attributed the eventual Soviet climb-down to the firmness of its stance. Equally it could have been the product of a deal hinted at by Qavam before he left Moscow. For on 18 March (the day of the formal appeal to the UN), a new ambassador was sent to Teheran with instructions to exchange a troop withdrawal for the promise of a joint Soviet–Iranian oil company. Agreement was reached in April, and withdrawal completed in May.[89] This left the autonomous Kurdish and Azerbaijani authorities in place, but the latter's leader, Pishevari, grumbled that Stalin had 'first raised' him 'to the skies and then let' him 'down into the precipice'.

Pishevari had clearly expected a permanent takeover of Azerbaijan. Whether Stalin, too, had intended this, then retreated in face of US pressure, we cannot say. He now explained that Soviet troops had 'had to leave' Iran lest they legitimate the British and American presence in a string of European and Asian countries. Iran was not in a 'profound revolutionary crisis'; rather 'We used the technique here that every revolutionary knows' of bidding high and threatening the government so as 'to achieve a certain minimum of demands'. The Iranian government now needed

---

[88] Natalia Yegorova, *The 'Iran Crisis' of 1945–6: a view from the Russsian Archives* (CWIHP Working Paper 15, 1996) esp. pp. 3, 6, 8, 14; Jamil Hasanli, 'New Evidence on the Iran Crisis 1945–46', *CWIHP Bulletin* 12/13 (2001) pp. 309–14.

[89] Louise L'Estrange Fawcett, *Iran and the Cold War. The Azerbaijan Crisis of 1946* (Cambridge, 1992) esp. pp. 125–8; Harriman and Abel, *Special Envoy*, p. 550; Yegoreva, *Iran Crisis*, pp. 17–20.

to 'seek support among democratic elements'; and these should use the 'conflict to wrench concessions from Qavam, to give him support, to isolate the Anglophiles . . . and to create some basis for the further democratization of Iran.'[90]

These themes played themselves out over the rest of the year. Qavam broadened his government to include Tudeh and Azerbaijani representatives. By the summer there were fears that, as in Eastern Europe, the communists would come to control its government. The growth of the communist Tudeh party led to strikes in the southern oil fields – and demonstrative British troop deployments across the river in Iraq – but also to serious trouble (conceivably fanned by the British) with the southern tribes. Partly as a result, the Shah and Quavam decided in October to swing against the USSR, dismissing the Tudeh ministers, applying to the US for financial aid, and finally, in December, suppressing the autonomous republics in the north. The Soviet oil concession was overwhelmingly rejected by a nationalist Parliament.[91]

In November 1940 Stalin had sought to enlist Bulgaria in a joint attack on, and partition of, European Turkey; the Turks also claimed that Soviet agents were stirring up minorities in eastern Turkey and Iran by dangling before them the prospect of a separate state.[92] In 1945 the USSR was again able to take up these threads, in March denouncing its non-aggression treaty with Turkey and in June intimating its terms for conceding a new one: not only the revision of the 1936 Montreux Convention governing the Black Sea straits (which Britain and the USA, at the Potsdam Conference, showed themselves ready to accept), but also the cession of Kars and Ardahan,[93] and the realignment of the Bulgarian frontier. For the next year

[90] Stalin to Pishevari, 8 May 1946 (in Yegoreva, *Iran Crisis*, pp. 23–4).

[91] The episode parallels events in 1920–1: Russia first established the south Caspian 'Gilan Republic', then withdrew following a treaty giving it a privileged position in Iran as a whole, only to see a nationalist grasp power and suppress Gilan – G. Lenczowski, *The Middle East in World Affairs* (Ithaca, NY, 1980 edn) Chap. 5; Barry Rubin, *The Great Powers in the Middle East 1941–1947: the Road to the Cold War* (1980) Chap. 9; R. Jervis and J. Snyder (eds) *Dominoes and Bandwagons: Strategic Beliefs and Great Power Competition in the Eurasian Rimland* (New York, 1991) pp. 56–60, 75–7; K. Roosevelt, *Countercoup – The Struggle for the Control of Iran* (New York, 1979) pp. 51 ff, 112.

[92] *FRUS 1941*, i, p. 336, also 288, 334–5.

[93] A strategic area conquered by Russia in 1877–8; its recovery after the First World War, when the destruction of independence in the Caucasus was a mutual Turkish and Bolshevik interest, was confirmed by treaty in 1921.

press and radio campaigns, and overbearing Soviet representatives in Turkey, reinforced (and expanded) these demands. They were, in themselves, quite unacceptable to Turkey, but were also viewed as a preliminary to bringing 'Turkey "like Poland" under direct Soviet influence'. They thus reawakened all Turkey's historic fears; and its leaders turned for aid to the United States, voicing sentiments that were to become the typical rhetoric of the Cold War: 'The Soviets have gone mad, they dream of world domination. They are crossing you and Britain at many points: Bornholm, Trieste, Albania, Greece, Turkey, Iran. Where they find a weak point they exploit it' (Prime Minister Saracoglu, July 1945). Given these convictions Turkey kept its large army mobilised, at a cost it could not sustain indefinitely.

In 1946, three elements heated things to a crisis: continued intimidation of Turkey; the faulty Western intelligence this gave rise to; and an American appreciation of the security interests involved. Soviet pressure was backed by hostile press campaigns, a substantial military presence in Bulgaria, and talk (whether loose or intentional) of a coming invasion. Such talk was picked up by, and sometimes deliberately relayed to, not only US but also British, French and Dutch intelligence; and fears were increased, at crucial times, by secret Soviet troop movements that may only have been geared towards re-equipment but that seemed to indicate a deliberate build-up of armour. That the US State-War-Navy committee should see control of the straits as strategically important is unsurprising; but they were not an area of historic American interest, and it is perhaps fortuitous that President Truman was a history buff who felt likewise as a result of his interest in the Middle East from Alexander the Great onwards. By December 1945 he was anticipating a seizure of the straits that would present the US with yet another 'accomplished fact', but added that he could 'send no divisions' to counteract it: 'I don't know what we're going to do.'[94] In February he signalled concern by sending the prestigious battleship *Missouri* to Istanbul, ostensibly to return the ashes of a former Turkish ambassador. Tension later ebbed, only to flare up again during the summer. In August Soviet demands for a 'joint' defence of the straits by the Black Sea powers prompted US, British and Turkish notes of rejection,[95] followed that autumn by the despatch of a US carrier force to the eastern Mediterranean. The expectation was that, if firmly confronted, the USSR would back down; but, warned that if it did not the outcome could be war,

---

[94] Joseph M. Jones, *The Fifteen Weeks* (New York, 1955) p. 66; Herken, *Winning Weapon*, p. 354, also p. 79.

[95] However, all accepted in principle modification of the Montreux convention.

Truman observed that 'we might as well find out whether the Russians [were] bent on world conquest now as in five or ten years'. In fact Stalin seems to have commissioned his spy Donald Maclean to 'find out exactly how far the West would go', and received the (correct) report that the US administration was in earnest. This may have prompted Soviet readiness to let Turkey gradually simmer down, and perhaps also to stand aside when Iran rolled up the communist 'autonomous regions' in the north.[96]

Soviet pressure on Turkey had had both historic and opportunistic roots. But it may also have reflected the view expounded in the September 1946 Novikov telegram that the USA was 'not interested in providing . . . support to the British Empire in this vulnerable point'. That view was wrong. As the Joint Chiefs put it in March 1946, Soviet domination of the 'vital Suez-Canal-Aleppo-Basra triangle' would mean 'Britain must ultimately fight or accept the disintegration of the Empire.' If the latter, Soviet potential might come to exceed that of the USA and 'allies bound to her ideologically'. 'Militarily [therefore] our present position as a world power is of necessity closely interwoven with that of Great Britain.' Stalin's August demands on Turkey accordingly prompted Anglo-Canadian-American military talks such that (one author writes) 'Britain and the United States had an informal alliance by December 1946'.[97]

The Baruch Plan, and the European peace treaties 1946–7

Two other topics loomed large in the diplomacy of 1946: UN discussions on atomic energy and negotiation of the European peace treaties. A surprisingly common view was that the USSR could be reassured by sharing atomic secrets with it, under UN auspices. Byrnes had broached the question at the December 1945 Moscow Conference; and many people (including Acheson, who was not usually a dove) believed the USA could share with Russia both scientific information and fissionable material so treated as to remove its weapons potential, while giving the UN a monopoly of bombs and the materials from which they could be made. The dangers were obvious, and the US plan hardened in the course of bureaucratic

---

[96] Eduard Mark, 'The War Scare of 1946 and its Consequences', *Diplomatic History*, xxi (1997); Modin, *My Five Cambridge Friends*, pp. 145–7; Rubin, *The Great Powers in the Middle East*, Chap. 10; Jervis and Snyder, *Dominoes and Bandwagons*, Chap. 3; Millis, *Forrestal Diaries*, p. 193.

[97] Mark, 'War Scare of 1946', p. 392; Ovendale, *English-Speaking Alliance*, pp. 45–6.

infighting. As melodramatically presented – 'We are here to make a choice between the quick and the dead' – by Baruch in June, it insisted on prior safeguards. Only when all countries had allowed surveys and controls of their reserves, mining and processing of nuclear materials would the US surrender its stockpile; to promote confidence there should be 'condign punishment' for infractions, and the UN's Atomic Development Authority should not be subject to veto. There can never have been any prospect of Stalin opening his country to such detailed inspection; nor could he have had any interest in suspending his own nuclear programme to leave a US monopoly in the transitional phase, a UN one thereafter. The Soviet counter-proposal, an initial uninspected sharing of scientific information and establishment of safeguards that would be subject to veto, was even less convincing. Baruch then settled down to playing subsequent negotiations for the propaganda value of Soviet rejection of a plan that would have so enhanced the UN's standing and ability to maintain peace.[98]

Meanwhile there were regular meetings of the Foreign Ministers Council to hammer out the peace treaties. These, though not always unsuccessful, generally tended to worsen the atmosphere. This was mostly due, no doubt, to substantive differences, but also to a Soviet negotiating style that has irritated others besides Westerners – Mao Zedong once compared prising concessions out of Stalin in 1950 to getting 'a piece of meat from the mouth of a tiger'.[99] For Soviet technique was, perhaps after initial warmth, to pile on the pressure and retract earlier concessions until it became clear that nothing more could be obtained; positions might then be suddenly abandoned and settlement reached in a euphoric atmosphere (though not necessarily implemented thereafter). One risk inherent in this approach was that the other side might give up in disgust before the Soviets judged the time ripe for a settlement – Hitler may have done so when Molotov proved stubborn in November 1940; Marshall probably did before the March–April 1947 Moscow Council at which Stalin appeared at his most forthcoming over Germany. Another danger was that, during the stage of deadlock, both sides might get angry. During the mid-1946 Paris Foreign Ministers Council Molotov was instructed 'to avoid . . . a defensive posture, but instead to hold a position of denunciation and attack'. Once he so got under Bevin's skin as to bring him to his feet 'saying "I've had enough of this, I 'ave," and for one glorious moment it looked as if the Foreign Minister of Great Britain and the Foreign Minister of the

[98] Herken, *Winning Weapon* Chaps 8, 9.
[99] D. Wilson, *Mao. The People's Emperor* (1979) p. 266.

Soviet Union were about to come to blows.'[100] The Americans were cooler. But they sometimes negotiated as much for public effect as for substance: the offer of a military alliance against Germany had originally been constructive, but by April 1946 it was being publicly suggested that if the Russians refused to sign, 'it will make them appear an outlaw nation before the eyes of the world.'[101]

Nevertheless, negotiations over the Italian and East European peace treaties eventually succeeded. Byrnes had already displayed his bargaining skills in securing a package deal at Potsdam. In 1946 his shrewd sense of timing, and apparent readiness to abandon proceedings, brought Molotov suddenly to reverse his position on a number of occasions. But it cannot be said that the treaties (formally signed in early 1947) mattered very greatly: the human rights clauses of the East European treaties were not adhered to, nor did the restrictions on Italian armed forces last. If anything, the enhanced legitimacy the treaties conferred on Romania, Bulgaria and Hungary probably facilitated the final extinction, in 1947, of non-communist politics.

The German question and possible Soviet perspectives

What mattered a good deal more, therefore, was the way the Powers handled the most important country that they (in theory) jointly occupied. Admittedly Germany was slow to emerge as a flash-point. Initial frictions were over Eastern Europe, while, in a press briefing Bevin gave in January 1946, 'neither Germany nor Western Europe was mentioned and Europe as a whole came a poor third after the Middle East and Far East'.[102] Later the first East–West 'crises' were those over Iran and Turkey. Still the USSR abandoned its position in Iran in 1946 and dropped claims on Turkey in 1953, while the West came quite soon to accept, at least tacitly, a Soviet sphere in Eastern Europe. Some say that similar 'agreement' might have been reached over Germany had the original plan to break it up been followed. But in 1945 it was decided to keep it together as a unit. So, given

---

[100] Pechatnov, *Correspondence between Stalin and Molotov*, p. 16; Bullock, *Bevin*, p. 282. Relations between Molotov and Bevin were particularly stormy, perhaps because both saw themselves as socialist leaders.

[101] Gaddis, *United States and the Origins of the Cold War*, pp. 328–9; Petchatnov, *Correspondence*, pp. 18–19.

[102] Bullock, *Bevin*, p. 216.

its size and potential strength, if East and West ever quarrelled, Germany's alignment could well prove decisive. Nor could either side readily dodge this competition, since both were present, and became increasingly committed, on the ground. From this geopolitical perspective, Germany lay at the heart of the Cold War – though debate continues as to whether this need necessarily have been the case.

Much depends on what Stalin's intentions and aspirations really were; and he held his cards so close to his chest that no *incontrovertible* evidence has yet emerged. He may initially have feared that the USSR would be excluded altogether from the post-war control of Germany, perhaps by the sort of Western deal with the relics of the Third Reich of which he showed himself so suspicious in the closing moments of the war; anxiety to prevent this may help explain his determination to secure Berlin, regardless of cost. Khrushchev says Stalin often spoke gratefully of Eisenhower's allowing the Russians to reach Berlin first; had he not done so 'the question of Germany might have been decided differently and our own position turned out quite a bit worse'.[103] One defector has also claimed that in 1944 'the Politburo had no confidence in the possibility of successfully sovietizing even those parts of Germany occupied by Soviet troops. It was considered probable that the United States and Great Britain would insist on conditions of peace under which the sovietization of Germany would be impossible.' This provided an added reason for the rapid dismantlement of German industry, even at the cost of gross inefficiency: 'If we can't ship it out, it's better to destroy it, so that the Germans won't have it' (July 1945).[104] In similar vein, Stalin insisted in April 1945 that Germany would recover in 'twelve to fifteen years' (actually no bad prophecy) and that there could well then be another round[105] – though he clearly did not so fear this as to accept the offer of a US guarantee that Byrnes put forward that autumn.

At the opposite extreme, 'Stalin and the Soviet leaders' were telling 'the Bulgars and Yugoslavs in the spring of 1946, that all Germany must be ours, that is, Soviet, Communist.' They did not explain how this goal would be achieved – Djilas attributed it to 'hopes for the economic and political dissolution of Western Europe.'[106] There was, too, talk – until

---

[103] *Khrushchev Remembers*, i, pp. 194–5.

[104] R. Slusser (ed.) *Soviet Economic Policy in Postwar Germany. A Collection of Papers by Former Soviet Officials* (New York, 1953), esp. pp. 19, 41–2, 46–7, 52.

[105] Djilas, *Conversations with Stalin*, p. 91.

[106] ibid. p. 119. In June 1946 the sceptical Litvinov privately remarked that since 'each side wants a unified Germany – under its control' the country would 'obviously be broken in two' (Taubman, *Stalin's American Policy*, p. 153).

mid-1948 – of 'a special German road to socialism',[107] very much in the mould of the Popular Front strategy prescribed for most other countries. This entailed communist dominance both of the working-class movement and of a looser grouping of 'anti-fascist parties'. As Stalin briefed German communists in June 1945, 'The unity of Germany to be ensured by a unified KPD a unified C[entral] C[ommittee], a unified party of labor [and] in the middle point a unified party.' Next spring the Communist [KPD] and Socialist [SPD] parties were forced to merge into a Socialist Unity Party [SED], in what became the usual East European model; Colonel Tiul'panov (head of the occupying forces' Propaganda Section) later explained that he had concluded the KPD could not win alone and had therefore 'devised the strategy of unification . . . as a way to win an eventual election in Germany.'[108] This emphasis on continuing on an all-German basis continued. Thus in January 1947 Stalin and Molotov stressed the desirability of an all-German government, and told SED leaders (to their discomfiture) that, to secure free SED operation in the Western zones, it would be worth allowing the SPD to function in the Soviet zone 'within confined limits'.[109] Even as late as December 1948 Stalin instructed that:

> *you should advance towards socialism not by taking a straight road*
> *but by moving in zigzags . . . The German people's attention should not*
> *now be concentrated on the questions which are posed in the people's*
> *democracies but on the question of Germany's unity, on the peace treaty,*
> *price cuts, wage raises and better nourishment. That will unite all*
> *Germany, and that is the main thing.*[110]

The goal may have been communist control over the whole of Germany, and Soviet pressure for German unification may have been presented, in communist circles, as a way of reaching this. But unification may also

---

[107] In September 1948 its chief protagonist, Anton Ackerman, was forced to recant: such a road 'allows room for anti-Bolshevism' – Norman N. Naimark, *The Russians in Germany. A History of the Soviet Zone of Occupation, 1945–1949* (Cambridge, Mass., 1995) p. 303.

[108] ibid. p. 258 (Wilhelm Pieck's notes), 276.

[109] In the Western zones the SPD had refused to merge into the SED, whose operation was thus confined to the East; but the KPD continued to function – in December 1948 Moscow enjoined that it should publicly deny, but secretly strengthen, its ties with the SED – Naimark, *Russians in Germany*, pp. 45, 299–300, 312.

[110] Mark, *Revolution by Degrees*, p. 38.

have had other attractions for the USSR. For it would provide improved access to reparations from the Western zones, deliveries of which were *de facto* subject to the discretion of their commanders and were indeed suspended by the American General Clay in 1946. More specifically, unification might bring a measure of Soviet control over the Ruhr. Stalin had tried for this at Potsdam, but been blocked by the British (in whose zone the Ruhr lay). When Molotov was asked (at the 1946 Paris Foreign Ministers Conference) what the Soviet Union really wanted, he replied $10 billion in reparations plus Four Power control of the Ruhr. Soviet involvement in such control would naturally have sought more dismantling and reparations. It might also have proved, as Byrnes (and the British) feared, 'an effective way of destroying the industries [there] . . . which, properly supervised, are vital to an economically healthy Europe'.[111] And this, presumably, reflected the final attraction to the USSR of a united Germany – it would at least prevent the incorporation of the greater part of that country into a hostile 'Western bloc', for which (as Soviet intelligence doubtless made clear) there were mounting US and British calls from 1946 onwards.

All the indications are that a communist or 'Socialist Unity' party would have fared very badly under a regime of *genuinely* free elections.[112] But a united Germany, operating broadly under the Weimar constitution, was at least ostensibly on the table in 1947, and was again proposed by Stalin in 1952 (below, pp. 192–3). Politicians and (later) scholars have argued as to whether these proposals were in fact genuine, and whether statesmen did well to give priority first to the construction, then to the integration into the West, of the Federal Republic. This priority did not in fact foreclose for all time the possibility of German reunion, as many feared during the Cold War; and it certainly facilitated economic recovery, German integration into Western Europe, and the management of the Western alliance. But it has been argued that acceptance of Soviet proposals for a united but disarmed (1947) or armed but neutral (1952) Germany would have been a reasonable price to pay for the installation of an elected all-German government. Of course nobody can determine what would have been the effect on the international system of such a united Germany. The

---

[111] James F. Byrnes, *Speaking Frankly* (1947), pp. 171–4, 194.

[112] One pitfall would have been divergent Soviet and Western understandings of precisely which were the 'democratic' parties whose rights were (according to e.g. Stalin's 1952 proposals) to be 'guaranteed' and which were the 'organizations inimical to democracy and to the maintenance of peace' that 'must not be permitted on the territory of Germany'.

necessity for watching it might have preserved a degree of East–West co-operation. Equally it might (as between the wars) have sought to play East off against West in pursuit of national revival.

Whatever attractions it saw in a united Germany, in practice the USSR did little to secure one. This was the case also in Korea, where the Soviets combined theoretical advocacy of an all-Korean government with a rapid sealing of the border between the two halves of the country. They were less drastic in Germany, but they certainly did not treat it as an economic unit (as agreed at Potsdam), and their non-delivery of the stipulated amounts of food from the agricultural east and interference with free movement provided much material for complaint and suspicion. 'Soviet officers,' Naimark writes, 'bolshevized the zone not because there was any plan to do so, but because that was the only way they knew to organize society.'[113] They retained concentration camps to serve as gulags. And when they encountered difficulties, they resorted instinctively to coercion: thus Marshal Zhukov told the Socialist Grotewohl in February 1946 that he had no choice but to enter the SED; that September Tiul'panov stressed the need for 'administrative methods' in handling the 'bourgeois' parties, explaining that 'this is not preelectoral terror, but only quite normal order'; and in 1947 Jacob Kaiser was bullied into quitting as CDU head in the east and fleeing west. Admittedly Tiul'panov was criticised on several occasions by emissaries from the CPSU Central Committee, but until 1949 he was apparently protected by yet more powerful figures, perhaps (Naimark speculates) even by Stalin himself.[114]

In January 1947 Molotov described the creation of a separate German government for the Soviet zone as an option, albeit a 'worst case' one. A year later Stalin told the Yugoslavs, 'The West will make Western Germany their own, and we shall turn Eastern Germany into our own state.' In fact eastern leaders were still being held back, that December, from an over-rapid transformation of the state for fear of the impact on opinion in western Germany. But by then the SED had been allowed to embark on its transformation into 'a party of a new type' akin to that of the USSR; and in September 1949 the 'German Democratic Republic' [DDR] was launched to parallel the Western 'Federal Republic'.[115]

---

[113] Naimark, *Russians in Germany*, p. 467. See also Naimark's judgements quoted on p. 626.

[114] ibid. pp. 277–9, 331–2, 336–8, 340–6.

[115] Naimark, *Russians in Germany*, pp. 300, 312, 346; Djilas, *Conversations with Stalin*, p. 119.

It is hard not to believe that this had not always been present in Stalin's mind, at least as an interim or a fall-back position. For it had very real advantages. It would reduce the population and resources at the disposal of the capitalist powers. Secondly, while evacuation of the zone was not inconceivable,[116] it would, as Zhukov had observed that May, have knock-on effects in Poland, where Soviet troops were supposedly stationed only to protect communications with their German occupation zone.[117] Thirdly, the USSR could, and did, extract resources from its own zone with far fewer constraints than it would have encountered in a united but non-communist Germany. Indeed, the Soviet atom bomb project was crucially dependent on uranium from the south of the zone, where in the late summer of 1946 Beria started mining on a massive scale.[118] It must be very doubtful whether all this could have been given up, or even put at risk, to secure any all-German state in which the communists were not extremely strongly placed. But this was not something that Stalin ever had to decide; he could afford the luxury of playing his cards only as the situation unfolded, even if tensions sometimes developed between a quick consolidation of the communist position in the east and the waning hope of taking over the whole country.

The German question, 1945–6

It would never have been easy to work the arrangements agreed in 1945 at Potsdam. Germany was to be treated as a single economic unit, and all-German administrative bodies were accordingly to be created. Overall policy was to be determined by a Four Power Control Council, subject to a veto and including a France that had not been admitted to the Potsdam Conference and disliked some of its policies. But actual control in each zone lay with the occupying Power. Each Power should look primarily to its own zone for reparations, and these should be taken by dismantling industrial plant surplus to the productive capacity the Four Powers adjudged appropriate for Germany as a whole; that determined, the first

[116] In September 1946 Tiul'panov told Central Committee visitors that, *in case the Soviets were to leave Germany*, it was very important to win over Grotewohl as he was the only figure of stature in the SED – Naimark, *Russians in Germany*, p. 331.
[117] Zhukov was advising against accepting Byrnes's Four Power treaty to enforce German disarmament – Petchanov, *Foreign Policy Correspondence between Stalin and Molotov*, p. 18.
[118] Naimark, *Russians in Germany*, pp. 238 ff.

charge on actual production (and one that was not to be met for several years) was to be the financing of the imports of food and raw materials needed to provide the German people with a low but acceptable standard of living. However, the USSR also held out for, and secured, agreement that 15 per cent of the equipment dismantled in the Western zones should be traded for food and raw materials from the East, 10 per cent despatched East as simple reparations; but the total figure of which these were percentages could not be known until after the permissible production capacity for Germany had been determined. Basically these reparations provisions represented Soviet concessions (alleviated by some western counter-concessions) in a package deal arranged by Byrnes at Potsdam that was in other respects (the Polish–German frontier) favourable to Russia; and some of the pitfalls they might occasion had in fact been foreseen.[119]

Four Power control did not have to lead to partition. In Austria the Soviets installed a coalition government presided over by a distinguished but very elderly Socialist. The Anglo-Americans were reluctant to recognise this, fearing a repetition of East European developments, but did so against a token reconstruction and a promise of free elections. These were held in November 1945, the Communists polling only 5 per cent and being relegated to a minor portfolio. A universally recognised government with authority throughout the country was thus in place; and in 1946 it secured (with British assistance) revision of the Control agreement so that laws could be vetoed only by the joint action of all the occupying powers, hence substantial self-government. (However, full independence was postponed until 1955 by a mixture of Soviet concern for economic advantage and the deteriorating international situation.) By contrast, in Germany the government that concluded the surrender was extinguished almost immediately

---

[119] The USSR would have liked $10bn (or at least $8bn) reparations, at least $2bn of which should have come from the Ruhr – which it wanted to see under joint Four Power control. Britain would not allow such control. Byrnes suggested that attempts to put an agreed value on the material the USSR had already stripped from its zone would only lead to trouble, and that it would therefore be best if each Power collected reparations from its own zone (by his calculations the 50% – Molotov said 42% – of German wealth that was located in the Soviet zone would cover the 50% share of total reparations Moscow sought); but the USSR insisted on receiving some reparations from the Western zones. That the financing of necessary imports should be the first charge on German production was to satisfy the absolute US and British refusal again to provide Germany with money so that it might pay reparations. These should therefore come from capital equipment, the limitation of which would also reduce the danger of Germany again emerging as a threat to her neighbours.

(as was not the case in Japan or Italy). No new one was ever appointed. It might, of course, have developed out of the all-German administrative bodies agreed at Potsdam. But France vetoed these when her wish to detach from Germany the Saar, Rhineland and Ruhr fell on deaf ears in the autumn of 1945. The USA regretted this, but did not pressurise France (then in a very shaky political condition).

By early 1946 both Washington and London privately wondered whether it was either possible or desirable to work out with the USSR a solution for Germany within a Four Power framework. Events that year certainly made such an outcome less likely. Agreement was reached in March, without too much difficulty, on the maximum level of industrial production to be permitted (about half that of 1938). This should have unlocked the door to the identification of the plants to be dismantled for reparations and to the drawing up of an import–export programme for the whole of Germany; but progress on the first was slow, on the second non-existent. The USA's response in May was to suspend reparations deliveries as a lever to force France and Russia to resume Four Power cooperation. It also determined, when the moment was right, to offer to merge their zone with the British.

Britain, too, was moving towards a harder line. Whitehall had been concerned about the Soviets from a very early date. Ministers took rather longer to be convinced. In March 1946 Bevin still favoured controlling the Ruhr through an international holding company with Soviet participation. But by May he felt that 'the danger of Russia has become certainly as great as, and possibly even greater than, that of a revived Germany. The worst situation of all would be a revived Germany in league with or domi-nated by Russia.' Against this background, he put to the Cabinet the question of whether 'we should continue to work towards a unified . . . Germany or . . . towards a West German State or States which would be more amenable to our influence'. The latter course:

would mean an irreparable breach with the Russians, who would go all out to destroy our policy in western Germany and turn the population against us. This task would not be too difficult in an industrial area in a period of acute food shortage. They would, no doubt, also redouble their attacks on us in all other parts of the world, and the prospect of UNO continuing in such circumstances would be slender.

. . . The Americans are probably not yet ready for this . . . In any case one could not count on continued American support even if they came to agree to it. But full American support would be essential.

For this and other reasons, Bevin did not favour such a drastic course, and sought, at the forthcoming Council of Foreign Ministers session in Paris, the best of both worlds, 'development along [very loose] federal lines' that would not 'exclude the possibility of splitting Germany into two parts'. Meanwhile it would be necessary 'to apply the economic principles of Potsdam to the western zones even if the Russians refuse to collaborate . . . to foster the solidarity of the western zones . . . [and] to act in the fullest collaboration with the Americans'. Lastly, were it ever decided 'to abandon the idea of a united Germany . . . it would be most important to ensure that responsibility for the break was put squarely on the Russians'.[120]

The Foreign Ministers made progress on several issues, but not on Germany. In July Bevin brought matters to a head by insisting on the full implementation of economic unity, with reparations subordinated to the elimination of the trade deficit that had to be met exclusively by Britain and the USA; otherwise the UK would go it alone and so organise its occupation zone that no further liability fell on the British taxpayer. Molotov responded with an unyielding statement that the USSR would continue to collect reparations from current production and would not send food from its zone west. At this point Byrnes made his offer to merge the US zone economically with any other. Britain agreed in late July to accept, and 'Bizonia' came into effect in January 1947. It would, the British realised, have important political implications: for if

our reforms are given some time to operate German opinion of the Western powers is likely to change for the better. The French are unlikely to stand out of the arrangements for the unification of the two zones for long, and a temporary split between Eastern and Western Germany will be complete. The long term result . . . given some kind of economic recovery, may well be that the Western zones are regarded by the Germans as 'Germany' and the Eastern zone as the lost provinces. A westward orientation of the Western zones might thus be effected, and a German desire stimulated for a Germany unified on our principles.[121]

The year 1946 also saw the start of the process, foretold by Hitler, whereby both the USSR and the USA would appeal for the allegiance of the German people. The USSR had certain initial advantages. It was at first

[120] 'Policy Towards Germany', 3 May 1946 (Public Record Office, Cab 129/9).
[121] Anne Deighton, *The Impossible Peace. Britain, the Division of Germany and the Origins of the Cold War* (Oxford, 1990) p. 134 and Chaps 3–5.

markedly more successful in restoring economic life in its zone; and, this being more agricultural and the Russians unwilling to send food west, they were able to feed their Germans better – General Clay observed that 'there is no choice between becoming a Communist on 1500 calories and a believer in democracy on 1000'.[122] The Russians also played up to national sentiments. They allowed their political party to question the new border with Poland; in May Marshal Sokolovsky asserted (incorrectly) that the dismantling and removal of German industry had ended; and at the Foreign Ministers Council Molotov stressed the desirability of a united German state, free to develop its civilian industry beyond the currently approved levels, while implying that the West sought to agrarianise[123] the country, dismember it and detach the Ruhr. This invited retaliation in kind, which came with Byrnes's Stuttgart speech in September: Byrnes favoured German retention of the Ruhr (though not the Saar), gave only partial support to Polish annexations in the east, undertook to help the Germans win back to 'an honorable place among the free and peace-loving nations', and, most importantly, promised that, as long as an occupation force was required, the US army would form part of it – thus scotching rumours that while the Russians would remain indefinitely, the Americans would soon go home.[124] Voting soon showed that, in this competition, the Russians were the less popular. In March a Socialist (SPD) referendum in the Western sectors of Berlin went heavily against Soviet-sponsored proposals to merge with the Communist Party. The merger still went ahead in (but only in) eastern Germany. However though the new Socialist Unity Party (SED) secured a plurality in the Soviet zone in October, it gained only an embarassing 20 per cent (to the SPD's 49 per cent) in Berlin. The Western Powers had contributed little to this result, beyond supervising the Berlin elections, but it was clearly encouraging for those who wished to go it alone.

Yet if 1946 saw growing division and disharmony on the ground in Germany, it did not necessarily close the door to an agreed peace treaty.

---

[122] W. Krieger, 'Was General Clay a Revisionist? Strategic aspects of the United States Occupation of Germany', *Journal of Contemporary History*, xviii (1983) p. 172. In Austria the USSR, at one point, deliberately obstructed the passage of food to the Western sectors of Vienna.

[123] A reference to the Morgenthau Plan to reduce Germany to a 'pastoral' state, which had been official American–British policy for some months in 1944–5.

[124] Beate Ruhm von Oppen (ed.) *Documents on Germany under Occupation 1945–1954* (1955) pp. 144 ff. (Molotov, 10 July 1946), 152 ff. (Byrnes, Stuttgart).

German questions did come before the Council of Foreign Ministers in July 1946. As he admitted privately to Byrnes, Molotov was not then ready to negotiate (hence, no doubt, the propaganda). But agreement was reached in December to proceed with discussion of a peace treaty; there were some signs of greater Soviet warmth (perhaps not unconnected with the conclusion of the other peace treaties); and this persisted in the initial phases of the Moscow Foreign Ministers Council in March.

British withdrawal from Greece and Turkey – the Truman Doctrine, 1947

In fact East and West moved in 1947 into full-scale Cold War, major road-marks being the Truman Doctrine, the failure of the Moscow Conference, American proposal and Soviet rejection of Marshall Aid, and the indefinite adjournment of the London Foreign Ministers Council that December.

To understand the first of these, we must return to the Balkans. We have seen that Soviet pressure led Turkey to keep its army mobilised at considerable expense. Further west Tito, despite much British aid during the war, was looking to advance his interests by a tough and ultra-communist line. In 1945 New Zealand forces had excluded the Yugoslavs from Trieste, an Italian port with a Slav hinterland; and in 1946 Yugoslavia and the USSR pushed hard, though unavailingly, for it in connection with the Italian peace treaty, Yugoslavia reinforcing its pressure by shooting down two American supply planes *en route* for Austria.[125] To the south, Yugoslavia (or its satellite Albania) mined the Corfu channel, blowing up two British warships. Later both backed a communist rising in a Greece that was in no shape economically to sustain the necessary military counter-measures. Greece, like Turkey, was in the British Middle Eastern sphere, and had in 1945–6 cost Britain some £132 million.[126] The Treasury disliked the expense, while Attlee saw bolstering the Greek regime as both provocative and ineffective. In February 1947 Bevin was brought to concede the sudden termination of aid to both Greece and Turkey.

Bevin had feared that too many withdrawals – the same month saw a fuel crisis and massive industrial shutdowns, the dumping on to the UN of the Palestine problem, and the announcement of Britain's intention to quit India in 1948 – would make Washington feel Britain was no longer worth

---

[125] This action apparently pleased Moscow, though Molotov also warned Yugoslavia not to go too far – Djilas, *Conversations with Stalin*, p. 102.

[126] K.O. Morgan, *Labour in Power* (Oxford, 1984) pp. 252–3.

supporting. In fact the decision over Greece and Turkey had the opposite effect. The US administration soon resolved on assistance. But it then had to secure approval of what some Congressmen saw as pulling British chestnuts out of the fire. Restrained advocacy by the new Secretary of State, Marshall, fell flat, so Acheson went over the top: not since Rome and Carthage had there been such a polarisation of power, and it was further exacerbated by an unbridgeable ideological chasm. Initial Soviet successes would spread by contagion, like apples in a barrel infected by one rotten one (the better-known 1950s metaphor was like a row of dominoes), until eventually even the United States was threatened. Aid for Greece and Turkey was not therefore a matter of bailing out the British but of building US security by strengthening free peoples against communist aggression and subversion. Impressed, Senator Vandenberg promised Truman support if he would publicly make the same plea to the Congress.

The result was the 'Truman Doctrine' of 12 March 1947, a request for $400 million for Greece and Turkey, buttressed by the potentially universalist prescription:

I believe it must be the policy of the United States to support free peoples who are resisting attempted subjugation by armed minorities or by outside pressures.

I believe that we must assist free peoples to work out their own destinies in their own way.

I believe that our help should be primarily through economic and financial aid which is essential to economic stability and orderly political processes.[127]

This Doctrine is often represented as a turning point, but its significance can perhaps be exaggerated. It might have torpedoed the important Council of Foreign Ministers meeting then being held in Moscow, but does not in fact seem to have upset Stalin. It did not commit the United States to military intervention. And, though the reference to free peoples resisting attempted subjugation was very broad, Acheson repeatedly explained to Congressmen that it was *not* meant either to encompass China or to sanction attempts to roll back Soviet control of Eastern Europe. It was, however, intended to pave the way for a further expansion of US aid to Western Europe – there had from the outset been acceptance that, though Greece and Turkey were the most urgent cases, they were not alone, and

[127] RIIA, *Documents 1947–8*, pp. 2–7 (esp. p. 6).

committees were set up in early March to study other countries in similar circumstances. On his return from what had proved an unsuccessful conference in Moscow, Marshall assigned this top priority.

Stalin's suggested Anglo-Soviet Treaty, 1947

1947 began with a Soviet attempt to woo Britain. Since 1943 the USSR had, when it distinguished between the major capitalist Powers, pressed more harshly on Britain than on the USA. Late in 1946 this changed, at least in propaganda terms. Molotov's demeanour also mellowed: Bevin was pleased by his remark in December that 'I think we are learning now to cooperate', and commented early in the Moscow Conference that he 'was beginning to come to a better understanding of the attitude of His Majesty's Government and to show some sympathy for it'. Stalin reinforced this impression, giving Field Marshal Montgomery red carpet treatment (and a Soviet Marshal's coat) during his visit to Moscow in January 1947, and urging on him a new treaty of Anglo-Soviet military alliance, independent of the UN. Stalin too proved gracious at an interview on 24 March, assuring Bevin that he appreciated Britain's wartime role in Egypt and 'had no intention of interfering in the carrying out of British policy' there or in India. Bevin was duly impressed.[128]

We can only speculate as to Stalin's motives. In a three Power situation, he instinctively tended to alternate between, and seek to divide, the other two. One aim of his post-war pressure on Britain's Middle Eastern 'sphere' may have been to force Britain to come to terms with the USSR. He may have known of the December 1946–January 1947 foreign policy confrontation between Bevin and Attlee (above, pp. 111–13), and presumably also of the public Labour back-bench pressure that winter to '*Keep Left*' and pursue a 'Third Force' policy distinct from the USA. Lastly, technical Anglo-American arms talks (triggered by the 1946 Turkey crisis) had leaked; Stalin described them to Montgomery as the prelude to an alliance – which his proposed Anglo-Soviet alliance probably sought to derail. That, certainly, was how Bevin saw it. He therefore sought so to handle the Soviet approach that 'it does not affect our relations with the Americans'. For if the UK gave priority to new Soviet negotiations, they would 'conclude that

[128] *FRUS 1947*, ii, pp. 282–3; Bullock, *Bevin*, pp. 381–2. Perhaps a better guide to Stalin's real outlook was his refusal (at that meeting) to permit the emigration of the handful of Russian war-brides, on the transparent pretext that the Supreme Soviet would not like it.

we had gone over definitively to the Russian camp and lost interest in military cooperation with them.' Washington did indeed show concern, which elicited copious Foreign Office reassurances; and formal diplomatic discussion of drafts for an Anglo-Soviet treaty were allowed to run into the sand during the spring of 1947.[129]

The Moscow Foreign Ministers Council, 10 March to 24 April 1947

Despite the enunciation of the 'Truman Doctrine' on 12 March, the opening phases of the Moscow Conference were marked by a degree of cordiality; after his interview with Stalin, Bevin could write that 'We are getting ahead. This week things will take shape, I have a quiet confidence of success, but it is too early yet to judge.'[130] But this was based on hopes that the USSR was coming closer to the British position. In the event few concessions were made by any of the four parties, and both the USSR and the USA sought to reopen questions they had tacitly conceded at Potsdam. France was alone in seeking to detach the Rhine and Ruhr and also in wishing to give German coal deliveries abroad priority over the level of German industrial production, but was now prepared to concede the central administrative agencies it had vetoed in 1945. However agreement was not reached on who should run these. The USA favoured a Provisional Government of delegates of the existing *Länder* (states), which could be put in place at once. Instead it was in principle decided to nominate a 'German representative body' to advise the Allied Control Council and draft a constitution. This was to lead on, Bevin hoped within a year, to elections and a Provisional Government. But the details were never agreed;[131] and discussion reverted to a Soviet wish to re-establish Weimar (bar its presidential powers) and Western insistence on entrenching the new *Länder* within a new German constitution, partly to ensure 'that

---

[129] Wayne Knight, 'Labourite Britain: America's "Sure Friend"? The Anglo-Soviet Treaty Issue, 1947', *Diplomatic History*, vii (1983) pp. 267–82; Ovendale, *English-Speaking Alliance*, pp. 43–5.

[130] Bullock, *Bevin*, p. 382.

[131] Molotov, but not Marshall or Bevin, wished to include in the Advisory body 'representatives of democratic parties, trade unions and other anti-Nazi organizations'; and Bidault insisted on the settlement of Germany's borders before the installation of any Provisional Government.

the election machinery should be controlled in the *Länder* and not in Berlin'.[132]

Records of the interminable meetings do not read as if success was ever very probable. Nor would agreements reached in Moscow necessarily have been implemented in practice. But some have argued that a pre-emptive Anglo-American acceptance of the Soviet position (on the German constitution, Four Power control of the Ruhr, and reparations from current production) would in fact secured the installation of an elected all-German government, and been a reasonable price to pay for it. In this connection it is worth noting that, admittedly within a Western framework, a supranational Ruhr authority was ultimately conceded to French pressure. And though Anglo-American distaste for subsidising Germany while the USSR extracted reparations from it is understandable, the USA was just coming to the point of proposing the even larger politico-economic subventions of the Marshall Plan.

All this, however, is speculation. The actual effect of the conference was to galvanise US foreign policy. A few Americans (notably General Clay) had been hopeful of a deal, but the State Department was pessimistic in the extreme – in late February its briefing ran that Marshall, the new Secretary of State, 'is going to Moscow knowing in advance that nothing would be decided there for the peace of the world ... Our experience ... has proved by now that it is impossible to negotiate with them. It is either to yield to them or to tell them no ...'[133] Intelligence intercepts supposedly convinced Molotov that Marshall 'would turn down all the Soviet proposals for the future of Germany.'[134] If so, he was mistaken. For Marshall was prepared to contemplate reparations from current production. In absolute terms, his proposal was limited; but he had had to overcome both State Department and Presidential opposition to put it forward at all, and, as he stressed in a radio report on the conference, he saw the absence of Soviet response as significant.[135] Still worse, Stalin seemed unmoved by a

[132] *FRUS* 1947, ii, esp. pp. 305–6, 311–13.

[133] Yergin, *Shattered Peace*, p. 297.

[134] Modin, *My Five Cambridge Friends*, p. 159.

[135] Philip Zelikow, 'George C. Marshall and the Moscow Council of Foreign Ministers Meeting of 1947', *Diplomacy and Statecraft*, viii (1997) esp. pp. 102–4, 107–13; *FRUS* 1947, ii, esp. pp. 298–9, 301–4, 306–7; Department of State, *Bulletin*, xvi (13 April 1947) pp. 652–3, which shows that Marshall's offer was only to 'study' a reparation from current production 'limited to compensation for the plants' earmarked for reparation that would remain *in situ* were permitted German production levels increased to aid a general European recovery.

frank exposition of US–Soviet differences and warnings that the conference was on the verge of failure: 'Differences,' he said,

> *had occurred before on other questions, and as a rule after people had exhausted themselves in dispute they then recognized the necessity of compromise. It is possible that no great success would be achieved at this session, but that should not cause anybody to be desperate. He thought that compromises were possible on all the main questions including demilitarization, political structure of Germany, reparations and economic unity. It was necessary to have patience and not become depressed.*

Stalin's reply may have been meant to be reassuring (though the Soviet record reads slightly more harshly).[136] According to Bohlen (a participant), Marshall perceived it as 'indifference to what was happening in Germany' and concluded 'that Stalin, looking over Europe, saw that the best way to advance Soviet interests was to let matters drift'. This view was presumably reinforced by the stolid time-wasting of 'Stone Arse' Molotov. As Marshall later put it, the Americans had originally thought the USSR 'could be negotiated with. [Ambassador] Harriman came back and said they could not be. I decided finally at Moscow . . . that they could not be.'[137]

Marshall Aid and the division of Europe

After the conference Marshall broadcast a sombre conclusion: 'Disintegrating forces are becoming evident. The patient is sinking as the doctor deliberates.' He felt, Bohlen says, that 'Economic conditions were bad . . . Millions of people were on short rations. There was a danger of epidemics. This was the kind of crisis that Communism thrived on. All the way back

---

[136] 'When the parties have exhausted each other, a moment will come for possible compromises' (quoted in Zelikow, 'Marshall and the Moscow Council', p. 114); for the US record, see *FRUS* 1947, ii, pp. 337–44.

[137] Charles E. Bohlen, *Witness to History 1929–1969* (1973) p. 263; Forrest C. Pogue, *George C. Marshall*, iv (New York, 1987) p. 196. Almost equally depressed, Bevin observed in May that he would give up hope of a settlement with the Russians should the next Foreign Ministers Council (in November) fail (Warner, 'From ally to enemy: Britain's relations with the Soviet Union, 1941–1948' in Michael Dockrill and Brian McKercher (eds), *Diplomacy and World Power. Studies in British Foreign Policy, 1890–1950* (Cambridge, 1996) p. 241.

to Washington, Marshall talked of the importance of finding some initiative to prevent the complete breakdown of Western Europe.'[138] The initiative was to be an increase of US aid, rendered the more urgent as UNRRA (under which e.g. Italy had received $589 million) was about to come to an end. State Department planning had, as we have seen, been in progress since March; the ground was prepared by a speech of Acheson's in May that estimated that Europe would need $5 billion a year for several years. At Harvard in June Marshall professed readiness to assist 'the revival of a working economy in the world so as to permit the emergence of political and social conditions in which free institutions can exist'; should the Europeans draw up a programme to that end, the USA would support it 'so far as it may be practical for us to do so'. It was a deliberately low-key launch, but the State Department was under no illusions as to the effect it could have in dividing Europe.

In fact the division of Europe was already proceeding very fast. In January 1947 Mikolajczyk's Peasant Party was crushed in Polish elections that Khrushchev admits were rigged – he enjoyed the joke, 'What sort of box is this? You drop Mikolajczyk in, but get Gomulka out'.[139] In Hungary a round of arrests, starting in December 1946, and the 'revelations' of conspiracy they produced, emasculated the Smallholders Party, whose secretary was interned in February; the screw was tightened again after the failure of the Moscow Conference, and the Prime Minister persuaded to retire into exile in late May. The opposite process occurred in Belgium, and in France and Italy, both of which had large Communist parties. Neither had tried to seize power at the Liberation, the French PCF believing itself too weak, the Italian PCI feeling that at best it could only take over in the north and that this would destroy national unity and entrench a reactionary regime in the south. So both embarked on what they envisaged as a long period of coalition government, within which they naturally sought to push their fortunes but not too dramatically; in September 1946 Stalin apparently endorsed such an approach in France. Nevertheless many people were suspicious, and the difficulties of working with the Communists increased over time, seriously hampering the conduct of economic policy. Early in May 1947 the Communists were dismissed from the French government after unwisely voting against its

[138] Bohlen, *Witness to History*, p. 263. Taubman notes Stalin's probing of Western visitors to establish whether an economic collapse was indeed imminent (*Stalin's American Policy*, pp. 136–9).
[139] *Khrushchev Remembers*, ii, p. 174.

(increasingly unpopular) incomes policy. At the end of the month an Italian political crisis was ended by the formation of an almost exclusively Christian Democrat (DC) government. In both cases the Communists, who had believed themselves indispensable, were taken by surprise and went quietly, though the French government had feared a coup and prepared against it. The initiative in shedding the Communists appears to have been local, taken by Socialist ministers in France, by the DC Premier De Gasperi in Italy.[140] The American ambassadors offered private encouragement (in the French case even assistance in contingency planning). Equally De Gasperi used the threat (that if his new government failed, the only alternative would be the far Left) to extract from the USA financial aid and a departure from its previously neutral stance on internal Italian politics.[141]

After Marshall's speech, Bevin and Bidault sought a European conference to draw up the recovery programme he had called for, and carefully invited Molotov to Paris in late June to discuss the joint issuing of invitations. Marshall's speech had surprised Moscow, and the USSR did not know what to make of it. As its Ambassador in Washington noted, the potential 'outlines of a Western European bloc directed against us are patently visible'; but the USA was seen as not really having many options – the economist Varga thought it faced a 20 per cent drop in production and 10 million unemployed, which Marshall was trying to stave off while at the same time seeking 'the maximum political benefits'. It was decided that Molotov should go to Paris to discover just what was on offer, while opposing any conditions limiting the sovereignty of (especially East) European states or seeking to draw them back into pre-war (i.e. Western-oriented) economic relationships. He should object to any use of German resources unless Soviet demands for reparations and Four Power control of the Ruhr were met in full; and aid should be limited to formerly anti-Nazi

---

[140] Eugenio Reale, *Avec Jaques Duclos au Banc des Accusés à la réunion Constituive du Kominform à Sklarska Poreba* (Paris, 1960), pp. 81–2 (France), 134 (Italy); Guido Pormigoni, 'De Gasperi e la crisi politica italiana del maggio 1947', *Ricerche di Storia Politica*, new series vi (2003) pp. 361–88. De Gasperi had sought to establish financial confidence by adding prestigious 'liberal' economists to the coalition government and downgrading, but not excluding, the communists. A disastrous meeting with Togliatti (following his newspaper denunciation of the US) led De Gasperi to press for exclusion. Anti-communist moves were seen as enhancing chances of a US loan; but Togliatti had not opposed seeking one.

[141] A. Platt and R. Leonardi, 'American Foreign Policy and the Postwar Italian Left', *Political Science Quarterly*, xciii (1978–9) esp. pp. 198–9; *FRUS 1947*, iii, esp. pp. 893–5, 904–13.

states. Molotov's subordinates have described this response to Marshall Aid as 'an attempt . . . at least to minimise its negative aspects and ensure that they should not impose any conditions on us. In a word, it should be something like Lend-Lease.'

This was not the model envisaged by the US envoy, Clayton, and Bevin in the course of – actually sometimes rather tense – talks. Three days after their conclusion, Soviet intelligence sent a summary to Molotov in Paris. He at once took steps to rebuff 'behind-the-scenes collusion of the USA and Great Britain', and further stiffened his opposition to Franco-British proposals to draw up a coordinated European economic plan that the USA could then be asked to fund. Crucially Bidault did not give way, though Bevin had feared, and Molotov presumably hoped,[142] that he could be influenced by the political strength of the French communists. So Molotov stalked out. Bidault and Bevin promptly extended formal invitations to a broader European conference on Marshall's offer. Initially Moscow still hoped to kill this. The USSR would make its displeasure clear by its absence; but on 5 July it instructed Yugoslavia (and the other East European countries) 'to take part . . . giving a rebuff to America, and its satellites, Britain and France, in order to prevent the Americans from unanimously pushing through their plan, and then . . . [to leave] the conference, taking with you as many delegates from other countries as possible.' But on 7 July this was countermanded, and a mass boycott enjoined.[143]

Moscow could hardly have played its cards worse. Both Bevin and Bidault had feared that, if the USSR continued to participate in Paris, it would certainly delay things and might get the conference to insist on conditions unacceptable to the United States. On the other hand, Bidault could not, politically, afford to exclude it from the outset; he hoped, therefore, that, if talks broke down, the blame would seem to rest with Molotov. In deciding to boycott proceedings, the USSR duly obliged. It should instead have cooperated, thus returning the ball to the American court. For the unspecific inclusion of all Europe in the US initiative had been 'a calculated

---

[142] That Molotov brought over 100 people with him to Paris is sometimes taken as indicating an intention to negotiate seriously; Bevin saw it as preparation to exert pressure on the French government via contacts with the political Left.

[143] The previous paragraphs derive chiefly from: Zubok and Pleshakov, *Inside the Kremlin's Cold War*, pp. 106–8; *New Evidence on the Soviet Rejection of the Marshall Plan, 1947: Two Reports* – by Scott D. Parrish and by Mikhail M. Narinsky – (CWIHP Working Paper no. 9, 1994), esp. pp. 13–26, 42–51; Bullock, *Bevin*, pp. 413–22.

risk both as regards the Russians and Congress', taken to prevent the USA incurring the blame for dividing the continent. The risk was that 'If the Russians came in the whole project would probably be unworkable because the amount of money involved in restoring both Eastern and Western Europe would be so colossal it could never be got from Congress, especially in view of the strong and growing reaction against the Soviet Union'.[144]

The Szklarska Poreba Conference and foundation of 'Cominform' (September 1947), French strikes (November–December 1947), Italian elections (April 1948) and covert US involvement

As Molotov left the Paris talks he warned that they 'would split Europe into two groups of states and . . . create new difficulties in the relations between them.' Bevin whispered in response, 'This really is the birth of the Western bloc'.[145] Stalin took the process one stage further by convening a conference in September of East European communist parties plus those of France and Italy. It was stage-managed by Malenkov and Zhdanov. The latter's keynote speech explained that, since the war, 'two diametrically opposed political lines' had taken shape; 'two camps were formed – the imperialist and anti-democratic camp having as its basic aim the establishment of world domination of American imperialism and the smashing of democracy, and the anti-imperialist and democratic camp having as its basic aim the undermining of imperialism . . .' The passage on the two camps was a late addition to drafts of Zhdanov's speech, probably inserted by Stalin himself. It was to be actualised in the East by the rapid completion of communist takeovers. In the West, communists were 'to destroy the capitalist economy and work systematically toward unity of live national forces' against US aid. This reversed the parliamentary-oriented policy the French and Italian Parties had adopted (with Soviet encouragement) since the war, and had continued even after their exclusion from office in hopes that they could force their way back into the government coalition.

---

[144] Acheson's recollections, as recorded in Jones, *Fifteen Weeks*, pp. 252–3; see also Bullock, *Bevin*, pp. 407–8, 417–21.
[145] *New Evidence on the Soviet Rejection of the Marshall Plan*, p. 25; Bullock, *Bevin*, p. 422.

At the conference both Parties were roughly harangued and forced to practice self-criticism – Duclos confessed to 'opportunism, legalitarianism, parliamentary illusions' and promised to 'mobilise the people of France against American imperialism'. Zhdanov ruled out an armed uprising as hopeless, but instructed the PCF to view itself as a party of opposition and demanded violent attacks on the socialists.[146] Proceedings ended with the symbolic re-establishment of a communist international, now named Cominform.

The order that communist parties should go into outright opposition in a last-ditch attempt to block the Marshall Plan had the effect of internalising the Cold War into the politics of (at least) France and Italy, in both of which, for over two decades, a substantial minority identified with Moscow rather than with their own government. (In Italy indeed the cleavage between Moscow and Washington was for many years the principal one in politics.) In November 1947 the communist-led French trades union federation called for general strikes. These soon had 3 million workers out and many factories occupied, and led later to explosions and train derailments. They brought down the government and created an atmosphere of crisis. But a new government mobilised army reservists, disbanded communist units of the riot police and deployed the remainder, and passed fierce anti-picketing legislation. With British encouragement, the USA helped by extending interim financial aid. America also provided more covert assistance – thus, responding *inter alia* to an appeal from Leon Blum, it financed a breakaway anti-communist trades union movement (the *Force Ouvrière*); the money came initially from the American unions,[147] but the cost (c. $1 million p.a. by the early 1950s) was later assumed by the CIA.

Italy, which was not evacuated by Anglo-American troops till December 1947, was quieter. But all manner of dangers were anticipated in connection with the 1948 elections, which the Communists and

---

[146] The Yugoslav Kardelj asserted that 'Peaceful development of socialism by parliamentary manoeuvres' was only possible in 'eastern countries like Poland and Bulgaria, where the directing role belongs to Communist Parties with solid positions acquired during the armed struggle'. For the conference generally, see: Zubok and Pleshakov, *Inside the Kremlin's Cold War*, pp. 132–3; *New Evidence on the Soviet Rejection of the Marshall Plan*, pp. 32–8; Reale, *Avec Jacques Duclos*, esp. pp. 23, 34, 81–2, 131, 134, 138–9, 153–4, 163, 175–7; RIIA, *Documents 1947–1948*, pp. 122 ff.

[147] These had worried as early as 1945 about a communist takeover of Europe, and so had assisted non-communist unions.

majority Socialists contested as a Popular Front – helped, it was believed, by both Soviet subventions and captured Fascist gold. A major operation was launched to influence the result; it included promises over Trieste, threats that US aid would end in the event of a Communist victory, co-ordinated lobbying by Italian-Americans, and the secret expenditure of some $10 million on electoral organisation, bribes and propaganda. Such involvement had its limits – military intervention was excluded except in response to a communist rising *after* electoral defeat.[148] But this question did not arise. For the DC (helped also by the Church, and by indigenous anti-communist sentiment) unexpectedly gained 49 per cent to the Popular Front's 31 per cent.[149] It went on to dominate Italian politics for over four decades; but for a good half of this period the Communists, aided until 1956 by the Socialists, were in unconditional opposition.

The London Council of Foreign Ministers meeting, November–December 1947

Contemporaneous with the French strikes was the London Foreign Ministers' meeting, held to resume discussion of Germany after the spring failure of the Moscow Conference. Bevin had said in May that he would abandon hope of a settlement with the USSR if this failed. Success was not expected; but Bevin continued to feel there was at least a chance that, once Molotov realised there would be no Western rifts or weakness, he would execute a sudden U-turn (as in 1946 over the Italian peace treaty). The worst possible outcome, though, and the one Moscow was thought to favour, would be endless indecision that would prevent German, hence West European, economic and political revival. The conference failed, its sticking point being Soviet refusal to agree, in advance of a general repara-tions settlement, that the Powers should account for the reparations they had so far removed. On 15 December, after three weeks of unproductive meetings, the Foreign Ministers all agreed to adjourn *sine die*. This was

---

[148] Though if the Communists obtained *domination* of the Italian government by legal means, the National Security Council recommended US support for 'the anti-Communist Italian underground'.

[149] R.W. Johnson, *The Long March of the French Left* (1981) Chap. 2; P.M. Williams, *Crisis and Compromise. Politics in the Fourth Republic* (1964) p. 347; Platt and Leonardi, 'American Policy and the Post-War Italian Left' pp. 201–2; Trevor Barnes, 'The Secret Cold War: the C. I. A. and American Foreign Policy in Europe, 1946–56' (2 parts), *Historical Journal*, xxiv and xxv (1981, 1982).

not quite the end of the Four Power framework, which struggled on in Germany for some months, or even of the Foreign Ministers Council (which met once more, largely *pro forma*, in 1949 after the lifting of the Berlin Blockade). But the era of regular negotiations was over, and little point was seen, at least until after Stalin's death, in attempting to resume them. Bevin's report to Parliament on the London Conference stressed that 'We cannot go on as we have been'. Instead he turned to the creation of what he rather opaquely described to Marshall as:

an understanding backed by power, money and resolute action. It would be a sort of spiritual federation of the West . . . If such a powerful consolidation of the West could be achieved it would then be clear to the Soviet Union that having gone so far they could not advance any further.[150]

[150] Bullock, *Bevin*, esp. pp. 490, 495, 498–9. The London meetings generated at least one memorable exchange: Molotov tried to patronise what he saw as the pseudo-socialist Bevin by recommending Hilferding's commentary on Marx, and drew the reply, 'You can tell Mr Molotov that I have read 'Ilferding and I found him tedious'.

CHAPTER 4

The nadir of the Cold War, 1948–1953

The years 1948–53 represent the harshest sustained period of the Cold War. There was East–West abuse and propaganda, but almost no negotiation. Instead each side unilaterally promoted the organisation of its own sphere, sometimes also trying to thwart that of the other side. In 1948–9 the focus was still on Europe, with a prolonged crisis over the Berlin Blockade. But 1948 also saw decisive communist victories in China north of the Yangtze, 1949 the takeover of all mainland China; a new, and highly militant, communist leader, Mao Zedong, had arrived. Scholars argue as to whether Stalin was emboldened by Mao's success, or merely moved by rivalry; either way, in 1950 he authorised North Korea to invade the South. The USA had already begun to involve itself in Indochina, extending financial aid to the colonial power, France, so as to prevent communist victory in the Chinese civil war being replicated in Vietnam. Now it intervened directly in Korea to prevent Northern conquest of the South, with China soon following suit to prevent the defeat and overrunning of the North. As a result of the Korean War, containment of China in Asia joined that of the USSR in Europe. A further development was the militarisation of the Cold War. After 1945 both East and West had cut defence. From 1948 armies again started to grow. In 1949 Soviet explosion, unexpectedly early, of a nuclear device led both to US development of the hydrogen bomb and to a policy review (NSC-68) advocating a massive increase in conventional forces. The Korean War secured its adoption. An ageing and increasingly paranoid Stalin responded on a scale that his East European satellite regimes could not have long sustained – some say with thoughts of a pre-emptive strike before rearmament in Western Europe could be completed.

West German currency reform 1948

Early 1948 saw one last initiative within a Four Power framework, an Anglo-American attempt to secure Allied Control Council agreement on an all-German currency reform. But relationships within the Council cooled rapidly in March 1948 (partly no doubt in response to the meeting of another, purely Western, London Conference on Germany) and the Russians walked out for good on the 20th. Thereafter both Western and Eastern currency reforms went ahead in parallel.

Even gaining Western agreement was not easy, and the extension of currency reform to the French zone needed eleventh-hour crisis negotiations. French consent stemmed mainly from the changed international situation (especially after the February–March Prague 'coup'), and from limited British concessions over control of the Ruhr – but also from the manifest Anglo-American readiness to go it alone in Bizonia, and from American hints that they would enter no commitments against either German or Russian aggression unless agreement was reached.[1] In the end, though, 20 June 1948 saw the implementation in all three Western zones of what turned out to be a spectacularly successful package of currency reform and economic liberalisation.

The London Conference had also called for the drafting of a constitution for what would presumably become a new West German state. Stalin must have expected this – in January and February he had told Yugoslav and Bulgarian delegations that 'The West will make Western Germany their own, and we shall turn Eastern Germany into our own state'. But such an outcome entailed risks since, if only for reasons of size, Western Germany was the more likely of the two to become the embodiment of German national sentiment. (Bevin had in fact written in January that, though the division of Germany was likely to deepen, it would not last indefinitely – 'The problem for us is to bring unity about as soon as possible but in such a way as to ensure that the forces of attraction operate from the West upon the East and not vice versa'.) So Stalin responded by squeezing Berlin, a city under Four Power occupation but deep within the Soviet zone.[2]

---

[1] *FRUS 1948*, ii, pp. 275–7.
[2] Milovan Djilas, *Conversations with Stalin* (paperback edn) p. 119; Alan Bullock, *Ernest Bevin. Foreign Secretary 1945–51* (1983) p. 515.

The Berlin Blockade 1948–9

The first months of 1948 saw growing Soviet interference with overland access to Berlin, and the spreading of rumours that the Western Powers would soon be pulling out.[3] Following the end of the (Western) London Conference in early March Marshal Sokolovsky was recalled from Berlin to Moscow for consultations, and plans drawn up for restrictions on communications between Berlin and the West. On 20 March Sokolovsky walked out of the Allied Control Commission, and on 1 April the restrictions started to be applied 'except for restrictions on communication by air, which we intend to introduce later'. On 17 April there were hopeful reports that these measures had 'dealt a serious blow to the prestige of the Americans and British in Germany. The German population considers that "the Anglo-Americans have retreated before the Russians" '.[4] Equally this hardened convictions that to abandon Berlin would be a great blow to Western prestige and thus to the growing Western alignment of the rest of Europe.

Further tightening followed, until in June the USSR shut off both electricity supplies and overland communication to the Western sectors. The immediate occasion was a dispute over which currency (the Soviet zone mark *tout court*, the Soviet mark but issued under Four Power supervision, or both the Soviet and Western marks)[5] should be used in Berlin. But the USSR indicated that its real concern was to stop the convocation of a West German constituent assembly and return the German question to a Four Power basis. Beyond that, a retrospective memorandum states, 'our

---

[3] (Sir) Percy Cradock, *Know Your Enemy. How the Joint Intelligence Committee Saw the World* (2002) pp. 73–4. Arrangements for overland access to Berlin's Western sectors had been agreed orally between the Americans and Russians in June 1945, with a supplementary written agreement that September about air corridors.

[4] Michail Narinsky, 'The Soviet Union and the Berlin Crisis, 1948–9', in Francesca Gori and Silvio Pons (eds) *The Soviet Union and Europe in the Cold War 1943–53* (Basingstoke, 1996) pp. 62–4.

[5] Britain and France had induced the USA to accept the Soviet mark – but only if it was printed under Four Power supervision, since the USSR had long been suspected (perhaps unjustly) of printing occupation currency that then had to be supported with dollars. (The suspicion, and insistence on supervision, had earlier blocked all ideas of joint currency reform for Germany as a whole.) The USSR rejected supervision and unilaterally introduced its currency to the whole of Berlin; on US insistence, the West mark was given equal legal status in the Western sectors. The Soviets replied with the blockade and a proclamation declaring the end of Four Power government of the city.

leading comrades in Germany assumed that, as a result of the . . . restrictions . . . the Western powers would be forced to retreat, to surrender their positions in Berlin to the Soviet Union', or at least that the inclusion of 'all Berlin in the economic system of the Soviet zone' and the restoration 'of unified administration of the city . . . would have served as basis for the winning over the population of West Berlin, and . . . created the preconditions for completely ousting the Western powers from Berlin.' How far Stalin shared these hopes is hard to say, though he had in late March encouraged an East German communist with the words, 'Let's try with all our might, and maybe we'll drive them out.'[6]

A blockade of Berlin had been forecast in the West, but no agreement sought as to how to counter it. General Clay believed the Soviets were only bluffing, and that they would not actually interfere with an army-escorted land convoy. In fact Stalin said the Red Army should stop such a probe, though he reserved his decision if the US seemed about to attack all along the border.[7] Cautiously the West did not attempt any overland move, but instead tried an airlift. This was a fairly desperate expedient to buy time, since West Berlin had stockpiles for only between one and two months and nobody in mid-1948 believed that 2.5 million civilians could be indefinitely supplied by air – on 27 June Marshall talked of zero hour not being reached for two to three weeks, and as late as 19 July it was thought the airlift would be viable only till October. But the hope that diplomatic discussions could be opened within this time was well founded.

The Western ambassadors in Moscow sought a high-level meeting, and were received by Stalin on 2 August. His message was, 'Stop applying the London [Conference] decisions and withdraw the . . . [Western] mark. There will be no difficulties. It could be done tomorrow. Think about it.'[8] Privately the ambassadors regarded these conditions for the lifting of the blockade as acceptable. But when it came to working out the details both sides hardened their positions, and though things again looked promising in late August, they stalled in September (when a Parliamentary Council was convened to draw up a constitution for a West German state). Nor was progress made at the UN in October–November, even though the

---

[6] Narinskii, 'The Soviet Union and the Berlin Crisis', pp. 65, 67, 69. A hint was also dropped that friction could be avoided if the West would swap its sectors of Berlin for a slice of the Soviet zone (an interesting idea that was never followed up).
[7] Stalin also excluded the possibility of the US using nuclear weapons over Berlin (Gromyko's recollections, recorded in Henry Kissinger, *Diplomacy* (1995) p. 436.
[8] Narinskii, 'The Soviet Union and the Berlin Crisis', pp. 68–70.

Western Powers were now prepared, in return for the calling off of the blockade, to accept the Soviet mark as the sole currency in Berlin.[9] On the ground, having failed to paralyse the elected Berlin government by mob violence, the USSR established a breakaway government for its sector and settled down to wait for the winter.

The Soviet plan of March 1948 had originally envisaged restrictions on Western flights to Berlin.[10] But these were never introduced, no doubt from caution, and perhaps also from an initial feeling that they would not prove necessary. Indeed the airlift's viability long remained in doubt. With the advent of fog in late December supplies fell very low, but recovered when fine weather returned in January. Stalin first hinted at the lifting of the blockade late that month – a counter-embargo on deliveries from western Germany had hit hard[11] – and, after leisurely back-channel negotiations, the blockade ended in May 1949 against an agreement to hold a Four Power meeting on Germany later that month. By now, though, new constitutions had been adopted in both eastern and western Germany; unsurprisingly the Four Power meeting brought no agreement.

In negotiations during the blockade France and Britain had sometimes favoured a softer line than the USA, which could have led to trouble had conditions become critical. Both, however, contributed energetically to the airlift. It succeeded, but only as a result of the concentration on Berlin of much of the Anglo-American transport capacity – over the protests of the ever-timorous US Chiefs of Staff. The decision to do so had been made possible by Western confidence (slightly dented in September–October 1948) that the Russians did not intend war and would therefore not allow things to escalate further. This confidence was reinforced by the US stockpile of fifty atom bombs. Truman still withheld these bombs' military control. But June–July 1948 saw British requests for the basing of nuclear bombers in the UK as a deterrent. The US *appeared* to comply.[12] Some at least of the Americans supporting these requests reckoned, correctly, that, once deployed, the planes would become an accepted fixture. One result of the Berlin Blockade, therefore, was to provide the USA with forward bases.

---

[9] *The Annual Register, 1948*, p. 163.

[10] Narinskii, 'The Soviet Union and the Berlin Crisis', pp. 62, 65.

[11] Also on deliveries through the US zone. But more forceful measures, like closing the exits to the Black and Baltic Seas, were never risked.

[12] Actually the aircraft despatched, though of the appropriate configuration, had not been converted to deliver A-bombs. Converted bombers did not come until 1949.

Still more important was its effect on relations between Berliners, and to a lesser extent West Germans, and the occupying Powers. For the latter Berlin was transmogrified into a symbol of freedom, while in December 1948 elections West Berliners overwhelmingly endorsed their occupiers as partners and protectors. In West Germany itself the effect was less marked – when in late 1949 the Opposition called Adenauer 'the Chancellor of the Allies' it was not a compliment. But Western refusal to abandon Berlin and the generally (though not universally) perceived need for protection against further communist expansion was one reason why relations in the 1950s ran more smoothly than they had in the 1920s. The blockade had proved another of Stalin's mistakes.[13]

The North Atlantic Treaty 1949

In June 1947 the US administration had proposed, and almost a year later Congress had legislated for, economic assistance to promote an Atlantic-oriented West European recovery. Security was the other side of the coin. Arguably the first country to seek a multilateral security system outside the UN was Canada. Be that as it may, in early December 1947 one Canadian reported his impression that the US authorities 'were casting about to see if proposals for a Mutual Defence Treaty could not be brought forward from some other source than themselves'.[14] If so, Bevin soon obliged them, floating, between December 1947 and January 1948, ideas of a 'Western democratic system' 'with the backing of the Americas and the Dominions'. The State Department was encouraging, and urged both on Bevin and on Spaak of Belgium the example of the September 1947 Rio Inter-American Treaty of Reciprocal Assistance. Bevin then publicly called for a Western Union based on treaties between the UK, France and the Benelux Powers. Within a couple of months he had secured both the multi-lateral Brussels Treaty between these countries (directed against any revival of German aggression but also providing for mutual assistance in the event of 'an armed attack in Europe') and the inauguration of secret Anglo-Canadian-US discussions 'on the establishment of an Atlantic security system'. The pace

[13] For the blockade as a whole, see (besides Narinskii, 'The Soviet Union and the Berlin Crisis') Avi Shlaim, *The United States and the Berlin Blockade 1948–1949* (Berkeley, 1983).

[14] J.W. Holmes, *Canada and the Search for World Order 1943–1957*, ii (Toronto, 1983) p. 105; also Martin Folly, 'Breaking the Vicious Circle: Britain, the United States and the Genesis of the North Atlantic Treaty', *Diplomatic History* xii (1986).

had undoubtedly been increased by the Prague 'coup' in February (below, pp. 147–8), which, though discounted in advance, nevertheless horrified the West when it actually happened, and by simultaneous Soviet pressure on Norway and Finland. Subsequent negotiations were slower and more difficult. There were differences as to which countries should be included in a North Atlantic Treaty, whether it should cover what was then the Algerian portion of metropolitan France, and above all as to how it could be made acceptable to Congress in view of the traditional US suspicion of entangling alliances. But a fillip was given to proceedings by the unexpected Democrat victory in the 1948 elections, and a treaty finally signed in April 1949.

Obviously the Treaty was meant to deter – in Bevin's words, 'to inspire the Soviet Government with enough respect for the West to remove temptation from them and so ensure a long period of peace'. But on both sides of the Atlantic people looked quite as much to its psychological effects *within* Western Europe. Bevin again:

Another essential thing . . . is to give confidence. That confidence would have very great repercussions and make the economic steps that have been taken more effective. Therefore the construction of a North Atlantic defence system would put heart into the whole of western Europe and would encourage them in their resistance to the infiltration tactics which they have had to face hitherto.

Kennan was more forthright: the basic Soviet intent was 'the conquest of western Europe by political means', military force playing 'a major role only as a means of intimidation': 'A North Atlantic Security Pact will affect the political war only insofar as it operates to stiffen the self-confidence of the western Europeans in the face of Soviet pressure'; indeed 'the need for military alliances and rearmament on the part of the western Europeans is primarily a *subjective* one . . .' Beyond this, both Bevin and Kennan had their eye on the treaty's broader implications for the German question, Kennan arguing that only a Western union 'holds out any hope of restoring the balance of power in Europe without permitting Germany to become again the dominant power', Bevin that 'if the new defence system is so framed that it relates to any aggressor [i.e. to Germany as well as the USSR] it would give all the European states such confidence that it might well be that the age-long trouble between Germany and France might tend to disappear'.[15]

[15] *FRUS* 1948, iii, esp. pp. 48, 78–9 (Bevin), 7, 285 (Kennan); on this occasion Kennan's views appear to have been generally accepted in the State Department.

Consolidation of communist rule in Eastern Europe

Meanwhile communist rule had consolidated itself in Eastern Europe. The process had been fastest in Yugoslavia and its satellite Albania. Here communist forces were in control from the time of the German withdrawals in late 1944. A year later they secured lop-sided majorities in elections where the choice lay only between supporting the 'bloc of communists and non-party sympathisers' and publicly placing one's vote in the opposition urn; overtly communist constitutions followed early in 1946.[16]

Elsewhere (with the possible exception of Greece)[17] communism was weaker, and could not have succeeded without support from Soviet occupation forces. We have argued above that, by 1944–5, Stalin viewed Poland, Romania and Bulgaria as non-negotiable. Even so, full transition to a 'People's Democracy' took time. In 1944–5 Polish relics of the anti-German but also anti-communist wartime 'Home Army' clashed, on the ground, with supporters of the (communist) Lublin government; in these conflicts the presence of the Red Army was decisive, and in October 1944 Stalin urged the communists to tougher action before it moved on west.[18] At a higher level, Stalin saw to it in 1945 that the Lublin government should not be too seriously diluted by politicians returning from the London government-in-exile; and both security and control over the resettlement of the ex-German Oder–Neisse territories remained in communist hands. Still in 1946 it was Mikolajczyk's Peasant Party that had the largest membership. The free elections promised at Yalta were repeatedly postponed. But in 1946 a referendum (on the abolition of the Senate) developed into a trial of strength between the communist Workers Party, with Socialist support, and Mikolajczyk's Peasants. The true result is unclear – Rothschild believes that voters rejected the proposition;[19] but after an embarrassing ten-day wait the government declared a favourable

---

[16] Joseph Rothschild, *Return to Diversity. A Political History of East Central Europe since World War II* (New York, 1993 edn) pp. 56, 73, 104–5, 119–20.

[17] It appears that the communist-dominated resistance movements EAM-ELAS could have taken over on the German departure, but were restrained by Stalin. When they did rise in December 1944 (rather than accept disarmament), it took considerable British force to check them.

[18] Antony Polonsky, *The Great Powers and the Polish Question 1941–45* (1976) pp. 44–5.

[19] Rothschild, *Return to Diversity*, p. 83.

two-thirds majority. In January 1947 it felt strong enough to hold what Khrushchev accepts were rigged elections; and in October Mikolajczyk abandoned the contest by fleeing the country. By then the communists had moved on to squeezing their (more numerous) Socialist allies, a process completed in December 1948 by the merger of the two parties.[20]

In Romania communist party membership had in 1944 been below 1,000. But takeover proved easier than in Poland. Government stemmed from King Michael, who had in August 1944 staged a coup and switched to the Allied side. After the Yalta conference, Vyshinsky descended on Bucharest and insisted on the installation in office of a communist-dominated coalition, albeit headed by a friendly pre-war politician, Petru Groza. In August 1945, encouraged by Truman's remarks that Romania should not be seen as in the sphere of any one power, King Michael dismissed Groza and appealed for US and British assistance. Groza simply refused to go, and the USA and Britain backed off, undertaking at the December 1945 Moscow Conference to recognise Groza's government once it had taken in two token non-communists and promised free elections. Romanian elections had traditionally been 'made' by the incumbents, and so were those of Novemeber 1946. In February 1947 the Romanian peace treaty was signed; freed from any further need to conciliate the Anglo-Americans, the government proceeded to a wave of political arrests, followed that autumn by trials of the top National Peasant leaders. In December King Michael was forced to leave, and Romania formally became a people's democracy.[21] In Bulgaria a communist-led coalition, the Fatherland Front, seized power shortly after the arrival of the Red Army in September 1944, and embarked on purges and executions. Their scale produced anti-communist revulsion; and from 1945–7 the Agrarian Nikola Petkov led a tenacious if ineffective opposition, injudiciously encouraged by the local US political representative. Elections were held in November 1945, but boycotted by the opposition. In December the USA and Britain agreed to recognise the Bulgarian, like the Romanian, government once it

---

[20] Rothschild, *Return to Diversity*, pp. 81–5; Nikita Khrushchev, *Khrushchev Remembers. The Last Testament* (1974) (hereafter *Khrushchev Remembers*, ii) pp. 173–4.

[21] Rothschild, *Return to Diversity*, pp. 107–12; Geir Lundestad, *The American Non-Policy towards Eastern Europe 1943–1947* (Oslo) pp. 231–48. Maniu was jailed 'on charges – not unfounded, albeit vastly exaggerated – of conspiracy with British and American intelligence agents', stemming largely from the time of the 1946 panics that the USSR was about to invade Turkey.

had taken in opposition figures. But Petkov refused to enter, save on terms that the USSR vetoed, so recognition was in practice withheld. Meanwhile the communists first purged their allies, and also the army, then staged elections in October 1946. Even the official voting figures conceded Petkov a respectable performance, and he continued to campaign against the frauds that had, he claimed, denied him victory. Washington endorsed his criticisms, but it also negotiated a Bulgarian peace treaty, signed in February 1947 and ratified by the US Senate on 4 June. Petkov was arrested the next day, and then hung. This did not end all political opposition – there were arrests of Social Democrats in mid-1948; but essentially only mopping up remained.[22]

Hungary and Czechoslovakia were different in that both experienced a longer period of genuine coalition government. In 1944–5 Hungarian leaders restrained their party's zeal, suggesting that the time might not be ripe for a takeover for another fifteen years. One reason for such caution was supposedly a wish not to alarm the Anglo-Americans while Poland was still being secured [above, p. 85]. Indeed they still wondered in 1946 whether 'Stalin might not let Hungary come under the political influence of the [Western] allies in exchange for Soviet demands on Poland and Germany'.[23] Their unpopularity had been borne in on them in 1945: in the parliamentary elections that November the Smallholders won 57 per cent of the vote, the Communists only 17 per cent. With the aid of the Soviet occupation authorities they recovered ground in 1946, by pressurising the Smallholders, in the name of anti-Fascism or by the discovery of 'conspiracies', into ejecting prominent members and dissolving party organisations and forcing resignations. (The technique came to be known as 'salami tactics'.) But even at the end of the year the Soviet commander, Marshal Voroshilov, gave instructions that 'Hungary will be a bourgeois democracy and therefore it is necessary . . . to place in the government apparatus and social organisations', communist sleepers, 'who could be trusted in future'. However such preparations were countermanded, our source recalls, at 'the beginning of 1947 – perhaps in February?'[24] February 1947 certainly witnessed the start of a communist offensive, with the Soviet arrest of the Smallholders' secretary; this continued in May with the

[22] Rothschild, *Return to Diversity*, pp. 115–19; Lundestad, *American Non-Policy*, Chap. 7.

[23] Zoltan Vas' unpublished memoirs, cited in Charles Gati, *Hungary and the Soviet Bloc* (Durham, N.C., 1986) p. 118.

[24] Tibor Szamuely, cited in ibid. p. 118.

announcement that he had incriminated the Prime Minister, Ferenc Nagy, who was intimidated into resignation and exile. By late August this pressure had so split and demoralised the Smallholders that they were overtaken by the Communists in new parliamentary elections. Nevertheless the latter had polled only 22 per cent; and at the September Sklarska Poreba Conference of communist parties (to found Cominform – above, pp. 138–9) the Hungarian representative Revai initially claimed only that the Hungarian system was a 'mixture . . . of elements of the people's democracy and bourgeois democracy'. But it soon 'became apparent that . . . communization . . . still only partial and uneven . . . was now to be carried out at top speed', 'easing the "National Front" allies out of power and establishing a Communist dictatorship in all countries of Eastern Europe'.[25] On his return Revai reported that there had been 'significant changes in the political and tactical direction', and required a more 'militant spirit'. Non-communist politicians were pressed into subordination or exile; in November parliament delegated its powers to the government; and by December 1947 communist leaders could claim to have 'caught up' other East European countries.[26]

There remained Czechoslovakia. In 1943 President-in-exile Beneš had concluded a deal with Moscow that effectively 'Finlandised' the country; it consistently endorsed Soviet foreign policy, but internally a Communist-led coalition government continued to operate a more or less liberal political system until 1948. The Communist leader, Gottwald, was later to say that 'We prepared [the] February 1948 [takeover] from 1945 on and particularly from 1947'. In May 1946 the Communists gained 38 per cent of the votes; they hoped to achieve an absolute majority, and with it full power, at the next elections – a distinctive road to socialism endorsed by Stalin that August. This electoral strategy was never abandoned.[27] But from mid-1947 one wing of the party came to doubt its wisdom and to look

---

[25] Eugenio Reale (an Italian delegate to the conference), 'The Founding of the Cominform', in Milorad Drachkovitch and Branko Lazitch, *The Comintern: Historical Highlights. Essays, Recollections, Documents* (New York, 1966) p. 260.

[26] Gati, *Hungary and the Soviet Bloc*, pp. 118–22; Rothschild, *Return to Diversity*, pp. 99–101.

[27] Both Communists and non-Communists expected to do well at the 1948 elections (a Communist poll in January forecasting 55%). Gottwald himself doubted whether the Communists would get 45%, though he did look also to using independently elected Socialist fellow travellers – Karel Kaplan, *The Short March. The Communist Takeover in Czechoslovakia 1945–1948* (1987) pp. 106, 115n, 148–9.

instead to their control of the security forces and to extra-parliamentary action – a process encouraged when the Czechs were rebuked at Sklarska Poreba for having overvalued the parliamentary approach and so let slip the right moment for seizing power. The non-communist parties were disunited, and also handicapped by their belief that Communist participation in government was a guarantee of Czech alignment with the USSR and hence a protection against direct Soviet intervention. Nevertheless some Communists feared that they might be excluded from government, as in France and Italy. As a political crisis mounted in February 1948 over the partisan behaviour of the police, the Soviet ambassador pushed Gottwald to take decisive action and invited him to turn for military help to the USSR. Gottwald declined, confident that the Communists were fully in control of the situation. This indeed soon proved to be the case – anti-communist ministers precipitated a crisis by resigning, and the Communists pressured Beneš into appointing a new government that rapidly established their monopoly of power.[28]

Stalin's growing radicalism, 1947–8; Stalin and Greek communist risings

This East European narrative serves to underline the importance, sometimes underrated in Cold War accounts that focus on the Marshall Plan, of the early part of 1947. The outcome in Poland, Romania and Bulgaria may never have been in real doubt; but the Polish elections that broke Mikolajczyk were staged in January 1947, while the signature (in February) and ratification (in June) of peace treaties opened the way to the execution of Petkov in Bulgaria and to a wave of arrests in Romania. February 1947 also saw the Soviet arrest of the Hungarian Smallholders' secretary, followed in May by the intimidation of the Prime Minister into exile. That said, things were further ratcheted up by the Marshall Plan, in response to which East European parties were instructed, at Sklarska Poreba, to hasten the completion of the process.

However, it was not clear how much further Stalin could go in Europe, at least in the short run. In 1948–9 he did try pressure on Berlin, but it proved counter-productive. Another possibility was Greece. The 1944 'Percentages' agreement with Churchill had left this in the British sphere.

---

[28] Kaplan, *Short March*, esp. pp. 14–15, 75–7, 105, 123–4, 138, 175–85; Rothschild, *Return to Diversity*, pp. 90–6. Soviet anxiety to afford military help may have stemmed from fears of US counter-intervention (*Khrushchev Remembers*, ii, p. 189).

Accordingly Stalin had first restrained the communists, then acquiesced in British suppression of their December 1944 rising. This rebellion alarmed moderate Greek opinion: it secured royalist victories at the 1946 election (internationally supervised, but boycotted by the communists who would perhaps have gained up to a quarter of the vote) and plebiscite. In 1945–6 Rightist reaction also took the form of police harrassment, and of vigilante attacks and murders. This drove some of its victims to the mountains, where a number of communist bands had never stood down. The summer of 1946 brought military sweeps by the government, the autumn large-scale communist guerrilla activity in the north and the creation (in concert with Belgrade) of a command structure that, in December, styled itself the 'Democratic Army of Greece'.[29] The rising, whose initial prospects seemed quite promising, had begun with Yugoslav rather than Soviet support. But in May 1947 Stalin sent Yugoslavia a message praising its actions; he also received the Greek communist Zachariades in Moscow, and overruled Zhdanov's refusal to supply him with arms.[30] However, the USSR then blocked Yugoslav attempts to have the Sklarska Poreba Conference pay tribute to the Greek insurrection in Cominform's founding declaration; and by February 1948 Stalin claimed to be getting cold feet, telling the Yugoslavs and Bulgarians the rebellion had:

no prospect of success at all. What, do you think that Great Britain and the United States – the United States, the most powerful state in the world – will permit you to break their line of communication in the Mediterranean? Nonsense . . . The uprising . . . must be stopped, and as quickly as possible.[31]

One may speculate as to how far Stalin really believed this – he allowed Bulgarian and Romanian aid to continue until the end a year later – and how far his primary concern was now to cut Tito down to size. Either way, Greece soon ceased to be worth pursuing, even as a probe.[32] Meanwhile, Tito's successful defiance in 1948 brought Stalin concerns nearer home,

---

[29] R.J. Crampton, *The Balkans since the Second World War* (2002) Chap. 6.

[30] Geoffrey Swain, 'The Cominform: Tito's International?', *Historical Journal*, xxxv (1992) esp. pp. 654–5; Vladislav Zubok and Constantine Pleshakov, *Inside the Kremlin's Cold War. From Stalin to Khrushchev* (Cambridge, Mass., 1996) pp. 127–9.

[31] Reale, 'Founding of the Cominform', p. 264; Djilas, *Conversations with Stalin*, pp. 102–3, 140–1.

[32] Tito withdrew assistance to concentrate on his own survival, and this, together with US aid to the government, doomed the insurrection.

and induced him to concentrate rather on eliminating all possibility of repetition elsewhere in Eastern Europe (below, pp. 537–8).

Outside Europe, though, other possibilities were opening up for forward policies. Some proved dead ends. In 1947–9 the USSR was the chief armourer of the Zionist movement/Israel in its 'War of Independence'. But whatever hopes had been dangled before Stalin by (deliberately chosen) Zionist Leftists, the state of Israel made clear by its alignment over the Korean War that it looked rather to the USA.[33] Nor did the 1948 communist insurgencies in Java and Malaya (if indeed they were authorised by Moscow) lead anywhere. But China was quite different; for communist success in its long-standing civil war both expanded the Cold War, hitherto primarily a European phenomenon, into East and Southeast Asia, and did much to heat it up.

China, 1945–9[34]

During the war it had looked as if China would be in the US sphere. With a view, as he admitted, to its future rather than its present power, Roosevelt had secured it permanent membership of the UN Security Council. But in the meantime Japan occupied much of northern and coastal China, leaving Chiang Kai-shek's Kuomintang (KMT) government confined to the interior and heavily dependent on US assistance; the commander of US forces in China, General Wedemeyer, acted also as Chiang's Chief of Staff, and Chiang had to put up with a succession of US military–political envoys. Also, to secure Soviet entry into the war against Japan, the Big Three decided at Yalta to confirm Outer Mongolia's independence of China (an inter-war Soviet gain) and to restore to the USSR most of the Tsarist rights in Manchuria that had been lost to Japan, notably control of the chief railways and the port of Dairen, and the lease of Port Arthur (Lushun) as a naval base. These concessions were to be confirmed by a treaty between the USSR and Chiang's Republic of China that 'The [US] President will take measures . . . to obtain'.[35]

On the Japanese surrender, Chiang could, as the internationally accepted government, reasonably expect US assistance in taking over their

---

[33] Arnold Krammer, *The Forgotten Friendship: Israel and the Soviet Bloc, 1947–53* (Urbana, Ill., 1974).

[34] See also volume ii, Chap. 5.

[35] John Wheeler-Bennett and Anthony Nicholls, *The Semblance of Peace. The Political Settlement after the Second World War* (1972) pp. 630–1.

positions. This was readily forthcoming; for official Washington was, at least temporarily, concerned about the spread of Soviet influence in the Far East.[36] Japanese forces were instructed to surrender only to the KMT, not to the Chinese communists. KMT troops were airlifted, first to beat the communists to the former capital, Nanking, and the chief commercial centre, Shanghai, then to Peiping (Beijing), and finally, after some hesitation, even to Manchuria. Some 50,000 US Marines were deployed in northern China, to repatriate Japanese troops, but also to occupy strategic positions in the KMT interest.

But if Chiang necessarily looked to the US, he also had an interest in maintaining relations with the USSR, since this would at least inhibit Soviet support for his chief challengers, the Chinese communists. True, the concessions promised to Stalin at Yalta were unpalatable, but, after prolonged negotiations, the KMT conceded them in the treaty concluded in August 1945. By this Stalin legitimated a considerable strengthening of the USSR's position along borders that had been dangerously exposed for over a decade. He could also hope that good relations with the KMT would reduce the likelihood of its needing to draw in US forces. Meanwhile his conquest of Manchuria gave him leverage. He could facilitate its recovery by the KMT, provided this kept its distance from the United States. But if America was allowed to station troops in China, Stalin warned Chiang's son, Chiang Ching-kuo, in December 1945, the Manchurian question would become 'more complicated'. Chiang Ching-kuo's mission to Moscow that month seems to have been an exploratory one on both sides. Little came of it beyond Stalin's acceptance of a KMT request that he postpone the withdrawal of his troops from Manchuria; and Chiang Kai-shek's disappointment led him to refuse several invitations in 1946 to come himself to Moscow to resume discussions.[37]

In 1946, however, both Soviet and American policy in China remained ambiguous. In Manchuria Stalin clearly meant to retain his Yalta gains, and to carry off as much economic equipment – one estimate is $2 billion – as he could under the heading of Japanese 'war booty'. Beyond that he would, he had told Chinese communist leaders in Yenan in September 1945, turn the major Manchurian cities over to the KMT but assist the

[36] Hence also the refusal to permit any Soviet share in the occupation of Japan, and the anxiety to confine it to the northern half of Korea.
[37] Odd Arne Westad, *Cold War and Revolution: Soviet-American Rivalry and the Origins of the Chinese Civil War* (New York, 1993) pp. 122, 141, 151.

communists elsewhere.[38] Spreading support among rival Chinese factions represented a *modus operandi* stretching back to the 1920s. Hopefully it would keep Chiang malleable, but without prompting a US intervention in his support large enough to counterbalance the security zone the USSR had just gained along its borders.

For their part, the Americans endorsed Chiang. But their chief aim was to broker a settlement between him and the communists. In any but the shortest of terms, the task was hopeless: they distrusted each other, with good reason, and each hoped sooner or later to triumph. But the USA believed a settlement would stabilise Chiang and prevent the communists serving as a vehicle for the spread of Soviet influence. The policy also reflected a common American assumption that bitter civil war opponents can smoothly convert into partners in government. Ambassador Hurley had secured talks to that end in 1944, then again in August–October 1945. In November he suddenly resigned, blaming US diplomats with communist sympathies for undermining his policies. Truman substituted the more prestigious General Marshall, with the mission of arranging for a ceasefire and a coalition under Chiang, and for Chiang's takeover of Manchuria from the Soviets. Marshall was at first successful, even securing in February 1946 an agreement for the integration of KMT and communist forces in a new US-trained army. He then left for consultations in Washington. Meanwhile a Soviet decision in March to withdraw troops from Manchuria sparked a scramble to replace them, with first communist then KMT successes. On his return to China in April, Marshall resumed his pressure for a ceasefire, which he secured in June. But Chiang warned that this would be 'his final attempt at doing business with the communists';[39] and when they refused to unblock railways in northern China, he resorted to military pressure not only in Manchuria but in China proper. Chiang expected this to lead to communist concessions, but it escalated into full-scale war.

It is generally accepted that the USSR had not wanted this. A Soviet representative at Yenan recalls that Moscow's post-war 'decision on non-interference [in the KMT–communist conflict] amounted to a refusal to support Mao's adventurist policies, which could have created a situation leading to global conflict.' Or, as Stalin himself put it in February 1948, 'I did not believe that the Chinese communists could win. I was sure that

[38] Sergei Goncharov, John Lewis, Xue Litai, *Uncertain Partners. Stalin, Mao, and the Korean War* (Stanford, California, 1993) pp. 10, 299n.
[39] *FRUS* 1946, ix, p. 978.

the Americans would do everything to put down an uprising. I told Mao Tse-Tung that it would be better if he came to terms with Chiang Kai-shek and formed some kind of coalition government.'[40] But during 1946 his hesitations crumbled. For direct US intervention came to look increasingly unlikely. The Marines left China in the summer of 1946. Further, Marshall tended to blame Chiang for the renewal of fighting, and even sought to restrain him by embargoing arms and ammunition deliveries from August. Equally Stalin's approaches to Chiang had not prospered – he reneged on an agreement to visit Moscow in September 1946; and when Chiang concluded a commercial treaty with the US in November, Stalin retaliated with one with the communists (for the supply of explosives) that undercut his recognition of Chiang's as the sole legitimate government of China. More seriously, he turned over to the communists a huge Manchurian arsenal of captured Japanese weapons.[41]

At the time the KMT was still in the ascendant. Indeed, the news was so bad that at one point in mid-1947 Stalin apparently offered Mao sanctuary in the USSR.[42] But in fact the military tide had turned, KMT advances in the north-west being counterbalanced by a communist offensive in Manchuria. By late 1948 the boot was very much on the other foot, with Chiang's loss of Manchuria, the surrender of his troops besieged in the capital of Shantung, and, above all, communist victory in the crucial battle of Huai-Hai, just north of the Yangtse.

All this, as Stalin had confessed as early as February 1948, represented unanticipated success. He responded by reinforcing strength; a substantial engineering mission, under I.V. Kovalev, was sent that summer to rehabilitate the railways in support of further communist pushes, and, if we can believe Soviet documents supposedly obtained by the KMT, orders were given in May 'to increase many times our assistance to the . . . People's Liberation Movement'. But much controversy has arisen as to how far Stalin felt victory should be pushed. For from September 1947 to August 1948 Soviet diplomats approached the KMT government, partly to lobby against US plans for a Japanese peace treaty (on which China's views had

---

[40] Goncharov, Lewis, Xue, *Uncertain Partners*, p. 7; Edvard Kardelj, *Reminiscences. The Struggle for Recognition and Independence: The New Yugoslavia, 1944–57* (1982) p. 108.

[41] Brian Murray, *Stalin, the Cold War, and the Division of China: A Multi-Archival Mystery* (Cold War International History Project [CWIHP] Working Paper 12, 1995) p. 9n; Goncharov, Lewis, Xue, *Uncertain Partners*, pp. 12, 14.

[42] ibid. p. 13 (July 1947).

some weight), but partly to proffer mediation in China's civil war. In 1948 Ambassador Roschin apparently explained this as influenced by fears that Mao Zedong could become an 'Asian Tito'. Acceptance of his offers would secure Soviet non-intervention in China's internal affairs, and even economic aid; rejection might force the USSR to establish a 'buffer zone' along its borders, presumably by detaching Manchuria.[43]

When these approaches were made, the KMT still controlled most of China, including the main northern and Manchurian cities. By January 1949 it had been heavily defeated in the north. Nevertheless, Chinese politicians and many scholars have contended that, during his visit then to the communist leaders, Mikoyan tried – unsuccessfully – to dissuade them from following up their successes by seeking to cross the Yangtse and liberate the south. This would have divided China at the Yangtse, as in the time of the fifth and sixth centuries' North–South Dynasties. The advice is explained partly by doubts as to communist capacity and fears that crossing the Yangtse would provoke US intervention, but partly also by a wish to keep China weak and dependable. However, no concrete evidence has ever been produced that Mikoyan did give such advice, and it has been strongly denied by Kovalev, Stalin's chief representative in China at the time.[44]

Be that as it may, the Yangtse was crossed without difficulty in April 1949, and KMT rule on the southern mainland disintegrated. Stalin had now to handle the victorious communists. He did so in part by playing to their continuing revolutionary sentiment – and the more readily because he himself shared it. He had, for instance, told Kovalev in May 1948 that 'If socialism is victorious in China and our countries follow a single path, then the victory of socialism in the world will virtually be guaranteed. Nothing will threaten us.' Earlier, if we can believe supposed KMT intercepts, he had treated the Politburo to a survey of 'the revolutionary struggle of the oppressed peoples of the dependent and colonial countries against the imperialism of America, England, and France': in this:

The most important of our trump cards is, and always should be, Asia . . . We have already exerted great efforts to accelerate the emancipation of Asiatic peoples, although I think henceforth we should increase our work tenfold in this direction. The example of China's liberation movement is enlightening to us and becomes for us a model of future work.

[43] Murray, *Stalin, the Cold War, and the Division of China*, esp. pp. 7–9, 24.
[44] Goncharov, Lewis, Xue, *Uncertain Partners*, pp. 25–6, 39–44, 306–7n. The relevant archives in both Beijing and Moscow remain effectively closed.

When Mao's deputy, Liu Shaoqi, visited Moscow in July 1949, Stalin picked up this theme, telling him that, after Marx's death, West European revolutionary leaders became 'arrogant' and their

movement began to fall behind . . . The center of the revolution moved from West to East, and now it is moving to China and East Asia.

. . . your role is now an important one, but you should . . . not become arrogant about it. At the same time . . . the responsibility placed on you is still growing. You must fulfill your duty with regard to the revolution in the countries of East Asia.[45]

This represented an obvious geopolitical calculation: as Stalin told Mao that December, 'The victory of the Chinese revolution will change the balance of the whole world. More weight will be added to the scale of the international revolution.' But such calculations were reinforced by conclusions drawn from US non-intervention in the Chinese civil war. The Chinese had always been rather more relaxed about this, Liu Shaoqi explaining to cadres in July 1948 that 'It is impossible for the United States to send one or two million troops. Fewer troops won't work', and would only enable them to 'occupy a few coastal cities'. But in considering the crossing of the Yangtse, Stalin had advised precautions against an Anglo-American landing in the rear of the communist armies; and indeed Mao's dispositions did provide against this.[46] In practice the response of the Truman administration was the publication of a lengthy account of *United States Relations with China* since 1944, designed to show that 'nothing this country did or could have done within the reasonable limits of its capabilities could have changed that result'. As Marshall later put it, to make the KMT work, 'we would literally have [had] to take control of the country . . . At that time . . . we had one and a third divisions in the United States.'[47] Further confirmation may have been provided by 'information

---

[45] 'Stalin's Dialogue with Mao Zedong' (1991 interview with Kovalev), *Journal of Northeastern Asian Studies*, x (1991) pp. 58–9; Murray, *Stalin, the Cold War, and the Division of China*, pp. 18, 20.

[46] Chen, Jian, *The Sino-Soviet Alliance and China's Entry into the Korean War*, CWIHP Working Paper 1 (June 1992) pp. 2, 15; Goncharov, Lewis, Xue, *Uncertain Partners*, pp. 43, 303n.

[47] *United States Relations with China* (State Dept, Washington, August 1949) p. xvi; John L. Gaddis, *The Long Peace. Inquiries into the History of the Cold War* (New York, 1987) p. 78.

coming from the United States' indicating that 'the prevailing mood is not to interfere.'[48]

Stalin did not lose his fear of a direct clash with the United States. But in 1949 he did not believe that the USA would take the initiative. While one could not exclude irrational action, he told Kovalev, and so the Chinese:

War is not profitable for the imperialists. Their crisis has begun and they are not ready to go to war. They try to scare us with the atomic bomb, but we are not afraid of it.

The objective conditions for attack and for unleashing war do not exist.[49]

Accordingly Stalin became increasingly ready to contemplate revolutionary moves, provided other countries took the direct risks. A minor instance was the January 1950 instruction to the Japanese communist party to reverse course and violently resist US military use of Japanese bases. More important was the decision that month by Stalin and Mao that China should respond to Ho Chi Minh's plea for weapons, military advisers and financial aid for his struggle in Indochina.[50] Yet more directly, Stalin changed his mind on Korea. In 1949 he had contemplated allowing a limited North Korean offensive, but rejected the idea lest it prompt American military interference. On 19 January 1950 Kim Il Sung 'began to speak about how now, when China is completing its liberation, the liberation of the Korean people in the south of the country is next in line', and again

---

[48] Soviet Central Committee report on Kim Il Sung's March–April 1950 visit to the USSR, cited in Kathryn Weathersby, *'Should We Fear This?' Stalin and the Danger of War with America*, CWIHP Working Paper 39 (July 2002) pp. 9, 11. Such information presumably included Acheson's 12 January 1950 speech describing the US 'defensive perimeter' as embracing only Japan, the Ryukyus and the Philippines. Weathersby speculates that Stalin may also have obtained (through Maclean) NSC 48/1 (December 1949); this had observed that communist success in China 'represents a grievous defeat for us; if southeast Asia also is swept by communism we shall have suffered a political rout the repercussions of which will be felt throughout the rest of the world', but it still advised against US military occupation of Taiwan (Thomas Etzold and John Lewis Gaddis (eds) *Containment: Documents on American Policy and Strategy, 1945–1950* (New York, 1978) pp. 257–9.

[49] 'Stalin's Dialogue with Mao', pp. 51–2.

[50] Goncharov, Lewis, Xue, *Uncertain Partners*, pp. 105–8; Yang Kuisong, *Changes in Mao Zedong's Attitude toward the Indochina War, 1949–1973*, CWIHP Working Paper 34 (February 2002) pp. 3–4. *Khrushchev Remembers*, i, pp. 441–2 says the Soviet contribution to Ho was chiefly quinine, and that Stalin stole back the autograph he had given Ho during the latter's secret Moscow visit.

sought permission for an offensive. Eleven days later Stalin invited him to come secretly to Moscow to discuss it. On his arrival in April 'Comrade Stalin confirmed . . . that the international environment has sufficiently changed to permit a more active stance on the unification of Korea'; and Kim's visit concluded with agreement that 'the offensive' should be planned and prepared by the summer. Stalin anticipated that the war would be over before the Americans had 'time to come to their senses', but he was careful to warn Kim 'that the USSR was not ready to get involved . . . directly, especially if Americans did venture to send troops to Korea.'[51]

Anglo-American covert propaganda and action, 1947–8; Attempts to destabilise Albania, 1949–53; Possible connections with the East European purges of 1949–53

In fact the USA and Britain were increasing rather than reducing their Cold War involvement. Their chief efforts were, admittedly, directed towards Western consolidation, notably through Marshall Aid and NATO. Indeed in the later 1940s the United States was operating rather as it had done in 1940–1, that is keeping what it perceived as indirect security threats at a distance by buttressing, with economic aid and off-shore military support, friendly powers that were geographically nearer the front line. In 1941 this policy had been finally destroyed by the US response to Japan's occupation of southern Indo-China. In 1950 events in Korea were to play a similar role. But even before this the policy had already started to broaden, both geographically and in terms of the tools employed.

In the latter context, the stabilisation of Western Europe was pursued through covert as well as overt means. Following the 1947 Sklarska Poreba conference, the communist-led union movement had mounted strikes to make France ungovernable. With British encouragement, the US responded by financing the breakaway anti-communist *Force Ouvriere*; the money came initially from the American unions, which had been assisting their non-communist counterparts since 1945, but the cost was later assumed by the CIA. Then in 1948 fears that the Communists and their allies might win the Italian elections triggered, besides more visible

[51] Weathersby, '*Should We Fear This?*' pp. 7–11, and 'Korea, 1949–50. To Attack, or Not to Attack? Stalin, Kim Il Sung and the Prelude to War', CWIHP *Bulletin*, 5 (Spring 1995) esp. pp. 8, 9.

pressures, a clandestine CIA expenditure of some $10 million (above, p. 140). This was deemed to prove the efficacy of covert action, which, from having previously been very small beer,[52] now grew fast both geographically and financially (the budget of the 'Office of Policy Coordination' increasing from $4.7 million in early 1949 to $200 million in 1953).

1948 saw not only attempts to influence the Italian elections and a revival of British wartime propaganda, albeit now directed against communists rather than fascists,[53] but also a mounting covert interest in Eastern Europe. One stimulus was military fear of renewed conventional war, in which case intelligence and sabotage capabilities would obviously be desirable. Another was Yugoslavia's break with Moscow, which suggested the possibility of 'loosening the Soviet hold' on other countries, or at least promoting sufficient 'confusion' to make Eastern Europe 'not a source of [Soviet] strength but a source of weakness'. The idea was pushed chiefly by the British military, by part of the CIA, and apparently by Kennan; Bevin and Marshall disliked it. But there seems to have been a compromise on Albania as a pilot project.

Yugoslavia's defection had left Albania geographically isolated from the rest of the 'camp'. Britain had been at odds with it since 1946 when 44 British sailors had been killed by mines in the (international) Corfu straits. Albania was, moreover, aiding the communist rebellion in Greece. Early in 1949 Bevin approved a plan 'to detach Albania from the [Soviet] orbit' by reactivating wartime Resistance networks there. The Americans agreed to join in; and in October twenty emigré Albanians were landed by boat to link up with anti-communists and recruit sympathisers in their home areas. 1950 and 1951 saw similar small-scale overland infiltration and US-managed parachute drops. The latter had clearly been betrayed to the Albanian authorities, who staged a broadcast trial of captured infiltrators in late 1951. The British then abandoned the operation in despair. But the USA persisted, having discovered a more effective leader, Matjani, and receiving apparently encouraging radio reports in 1952–3. These turned out

[52] The Church Committee dated the first covert action to 1947; Trevor Barnes, 'The Secret Cold War: the CIA and American Foreign Policy in Europe, 1946–56' (2 parts), *Historical Journal*, xxiv and xxv (1981, 1982) suspects 1946, and mentions that subsidies for the centrist French press date from an approach by a resistance hero in 1945.
[53] Richard J. Aldrich, *The Hidden Hand. Britain, America and Cold War Secret Intelligence* (2001) Chap. 5. Among the anti-communist material diffused and funded were translations into innumerable languages of Orwell's *Animal Farm* and *1984*.

to be disinformation that lured Matjani to his doom in May 1953, and Albania broadcast the whole episode in December.

In the words of a CIA officer of the time, 'The Albanian was the first and only attempt by Washington to unseat a communist regime within the Soviet orbit. It taught a clear lesson . . . Even a weak regime could not be overthrown by covert military action alone.' Actually the lesson is not clear – covert action proved successful in Iran and Guatemala, and Hungary was to show in 1956 that communist regimes can simply disinteg-rate. But the wartime Resistance movements, on experience of which Britain had been drawing, had not by themselves liberated any state.[54] Moreover, the Albanian intervention was limited by Anglo-American determination to provide 'capacity for plausible denial'; sympathisers within Albania noted the contrast with the Second World War operations, and indicated that they would rebel only when there were substantial drops of men and supplies. In any case information as to the incursions leaked through the emigré community, and perhaps also through Kim Philby, British diplomat and KGB agent in Washington, which may explain the Albanian government's excellent preparedness.[55]

Nothing as ambitious as the Albanian operation was ever attempted elsewhere. But agents were similarly infiltrated and occasional supplies dropped into the Baltic States and the Ukraine (1949–56) to establish con-tact with the nationalist resistance, though more to gather intelligence than to sustain fighting. From 1950 equipment and money was also dropped to a Polish organisation, WIN, to create an underground that could, by sabotage, delay any Soviet invasion of Western Europe; in December 1952 the Polish authorities revealed that WIN had been a hoax, operating entirely under their control.[56]

So far, so ineffective. But debate has arisen as to whether policies of creating 'confusion' did not achieve at least a partial success in intensifying

[54] Both Yugoslavia and Albania claim to have liberated themselves. But the German withdrawal was due not to local partisans but to the need to pull troops back to defend Germany itself from direct invasion. Also, as the USSR often insisted, the Red Army played a considerable role in the liberation of northern Yugoslavia.

[55] Aldrich, *The Hidden Hand*, Chaps 6, 7; N. Bethell, *The Great Betrayal. The Untold Story of Kim Philby's Biggest Coup* (1984); Harry Rositzke, *The CIA's Secret Operations* (New York, 1977) p. 173.

[56] John Prados, *Presidents' Secret Wars* (New York, 1986) esp. pp. 40–4, 52–9; John Ranelagh, *The Agency. The Rise and Decline of the CIA* (1986), p. 227; Thomas Powers, *The man who kept the secrets. Richard Helms and the CIA* (paperback edn, 1979) pp. 46 ff.

the purges of high-level communists that swept Eastern Europe in Stalin's closing years. There were certainly aspirations to do this; in September 1949 NSC-58 noted, in connection with the aim of bearing down on 'Stalinist' (as opposed to nationalist) elements in East European parties, that 'The propensity of the revolution to devour its own, the suspicions of the Kremlin regarding its agents and the institutions of denunciation, purge and liquidation are grave defects in the Soviet system which have never been adequately exploited.'[57] No hard evidence has been produced to support the hypothesis; but some scholars believe Western disinformation was fed in to exacerbate the East European purges (below, pp. 537–8) that were set off by Tito's defection and continued until after Stalin's death.[58] (If so, the purges' immediate effect was to tighten, not loosen, Stalin's control over Eastern Europe; but the USSR's subsequent reversal of course discredited many of the 'Stalinists' who had administered the purges, and so strengthened the 'national' communist tendencies against which these had been directed – and which Kennan had hoped to encourage.)

American responses to the 'loss of China'; The extension of 'containment' to Indo-China, 1949–50

From 1946 to 1949 US Cold War concerns centred on Western Europe. Indeed, Acheson found it necesary to reassure Congress that the Truman Doctrine of support for 'free peoples . . . resisting attempted subjugation by armed minorities' did not apply to China. Admittedly the US military were worried by communist successes there in mid-1947; but a strategic study that May had placed China 'very low on the list of countries which should be given . . . assistance', and Marshall's State Department used this to head off pressures for significant aid to Chiang Kai-shek. Just possibly things might have been different had the Republicans won the 1948 presidential elections. But the Truman administration was terminally disillusioned with the KMT; and it seems, after communist victory on the mainland in 1949, to have been 'waiting for the dust to settle' in hopes that

---

[57] Etzold and Gaddis, *Containment: Documents*, p. 221; the passage immediately before this quotation is withheld for security reasons.

[58] Many purge victims were fingered for real or alleged contacts with an American communist, Noel Field; and the Field brothers could have been unwitting conduits for Western disinformation, *if* this was supplied – Aldrich, *Hidden Hand*, pp. 174–9.

the new regime would soon turn against the USSR.[59] Not everybody, however, took developments so calmly. For China, or more accurately a romanticised and often missionary image of it, had long held a special place in American hearts. The collapse of Chiang's friendly client regime came to be seen – even by many people opposed to direct US intervention to prevent it – as the 'loss of China'; and there developed a right-wing 'China Lobby' that remained for two decades supposedly capable of punishing any administration that 'lost' further countries in Asia.

Nor was the Truman administration itself prepared to see the Chinese communist revolution spread south. (So it was in effect setting itself up for at least an indirect conflict with Mao, who told a Chinese 'military assistance group' leaving for Vietnam in June 1950 that 'Since our revolution has achieved victory, we have an obligation to help others. This is called internationalism.')[60] In 1948 the British had failed to interest the USA in backing an orchestrated response to communist insurgencies by local states in Southeast Asia. But in February 1949 the State Department's Policy Planning Staff (still headed by Kennan) declared the area to be 'the target of a coordinated offensive plainly directed by the Kremlin', whose loss would affect Japanese, Indian and Australian security; the region was, therefore, 'a vital sector on the line of containment'. In June the National Security Council found that the fall of China threatened all of Southeast Asia; and Secretary of State Acheson wrote that the US would not allow another Asian nation to fall to the communists. Nor did he accept the idea that Asian communism was different from European and more properly viewed as just another manifestation of local nationalism – 'Question whether Ho . . . nationalist or Commie', he had cabled, 'is irrelevant. All Stalinists in colonial areas are nationalists. With achievement of national aims (i.e. independence) their objective necessarily becomes subordination state to Commie purposes and ruthless extermination [of] not only opposition groups but all elements suspected [of] even slightest deviation.' Accordingly he favoured strengthening China's neighbours by building up their internal stability and living standards, and, above all, getting 'on

[59] Dean Acheson, *Present at the Creation: My Years in the State Department* (1969) p. 225; *FRUS 1947*, vii, pp. 843–4, 849; Gaddis, *Long Peace*, pp. 164 ff.
[60] Douglas J. MacDonald, 'Communist Bloc Expansion in the Early Cold War. Challenging Realism, Refuting Revisionism', *International Security*, xx (1995–6) p. 183; cf. Mao's 1945 dictum that 'when you are making revolution, you need foreign aid; after you have achieved victory, you ought to support foreign revolution' (Yang Kuisong, *Mao Zedong's Attitude toward the Indochina War*, pp. 2–3).

the side of Nationalist movements'. So, when the British again raised the question in December, he was able to tell them he had 'scratched together' the symbolic sum of $75 million for the purpose; he would provide some military assistance to France in Indo-China, while pressing it to remove 'barriers to the obtaining by Bao Dai or other non-Communist nationalist leaders of the support of a substantial proportion of the Vietnamese'.

Actual disbursements were slow – a mere $48.5 million for Southeast Asia by June 1950[61] – and we cannot say how far things would have gone but for the Korean War. The USA was not binding itself to direct military intervention (indeed it decided against this more than once before 1965). But support for the French in Indo-China clearly represented an extension of the geographical scope of 'containment'. Admittedly this had never been as limited, even at the outset of the Cold War, as was sometimes claimed by advocates of the so-called 'strong point' approach. Kennan may once have claimed that, besides the USA and USSR, there were only three 'centers of industrial and military power . . . which are important to us from the standpoint of national security', Germany, Britain and Japan, and that containment should concentrate on keeping them out of Soviet hands. But the crises of 1946 had related rather to Iran and Turkey; and in 1948 Kennan himself included, among the areas it was necessary to safeguard, 'The countries of the Mediterranean and the Middle East . . . including . . . Iran'. Now both he, and more importantly Acheson, were beginning to resile from the view that 'you can theoretically content yourself with permitting most of these [Eurasian] land areas to be in the hands of people who are hostile to ourselves as long as you exercise that power of inhibiting the . . . launching of amphibious forces from . . . Asian ports.' Further, while Kennan had argued for a degree of selectivity on the grounds that US resources were more limited 'than we are often inclined to remember', by early 1950 Acheson was seeking (in NSC-68) to stand this argument on its head: 'our present weakness [in conventional arms] would prevent us from offering effective resistance at any of several vital pressure points', resulting in 'a gradual withdrawal under the direct or indirect pressure of the Soviet Union, until we discover that one day we have sacrificed positions of vital interest' and fallen back on an unviable 'isolation in the Western Hemisphere.' What was needed, therefore, in Acheson's view, was greater

---

[61] Douglas Macdonald in Jervis and Snyder, *Dominoes and Bandwagons*, pp. 120, 126–30; *FRUS* 1949, ix, p. 465; Ritchie Ovendale, 'Britain, the United States and the Cold War in South-East Asia 1949–50', *International Affairs*, lviii (1982).

defence spending to secure the capabilities for a wider geographical range of response.[62]

NSC-68 and US rearmament

Once fighting was over in 1945, the American public had insisted on demobilisation on a first-in-first-out basis. This had devastating effects on efficiency – two months after VJ day most units are supposed to have lost 50–75 per cent of their combat value.[63] Effectively the USA reverted to 'off-shore' naval and air power. Nor, despite its continuing concern to preserve its nuclear monopoly, did it build its nuclear arsenal with any urgency – in July–August 1945 one bomb was tested, two dropped on Japan with the intention that a third should follow by the end of the month if there were no surrender; but in April 1947 there were no bombs actually assembled for use.[64] The USA was certainly not then in the business of crude 'nuclear blackmail'; and the Joint Chiefs of Staff did not in fact believe the Soviet Union could be conquered, even given the use of nuclear weapons.[65]

The Berlin Blockade brought a crash programme to expand the number of available atom bombs. Overall military expenditure also rose, but was still kept low – a ceiling of $15 billion per year was imposed in 1948 –

[62] John Lewis Gaddis, *Strategies of Containment. A Critical Appraisal of Post-War American National Security Policy* (New York, 1982) pp. 30–1, and *Long Peace*, p. 76; Etzold and Gaddis, *Containment: Documents*, pp. 414, 428 (NSC-68). Some historians hold that one reason for America's (and Kennan's) concern over Southeast Asia was the wish to preserve the area as an economic partner for a Japan whose international outlook might otherwise be swayed by trade dependence on communist China and Korea.

[63] *History of the Joint Chiefs of Staff* (National Archives, Washington, DC), i, pp. 212, 214.

[64] Two more bombs were tested in 1946. In April 1947 the stockpile contained about twelve bombs, none assembled and some probably inoperable. New 'shaped' high explosive charges (necessary as triggers) were devised later that month, which facilitated assembly. But the real increase did not come till after the Berlin Blockade. By 1953 the US arsenal was apparently 1600, while the USSR is not believed to have had any operationally deployed. (G. Herken, *The Winning Weapon: The Atomic Bomb and the Cold War 1945–50* (New York, 1980) pp. 197, 199; D. Yergin, *Shattered Peace: the Origins of the Cold War and National Security State* (paperback edn) pp. 266, 465–6; *History of the JCS*, i, pp. 294–5; S.E. Ambrose, *Eisenhower the President* (1984) p. 93).

[65] *History of the JCS*, esp. i, Chap. 4; ii, Chaps 9, 10. The appreciation that the USSR could not be conquered dates from 1944 (i, pp. 14–16), but subsequently the use of nuclear weapons was only expected to hamper Soviet overrunning of Western Europe and the Middle East and assist their eventual recovery.

partly in the belief that the USSR was not seeking a hot war, but also through confidence stemming from the US nuclear monopoly. In theory people accepted that this monopoly would not last, but in practice they behaved as if it would, and were correspondingly jolted by the Soviet explosion of an atomic device in September 1949. This served as a further stimulus to American spy-mania; for the Soviet programme had indeed benefited (though perhaps only by a couple of years) from espionage, and this was highlighted by the arrest next February of Klaus Fuchs.[66] It also led to Truman's rapid authorisation of the development of a hydrogen bomb; a device was tested in November 1952, and a deliverable weapon in March 1954.

Another response was a general survey of the USA's strategic position and needs. This survey (NSC-68), drafted in February–March 1950, has become famous, perhaps too much so.[67] Its purpose, Acheson has recalled, 'was to so bludgeon the mass mind of "top government" that not only could the President make a decision [for rearmament] but that the decision could be carried out'. Accordingly it did not understate the drive of Soviet military spending, and, while admitting that the USSR 'followed the sound principle of seeking maximum results with minimum risks and commitments', stressed that there was no ground 'for predicting that, should the Kremlin become convinced that it could cause our downfall by one conclusive blow, it would not seek that solution'; it guessed that the USSR might have sufficient bombs for a surprise attack on the USA by mid-1954. The recommendation was a rapid US build-up, both to limit this danger and, by acquiring non-nuclear options, to preclude the risk of having either to capitulate 'at any of a number of pressure points' or to precipitate a global war. The nature and cost of this build-up was deliberately left unspecified – the State Department was thinking of a $35 billion or even $50 billion defence budget, service planners of perhaps $18 billion[68] – but NSC-68 did challenge the conventional economics then dominant, observing that

---

[66] David Holloway, *Stalin and the Bomb. The Soviet Union and Atomic Energy 1939–1956* (New Haven, 1994) pp. 220–3; Aldrich, *Hidden Hand*, pp. 378–9. A German communist refugee who had worked in the British contingent on the Manhattan Project, Fuchs attracted more public attention than did American nuclear traitors.

[67] Text in Etzold and Gaddis, *Containment: Documents*, pp. 252–69. Its bureaucratic fortunes and significance are discussed by Paul Hammond in W.R. Schilling, P.Y. Hammond, and G.H. Snyder, *Strategy, Politics and Defense Budgets* (New York, 1962) Chap. 2. See also Acheson, *Present at the Creation*, pp. 343, 347–9, 373–5.

[68] Hammond *et al.*, *Strategy, Politics and Defense Budgets*, p. 319.

the programme might even boost the American economy and increase personal consumption (as had occurred between 1939 and 1944). Truman referred the document for further detail and costing. There is no evidence that it affected his response to the outbreak of fighting in Korea in June 1950. So it was not, in itself, a cause of the 'globalisation' of containment as is sometimes suggested. Indeed it is far from clear that, but for the Korean War, NSC-68 would even have produced a great change in defence spending. Truman continued to talk of the possibility of a *reduced* defence budget, the Chairman of the Senate Finance Committee seems to have regarded NSC-68's arguments as sound but politically unrealistic,[69] and its military sponsors would have been satisfied with comparatively small increases. However the Korean War appeared to validate NSC-68's forebodings. The war would in any case have led to significant rearmament. The existence of NSC-68 further eased the way, stilling doubts as to the economic consequences and providing a framework in which rearmament appeared not as a panic reaction but as the response to a considered appraisal of need.

Korea, 1945–50: Stalin authorises the invasion of South Korea, 1950

But though shifts towards greater defence spending and the geographical expansion of containment can be discerned before the Korean War, the war was at least the catalyst, perhaps the necessary condition, for their consolidation. To understand it we must go back to 1945.

There had been agreement at Yalta that Korea, then a Japanese colony, should proceed to independence 'in due course'. But for the purpose of receiving the surrender of Japanese troops, it was divided between the US and Soviet armies. In mid-1945 the USA was anxious to check the spread of Soviet influence in the Far East, and Secretary of State Byrnes had sought a dividing line 'as far north as possible'. Accordingly the USA had, without any very deep thought, suggested the 38th parallel, which Stalin accepted without demur: it left two-thirds of the population in the south, but the more industrialised areas in the north.[70]

---

[69] ibid. pp. 329, 331.

[70] This and subsequent paragraphs draw on David Rees, *A Short History of Modern Korea* (Port Erin, Isle of Man, 1988) Chaps 8–9, also 1–2; Callum A. MacDonald, *Korea. The War before Vietnam* (Basingstoke, 1986) Chap. 1; Andrew C. Nahm,

It now seems that the USSR had potentially conflicting interests in the peninsula. In strategic terms it was, in September 1945, chiefly concerned with acquiring sufficient control of parts of *southern* Korea (Pusan, Cheju Island – and Tsushima island, which it wished transferred from Japan – and Inchon) that it regarded as 'of essential importance for securing dependable sea communications to the [recently re-acquired] Soviet military-naval base at Port Arthur'; it looked to do this in the context of a joint Four Power trusteeship over the whole country. Equally 'the Japanese military and heavy industry in North Korea must be transfered to the Soviet Union as partial payment of reparations, and also as compensation for the huge damage inflicted by Japan on the Soviet Union throughout the time of its existence, including the damages from the Japanese intervention . . . from 1918 to 1923'. This too could be achieved within the context of an single Korean government, if an acceptable one could be arrived at. But it could equally be effected by partition, and on the ground the USSR moved in that direction far more rapidly than in Germany: by October 1945 it had sealed off its zone.[71]

Unsurprisingly Soviet actions resembled those in Eastern Europe. Initially the USSR worked through the Leftist committees that had sprang up at provincial level throughout Korea after Japan's decision to surrender, but in October 1945 it grouped them into an embryo state government. October also saw the foundation (under Soviet supervision and guidance) of a Communist Party whose First Secretary, Kim Il Sung, had returned in the entourage of the Red Army; and reports to the CPSU Central Committee show that, that autumn, the 'occupation authorities were very active in creating Soviet-style social and political structures in northern Korea'. The winter saw the repression of a number of anti-communist riots and risings. On the other hand no effort seems to have been made to help the 'Korean Communist Party' in the south, and its members were told that 'The ideals of the United States, the leader of capitalism, and

---

Korea. Tradition and Transformation (Elizabeth, N.J., 1988) Chap. 9; and Kathryn Weathersby, *Soviet Aims in Korea and the Origins of the Korean War, 1945–1950: New Evidence from Russian Archives* (CWIHP Working Paper no. 8, 1993).

[71] Any economic incentive to reopen it evaporated in early 1946. For the disappearance of southern rice surpluses (as a result of market reforms) prevented the USA from acceding to a Soviet request for a return to the traditional barter of southern rice for northern coal (Peter Lowe, *The Origins of the Korean War* (1986) p. 26). In Germany it had been the Soviets who occupied the agricultural areas but could, or would, not supply the industrial West with grain.

the Soviet Union, the fatherland of the proletariat, are to be expressed in Korea without contradiction'.[72]

Korea was among the subjects considered at the December 1945 Moscow meeting of the Council of Foreign Ministers. Soviet briefing papers continued to assume the 'Necessity for the Restoration of the Unity of Korea' – one declared that 'it would be politically inexpedient for the Soviet Union to oppose the creation of a single Korean government' – while noting that this would not be easy given the divergent Soviet and American policies. In the event the Council called for the establishment of 'a four-power trusteeship for Korea for a period of up to five years'. 'Trusteeship' was an unfortunate term, given that Japan's post-1905 takeover had initially assumed that form; and the idea was repudiated by all Korean politicians except the communists. This seems to have brought the USSR to decide definitely in favour of partition. At the Joint Soviet–American Commission meetings in Seoul in early 1946, it insisted that only groups accepting the Moscow agreement – i.e. communists – be consulted on the formation of a provisional government; the USA refused, and talks were adjourned. Meanwhile, the Soviet authorities moved in February to create (and closely supervise) a government (under Kim Il Sung), constitution and laws for North Korea.[73] Thereafter there was little doubt that the north had passed under communist control, though with continued competition (as in Eastern Europe) between rival communist leaders who may have been marked by the different ways in which they had spent the years before 1945.

The interlude between the Japanese decision to surrender and the US arrival in the south had seen the proclamation of a 'Korean People's Republic', which sought to unite all politicians who had been opposed to the Japanese, but whose aims were broadly leftist though not necessarily communist. General Hodge, the US commander, refused to recognise it, and instead operated first through the Japanese authorities, then through his own military government. Fear of communism led him, in conditions of sporadic risings and considerable social disturbance, to a tough maintenance of order that some historians see as a counter-revolution. Also though Washington favoured trusteeship, its men on the ground seem to have been looking, by the winter of 1945–6, to devolve power progressively to conservative nationalists who had opposed the Japanese from

---

[72] Weathersby, *Soviet Aims in Korea and the Origins of the Korean War*, pp. 9–12, 15; see, however, note 74 below.

[73] ibid. pp. 13–18.

exile in China. Accordingly February 1946 saw the constitution of an advisory body, chaired by Syngman Rhee, the 'Korean Representative Democratic Council' (KRDC). This process of the parallel evolution of potential Northern and Southern governments might have been halted by the Joint Soviet–American Commission; but, as we have seen, the 1946 negotiations failed: despite occasional signs of flexibility, the USSR would contemplate only 'democratic parties and organizations' who accepted the idea of a trusteeship, while the US pushed the KRDC, which vehemently opposed it.

Ironically Hodge spent the next year quarrelling with Syngman Rhee, who was campaigning for the early establishment of an independent anti-communist South Korean government. Hodge wished to draw together all non-communist southern politicians; and when Rhee's supporters dominated the indirect (and rather questionable) October 1946 elections to an Interim Legislature, Hodge balanced them through his choice of nominated members; but the result was deadlock. Meanwhile the government apparatus was gradually gaining power. A constabulary had been established in January 1946; communist and harvest risings were put down in October.[74] The administration was 'Koreanised' in early 1947, then designated in May the South Korean Interim Government; it was bolstered by a grant of $600 million over three years, decided on in parallel to the 'Truman Doctrine' aid to Greece and Turkey.

This did not quite close the door on the official policy of agreeing a provisional government for the entire peninsula. Indeed the Joint Commission was reconvened in May 1947 to search for such a government, and initially seemed to be making progress. But it then bogged down – possibly as a by-product of the Soviet decision to turn against Marshall Aid. Meanwhile the USA was coming to doubt whether its administration of south Korea could be sustained in the face of Rhee's campaign for independence. One option 'would be to arrange with the Soviet Union for mutual withdrawal of troops and let nature take its course which will eventually mean another Soviet satellite in Korea'. This prompted debate in Washington as to how much Korea mattered. Some held that 'If we allow Korea to go by default and to fall within the Communist orbit, the

---

[74] General Shtykov's diaries show that he subsidised and 'advised' on these disturbances (Hyun-su Jeon with Gyoo Kahng, 'The Shtykov Diaries: New Evidence on Soviet Policy in Korea', CWIHP *Bulletin* 6–7 (1995–6) pp. 92–3). Were such material available for the period before September 1946, it might modify the picture of Soviet non-interference in the south in 1945.

world will feel that we have lost another round in our match with the Soviet Union, and our prestige and the hopes of those who put their faith in us will suffer accordingly.' But the Joint Chiefs of Staff judged that 'the United States has little strategic interest in maintaining the present troops and bases in Korea'. The eventual decision was that, since 'the US position in Korea is untenable' but since, equally, America could not ' "scuttle" and run from Korea without considerable loss of prestige and political stand-ing', it should seek a settlement 'which would enable the US to withdraw from Korea as soon as possible with the minimum of bad effects'.[75]

This meant installing an indigenous government, withdrawing, and hoping that South Korea did not collapse too quickly. Washington's chosen medium was the United Nations General Assembly; in late 1947 this appointed a Commission (on which the Ukraine declined to serve) to observe elections and advise on the installation of a government for the whole peninsula. The Commission was firmly excluded from the north, and recommended against holding elections only in the south lest this perpetuate the peninsula's partition. But the UN decided to go ahead. Elections were held in May 1948 under very disturbed conditions – the police tried to make people vote, while the far Left attacked polling booths and killed candidates. UN supervisors were thin on the ground, but the results were recognised as a 'valid expression of the free will of the elect-orate in those parts of Korea which were accessible to the Commission and in which the inhabitants constituted approximately two-thirds of the people of all Korea'. The Right had won; the new National Assembly quickly elected Syngman Rhee as President of the 'Republic of Korea' (ROK); in December the UN recognised it as 'the only' 'lawful govern-ment' 'in Korea'. By implication the 'Democratic People's Republic of Korea' that had been proclaimed in the North in September was not lawful. But there were now, *de facto*, two Korean regimes both claiming authority throughout the peninsula.

The USSR withdrew its troops from the North in December 1948, and the USA followed suit next June, being determined not to be sucked into hostilities by a Northern invasion (which it thought quite possible). However, it did not want to see South Korea collapse, and so continued to provide both economic and military aid. The new Republic got off to a bad start, with a major rebellion on the island of Cheju and a mutiny among the police sent to suppress it in October 1948. Next autumn the number of active guerrillas is supposed to have peaked at over 3,000; but by the

---

[75] Lowe, *Origins of the Korean War*, pp. 34–6; Gaddis, *Long Peace*, pp. 94–5.

spring of 1950 they had been worn down, despite substantial infiltration from the North. This success, though, had been won at the cost of pushing public expenditure out of control; by 1950 the US was worried that South Korea would follow Kuomintang China into hyperinflation. In the May 1950 elections (held at US insistence) Rhee's party suffered an appreciable if limited set-back, while in June the price of rice rose by a third (which could have had serious political repercussions).

Officially the USA held that South Korea could now handle anything short of an invasion actively supported by the USSR or China, and that this was unlikely. But the British (always rather sceptical observers of US Korean policy) produced a report in December 1949 to the effect that the North's 'ultimate object is to overrun the South; and I think in the long term there is no doubt that they will do so'. A little later the commander of the American Military Advisory Group also doubted Southern military capabilities, though admittedly by way of lobbying Washington to improve them. Further in May 1950 the chairman of the Senate Foreign Relations Committee told the press that he expected the communists to overrun Korea (and probably Taiwan).[76]

These views appear to have been held also by Kim Il Sung, who was from 1949 advocating invasion of the South. Stalin had that September been prepared to investigate a limited operation to squeeze out the Ongjin border salient, but decided to advise Kim rather to concentrate on fostering guerrilla activity in the South and on strengthening his own army. However, when Kim next raised the subject in January 1950, he was invited to Moscow and told that 'the international environment has sufficiently changed to permit a more active stance on the unification of Korea.' The Korean delegation expressed confidence that:

The attack will be swift and the war will be won in three days; the guerrilla movement in the South has grown stronger and a major rising can be expected. Americans won't have time to come to their senses, all the Korean people will be enthusiastically supporting the new government.

Stalin promised to supply arms and armour, and it 'was agreed that the North Korean army would be fully mobilised by the summer' and a 'concrete plan for the offensive' drawn up 'with the assistance of Soviet

[76] ibid. p. 96; Lowe, *Origins of the Korean War*, pp. 57–67; R.R. Simmons, *The Strained Alliance. Peking, Pyongyang, Moscow and the Politics of the Korean War* (New York, 1975) p. 115.

advisers'. However, Stalin made it clear the USSR would not itself commit troops,[77] 'especially' in the event of a US intervention; and he insisted that, before finally committing himself, Kim should also get the go-ahead from Mao – which, however, Mao could hardly refuse given his general revolutionary stance. Mao gave it in May, though there is a conflict of evidence as to whether he warned obliquely against possible US involvement or promised Chinese military assistance in that event. In June all was in readiness for a general invasion, to be disguised by a diversionary attack on the Ongjin peninsula. But fearing intelligence leaks and a Southern reinforcement of Ongjin, Kim sought and obtained Stalin's permission for, 'Instead of a local operation [there] as a prelude to the general offensive', 'an immediate advance along the whole front line.' This was launched on 25 June 1950.[78]

The Western response

The invasion thus shed the disguises with which it could easily have been surrounded; nor did the general Southern uprising that the North Koreans had promised Stalin ever materialise.[79] Their attack therefore appeared a clear-cut case of 1930s-style military conquest. It caught Truman on holiday. He later wrote that, as he flew back to Washington, he recalled Manchuria (1931), Ethiopia (1935–6) and Austria (1938) where the democracies' inaction had simply encouraged further aggression:

If this was allowed to go unchallenged it would mean a third World War, just as similar incidents had brought on the Second . . . It was also clear to me that the foundations and the principles of the United Nations were at stake unless this unprovoked attack on Korea could be stopped.

[77] He even stopped Soviet advisers from accompanying North Korean invasion forces lest they be captured and provide proof of Soviet involvement, a decision Khrushchev strongly criticises (*Khrushchev Remembers*, i, p. 335; iii, p. 146).

[78] Weathersby, '*Should We Fear This?*' esp. pp. 6–15. The Soviet documents now released seem to disprove revisionist contentions that the Korean War was the product either of a botched *Southern* offensive or of a Northern operation aimed only at Ongjin that got out of control. Admittedly Syngman Rhee was as eager as Kim Il Sung to secure reunion by force (Simmons, *Strained Alliance*, pp. 115–16); but the USA did not give him the go-ahead.

[79] Kim Il Sung said 'a major uprising can be expected', while Pak Hon-yong 'predicted that 200,000 party members will participate as leaders of the mass uprising' – Soviet summary of the March–April 1950 talks, cited in Weathersby, '*Should We Fear This?*' p. 10.

Such perceptions were not confined to America – a leading French official thought the loss of Korea would 'irretrievably impair' Western prestige and drew parallels with 1938. According to Acheson, 'the governments of many Western European nations appeared to be in a state of near panic, as they watched to see whether the United States would act or not'; and there were US fears that, if it did not, Europe would go neutralist.[80] Washington's decision to respond, therefore, was taken in the light not of feelings about Korea itself, or even about its strategic significance (which, in Japan at least, is seen as considerable), but of a general view of the international system.

The USA instantly referred the question to the UN Security Council, which (as a result of the then Soviet boycott)[81] was able to condemn the invasion and call on North Korea to withdraw. To nobody's surprise nothing happened. The USA then extended air and naval support to South Korea in the knowledge that the UN would endorse the action, but before it had actually called on its members to help repel the attack. The USA would presumably have acted as it did even had the Soviet delegate been present to cast a veto. But the view that the UN should be able, and that the League of Nations should have attempted, to provide collective security in such situations was an important component of the Truman Administration's outlook. Equally UN support did much to legitimate, at home and abroad, a war in which the command, and all the crucial decisions, were taken by Americans – eventually (and after some US pressure) fifteen other countries (besides South Korea itself) contributed troops, though only those from the British Commonwealth and Turkey had much military value.[82]

The initial US (and British) contribution was of naval and air support, in line with the off-shore nature of its then defence posture. Originally it was hoped (despite US Army scepticism) that this would suffice. By the end of June it was clear that it would not; and Truman authorised the commitment of combat troops. Assessments of the forces needed steadily escalated, but by mid-July General MacArthur was confident: 'I intend to

---

[80] Harry S. Truman, *Years of Trial and Hope, 1946–1953* (1956) p. 351; Deborah Larson in Jervis and Snyder, *Dominoes and Bandwagons*, pp. 96–8.

[81] To please Mao, the USSR was boycotting the Security Council until the UN recognised Mao's rather than Chiang's government as representing China. When the Security Council was summoned to consider the outbreak of war in Korea, Stalin rejected Gromyko's advice that the USSR attend and cast its veto – Andrei Gromyko, *Memories* (paperback edn) pp. 131–2.

[82] *History of the JCS*, iii, pp. 94–5, 1103–4.

destroy and not to drive back the North Korean forces . . . I may need to occupy all of North Korea. In the aftermath of operations, the problem is to compose and unite Korea.'[83] MacArthur's strategy, an amphibious landing at Inchon hundreds of miles behind the current front, had technical flaws. But he staked his reputation on it; and, when executed on 15 September, it succeeded brilliantly – a fortnight later North Korean forces south of the 38th parallel had been destroyed. This must have enhanced yet further Washington's disposition to defer to MacArthur.

The UN invasion of North Korea, China's intervention and US responses 1950–51

Victory raised the question of what to do next. Initially the US administration had proclaimed, publicly and privately, that its intervention was intended only to restore the pre-war position. But opinion had been hardening during the summer in favour of overrunning the North; and on 27 September MacArthur was directed to do so provided there was no likelihood of major Soviet or Chinese intervention. In retrospect this was a disastrous mistake. At the time it was seen as a natural punishment for aggression (the Allies had not halted in 1944–5 on reaching Germany's frontiers), as the simplest way of preventing the regrouping of North Korean forces and another round of fighting, and, above all, as the implementation of the 1947 UN policy of re-uniting Korea through free elections. On 7 October a British resolution was carried overwhelmingly in the General Assembly calling on UN forces to cross the parallel, restore 'stability throughout Korea' and hold elections.[84] They then followed the South Koreans over. No restrictions were placed on MacArthur's deployments. In late September he had envisaged halting foreign troops at the narrowest point (the 'neck') of the peninsula and using only Koreans beyond it. Such a deployment might well have enabled him to withstand even Chinese intervention.[85] But on 17 October MacArthur ordered a further bound,

[83] *History of the JCS*, iii, p. 222.

[84] With this in mind, the UN Command itself administered, until the 1953 armistice, occupied territory north of the parallel, rather than simply turning it over to South Korea.

[85] It was to be urged by the UK, but unfortunately not till after UN forces had passed the neck. They would therefore have had to withdraw, and, for this and other reasons, the proposal was unacceptable in Washington – P.N. Farrar, 'Britain's Proposal for a Buffer Zone south of the Yalu in November 1950', *Journal of Contemporary History*, xviii (1983).

and thereafter he headed hard for the international frontier along the Yalu river. The orders given him on 27 September to proceed north had been conditioned on the absence of any entry, or threatened entry, into North Korea of either Soviet or Chinese forces, though on 9 October he was authorised to disregard minor Chinese involvement. In Washington there was increasing concern (since retrospectively magnified); but the consensus was that China would not strike unless its border and power stations on the Yalu were threatened. On the ground, however, MacArthur's Eighth Army seems to have expected resistance from the 150,000 Chinese troops it understood to have crossed into North Korea.[86] But it had grossly under-estimated their numbers; and it expected them to fight in Soviet style, like the North Koreans, and to be similarly vulnerable to US air power. In combination with American over-extension and front-line sloppiness, this overconfidence nearly proved disastrous.[87]

In fact Chinese intervention had always been likely if North Korea got into difficulties. Troop concentrations to provide that option had begun as early as late June, and were pushed ahead rapidly. In early September one observer felt the leaders had decided that 'China would surely send troops to Korea; what remained a problem was when to issue the final order'. Their discourse was certainly suffused with hostility to the USA, and one scholar sees them as regarding as inevitable an eventual 'Chinese-American confrontation, most likely in Taiwan, Indochina or Korea'. On this analysis the UN's decision to cross the 38th parallel was no more than one cause among many of Chinese intervention.[88] More usually it is seen as crucial: 'We originally planned,' Mao telegraphed on 2 October, '. . . to render assistance to the Korean comrades when the enemy advanced north of the 38th parallel'; and, according to Zhou Enlai's subsequent account, 'Before the Inchon landing . . . we thought that the US imperialists might halt when they reached the 38th parallel, and shift to diplomatic negotiations'.[89] On 3 October, indeed, Zhou Enlai warned the Indian

[86] MacArthur's rapid advance was partly meant to secure the Yalu before the river froze and Chinese reinforcements could no longer be interdicted by bombing its bridges.

[87] See the discussion in Eliot A. Cohen and John Gooch, *Military Misfortunes. The Anatomy of Failure in War* (New York, 1991 edn) Chap. 7.

[88] Chen, Jiang, *China's Road to the Korean War* (New York, 1994) esp. pp. 121, 153, 213–19.

[89] Mao to Stalin (version actually sent), cited in Shen Zhihua, 'The Discrepancy between the Russian and Chinese Versions of Mao's 2 October 1950 message to Stalin on entry into the Korean War . . .' CWIHP *Bulletin* 8–9 (1996–7) p. 238; Zhou, 24 October 1950,

ambassador (and declared on the radio) that China would intervene if UN, as opposed to South Korean, troops crossed the parallel. But he never sought to convey this formally and convincingly (e.g. through the British chargé in Beijing), probably because achieving surprise was a prerequisite for any Chinese military success.

In August a military appreciation had suggested that intervention would come best when UN forces had penetrated far to the north, partly because this would 'gain more political capital', but also because logistics would be easier and 'the enemy's disposition will be lengthened and widened'. Stalin had always made it clear that the USSR would not itself directly intervene in Korea. But on 1 October he cabled that the North Koreans' situation 'is getting desperate' and asked for immediate Chinese intervention to enable them to regroup. At this point, much of the Chinese leadership developed cold feet: China's forces might simply be shredded, or things develop into full-scale hostilities with America, upsetting con-solidation and reconstruction after the recent civil war. Such fears were real enough for Lin Biao to refuse the command of Chinese forces (which went instead to Peng Dehuai); but at an expanded Politburo meeting Mao forced through the decision to intervene.

There followed, however, a puzzling diplomatic minuet, since the Chinese emissaries to Stalin (Zhou Enlai and Lin Biao, both opponents of intervention) took the position that nothing could be done. Years later Mao explained this as a device to extract guarantees of Soviet air cover. On this, though, Stalin seems (despite later Chinese claims) to have been consistent; he would provide cover, but not 'far behind enemy lines in case our pilots were shot down and captured'; and its organisation might take a couple of months. While reluctant to risk the capture of his own airmen, Stalin pressed hard for Chinese ground intervention: the USA was not ready 'for a big war', nor could Japan yet give it any military assistance. It would accordingly 'be compelled to yield in the Korean question'; further:

I believe that the USA would be compelled to return Taiwan to China and, ultimately . . . to give up also on the separate treaty with the Japanese reactionaries as well as the conversion of Japan into its satellite.

cited in C.W. David Tsui, *Chinese Military Intervention in the Korean War* (Oxford D. Phil thesis, 1998) pp. 241–2. Perhaps with a view to such negotiations, China had bombarded the UN that summer with proposals on Korea (always including the with-drawal of foreign troops – i.e. the restoration of North Korea's advantage), Taiwan, and Chinese representation at the UN.

I do not believe that China could obtain these concessions as a result of passive temporizing and patience . . . on the contrary . . . without serious struggle and without new imposing display of its force China will not obtain these and similar concessions, as well as it will not obtain Taiwan, which the Americans will keep in their hands . . .[90]

When the Chinese emissaries seemed set against committing troops, Stalin called their bluff by making it clear that, if so, he would write the North Koreans off; on 13 October he even told Kim Il Sung to evacuate Korea. At that point Mao reconsidered, and ordered intervention even in the absence of agreed arrangements for Soviet air cover; so the evacuation instructions were suspended.[91]

Mao seems to have envisaged standing on the defensive, assimilating Soviet weapons, and then attacking in 1951; but the pace of the UN advance compressed this timetable. So in late November MacArthur's final move to the Yalu coincided with China's counter-offensive. This failed to trap and annihilate UN forces, but it did force them into headlong retreat. As before North Korea (backed by Soviet diplomats) favoured going for broke in hot pursuit; Peng Dehuai wanted to regroup and consolidate. For political reasons, Mao insisted on crossing the 38th parallel and reoccupying Seoul (which fell on 4 January), but otherwise supported Peng and eventually secured Stalin's backing. Two to three months of pause and preparations, Mao held, 'can secure the final victory'.[92] Meanwhile it was decided on 7 December to stake out a tough position at the UN, implying

[90] Stalin admitted, as a worst case scenario, that the USA might be drawn into 'a big war' with China, and hence (given their 1950 treaty) the USSR; but the USSR and China together were stronger than the USA and England, while 'the other European capitalist states . . . do not present a serious military force' (message delivered to Mao on 6 October – CWIHP *Bulletin* 14/15 (2003–4) pp. 370, 375–6). In the version passed to Kim Il Sung, Stalin added that 'if a [general] war is inevitable, then let it be waged now, and not in a few years when Japanese militarism will be restored as an ally of the USA', etc. (*Bulletin* 6–7 (1995–6) p. 116).

[91] These exchanges are discussed in e.g. Shen Zhihua, 'Sino-North Korean Conflict and its Resolution during the Korean War', and 'The Discrepancy between the Russian and Chinese Versions of Mao's 2 October 1950 Message', CWIHP *Bulletin* 14–15 (2003–4) and 8–9 (1996–7); Bajanov, 'Assessing the Politics of the Korean War'; and Alexandre Mansourov, 'Stalin, Mao, Kim, and China's Decision to Enter the Korean War, Sept. 16–Oct. 15, 1950: New Evidence from the Russian Archives', *Bulletin* 6–7 (1995–6); Tsui, *Chinese Military Intervention*, pp. 249–69, and Zubok and Pleshakov, *Inside the Kremlin's Cold War*, pp. 65–9.

[92] Shen Zhihua, 'Sino-North Korean Conflict', pp. 14–15.

that there could be no ceasefire without the withdrawal of all foreign troops from Korea and of US forces from Taiwan, and the seating of Communist China in the UN.

Here an opportunity was missed. For in December Washington was in a flat spin, without a policy but revolving ideas of evacuating Korea and/or expanding the war beyond the peninsula. It would have jumped at a ceasefire, and endorsed attempts to secure one through the UN. On 11 January a UN committee put to the General Assembly a second ceasefire plan, in many ways rather nebulous but involving withdrawal of foreign troops and a conference to settle the status of Taiwan and Chinese representation at the UN. The US administration accepted, preferring domestic political trouble to the risk of alienating its allies, and hoping that the Chinese would decline – which on the 17th they did, with Stalin's encouragement.[93] By then the USA had become militarily more confident, and at the end of the month it proceeded to have China declared an 'aggressor' under the new UN 'uniting for peace' procedure (below, p. 186),[94] despite Chinese warnings that this would 'close the door' on any possibility of peace.

In mid-January Mao was envisaging either a UN withdrawal from South Korea or one to two further offensives to compel this. On the 28th Peng suggested broadcasting a ceasefire offer, but Mao overruled him and looked to advancing halfway down South Korea before opening peace negotiations.[95] In fact late January brought an unexpected UN offensive. By March UN forces were approaching the 38th parallel, and there was concern, both in Washington and still more among its allies, that General MacArthur would again cross it. Truman had intended a reassuring public statement of readiness to 'conclude the fighting' with a view to a Korean settlement and consideration of 'other problems' in the Far East. But MacArthur pre-emptively declared that the enemy must realise that 'an

---

[93] Tsui, *Chinese Military Intervention*, pp. 284–98; CWIHP *Bulletin* 6–7 (1995–6) esp. pp. 32, 34, 51–3; Callum A. MacDonald, *Korea. The War before Vietnam* (Basingstoke, 1986) pp. 81–3.

[94] This could have led to the imposition of serious sanctions, but in practice America's allies declined to go so far. *History of the JCS*, iii, pp. 385, 428–30; Acheson, *Present at the Creation* p. 513; Robert R. Simmons, *The Strained Alliance. Peking, Pyongyang, Moscow and the Politics of the Korean War* (New York, 1975) pp. 188–90.

[95] Tsui, *Chinese Military Intervention*, pp. 298–9; CWIHP *Bulletin* 6–7 (1995–6) pp. 55–7, 90.

expansion of our military operations to his coastal areas, and interior bases, would doom Red China to the risk of imminent military collapse'; the Korean problem need not therefore be bound up with 'extraneous matters' like Taiwan or Beijing's claim to UN representation; and he invited the opposing commander to meet him to arrange the bloodless realisation of UN 'political objectives'. London and Ottawa were appalled; but if Truman moved against MacArthur, he risked Republican backlash against his controversial military build-up of NATO. His difficulties were resolved when a leading Republican Congressman released a letter of MacArthur's attacking those who gave priority to Europe: 'If we lose the war to Communism in Asia, the fall of Europe is inevitable . . . We must win. There is no substitute for victory.' On 10 April MacArthur was sacked for this entry into the political arena.[96]

China had operated all along on the basis that the war would be largely confined to Korea, and MacArthur's dismissal seemed to confirm this. However, it felt the UN might well wish to secure the neck of the peninsula. So on 22 April China launched the 'Fifth Campaign', hoping to destroy five divisions and drive south to the 37th parallel. At one point this came within five miles of Seoul. But at the end of May it was repulsed with such heavy losses that the new UN commander could report that for the next two months the 'military situation' would offer 'optimum advantages in support of . . . diplomatic negotiations'. Various soundings of the USSR and China had already been made, but to no purpose. So Kennan was asked to speak ominously but unofficially on 31 May to the Soviet UN ambassador: the present Chinese course seemed to be leading the US and USSR towards an unwanted but potentially 'most dangerous collision . . . If the drift to serious trouble was to be stopped, the method would seem to be an armistice and cease-fire in Korea at about where the forces stood.' He need not have worried: China was in military trouble, fearful of a second amphibious landing behind its lines, and anxious for a period of calm to allow its forces to regroup. On 13 June Stalin agreed with Gao Gang and Kim Il Sung that an armistice was indeed desirable, though it took till 10 July for talks actually to convene.[97] Both sides then dug into defensive positions, and the war ceased to be one of movement.

[96] MacDonald, *Korea*, pp. 91–8.
[97] Tsui, *Chinese Military Intervention*, pp. 247–9, 305, 308–9; *History of the JCS*, iii, pp. 502, 527, 564; Acheson, *Present at the Creation*, p. 532; CWIHP *Bulletin* 6–7 (1995–6) pp. 34, 60 ff.

Ceasefire talks 1951–3 and the 1953 armistice

Fighting eased off but did not end, owing to an American concern that, if it did, public opinion would insist on bringing the boys home as in 1945, leaving the UN Command helpless if the communists chose to break off talks. In fact the talks dragged on for two years – which greatly soured the US domestic response to 'Truman's War' – and almost half of all US casualties were incurred after they had started, many (admittedly) at the very end when the talks were at last making progress. Negotiations were always difficult, but in November 1951 agreement was reached on an armistice line along the current front (a position slightly more favourable to South Korea than the 38th parallel). Thereafter the chief, and from May 1952 the only, issue was that of the repatriation of prisoners against their will. About half of all communist, two-thirds of all Chinese, prisoners refused to return; the UN command would not compel them to do so, partly for propaganda reasons but also because it did not want to expose them to the fate of the Russians returned after Yalta; and though the Chinese often seemed prepared to overlook Korean prisoners, they insisted on getting all theirs back.

By October 1952 the UN Command had made a final offer, and, as it was not accepted, recessed the armistice talks indefinitely. Thoughts then turned to possible coercive action. But most US generals doubted the chances of any significant victory on the ground without major reinforcements – and renewed heavy fighting in October–November confirmed this judgement. The new UN commander favoured a large troop build-up and a drive for either the neck of the peninsula or the Yalu, backed by strikes against supply centres and airfields in China. But, given the calls on US troops elsewhere, the Chiefs of Staff were unenthusiastic. During his visit to Korea in December, President-elect Eisenhower made it clear that he favoured a ceasefire in place. Once President, he made no definite plans for major operations, but hinted discreetly in a number of quarters 'that, in the absence of satisfactory [negotiating] progress, we intended to move decisively without inhibition in our choice of weapons, and would no longer be responsible for confining hostilities to the Korean peninsula'. Eisenhower (and others) later cited this as a successful use of a nuclear threat.[98]

---

[98] Dwight D. Eisenhower, *Mandate for Change* (1963) p. 181. In May he told the NSC that, if talks failed, he favoured decisive atomic strikes against China – 'the quicker the operation was mounted, the less the danger of Soviet intervention' (*The (London) Times*, 9 June 1984, p. 3).

Probably, though, Stalin's earlier death on 5 March 1953 was more important. Stalin had exercised a tight control over the armistice negotiations. In mid-1952 he was unimpressed by North Korean urging of an early armistice: 'The North Koreans have lost nothing, except for casualties that they suffered during the war'. China then endorsed, albeit some say rather wistfully, Stalin's judgement that 'this war is getting on America's nerves', and claimed that it was 'helping to stave off the [world] war for 15–20 years'. But at Stalin's funeral, Zhou apparently 'proposed that the Soviet side assist the speeding up of the negotiations and the conclusion of an armistice'. Stalin's successors agreed, and on 19 March the Council of Ministers approved moves to resume negotiations.[99] Once again these were slow; they were complicated by the resistance of Syngman Rhee to any armistice that left Korea divided, and marred both by the escalation of US bombing and by heavy final communist offensives. But ultimately the communists dropped their demand for the forcible repatriation of prisoners,[100] and an uneasy but indefinite ceasefire ensued.

The cost of the war had been horrific – perhaps 0.5 million Chinese, and *many* more North and South Korean, casualties (the latter largely civilian), plus 34,000 US dead (and over 100,000 wounded).[101] The peninsula ended, as it had begun, far more harshly partitioned than Germany. The possibility of another Northern invasion remained; partly for this reason, partly to induce Rhee to accept the armistice, the US concluded a defence agreement with South Korea and has retained troops there. Nevertheless the Northern threat provided a rationale for continued authoritarian rule in the south – though this may also have been a necessary condition for the spectacular economic growth that began in the 1960s.

[99] CWIHP *Bulletin*, 3 (1993) p. 17 (1966 Soviet account), 6–7 (1995–6) esp. pp. 34–5, 77 (16 June 1952), 12–13 (20 August), 80–2 (19 March 1953).

[100] Face-saving arrangements were made for each power to interview those of its prisoners who did not wish to return, under the supervision of neutral Indian troops. Very few changed their minds as a result.

[101] The Chinese figures come from Tsui, *Chinese Military Intervention*, pp. 398–9. Simmons, *The Strained Alliance*, pp. 213, 242 puts North Korean casualties at 1.5m; this may be too high, but war and refugee movements left the North Korean population 1m lower in 1953 than it had been in 1949.

Implications of the Korean War: 'Limited war'; China's relations with the USSR and the USA; Taiwan; The Japanese peace and security treaties, 1951–2

The war had, in part, been fought to demonstrate the UN's ability to provide collective security. Indeed, in 1950 the US secured the (legally dubious) 'Uniting for Peace' resolution that enabled the UN General Assembly to act by a two-thirds majority when the Security Council was deadlocked by a veto. But the 'Uniting for Peace' procedure has never led to anything concrete. Nor, after Korea, did the UN show any further disposition to embark on coercive military action until Iraq's 1990 annexation of Kuwait, after the 'end of the Cold War'. However, if the war did not constitute the hoped-for precedent for the successful operation of collective security, it did set others. Crossing the 38th parallel had brought China into the war. The Americans were not going to make that mistake again; so, though they bombed North Vietnam in the 1960s and 1970s, they never invaded it. More generally, Korea was, for most of its course, a 'limited war' in the sense that the UN fought not for outright victory but only to induce the enemy to conclude an armistice broadly along the pre-war border. This is the response prescribed by the international law doctrine of the right to self-defence. But much US public opinion, prone to viewing international relations in more black and white terms, found fighting for such restricted objectives uncongenial, even immoral. Nor did it relish according immunity to communist supply and air bases just over the Chinese border, which appeared to expose UN forces to unnecessary risks in deference to half-hearted European allies. Nevertheless both North Korean immunity from invasion and the existence of 'sanctuary' areas outside the combat zone came to constitute precedents. These have certainly not always been followed; but they have often affected military operations, and world opinion tends to regard it as illegitimate when they are breached.

Initially the Korean War strengthened the Sino-Soviet alliance, removing (as a Chinese official history has it) 'Stalin's last suspicion of China taking "a nationalistic path"', and leading to the Soviet decision 'to supply China with the 156 whole [industrial plants] and the vast amount of military equipment'; Mao too was to say that 'It was from the Korean War' that the Soviets began 'to trust the Chinese'. In all, Stalin re-equipped 100 Chinese divisions; and China's self-esteem was clearly boosted by her military performance against the USA.[102] Nevertheless her losses were such that in 1954, Zhou Enlai told Khrushchev, she was in no condition to intervene in Indo-China to rescue the Vietminh if the French got the upper hand.[103]

More intangible were the consequences for relations with Taiwan and the USA. In 1949 Chiang Kai-shek had transferred to Taiwan the government, gold reserve, and some of the army of his Republic of China. The communists naturally wished to round off their victory by eliminating his rule. So their main military preparations, in the first half of 1950, were for the invasion of that island. Washington readily accepted that Taiwan's fall was not in the US interest, but the predominant view was that the US should not, in time of peace, take the island over to defend it. Nor was there any confidence in the KMT's determination or ability seriously to defend itself; so the Truman administration was, before the outbreak of the Korean War, prepared to write Taiwan off. There were, though, some contrary voices, notably that of General MacArthur. In the immediate aftermath of the North Korean invasion, MacArthur's memorandum (urging Taiwan's defence or neutralisation) was discussed, and on 27 June 1950 Truman announced the interposition of his fleet between Taiwan and the mainland. Supposedly this was to prevent the further spread of conflict in East Asia, and the fleet was charged to prevent not only communist invasion of Taiwan but also any attempt by Chiang's forces to 'return to the mainland'. Practically, though, the Korean War had led to the incorporation of Taiwan into the US defensive perimeter, and (soon) to the resumption of US aid on a large scale. This time the KMT used it well. It may be that the communists could never have conquered Taiwan anyway (it is over 100 miles offshore). But the USA had now intervened directly to prevent the termination of the Chinese civil war; and the status of Taiwan remains a serious international question.[104]

Even before this, Mao had in 1949 embraced the Soviet side in the Cold War and stridently denounced US imperialism. Then, later in 1950, 'Red

---

[102] Tsui, *Chinese Military Intervention*, pp. 116–17, 119, 315. However China had to *buy* the military equipment, and when Sino-Soviet relations cooled this was brought forward as a grievance.

[103] *Khrushchev Remembers*, i, p. 443.

[104] *FRUS 1950*, vi, pp. 349–51, 366–7; vii, pp. 157–8, 161–5; He Di, ' "The Last Campaign to Unify China": the CCP's UN-materialized Plan to Liberate Taiwan, 1949–50'; *Chinese Historians*, v (1992) pp. 1–16. Taiwan's subsequent history is discussed in *The Post-Imperial Age*, Chap. 8.

China's' entry into the Korean War sealed its hostility to the USA, and, by bringing it into armed conflict with US forces, elevated it, for two decades, into prime position in American demonology. This rift was admittedly overcome in the 1970s by a common fear of, and hostility to, the USSR. But the residual US commitment to Taiwan periodically reemerges as a significant problem.

Still more important, perhaps, was the effect of the Korean War on two ex-enemy states, Japan and West Germany. Truman had already decided before the outbreak of the Korean War to push for a peace treaty with Japan that would preserve US bases there, even if it meant (as in the event it did) that the USSR would not sign. But the war both added urgency and provided a propitious environment for such a policy. It also hardened US determination that Japan should not risk becoming dependent on trade with mainland China, and that it should make peace with Chiang Kai-shek not Mao Zedong. All this the USA achieved in 1951–2 through linked peace and security treaties, thereby ensuring that, even after independence, Japan was locked firmly into the American sphere.[105]

German rearmament – the European Defence Community, 1952

More complicated, but (as people then thought) more important, were moves towards West German rearmament. Soviet military strength in Central Europe was vastly greater than NATO's: at the time 175 Soviet divisions were believed ready for use; and though this estimate has since been cut to about 60, they still out-classed the (at best) 6 Western divisions on the German front.[106] US war plans called for the evacuation of Europe to the Pyrenees and the establishment of off-shore bases in the UK and North Africa. So it is not surprising that the earliest advocates of German rearmament were to be found among the US, British and indeed French military. Both Washington and London had begun to contemplate some *eventual* West German rearmament within a NATO framework. But the

---

[105] The September 1951 San Francisco Peace Treaty ending the occupation of Japan was accompanied by a US–Japanese Security Treaty; and US ratification of the former in 1952 was conditioned on a Japanese pledge to seek peace with the Republic of China (on Taiwan) not the Beijing People's Republic. US–Japanese relations are discussed more fully in *The Post-Imperial Age*, Chap. 7.

[106] R. McGeehan, *The German Rearmament Question. American Diplomacy and European Defense after World War II* (Urbana, Ill., 1971) pp. 6–7, 102.

idea was generally unpalatable, and Acheson concluded from the May 1950 NATO council that moves towards it could destroy the welcome new French plan for a European Coal and Steel Community (ECSC). Nor did there seem any urgency; none of the NATO Foreign Ministers had seen any immediate threat of war.[107]

Korea changed things. There were uncomfortable (though not exact) parallels with a divided Germany. 'One thing is certain, they [the North Koreans] did not do this purely on their own but as part of the world strategy of international communism',[108] which could, presumably, no longer be counted on not to exploit conventional force superiority. The United States, which had already been cogitating major rearmament (NSC-68), at once decided on it, and remained very apprehensive of Soviet intentions for the next two and a half years. So initially were Western Europeans.[109] In July reports from US missions in Europe converted Acheson to the view that West Germany would have to be rearmed and that the USA would have to give an immediate lead.

At first it tried to insist on a 'single package', US troop reinforcements for Europe, the redesign of the NATO command structure to secure strategic integration, and German rearmament. In response to strong French criticism a less rigid posture was adopted; but it was always clear that refusing German rearmament would jeopardise US protection. Equally the American decision to commit troops to Europe was not easily made. For in the aftermath of Republican victories in the November 1950 elections and of Chinese intervention in Korea, some Republicans sought a 're-examination' of foreign policy – concentration on air and sea power to 'preserve this Western Hemisphere Gibraltar of Western Civilization', holding the off-shore islands of Britain and Japan but largely leaving Europe to defend itself. Hearings on these ideas took up the first quarter of 1951, the most persuasive testimony to the contrary being given by the newly designated Supreme Allied Commander Europe (SACEUR), General Eisenhower, who maintained that 6 US and 34 other NATO divisions would suffice to protect 'rather significant portions' of Western Europe. Eventually the Senate grudgingly approved both Eisenhower's new post and the despatch

---

[107] *History of the JCS*, iv, p. 193; McGeehan, *German Rearmament*, p. 3; Anne Deighton (ed.) *Britain and the first Cold War* (Basingstoke, 1990) pp. 276–8.

[108] Dulles, July 1950 (McGeehan, *German Rearmament*, p. 21).

[109] Acheson recalls both French and Belgian queries in December 1950 as to whether there would be war in three months (*Present at the Creation*, p. 487), though such feelings subsided faster than in the USA.

of 4 divisions (taking the US total in Europe to 6).[110] By the end of 1951 they had arrived. Eisenhower viewed them as a temporary expedient to cover European rearmament, but US troops are still (2006) there – a symbol of determination to defend Western Europe, or, as strategic commentators had it during the Cold War, 'hostages' to ensure the commitment of US nuclear deterrence. It took until 1952 to negotiate a satisfactory NATO command structure. How much this amounted to could only have been shown in war – certainly not to the standardisation of equipment or even the effective control of force levels, but equally clearly to far more than say the pre-war Franco-Czech alliance or Franco-British partnership. De Gaulle was to see it as a vehicle of American 'hegemony' incompatible with French national sovereignty.

German rearmament proved more thorny. East–West relations apart, there was no urgency. Probably most West Germans were opposed: their ideal would have been the deployment of more Anglo-American troops. But since much of the Christian Democrat leadership favoured a German military contribution, the issue would presumably have come up some time. Adenauer apparently said privately in 1949 that within four years there would again be Germans in uniform, and in December he made several pronouncements about the possibility of a German contribution to a European army. He says he saw that 'Rearmament might be the way of gaining full sovereignty for the Federal Republic'.[111] In August 1950 he first proposed a West German paramilitary police force of 150,000 (to counter the 50,000 already raised in East Germany), then urged a German military contribution to a European army linked with a drastic modification of the occupation regime. The chief obstacle was France's continuing fear of a country that, even partitioned, was more populous and industrialised than itself. Adenauer's bids might have been disregarded; US proposals, made formally in September, could not. Things might, as Bevin suggested, have gone more smoothly had the USA simply pushed the paramilitary police proposal. Instead it conditioned its enhanced support for NATO on acceptance of a force containing German units. France's counter in October was the 'Pleven Plan', a European army (linked to the ECSC but at the disposal of SACEUR) that would include, within an integrated structure, German 'combat teams' 800–1,200 strong,

---

[110] Acheson, *Present at the Creation*, pp. 488–96; S.E. Ambrose, *Eisenhower 1890–1952* (1984) pp. 496–510.

[111] T. Prittie, *The Velvet Chancellors* (1979) p. 80 and *Konrad Adenauer* (1972) pp. 157–8; K. Adenauer, *Memoirs 1945–53* (English translation, 1966) p. 270.

that is too small to be dangerous. The plan prompted jibes about creating German forces that should be stronger than Russia but weaker than France; but it certainly served the purpose of delaying things.

Intensive negotiation gradually modified both the French and the American stances – France eventually accepting division-sized (12,000) German units and eliminating many obviously discriminatory provisions, the United States recognising in July 1951 that progress could only come through a European army and Defence Community (EDC).[112] Meanwhile, West Germany bargained (hard) its readiness to make a defence contribution against successive relaxations of occupation controls. The USA had originally hoped to start recruiting German units in 1951, and France came under pressure to reach a conclusion by the end of the year. Inevitably things took a little longer. But after further negotiations (especially in London and Lisbon in February 1952) and Anglo-American reassurances to France of assistance were West Germany to break from the EDC, the treaty was signed in May 1952, as part of a package providing for the restoration of sovereignty to West Germany when it was ratified.

Thereafter US diplomatic pressure eased, and ratification stalled (below, pp. 217–18). The first West German conscripts were not called up until 1957. If 1954 had really been, as the Americans feared, the 'year of maximum danger', they would have come too late. The decision for rearmament remains controversial. Did it, as the SPD maintained at the time, seal the partition of Germany (at least until 1990)? Or was it essential for the credibility of NATO's conventional defence, and indeed for NATO's survival after de Gaulle's withdrawal in 1965? Lastly, was it important for Germany's smooth reintegration into Western Europe that the traumatic issue of rearmament was pushed not, as after the First World War, by the Germans themselves but by the Americans?

Stalin's 1952 'offer' of German reunification

West Germany's rearmament and incorporation into the Western alliance would clearly be a blow to Soviet interests, and the USSR sought until 1955 to prevent it. There has been much debate over what Stalin, and his successors, were prepared to concede in order to do so: were they ready,

---

[112] As agreed in November 1951, this was to have 14 French, 12 German and 12 Italian, and 5 Benelux divisions, all with a common logistics system but with integrated international command only at corps and army level. France would have 6 extra, purely national, divisions (McGeehan, *German Rearmament*, pp. 155–6).

either in 1952 or after Stalin's death in 1953, to give up communist control of East Germany so as to secure German neutrality? On 10 March
1952 the USSR proposed 'a unified democratic and peace loving [German]
government in accordance with the Potsdam provisions', with all foreign
troops withdrawn from its territory; it would be permitted armed forces on
a scale 'necessary for the defense of the country', but debarred from joining 'any kind of coalition or military alliance directed against' any of the
powers that had fought it in the Second World war.[113] Many historians
have taken this proposal at face value, or argued that it represented at least
a possible chance of reunification within a liberal democratic context
that Adenauer rejected out of hand in his blind pursuit of a West Germany
constrained to alignment with the West. By way of confirmation they can
cite Stalin as telling the Italian fellow-traveller Nenni in July 1952 that,
though he had now come to think unification impossible, he would earlier

*have sacrificed the East German Communists so as to bring about a
Germany ruled by a government friendly to the West but containing a
strong leftist opposition as in Italy today. Stalin felt a weak Germany
containing strong political forces looking both to the West and to the
Soviet Union would bring about a political equilibrium sufficient to
stop any drift to war.*[114]

This, however, now looks unlikely. The Soviet bureaucracy had since 1951
been preparing an East German initiative that was to be followed up
by a formal Soviet proposal for a German peace treaty. In January 1952
Gromyko suggested to Stalin that the time was now ripe; the move would
have 'great political significance for the strengthening of the struggle for
peace against the remilitarization of West Germany, thus helping the supporters of the unity of Germany . . . to expose the aggressive intentions of
the three Western powers.' He also transmitted a draft peace treaty so

[113] Soviet notes of 10 March, 9 April and 24 May (*FRUS 1952–1954*, vii, nos. 65, 82,
102), US notes of 25 March and 13 May (ibid. nos. 78, 101).
[114] Canadian report of what the Italian ambassador in Moscow said Nenni told him –
Rolf Steininger, *Eine Chance zur Wiedervereinigung? Die Stalin-Note von 10 März
1952* (*Archiv für Sozialgeschichte*, Beiheft 12, 1985) p. 282. (Steininger's book, arguing
that the West should have taken the 1952 offer more seriously, is translated, with fewer
documents, as *The German Question. The Stalin Note of 1952 and the Problem of
Reunification* (New York, 1990). However, a colourful Nenni account to Western
diplomats of what Stalin had told him on another topic is not borne out by his
own diaries (Vojtech Mastny, *The Cold War and Soviet Insecurity. The Stalin Years*
(New York, 1996) p. 144).

biased towards Soviet interests that it was in fact discarded, the Soviet note of 10 March only advancing nebulous treaty principles, not an actual text. In East Berlin the proposals were explained to party activists and officials as intended to derail the EDC treaty that was expected to be concluded in May, or at least to bring down Adenauer's government. Years later Vladimir Semyonov (in 1952 Political Counsellor to the Soviet High Commissioner in East Germany) said Stalin had asked whether he could be sure the USA would turn the proposals down, and had only launched the 10 March note on being assured that it would.[115] The Western response of 25 March was certainly cool, but instead of outright rejection it directed attention to the need for genuinely free elections.[116] At this point, Stalin apparently lost interest, and in early April told high East German officials to 'organise your own state', proceding to socialism and creating 'a People's Army – quietly'; the 'demarcation line' with West Germany was a 'dangerous frontier' behind which should stand 'in the first line German-Stasi' and then Soviet troops.[117]

Not that Western governments were enamoured of the 10 March proposal, whether viewed as a manoeuvre to preclude West Germany's incorporation into the EDC that would evaporate as soon as it had served its purpose, or even as a genuine offer.[118] Either way it might undercut Adenauer and his policy of westwards integration. Accordingly the chief

[115] Ruud van Dijk, *The 1952 Stalin Note Debate: Myth or Missed Opportunity for German Unification* (CWIHP Working Paper no. 14, May 1996) p. 35n.
[116] To be monitored by a commission answering to the UN General Assembly (i.e. not subject to a Soviet veto); in reply the USSR insisted on Four Power control. The US also insisted that the projected 'all-German' government be free to join any association 'compatible with the principles . . . of the United Nations', including the EDC, something the USSR would not concede.
[117] This account chiefly follows Gerhard Wettig, 'Stalin and German Reunification: Archival Evidence on Soviet Foreign Policy in Spring 1952', *Historical Journal*, xxxvii (1994) pp. 411–19 and Mastny, *Cold War and Soviet Insecurity*, pp. 135–9; cf. also Wettig, 'Die Stalin-Note vom 10 März 1952 als geschichtswissenschaftliches Problem', *Deutschland Archiv*, February 1992, esp. pp. 161–3, citing Pieck's notes of the meetings. (The Stasi were the East German security police.)
[118] Some feared a reunited Germany *per se*. Others felt it might be vulnerable to Soviet attraction through trade and (at the crucial moment) an offer to restore territory east of the Oder, especially were economic adversity to displace the likely initial SPD government by a more adventurist and Rapallo-minded Right-authoritarian one. A few felt that any unattached Germany would be vulnerable to minority Communist takeover, East European style. Lastly the appearance of detente with the USSR might inhibit consolidation and rearmament of the rest of Western Europe.

(and successful) thrust of Western diplomacy was so to reply to Soviet notes as not to disturb either the completion of the EDC or political support in West Germany for this cause and its embodiment, Chancellor Adenauer. Nevertheless Acheson came by late April to favour talks with the Russians: 'it is in our interest to expose Soviet insincerity at the earliest possible date and in any event before [West German] legislation debates are concluded'; but 'If Soviets are really prepared to open [the] Eastern Zone, we should force their hand. We can *not* allow our plans to be thwarted merely by *speculation* that Soviets may be ready actually to pay a high price'. London and Paris were cool, but the decisive opposition was probably that coming from Adenauer after he had considered the question all day and 'through half the night'.[119]

Stalin's final years

In 1951 Stalin was overheard to soliloquise, 'I'm finished. I trust no one, not even myself.' Distrust was a feature of his closing years – was Voroshilov an English spy, had Molotov travelled by train in the United States and did that mean that he had his own private railway car bought with American money? Stalin kept his cards so close to his chest that there is much disagreement as to what his foreign policy really was. Nor need one assume that he was necessarily consistent. Earlier his 1937 purge of the officer corps had seriously undercut Soviet foreign policies in other directions; and everybody agrees that, by the end of his life, Stalin was 'weakening mentally as well as physically', albeit not to the point where he had lost the ability to express himself, when dictating, 'clearly and concisely'.[120]

Some say that, at the end of his life, Stalin was coming round to seeking rather warmer relations with the West. This seems unlikely. The only tangible evidence advanced is the apparent offer in March 1952 of a neutral reunited Germany; and, as we have seen, this should probably not be taken at face value. We know, too, that in 1952 Stalin set himself against the ending of the Korean War (above, p. 185). He also repeatedly warned his

---

[119] Steininger, *Eine Chance?* esp. pp. 233, 241.
[120] Djilas uses the word 'senility' of Stalin's decline between 1945 and 1948 (*Conversations with Stalin*, p. 118); Khrushchev says that later his deterioration became 'Every year . . . more and more obvious' (*Khrushchev Remembers*, i, pp. 242, 273–4). It will not have helped that, from early 1952, Stalin refused medical attentions (Holloway, *Stalin and the Bomb*, pp. 288–9).

colleagues that 'when I'm gone the imperialistic powers will wring your necks like chickens'.[121]

Another interpretation would accept Stalin's palpable suspicion and fear of the West. He lived, Khrushchev says, 'in terror of enemy attack. For him foreign policy meant keeping the anti-aircraft units around Moscow in a twenty-four-hour alert.' There were periodic panics, e.g. that the United States would send in troops to contest the communist takeover in Czechoslovakia in 1948 or that (at US instigation) Turkey was about to attack Bulgaria. Khrushchev further maintains that, 'In the days leading up to Stalin's death, we believed that America would invade the Soviet Union and we would go to war. Stalin trembled at this prospect [having never got over the ghastly experience of the German attack in 1941] . . . He knew that we were weaker than the United States [in nuclear, if not conventional, weapons] . . . [and] never did anything that might provoke a war with the United States.'[122] But political counter-measures did not go beyond a barrage of propaganda, designed to appeal to West European peoples and 'peace movements' over the heads of their governments, perhaps also to drive wedges between these governments and the United States. Such initiatives were commonly launched shortly before major measures of Western consolidation, like the signing of NATO in early 1949, the establishment of West Germany that summer, or the 1952 treaties to end its occupation and create the European Defence Community. They were handled badly, perhaps because Stalin had discarded diplomatic advisers with experience of foreign countries, perhaps because he himself now lacked energy. Certainly Americans counted themselves lucky that 'the Soviets played their cards all the wrong way'. Friendly gestures were cancelled out by automatic reversions to a strident and hostile tone; and important overtures (like the apparent offer of German reunification in 1952) were simply dropped when they met no immediate response, instead of being so pressed as to force Western governments to address them or at least to pay a political price for not doing so.

A much harsher picture comes from the Czech historian, Karel Kaplan. Though in 1946 Stalin was talking about another war with *Germany*, in September 1948 he told Gottwald that sooner or later the USSR would have to fight America. 1949 brought massive rearmament; and in January 1951 (according to the then Czech Defence Minister, Cepicka) East

---

[121] *Khrushchev Remembers*, i, pp. 356, 545 ('Secret Speech'); cf. also Edvard Radzinsky, *Stalin* (paperback edn) pp. 544–6.
[122] *Khrushchev Remembers*, i, pp. 273–5, 356–7; ii, pp. 188–9; iii, pp. 100–1.

European leaders were summoned to Moscow, where Stalin portrayed a window of opportunity. By 1955 at the latest the USA would have completed the ring of bases needed for an atomic assault on the USSR and acquired the means for the rapid reinforcement of Western Europe; in the meantime there was a heavy Soviet military predominance. No European army could resist effectively, and there might well be no attempt to do so; the existing US forces were not great, and, despite their advanced technology, had been shown up in Korea (this was at the time of maximum Chinese success there). Accordingly there should be a complete mobilisation of resources to permit the military occupation of Western Europe – before it was too late.[123] Recently discovered Romanian minutes of the conference confirm that Stalin led off by speaking of the US as 'unable even to cope with a small war such as the one in Korea'; the 'fact that the US will be tied down in Asia for the next two or three years constitutes a very favorable circumstance for us, for the world revolutionary movement. These two-to-three years we must use skilfully.' Within that time, the People's Democracies should develop forces of '3 million, to be ready on first alert, well organized and equipped.' But, at the conclusion of the conference three days later, Stalin justified the undertaking in more defensive terms than Cepicka later recollected: the imperialists were:

in the habit of attacking . . . weakly armed countries in order to liquidate them, but they keep away from well armed countries. This is why you need to arm during this respite . . . in order that the imperialists respect you and keep away from you.[124]

[123] Much of Kaplan's account derives from his 1960s interviews with Cepicka, who regretted that the plan had been abandoned: 'Il piano di Stalin', *Panorama* (Milan) 26 April 1977, pp. 169–89, and his *Dans les Archives du Comité Central* (Paris, 1978) pp. 164–6. Some see Kaplan's picture as confirmed by Stalin's January 1951 request that the Italian communist Togliatti come East to run a beefed-up Cominform and, through it, the West European parties, since 'from one moment to the next one could face an international conflict or the banning of the communist parties in all western countries' (Enzo Collotti (ed.), 'Archivio Pietro Secchia 1945–1973', *Annali – Fondazione Giangiacomo Feltrinelli* xix (1978) pp. 229–30). But Stalin's fears that Togliatti would be arrested or murdered may have been genuine; alternatively he may have 'thought that in Italy Togliatti would be a restraint on a policy of more decisive struggle against American imperialism' or suspected Togliatti's partner of being a Vatican agent.

[124] 'Did NATO win the Cold War? Documentary supplement to the article . . . by Vojtech Mastny . . . April 23, 1999' (National Security Council, Electronic Briefing Book no. 14, Document 3). Edvard Ochab, then a Polish central committee secretary, also described the meeting and Stalin's insistence, 'given the international situation',

Whatever his motives, Stalin continued with massive rearmament, perhaps designed to get the Soviet Union through the dangerous period when
the United States would see its nuclear 'window of opportunity' closing as
the USSR converted its 1949 test into deliverable atom bombs. He also
constantly described the international situation in sombre terms. Against
this background, he published, in October 1952, *Economic Problems of
Socialism in the USSR*, in part to attack a memorandum by the economist,
Varga. Varga saw the USA as having consolidated the various countries of
the imperialist camp into a durable unit, in which 'The mutual interest of
the big bourgeoisie' was 'stronger than its internal contradictions'; moreover this 'alliance' recognised that 'the potential winnings' in a war with
socialism 'do not match the risk of the destruction of the capitalist system'.
This pointed, presumably, towards at least coexistence and a cold peace.
Against this, Stalin decreed that though 'Some comrades believed that wars
between capitalist countries had ceased to be inevitable, they . . . were
mistaken.' Capitalist countries would find their industries operating 'more
and more below capacity' as a result of the breakaway of, and competition
from, the socialist camp. Attempts (like 'the "Marshall Plan", the war in
Korea, frantic rearmament') to offset this were merely clutching at straws.
In this 'general crisis of the world capitalist system', the other capitalist
countries would not 'tolerate the domination and oppression of the United
States endlessly', but would 'endeavour to tear loose from American
bondage and take the path of independent development'. *Intra-imperialist*
wars were therefore inevitable.

Stalin accepted that capitalist–socialist contradictions were in practice less urgent. For war with the USSR might destroy capitalism itself,
whereas 'war between capitalist countries puts in question only the supremacy
of certain capitalist countries over others'. But he did not seem particularly reassured by this diagnosis, and treated the newly elected Central
Committee in October 1952 to a warning that:

*the situation in the world was complex and a difficult struggle with
the capitalist camp lay ahead and that the most dangerous thing in this
struggle was to . . . take fright, to retreat, to capitulate. That was the
main thing he wished . . . to instill into those present and that in its turn
was connected with the theme of his own [old] age and possible departure
from this life.*

that the East Europeans boost arms production and defence spending way beyond what
they regarded as economically or politically safe (Teresa Toranska, *Oni. Stalin's Polish
Puppets* (1987) pp. 46–7).

He then tore into Molotov and Mikoyan, accusing them of 'cowardice and defeatism'.[125]

This was a prelude to the unleashing, from November onwards, of another purge, the 'Doctors' Plot', in which much of the old Politburo (almost certainly including Molotov, Mikoyan and Beria) would have perished, and Soviet Jewry probably have been dumped in Siberia. In itself this did not entail war with the West. Indeed if Stalin was to turn again on his own people, detente should logically have suited him better. But many have seen it as a rerun of the 1930s, when internal purges had paralleled a darkening international scene. The wars then were initially intra-imperialist, of the kind again forecast by the *Economic Problems of Socialism*. But they had issued in an attack on the USSR, for which, despite frenzied last-minute rearmament, it had been underprepared. Now Stalin was once more preparing for this, and on a scale that led at least some of his Air Staff to believe that he actively anticipated war.[126]

---

[125] Holloway, *Stalin and the Bomb*, pp. 289–92; W.C. Wohlforth, *The Elusive Balance* (Ithaca, NY, 1993) pp. 84–7; Radzinsky, *Stalin*, pp. 532–3. Though *Economic Problems* covers a range of topics (including Stalin's thoughts on linguistics), it chiefly relates to a prospective authoritative economics textbook, in whose ideological correctness Stalin took considerable interest (Ethan Pollock, *Conversations with Stalin on Questions of Political Economy* (CWIHP Working Paper no. 33, July 2001); Varga had sent his memorandum to the panel charged with submitting a draft of this book to Stalin.

[126] Holloway, *Stalin and the Bomb*, pp. 292–3, 431n. Radzinsky records ominous remarks, on the eve of Stalin's death, to the effect that 'they *will* attack us, they're imperialists, and they will certainly attack us. If we let them,' and that 'Either we shall liquidate them, or after my death they will liquidate you like blind kittens' (*Stalin*, pp. 545, 551).

CHAPTER 5

The Khrushchev years – detentes, challenges, crises

Stalin's death and detente

Stalin's death in March 1953 represented a major turning point. Unsure of itself, the new leadership sought a period of internal and external calm; and it proceeded to reverse his more obvious mistakes, notably the blocking of a ceasefire in Korea and the territorial demands on Turkey. It was, of course, divided over how far this process should go, and over which of Stalin's policies had been mistakes. But it tried to lower the rhetorical temperature, and to pursue at least some negotiations. Thus in the summer of 1953 Malenkov (then apparently the leading figure) listed Soviet efforts to lessen international tensions, and declared that 'We stand, as we have always stood, for the peaceful coexistence of the two systems. We hold that there are no objective reasons for clashes between the United States of America and the Soviet Union.' This new approach, though characterised by the British Foreign Office only as 'leaving off doing things which we have not been doing to them', forced the West to consider how it should respond.

The leader most disposed to be forthcoming was the British premier Winston Churchill, the most cautious the US Secretary of State John Foster Dulles. But the changed Soviet stance eventually gave rise to negotiations at Foreign Minister level, to the 1955 Geneva Summit, and to the 1956 state visit to Britain by Khrushchev and Bulganin. The period represented the first of what were to prove a series of 'detentes' (a term used at the time). Some of these had more concrete achievements than others.[1] But every detente before that beginning in 1985 evaporated as a result of a crisis or crises (in 1956 those of Hungary and Suez) that revealed and restimulated the two sides' mutual antagonism, and/or because detente itself proved a disappointment and support for it evaporated in Moscow, Washington or both. The East–West history of the three decades following Stalin's death is therefore cyclical, though many would also see in it a process of incremental gains and the construction of mutual links that were never wholly eroded by the collapse of the detentes from which they sprung.

Western approaches

From 1948 the leading Western policy had been that of creating facts. People who had had the experience of negotiating with the Soviets after 1945 were in no hurry to resume. Acheson, admittedly, was prepared for talks on Stalin's 1952 German reunification proposals. More usually, though, he claimed that 'all important outstanding issues' had been repeatedly discussed, and that the Russians clearly did not want to settle 'as long as they feel there is any possibility they can exploit them for their own objectives of world domination. It is only when they come to the conclusion that they cannot . . . that they will make agreements, and they will let it be known when they have reached that decision.' For:

the Soviet Government is highly realistic and we have seen time after time that it can adjust itself to facts when facts exist . . . So it has been our basic policy to build situations which will extend the area of possible agreement, that is to create strength instead of the weakness which exists in many quarters. (He cited the rebuilding of Germany, E[uropean] R[ecovery] P[rogam], the arms programme and Point 4 aid as ways in which this was being done.)[2]

The corollary of such an approach was the belief that if Western unity and power continued to build, the Soviets would become too overstretched to maintain all their post-war gains, and so be forced to offer major

---

[1] Thus 1953–6 brought the ending of the Korean war, the Geneva agreements on Indo-China, and in 1955 Austrian independence, 1958–60 only a US–British–Soviet moratorium (broken in 1961) on nuclear testing and Khrushchev's visits to the USA (with the delusive 'spirit of Camp David') and France.
[2] Coral Bell, *Negotiation from Strength* (1962) pp. 13–14 (citing the *Department of State Bulletin*, 20 February and 20 March 1950).

concessions. The leading exponent of this view was Acheson's successor, Secretary of State John Foster Dulles. Appearances notwithstanding, Dulles was mentally agile, even volatile, and his attitudes towards the USSR certainly evolved over time. He did not categorically oppose negotiation, but his underlying predisposition was towards policies of pressure. 'Dictatorships,' he once wrote, 'usually present a formidable exterior . . . hard, glittering, and irresistible,' but within 'they are full of rottenness'. Soviet power, he advised in 1953, was 'already overextended and represents tyrannical rule over unwilling peoples. If we keep the pressures on, psychological or otherwise, we may either force a collapse of the Kremlin regime or else transform the Soviet orbit from a union of satellites dedicated to aggression, into a coalition for defense only.' Communist regimes were 'bound to crack': the break-up, he told a Chinese nationalist in 1955, could well come within a year, though equally 'it might be some years away'; that autumn he was talking of German reunification, 'if we are stout', within a 'couple of years', and of the possibility of the retraction of Soviet political influence throughout the satellites within five. In more pessimistic moments Dulles mentioned twenty-five or even a hundred years; and after 1956 he came to look increasingly to the evolution rather than the simple collapse of communist rule. But he still saw the 'future' as 'predictable in its broad outlines'. The West could not directly disrupt communist rule, 'for we renounce the destructive power of so-called "preventive war". But we can prevent that pattern from prevailing and we can confidently expect that in due course it will be altered from within' – by local nationalisms, by the ratchet effect of internal liberalisations, and by economic difficulties that could be addressed only by abandoning 'this fantastic dream of world conquest', placing 'more emphasis upon national welfare', and extending the kind of education that would also lead people to 'penetrate the fallacies of Marxism and increasingly resist conformity'.[3]

Churchill stood at the opposite extreme. He had been habituated to summits, and he felt 'the three victorious Powers, who separated at Potsdam in 1945, should come together again'. He certainly hoped to crown his career with a last great foreign policy achievement: 'I must see Malenkov. Then I can depart in peace.' He may also have been impelled by

---

[3] cf. John Lewis Gaddis, 'The Unexpected . . . Dulles' in Richard H. Immerman (ed.) *John Foster Dulles and the Diplomacy of the Cold War* (Princeton, NJ, 1990) pp. 61–6, and R.H. Immerman, *John Foster Dulles. Piety, Pragmatism, and Power in US Foreign Policy* (Princeton, NJ, 1999) p. 143.

nuclear fear. In and after 1945 Churchill had sought a showdown with the USSR in negotiations backed by US nuclear superiority. After the Soviet test of 1949 that superiority remained. But Britain, if not the USA, now seemed exposed; and Churchill had, at least at the back of his mind, fears that the USA might, in its current combination of (temporary) nuclear immunity and over-the-top anti-communism, press to the point of triggering devastating reprisals against those countries the USSR could reach.[4] In this context, 'jaw-jaw' was better than 'war-war'. That apart, Churchill had often been early to sense new international configurations, whether as an anti-appeaser or an early Cold Warrior. Now he was seeking a negotiated European detente, and looking to the effects of mutual nuclear deterrence – in which 'safety will be the sturdy child of terror, and survival the twin brother of annihiliation'.[5] Lastly, personalities apart, British premiers, representing what was still a world Power but a declining one, naturally sought the status conferred by visible participation at the summit, and were drawn to the role of mediating between the two emerging superpowers.

Eisenhower was always concerned by the possibility that Churchill might launch some maverick initiative. But he too wanted 'to do something'. He was, however, exposed to advice, from Dulles and others, that 'Discussion of German unity . . . would ruin every possibility of the ratification of the European Defense Community' and so undermine the French, Italian, and West German governments; 'the Soviets would resort to all their devices for delay and obstruction . . . and meanwhile the neutralists and all those who were hostile to a more united [Western] Europe, would take new heart.'[6] So, though, in an April 1953 speech billed as a 'Chance for Peace', Eisenhower professed readiness to meet any Soviet leader to seize the 'precious opportunity' 'to turn the tide of history', he required prior Soviet deeds: 'Even a few such clear and specific acts . . . as . . . signature upon an Austrian [peace] treaty or . . . release of thousands of prisoners still held from World War II, would be impressive signs of sincere intent . . . The first great step must be the conclusion of an honorable

---

[4] For such fears, see esp. Richard Aldrich, *The Hidden Hand. Britain. America and Cold War Secret Intelligence* (2001) Chap. xv.

[5] 21 April and 5 November 1953, 1 March 1955 (Martin Gilbert, *Winston S. Churchill*, viii (1988) pp. 819, 909, 1100.

[6] 11 March 1953, opposing C.D. Jackson's proposal to reconvene the Foreign Ministers Conference for negotiation of 'all the major outstanding issues' (*FRUS 1952–4*, viii, p. 1121).

armistice in Korea.'[7] Meanwhile, he told Churchill, they 'should not rush things too much' in the absence of 'concrete Soviet actions'; 'we would risk raising hopes of progress toward an accommodation which would be unjustified.'[8]

German reunification – Adenauer, Churchill, and Beria

Any real accommodation would have involved a German settlement. Stalin had raised the 'German Question' in 1952, and with his death it returned to the international agenda. Both Eden and Adenauer feared Stalin's apparent offer of German reunion. Both therefore successfully put it to their countries' cabinets that, in Eden's words, the proposals

had doubtless been prompted by the progress . . . towards the establishment of a European Defence Community . . . the wise course was for the Western Powers to go forward . . . with a view to bringing Western Germany into the European Defence Community . . . When these negotiations were even nearer to completion, the Soviet Government might come forward with a more satisfactory offer. The test of their sincerity would be their willingness to agree to the holding of free elections under independent supervision throughout Germany.

Privately, though, Eden was wondering whether, even if the Soviet Union met all Western requirements about free German elections, it might not still be possible, by introducing 'other conditions . . . e.g. Austria', to block the dangerous prospect of an agreement that would probably bring to power a neutralist SPD government.[9]

Adenauer's position is more controversial. German reunification was certainly not his top priority. In 1951 he had told the Allied High Commissioners that:

The Federal Government wants a German unity whereby the whole of Germany is integrated into the West. The Soviets want Germany's unity

---

[7] More was asked in the original draft, but the passage was softened to meet British objections (Henry Pelling, *Churchill's Peacetime Ministry, 1951–55* (Basingstoke, 1997) pp. 91–2).

[8] Immerman, *Dulles* (1999) p. 133.

[9] Cabinet Conclusions, 12 March 1952, and Eden's marginal notes on a 15 March internal F.O. minute (Rolf Steininger, *Eine Chance? Die Stalin-Note von 10 März 1952*, *Archiv für Sozialgeschichte* (Beiheft 12, 1985) pp. 120, 142).

but without integration into the western community. They do not
want this because it is clear that an integration of Europe is impossible
without a simultaneous integration of Germany . . . To stop Germany's
integration into Europe would be a great success for which it would be
worth paying a price. If one believed – and he, the Chancellor, was of this
opinion – that such integration was in the long term imperative, then one
must set out on this route regardless of what Russia did or did not do.
Soviet Russia had met a decisive defeat [over the Japanese peace treaty]
at San Francisco. It would meet further defeats when it failed to prevent
the integration of West Germany into the West.

Similarly in late 1955 he told the British that 'when he disappeared
from the scene a future German government might do a deal with Russia
at German expense. Consequently, he felt that the integration of West
Germany into the West was more important than the reunification of
Germany'.[10]

Adenauer saw Stalin's 1952 note as a propaganda move against the
EDC; in any case he held that even a united Germany could not stand
alone, neutral between East and West, without eventually succumbing
to the Soviet Union. So he discouraged all attempts to probe the 'offer',
treating it merely as confirmation of the correctness of existing policy 'to
help make the West strong enough to induce the Russians to want to
compromise . . . I believe . . . that if we continue to do this the point will
soon be reached when the Russians are ready to negotiate sensibly'. 'When
these talks come, they will have to deal not only with the German Soviet-
Zone but with the whole of Eastern Europe. That is why talks . . . should
not come too soon as things are not yet that far advanced. We must
get into talks with the Soviets at exactly the right moment.' Adenauer's
outlook closely resembled that of Dulles: perception of 'overwhelming
[Soviet] problems at home',[11] and confidence in Western consolidation,
led him to claim that this moment would come surprisingly soon – to
British journalists' questions as to whether it 'would be twenty-five or
100 years from now, the Chancellor replied that it would be in five or
ten years' time. By 1955 America would be strong and Europe relatively

---

[10] 24 September 1951 (in response to an East German overture on reunification) –
Hans-Peter Schwarz (ed.), *Akten zur Auswartigen Politik der Bundesrepublik*
Deutschland, i, *Adenauer und die Hohen Kommissare 1949–1951* (Munich, 1989)
p. 381 – cf. also p. 307; Steininger in Immerman (ed.), *Dulles* (1990) pp. 107–8.
[11] To which, after 1955, Adenauer added the likelihood of a major clash with China.

so . . . what matters is to choose the right moment, not too soon and not too late'.[12]

Clearly many people genuinely believed this; for Adenauer retained the support of his cabinet, coalition, and electorate. In the long run, the events of 1989–90 proved him right. But from the mid-fifties to the late eighties such a development looked highly unlikely; and much controversy was devoted to the question of whether (as the SPD maintained at the time) Adenauer had thrown away the last chance for reunification by his rejection of German neutrality and holding out for the whole loaf of full integration into the West.

Churchill accepted that there would always be a ' "German problem" and a "Prussian Danger",' but he felt 'that a United Germany would not become allies of Soviet Russia'.[13] In the spring of 1953 he was working on ideas, bitterly contested by the Foreign Office, for an agreement with the USSR on the basis of its own ostensible policy – a reunited and (in the Western sense) free, but neutral, Germany – with some kind of provision (whether a strengthened UN or a new Locarno)[14] for Soviet security.[15]

There are those who believe a historic chance was missed by not following Churchill's advice. This cannot be conclusively disproved, but though there may conceivably have been a 'window of opportunity' immediately after Stalin's death, it closed in June 1953 with the East German workers' uprising and Beria's arrest – well before the 'West' could reasonably have been expected to agree and propose an overture along Churchill's lines. We now know that the Soviet Praesidium was deeply divided. This emerged as it was preparing, in late May, for a visit by East

[12] Karl-Günther von Hase, Hans-Peter Schwarz, Christian Watrin, *Adenauer at Oxford* (Oxford, 1983) pp. 34–5; Steininger, *Eine Chance?* pp. 28–36; Coral Bell, *Negotiation from Strength* (1962) p. 98n.

[13] He felt 'the character of the German people rises superior to the servile conditions of the Communist world'; 'they have had a potent object-lesson in the fate of the Eastern Zone'; and 'the hatred which Hitler focussed upon Bolshevism is stony in German hearts' – Anthony Glees, 'Churchill's Last Gambit', *Encounter*, lxiv (April 1985) p. 33.

[14] The 1925 Locarno Treaties, involving mutual Franco-German acceptance of their post-war frontiers and an Anglo-Italian guarantee of military assistance to whichever country suffered aggression, enormously improved Western European relations at the time – but did not last. Now, Churchill felt, 'America must be ready to attack Germany if she should attack Russia, while if Russia is the aggressor America would declare war on her' (July 1953 – Gilbert, *Churchill*, viii, p. 869).

[15] See e.g. J. Foschepoth, 'Churchill, Adenauer und die Neutralisierung Deutschlands,' *Europa Archiv*, xvii (1984) pp. 1286–1301; also Glees, 'Churchill's Last Gambit'.

German leaders. When a Foreign Ministry draft argued, on economic grounds, for a slow-down in the rate of building socialism in the DDR, Beria cut in to the effect that this is 'not even a real state. It's only kept in being by Soviet troops', and suggested that socialism there could be abandoned so long as a reunified Germany remained 'peace-loving'. Molotov and Khrushchev appear to have dissented, and the issue was referred to a committee. But Malenkov was at the time very close to Beria. His (recently discovered) draft of an opening speech for the conference with the East Germans is blunt. Though past DDR policy had been approved by the Soviet politburo,

The analysis of the internal and political situation . . . [there], the . . .
mass flight of the population to West Germany (about 500,000 have
already fled!) show conclusively that we are really heading at full
steam . . . not towards socialism . . . but towards an internal disaster.

And not merely 'internal', for the East German mistakes provided persuasive ammunition for attacks in the West on 'socialism' and the USSR. Worse still, 'the dismembered Germany in the middle of Europe means nothing else than an extended remilitarization of West Germany, an open preparation for the unleashing of the new war . . .' This could be foiled by 'uniting East and West Germany into a united peaceful and democratic state', but 'in the current situation' that could be achieved only 'on the basis that Germany will be a bourgeois-democratic republic.' The East German leaders should therefore implement the measures 'we are recommending for the rehabilitation of the political and economic situation in the DDR and for the subsequent . . . task of unifying Germany and transforming it into a peaceful and democratic state.'[16]

As finally transmitted, these recommendations were (perhaps as a result of Molotov's and Khrushchev's opposition) a little less specific. On the ground in East Germany, their effect proved disastrous. Discontinuance of the 'accelerated construction of socialism' shook the regime's prestige. But its recent enhancement of work norms was – perhaps inadvertently – allowed to stand. The result, on 16–17 June, was massive strikes,

---

[16] Vladislav Zubok and Constantine Pleshakov, *Inside the Kremlin's Cold War. From Stalin to Khrushchev* (Cambridge, Mass., 1996) pp. 159–62; Alexey Filatov, '"Germany will be a Bourgeois-Democratic Republic": the New Evidence from the Personal File of Georgiy Malenkov', *Cold War History*, pp. 350–5, which has the advantage over other accounts of Praesidium alignments in May–June 1953 that it is less dependent on retrospective reminiscences.

developing into calls for free elections and German reunification, that had to be suppressed by Soviet troops. Beria strongly supported such suppression; equally he wanted to purge the local framers of past policy in East Germany. Whether he would have continued to press for German unification, we shall never know, for he was arrested (as a danger to his colleagues) on 26 June. From 2 to 7 July a Central Committee Plenum was treated to denunciations of Beria and all his works, among them his German policy. Malenkov took the opportunity to resile from his former approach: he still urged correction of the 'course of the accelerated building of Socialism', but Beria 'had proposed that any course for the building of Socialism in the DDR be abandoned . . . this fact characterizes him as a bourgeois renegade.' Khrushchev went further: Beria's policy would have placed '18 million Germans under the mastery of American imperialism', and no treaty could really guarantee Germany's neutrality since 'if a treaty is not reinforced by strength, then it is nothing, and others will laugh at us and consider us naive'.[17] The chief beneficiary of this shift in Soviet policy was Ulbricht: after the Berlin workers' rising, his opponents had sought to pin the blame on him and oust him from his position as East German General Secretary; now he could turn the tables, accusing them of aligning with Beria and planning to 'restore capitalism' in the DDR.[18]

Whatever might have been the prospects of an initiative on Churchill's lines, the British Prime Minister (partially disabled by a stroke in late June) was unable to sell, even to his own Cabinet, his German policy of *insisting* on immediate French ratification of the European Defence Community, armed with which the West could then urge German reunification on the USSR as the only alternative. The prevailing view was still fear of jeopardising the linked goals of West German integration into the EDC and of Adenauer's victory in the 1953 elections, and instead reaching a situation where the Soviets could endlessly string out negotiations on Germany as they had on Austrian independence. They would probably not

---

[17] James Richter, *Re-examining Soviet Policy towards Germany during the Beria Interregnum* (CWIHP Working Paper 3, Washington 1992), esp. pp. 11–13, 18–20.

[18] Filatov, 'New Evidence', *Cold War History*, pp. 351, 355–6; Zubok and Pleshakov, *Inside the Kremlin's Cold War*, pp. 162–3; James Richter, *Reexamining Soviet Policy towards Germany during the Beria Interregnum* (Cold War International History Project Working Paper 3, Washington 1992) pp. 11–22; Vladislav Zubok, *Soviet Intelligence and the Cold War: The 'Small' Committee of Information, 1952–3* (CWIHP Working Paper 4) p. 16; Andrei Gromyko, *Memories* (paperback edn, 1989) pp. 407–8; Amy Knight, *Beria. Stalin's First Lieutenant* (Princeton, NJ, 1993) pp. 191–5.

gamble on free elections, which might merely 'add another 18 million anti-Communist Germans to the Federal Republic . . . [and] set a dangerous precedent for retreat in Eastern Europe'. But if they did, the result could

be highly dangerous for the West. A neutralised Germany with no ties with the West would, if disarmed, soon fall a prey to Russia. If armed, as proposed last year by the Russians, it would soon fall back on the traditional German policy of balancing East against West, or, still worse, into a modern version of Rapallo under which the Germans would attempt to regain their lost Eastern territories by aligning themselves with the Soviet Union. Before long such a Germany might be little better than a Soviet satellite and the balance of power within Europe would have been fatally shifted to our disadvantage.[19]

Further, as Selwyn Lloyd contended in less official language,

Germany is the key to the peace of Europe. A divided Europe has meant a divided Germany. To unite Germany while Europe is divided even if practicable is fraught with danger for all. Therefore, everyone – Dr Adenauer, the Russians, the Americans, the French and ourselves – feel in our hearts that a divided Germany is safer for the time being. But none of us dare say so openly because of the effect on German public opinion. Therefore we all publicly support a united Germany, each on his own terms.[20]

In these circumstances the issue of German reunification was bound to be aired, albeit with great caution. Churchill would have liked to raise it at a resumed Potsdam summit meeting, and periodically threatened himself to hold conversations with Malenkov if the Americans would not accept an East–West summit. Eisenhower restrained him, but agreed to a Western (US–British–French) summit. Churchill's stroke, however, forced its postponement (to Bermuda in December) and the substitution of more workmanlike tripartite talks in Washington in July at Foreign Secretary level. This meeting invited the USSR to a Foreign Ministers' conference to discuss the holding of free elections and the constitution of an all-German government. In August the Soviet Union accepted in principle, but urged a Five Power conference (including the Chinese People's Republic) and a wider agenda, and continued (as it had in August 1952) to resist external

[19] Cabinet Memoranda, 3 July 1953 (P.R.O. Cab. 129/161).
[20] To Churchill, 22 June 1953 (P.R.O., PREM 11/449 – quoted by Foschepoth, *Journal of Contemporary History*, xxi (1986) p. 411).

supervision of the elections. The omens for agreement were not promising. But a Four Power Foreign Ministers' meeting in Berlin, the first since 1949, was eventually settled on for January 1954. Its discussion of Germany went nowhere fast – the West insisted that a reunited Germany be free to adhere to the European Defence Community, Molotov that the East and West German parliaments should begin by establishing an all-German government that would then conduct elections without external supervision.

The Geneva Conference on Korea and Indo-China 1954

Complete deadlock was thus reached in Europe. But the Russians did secure agreement on a further conference to meet in Geneva in April and discuss, with Chinese communist participation, both Korea and Indo-China. They owed this success partly to common sense. The Korean Armistice Agreement of July 1953 had called for a peace conference, but all attempts to agree its composition had failed; so it was natural to hitch it on to the Foreign Ministers' meeting with the addition of all countries whose armed forces had participated in the war. That the Geneva Conference was also to discuss Indo-China was chiefly due to the French. By 1953 France had tired of the fighting there,[21] and Bidault suggested at the tripartite talks in Washington that the anticipated Korean Conference should also discuss Indo-China. The idea met with initial British, and more durable US, reluctance (both countries hoped to keep the French fighting). But France returned at intervals thereafter to the idea of a *Five* Power Conference – their hope was that the inclusion of communist China for the first time in a major international gathering would lead it in exchange to press restraint on the insurgent Vietminh. The Americans, of course, disliked thus conferring status on China. But at Berlin they had to give way for fear of undermining the only French government that seemed likely at least to continue fighting in Indo-China meanwhile, and also to ratify the EDC that was so central to US policy on Germany. Dulles privately doubted whether this Geneva Conference would have important consequences.[22] As far as Korea was concerned he was quite right –

---

[21] Indo-China is discussed more fully in *The Post-Imperial Age*, Chap. 2.
[22] Sir James Cable, *The Geneva Conference of 1954 on Indochina* (1986) pp. 22–4, 35–8, 43–4, 50; Historical Division Joint Chiefs of Staff, *The Joint Chiefs of Staff and the War in Vietnam. History of the Indo-China Incident 1940–54* (Washington, National Archives) pp. 362–3.

disagreement on Korean reunification closely parallelled that at Berlin on Germany. But Indo-China was another matter.

The approach to the conference had been ominous. France had sought to entice the Vietminh into a set-piece battle in which they would be destroyed by superior fire power. So in November 1953 French and Vietnamese forces were airlifted to Dien Bien Phu, deep in the interior, where from March to May they were attacked by a combination of remarkably effective close-quarters fighting and long-range shelling by artillery (probably recently brought in from China) that the French simply had not anticipated.

On 22 March 1954 the French Chief of Staff General Ely visited Washington to seek help, thereby inaugurating a period of intense and bad-tempered triangular diplomacy between Paris, Washington and London. Ely's counterpart Admiral Radford, a partisan of US intervention, was told by Eisenhower (in Ely's presence) to respond quickly to his requests on Dien Bien Phu. The upshot was the drafting of a plan (Operation Vulture) for non-nuclear US air strikes to seek to lift the siege; there was no US commitment, but Radford's manner may have given France cause to expect its implementation.

Eisenhower was only briefly tempted by the idea of air strikes to save Dien Bien Phu. But he was concerned over Indo-China in general: when his Defense Secretary suggested forgetting about it and concentrating on the defence of the rest of Southeast Asia, Eisenhower replied that 'the collapse of Indochina would result in the fall of all Southeast Asia to the Communists'. He was not, however, prepared for sustained unilateral US action; and Congressional leaders were to insist (on 4 April) that there be 'no more Koreas with the United States furnishing 90 percent of the manpower'. Instead Eisenhower's solution was 'United Action'. He had come, he told Churchill that evening in a personal letter,

to the conclusion that there is no negotiated solution to the Indochina problem which in its essence would not be either a face-saving device to cover a French surrender or . . . [one] to cover a Communist retirement . . .

He therefore proposed a coalition of the US, UK, France, Australia, New Zealand, Thailand and the Philippines. He clearly hoped that the mere existence of such an alliance would suffice – as he later put it, 'The general security and peaceful purposes . . . of such a concert of nations should be announced publicly – as in NATO. Then we possibly wouldn't *have* to fight.' But, his letter to Churchill continued, it

must be willing to fight if necessary . . . If the members of the alliance
are sufficiently resolute it should be able to make it clear to the Chinese
Communists that the continuation of their material support for the Viet
Minh will inevitably lead to the growing power of the forces arrayed
against them.

. . . If we grasp this . . . [nettle] together I believe that we will
enormously increase our chances of bringing the Chinese to believe that
their interests lie in the direction of a discreet disengagement. In such a
contingency we could approach the Geneva conference with the position
of the free world not only unimpaired but strengthened.[23]

One historian speculates that Eisenhower may have been right – 'In the
light of what we now know from Communist sources' of Vietminh weakness and Chinese unwillingness to rescue them, 'it seems unlikely that
either the Russians or the Chinese would have risked a world war for the
sake of the Vietminh'.[24] At the time Eden thought otherwise: 'warnings
might deter China from 'some unspecified future action' but not 'from
action in which she is already engaged. It is hard to see that threat would
be sufficiently potent to make China swallow so humiliating a rebuff as the
abandonment of the Vietminh without any face-saving concession in
return'. So 'the coalition would have to withdraw ignominiously or else
embark on warlike action against China' that would probably be ineffective but that would give China 'every excuse for invoking the Sino-Soviet
treaty and thus might lead to a world war'. A visit from Dulles produced
only agreement on negotiations to establish a coalition, with the proviso
that no announcement be made until after it was clear how the Geneva
Conference was going; even these fell through with considerable mutual
acrimony.

---

[23] These paragraphs derive chiefly from Lawrence S. Kaplan, Denise Artaud, Mark
R. Rubin (eds) *Dien Bien Phu and the Crisis of Franco-American Relations, 1954–5*
(Wilmington, Del, 1990), Chaps 3–5 and Geoffrey Warner, 'The United States and
Vietnam: two episodes', *International Affairs*, lxv (1989) pp. 516–18; Eisenhower's
4 April 1954 letter to Churchill is printed in *FRUS 1952–4*, xiii, pp. 1239–41; Stephen
Ambrose maintains that Eisenhower intended only to apply the 'United Action' threat
to a Vietnam partitioned by the upcoming Geneva Conference (*Eisenhower. The
President*, ii (1984) pp. 179–80), but this fits ill with the text of a powerfully drafted
appeal.
[24] Geoffrey Warner in Kaplan, Artaud, Rubin, *Dien Bien Phu*, p. 74, referring implicitly
to *Khrushchev Remembers*, i, pp. 442–3 and J. Radvanyi, *Delusion and Reality* (South
Bend, Indiana, 1978) pp. 8–10.

Meanwhile the French position in Dien Bien Phu was weakening, and France had begun to beg for the implementation of Operation Vulture. At the same time feeling was growing in Paris in favour of a pull-out, especially as the condition of US aid appeared to be the internationalisation of the war and the displacement of French control. During a second visit to Europe Dulles seems to have been desperate to stimulate French resistance. On 22 April the French understood him to have offered them two atom bombs for use in Vietnam. On 24–5 April Britain was placed under considerable pressure to join, Dulles indicating that the US would give the French immediate military help providing the UK did so too. Eden, however, persuaded his colleagues that 'large parts of Indo-China' would inevitably

fall under Communist control, and the best hope of a lasting
settlement lay in some form of partition. Our object should
therefore be to strengthen the negotiating position of the French
at the Geneva Conference. Their position would not be strengthened
by a premature military intervention which would soon be seen to
have been ineffective . . . France's Allies could at the moment make
a better impression on the Chinese if they left them to guess what
action they might subsequently take to help the French . . .

The ministerial meeting was, however, prepared to join a collective defence of Southeast Asia *after* the Geneva Conference, hopefully by way of guaranteeing the resultant settlement.

The British refusal was decisive. Both Dulles and Eisenhower told the French there could be no US intervention without a preliminary multilateral treaty. On 29 April the National Security Council decided to 'hold up for the time being any military action on Indo-China' pending developments at Geneva, while exploring the posssibility of a coalition without Britain. There were US–French talks on this. But the US insisted on the internationalisation of the conflict and stressed that the French Associated States (Vietnam, Laos and Cambodia) would only fight if accorded full independence. France had never been attracted by the idea of thus fighting somebody else's war. It just might have accepted in late April to save Dien Bien Phu, but this fell on 7 May. So France would only 'discuss' US conditions, while itself insisting on a promise Eisenhower would not give of the commitment of American ground troops. The talks, therefore, achieved little; they stopped when Mendès France became Prime Minister in mid-June.

After all this, and a slow and sticky start, the Geneva Conference went quite well. Arguably most of the participants were resigned to the partition of Vietnam. Eden had accepted the idea by 1 April, while Eisenhower suggested at the end of the month that something along the lines of Germany 'was the most you could ask' in existing circumstances. At a preparatory meeting in Moscow China showed itself very concerned at the possibility of being drawn in by an expansion of the fighting; quite apart from its losses in Korea, 'this would oppose China to the other peoples of South East Asia and allow the USA the possibility of creating a bloc extending from India to Indonesia'. At the conference Zhou Enlai spoke positively to Bidault and Eden of Laos and Cambodia as neutral countries under their existing monarchies, and left Mendès-France with the impression that he preferred even the prolonged existence of two separate states in Vietnam provided the South did not fall under a foreign power.[25] The French attitude was mercurial, unnerved by the fall of Dien Bien Phu but finding it difficult to make concessions and continuing to explore (though not to wish to trigger) the option of US intervention. But on 13 June the new Prime Minister, Pierre Mendès-France, publicly determined to secure a ceasefire by 20 July, and began direct talks with the Vietminh. The Vietminh themselves did *not* want partition; but they had been much harder pressed early in the year than Westerners had realised, and had, before the start of the conference, been looking for no more than a ceasefire in place.[26] On 10 June they first indicated a readiness to settle for French evacuation of the North; and over the next month concessions appear to have been extracted from them by China, their chief source of weapons. By Mendès-France's deadline it had been agreed that Vietnam should be temporarily divided near the 17th Parallel, subject (on paper) to reunification by free elections two years later; neither zone should form part of any military alliance. Cambodia and Laos were to be independent and to abstain from seeking any military aid bar a small French training mission in Laos.

These terms were in fact not far short of the seven points agreed in June between Dulles and Eden, which (Dulles told Mendès-France) 'constitute a minimum as far as the US is concerned' though, he feared, 'merely an optimum solution as far as your Government and perhaps the UK are concerned'. However, the United States was not enamoured of the neutralisation provisions. Since it was not itself prepared to intervene militarily, there was little it could do at Geneva to stop France settling for whatever

---

[25] F. Joyeaux, *La Chine et le règlement du premier conflit d'Indochine (Genève, 1954)* (Paris, 1979) pp. 70–1, 322–3, 346; Cable, *Geneva Conference*, pp. 97–8.
[26] *Khrushchev Remembers*, i, pp. 442–3.

was obtainable. But it would not itself sign, merely undertake to note the agreements and not to use force to upset them.[27] The other unreconciled party was the new government of French (after the armistice, of South) Vietnam, headed by Ngo Dinh Diem, which had been kept apart from the Franco-Vietminh negotiations. The two rapidly drew together, and by November Eisenhower had agreed on a military mission and a $400 million aid package 'to maintain and support a friendly and independent non-Communist government in Vietnam and to assist it in diminishing and ultimately eradicating Communist subversion and influence'.

The other half of US policy to limit the spread of communism was 'the rapid organization of a collective defense in South-east Asia'. This had been one purpose of the administration's earlier pursuit of 'United Action' in Vietnam; and while the British had refused to commit to anything that would pre-empt the holding of the Geneva Conference, they were agreeable to the collective guarantee of its outcome. Such a guarantee might have taken a 'Locarno' form, that is a guarantee of all the parties by both China (and allies) and the USA (and allies) and, possibly, by Asian states like India. This would have been agreeable to the People's Republic (which would, *inter alia*, have gained further recognition thereby); but it was rejected by the USA as expressing a moral approval of a communist success. Instead there was to be a defensive Southeast Asia Treaty Organisation (SEATO), modelled on NATO. Few newly independent states were keen to join, so it came into existence in September 1954 with only three Asian members, the heavily aligned Philippines, Thailand and Pakistan, plus the USA, UK, France, Australia and New Zealand. Although the Geneva Conference had precluded Laos, Cambodia, and (South) Vietnam from membership, the area covered by the pact's obligations was so defined as to include them.

The Chinese offshore islands crisis 1954–5

SEATO never amounted to much; it has been described as a whole 'zoo of paper tigers'. But, together with South Vietnam's rapid shift from French to American tutelage, it destroyed one of the chief gains China thought it had secured from the Geneva Conference – the exclusion of US influence from Southeast Asia, which would be divided between weak neutral states accepting a loose Chinese hegemony. This disappointment may have

---

[27] Even this pledge was somewhat stretched by the despatch of a CIA sabotage team to disrupt the Vietminh's takeover of Hanoi.

underlain the next crisis, though it may simply be that, following the end of fighting in East Asia, Mao now felt it safe to return to return to the problem of Taiwan. Either way, the resultant 'offshore islands crisis' was to prove one of the most alarming in the entire post-war period.[28]

These islands, Quemoy, Matsu and the Tachens, were very close to the Chinese mainland but still held by the nationalists. The communists started shelling them in September 1954, and were apparently building towards an invasion. The islands themselves were of little military value, and European statesmen (in Eisenhower's words) considered 'America reckless, impulsive and immature' in not letting them go. But Chiang Kai-shek had stationed 70,000 troops there, and Eisenhower worried that, if Chiang lost them, his regime might again unravel (as it had done only a few years earlier on the mainland). Eisenhower recognised the dangers if the US got deeply involved in defending them: 'When we talk of general war with Communist China, what we mean is general war with the USSR also'. For 'If the Soviets did not abide by their treaty . . . and go to war in support of their Chinese ally, the Soviet empire would quickly go to pieces.' But initially he felt fairly confident he could prevent matters coming to such a pass. One tactic was to get New Zealand to refer the question to the UN Security Council with a view to securing the islands' demilitarisation. This might split the Soviet Union from China should it decide not to use its veto and so spoil its new peace-loving image. However, Chiang's 'Republic of China' also had a veto. To prevent Chiang using it, he was offered a defence treaty that committed the US to defending Taiwan and the Pescadores and left deliberately vague whether it would also protect the offshore islands. But China then jailed thirteen US airmen shot down over its territory during the Korean War; and this created such a domestic storm in the USA that it was thought best to postpone the UN initiative until the dust had settled.

In January 1955 China overran one of the Tachen islands. The others (which were too distant for air cover from Taiwan) were thought to be indefensible; so the USA bribed Chiang into permitting their evacuation by promising to protect Quemoy and Matsu. The administration had

---

[28] It is correspondingly controversial. My account derives from Gordon Chang, 'To the Nuclear Brink. Eisenhower, Dulles, and the Quemoy-Matsu Crisis' (which has a map) and H.W. Brands, 'Testing Massive Retaliation. Credibility and Crisis Management in the Taiwan Strait' – both in *International Security*, xii (1988); cf. also Ambrose, *Eisenhower*, Chaps 9, 10.

originally decided to make this promise public for its deterrent effect. But it eventually decided not to – perhaps to ease the passage through Congress of a resolution giving Eisenhower the authority, if he judged it necessary, to commit US forces to action in defence of Taiwan and 'closely related localities'. Chiang felt betrayed.

By March things were worse, and Dulles returned from a Far Eastern visit convinced there was 'at least an even chance' that China would attack Quemoy and Matsu and that the US would have to fight. He and Eisenhower started to prepare American – and Chinese – opinion for the use of nuclear weapons: 'Yes, of course they would be used. In any combat where these things can be used on strictly military targets and for strictly military purposes, I see no reason why they shouldn't be used just exactly as you would use a bullet or anything else.' (Privately, though, Eisenhower sought to bolster Chiang's own forces to avoid the need for direct intervention, and said that if America had to join in it would do so first with conventional weapons; atomic ones 'should only come at the end'.) Tension was further raised when the Chief of Naval Operations told the press the USA had plans for all-out nuclear attack on China and that he personally expected hostilities by 15 April.

On 5 April Eisenhower wrote that they could no longer inertly await the moment of decision 'between two unacceptable choices', war or a retreat in the face of Chinese attack that could lead to the disintegration of 'all Asian opposition' to communism, and asked for ideas. This led to a mission being sent to Taiwan to consider whether Chiang should be pressed to withdraw his troops from the remaining islands in return for a US blockade of the Chinese coast opposite Taiwan – which would have proved both provocative and dangerous.

Fortunately China changed course. Washington later heard, and credited, a rumour that Zhou Enlai had secretly flown to Moscow and been told that the USSR would not support China in a war over the islands. Another view is that China had never meant to expel the nationalists from *all* the offshore islands. For these were indubitably Chinese, whereas links between the island of Taiwan and China had been surprisingly tenuous before 1895; Taiwan had then for fifty years been ceded to Japan; and the majority of its inhabitants were in the 1950s probably quite prepared to embrace a specifically Taiwanese, as opposed to Chinese, political identity. From this perspective Chiang's retention of Quemoy and Matsu, and claim to be the ruler of all China, may also have been a communist Chinese interest. For it would anchor Taiwan/nationalist China to China proper in a situation of 'one country/two systems' that still afforded some hope of future reunion.[29] Anyway, at the Bandung Conference,[30] Zhou made friendly noises towards the USA and offered negotiations. Eisenhower responded; and Zhou went halfway towards giving the assurance the US had been appealing for via friendly Asian states, declaring that China was 'willing to strive for the liberation of Formosa by friendly means as far as this is possible'. Tension was gradually wound down, the imprisoned US airmen released, and talks started in August – though apart from bestowing a modicum of US recognition on communist China, they achieved nothing.

French opposition to the European Defence Community

By this time events in Europe were moving rapidly towards detente. In 1954 the chief Anglo-American concern had been to secure, and Soviet to prevent, the achievement of the linked goals of West German independence and incorporation into the Western defensive structure. To this end the Soviets constantly floated alternative schemes for European security; in March they even suggested that they too should join NATO; more usually they proposed some form of pan-European pact ideally without, but probably including, the United States. The West was not prepared to consider anything of the kind until after a West German settlement.

In the first half of 1954 such a settlement was looked for from the European Defence Community, which still needed French ratification. As we have seen the EDC had originally been a French idea to delay and water down German rearmament. Now things had come to the point, it no longer looked attractive; the French still feared German rearmament and were not prepared to relinquish (to the EDC) control over their own army. Knowing that the chances of ratification were slim, French governments (to the fury of their partners) kept putting off submitting the EDC to parliament. Mendès-France was more decisive: after a vain plea to renegotiate

---

[29] In late 1955 China charged the USA with wanting to 'hoodwink world public opinion by arranging for the traitorous Chiang Kai-shek group to "quit" the coastal islands'; later, after the 1958 crisis, Mao praised the Taiwanese public for its loyalty to the concept of a single China and claimed the Americans were trying 'to force on us [both] a Two China policy' (Nancy Bernkopf Tucker, in Immerman, *Dulles and the Diplomacy of the Cold War*, pp. 259–60).

[30] Taiwan's secret service blew up the flight on which Zhou had originally intended to travel to Bandung (Aldrich, *Hidden Hand,* p. 311).

its terms, he put the EDC to a free vote of the National Assembly, which buried it on 30 August.[31] This was, potentially, a disaster, and both the US and Britain moved rapidly to counter it. The United States leaned towards a NATO conference that (faced with a US ultimatum) would simply admit West Germany as an equal partner.[32] Eden proceeded with a round of diplomatic visits, securing the support of both Dulles and Mendès-France for a more elaborate approach via German adhesion not only to NATO but also of the 1948 Brussels Treaty in a 'Western European Union' (WEU). This had the effect of making possible the imposition of limits (some, but not all, apparently multilateral) on German rearmament.[33] The way was further smoothed by a West German pledge never to use force to achieve reunion or territorial revision, and by a British promise, not unbreakable but firmer than ever before, as to the continued maintenance of substantial forces on the continent. The result was the conclusion in October of the Paris Agreements, which, if ratified, would incorporate a sovereign West Germany into the NATO alliance.

Though it is hard to square with their ostensible proposal of a neutral, united and armed Germany, the Russians appear to have been genuinely worried at the prospect of a rearmed and revisionist West Germany. Mikoyan once said they had considered a range of responses, including the

[31] There is a view that Mendès-France's despatch of the EDC was a *quid pro quo* for Soviet helpfulness over Indo-China at the Geneva Conference, but this is apparently a myth (Cable, *Geneva Conference*, pp. 129–32). Mendès-France himself told Churchill on 23 August that France would reject the EDC, but would 'never dare to reject an alternative, even that of German entry into NATO' (Immerman, *Dulles and the Diplomacy of the Cold War*, p. 100).

[32] Ambrose, *Eisenhower*, pp. 210–11.

[33] All WEU members accepted maximum levels for their forces *on the continent* and agreed not to deploy these without the consent of the Supreme Allied Commander Europe (an American); Germany, unlike France, had no other forces. Germany undertook not to manufacture atomic, biological or chemical weapons, nor, without the consent of a two-thirds majority in the WEU to build long-range missiles, heavy bombers, or warships/submarines of any appreciable size. The WEU was to monitor compliance with these conditions (Beate Ruhm von Oppen, *Documents on Germany under Occupation 1945–54* (1955) esp. pp. 642–4). These constraints were to some extent paper ones: in the 1960s France withdrew all its troops from SACEUR's control, while limitations on German submarines had been relaxed. But they served their purpose of producing a feeling of security; in fact no states have wished to exceed their maximum force levels, and concern more usually arose from their reluctance to spend enough on conventional defence.

absorbtion of their zone of Austria into the Eastern bloc.[34] Probably the chief purpose of the more relaxed tone of Soviet diplomacy in the first half of 1954 had been to convince Western opinion that West German rearmament was no longer necessary. When the French National Assembly rejected the EDC this appeared to have been achieved. The Paris agreements therefore came as a disappointment. This may be sufficient explanation of the subsequent sharpening of the Soviet tone: 'The carrying out of the ... Paris Agreements would mean that the unification of Germany through the holding of free all-German elections would be sacrificed for the present plans to restore German militarism – that mortal enemy of all the peoples of Europe, including the German people themselves.'[35] Or it may be that the harshness resulted from a Molotov–Khrushchev alignment in a Kremlin power struggle against Malenkov. In any case it failed. The French National Assembly nearly rejected the Paris Agreements on 24 December 1954, but finally accepted them after Christmas when Mendès-France made them a question of confidence.

Austrian independence 1955

There still remained a possibility of rejection by the French Senate. This may have led the Soviets to seek yet another conference, with the bait of discussing internationally supervised elections for Germany and also that of ending the occupation of Austria (on which they had been distinctly unforthcoming of late). Accordingly in February 1955 (despite the off-shore islands crisis) Molotov started pressing, both publicly and through the Austrian ambassador in Moscow, for an Austrian settlement on the basis of neutrality and guarantees against future union with Germany. These overtures gained momentum despite both Western disinterest in any conference on Germany and the increasing likelihood that the French Senate would ratify the Paris Agreements (as it did on 27 March). By April the Soviets were negotiating with the Austrians the outlines of a settlement (providing for the withdrawal of all occupation forces, Austrian adoption of 'Neutrality after the Swiss model', and delivery of petroleum and other products to the USSR). As Bulganin explained, the Soviets had for five years stalled on Austria so as to be able to link its fate to progress on the German question. 'Now a solution to the German problem has been found

---

[34] Sven Allard, *Russia and the Austrian State Treaty. A Case Study of Soviet Policy in Europe* (Pennsylvania State University, 1970) p. 141.
[35] 13 November (RIIA, *Documents ... 1954* pp. 58–9).

that is unfortunate. We had to take this into account and draw the consequences for ourselves.'[36] The Austrian State Treaty was signed on 15 May
1955; on the 14th Molotov had informally agreed to a summit meeting in
Geneva in July.

Khrushchev's foreign policy, 1955

The neutralisation of Austria came during a period of important new
initiatives in Soviet diplomacy. Khrushchev recalls that at the time of
Stalin's death 'we believed that America would invade . . . and we would go
to war.'[37] Everybody, even Molotov, had agreed on the need for some
changes. For Molotov, though, this meant little more than disengaging
from some of Stalin's unwise probes, notably his pressure on Turkey and
the Korean War. In other respects Molotov was both defensive of Stalin's
past record and very cautious. It was, he felt, a pity that pressure on Tito
had not been more successful in 1948, but it had prevented Poland from
going the same way under Gomulka. Formal diplomatic relations would
now be appropriate with Yugoslavia, as with other hostile states, but not
party-to-party dealings in an attempt to draw it back into the 'camp'. Nor
was it worth evacuating eastern Austria and foregoing the military advantages of the link between forces in Hungary and in western Czechoslovakia
in order to gain the disjunction of Western forces in Germany and Italy
plus the intangible benefits of Austrian neutrality. A bird in the hand was
worth two in the bush.

Both Beria and Malenkov wanted to go much further, though how far
we shall never know.[38] Khrushchev had not hitherto thought much about
foreign affairs, and was initially disposed to look up to Molotov. They
were, too, drawn together by their common opposition to Beria; and this
friendship continued politically useful until Malenkov could be forced out
of the Chairmanship of the Council of Ministers in February 1955. Against
Malenkov Khrushchev had cultivated a conservative coalition; now he
changed course to deal with Molotov. In his rise, Khrushchev adopted
policies (as Stalin had done before him in the 1920s) largely for their
political utility. But there seems no reason to doubt his subsequent claims

---

[36] Allard, *Russia and the Austrian State Treaty*, p. 107; V. Mastny, 'Kremlin Politics
and the Austrian Settlement', *Problems of Communism*, xxxi (July–August 1982) p. 46.
[37] *Khrushchev Remembers*, iii, *The Glasnost Tapes* (Boston, 1990) p. 100.
[38] Zubok and Pleshakov, *Inside the Kremlin's Cold War*, Chap. 5.

that, with growing exposure to foreign affairs, he became shocked by Molotov's lack of imagination – 'A man of such limits, so closed-minded'.[39] Molotov had already been overridden or bypassed on a number of issues; at a July 1955 Central Committee Plenum he was now subjected to a barrage of criticisms, which he had formally to accept. These concentrated on Yugoslavia, Austria, and the need for a more sensitive management of Eastern Europe. But Khrushchev also apparently explained that, with revolutions impracticable in the West, the European situation had stabilised. Instead the capitalist world's weak points lay in its former colonies, with India, Egypt and other Arab states ready for an 'anti-imperialistic' revolution and potentially willing to 'isolate themselves' from the 'capitalist camp'.[40]

The policy of cultivating anti-imperialist sentiment in the Third World was very much Khrushchev's own. Its consequences were quickly apparent in the 1955 arms deal with Egypt and the Soviet penetration of the Middle East that ensued (below, pp. 237–9). In Europe, Khrushchev was rather drawing on ideas earlier favoured by Malenkov (and perhaps also Beria). These entailed the presentation of a softer face than before. The USSR should drop its economic exploitation of the communist East[41] and the proconsular involvement of Soviet ambassadors in local politics and administration. In May 1955 the Soviet military presence was regularised by the conclusion of the Warsaw Pact, represented as a defensive reaction to be dissolved if the West would abandon NATO; 'in setting up the Pact,' Khrushchev recalls, 'we wanted to make an impression on the West.' The USSR also closed its military bases in Finland and China, mostly to improve relations with these countries, but also to point a contrast with the global proliferation of US bases. Withdrawal from a neutral Austria fitted with this policy of cultivating non-communist opinion in (particularly) Western Europe. It also left Khrushchev childishly gratified by the demonstration that, Stalin's forbodings notwithstanding, 'We . . . were able to force other countries – capitalist countries . . . to agree to our way of thinking. Austria became a neutral country' and 'we celebrated

---

[39] *Khrushchev Remembers*, iii, esp. pp. 75–7, 85–7.

[40] Minutes of the Central Committee meeting were seen by a Polish official, Seweryn Bialer, who subsequently defected. His account has been used by Allard (*Russia and the Austrian State Treaty*, pp. 216–19) and by Wolfgang Leonhard, *The Kremlin since Stalin* (1962) pp. 106–10.

[41] Exploitation through 'joint-stock' companies was denounced at the July 1955 plenum.

a great international victory.'[42] Readiness, even eagerness, for a summit meeting was a further manifestation of this pattern.

The Geneva Summit 1955

On the Western side the United States had always been the country most reluctant to contemplate a summit. But Eisenhower had in November 1954 reduced his preconditions to one – agreement on an Austrian Treaty 'would indicate real sincerity on the part of the Communist world to go into further negotiations'. In April 1955 the new British Prime Minister, Eden, in his run-up to elections, resumed pressure for a summit; and in May Dulles reported to Eisenhower that 'a passionate eagerness' for a summit was evident throughout Europe. For his part, Eisenhower was attracted, by the light such a meeting might shed on the real distribution of power within the post-Malenkov Soviet leadership. He may also have hoped to secure Soviet acceptance of his 'open skies' proposal (of mutual aerial inspection by the two sides as a security for disarmament), which he sprang on the conference in a dramatic speech. The proposal did at least pinpoint the true location of power on the Soviet side; the reply of the delegation's ostensible leader, Bulganin, was not unsympathetic, but after the session Khrushchev came up to Eisenhower and turned the idea down flat.

However, the Geneva Summit had been billed not as one at which agreements would be reached (like the wartime Teheran, Yalta and Potsdam meetings) but as a device to improve the atmosphere and encourage more detailed discussions at Foreign Secretary and diplomatic levels. As far as atmosphere went the effect was, for a time, remarkable. Eisenhower's final words at the conference were, 'the prospects of lasting peace with justice, well-being and broader freedom, are brighter. The dangers of the overwhelming tragedy of modern war are less'. Unsurprisingly there was much talk of the 'spirit of Geneva', which was also encouraged by the new and less barbaric face the Soviet Union now presented. Even Dulles, who had been acutely conscious both of the dangers this might pose to the American alliance and of those that might result from a sudden puncturing of unrealistically high expectations, is reported as saying privately in 1956:

---

[42] *Khrushchev Remembers*, iii, pp. 70–1, 80. In fact Soviet eagerness in the final Austrian negotiations had been such that the other occupying powers secured several minor concessions they had been prepared to forego in earlier discussions.

So long as the Soviets under Stalin continued to behave so badly . . .
it was relatively easy for our side to maintain a certain social ostracism
toward them . . . The man who spits in your eye, puts poison in your
soup . . . is the kind of person you just don't want around . . . And
what is more important, everybody else understands.

Now . . . Frowns have given way to smiles. Guns have given way
to offers of economic aid . . . with the repudiation of Stalin, with the
rehabilitation of scores of officials, scientists, soldiers . . . with the
apparent acceptance of Tito, and therefore of Titoism with all these
things going on, it is very difficult for the US to say to its allies that
all of this means nothing, that it is a trick, that the ostracism must be
maintained.

I don't think anyone wants to turn the clock back . . . and furthermore
I doubt if anyone could if he tried. We may be in very grave long-term
danger because of the Soviets' new economic competition, but I would
rather be trying to work out the answers to that one instead of trying to
find an answer to H-bomb competition.

Back in 1950 or '51, I spent $1,000 to build a bomb-proof cellar in
my New York house . . . today I just would not spend that thousand
dollars . . . because I don't think that is the way the struggle is shaping
up any more . . .[43]

But if the Geneva Summit improved the atmosphere, it also showed further agreements on high politics to be unlikely (whereas the previous two years had seen such agreements on Korea, Indochina and Austria). We have noted the failure of proposals for inspection, without which there would clearly be no nuclear disarmament. A fortnight after the conference the Russians staged a series of H-bomb tests that showed their ability to drop such bombs from aircraft (as opposed to simply exploding them on the ground) and led to fears that they had acquired a technological lead. Meanwhile on Germany Bulganin had declared at Geneva that the inclusion of the Federal Republic in NATO had made reunification impossible. Admittedly the conference communiqué (perhaps reflecting Bulganin's diplomatic inexperience) appeared to suggest otherwise.[44] But

[43] April 1956 – Blanche Cook, *The Declassified Eisenhower* (Garden City, NY, 1981) p. 200.
[44] 'the settlement of the German question and the reunification of Germany by means of free elections shall be carried out in conformity with the national interests of the German people and the interests of European security'.

Khrushchev's speech in East Berlin on his way home cast doubt on this; and in September the Soviets accorded East Germany full independence. So discussion of German reunion at the Foreign Ministers' conference (also at Geneva) in October was not a success.

East-West summits and their limitations

This dented, but did not wholly destroy, the 'spirit of Geneva'. The summit had established the principle that East and West should both talk and be seen to talk. Adenauer went to Moscow in September 1955, and, after extremely tense negotiations (in which he apparently offered loans and reparations payments in exchange for unification),[45] established diplomatic relations between West Germany and the USSR, securing in exchange the release of some 30,000 prisoners of war/civilian deportees.[46] In 1956 (as arranged at Geneva) the Soviet leaders made what seemed a highly successful visit to Britain – though in retrospect its most significant aspect was the warnings each side gave about the other's policies in the Middle East.[47] There was meant to follow a return visit by Eden to Moscow, also a Soviet visit to the United States. Hungary and Suez interrupted the process. But the idea of summit meetings remained. Khrushchev suggested one in connection with the 1958 Middle East crisis. In 1959 Macmillan resurrected the invitation to Moscow in response to an apparent ultimatum over Berlin; later that year the same problem led Eisenhower to invite Khrushchev to the USA; and a Four Power summit was arranged for Paris for 1960, its collapse being followed in 1961 by a Kennedy–Khrushchev meeting in Vienna.

It was less clear what should be the content of these meetings and, more generally, of the East–West relationship. Certainly not negotiation from Western strength. Khrushchev ends his account of the Geneva Summit with the claim that it had been 'an important breakthrough', he concluded that:

---

[45] *Khrushchev Remembers*, ii, p. 358; Martin McCauley, *Nikita Sergeevich Khrushchev* (1991) p. 53.

[46] Distinctly more than the 10,000 'war criminals' who were all the Soviets had previously admitted holding, though markedly fewer than the 130,000 the West Germans attributed to them. For years West German public opinion regarded the prisoners' release as Adenauer's principal achievement.

[47] See e.g. Harold Macmillan, *Memoirs*, iv, 'Riding the Storm' (1971) pp. 95–6; *Khrushchev Remembers*, i, p. 367.

our enemies probably feared us as much as we feared them . . . [they]
now realized that we were able to resist their pressure and see through
their tricks . . . that they had to respect our borders and our rights,
and that they couldn't get what they wanted by force or blackmail . . .
they would have to build their relations with us on new assumptions
and new expectations if they really wanted peace.

If not negotiation from strength, then there might be a limited scope for
crisis management. The idea was around in 1958–9. But in general there
has been a marked, and laudable, preference for crisis avoidance rather
than crisis management – Khrushchev never did act on his threat to transfer to East Germany control over access to West Berlin. The few direct
East–West crises, notably the Cuban Missiles Crisis of 1962, were not in
fact handled at the summit. Nor, finally, were East–West relations good
enough (at least until the later 1980s) to permit attempts to manage other
people's crises by a superpower condominium.

What remained was more humdrum. Participants naturally claimed
that they gained a better understanding of each other's positions, and this
may sometimes have been useful in avoiding trouble.[48] High-level meetings
will also have given a certain stimulus to contacts and consultations at
lower levels – Khrushchev and Bulganin took an eminent scientist with
them on their British visit 'because we wanted to establish contacts with
the British scientific community'. In the long run such contacts can significantly alter countries' perceptions of each other; and they may indeed
have proved a factor in changing the image many Soviet citizens had
of the West.[49] But this process, necessarily slow, proved even slower in the
East–West case since it was often so obviously subject to politics and
official management. In the 1950s even National Exhibitions were rather
the subject of competition and controversy, leading to a heated set-to
between Khrushchev and Vice-President Nixon in 1959 over the usefulness
or otherwise of American household gadgets (the 'kitchen debate').

One subject, however, is far more eye-catching – nuclear weapons.
These have been peculiarly the province of the Great, to a very considerable extent of the two Super, Powers; and once the USSR had gained
approximate strategic parity, their management proved the least difficult

[48] Equally both Khrushchev's 1958 summit call and his 1959 visit to America strained
Sino-Soviet relations.
[49] Of course we do not know how widespread favourable images were even in the USSR
of the 1950s.

element in what had become a curious US–Soviet adversary partnership. As such, it dominated discussion at summits from 1972 until 1987 – after which relationships so far improved that other issues, now become tractable, came to overshadow, though never wholly to displace it, at the summit.

Eisenhower's 1953 decision against 'roll-back'; US quiescence during the 1953 Berlin and 1956 Polish disturbances

A precondition of Khrushchev's foreign policy was that Soviet hegemony in Eastern Europe remain sacrosanct: during the crises of 1956 he declared that 'recognition of the present status quo in Europe was the essential condition for any talks and that this must be made quite clear to the West'.[50] In the 1950s the USA never accepted the legitimacy of this hegemony, but it abandoned all ideas of direct action against the regimes there. It had, of course, never been intended to overthrow them militarily. But the USA and Britain had dabbled in covert action 'to detach Albania from the [Soviet] orbit' by infiltrating anti-communists in order to spark a general rebellion. These attempts had proved disasters, as had the support of a putative Polish underground and of various nationalist resistance movements (above, pp. 163–4). Such fiascos led to gradual disillusion; and in 1953 the new Director of Central Intelligence, Allen Dulles, reluctantly suspended the construction of East European networks,[51] though paramilitary training of emigrés continued.

To judge by political rhetoric, one would have expected a rather different pattern. For, despite these dabblings, the Truman administration had favoured 'containment' – a policy that, whatever its hopes for an ultimate internal collapse of Soviet power, implied leaving Eastern Europe to its fate. In 1952 the Republican platform described it as a 'negative, futile and immoral policy . . . which abandons countless human beings to a despotism and godless terrorism which in turn enables the rulers to forge the captives into a weapon for our destruction'; and John Foster Dulles promised 'to shift from a purely defensive policy to a psychological offensive, a liberation policy, which will try to give hope and a resistance mood

---

[50] V. Micunovic, *Moscow Diary* (1980) pp. 87, 337–8.
[51] Thomas Powers, *The man who kept the secrets. Richard Helms and the CIA* (paperback edn, 1979) pp. 54–5; John Prados, *Presidents' Secret Wars* (New York, 1986) p. 59.

inside the Soviet empire'.[52] This declaratory policy (now commonly called 'roll-back') seemed to go well beyond 'containment', but was in fact very similar. For privately Dulles saw 'total war' as 'an incalculable disaster', and felt that any overt attempt to detach Eastern Europe from Soviet control might set it off. So it was better to wait for time and local nationalisms to bring changes – albeit with the assistance of as much pressure as could safely be applied.

Such a policy was set by the mid-1953 'Solarium' study, in which White House task forces considered options ranging from the continuation of containment to much increased 'efforts to disturb and weaken the Soviet bloc'. Eisenhower's preference was for a course closer to the first alternative, but not excluding some 'Actions to Exploit the Unrest in the Satellite States'.[53] Most of these actions were probably rather minor – a further enhancement of Radio Free Europe and Liberation (started in 1950–1) and of the eastwards despatch of propaganda leaflets (ultimately 300 million) by balloon. Some represented conventional intelligence coups, and perhaps the spreading of important disinformation, via Eastern informants and defectors. The most visible success was the acquisition and publishing of Khrushchev's Secret Speech denouncing Stalin to the 20th Party Congress.[54] Khrushchev had intended this to be released only within party circles and under heavy explanatory guidance; its broadcasting by the West must have put the Stalinist leaders of Eastern Europe even more on the defensive and added to Mao Zedong's irritation that he had not been consulted about it beforehand.

But when things came to a real rising in Eastern Europe, the USA drew back. In June 1953 news of the Berlin riots and their demands was beamed to East Germany by the American Sector Radio; but the CIA's Berlin station chief was refused permission to arm the rioters, the US tacitly acquiesced in their suppression by Soviet troops and then offered the USSR food aid for East Germany. The CIA was later asked to study possible counter-measures and sanctions in the event of renewed East European unrest, but concluded that little could be done.[55] This conclusion was to be more seriously tested in 1956. The then developments in Poland (below,

---

[52] Townsend Hoopes, *The Devil and John Foster Dulles* (1974) pp. 130–1.

[53] Prados, *Presidents' Secret Wars*, pp. 120–1.

[54] John Ranelagh, *The Agency: The Rise and Decline of the CIA* (1986) pp. 255–6, 185–8; Powers, *The man who kept the secrets*, pp. 405–6.

[55] Prados, *Presidents' Secret Wars*, p. 120; Ranelagh, *The Agency*, pp. 258–9, 287; Powers, *The man who kept the secrets*, pp. 55–7.

pp. 540–2) seem to have owed nothing to the West, nor, in the event, did they demand any Western reaction. But John Foster Dulles declared publicly that, in what he regarded as the unlikely event of Soviet coercion, the USA would not intervene militarily.[56]

The 1956 Hungarian and Suez crises and detente

Russian leaders did recognise that local factors, even Soviet mistakes, had contributed to their problems in Eastern Europe. But they naturally preferred to blame Western machinations. In July 1956 Khrushchev attributed turmoil in Poland and Hungary to 'the subversive actions of the imperialists', who 'want to ferment disunity' and 'destroy the socialist countries one by one'. Hardliners went further, Molotov's ally Voroshilov claiming on 28 October that 'The American secret services are more active in Hungary than [the Praesidium's envoys] Suslov and Mikoyan'.[57]

Nor was it only communists who perceived external backing for the Hungarian revolution that developed with remarkable speed in October 1956 (below, pp. 544–7). Its outbreak set off a good deal of fighting, and the apparent defeat of the Soviet forces that had occupied Budapest on 24 October. So there was plenty for Radio Free Europe to report. A post mortem study found that the radio had not deliberately sought to inspire revolution; but it had sometimes passed from simply reporting revolutionary demands to identifying with them, and had occasionally even offered tactical advice. Its audiences no doubt exaggerated the degree of US support this implied, and refugees later told Vice-President Nixon that the radio had played a part in encouraging the revolution.[58] But the United States never went beyond broadcasts. There were those in the CIA who wished to, but Allen Dulles was hostile and Eisenhower adamant – twice vetoing proposals to drop arms. (Instead the USA again offered food aid.)

26 October had in fact seen a decision to try to reassure the USSR. Eisenhower doubted whether Soviet leaders genuinely anticipated a Western invasion; but Khrushchev appeared insecure; and, faced with

[56] Brian McCauley, 'Hungary and Suez, 1956: The Limits of Soviet and American Power', *Journal of Contemporary History*, xvi (1981) p. 781.
[57] Mark Kramer, 'The Soviet Union and the 1956 Crises in Hungary and Poland: Reassessments and New Findings', *Journal of Contemporary History*, xxxiii (1998) pp. 179, 186.
[58] Prados, *Presidents' Secret Wars*, pp. 125–6; Ranelagh, *The Agency*, pp. 308–9; Richard Nixon, *Memoirs* (paperback edn, 1979) p. 183.

the weakening of its hold over its satellites, 'might not the Soviet Union be tempted to resort to extreme measures, even to start a world war?' Also (as Eisenhower was later to emphasise to critics) since NATO had no common frontier with Hungary and no way of intervening on the ground, his only available option was to use (or, presumably, threaten to use) nuclear weapons.[59] So it was decided to tell the USSR that 'We do not look upon these nations as potential military allies'. But the message may have seemed to the Kremlin less than reassuring, since it also said they 'should have sovereignty restored to them, and that they should have governments of their own free choosing . . . We see them as friends and as part of a new and friendly and no longer divided Europe'. Dulles had, too, earlier spoken of according aid to East European nations during their 'economic adjustment' away from exclusive dependence on the USSR, albeit without any preconditions that they renounce communism. The State Department was looking, as a 2 November internal circular shows, to a transformation of Eastern Europe into a collection of 'national Communist regimes' presumably on the Yugoslav model.[60] This accorded with a Soviet Declaration on 31 October that the socialist states could build their relations 'only on the principles of complete equality . . . and of non-interference in one another's internal affairs'. But it had very little in common with the real Soviet view of the 'camp'. Nor did it address what Khrushchev saw as the problem of the likely restoration of capitalism in Hungary:

If we let things take their course the West would say we are either stupid or weak, and that's one and the same thing. We cannot possibly permit it, either as Communists and internationalists or as the Soviet state. We would have capitalists on the frontiers of the Soviet Union.[61]

Eisenhower says that (unlike Allen Dulles) he always suspected the 31 October Declaration; and in the first days of November there was much evidence that Soviet troops were not really withdrawing but regrouping for a new offensive. Eisenhower decided, though, on 1 November, not 'to take up the situation in the Soviet satellites', but rather to concentrate on the

---

[59] Ambrose, *Eisenhower*, p. 372; some people in the CIA deployed the case for a nuclear ultimatum to Russia (Ranelagh, *The Agency*, p. 306).
[60] McCauley, 'Hungary and Suez' pp. 782–4, 791; Dwight D. Eisenhower, *White House Years*, ii *(Waging Peace, 1956–1961)* (1966) p. 70 – cited as Eisenhower, *Memoirs, ii*.
[61] For Khrushchev's explanation to the Yugoslavs of his decision to use force in Hungary, see Micunovic, *Moscow Diary*, pp. 132–40 (esp. p. 133).

Middle East, where hostilities were actually in progress and where the USA was far better positioned to determine the outcome.[62] An opportunity for further diplomatic involvement was presented by the Hungarian Premier's appeals of 1 and 2 November to the United Nations and the 'four great Powers' to guarantee Hungarian neutrality. But the US resisted Anglo-French attempts to transfer the Hungarian question from the UN Security Council to the General Assembly, which had been seized of the 'Suez' war since 31 October, and so delayed UN proceedings on Hungary until after the actual 4 November Soviet invasion.[63]

The public US decision not to intervene in the event of Soviet coercion of Poland and that of 26 October to try to reassure the USSR over Hungary both antedate the start of Middle Eastern hostilities. So American, hence Western, inaction over Hungary cannot really be blamed on the simultaneous Suez crisis. Equally what is perhaps the fullest account of the Soviet Praesidium's deliberations is clear that the 'invasion of Hungary would have been approved even if there had been no Suez crisis'. It was precipitated by reports on 30 October that the Hungarian army was unreliable, by pressure on the part of the new government for complete Soviet troop withdrawal and Hungarian departure from the Warsaw Pact, and by the seizure of party headquarters in Budapest and the lynching of secret policemen. More generally it was held that 'If we don't embark on a decisive path [in Hungary], things in Czechoslovakia [and elsewhere] will collapse'; nor, probably, could Khrushchev personally have survived the loss of Hungary.[64]

However, Middle Eastern hostilities and extra-European rivalries did influence both superpowers. Eisenhower held that:

at all costs the Soviets must be prevented from seizing a mantle of world leadership through a false but convincing exhibition of concern for smaller nations. Since Africa and Asia almost unanimously hate one of the three nations [that had attacked Egypt], Britain, France, and Israel, the Soviets need only to propose severe and immediate punishment of these three to have the whole of two continents on their side.

---

[62] Ambrose, *Eisenhower*, p. 363. For the Suez crisis see below, pp. 231, 238–9 and *The Post-Imperial Age*, Chap. xi.

[63] Csaba Bekes, 'New Findings on the 1956 Hungarian Revolution', *Cold War International History Project Bulletin*, 2 (1992) p. 3.

[64] Kramer, 'The Soviet Union and the 1956 Crises in Hungary and Poland' pp. 188–92, 194, 213.

This he sought to head off by forcing an early Suez ceasefire.[65]

For its part, the Soviet Praesidium had, on 31 October, decided on military intervention in the context, not only of reports from Hungary, but also of the Israeli attack on, and Anglo-French ultimatum to, Egypt. That country appeared lost. But:

If we depart from Hungary, it will give a great boost to the Americans, English and French – the imperialists. They will perceive it as weakness on our part and will go onto the offensive . . . To Egypt [they] will then add Hungary.

Khrushchev had, moreover, noted the way in which, after Egypt's nationalisation of the Suez Canal, Britain and France had become entangled in endless negotiations. This had not, in fact, precluded Soviet readiness to talk, in October, both in Poland and Hungary; indeed, at the end of the month, Mikoyan wished to continue, still hoping that the Hungarian government could control events. But his colleagues would wait no longer, determining instead to 'take the initiative in restoring order'. At first Khrushchev saw a degree of parallelism: the British and French 'are bogged down in Suez, and we are stuck in Hungary'.[66] But once his troops had actually moved, he felt confident enough to try also to score points by intervening, at least verbally, also in the Suez crisis; on 5 November the USSR hinted that it might commit troops to the Middle East and warned Britain and France of their vulnerability to Soviet rockets. This latter threat was seen, correctly, as a bluff. But both Britain and the US took seriously the possibility of the despatch of Soviet troops, and mounted surveillance flights over Syria to detect them. Indeed Eisenhower was briefly worried that the 'Soviets, seeing their failure in the satellites, might be ready to undertake any wild adventure . . . [they] are as scared and furious as Hitler was in his last days'[67] They were not. But it is not surprising that, between them, Hungary and Suez brought the first detente to a distinctly chilly close.

Khrushchev and the policy of 'peaceful coexistence'

The USSR's action over Hungary made clear its readiness to maintain communist rule in Eastern Europe; and for over three decades this was

---

[65] 1 November 1956 – Ambrose, *Eisenhower*, p. 364.
[66] Kramer, 'The Soviet Union and the 1956 Crises', pp. 190–2, 199.
[67] Eisenhower, *Memoirs*, ii, p. 90; Aldrich, *Hidden Hand*, pp. 489–90.

accepted as a basic fact in international relations. But if Eastern Europe constituted the Soviet sphere, much of the rest of the world was under, or just emerging from, colonial rule. Stalin had in fact conducted some post-war probes, by supporting Israel's emergence in 1947–8 and probably also by encouraging insurgency in Southeast Asia in 1948. But Khrushchev tells us Stalin's expectations were very limited: he had qualms about having recognised Ho Chi Minh's revolutionary government as he 'did not believe in the possibility of victory for Vietnam'; and he refused to send arms to King Farouk of Egypt, declaring 'in my presence that the Near East was part of Britain's sphere of influence and that therefore we couldn't go sticking our noses into Egypt's affairs'.[68] After Stalin's death Molotov continued to defend and advocate Stalin's policies. Khrushchev used his support against Malenkov, then turned on him in 1955. Despite Khrushchev's initial success, the antagonism rumbled on until 1957, when it flared up again in the so-called 'Anti-Party Group' attempt to depose Khrushchev. As Khrushchev described this to Nasser in 1958, Molotov 'thought we should go back to traditional policies':

first . . . we should draw a line in Europe beyond which we should allow no retreat. Second, we should refuse to discuss anything affecting countries on our side of that line. Third, we should stop what he called 'adventurism', in which he included our interest in your part of the world . . . I told Molotov that to adopt a purely defensive position in Europe would be a mistake, because there are so many currents flowing over Europe, and the socialist movement in western Europe is becoming very important. Offence is the best form of defence. I said that we needed a new, active diplomacy because the impossibility of a nuclear war meant that the struggle between us and the capitalists was taking on new forms. I told them: 'I'm not an adventurer, but we must aid national liberation movements, and if imperialism controls somewhere like the Middle East it could liquidate the national liberation movements there and bring to power reactionary forces which would be ready to play their part in a policy of encirclement of the Soviet Union.'[69]

Khrushchev was no doubt putting special stress on those aspects of the dispute that most concerned Nasser,[70] but they did go to the heart of his

---

[68] *Khrushchev Remembers*, iii, pp. 155–6; i, p. 394.

[69] M. Heikal, *Sphinx and Commissar. The Rise and Fall of Soviet Influence in the Arab World* (1978) pp. 91–2.

[70] The chief issue had been the handling of Yugoslavia, which had major implications for the rest of Eastern Europe; and there were many other differences besides those here

foreign policy. This he set out at length in the Central Committee report to the 1956 Twentieth Party Congress.[71] A 'vast zone of peace has emerged in the world, including the peace-loving States, both Socialist and non-Socialist, of Europe and Asia . . . inhabited by . . . the majority of the population of our planet'. This meant that, despite the earlier Marxist-Leninist thesis, war with imperialism was no longer 'fatalistically inevitable', which was just as well, 'for in present-day conditions . . . there are only two ways: either peaceful co-existence or the most destructive war in history.' So 'when we say that the Socialist system will win in the competition' with capitalism, 'this by no means signifies that its victory will be achieved through armed interference'.

One ground for Khrushchev's confidence was economic: 'Our certainty of the victory of Communism is based on the fact that the Socialist mode of production possesses decisive advantages over the capitalist mode'. He had begun his report by claiming a 1,949 per cent increase in Soviet industrial production since 1929, as against one of 134 per cent for the US and 93 per cent for capitalist states in general. He seems to have looked for the sort of phenomenon that did actually occur in 1989–91, only in the opposite direction: the internal disintegration of a system that had, comparatively speaking, failed to deliver the goods. He often rubbed this in to foreigners; thus he told Adenauer in 1955 that ' "You are condemned to go under and we will be master of the world!" I think it was really important to him.' Similarly Khrushchev explained to the London *Times* that he did not need to teach the British

to effect a revolution and establish a socialist system in their country. They will do it themselves when they come to realise that the system which we have here . . . presents greater advantages to the peoples than the capitalist system, that the socialist system offers unlimited possibilities . . .[72]

The other basis for Khrushchev's confidence lay in 'the disintegration of the imperialist colonial system', which he described to the Twentieth

---

mentioned. But Molotov was made to confess to the Twentieth Party Congress that the Foreign Ministry had not appreciated the importance of the 'colonial liberation movements' (*Keesing's*, 14748); and it was later claimed that he had opposed the 1955 Egyptian arms deal (Karen Dawisha, *Soviet Foreign Policy towards Egypt* (1979) p. 142).

[71] *Keesing's*, 14745–6.

[72] K. Adenauer, *Erinnerungen*, ii, *1953–5* (Stuttgart, 1966) pp. 520, 554; N.S. Khrushchev, *For Victory in Peaceful Competition with Capitalism* (1960) p. 88.

Party Congress as a 'development of world historical significance' and which the 1960 Moscow Conference of 81 Communist Parties was to rate as 'second only to the formation of the world socialist system'. Khrushchev implied in 1956 that the newly emancipated states were natural allies of the 'world camp of Socialism': in 1959 he spelt things out more fully to the next Congress:

... if we take the countries forming the world socialist system and the countries waging a courageous struggle against imperialism . . . for their freedom and independence, we shall find that the scales have already turned in favour of these peace-loving countries . . .

One of the cardinal conclusions to be drawn from an analysis of the present balance of forces in the world is that most colonial and semi-colonial countries, which have only recently been the reserve and the rear of imperialism, are no longer that.[73]

To Khrushchev this was an inevitable process: Iran, he told Kennedy at the 1962 Vienna Summit, was a typical unstable pro-Western country about to experience political upheaval; the USSR would no doubt be blamed, but it would not in fact have been involved.[74] But the process was also desirable and to be forwarded. Many of his early 1960s polemics with the Chinese revolved around their refusal to accept his contention that peaceful coexistence provided a more favourable context than hardline confrontation for the development of the 'national liberation movement'.[75] His 1961 Party Programme declared it the CPSU's duty 'to support the sacred struggle of the oppressed peoples and their just anti-imperialist wars of national liberation'. When, at the Vienna Summit, Kennedy sought to dissuade him from eliminating free systems in areas hitherto associated with the West, Khrushchev categorically rejected any such attempt to 'freeze' existing conditions. As he later told a visiting US Senator:

We in the USSR feel that the revolutionary process should have the right to exist . . . the right to rebel, and the Soviet right to help combat reactionary governments . . . is the question of questions.

---

[73] *Keesing's*, 14745; RIIA, *Documents 1960*, p. 230; N.S. Khrushchev [sic] *World Without Arms, World Without Wars*, i (Moscow, 1959) p. 65.

[74] Barry Rubin, *Paved with Good Intentions. The American Experience and Iran* (New York, 1980) p. 107.

[75] RIIA, *Documents 1963*, pp. 231 ff. (Chinese polemic), and 250 ff. – esp. pp. 267, 275 (Soviet reply).

This question is at the heart of our relations with you . . . Kennedy could not understand this.[76]

Implications of Soviet aid to, and trade with, the Third World

Khrushchev began his new policy in 1955 by visiting, and offering aid to, India, Burma and Afghanistan. This offer of economic assistance introduced a new dimension into East–West competition. At the time it occasioned much Western concern. For the socialist planned economies appeared to have the advantage that they could easily direct the giving of aid or the purchase of products that might not be in demand on the open market. Such barter deals had been practised in the 1930s by Nazi Germany; they had gone far to bind Eastern Europe to it economically, and in the 1950s there was a tendency to exaggerate their political consequences. The 1950s also tended to exaggerate the economic achievements of the planned Stalinist economic system with its accent on heavy industry; for the Soviet growth-rate was high and Khrushchev was continually looking forward to overtaking the USA. So it was natural for countries like Egypt and India to wish to move in this direction, and for the USSR to encourage them. But in the longer run this economic approach came to look less impressive, leading some politicians (notably Sadat) to seek to break with it and try other systems. Soviet aid, too, had certain limitations: Mohamed Heikal's instruction manual for Third World leaders (derived largely from Nasser) recalls that 'agriculture is the Soviets' Achilles heel. You can ask them for arms, or factories, but, unless you are in a real crisis, never ask for wheat. They will almost certainly be unable to provide it.' Heikal also mentions that, in the late 1960s, Soviet teams (in contrast to American) could not drill deep enough to find oil.[77] Even setting such

---

[76] *Keesing's*, 18468; *Khrushchev Remembers*, ii, pp. 495–7; Arthur M. Schlesinger, *A Thousand Days. John F. Kennedy in the White House* (London edn, 1965) pp. 325–33. Khrushchev's chief concern was to wean countries from their Western orientation – he had little use for 'temporary people' like Sir Abubaker Tafawa Balewa of Nigeria, who was 'building a new independent state' but who 'went out of his way to be accommodating to Great Britain'. The question of whether Third World leaders persecuted their own communists was distinctly secondary. But where occasion arose, he encouraged development along socialist lines (cf. his advice to Nasser on agriculture). He was also prepared to deal with communist generals behind the back of the friendly Indonesian leader Sukarno (*Khrushchev Remembers*, i, pp. 410–12; ii, pp. 323, 480).

[77] Heikal, *Sphinx and Commissar*, pp. 30, 212.

considerations aside, the socialist economies were always both smaller and more self-sufficient than the 'advanced capitalist' OECD ones; so their international economic weight was inevitably less.

But if Soviet economic competition was less serious than originally feared, it was still significant. At the least it enabled Third World states to play East off against West. Nasser wanted the West to build him the Aswan Dam, and used the possibility of turning to the Soviet Union to secure Western credits. Admittedly these were later withdrawn; but the USSR then stepped in to undertake the project. For though Soviet economic aid was not extensive,[78] the Russians (and occasionally also the Chinese)[79] were capable of replacing the West in an emergency. Thus in 1969 the USSR offered Iraq technical assistance and loans to develop the North Rumaila oilfield, whose nationalisation the Western-owned Iraq Petroleum Company (IPC) was contesting; the USSR was also among the countries prepared to take oil from the Kirkuk field when this was nationalised in 1972 and the IPC sought to have it boycotted.[80] Similarly as the USA imposed sanctions on Castro's Cuba, the USSR stepped in to counteract them. In *this* instance it was rewarded by the acquisition of a new member of the socialist camp – but at a cost that had risen to some $4.6 billion per annum by 1984 (and that some say made the USSR think twice in the 1960s about picking up more such clients).[81]

Khrushchev's other major Third World initiative in 1955 was the sale of (ostensibly Czech) arms to Egypt. Supplying arms has its problems. For the recipients are likely to seek modern weapons, but may well lose them to your enemies (over the years Israel deliberately captured from Egypt a range of Soviet weaponry for transfer to the USA). Refusal to supply up-to-date equipment can give offence, however, and a country's prestige can (and in the Middle East did) become tied in with the military success of the purchasers of its arms. But, when all is said, arms sales are profitable; and they constituted a field in which the USSR was well equipped to compete.

---

[78] The CIA calculated 'Gross Official Bilateral Capital Flows to the Less Developed Countries' from 1954–78 as $193bn from OECD countries, $21bn from OPEC countries, and $14bn from Communist countries (*Handbook of Economic Statistics, 1980*, Tables 70, 74).

[79] When Western powers declined fo finance a Tanzania–Zambia railway (regarding it, correctly, as a waste of money), the two countries reluctantly turned to China, who built it between 1970 and 1976 on very easy terms (*Keesing's*, 27900).

[80] *Keesing's*, 24648, 25201, 25455.

[81] Richard F. Staar, *USSR Foreign Policies after Detente* (1987 edn, Stanford, CA) p. 145.

From at least the early 1960s, therefore, it was almost always the leading weapons exporter to the Third World.[82] Both buyers and sellers perceive arms sales as not merely financial but also political transactions, and they also provide a constituency within the recipient military that should be favourably inclined towards the supplier. This can only be a slippery source of influence, but then most sources of influence are slippery. It was to its readiness to supply arms that the Soviet Union owed much of its position in the Middle East.

The USSR and Egypt 1955–6

In 1955 the Middle East still seemed a largely British sphere, but it was in considerable turmoil.[83] It had been rent by the establishment of Israel and the humiliating 1948–9 Arab defeat; thereafter Arab–Israeli frontiers had stayed closed, save only for frequent and bloody border incidents. Also Egypt had only just managed (after a long struggle) to force Britain to give up its Suez Canal bases, and Anglo-Egyptian relations were still fragile – especially as Nasser hoped to use his enormous charisma and appeal to Arab nationalism to destroy the traditional (and mostly pro-British) regimes in other countries in an extension of his own Egyptian revolution. Nasser had originally sought arms from the United States. But he ran up against the 1950 Tripartite Declaration in which the major Western suppliers, Britain, France and the USA, had undertaken to maintain a rough arms balance between Israel and the Arabs. By approaching the USSR, Nasser introduced a new player and broke out of the Western strait-jacket. The approach was made via Zhou Enlai, who recommended it to Moscow with the advice

that we must expect a major collision in the Middle East between what
. . . [Nasser] calls the new forces of Arab nationalism and the colonialists
and reactionaries who oppose it.
*   . . . It is impossible for the socialist camp to adopt the role of a*
spectator . . . As I see it, our position obliges us to assist the nationalist
forces in this battle for two reasons – because their victory would be in
the interest of the socialist camp and because it would thwart all attempts
of the western imperialists to complete the encirclement of the eastern

---

[82] *SIPRI Yearbook, World Armaments and Disarmament* (Oxford) *1983* p. 272, *1987* p. 184 – the exception is the period 1973–7.
[83] For a fuller discussion, see *The Post-Imperial Age*, Chaps 10, 11.

*camp. My conclusion is that the logic of history points to the nationalist
movement as the coming force in the Middle East, and that we should
make our approach to it as [early and] as friendly as we can.*

Acting on this advice, Moscow initiated military discussions, and sent the
editor of *Pravda* to check Nasser out. Nasser made it clear that he was *not*
a communist, but Shepilov was able to report that he seemed both determined and reliable. The deal went ahead, and was hurriedly announced by
Nasser in September to forestall US pressure to cancel it.[84]

The Egyptians maintain that, at this stage, Soviet commitment was still
distinctly conditional, and that Khrushchev and Bulganin were tempted
(during their 1956 visit to London) by Eden's invitation to subscribe to
the Tripartite Declaration – which would have accorded them a new standing in Middle Eastern affairs. It was partly to circumvent this possibility
and gain access to another arms supplier that Nasser recognised communist China in May.[85] Whether to punish Nasser for thus working both
sides in the Cold War or for the spurning of a US attempt to mediate
over Israel, Dulles then brusquely withdrew the offer of aid for the Aswan
Dam. Nasser's response was to nationalise the Suez Canal. A surprised
but delighted Khrushchev accelerated military deliveries to Egypt, while
threatening the British and French ambassadors 'that Egypt would not be
left alone in an armed battle if the West launched it'. But, despite Eden's
April 1956 warnings that Britain would if necessary fight for its vital
Middle Eastern interests, it does not look as if Khrushchev anticipated
having to make his threat good.[86]

When war actually broke out, Khrushchev and Zhukov were profuse in
their explanations that it was geographically impossible for them to intervene. Eisenhower felt much the same about Hungary. But whereas this had
led the USA to eschew threats, the fact that the Anglo-French invasion of
Egypt was opposed also by the United States gave Moscow an opening.
So late on 5 November it approached the UN and USA to suggest a joint
Soviet–US military force to end the invasion, and sent ferocious letters
to Britain, France and Israel apprising them of this; Eden was also told
that, 'Were rocket weapons used against Britain and France, you would,
most probably, call this a barbarous action. But how does the inhuman

---

[84] Heikal, *Sphinx and Commissar*, pp. 58–63.
[85] ibid., pp. 66–7; Heikal, *Cutting the Lion's Tale. Suez through Egyptian Eyes* (1986)
pp. 102–3.
[86] Micunovic, *Moscow Diary*, pp. 103–4, 117.

attack launched . . . against a practically defenceless Egypt differ . . . ?' All this committed the USSR to very little. Khrushchev was later to say he had never contemplated unilateral action in the Middle East and that the proposal for joint action with the US was advanced for propaganda purposes;[87] and though the reference to rocket attacks was obviously meant to be alarming, it was not a direct threat. The White House promptly termed the suggestion of joint US–Soviet action 'unthinkable' and observed that it would 'oppose' the introduction of any new forces into the Middle East other than that already authorised by the UN. Eisenhower's private language was distinctly stronger, and he prepared to place US forces on the alert as a warning to Khrushchev.[88] But he continued his financial pressure on London; and it was this that induced Eden to call a ceasefire on 6 November while he still controlled only half the Suez Canal, too little to give him any leverage over the subsequent settlement.

The Eisenhower Doctrine, 1957

It was, then, not the USSR that had saved Egypt. Privately Nasser recognised this.[89] But he had no interest in contesting the enormous popularity the Soviet démarche earned in the Arab world, especially as Moscow soon promised to make good Egyptian arms losses in the war, whereas Washington combined legalistic determination to secure Britain, France and Israel's total withdrawal with deep hostility to Nasserism. Just as Zhou (and Khrushchev) had looked enthusiastically to 'a major collision . . . between . . . the new forces of Arab nationalism and the colonialists and [local] reactionaries who oppose it', so Eisenhower felt that 'radical elements of pan-Arab nationalism, as symbolized by Nasser, are characterized by many elements inimical to basic US objectives in the Near East.' The tendency, indeed, was to elide Nasserism into communism. So as soon as it had halted the Suez hostilities, Washington turned to devising 'plans whereby the Western countries can work together in making the Middle East secure from Communist penetration'; for, as Dulles put

---

[87] McCauley, 'Hungary and Suez', pp. 786–8; Bohlen, *Witness to History*, p. 434; *Khrushchev Remembers*, i, pp. 397–8.

[88] Eisenhower, *Memoirs*, ii, p. 91; Ambrose, *Eisenhower. The President*, pp. 368–9.

[89] M. Heikal, *Nasser. The Cairo Documents* (1972) pp. 139, 142; O. Smolyansky, 'Moscow and the Suez Crisis: A Reappraisal', *Political Science Quarterly*, xxx (1965) p. 602; McCauley, 'Hungary and Suez', pp. 786, 797.

it, 'if we do not act, the Soviets are likely to take over the area, and they could thereby control Europe through oil on which [Western] Europe is dependent.'

To prevent this, the administration hoped to bring round, and 'build up', King Saud (who had been flirting with radicalism) and 'to assist Jordan financially and perhaps militarily in the context of a closer federation with Iraq' that might, hopefully, also include Syria. In all this, Eisenhower looked to re-establish cooperation with Britain, which retained important assets in the area. But, having badly dented British prestige, the USA would inevitably now play a more conspicuous role; and to secure a free hand from Congress, Eisenhower stressed that 'The existing vacuum in the Middle East must be filled by the United States before it is filled by Russia'. He thus (with some difficulty) obtained approval, in March 1957, of what became known as the 'Eisenhower Doctrine', whereby the US undertook 'to secure and protect the territorial integrity and political independence of . . . nations, requesting such aid, against overt armed aggression from any nation controlled by International Communism.'[90]

Both Eisenhower and Dulles conceded that the Middle East also had 'Problems other than of Communist Source', but they clearly saw it as having become a key arena of East–West rivalry. So did the Soviets. Admittedly they were attracted, then and later, by the idea of entering into a partnership to control the region. But the West did not respond, and probably Khrushchev did not expect it to.[91] Failing such a development, Mikoyan told the US ambassador in 1957, 'We are going to do everything we can to oppose the establishment of Western military strength in that area, and particularly yours'.[92] The stage was therefore set for a US–Soviet clash.

---

[90] Ray Takeyh, *The Origins of the Eisenhower Doctrine. The US, Britain and Nasser's Egypt, 1953–57* (Basingstoke, 2000) Chap. 7 (esp. pp. 144–5, 149–52); also Nigel John Ashton, *Eisenhower, Macmillan and the Problem of Nasser. Anglo-American Relations and Arab Nationalism, 1955–9* (Basingstoke, 1996) Chap. 6 (which stresses that, despite substantial convergence, frictions still resulted from US emphasis on Saudi Arabia, and British on Iraq).

[91] He told a worried Egyptian delegation in 1957, 'We are quite aware that they have no intention of allowing us any role in the Middle East – or anywhere else for that matter – unless we completely change our skins; and that is a day which they will no more see than a man can see his ears' (*Sphinx and Commissar*, p. 83).

[92] Bohlen, *Witness to History*, p. 450.

Jordan, Syria and the Lebanon 1957–8

For this the condition of the Middle East afforded many opportunities. The sense that there existed a single Arab nation legitimated, and similarities of language and culture facilitated, intervention by one Arab state in the internal politics of another, generally through a mixture of propaganda and subversion. Such an environment also encouraged the involvement of external 'intelligence' agencies. This state of affairs continued throughout the 1950s and 1960s. But its international importance was probably greatest in the period 1956–8, when 'It was to a very large extent on the plane of internal Syrian politics that were fought the decisive battles over the Baghdad Pact, the Eisenhower Doctrine, and Russia's bid to bring Syria within the Soviet sphere of influence in 1957.' The future also of Jordan and the Lebanon seemed equally at stake. In April 1957 King Hussein managed to stabilise Jordan, dismissing his cabinet after it had decided to open relations with the USSR. He was assisted by a reconciliation with King Saud of Saudi Arabia (who had himself been assiduously courted by Eisenhower but subjected to assassination plots from elsewhere), by a $10 million US loan, and by protective movements on the part of the US Sixth Fleet. Then in June status quo parties, with some Western assistance, did well in the Lebanese elections, despite the alleged commitment by Egypt and Syria of $0.7 million on the other side.[93]

In the autumn of 1956 what the Syrians termed 'the Iraqi Plot', a coup and rising with Anglo-American backing, had been pre-empted only by the outbreak of the Suez hostilities.[94] This was followed by internal disturbances, then by a poorly planned CIA coup that the Syrian authorities discovered and denounced in August 1957. Each episode moved Syrian politics further left, amid precautionary purges. In July Syria had secured massive Soviet aid and arms promises, in August Soviet assistance in re-organising its security services. The British saw in this 'the final obliteration of elements in the Army prepared to oppose complete control by the left-wing officers around [the Security chief] Sarraj', Dulles the prelude to a Czech-style communist takeover.

---

[93] Andrew Rathwell, *Secret War in the Middle East: the Covert Struggle for Syria, 1949–61* (1995) p. 4 (quoting Patrick Seale, *The Struggle for Syria* (1965)), 128–33; Eisenhower, *Memoirs*, ii, esp. pp. 190–1, 194; R. Lacey, *The Kingdom* (New York, 1981) pp. 315–17; RIIA, *Survey of International Affairs 1956–1958*, pp. 171–5.

[94] Rathmell, *Secret War in the Middle East*, pp. 112–23; the coup's Anglo-American code-name was 'Operation Straggle'.

Dulles concluded that 'there is now little hope of correction from within and that we must think in terms of the external assets reflected by the deep concern of the Moslem states having common borders with Syria'. Of these, Iraq had been predisposed towards intervention since 1954; the Turkish premier now saw Syria as 'a Soviet satellite' 'on her way to becoming a spring-board for covert aggression'; and the Lebanese Foreign Minister forecast that, if the current Syrian government became entrenched, Jordan would fall in one month, the Lebanon in three, Iraq in six, and Saudi Arabia in 'perhaps a year'. Dulles accordingly promised US support to Syria's neighbours acting in 'self-defence'. They agreed to mobilise to induce her to disperse her forces, after which Iraq would attack. The United States' part was to 'see that no outside countries – for example, Israel or the USSR – would interfere', and it staged demonstrative fleet and air movements. However, the Arab countries involved then got cold feet. Turkey would have been prepared to go ahead on her own with the 50,000 troops concentrated for 'manoeuvres' on her Syrian border; but, in the absence of any Arab support for intervention, the USA then shifted to restraining her. So, more openly, did the USSR, warning Turkey she would 'suffer' if she attacked Syria, and sending token warships to Syria. Later, in October, buoyed by the prestige of the first ever successful launch of a satellite ('sputnik'), Khrushchev renewed the threats, and was in turn reminded by Dulles that the United States would respond by hitting the USSR. But by then the crisis was subsiding, and many of these statements were being made for the record.[95]

Nasser's contribution to this phase was to airlift troops into Syria in October. He had, thus far, been working on the same side as the communists. The two now diverged. In November a meeting of Syrian and Egyptian parliamentarians advocated a federal union of the two countries. They were strongly supported by the Syrian military. But December saw a struggle between partisans of the USSR and those of Arab unity that apparently led Nasser to ask the US for a three-month propaganda truce to enable him to concentrate on opposing the Syrian communists; this was supposedly forthcoming, and some intelligence even shared. January 1958 brought a mission to Cairo, and in February the 'United Arab Republic' [UAR] was proclaimed in Damascus, with Nasser swearing at Saladin's tomb 'to follow Saladin's example to realize total Arab unity'.[96]

[95] Rathmell, *Secret War*, pp. 136–42; Prados, *Presidents' Secret Wars*, pp. 128–30; Eisenhower, *Memoirs*, ii, pp. 196–203.
[96] Rathmell, *Secret War*, pp. 142–4, 147; Tabitha Petran, *Syria* (1972) p. 128; Ashton, *Eisenhower, Macmillan, and the Problem of Nasser*, Chaps 7–9.

The Iraqi revolution 1958

Trouble next struck in the Lebanon, whose President Chamoun had sought to amend the constitution to gain himself a second term of office. Chamoun saw the resulting disturbances in (oversimplified) terms of a cleavage between conservatism and Nasserite Arabism, sounded out American willingness to intervene, and also appealed to the UN claiming UAR subversion. But by early July the crisis appeared to have passed, with Chamoun declaring his readiness to retire at the end of his constitutional term.

Then on 14 July 1958, Iraqi units that had been ordered into Jordan (whether to stabilise it or, the Egyptians claimed, as a preliminary to an attack on Syria) staged a coup as they passed through Baghdad. The King, Crown Prince, and political strong-man Nuri es Said were killed, and a Republic proclaimed. Iraq had long been one of the pillars of the pro-British and pro-Western configuration of the Middle East; its sudden revolution seemed to sweep all this away, leaving Nasserism triumphant. The obvious question was whether the West would take it lying down. Saud (whose family had admittedly now forced him to relinquish much of his power) secretly demanded 'that the Baghdad Pact powers intervene in Iraq, on pain of Saudi Arabia's having to "go along" with the United Arab Republic'. Turkey was very anxious to oblige. And countries that felt themselves more directly at risk sought stabilisation by US or British troops. The now neurotic Chamoun appealed to Eisenhower on the 14th, Hussein to Britain on the 16th.[97] On the 15th US troops landed on the crowded Beirut bathing beaches (supposedly much to the profit of local ice-cream vendors), in what was intended chiefly as a demonstration of strength – by early August they totalled 14,000, including tanks and atomic-capable artillery.[98] The British drop of 2,200 paratroops on the 17th was a more risky affair, large enough to secure Amman airport and if necessary to take on the mob, but not enough to handle Jordanian armour had the army mutinied. Both forces in fact achieved their goals. But given the logistic difficulties of putting them in place,[99] neither the USA nor Britain would have had any spare capacity to invade Iraq. Nor were they

---

[97] Eisenhower, *Memoirs*, ii, pp. 265–72; Harold Macmillan, *Memoirs*, iv (*Riding the Storm 1956–1959*) esp. pp. 513, 516, 522.

[98] Eisenhower, *Memoirs*, ii, p. 286. Though chiefly demonstrative, US strength may also have reinforced diplomacy in dissuading elements of the Lebanese army from resisting.

[99] The original contingency plan had called for joint Anglo-American action in the Lebanon. When Eisenhower determined that it should be all-American (perhaps to leave British troops for use elsewhere), the intervention force could only be assembled in time

anxious to give the go-ahead for a Turkish invasion or risk provoking an
Iraqi attack on Jordan or Kuwait.

Khrushchev, however, was highly concerned. He had been delighted by
the Iraqi revolution, and did not wish to jeopardise it. So he pressed Nasser
(who happened to be in Yugoslavia) to fly to Moscow, and, after some
bravado, told him of Eden's 1956 threat to fight if his oil was endangered.
Khrushchev therefore counselled prudence and reassurances to the West
that oil supplies would be maintained: 'Remember, this is a game of nerves
. . . The possibility of nuclear war is always there, but the moments of
greatest risk are in the first shock of new events. If you can get through this
period all right, you will be safe'. Khrushchev's own contribution to this
process was, on the one hand, to stage manoeuvres (but, as he emphatic-
ally reminded Nasser, 'nothing more than manoeuvres'),[100] and, on the
other, to call on 19 July for an urgent summit meeting. Both France and
Britain would have been happy to hold one, but the United States was not
– and succeeded in stalling. As far as the Middle East was concerned, this
did not matter, for things settled down very quickly. A US envoy managed
to negotiate a political settlement in the Lebanon, and the army commander, General Chehab, was elected to succeed President Chamoun when he
retired in September. Meanwhile the new regime in Iraq had proved conciliatory. On 28 July a Baghdad Pact meeting in London decided that it
should be recognised. At a special session of the UN General Assembly the
Arab states all agreed on 21 August to propose a moderate resolution
inviting Secretary-General Hammarskjöld to make practical arrangements
to consolidate Jordan and the Lebanon. Accordingly he toured the Middle
East, and the autumn saw US and British withdrawals.[101]

by over-flying neutral Austria (which protested) – *The Joint Chiefs of Staff and National
Policy 1957–60* (National Archives, Washington) esp. pp. 426–7, 445, 454. British
forces for Amman had to overfly Israel, which made difficulties about their resupply
(as did Saudi Arabia); to avoid using the Suez Canal, the further battalion that reached
Akaba in early August had to be drawn from Aden, reducing reserves that might be
needed to hold Kuwait (Macmillan, *Memoirs*, iv, pp. 519–25). US Marines were sent
to the Gulf as a possible reinforcement (Barry M. Blechman and Stephen Kaplan (eds)
Force without War. US Armed Forces as a Political Instrument (Washington, 1978)
p. 238).
[100] Heikal, *Sphinx and Commissar*, esp. p. 98, *Nasser. The Cairo Documents*,
pp. 131–2.
[101] RIIA, *Survey 1956–8*, pp. 374–92; Ashton, *Eisenhower, Macmillan and the
Problem of Nasser*, Chaps 10–13.

Soviet–Egyptian coolness 1959

This proved to inaugurate something of a lull in the Arab world. For the remaining conservative regimes proved far more stable than most people had expected, while 1959 brought a temporary Soviet–Egyptian estrangement. The chief cause was Iraq's swing to the left after Brigadier Kassem ousted the more Nasserite President Arif in September 1958. In an attempt to topple him, the UAR was, by March 1959, backing an unsuccessful rising in Mosul. Kassem came to lean increasingly on the communists;[102] and the USSR viewed him as a still more promising leader than Nasser, whom Khrushchev started to criticise for talking about socialism but attacking communists. Nasser saw this as dictation and replied in kind, which led to a vitriolic exchange of letters raking up past incidents. As a result Nasser moved some way back towards the United States, transferring thither in October 1959 all the 250 Egyptian students who had gone to Soviet universities. The resultant coolness was only gradually cleared up; and, for the time being, the Middle East ceased to be the major arena of East–West competition.[103]

The Chinese offshore islands crisis 1958

No sooner did tension die down in the Middle East than it flared in East Asia. This was 'not by accident': action had clearly been prepared for some time, and, to domestic audiences, Mao linked it to the Middle Eastern crisis. But on 27 July he told General Peng Dehuai 'to hold our [plans] to attack Jinmen [Quemoy] for several days . . . The solution of the problem in the Middle East takes time. Since we have time, why should we be in a big hurry?'[104] Mao may have been displeased by Khrushchev's 19 July 1958 call for a summit comprising the US, USSR, Britain, France and India – but not China. On 22 July he exploded when presented with a Soviet proposal for a joint submarine and communications base on Chinese territory that seemed reminscent of past extra-territorial imperial encroachments. Mao abruptly summoned Khrushchev to Beijing, vented

---

[102] In 1963, however, he was killed in a coup.
[103] Heikal, *Nasser. The Cairo Documents*, Chap. 4; *Sphinx and Commissar*, pp. 101–14.
[104] Li Xiaobang, Chen Jian, David Wilson, 'Mao Zedong's handling of the Taiwan Straits Crisis of 1958: Chinese Recollections and Documents', CWIHP *Bulletin* 6–7 (1995–6) pp. 209, 215.

his displeasure, and discoursed on socialist superiority to the capitalist world in terms of population and size of armies.

Mao claims he added that 'whether or not we attack Taiwan is our domestic affair. . . . [Khrushchev] shouldn't try to interfere'. On 23 August China began an artillery bombardment of Quemoy, soon accompanied by broadcasts about its imminent invasion and Chinese determination to liberate Taiwan. A visit by the Soviet Foreign Minister, Gromyko, in September to learn more of Beijing's intentions went badly; and indeed the leadership's subsequent explanations of the crisis proved both vague and varied. They included providing the army with combat experience, enhancing the popular 'feeling of not being afraid of war and . . . hatred toward American imperialism', getting the US 'stuck' in Taiwan 'just as they have already "gotten stuck" in the Middle and Near East', and, by exerting pressure on both, promoting 'more acute contradictions' between Dulles and Chiang Kai-shek. Probably, though, Mao's chief purpose was to complicate Khrushchev's foreign policy – 'He wants to improve relations with the United States? Good, we'll congratulate him with our guns' – and simply to demonstrate his own ability to take independent action: Quemoy and Matsu 'are two batons that keep Khrushchev and Eisenhower dancing . . . Don't you see how wonderful they are?'[105]

Chiang Kai-shek had again concentrated on the offshore islands far more men than were optimal for defence, and their resupply was not easy. As in 1955 Eisenhower supported Chiang, convoying nationalist supplies in international waters but reserving to himself the decision as to further military action. This time he was more confident he would not be pushed to extremes; but the apparent prospect of a major war for the offshore islands was even more unpopular – at one point Eisenhower told Dulles that 'as much as two-thirds of the world, and 50 per cent of US opinion, opposes the course which we have been following', and he worried that NATO might be 'beginning to fall apart'. Nevertheless, he was successful. In part this was because Mao was satisfied with creating an international stir. To one of his journalists he explained that, though he was 'not unwilling to take over' Quemoy and Matsu, essentially he was probing 'American responses . . . to our shelling, and then we could decide on our next move.' Moreover, though he talked (to Gromyko and others) of not fearing war

---

[105] Zubok and Pleshakov, *Inside the Kremlin's Cold War*, pp. 219–27; William Taubman, *Khrushchev. The Man and his Era* (2003) pp. 389–92; *Khrushchev Remembers*, ii, pp. 258–61; Andrei Gromyko, *Memories* (paperback edn, 1989) pp. 321–3.

and of the USSR and China together outweighing the West, he also told his Supreme State Council that 'We have only grenades and potatoes in our hands right now. A war of atomic and hydrogen bombs is of course terrible . . . That is why we oppose a war'; and on 10 September he wrote to Ho Chi Minh that 'it is highly unlikely that a big war will break out'.[106]

Locally the nationalists established air supremacy (using US Sidewinder missiles) and (with US-supplied landing craft) managed to fight supplies through to Quemoy, thus dampening the crisis. Moreover, in a flying visit to Taiwan, Dulles read the riot act, emphasising Chiang's political isolation and the suspicion that he positively 'wants to endanger the peace and involve the US, as the only means of returning to the mainland'. The Korean and Indo-Chinese 'civil wars' had been 'ended by armistice', and Chiang should in future behave as if an armistice were in effect. On 23 October Chiang renounced the use of force to return to the mainland.[107] Beijing read Dulles as seeking 'to freeze the Taiwan Straits' into a 'two Chinas' policy; 'Mao believed that Dulles' mission to Taiwan was to persuade' Chiang Kai-shek 'to withdraw his troops from Jinmen-Mazu in exchange for our commitment not to liberate Taiwan so that America could gain total control of Taiwan's future.' He preferred leaving nationalist forces on the islands, where they could be shelled – 'Whenever we needed tension, we could pull the noose tighter. Whenever we wanted a relaxation, we could give the noose more slack.' Accordingly October saw both pauses in the shelling and two appeals 'to the compatriots in Taiwan' stressing that 'We are all Chinese', warning them that American protection would not last indefinitely, and suggesting talks on reunion. This led on 25 October to the announcement that the islands would be bombarded only on odd days of the month.[108]

---

[106] 'Mao's handling of the Taiwan Staits Crisis', CWIHP *Bulletin* 6–7 pp. 209, 211, 218, 221.

[107] P.P.P.C. Cheng, *Truce Negotiations over Korea and Quemoy* (Washington, 1977) Chap. 3; Ambrose, *Eisenhower*, pp. 482–5; Hoopes, *The Devil and John Foster Dulles*, Chap. 17; R.L. Garthoff (ed.) *Sino-Soviet Military Relations*, pp. 109–11, Chap. 7.

[108] Wu Lengzi's recollections of the crisis, and Zhou Enlai's 5 October 1958 conversation with the Soviet chargé – 'Mao's handling of the Taiwan Straits Crisis', CWIHP *Bulletin* 6–7 (1995–6) esp. pp. 212–15, 221–3. Shelling was particularly heavy on 3 November, so as 'to affect the American [mid-term] election, promoting the Democrats' victory'.

Khrushchev's view of the international scene 1957–8

In 1957 and 1958 there were not only very serious international crises but also a number of more hopeful signs (notably the moratorium on nuclear tests), a mixture that was to persist for some years. At a party on 31 December 1957 Khrushchev toasted Eisenhower and declared that a US–Soviet understanding could only be to everybody's advantage. This was followed up by proposals in January for an East–West conference, in June for talks on economic cooperation (and US credits), and in July for a Five Power summit on the Middle East. Khrushchev seemed to wish to establish the USSR as the second 'superpower', with the same sort of standing as the United States; and he was to be delighted when Macmillan and de Gaulle later admitted that they were no longer in the same league.[109] He probably also hoped to exploit contradictions between the United States and its allies; and he was prepared to offend China in the pursuit of these goals. But Khrushchev always saw East–West relations as adversarial. Thus he told the Yugoslav ambassador in October 1958 that he

did not believe there was a danger of serious conflict breaking out. He said that capitalism was getting steadily weaker. Africa was the centre of the struggle between socialism and imperialism.

If we weren't strong . . . would it really be possible for Nasser, Sukarno, or the new government in Iraq . . . to hold on to power? The United States would send troops in . . . The Soviet Union will continue to fight stubbornly for peace, which we have especial need of for the next fifteen or twenty years. After that no one will be able to go to war even if he wants to. The United States doesn't yet want any relaxation in Europe because that would lead to a general relaxation, would weaken the system of American domination [and military alliances/bases] in vast areas around the world . . . and that would in turn produce political problems at home.

. . . He mentioned certain [recent] events [Suez, the Iraqi revolution, etc.] which were of special importance for the relation of forces on the world scene and said all of them had been bad for imperialism and the Americans.[110]

---

[109] *Khrushchev Remembers*, ii, pp. 439, 460.
[110] Micunovic, *Moscow Diary*, pp. 335–8, 342, 391, 431–2.

The Berlin question 1958–9

Khrushchev's next move came over Berlin. Since the Blockade the city had been administratively divided, with the Soviet sector under communist local government while the three Western sectors formed a unit with an elected mayor and senate. Each side was broadly assimilated into its own Germany; but the city remained open, with people passing readily from one side to the other, and was in law still subject to Four Power military occupation. Access from West Germany was governed by a complex of arrangements, written and unwritten. Land access was subject to periodic interference that could be alarming but that never in fact proved damaging; even after the USSR had in 1955 conceded independence to East Germany [the DDR], it continued to be run or supervised on a Four Power basis. Since the Blockade West German subsidies had built West Berlin into a showcase far richer than the East. But it could not have been maintained at this level by an airlift alone. Nor, despite a good deal of contingency planning, was there ever much likelihood of NATO forces being able to open the motorways across East Germany if the USSR really decided to close them. So, in the last analysis, the Western position in Berlin rested on Soviet restraint and/or on the ability of Western nuclear power to deter the USSR from taking (or allowing East Germany to take) any sustained disruptive action. To add to the difficulties, the West did not officially accept either the partition of Germany or the (undoubtedly unrepresentative) East German regime; and West Germany, which had now emerged as a key component of NATO, was adamant that this state of affairs should continue (even though it itself concluded *de facto* trade agreements with the DDR). Yet from 1958 onwards the USSR threatened to transfer all control over Berlin access to the DDR, which could then compel the West either to recognise it or to precipitate a blockade by refusing to accept DDR management of the access routes. 'When I go to sleep at night,' Secretary of State Dean Rusk was to say, 'I try not to think about Berlin.'

It is not entirely clear why Khrushchev decided to reopen the question in 1958. In his memoirs, he put the question in the light of what he saw as the unfair competition between the two Germanies in the struggle

to win the minds of the people by using culture and policies to create better living conditions . . .

. . . given the conditions that developed in the two German states, there was no real . . . choice . . . [since] West Germany was richer, with more industrial potential . . . It was hard for East Germany to compete.

> *. . . The West's goal was to turn West Berlin into what it called a mirror of Western life, a showcase for the capitalist world, in order to attract the people of East Berlin into resisting the steps towards socialism taken in the GDR.*
>
> *It was my dream to create such conditions in Germany that the GDR would become a showcase of moral, political and material achievement.*[111]

In pessimistic moments, indeed, the Soviet leadership feared the impact of the West German 'economic miracle', not only on East Berlin and the DDR, but also on Poland and Czechoslovakia. Nor was it happy with indications that West Germany might be pursuing nuclear weapons. 'If that happened without any Kremlin opposition,' Khrushchev's aide Troyanovsky later recalled, 'it was obvious that Khrushchev's prestige would plummet.'[112] To prevent this, and also to prove – in the context of burgeoning Chinese pressure – that he was neither 'soft' or 'naive' in dealing with the West, Khrushchev decided to bring things to a head.[113]

'Germany was a sort of barometer. The slightest fluctuation in the pressure of the world political atmosphere registered at the point where the forces of the two sides were squared off against each other.' So, by threatening to step on this American 'blister', Khrushchev hoped to end a situation where, despite a number of his informal personal overtures, there had been (in Troyanovsky's later words) 'no breakthrough' in East–West relations, with 'the situation . . . getting even worse.' By setting a time limit after which current Western access rights to West Berlin would lapse, unless renegotiated, Khrushchev could perhaps force a summit on his own terms – and thereby also gratify his by now insatiable appetite for foreign travel and wish to visit the USA. His colleagues had cold feet, but Khrushchev overrode their warnings. It would, he told his son, be perfectly safe, since 'no one would start a war over Berlin'. 'He intended to act in accord with circumstances and depending on our partners' reactions. He

---

[111] *Khrushchev Remembers*, iii, pp. 163–4; i, p. 419.

[112] Taubman, *Khrushchev*, pp. 403, 747n. The West German government had in fact displayed interest in a French–German–Italian nuclear project (above, p. 51); independently of this the *Bundeswehr* was being equipped with nuclear weapons (albeit subject to continued US control of their warheads, a safeguard the East tended to neglect or regard as unreal). Most scholars believe Khrushchev was concerned about its nuclearisation, though he did once doubt whether Adenauer would want nuclear weapons that would alarm not only the USSR but also many Western countries.

[113] Zubok and Pleshakov, *Inside the Kremlin's Cold War*, pp. 195–6, 199.

hoped to give them a good scare, and thereby extract their agreement to negotiate.' Should negotiations not work, 'Then we'll try something else. Something will always turn up.'[114]

In November 1958 the Soviet ambassador told Adenauer the USSR intended 'to liquidate the occupation statutes concerning Berlin'. The message was then spelt out in a long note: there should be general negotiations on a German peace treaty, and on the reconstitution of West Berlin as a Free City that would arrange 'guarantees of unhindered communications' with East Germany and in return 'commit itself not to tolerate on its territory hostile subversive activity' against that state; six months should be adequate for these negotiations; but if the time was not used to reach 'an appropriate agreement' the Soviet Union would sign a peace treaty with East Germany that would leave the latter in full control of all movement across its territory; the entire Warsaw Pact would support it in the event of any 'aggressive action' (i.e. Western attempt to enforce previous rights).[115] What really caused alarm was the fear that, by specifying a six months time limit, Khrushchev might have left himself no option but to take some drastic action if his wishes were not met. The Western reply (on 31 December) professed readiness for Four Power negotiations provided they were not conducted under time limits and threats of unilateral action. In January Mikoyan made soothing noises; but a Soviet note reiterated that Western refusal to negotiate would lead to a direct Soviet settlement with the DDR. Macmillan, the Western leader most alarmed by the crisis's potential for war and most anxious to revive summit diplomacy, then invited himself to Moscow for a personal exploratory visit (a move de Gaulle regarded as unwise, Adenauer as an electoral gimmick). During his visit Macmillan was accorded the classic friendly-hostile-then-again-friendly treatment; at its end Khrushchev agreed to shelve the time limit and accept negotiations initially at Foreign Minister level, while Macmillan appears to have promised to work for a summit.[116]

Foreign Ministers met in May in Geneva, where they continued (with intermissions) until August. Despite Eisenhower's threat to put them in a plane and keep them airborne until they settled, they failed to make progress – on Berlin, the broader German question, European military security, or an atomic test ban. On Berlin the Russians insisted on their 'free city' proposal, and went no further than offering the West the choice

---

[114] Taubman, *Khrushchev*, pp. 398–9.
[115] RIIA, *Documents 1958*, pp. 146–64.
[116] For Macmillan's promise, Eisenhower, *Memoirs*, ii, p. 401.

between withdrawing their garrisons altogether, replacing them with UN troops, or keeping them but adding a Soviet contingent; the USSR was also prepared to permit the current Western occupation to continue for a further eighteen months while the two Germanies worked out a peace treaty. The West rejected all these proposals; it was prepared to offer minor reductions in the size of its garrison, and to discuss the prohibition of intelligence and propaganda activities in West Berlin;[117] and it floated the idea of a Four Power Commission, advised by East and West Germany, to manage access to the city. Faced with this deadlock Eisenhower sent Khrushchev an invitation to visit the USA. The invitation was meant to be accompanied by an oral message making it conditional on progress at Geneva, but this was never delivered; so Khrushchev could accept the invitation (for which he had been angling since January) without making any concessions. Still, the fact that he was looking forward to touring the USA made any dangerous Soviet move unlikely in the meantime.

Khrushchev's visit to the USA 1959

Khrushchev's US tour in September 1959 was not without upsets – over the refusal to let him visit Disneyland for fear of assassination, and, more revealingly, a row with organised labour[118] – but in general it went well and his extrovert ebullience made a good impression. Public relations apart, by admiring the helicopter in which Eisenhower took him for a ride Khrushchev managed to purchase (and then copy) two such machines, whose export would otherwise have been embargoed; Eisenhower also gave him a couple of his own prize cattle. But Khrushchev was less impressed than Eisenhower had hoped with the American way of life – individual houses and cars were simply wasteful, while as for leisure motoring, 'Your people do not seem to like the place where they live and always want to be on the move going some place else.' Nor did they agree in discussions of disarmament or of ways to police a nuclear test ban. But

---

[117] Jack M. Schick, *The Berlin Crisis 1958–62* (Philadelphia, PA, 1971) esp. pp. 72–85. The renunciation of intelligence gathering (e.g. by radio monitoring) would have been a real loss to the West; that of 'propaganda activities' could conceivably have given the East some standing in West Berlin to determine what constituted 'propaganda'.

[118] The mainstream deliberately ignored him. He had a meeting with liberals like Walter Reuther, but it degenerated into a row over trade union and other civil liberties in the East – Khrushchev later remarked that 'We hanged the likes of Reuther in Russia in 1917'.

on Berlin Khrushchev lifted his deadline, while in return Eisenhower said the United States 'was not trying to perpetuate the situation' there, and agreed to attend a Four Power summit (and then visit the USSR) next year. Khrushchev returned to Moscow in what his son later termed a 'euphoric' mood, convinced that West Berlin and other questions would be settled there 'on an agreed basis'.[119]

In August 1959 Adenauer had conceded privately to Eisenhower 'that no one could or should carry on a nuclear war' over Berlin; so, though Khrushchev's proposals should at first be flatly rejected (since Adenauer did not believe 'the Soviets would let it come to war over Berlin'), 'For the most extreme emergency' the idea of converting Berlin into a free city 'must be carefully studied'.[120] Eisenhower was clearly drawn to this; for, he observed in March 1960 during preparations for the Chancellor's forthcoming visit, 'The Soviets and East Germans could observe the letter of existing commitments and still starve West Berlin'. He did not know 'what he could do if access to West Berlin were restricted for civil transit'; the 'Berlin situation' was 'something over which a war could occur'. So Eisenhower thought Germany 'would be better off with UN control of Berlin, with the UN guaranteeing access'. However, the US ambassador in Bonn had made it clear that West German opinion had hardened, with unusual unanimity, behind the view 'that any change in Berlin status can only be for worse'; he 'did not think it would be wise to push Adenauer too hard on the subject of Berlin'. Instead Eisenhower assured Adenauer 'the American flag would continue to fly over Berlin as long as . . . no agreement acceptable to the populations of West Berlin and West Germany had been concluded.'[121] The hope, the British were told, was that 'starting from this basis, it should be possible to consider realistically the various options open to the West'.[122] But essentially Adenauer had gained his point.

The Paris Summit and the U2 incident 1960

Arranging a summit took a long time, partly due to the *wanderlust* that seems to have seized all the principals. But there was growing agreement that the summit, when it came, would be merely the first of a series that

---

[119] *Khrushchev Remembers*, p. 37 and Chap. 16; Taubman, *Khrushchev*, pp. 415–16, 419 ff. (esp. 438–40, 448).
[120] *FRUS 1958–60*, ix, pp. 19, 23.
[121] ibid. pp. 217, 219–20, 660.
[122] ibid. p. 249. These options also included seeking an interim solution.

would rotate around the capitals of the Big Four. Macmillan was the principal proponent of such a system, hoping, rather unrealistically, that such meetings might eventually succeed, where the UN Security Council had failed, in regulating the major problems of the world. (He told Khrushchev he hoped to reach a position 'in which the four Heads of Government could sit down together . . . to make a start in solving those questions on which unhappily there are still differences of view between us. Such discussions are the only hope which I can see for progress for our peoples and for the world.')[123]

What the statesmen were actually going to say at these summits is less clear. For months Khrushchev had hyped his Camp David visit, his regard for Eisenhower, and his expectations for the summit. But by April 1960 his mood had changed, and he was again stressing obstacles. American speeches on Berlin had also hardened. Privately de Gaulle had appealed to Khrushchev, during his state visit to France, to let sleeping dogs lie; the current situation in Germany really did not threaten anybody.[124] Macmillan maintains that de Gaulle expected Khrushchev eventually to accept something along the lines the Western Foreign Ministers had proposed at the 1959 Geneva Conference, while Eisenhower hoped to get a Berlin settlement in exchange for promising to accept the Oder–Neisse line for ever.[125] De Gaulle paints a more lurid picture: on the eve of the summit he found the Anglo-Saxons inclined to compensate for Eisenhower's U2 gaffe by making concessions, with Macmillan leaning towards troop withdrawals and the reconstitution of West Berlin as a free city under UN guarantee. However, he persuaded them that abandoning Berlin in the current state of tension would have disastrous consequences, and that attempts to resolve the German question could only be fruitful after detente and cooperation had been restored.[126]

In the event the U2 incident shipwrecked the summit before it had really started. Ever since the onset of the Cold War the Pentagon had been alarmed by its ignorance of what was going on inside the USSR and had sought both general intelligence and the ability to monitor the rise

[123] Macmillan, *Memoirs*, v, pp. 105, 107, 114, 188, 199.

[124] *Khrushchev Remembers*, ii, pp. 441–2; Charles de Gaulle, *Memoirs of Hope* (1971) pp. 226–9.

[125] Macmillan, *Memoirs*, v, pp. 191, 193. To oblige the Federal Republic, the West had hitherto withheld recognition of Poland's 1945 acquisition of the lands east of the Oder–Neisse line.

[126] De Gaulle, *Memoirs of Hope*, p. 249 (cf. also pp. 222–4); Eisenhower recalled 'no major disagreements' on Berlin, Macmillan that 'no one got down to brass tacks'.

of day-to-day military activity that would presage a sudden attack. This concern had led, between 1949 and 1954, to the overflights and parachuting in of agents that we have already noticed. After their discontinuance, planning turned instead to the development of a spy plane that could fly so high as to be invulnerable; and from 1956 to 1960 the CIA conducted some twenty such U2 overflights, which the USSR could detect but not shoot down. All were personally authorised by the President, who valued them as reassurance that the much-vaunted Soviet lead in missiles did not exist, and who also saw such a capability as essential to monitor any nuclear test ban that might be negotiated. Eisenhower was, however, cautious, the CIA thought too cautious,[127] in authorising such flights, and aware that they could have disastrous diplomatic consequences – in February 1960 'The President said that he has one tremendous asset in a summit meeting . . . his reputation for honesty. If one of these aircraft were lost when we are engaged in apparently sincere deliberations, it could be put on display in Moscow and ruin the President's effectiveness.'[128] This is exactly what happened.

A flight on the last permitted day before the summit, 1 May, was shot down, and the plane and pilot recovered more or less intact. Khrushchev trapped the Americans, by announcing the shooting but displaying a photograph of the wrong type of plane. Believing the U2 would have auto-destructed, the US made disingenuous statements about weather research and accidental violation of Soviet territory, whereupon Khrushchev put on show both plane and pilot. At one level, he was enjoying the game. At another, he was working off the humiliation of the USSR's inability to prevent past overflights. Lastly, he hoped Eisenhower would respond by denying all knowledge and blaming rogue elements in the US military; this would enable Khrushchev to embark on the summit from a position of strength. Instead Eisenhower admitted on 11 May that he had personally authorised the overflights, which, while 'distasteful', were (given Soviet secretiveness) needed to ensure against another Pearl Harbor. This seems to have left Khrushchev in two minds about the summit. But on the flight to Paris, he told his aides he would demand a personal apology from Eisenhower as a prerequisite for further discussions, and that this would probably collapse the summit. Although it now belatedly emerged

[127] Ranelagh, *The Agency*, pp. 31–48. To circumvent Eisenhower's caution the CIA transferred some U2s to Britain to operate independently. U2s were also flown over China by the Nationalists.

[128] Ambrose, *Eisenhower. The President*, p. 568.

that Eisenhower had called the U2 programme off, neither Macmillan nor de Gaulle could dissuade Khrushchev; and that was the end of the conference.[129]

There was, however, one side-effect. De Gaulle asked Khrushchev how he distinguished between the U2 overflight and the much vaunted tran-siting of France eighteen times a day by Soviet satellites that probably also contained cameras; Khrushchev could only protest that the two cases were quite different, adding (according to Eisenhower) that any country was welcome to photograph the Soviet Union from satellites.[130] Satellite photography would, of course, have come anyway – there was then no way of shooting satellites down, and the US programme was well advanced, becoming fully operational in 1961. But it was from the outset regarded as internationally acceptable; and the superpower arms limitation agree-ments of the 1970s were explicitly postulated on such 'national technical means of verification'. The USSR still rejected on-site inspection, but it was sometimes at pains to facilitate satellite photography that would reassure the US it was not cheating.

The summit's collapse undoubtedly poisoned the international atmo-sphere. In June a major KGB 'dirty tricks' programme was approved to discredit Alan Dulles personally and the CIA generally. In the autumn Khrushchev attended the UN General Assembly to press his anti-imperialist message, arriving in the Port of New York to a virulent reception from the longshoremen ('Roses are red, Violets are blue, Stalin dropped dead, How about You?'). While there he distinguished himself by boorish and unparliamentary behaviour in the UN sessions, though whether he actually interrupted a Filipino attack on Soviet imperialism in Eastern Europe by banging his shoe on the table is still debated.[131]

Nevertheless, Khrushchev had not given up on diplomacy, only on Eisenhower. Indeed, even on the way home from Paris, he told an East German audience that he 'would like to believe that a summit conference will be held in six to eight months [i.e. with Eisenhower's successor]. Under the circumstances, it makes sense to wait a little longer'.[132] Meanwhile Gromyko was promising Western Foreign Ministers there would be no unilateral action against West Berlin. The East Germans,

[129] Taubman, *Khrushchev*, esp. pp. 455–67.
[130] Eisenhower, *Memoirs*, ii, p. 556.
[131] Vladislav Zubok, 'Spy vs. Spy: The KGB vs. the CIA, 1960–1962', CWIHP *Bulletin*, iv (Fall 1994) pp. 25–7; Taubman, *Khrushchev*, pp. 473–9, 657.
[132] Taubman, *Khrushchev*, p. 467.

however, were becoming impatient. In October their talk about closing the border between East and West Berlin alarmed the Soviet embassy. But their position was weakened by their vulnerability to the cut-off of West German trade they expected would follow the signature of a Soviet–East German treaty; to counter this they asked for massive Soviet aid (including a quite unacceptable 68 tons of gold). The upshot was a meeting between Khrushchev and Ulbricht on 30 November, at which it was agreed that the DDR's economy should be disengaged from West Germany's and integrated instead into that of the 'socialist camp'. East Germany would take no precipitate action. But Khrushchev undertook to settle the Berlin question in 1961. He would offer an interim agreement, at the end of which Western rights would lapse and the USSR sign a peace treaty with East Germany. Were this refused, the USSR would proceed directly to an East German treaty, and 'work out with you a tactic of gradual ousting of the Western powers from West Berlin, but without war'.[133]

The Vienna Summit 1961

In February 1961 the USSR declared that the Berlin question could not wait till after the West German elections in September. In March the Kennedy administration indicated that it was approaching Berlin *de novo*, so was not bound by the concessions offered at Geneva in 1959 (or contemplated for Paris in 1960).[134] There ensued a round of intense US and Western planning. Kennedy had already suggested a summit to Khrushchev; and in May, after his Bay of Pigs bungle over a guerrilla invasion of Cuba (below, p. 266), Moscow took him up on this and it was agreed to meet in June in Vienna.[135]

Kennedy was briefed that there would 'probably be considerable flexibility' in Khrushchev's position. This is odd, as Khrushchev had stressed to the US ambassador that 'when we have the [East German] peace treaty signed, we will in no way tolerate the existing regime in Berlin . . . access etc. will . . . be allowed only in accordance with agreements with the GDR.' Khrushchev told his colleagues that 'Apparently, we will

---

[133] Hope M. Harrison, *Ulbricht and the concrete 'Rose': new archival evidence on the dynamics of Soviet-East German relations and the Berlin crisis, 1958–1961* (CWIHP Working Paper no. 5 – Washington, DC, 1993) pp. 27–31 and Appendices A to C.

[134] Blechman and Kaplan, *Force without War*, pp. 348, 409.

[135] Harrison, *Ulbricht and the concrete 'Rose'*, p. 37; Vladislav Zubok, *Khrushchev and the Berlin Crisis (1958–62)*, (CWIHP Working Paper 6) pp. 17–19.

not be able to come to an agreement . . .' 'They will threaten us with war – and, of course, they do now.' Neither West Germany, France nor the UK would wish to unleash a war, since they knew 'the greatest detonation of nuclear weapons' would be on their territory. But the Americans were another matter:

their decisions are not based on logic, they are made under the influence of some groups and the combination of random phenomena . . .

Therefore, I think that . . . there is a [small] risk and the risk that we are taking is justified [as] there is more than a 95 per cent probability that there will be no war . . .

. . . Our position is very strong, but of course we will have to really intimidate them now. For example, if there is any flying around, we will have to bring airplanes down. Could they respond with a provocative act? They could. [But] if we don't bring the plane down, this would mean that we are capitulating. I think that they will put up with it . . .

In a word, politics is politics. If we want to carry out our policy . . . it is necessary to be firm.

On his way to Vienna, Khrushchev told Czech leaders 'we are 95 per cent sure that there will not be a war because of West Berlin', and put the chance of the USA breaking off relations at 30 per cent; Lenin had taken greater risks.[136]

The Vienna Summit went badly. Kennedy had been advised to avoid discussing ideology. But his claims that there were geopolitical changes neither side could accept exposed him to a lecture on the impossibility of blocking historical evolution; there followed an explosion when Kennedy warned, as Khrushchev believed patronisingly, of the dangers of 'miscalculation'. That apart, Kennedy had two specific concerns, Laos and the conversion of the 1958 moratorium into a nuclear test ban treaty. On the former Khrushchev proved relatively unconcerned, and agreeable to the Soviet–American–British diplomatic coordination that was temporarily to resolve that country's crisis (below, pp. 291–2). But though promising not to be the first to resume testing, he showed no immediate interest in the treaty. He had, in fact, told the Czechs, 'We will not agree to this now.'

---

[136] Praesidium meeting, 26 May 1961 (http:/millercenter.virginia.edu/pubs/Kremlin_steno.pdf) pp. 2–5; 1 June 1961, 'Notes on the meeting of N.S. Khrushchev with Leading Representatives of the Central Committee of . . . Czechoslovakia . . .' (www.ethz.ch/php/documents/collection_8/docs/KhrSmolenice_610601.htm) pp. 2–5.

What he wanted to talk about was Berlin. Over this, tempers flared, with Khrushchev saying that 'Perhaps the USSR should sign a peace treaty [with the DDR] and get it over with.' Then, if the USA wanted to start a war over Germany, 'let it begin now' rather than later when weapons had become still more horrible. In a final session, Kennedy warned against presenting the USA 'with a situation so deeply involving our interests'; Khrushchev responded that 'the US wants to humiliate the USSR and this cannot be accepted'. He offered a face-saving two-year interim agreement, but thereafter US rights would lapse. To Kennedy this seemed a choice between American retreat and confrontation. Khrushchev replied that 'if the US wanted war, that was its problem'; if it refused an interim agreement, the USSR would sign the peace treaty in December. Kennedy had the last word: 'If that's true, it's going to be a cold winter.'[137]

Kennedy emerged from the conference dazed: 'I never met a man like this . . . [I] talked about how a nuclear exchange would kill seventy million people in ten minutes and he just looked at me as if to say, "So what?" ' He believed Khrushchev regarded him as weak, and was challenging him accordingly. It took until 25 July to formulate the US position, a hard one, though less so than Acheson had originally suggested. Kennedy professed himself ready for further negotiations, but depicted the Soviet approach as 'what's mine is mine and what's yours is negotiable'. 'We cannot and we will not permit the communists to drive us out of Berlin, either gradually or by force'; and he announced enhanced military measures to prevent it.

Khrushchev was now worried in his turn: 'When our "friend" Dulles was alive, there was more stability'; he 'would reach the brink . . . but he would never leap over the brink, and still retained his credibility,' whereas if Kennedy drew back 'he will be called a coward'; he might be 'too much of a light-weight' to control 'the dark forces' in his enormously powerful state machine.[138] At one level this simply inspired Khrushchev to ratchet up the tension by planning the biggest nuclear explosion ever: 'We have to conduct our policies from a position of strength . . . Our opponents don't understand any other language.' Privately, though, he was, his son says,

---

[137] Taubman, *Khrushchev*, pp. 496–500; Zubok and Pleshakov, *Inside the Kremlin's Cold War*, pp. 243–8; H.M. Catudal, *Kennedy and the Berlin Wall Crisis* (Berlin, 1980) pp. 114–18.
[138] Taubman, *Khrushchev*, pp. 500, 502; Zubok, *Khrushchev and the Berlin Crisis*, pp. 21–2; Zubok and Pleshakov, *Inside the Kremlin's Cold War*, pp. 252–3; Khrushchev had similarly praised Dulles to his Praesidium and to the Czechs.

'far less resolute than he seemed on television'. For, Dobrynin maintains, he feared war

and never considered a possibility of one waged over Germany or other international issues.

This check on Khrushchev's temper was never fully understood in the West. An unnecessary fear of war over Berlin affected US diplomacy for many years, starting with Kennedy himself.[139]

The Berlin Wall and its sequel, 1961–2

Failing an agreement, Khrushchev had proposed waiting until December before concluding a treaty with the DDR. But meanwhile matters were getting out of control on the ground, with a sharp increase in the number of East German refugees. These were disproportionately young, male, educated, and therefore economically valuable. Almost all came through Berlin, since the DDR's other borders were controlled; and the more Khrushchev pressed the Berlin issue, the greater the rush to get out while there was still time – *Torschlußpanik*.[140] By 1961 this exodus may have come to threaten the viability of the DDR; by July 1961 Ulbricht was sending messages to the effect that 'if the present system of open borders remains, collapse is inevitable' and that 'he refuses all responsibility for what would then happen'.[141]

With hindsight it would seem that Khrushchev concluded from a careful reading of Kennedy's speeches, and perhaps from KGB informants, that the United States really would go nuclear to defend West Berlin but *not* the undivided status of the city as a whole; and Kennedy had indeed directed military reaction only if 'our presence in' or 'our access' to West

---

[139] Lawrence Freedman, *Kennedy's Wars. Berlin, Cuba, Laos, and Vietnam* (New York, 2000) p. 71; Taubman, *Khrushchev*, pp. 503, 506; Anatoly Dobrynin, *In Confidence: Moscow's Ambassador to America's six Cold War Presidents (1962–1986)* (New York, 1995) p. 45 – the nuclear tests were actually staged in September–October.

[140] Refugee numbers went from 10,000 a month in September 1958 (before the crisis) to: 140,000 in 1959; 200,000 in 1960; 80,000 (January–May 1961); 20,000 (June); over 30,000 (July), and 20,000 (1–12 August) – Catudal, *Kennedy and the Berlin Wall*, pp. 23, 29, 48, 164; Schick, *The Berlin Crisis*, p. 159; R.M. Slusser, in Blechman and Kaplan, *Force without War*, p. 347.

[141] Harrison, *Ulbricht and the concrete 'Rose'*, p. 47; Western intelligence, though, suspected that the East Germans might actually be encouraging the flight so as to build up their case for immediate Soviet action (ibid. p. 35).

Berlin were threatened.[142] The DDR had long been pressing for movement between East and West Berlin to be controlled, and Khrushchev suddenly had his ambassador tell Ulbricht to work out (with the Soviet military commander and diplomats) ways of effecting this. Ulbricht brought the plans to Moscow, where (by one account) Khrushchev vetoed the idea of closing the air corridors out of West Berlin. The general situation was discussed at a Warsaw Pact meeting of 3–5 August 1961. Here, in response to another desperate plea by Ulbricht for the refugee flood to be curbed, Khrushchev is reported (by the same source) as having authorised him to erect barriers within Berlin at the sectoral border – 'but not one millimeter further'.[143] In the early hours of Sunday 13 August the East Germans strung barbed wire along the border, catching the West completely by surprise (as the crisis had not been expected to break until September). Kennedy was not reached for a good eight hours; he then instructed Secretary of State Rusk to make a statement but do nothing to aggravate the situation further – 'Go to the ball game as you had planned, I am going sailing'.[144]

West Berlin politicians felt let down by the sluggish and low-key Western response. Intellectually they knew there was no deep commitment to the undivided nature of the city – Brandt's Press Secretary, Egon Bahr, is said to have exclaimed over NATO's May 1961 reaffirmation of rights in West Berlin, 'That is almost an invitation to the Soviets to do what they want with the Eastern sector'.[145] Nor did they have any constructive suggestions beyond measures to boost West Berliners' confidence. But they had never really expected the 'West' to allow itself to be so pushed around. As the then Mayor, Willy Brandt, later put it:

We lost illusions . . . Ulbricht had been allowed to take a swipe at the Western super-power, and the United States merely winced with

---

[142] Andrew and Gordievsky, *KGB*, p. 368; Catudal, *Kennedy and the Berlin Wall Crisis*, pp. 175, 244–5. It has been alleged that an arrangement was secretly worked out with Khrushchev in late July (through a private visit by John McCloy, the former US High Commissioner in Germany); but the claim is backed by no evidence and does not fit McCloy's cabled report of the meeting (ibid., pp. 198–200).

[143] Zubok, *Khrushchev and the Berlin Crisis*, pp. 22–4; Harrison, *Ulbricht and the concrete 'Rose'*, pp. 47–50, Appendices G, H, I; Catudal, *Kennedy and the Berlin Wall*, pp. 208–12 – the authority for Khrushchev's vetoing the closing of the air corridors and for his 'not one millimeter further' is the controversial Czech defector, General Séjna.

[144] Catudal, *Kennedy and the Berlin Wall*, p. 38.

[145] ibid. p. 145.

annoyance. My political deliberations in the years that followed were substantially influenced by this day's experience, and it was against this background that my so-called Ostpolitik – the beginning of detente – took shape . . . My new and inescapable realization was that traditional patterns of Western policy had proved ineffective, if not downright unrealistic.[146]

Inevitably there have been suggestions that the West should have reacted more strongly, that if its troops had simply torn down the barbed wire they would not have been resisted. One cannot know for certain, but I doubt it.[147] Anyway no interference was attempted. The wire progressively hardened into a Wall, the concrete embodiment of the division of Europe, guarded by troops who right up to 1989 shot would-be escapers, and shown off to Western visitors and (surprisingly) also by Ulbricht to Eastern delegations.

Tension did not subside after the erection of the Wall. In the autumn the USSR broke the 1958 moratorium with a sequence of fifteen massive nuclear tests. September also saw – as a gesture to reassure the West Berliners – the appointment as US Commander of General Clay, the hero of the Blockade; he alarmed the Soviets by rehearsing the bulldozing of a replica of the Wall. On 27 October he deployed US tanks at Checkpoint Charlie to maintain the vestigial rights of Western military personnel freely to enter and drive around East Berlin; the Soviets replied in kind, and for two days tanks faced each other in the most dramatic moment of the crisis before back-channel negotiations secured their phased withdrawal.[148] Earlier, in late August, Moscow had threatened to interrupt air access to the city and drawn an immediate warning from the White House. The air corridors were accordingly never closed, but there was a good deal of harassment of Western airliners, declining in late 1961 but resuming in February–March 1962 with Soviet military flights in the corridor (partly to influence the negotiations then in progress).

---

[146] W. Brandt, *People and Politics: The Years 1960–1975* (1978) p. 20.

[147] Apparently the East German troops actually erecting the wire had no ammunition. Beyond that there are different stories. Séjna says Khrushchev gave instructions that, if interfered with, they should drop back up to 300 metres, trying again each 100 metres; at 300 metres they should await the arrival of Soviet troops. The *Penkovskiy Papers* (another problematic source) claims that there was fear of an East German rising, but also preparations to fight over Berlin if necessary, initially with DDR troops but, if they failed, also with Soviet ones.

[148] Freedman, *Kennedy's Wars*, pp. 89–91.

Discussions of the Berlin problem were quietly resumed in the autumn, though Kennedy rejected a Soviet offer to guarantee access to West Berlin if the US signed a treaty recognising the DDR; and in October 1961 Khrushchev withdrew his December deadline for concluding a unilateral treaty with the DDR. In December NATO formally agreed, over French opposition, on active negotiations, which were pursued at various forums – notably the fringes of the perennial Geneva disarmament conference in March 1962. But West Germany became increasingly stubborn, and the Soviet position also hardened. As one official remarked of the final meeting, 'They really just keep going round in circles.' Tension accordingly rose in the summer with further incidents. And in September a Soviet note again stressed the necessity, 'at long last, to liquidate the occupation regime in West Berlin on the basis of signing a German peace treaty' and withdrawing Western troops. Kennedy responded by seeking Congressional authority to mobilise 150,000 reserve soldiers. But the Russians then indicated that they would not propose new Berlin negotiations till after the November Congressional elections.

By then they expected to have in place in Cuba missiles that could, for the first time, provide a credible capability to mount nuclear strikes on the United States. Khrushchev let it be known that he proposed to address the UN in November, and that he hoped then to reach agreement with Kennedy on West Berlin; the assumption is that he meant to reveal the changed balance of power and make new demands on the subjects currently in contention.[149] In fact the United States discovered the missiles while they were still being secretly installed, and forced their withdrawal. In so doing the USA had the advantage of overwhelming local military supremacy, and the ability to impose a naval blockade on Cuba. But it was always aware the USSR could retaliate by interfering with access to Berlin, where it enjoyed a comparable superiority. Kennedy's speech announcing the blockade sought to head this off: 'Any hostile move anywhere in the world against the safety and freedom of peoples to whom we are committed – including in particular the brave people of West Berlin – will be met by whatever action is needed.' A counter-blockade of Berlin was nevertheless proposed, but Khrushchev slapped it down: 'We're just beginning

---

[149] Berlin; Germany; a nuclear-free zone in the two Germanies that would eliminate the tactical nuclear weapons on which NATO relied; troop disengagement; nuclear testing and inspection; probably also Cuba; the Congo, and the structure of the UN. For different views on the 1962 Berlin negotiations, see e.g. Freedman, *Kennedy's Wars*, Chap. 12 and Taubman, *Khrushchev*, pp. 537–41.

to get ourselves out of one adventure, and you're suggesting we climb into another.'[150] Berlin remained quiet throughout the Cuba crisis; and its resolution ushered in a period of detente, during which the Berlin issue gradually receded from the centre-stage of world politics. Minor incidents continued, as did interferences with access (particularly when official West German functions were staged in West Berlin). But the city's situation came increasingly to be accepted by all parties as routine – artificial and undesirable no doubt, but not something that could readily be changed. Moreover, once the Wall had ended the East German exodus, the Ulbricht regime recovered confidence and managed to restore and develop the economy, if not to anything like West German standards at least as the wealthiest per capita in Eastern Europe. The DDR had come to stay, and the next phase in the unfolding of the German question (see Chapter 7) would be West Germany's gradual accommodation to that fact.

Latin America in the 1950s: the Cuban revolution

I have suggested that the Cuban missile crisis was, with the erection of the Wall, the chief factor in the resolution of the Berlin crisis. It was also probably the most dramatic post-war crisis, and arguably the only one where one superpower was seeking not simply to deter the other from taking action but rather to compel the retraction of action already taken. To understand the background, we need to glance briefly at earlier history. Since the 1820s it had been a fixed aim of United States policy (enshrined in the Monroe Doctrine) to exclude from the Americas external rule or military involvement. The USA had taken advantage of both World Wars to acquire insular possessions and military bases that would keep hostile forces at a distance. Early in the Second World War it had successfully organised most of Latin America to extrude fascist influence and penetration. After 1945 it was equally anxious to keep out 'international communism'. This was, at first, even easier, since communism had few governmental sympathisers. The isolation of Latin American politics from East–West rivalry is very striking: Colombia was devastated, between 1948 and 1958 (or 1962), by the *violencia*, civil disorder that cost some 200,000 lives; but though local communists are accused of having exacerbated it, there is general agreement that it was basically a struggle between the Liberals and the Conservatives, leading eventually to agreement that

---

[150] Schick, *The Berlin Crisis*, p. 219; Taubman, *Khrushchev*, p. 538.

they should alternate in office for sixteen years from 1958.[151] To Washington the *violencia* appeared less threatening than the leftwards trend in Guatemala, which Eisenhower's brother reported as having 'succumbed to Communist infiltration'; if the Soviets ever obtained a base there, they could export subversion and revolution to neighbouring countries. 'My God,' Eisenhower remarked, 'just think what it would mean to us if Mexico went Communist.'[152] To foreclose such a possibility, he covertly helped install a new military regime in Guatemala.[153]

Washington may have been too prone to see reds under the bed in Guatemala. Surprisingly it was not ready enough to see them in Cuba. Early in 1958 the authoritarian Batista regime had seemed reasonably in control. It was faced with urban terrorism (which it handled brutally) and a diaspora of small guerrilla groups in the mountains, mostly traditional bandits but including a few hundred men under Fidel Castro who had emerged (through skilful publicity and the division and discrediting of more orthodox politicians) as the leading opposition figure. Batista had enjoyed widespread sympathy after the assault on his palace in 1957, and as late as April 1958 the opposition's call for a general strike was a complete failure. But when Batista followed this up with a major assault on Castro's Sierra Maestra stronghold, first his army and then his regime disintegrated without any very serious fighting. Parts of the US administration had for some time been anxious to edge Batista out. But the exercise was badly handled, probably because it was not accorded priority or high-level political attention – in December 1958 Eisenhower was obviously not au fait with the Cuban situation.[154] When Batista was finally pressured into leaving on 1 January 1959, there had still been no clear US planning for the succession. This therefore fell into Castro's lap.

Historians are still divided as to when and why Castro became communist. The usual view is that, during his rebellion against Batista, he had had no distinctive views on government beyond a general liberal nationalism. Between January 1959 and early 1961 he decided, probably by stages, that, in the face of internal opposition and US economic pressure, he could best conduct his revolution by taking over, and then working through,

[151] *Encyclopaedia Britannica*; Richard Gott, *Rural Guerrillas in Latin America* (Harmondsworth, 1973) Part 3.

[152] Ambrose, *Eisenhower. The President*, pp. 192, 197.

[153] Post-1945 Latin America is more fully discussed in *The Post-Imperial Age*, Chap. 16.

[154] Ambrose, *Eisenhower. The President*, p. 505.

the Communist Party. From December 1961 onwards, however, Castro was to proclaim that he had always been at least loosely Marxist-Leninist but had disguised these views in order to seize power. Partly, though not entirely, on the basis of such retrospective information, Tad Szulc argues that at the January 1959 takeover Castro paralleled the new official administration with a 'hidden government', the Office of Revolutionary Plans and Coordination.[155] Whatever the truth, by November 1959 Castro's domestic nationalisations, stridently anti-USA tone at the United Nations, and subversion elsewhere in Latin America had alarmed Washington. And in March 1960 Eisenhower approved the creation of 'a paramilitary force outside of Cuba for future guerrilla action', while planning also started (later that year) for Castro's assassination.[156]

The Bay of Pigs 1961

Little had come of all this by the time Kennedy succeeded Eisenhower in January 1961. But Cuban emigrés were receiving military training in Guatemala, and their morale would suffer if they were not used soon. Kennedy thus inherited a bad situation, and soon made it worse. He decided to go ahead with the invasion (in April); but he tinkered with the plan's details, moving the proposed landing site to the Bay of Pigs (an unsuitable choice). Worse still, when the cover story for the preliminary CIA bombing of the Cuban air force fell apart, Kennedy refused to authorise the second strike that would have completed the job. The landing was accordingly shot up by the surviving Cuban planes, and the forces that came ashore destroyed by the unexpectedly rapid deployment of the Cuban army. Kennedy's refusal to provide proper air cover stemmed, as he later explained to Eisenhower, from a fear that 'if it was learned that we [the United States] were really doing this rather than these rebels, the Soviets would be very apt to cause trouble in Berlin'. Eisenhower regarded this as ridiculous: US involvement in so large an invasion could never have been hidden; the Soviets would have respected such a show of strength, but

---

[155] Hugh Thomas, *Cuba or the Pursuit of Freedom* (1971) *passim*; Tad Szulc, *Fidel. A Critical Portrait* (New York, 1986) esp. pp. 472–80.
[156] Stephen Rabe, *Eisenhower and Latin America. The Foreign Policy of Anticommunism* (Chapel Hill, N.C., 1988) Chaps 7, 9; Ranelagh, *The Agency*, p. 357; Szulc, *Fidel*, p. 672; Ambrose, *Eisenhower. The President*, p. 557; Powers, *The man who kept the secrets*, pp. 186–92.

would now probably be emboldened 'to do something that they would otherwise not do'.[157]

The Cuban missile crisis 1962[158]

The Bay of Pigs fiasco did not end US attempts to topple Castro. Over the next eighteen months Washington was constantly turning over schemes for assassination, the creation of economic difficulties, or the encourage- ment of insurrection. There was more talk than action, and on the ground 'Operation Mongoose' amounted to little more than isolated acts of sabotage and the creation of a limited intelligence network. But Robert Kennedy's talk, in particular, was often extreme; military plans were drafted to make possible rapid intervention (for instance in support of a Cuban insurrection), and large amphibious landing exercises were staged in April 1962. The USSR's intelligence evaluation seems to have been quite restrained, but Castro naturally pressed for the stationing of defensive Soviet troops.[159]

In May Khrushchev decided to go one better, sending to Cuba not only defensive forces but also nuclear missiles capable of targeting the major cities of the eastern USA. To do so, he overrode both his colleagues' muted caution and Castro's own reluctance to accept such offensive weapons. There have been many interpretaions of Khrushchev's motives, probably all to some extent true.[160] His message of May 1962 to Castro was

---

[157] Freedman, *Kennedy's Wars*, Chaps 14, 15; Ambrose, *Eisenhower. The President*, pp. 608–10, 638–9. Eisenhower told Kennedy that 'when you go into this kind of thing' 'It must be a success'; but, unlike Nixon, he warned that only in exceptional circum- stances would the American people approve direct military invasion of Cuba by their own forces.

[158] Following the end of the Cold War, this crisis, as its most dramatic moment, generated innumerable conferences, memoirs, and books. Perhaps the best treatments are Aleksandr Fursenko and Timothy Naftali, *'One Hell of a Gamble'. Khrushchev, Castro, Kennedy and the Cuban Missile Crisis 1958–64* (1997); Freedman, *Kennedy's Wars*, Part 3; and Taubman, *Khrushchev*, Chap. 19.

[159] Freedman, *Kennedy's Wars*, Chaps 16, 17; Fursenko and Naftali, *'One Hell of a Gamble'*, pp. 149–60, 166, 179.

[160] *'One Hell of a Gamble'*, pp. 182–3 lists: papering 'over the USSR's strategic inferi- ority'; concern 'about the likelihood of an American invasion'; 'anger at the American decision to station Jupiter missiles in Turkey'; 'an attempt to guarantee the [pro-Soviet as opposed to pro-Chinese] status quo in Cuba and to prevent any attempt by the Chinese to dislodge him from the leadership of international communism'.

essentially that 'an attack on Cuba is being prepared. The correlation of forces is unfavorable to us, and the only way to save Cuba is to put missiles there.' Being 'intelligent', Kennedy 'would not set off a thermonuclear war if there were our warheads there, just as they put their warheads on missiles in Turkey . . . [that] are aimed at us and scare us.'[161] After the event, it was naturally this motivation that Khrushchev stressed.

But it is hard to believe that was all. In late 1961 the USA had called the bluff of Khrushchev's constant boasts that his rockets had given the USSR at least nuclear parity: Defense Secretary McNamara claimed 'nuclear power several times that of the Soviet Union'. In February 1962 Marshal Malinovsky confirmed this to Khrushchev: a Soviet ICBM took hours to prepare, and 'Before we get it ready to launch, there won't be even a wet spot left of any of us.' Khrushchev asked his Defence Council 'to think about the amount of time it would take to catch up with the Americans'. In April he himself came up with a solution: 'what if we throw a hedgehog down Uncle Sam's pants?' Over May and June plans were finalised for the despatch to Cuba of 36 1,200–mile and 24 2,200–mile rockets, plus nuclear-equipped bombers, to be accompanied by air defence missiles, combat troops, and 'tactical' nuclear missiles.[162]

Khrushchev further insisted that the whole deployment be kept secret until (after the US Congressional elections in November) he visited the UN and revealed the *fait accompli*; hopefully he could then, from this position of strength, strike a deal with Kennedy over Berlin, and so confound his Chinese critics. Castro told his representatives to ask, 'what would happen if the operation were discovered while it was in progress?' But Khrushchev avoided discussion; almost certainly he had not thought things through.[163] He may have believed that the US would never permit any open reinforcement of Cuba; and the USSR gave copious assurances that 'no missile capable of reaching the United States will be placed in Cuba'.[164] The revelation of these lies gravely damaged the USSR's position in the subsequent crisis.

[161] ibid. p. 182. The 15 Jupiters in Turkey were (prematurely) reported as operational by Malinovsky in April 1962; 30 were based in Italy the previous year. There had also been 60 Thors in the UK following a 1957 agreement; but they were removed in the second half of 1962 – Raymond L. Garthoff, *Reflections on the Cuban Missile Crisis* (Washington, 1987) p. 43n; Taubman, *Khrushchev*, p. 541.
[162] Freedman, *Kennedy's Wars*, pp. 83–5; Taubman, *Khrushchev*, pp. 537, 541, 547.
[163] ibid. pp. 539, 552–3.
[164] Garthoff, *The Cuban Missile Crisis*, p. 27; Philip Knightley and Peter Pringle, 'The Cuban Missile Crisis 1962', *The Independent*, 5 and 6 October 1992, p. 19.

But the attempt to proceed secretly was very nearly successful; for most Americans were convinced, even after the detection of anti-aircraft missiles, that the USSR would never embark on anything so foolhardy. One exception was the new head of the CIA, McCone. From his honeymoon in Paris he badgered Washington with telegrams; but it was reluctant to risk the loss of another U2 – one was shot down over China in September – and western Cuba was left unsurveyed from 5 September to 14 October 1962. Ultimately McCone got his flight; and early on 16 October Kennedy was presented with clear evidence of the presence of Soviet ballistic missiles.[165]

The next few days were spent deciding what to do, in the knowledge that little time remained before the missiles became operational. Acquiescence was ruled out by Kennedy's earlier statements,[166] and would not anyway have been tolerated by US public opinion. The idea of taking the question up privately with Khrushchev was considered, but it seemed impossible to draft a letter that would be forceful enough to be effective without at the same time provoking a crisis.[167] There remained only the options of direct or indirect action. Many were attracted to the idea of simply bombing the missile sites. But it became clear that this would not be easy: it would kill appreciable numbers of the Russians working on them; some missiles might be missed; and if any were already armed, it might provide an incentive to fire them. In any case it might lead to a Soviet response, and thence escalate via US reprisals into the full-scale war that neither side originally wanted – in Kennedy's view the First World War had begun like this.[168] Alternatively the US might invade Cuba; this would encounter the same difficulties on a larger scale, but would (if resolutely

---

[165] McCone suspected that the SAMs were there to protect something even more valuable; he may also have been primed by French intelligence – Knightley and Pringle, *Independent*, 5 October 1992; G.T. Allison, *Essence of Decision. Explaining the Cuban Missile Crisis* (Boston, 1971) pp. 190–2, 317n.

[166] Less because he then believed it to be necessary than to head off pre-election claims that he was covering up the existence of missiles there, Kennedy had twice warned that he would not permit Cuba to 'become an offensive military base of significant capacity'. This was reinforced by Congressional resolutions and by a statement by 20 Latin American Foreign Ministers – Garthoff, *The Cuban Missile Crisis*, pp. 14–19.

[167] ibid. pp. 28–9.

[168] He had been reading Barbara Tuchman's *The Guns of August*. The other influential analogy was 1941 – for opponents of a sudden air strike labelled it 'a Pearl Harbor in reverse', a course alien to all America's traditions and history – Allison, *Essence of Decision*, pp. 217–18, 197.

proceeded with) eliminate the Castro problem once and for all. Inevitably there were inconsistent shifts of position, but the general tendency was for attitudes to soften as discussion proceeded; most importantly this was true of Kennedy himself. The final decision was to prepare to stage an invasion and to place Strategic Air Command on high alert to deter the Russians, but first to try the effect of indirect action in the form of a blockade.

So on 22 October Kennedy announced the imposition of a 'quarantine' under which the US Navy would check all cargoes for Cuba.[169] He also embarked on a public relations campaign and the briefing of allies and neutrals. Partly because the USSR persisted (at the UN and elsewhere) in denying the missiles' existence, this proved a great success – on 23 October the Organisation of American States endorsed the 'quarantine' *nem. con.* On the 24th sixteen Soviet freighters stopped just before meeting the quarantine line, and five (thought to be those carrying nuclear warheads) soon turned back. This was taken to be encouraging. But work on the launching sites proceeded apace. Since the United States could not be sure the missiles there were not armed, it still felt the need to insist on their dismantling and to prepare to take direct action on the 30th to effect this. It seems, though, that, before any invasion, a last-minute attempt would have been made to get the UN to propose a compromise, the removal of the Soviet missiles in exchange for that of the American Jupiters in Turkey.[170]

During the late summer there had been fears in Moscow that the operation was bound to be discovered. Despite these, and Kennedy's September warnings, Khrushchev determined to press on, and to keep it secret as long as possible. On 22 October news came in that Kennedy would be addressing his nation. Khrushchev was alarmed – the missiles were still 'defenseless, they can be wiped out from the air in one swipe' – and summoned an emergency Praesidium meeting on 'further measures in connection with Cuba and Berlin'. This opted for toughness; the Soviet commander was initially authorised to use tactical nuclear weapons in the event of an invasion.[171] That Kennedy only announced a 'quarantine' was seen as reassuring, especially as five ships with warheads and rockets were

---

[169] Technically this breached international law, as war had not actually been declared on Cuba; but the US had already thus proceeded against Guatemala in 1954.

[170] Garthoff, *The Cuban Missile Crisis*, pp. 54, 59–60; Freedman, *Kennedy's Wars*, p. 215.

[171] However, at Malinovsky's instance, authorisation was then withheld in default of further instructions from Moscow, a position reaffirmed on 27 October (Fursenko and Naftali, *One Hell of a Gamble*, pp. 242–3, 276).

just able to beat the deadline; so little should be read into the decision not to test it with further suspicious cargoes. On both 22–3 and 24 October firm letters were sent demanding that Kennedy 'renounce actions . . . which could lead to catastrophic consequences for peace throughout the world'. But Khrushchev was probably impressed by the very visible US military preparations, with nuclear bombers airborne and poised to strike. On 25 October Khrushchev first talked to the Praesidium of dismantling the missiles, but decided to 'look around' to see if Kennedy would settle for less.

It seemed not. Soviet intelligence reported, inaccurately, that the US had decided 'to finish with Castro'. So on 26 October Khrushchev wrote urging mutual restraint in pulling 'the rope in which you have tied the knot of war', and suggesting that a US pledge not to invade Cuba would remove the need for Soviet 'military specialists' there. Next day he was more relaxed about Kennedy's immediate intentions, and moved to tie up the deal, but also to get something more out of it. Whether under instructions or not, various American intermediaries had suggested the USA might be prepared to trade the Turkish Jupiters. These had not featured in earlier Praesidium discussions, but Khrushchev now suggested that 'If we could achieve additionally the liquidation of the bases in Turkey, we would win.' This upset Washington, which concluded that Kremlin hawks had forced a hardening of Soviet terms or perhaps even a disavowal of Khrushchev. Furthermore the (unauthorised) shooting down of a U2 overflight alarmed both Washington and Moscow. President Kennedy deliberately answered not the Praesidium's letter of the 27th, but Khrushchev's one of the 26th (a move that was subsequently spun as a master stroke). Still, he felt that 'We're going to have to take our missiles out of Turkey'; his problem was how to do this without upsetting the Turks. He therefore had his brother tell Ambassador Dobrynin that 'Time is running out': should another U2 be attacked, the US would respond, which might set off a chain reaction; military 'hot-heads . . . were spoiling for a fight'; so the Soviet missiles had to go, or 'we would remove them'. But if they went, the US would undertake to permit no invasion of Cuba 'from American soil', and also to remove the Jupiters within a few months provided this did not seem to be done under duress. Dobrynin's account arrived during a Praesidium meeting at which Khrushchev had already urged concession by invoking Lenin's climb-down at Brest-Litovsk. A new letter agreeing to remove the missiles was rapidly agreed, and its text put out by Moscow radio so as to pre-empt a broadcast that evening at which it was feared that Kennedy would announce either air strikes or an invasion.

We cannot say how close the world came to war. One danger was of an unintended incident. One U2 strayed across the Bering Straits, occasioning a fighter scramble by both sides but then escaping intact. Soviet escort submarines with nuclear torpedoes showed restraint when depth-charged and forced to surface. Soviet forces in Cuba did not when, at the height of the crisis, they downed a U2. Trouble could also have ensued had the US, instead of adopting the delaying tactics of the 'quarantine' (and thereby allowing the missiles to become operative), followed its first impulse to eliminate them by air strikes; this might well have succeeded, but would have dangerously humiliated Khrushchev. Actual invasion would have been still worse; for one thing the USSR had four times as many troops on Cuba as the USA realised; for another, these might, with or without authorisation, have used tactical nuclear weapons, of whose presence the US was completely unaware. That there was a peaceful resolution chiefly reflects Kennedy's reluctance to risk any such outcome, despite the United States' overall military superiority. Khrushchev had initially been less risk averse – he had, after all, created the situation, and had in September pressed on rather than pulled back. But when it came to the point, he too was scared. He had no intention of firing his missiles at the United States in the pre-emptive attack Castro urged when he saw an American invasion as imminent;[172] and he preferred withdrawal to expanding the crisis by moving on Berlin (or Iran) as the US feared. Kennedy's diplomacy, in particular the informal assurance on the Turkish missiles, eased Khrushchev's path. Equally US superiority in the Caribbean placed the onus on Khrushchev, who, by 28 October, felt he had to move hurriedly to prevent its exercise, whereas Kennedy had not in fact come to the point of having to make his final decision.

The acute phase of the crisis accordingly ended on 28 October. Tidying up the details took another month, and loose ends were left that were later to be of some importance. (Thus the USSR undertook to withdraw its Ilyushin bombers from Cuba, but was vaguer on the combat troops originally introduced to defend the missiles. The legitimacy of any Soviet submarine base was left unsettled once it was clear that none was under construction.)[173] The chief difficulty proved to be Castro: he was so angry at what he saw as Moscow's betrayal that he agreed to talk to the Soviet emissary Mikoyan only when the latter threatened to cut off his oil

[172] Taubman, *Khrushchev*, pp. 572–3; *Khrushchev Remembers*, iii, p. 177.
[173] Garthoff, *The Cuban Missile Crisis*, pp. 65–78, 99–101; Kissinger, *Memoirs*, i, p. 633; J. Radvanyi, *Hungary and the Superpowers* (Stanford, 1972) pp. 137–8.

supplies; even so he adamantly refused to allow UN verification of the missiles' departure. Other ways of satisfying the US on this were eventually found. But, in the absence of UN inspection, Kennedy would not officially promise not to invade Cuba; so the 1962 understanding with Khrushchev remained informal until 1970. The Soviets then secured its written reaffirmation in August, the month before they were discovered to be rapidly constructing an SLBM base at Cienfuegos.[174]

Khrushchev's position after the crisis

Kennedy's prestige gained enormously from the outcome of the Cuban missile crisis. Khrushchev's did not. For Kennedy had insisted that his undertaking to trade the missiles in Turkey and Italy for those in Cuba be kept secret,[175] and Soviet action had appeared either adventurist, or capitulationist, or (the Chinese said) both. But Khrushchev was not as much weakened as is sometimes suggested – in November 1962 he was able to push through his most disruptive organisational reform ever, the division into two of most levels of the Communist Party. What did change was the confrontational approach to the West of 1961–2 (Berlin, the resumption of massive and demonstrative nuclear testing, Cuba). At one stage in the crisis Khrushchev had sought reassurance from his military that calling Kennedy's bluff would not lead to a nuclear holocaust, and been appalled at their response.[176] Now, he told the Hungarian Kadar, 'the Soviet leadership felt it was in the interest of the socialist "commonwealth" to work for a temporary reduction of international tensions . . . to achieve this goal the Soviet Union would adopt a more flexible position in the on-going nuclear test-ban talks.'[177]

In November 1962 Khrushchev told Kennedy he could look forward to six more years of power, 'a long period' during which 'we could

[174] Nixon insisted, in secret, that it be scrapped – Radvanyi, *Hungary and the Superpowers*, pp. 135–6; Garthoff, *The Cuban Missile Crisis*, pp. 95–7; Kissinger, *Memoirs*, i, Chap. 16.

[175] When on 29 October Khrushchev tried to tie Kennedy down in writing, he was told that the deal would be off if the USSR ever publicly alluded to it (Garthoff, *The Cuban Missile Crisis*, p. 55).

[176] 'They looked at me as if I was out of my mind, or what was worse, a traitor. The biggest tragedy as they saw it was not that our country might be devastated and everything lost, but that the Chinese or Albanians might accuse us of appeasement or weakness' (Knightley and Pringle, *The Independent*, 6 October 1992).

[177] Radvanyi, *Hungary and the Superpowers*, pp. 140–1.

create conditions for peaceful coexistence'. Thereby, as Khrushchev put it defensively to Castro, they would gain time, and 'gaining time is a very important factor, because the correlation of forces is everyday more favorable to socialism.' Initially Khrushchev talked of a German peace treaty, disarmament, and a NATO–Warsaw Pact non-aggression treaty. But by April 1963 he had dropped the first, observing to Harriman that 'Berlin is no longer a source of any trouble'.[178] Discussions also moved from propaganda about general and complete disarmament to a test ban treaty. Admittedly they stalled when Khrushchev believed he had been double-crossed over US requirements for inspections. But they were got back on course, partly by Kennedy's 'peace speech' in June to the American University: 'history teaches us that enmities between individuals, as between nations, do not last for ever'; 'If this pause in the Cold War merely leads to its renewal and not to its end, then the indictment of posterity will rightly point its finger at us all.' Khrushchev called it 'the best statement made by any President since Roosevelt',[179] and was not put off by Kennedy's very different speech on visiting the Berlin Wall.[180] June 1963 also saw the collapse of fence-mending Soviet talks with the Chinese party; both superpowers could now find common ground in condemning Chinese rashness and irresponsibility. There followed in quick succession agreement on a Moscow–Washington hot line (to remedy communications difficulties highlighted by the Cuban crisis), a US–British–Soviet treaty banning nuclear tests in the atmosphere (removing a health risk, and at least complicating life for would-be nuclear powers like China), and United States agreement *in principle*[181] to sell wheat to the USSR.

Both Kennedy and Khrushchev hoped more would follow; but in November 1963 Kennedy was shot. Khrushchev did not have the same feelings for Lyndon Johnson, about whom he received derogatory reports from both the KGB and former Kennedy associates; he also believed Johnson would be fully absorbed in the 1964 election contest. Typically Johnson sought to realise and expand Kennedy's policies; but though

---

[178] Zubok and Pleshakov, *Inside the Kremlin's Cold War*, pp. 267–9; Freedman, *Kennedy's Wars*, p. 262.

[179] ibid. pp. 267–8; Schlesinger, *A Thousand Days*, pp. 785–6; *Keesing's*, 19537–8.

[180] 'There are many people . . . who do not understand what is the grand issue between the free world and communism. Let them come to Berlin, And there are some who say in Europe and elsewhere that we can work with the Communists. Let them come to Berlin': *Keesing's*, 19519.

[181] In fact US unions blocked sales by banning the loading of Soviet Ships, until bought off in 1971 (below, p. 366).

his overtures sparked no hostility, they also received little attention in Moscow. By then Khrushchev was showing increasing signs of age and tiredness. Colleagues were indeed concerned that his son-in-law's visit to Bonn might represent an important move behind their backs; but Khrushchev may no longer have been up to new initiatives. He spent 150 days away from Moscow in 1964, and was indeed on holiday when toppled by a Praesidium coup in October.[182]

[182] Fursenko and Naftali, *One Hell of a Gamble*, Chap. 17; Taubman, *Khrushchev*, Chap. 20.

CHAPTER 6

The Vietnam War and other proxy conflicts of the 1960s and 1970s

Since the Cuban missile crisis of 1962, East–west crises involving any prospect of superpower collision have been very rare; examples include the Cienfuegos affair, the 1967 and 1973 Arab–Israeli wars (at the end of both of which the USSR threatened direct action if Israel pushed her victory any further), and perhaps the 1971 Indo-Pakistani war (which, the USA feared, might expand to involve China, the USSR and the USA itself if India did not stop). Instead the chief theme now becomes that of attempts to construct East–West relationships involving cooperation as well as competition, notably Brandt's *Ostpolitik* and the detente policies of the Brezhnev and Nixon administrations. The shift was both gratifying and important, but it must not lead us to overlook the extent to which rivalry proceeded through struggles – often, but not always, clandestine or by proxy – outside Europe.

The idea that anti-imperialist movements could make an important contribution to the Bolshevik cause goes back at least to 1920, when the Comintern staged a Congress of Oppressed Peoples in Baku. It was at first eagerly promoted, but setbacks then led Stalin to back off. After his death, the idea again returned to favour in the Kremlin. In 1955 Nasser and Zhou Enlai put it to Khrushchev 'that the logic of history points to the [Arab] nationalist movement as the coming force in the Middle East' (above, pp. 237–8); and he was at pains to cultivate it. Equally transfer of power from colonial to friendly nationalist rulers was often seen, especially by the USA, as the surest bulwark against communism. Of course many newly independent states sought, and some managed, to stand well with both East and West. Quite as many came to incline one way or the other, and, indeed, to seek, through such alignment, to attract external assistance in order to realise local goals and confound local enemies. Nasser himself, though at first close to the CIA, ended by demanding the deployment of Soviet missiles as protection against Israel and by according the USSR naval and air bases as an incentive. His successor, Sadat, concluded that the Soviet Union could not recover the Sinai peninsula Nasser had lost, and aligned with the USA to secure its return.

Such developments were closely entwined in local circumstance and are often best viewed in their own right. But the attempt to use, or manipulate, them was also central to the Cold War, especially in the 1960s and early 1970s, and again, with the decline of detente, in the late 1970s and early 1980s. Some idea of Soviet aspirations (achievements were much less) is given by a KGB plan advanced during the 1961 Berlin crisis. This sought to distract 'the USA and their satellites, and . . . tie them down during the settlement of the question of a German peace treaty'. Shelepin suggested activating through 'the KGB [and through Cuban assistance] armed uprisings against pro-Western reactionary governments' in Latin America, notably Nicaragua, El Salvador, and Guatemala. In Africa, rebels were to be armed and trained, and risings promoted in Kenya, Rhodesia, and Portuguese Guinea. In the Middle East Mustafa Barzani's movement 'for . . . an independent Kurdistan' should be revived 'to cause uncertainty . . . in the USA, England, Turkey and Iran about the stability of their positions' and access to oil. In the Far East 'disinformation' should be spread about joint Soviet, Chinese, North Korean and North Vietnamese plans 'to liberate South Korea, South Vietnam, and Taiwan in case of armed conflict in Germany', and military 'demonstrations' arranged accordingly.[1] We cannot examine such projects, and their Western counterparts, in any detail; but it may be helpful to give a brief *tour d'horizon* of the 1960s and early 1970s, followed by a slightly longer look at the greatest of these struggles, the Vietnam War.

Cuba and Latin America in the 1960s

Kennedy had more or less promised not to *invade* Cuba. But attempts to assassinate Castro did not stop until the succession of President Johnson. Castro, for his part, had been interfering abroad ever since 1959, when he sponsored an exile invasion of the Dominican Republic;[2] he continued

---

[1] Vladislav Zubok, 'Spy vs. Spy: The KGB vs. the CIA, 1960–1962', CWIHP *Bulletin* 4 (Fall 1994) pp. 28–30.
[2] Hugh Thomas, *Cuba: the pursuit of freedom* (New York, 1976) p. 1228.

to do so with gusto. Much of Cuba's destabilising effect was simply that of example and propaganda; and it must be remembered that insurgencies were common in Central America, as was cross-border involvement. But the Cuban revolution had been deceptively easy, and there were hopes that it could be generally replicated – 'Given suitable operating country, land hunger, and injustices', Che Guevara wrote in 1960,[3] 'a hard core of 30 to 50 men [Castro had originally had about 20 in the Sierra Maestra] is enough to set off armed revolutions in any Latin American country'. Not so. In the mid-1960s there appears to have been Cuban involvement in insurrections in Venezuela, Guatemala, Peru, Bolivia, and perhaps Colombia. None succeeded; and Guevara's failure and death in an ambitious 1966–7 attempt to establish 'the continental command' in Bolivia became well chronicled when Castro published his diary.[4] Among the reasons for these failures were a lack of peasant support, greater strength on the part of most governments than had been anticipated, and the readiness of weaker ones (like Peru and Bolivia) to turn to the CIA for help. Cooperation with local communists was at best limited. For they often did not relish submitting to Cuban command. Also guerrilla insurgency appeared closer to the Chinese than to the Soviet approach; so, as Sino-Soviet rivalry deepened, Moscow-oriented parties might condemn such rebellion as 'an erroneous form of revolution'. Nevertheless they too practised it; and the KGB appears sometimes to have funded insurrection, and indeed itself to have planted North Korean trained guerrillas in Mexico.[5]

The former Belgian Congo

The other great venue for clandestine operations was newly decolonised Africa. The biggest prize was the former Belgian Congo,[6] which was

[3] Keesing's, 23108. See also Guevara's influential Guerrilla Warfare (paperback edn) p. 123.

[4] Keesing's, 23108 ff, 23235, 23855 (Bolivia – and Peru, for which cf. also 23101), 20071, 22119 (Venezuela), 24828 (Colombia); Richard Gott, Rural Guerrillas in Latin America (Harmondsworth, Middlesex, 1973) esp. pp. 52–6, 295–6; John Ranelagh, The Agency: The Rise and Decline of the CIA (1986) p. 424; V. Marchetti and J.D. Marks, The CIA and the Cult of Intelligence (1974) pp. 123 ff.

[5] Money from the Italian communists (very probably a conduit) for Venezuela, Keesing's, 20875; from the KGB for Colombia, John Barron, KGB (1974) p. 256; the destabilisation of Mexico, ibid. Chap. 11, Keesing's, 24899–90.

[6] Mao was quoted as saying in 1964 to a Chinese diplomat (who subsequently defected), 'If we can take the Congo, we can have all of Africa' – Bruce D. Larkin, China and Africa 1949–1970 (Berkeley, 1971) p. 72.

suddenly decolonised in July 1960, and almost immediately disintegrated into military mutinies and governmental fragmentation. Belgian troops intervened to protect expatriates and restore order; and Moise Tshombe, who valued continued Belgian assistance, took the opportunity to declare himself the independent President of the richest province, Katanga. The mercurial Prime Minister, Patrice Lumumba, sought first US, then, when that was refused, UN aid to reverse this. The UN despatched a stabilisation force, but would not allow Lumumba to direct it. So he turned increasingly to the USSR, which clandestinely supplied him with arms, technicians, and some transport facilities. This led both the USA and UN Secretary-General Hammarskjöld to see Lumumba as part of the problem. (He was later murdered in January 1961.)[7] By January 1963 the UN had superficially reunited the country, extinguishing a breakaway Lumumbist regime in the north-eastern city of Stanleyville and (rather messily) reconquering Katanga. The UN had undoubtedly been influenced by the decolonised countries that now constituted a new majority in its General Assembly. But the determining voice had been that of the United States, which saw things chiefly in Cold War terms – Kennedy 'used to say that, if we didn't have the UN operation, the only way to block Soviet domination in the Congo would be to go in with our own forces.'[8]

Following its Katanga success, the UN pulled out. But by the time its forces had left in mid-1964, Lumumba's successor Gizenga had again risen in Stanleyville, half the country was in revolt, and the 'Congolese army' was collapsing. The United States' first thought was to press the Belgians to intervene.[9] Following Belgium's refusal, a 'mercenary brigade is second best alternative'. Tshombe, who had – somewhat improbably – assumed

---

[7] The CIA did make plans for his assassination; but the January murder seems to have been a Congolese/Katangan affair, with no foreign encouragement (though Belgian direction has been claimed).

[8] Arthur M. Schlesinger, *A Thousand Days: John F. Kennedy in the White House* (1965) p. 501; Madeleine G. Kalb, *The Congo Cables. The Cold War in Africa – From Eisenhower to Kennedy* (New York, 1982); Stephen E. Ambrose, *Eisenhower. The President* (1984) pp. 586–9. The Congo is further discussed in *The Post-Imperial Age*, pp. 463–8.

[9] In February 1964 it had similarly asked Britain (in vain) to 'frustrate Communist takeover in Zanzibar' – Piero Gleijeses, ' "Flee! The White Giants are Coming!": The United States, the Mercenaries, and the Congo, 1964–5', *Diplomatic History*, xviii (1994) p. 212.

the Congolese premiership in July 1964, was agreeable. So, to Tshombe's own ex-Katangese gendarmes were added over 1,000 white mercenaries, recruited chiefly from southern Africa. They were supplied and transported by the CIA, and assisted by both a CIA air force (flown by Cuban exiles) and a November 1964 Belgian paratroop drop on Stanleyville (largely, but one suspects not entirely, to rescue European hostages). By mid-1965 they had triumphed, scattering the surviving Gizengists into the bush.[10]

The US ambassador observed that 'For the last five years, Congo has been the principal insurgent theater in Africa, and second only to Vietnam'. The Vietnam comparison is overblown – the forces (if not the atrocities) involved in the Congo had been miniscule. But the Gizengists had attracted foreign 'progressive' support: by February 1965 29 aircraft loads of supplies had reached the southern Sudan for onwards transit, while Chinese and other equipment arrived via Tanzania/Uganda and Egypt claimed to have trained over 2,000 Congolese fighters; following requests from Tanzania and Egypt, Che Guevara also visited the rebellion for several months in 1965 with a hundred Cuban 'instructors', but decided its prospects were hopeless. Such assistance had, however, been dwarfed by US 'covert action' on the other side, and the outcome was probably widely noted in Africa – President Kenyatta of Kenya summoned the US ambassador and declared, 'The Congo is finished. Now we can be friends again.'[11]

In the Congo itself, victory had no sooner been gained than Tshombe and President Kasavubu fell out; but both became irrelevant in November 1965 when the army commander General Mobutu seized power in a coup. For a time he seemed to have stabilised the situation, and to be building the Congo (with its plentiful natural resources) into a state of significant potential. In fact he proved one of the continent's chief kleptocrats; and in 1977–8 his Zaire was revealed as a Potemkin structure when it could not handle incursions from Angola and had to be rescued by Morocco, Belgium and France (below pp. 389–90).

---

[10] In 1996–7 Rwandan and Ugandan intervention plucked one of them, Laurent Kabila, from obscurity and propelled him to the Presidency.
[11] Gleijeses, 'The White Giants', esp. pp. 209, 213–14, 216, 221, 227; also Keesing's Research Report, *Africa Independent. A Survey of Political Developments* (New York, 1972) pp. 252–67; *Keesing's*, 20561–4, 20803; Ranelagh, *The Agency*, pp. 338–44; Barron, *KGB*, p. 256; Larkin, *China and Africa*, pp. 73–4, 181.

Africa in the 1960s: The OAU; The Nigerian civil war; Kenya; Ghana

Over much of the rest of Africa decolonisation had proceeded more smoothly. The newly independent states were at first assiduously wooed – left-leaning Guinea, in particular, was showered with attention by a Kennedy administration anxious to prove that (unlike its predecessor) it could befriend progressive and neutralist countries. Many of the early diplomatic alignments reflected personal, local, or Pan-African issues and rivalries. But from 1960 to 1963 there appeared to be a broad division between a moderate Brazzaville and a more radical Casablanca group of states. In 1963 they came together to form a single Organisation of African Unity (OAU), whose Charter affirmed 'a policy of non-alignment with regard to all blocs'. This dampened, though it certainly did not end, the extension into Africa of East–West rivalries. But for a time it seemed that these would be supplemented by Sino-Soviet competition. For China was anxious to round up Third World support and secure the USSR's exclusion from the projected June 1964 Afro-Asian Conference in Algiers. To this end Zhou Enlai toured ten Arab/African countries in the 1963–4 winter with an enormous entourage. Unfortunately China also wished to appear the patron of real revolution, as opposed to the USSR's moderate revisionism; and Zhou's ritual remarks to the effect that 'an excellent revolutionary situation exists in Africa' seemed a threat to many of the newly established governments.[12]

Nor were their fears unreasonable. For most governments were insecure, subversion was rife, and plotters naturally sought external aid. Ruth First lists 36 military coups (successful and attempted) in the 1960s.[13] These obviously all had a local context, and it should be stressed that the issues could be quite other than those of East–West rivalry. Thus the largest African state, Nigeria, fell victim to tribally motivated coups, leading to massacres of Ibos, then to the attempted secession of the predominantly Ibo 'Biafra'. Biafra was reconquered in the 1967–70 civil war; during this, Nigeria drew arms from Britain, the USSR and Egypt, while Biafra enjoyed Tanzanian and Chinese endorsement, Roman Catholic publicity assistance and humanitarian aid, and initially more clandestine

---

[12] James Mayall, *Africa. The Cold War and After* (1971) pp. 29, 122, 148; Keesing's Research Report, *Africa Independent*, p. 3; Larkin, *China and Africa*, esp. pp. 69–70, 80–1.

[13] *The Barrel of a Gun* (1970) pp. xii–xiv.

support from France and Portugal.[14] But many internal convulsions were accompanied by allegations of communist subversion and by expulsions of Soviet or Chinese personnel. To take only two examples, during 1965 the Vice-President of Kenya, Oginga Odinga, attacked government policy as too pro-Western and so was gradually stripped of his offices; during this process it was announced that China, the USSR and other countries had been training prospective rebels and that in 1964–5 $400,000 had been spent on undermining the Kenyan government; in March 1966 communist diplomats and journalists were expelled, and further expulsions followed in 1967, 1968 and 1969.

In Ghana, the first President, Kwame Nkrumah, succumbed to megalomania. This led him to recruit 'freedom fighters' to promote 'Nkrumaism' ('African in context, but Marxist in form') not only in reactionary states but also in countries like Tanzania. For their training he turned first to Soviet and then to Chinese instructors (his successors accused him of cribbing their lecture notes to prepare a book on the *Strategy and Tactics of Revolutionary Warfare with Particular Reference to the African Revolution*). He also sought East German assistance with the creation of an All-African Intelligence Service and the development of Ghanaian security, while Russians trained a rapidly expanding Presidential guard. Nkrumah was, however, overthrown by what he regarded as a Western-promoted military coup in 1966, following which 1,100 Russians, 430 Chinese, and 'scores' of other communists were expelled.[15] One commentator sees his fall, together with that of Ben Bella in Algeria (1965) and of Modibo Keita in Mali (1968), as having transformed the Cold War contours of the continent.[16]

The Middle East

We have already noted the 1955–8 struggle for influence in the Middle East, and shall return in due course to the crises connected with the

---

[14] A.H.M. Kirk Greene, *Crisis and Conflict in Nigeria. A Documentary Sourcebook*, ii (1971) pp. 46–9, 56, 76, 79, 85, 88, 111, 140, 245–6, 329.

[15] Admittedly some of those expelled were *bona fide* development technicians. Larkin, *China and Africa*, p. 136; Keesing's Report, *Africa Independent*, pp. 131–4; *Keesing's*, 21345, 22277, 23423 (Kenya), 21273–4 (Ghana); Ghana Ministry of Information, *Nkrumah's Subversion in Africa* (Accra, 1966); John Prados, *Presidents' Secret Wars: CIA and Pentagon covert operations since World War II* (New York, 1986) p. 237.

[16] Gleijeses, 'The White Giants', p. 208; *Keesing's*, 20965–8, 23203.

1967–73 wars (see pp. 363, 379–82). Here we need only note that, in April 1967, a bibulous Brezhnev assured Gomulka and Ulbricht that 'Even our opponents cannot deny that we have achieved major successes in the Near East. We have already partially succeeded in driving the Americans out of this part of the world and we shall soon be in a position to deal them a decisive blow.' He proved over-sanguine. But Eugene Rostow, then responsible for the Middle East within the State Department, saw things in much the same light:

The Middle Eastern crisis is not a regional quarrel about Israel's right to exist. It is . . . a fissure in the foundation of world politics – a Soviet challenge . . . The first purpose of the Soviet effort is to achieve . . . control of the Mediterranean, the Middle East and the Persian Gulf area. On that footing, the next step would be to drive the United States out of Europe, and to have NATO dismantled.[17]

India and Pakistan

In the Indian sub-continent East–West rivalry was more subdued, but still evident. The basic fact of politics was Indo-Pakistani enmity, particularly over the disposition of Kashmir. In the 1950s Pakistan had turned for arms and sympathy to the Western alliance, and in the 1960s it had added the friendship of China (whose border disputes with India had led to two small frontier wars). India, despite some US attempts to woo it (especially after its 1962 defeat by China), looked most readily in geopolitical (though not domestic) terms to the Soviet Union, Pakistan's enemy and by the 1960s also China's. The 1965 Indo-Pakistani war had no direct East–West repercussions. But it was something of a blow to Pakistan's oddly assorted patrons, China and the USA, that in January 1966 it allowed the USSR to mediate its dispute with India (at Tashkent). However, Pakistan's relations with both China and the USA improved later in the decade, and it arranged the secret Kissinger visits that brought detente between the two. So when Pakistan ran into trouble its President, Yahya Khan, was confident that 'both Chinese and Americans will help us, how could they forget our

---

[17] Erwin Weit, *Eyewitness. The Autobiography of Gomulka's Interpreter* (1973) p. 139; E. Rostow, 'The Middle Eastern Crisis in the Perspective of World Politics', *International Affairs*, xlvii (1971) pp. 275–6. The Middle East is further discussed in *The Post-Imperial Age*, esp. Chaps 12–13.

services over the last two years?'[18] Trouble had come in 1971, when Yahya Khan responded to the overwhelming electoral success of the East Pakistan autonomist party with bloody repression. India did not intend either to saddle itself indefinitely with the millions of refugees this precipitated or to pass up a golden opportunity to break up Pakistan and achieve indisputable primacy on the sub-continent.

In July 1971 Kissinger warned the Indian ambassador that China, which had apparently cautioned India against invading East Pakistan during the 1965 war, might intervene in the event of another conflict. In August India countered by concluding with the USSR a treaty whose literal terms were anodyne, but which in effect assured it Soviet protection against third-party intervention. The resulting crisis has been very differently interpreted. Nixon and Kissinger suggest that the problem of East Pakistan might have been sorted out by secret negotiations, had India been prepared to give these time. They also had intelligence from within the Indian cabinet that the Prime Minister, Mrs Ghandi, was really seeking not only the liberation of East, but also the break-up of West, Pakistan. Their critics doubt both the prospects of the negotiations and the trustworthiness of the intelligence reports from Mrs Ghandi's rival, Moraji Desai; they also depict the US administration as so obsessed by global politics that it could see South Asia only in this light. 'The Indo-Pakistani conflict,' two of Kissinger's aides wrote after the Soviet–Indian treaty, 'becomes a sort of Sino-Soviet clash by proxy.' So, Kissinger remarked, 'We don't really have any choice. We can't allow a friend of ours and China's to get screwed in a conflict with a friend of Russia's.' Or, as another Kissinger aide explained in a more formal context, 'We had to show China that we respect a mutual friend and opposed the crossing of international borders. So it was not so much a "thanks, Yahya, for helping us with China" as demonstrating to China we were a reliable country to deal with.'

Indian troops started to penetrate East Pakistan in late November, making excellent progress with the aid of local guerrillas. The crisis heightened when on 3 December President Yahya launched air strikes from, and so extended the fighting to, West Pakistan. There was, clearly, some potential for even wider trouble: China alerted troops on the Indian border; the USSR blocked UN calls for a ceasefire and moved troops to the Chinese border; and the USA ordered an aircraft carrier into the Bay of Bengal.

---

[18] D.K. Hall, in Barry M. Blechman and Stephen Kaplan (eds) *Force without War: US armed forces as a political instrument* (Washington, 1978) p. 208.

Washington's chief worry was probably of some definite Chinese intervention that it would have either to support, which might be risky, or to back away from and so halt the current Chinese realignment towards the US side in the Cold War. To pre-empt this the administration pressed the Soviet Union[19] (which it saw as trying to drag things out and so allow time for an Indian victory) to restrain India and to guarantee that there would be no territorial annexations in the West. Opinion differs as to whether these had ever been intended.[20] But by 16 December the USSR was able to offer private assurances. On the 17th Pakistan's forces in the East surrendered, leaving India free to reconstitute it as the independent country of Bangladesh. The crisis subsided, without, as it turned out, any major geopolitical consequences outside the sub-continent.[21]

Indonesia

Southeast Asia's troubles were more protracted. They are usually seen in connection with Vietnam, but the region's largest country is Indonesia. In 1961 the US Chiefs of Staff observed that 'Indonesia's large population ... wealth of natural resources, and strategic location constitute a major prize in the East–West struggle ... The loss of Indonesia to the communists would gravely undermine the Free World military position in the West Pacific.'[22] The United States had long been conscious of the country's potential. After 1945 it had leant on the colonial power, the Netherlands, to leave. In the mid-1950s the Indonesian President, Sukarno, turned increasingly to a flamboyant neutralism in foreign relations – he was, with Nehru, Nasser and Tito, one of the leaders of the non-aligned movement – while domestically he improved the position of the communist party and

---

[19] By using the hotline, and by implying that the planned 1972 Nixon–Brezhnev summit was at risk.

[20] Guarantees were forthcoming that there would be no annexations from West Pakistan proper. But in India's eyes this did not include Azad Kashmir, and there were fears that its loss would be enough to trigger West Pakistan's disintegration.

[21] Richard M. Nixon, *The Memoirs of Richard Nixon* (paperback edn) pp. 525–30; Kissinger, *Memoirs*, i, Chap. 21; Seymour Hersh, *The Price of Power: Kissinger in the Nixon White House* (New York, 1983) Chap. 32; Blechman and Kaplan, *Force without War*, pp. 176–210; Y.Y.I. Vertzberger, *China's Southwestern Strategy* (New York, 1985) pp. 40, 58.

[22] John Subritzky, *Confronting Sukarno. British, American, Australian and New Zealand Diplomacy in the Malaysian–Indonesian Confrontation, 1961–5* (Basingstoke, 2000) p. 23.

distanced himself from the largely pro-Western forces that had previously been dominant. This led to military dissatisfaction, and regional commanders gradually drifted into revolt in 1956–7; they approached the USA, and, on being accorded arms and CIA aeroplanes, declared their independence in 1958. Dulles privately explained that 'as between a territorially united Indonesia which is leaning toward Communism and a break-up of that country into geographical units, I prefer the latter'. The revolt was soon suppressed,[23] and the episode produced an understandable coolness.

However, Sukarno needed outside support for territorial expansion. The Dutch had continued to occupy Western New Guinea (West Irian, now 'West Papua'), which was contiguous to Indonesia but ethnically very different; and from 1960 Sukarno brought the question to a head. In 1961 he secured from the Soviet Union warships, aircraft, and military technicians, then used this to put pressure on the USA. He further raised tension in 1962 by seeking, albeit with total lack of success, to infiltrate small bodies of troops into West Irian. And he rejected the Dutch offer of a UN-conducted plebiscite, which would almost certainly have gone against him. Washington was divided between those who saw Sukarno as, potentially, a serial aggressor like Hitler, and those who felt the Dutch would inevitably be compelled to yield West Irian – 'The only question is will it go with our help, and in such a way that we get some credit for it, or will this issue be left on a silver platter for the Bloc?' President Kennedy favoured the latter school. So he conducted an exercise in appeasement, pressing the Dutch into agreeing in August 1962 to turn West Irian over (via the UN).[24]

Sukarno's next target was the British colonies in North Borneo (Sabah, Sarawak, and the protectorate of Brunei). Their destiny had become linked to the decolonisation of Singapore. For Singapore's Prime Minister, Lee Kuan Yew, agreed with his Malayan counterpart, Tunku Abdul Rahman, that, while Singapore could not remain a British dependency, it would be dangerously exposed (in terms of both security and economics) if it proceeded to independence on its own: it should therefore join Malaya. But the adhesion of so many ethnic Chinese might upset Malaya's political equilibrium, and the Tunku insisted that it be balanced by the simultaneous accession of the north Borneo colonies to what would then be known

[23] Prados, *Presidents' Secret Wars*, Chap. 8.

[24] Subritzky, *Confronting Sukarno*, pp. 24–5; Arthur M. Schlesinger, *A Thousand Days*, pp. 464–6, and *Robert F. Kennedy and his Times* (1978) pp. 569–70; *Keesing's*, 18845 ff.

as Malaysia. The British were keen, provided they could retain the military basing rights they currently enjoyed. But this made the whole scheme all the more obnoxious to Sukarno; it smelt of 'neo-colonialism', and would constitute a barrier to future Indonesian expansion. Preparations were pushed forward over-rapidly in 1962, partly in response to Lee's domestic difficulties. In December there followed a small revolt in Brunei, probably with covert Indonesian support; although this was rapidly suppressed, in January 1963 Indonesia announced a policy of 'Confrontation' against Malaysia. There followed raids into, and guerrilla infiltration of, the north Borneo territories (and on one occasion Malaya proper) – initially interspersed with negotiations for an Indonesian-led federation of itself, Malaya and the Philippines (Maphilindo).

Many in Washington were unhappy, feeling that 'it's worth every resource of preventive diplomacy to forestall the kind of blow-up over Malaysia in which our very success in blocking Sukarno may lose us Indonesia.' So, Harriman told the British in October 1963, it was 'essential to save Indonesia from communist influence. If Indonesia did go Red, there was no hope for the other countries in Southeast Asia.' By contrast London felt 'an army coup d'etat [there] would become a real possibility if it were evident that Malaysia could not be broken up and the Indonesian economy were on the point of collapse.'[25] Neither Britain nor Malaysia bowed to US pressure for appeasement. Under President Johnson the USA came round to their position: in February 1964 he 're-affirmed' US support 'for the peaceful national independence of Malaysia' in return for a declaration of 'British support for US policy in South Vietnam'. A year later, and against the background of Sukarno's cultivation of communist China, Johnson had moved on to promising Britain military support in the event of 'major war against Indonesia'; 'we will back you if necessary to the hilt and hope for your support in Vietnam.'[26] By September 1965, indeed, the reversal was complete: US threats to stop supporting sterling on the exchanges helped dissuade Britain from sounding Indonesia out on negotiations.[27]

---

[25] Subritzky, *Confronting Sukarno*, pp. 78, 76.

[26] British and Malaysian forces easily handled the small-scale Indonesian probes; and the Tunku decided, in September 1964, to respond to all but major attacks by appealing to the UN rather than by direct retaliation. However, by 1965 over 60,000 British troops were needed in the theatre; and real war would have required early British destruction of the Indonesian air force, which would not have played well internationally – Subritzky, *Confronting Sukarno*, pp. 116, 118–19, 121, 137.

[27] ibid. pp. 103, 144, 172–3.

Sukarno clearly hoped to replicate his success over West Irian. But since Malaysia was an indigenous state and the UN had certified that Sabah and Sarawak's adhesion to it had popular support,[28] Malaysia's diplomatic position was a good deal stronger than the Dutch one had been. In 1964 Indonesia gained little sympathy either from Moscow or from the conference of non-aligned countries in Cairo; in January 1965 Malaysia was elected to the UN Security Council, and Indonesia withdrew from the UN in disgust.[29] So from late 1964 onwards Sukarno threw himself into the arms of China. The two countries talked of the emergence of 'one Asian bloc of more than 700 million people', of the creation to replace the UN of a 'Conference of New Emerging Forces' based on opposition to imperialism and neo-colonialism, and, of course, of the need to crush Malaysia. China seems to have been prepared to play up to Sukarno's vanity by staging its next nuclear test on his territory and allowing him to claim it as Indonesian. It also pressed on him small arms for the formation of a 'Fifth Force' militia to counterbalance the largely anti-communist Indonesian army.

Internally, too, Sukarno was becoming increasingly radical, toying with the idea of a 'Fifth Force', and tolerant of the large Indonesian communist party (PKI). This in turn supported him, made further demands, and seized every opportunity of enhancing its position. The army's unhappiness mounted, and there was much alleged plotting by, and counter-plotting against, the 'Council of Generals'. Then in September 1965 a Palace Guard colonel staged a pre-emptive coup, murdering six generals. The details are obscure. But it is likely that Sukarno was at least partially implicated in the coup, and that it was either associated with, or triggered the parallel plans of, the PKI.[30] The coup failed, as General Suharto rallied the army. He then proceeded (with some US help)[31] to root out communists – the CIA

[28] *Keesing's*, 19718–9; the UN investigation seems more cursory than that of the earlier Anglo-Malay Cobbold Commission (*Keesing's*, 18937). Brunei finally decided to remain aloof after disagreement over the future of its oil revenues.

[29] Macmillan, *Memoirs*, vi, Chap. 8; D.P. Mozingo, *Chinese Policy toward Indonesia* (Ithaca, NY, 1976) pp. 201–2; *Keesing's*, 20576, 20591 ff.

[30] A.C.A. Dake, *In the Spirit of the Red Banteng. Indonesian Communists between Moscow and Peking 1959–1965* (The Hague, 1973) pp. 326–420; Mozingo, *Chinese Policy toward Indonesia*, esp. pp. 221–6, 234 ff; J.D. Legge, *Sukarno. A Political Biography (1972)* Chap. 15.

[31] This took the form of passing on lists of several thousand communist cadres and then checking on their arrest – *Washington Post*, 21 May 1990, p. A5.

later reported that 250,000 people were killed during their repression – and more gradually down-graded Sukarno. Suharto thus secured special powers in March 1966 and took over the Presidency himself a year later. The army had never much liked the confrontation with Malaysia; once firmly in power, it readily accepted Thai mediation to end it, a process formally completed (despite Sukarno's opposition) in August 1966. The following August Indonesia, Malaysia, the Philippines, Singapore,[32] and Thailand came together to form the Association of South-East Asian Nations (ASEAN) – an amorphous grouping, but one that proved, at a political level, surprisingly successful.

In 1965 the outlook had seemed very different – Khrushchev comments wistfully:

Indonesia might have chosen the correct course and become a socialist country. It would have been one of the most powerful socialist countries in the world, occupying a strategic position in the struggle against imperialism.[33]

What had prevented this was partly the denial to Sukarno of a quick victory over Malaysia, but chiefly his own military, once given (by the 1965 coup) a green light to mobilise an intense local hostility to both communists and ethnic Chinese (two heavily overlapping groups). The CIA had hoped for some such outcome. But even in the privacy of US bureaucratic politics, it refrained from claiming credit, suggesting rather that the result 'evolved purely from a complex and long-standing domestic political situation'.[34] The CIA might also have added that it had transpired in a context in which (unlike Vietnam) there had been no fusion between communism and nationalism.

Indo-China

In the troubles we have recounted, external superpower involvement was only indirect, or at most limited and clandestine. In Indo-China large

---

[32] Singapore had seceded from Malaysia in August 1965, following an irremediable dispute as to the freedom to be accorded to political action outside the Malay-dominated ruling coalitions.

[33] *Khrushchev Remembers*, ii, p. 330 – typically he blames the PKI's disasters on following Chinese advice.

[34] H.W. Brands, 'The limits of manipulation: how the US didn't topple Sukarno', *Journal of American History*, lxxvi (1989) p. 805.

numbers of US combat troops were to be committed in the 1960s and early 1970s. The USSR did not reciprocate, but (with China) it poured in, albeit surprisingly inconspicuously, the weapons and supplies without which North Vietnam's ultimate victory would have been impossible. Accordingly the 'Vietnam War' developed a far greater hold on international consciousness and public opinion than did, for instance, the Indonesian turmoil of 1965–6, even though it could be argued that Indonesia's destiny was of more geopolitical importance.

As we have seen (above, pp. 166–7), the USA first came to feel the need to contain Southeast Asian communism in 1949 (after the collapse of Kuomintang rule in China). There were prophesies that, if Indo-China went communist, Thailand and Burma would also fall.[35] The USA accordingly provided increasing financial support for the French war effort. True it did not intervene militarily in 1954 when France was on the verge of major defeat at Dien Bien Phu. But it was unhappy with the French decision, reached during the Geneva Conference, to pull out, and it sought to prevent any more countries following North Vietnam to communism by intrusively offering economic support and political training to South Vietnam and Laos. Trouble first developed in Laos.

Laos

The Geneva Conference had provided for Laos to become a non-communist neutral state, but it faced the problem of integrating the communist Pathet Lao forces that had ended the war controlling (with Vietminh backing) substantial areas in the east of the country. Prince Souvanna Phouma irritated the USA by his conciliatory stance towards the Pathet Lao. Although he had become disillusioned with it by mid-1958, he encountered opposition from right-wing parties, lost his parliamentary majority, and was replaced (probably with CIA encouragement) by a strongly anticommunist premier – who in turn was ousted in December 1959 by a coup led by Phoumi Nosovan. When, from mid-1959, these rightist governments faced a Pathet Lao rebellion, the USA supported them and established a military training mission. In August 1960 a further coup by a young neutralist captain, Kong Le, reinstated Souvanna Phouma. Phoumi Nosovan took up arms, with Thai and CIA assistance. So Souvanna Phouma turned to the Pathet Lao, and by December was receiving airlifted Soviet supplies.

[35] *Pentagon Papers* (Boston, Senator Gravel edn, 1971) i, pp. 361–2.

This open external support for rival sides in the civil war was extremely ominous; and the US was under strong Thai and some Filipino pressure to intervene militarily to keep the communists at a safe distance. Eisenhower contemplated a SEATO intervention, but did not wish one. Kennedy, too, was deeply suspicious of the communists – Congressmen were briefed that 'if Laos goes Communist' it would probably infiltrate guerrillas into Thailand. In March 1961 he secured SEATO agreement to the defence of western Laos, and in April (after rumours of a neutralist–Pathet Lao offensive) he seriously considered intervention. Unlike Eisenhower, however, Kennedy was ready to accept Laotian neutrality: 'If in the past there has been any possible ground for misunderstanding of our support for a truly neutral Laos,' he announced, 'there should be none now'.[36] So Kennedy supported Britain in approaching the USSR to reconvene a Geneva Conference on Laos. Khrushchev was not unwilling. In 1959 he had told Mao he had 'not the slightest interest in this [Laos] affair, because this affair itself is small, but there is much noise about it'; for if the fighting intensified, the USA might intervene directly, appearing on or even crashing over the North Vietnamese border. In March 1961 he told the US ambassador he would welcome 'a Laos that pursues neutral policy on the model of Austria'. Khrushchev's eyes were fixed rather on Germany; indeed, the Chinese were told in 1962 that any violation of the recent agreements on Laos would discredit Soviet initiatives on Berlin by enabling '[our enemies] to say in their propaganda that socialist countries do not meet their obligations.'[37] In April 1961 the UK and USSR, as co-chairmen of the 1954 Conference, jointly called for a ceasefire and conference. The conference convened in Geneva; and the three Laotian factions (rightist, neutralist, and Pathet Lao) met periodically to discuss the formation of a unified government. The difficulty came over who should get which portfolios; in 1962 Washington began exerting financial pressure on the rightists to induce them to cooperate. This policy of backing Laotian neutralism alarmed Thailand, which had to be reassured (in early 1962) by guarantees of its security and promises that the USA would prevent a Communist takeover of Laos.[38] The occasion to redeem these undertakings appeared to have come in May 1962, when the Pathet Lao routed the rightist army. The United States duly sent further troops to Thailand, but it was made

[36] Martin E. Goldstein, *American Policy toward Laos* (Cranbury, NJ, 1973) p. 236.
[37] Ilya Gaiduk, *Confronting Vietnam. Soviet Policy toward the Indochina Conflict, 1954–1963* (Washington and Stanford, 2003) esp. pp. 122, 134, 149, 164, 179–80.
[38] Blechman and Kaplan, *Force without War*, p. 141.

plain that they would not support Phoumi. Thus weakened, he finally agreed to a coalition. The Pathet Lao, too, were restrained from further exploiting their – or more probably North Vietnam's – military victory. So in June 1962 a united neutralist government under Souvanna Phouma came into being, and the Geneva Conference was able to conclude with a Declaration on the Neutrality of Laos.

Inasmuch as the civil war had been prevented from escalating into major conflict between outside communist and anti-communist powers, this was a success, but in Laos itself not much had changed. By late 1962 cooperation between Pathet Lao troops and Kong Le's 'neutralist' forces had broken down, and the USA began supplying the latter. In April 1963 the Pathet Lao left the government, and sporadic fighting resumed. The USA now supported Souvanna Phouma's 'neutralist' government, and successfully blocked attempted 'rightist' coups in 1964 and 1965. But outside involvement steadily deepened in response to the intensification of the war in Vietnam. In June 1962 Hanoi had told Souvanna Phouma that, though happy to see him lead a united Laotian government, it insisted on continued freedom to use the trails through Laos to South Vietnam; so the 1962 Geneva provision prohibiting such use was bound to be a dead letter. By the end of the decade Hanoi had 67,000 troops in Laos to operate and defend the trails, and this led to the gradual extension of the area under Pathet Lao control. From 1965 the USA, with Souvanna Phouma's permission, embarked on massive bombing in an attempt to cut the trails.[39] It had already been drawn into air strikes to bolster the government in the north, to which end it later came to finance small numbers of Thai 'volunteers'. Finally the CIA came during the 1960s to recruit a private army from the minority Hmong (or Meos). This was, all too probably, partly financed by drug trading; and though it at first brought great prosperity, in the end Pathet Lao counter-offensives killed or drove into exile an alarmingly high proportion of the Hmong.[40] The Laos civil war accordingly remained very much alive. But it was conducted clandestinely, and attracted little international attention – partly because for both the Americans and the North

---

[39] Over two million tons of munitions were supposedly dropped in 1964–73; many did not detonate, bequeathing a continuing explosives problem (*Daily Telegraph*, 9 December 2004 p. 14).

[40] Goldstein, *American Policy toward Laos*, p. 330; Prados, *Presidents' Secret Wars*, pp. 292, 296; Thomas Powers, *The Man Who kept the Secrets: Richard Helms and the CIA* (paperback, 1981 edn) pp. 226, 451.

Vietnamese (who provided most of the fighting power of the rival parties) it was essentially subsidiary to the struggle for South Vietnam. Once that was over, the remainder of Laos fell (as Khrushchev had forecast in 1961)[41] to the Pathet Lao 'like a ripe apple'.

South Vietnam 1954–64

When Kennedy became President he was prepared for trouble over Laos, but he was shocked by the condition of South Vietnam: 'This is the worst yet. You know, Ike never briefed me . . .'[42] From 1954 South Vietnam was controlled by what had previously been a (theoretically independent) French puppet government. This was headed by Ngo Dinh Diem, a non-communist nationalist of the kind the USA had been looking for; despite some initial hesitations, the USA proceeded from late 1954 to back him in the hope of building a viable non-communist state. In so doing the USA and what we can now call South Vietnam were disregarding the Geneva Agreements, which prescribed the holding of elections in 1956 to reunite Vietnam. This sat ill with US advocacy of elections to reunite Germany and Korea but was not otherwise remarkable. Neither the USA nor South Vietnam were a party to the agreements. China (which had negotiated them) apparently favoured Vietnam's continued partition, provided South Vietnam did not become a vehicle for American influence (see p. 213). North Vietnam itself broke the provision that any civilians who wished to leave for the other part of the country 'shall be permitted and helped to do so'; for the resulting exodus might, as Ho and Giap admitted, have tilted the numerical balance from North to South Vietnam.[43] Diem's refusal to contemplate elections cannot be said to have harmed his legitimacy in the short run. But the general assumption had been that the communists would have won elections in 1954;[44] Diem's refusal to hold them did much, in the 1960s and 1970s, to undercut his state's appeal in the West.

---

[41] Goldstein, *American Policy toward Laos*, pp. 245–6. The previous paragraphs are drawn chiefly from Goldstein, from David Hall, 'The Laotian War of 1962 and the Indo-Pakistani War of 1971', in Blechman and Kaplan, *Force without War*, and from Prados, *Presidents' Secret Wars*, Chap. 14; see also Gaiduk, *Confronting Vietnam*, Chap. 7.

[42] Schlesinger, *Thousand Days*, p. 291.

[43] D.A. Ross, *In the Interests of Peace: Canada and Vietnam 1954–73* (Toronto, 1984) p. 111 and Chaps 4, 5.

[44] *FRUS 1952–4*, xiii, Part 2, pp. 1794, 2191, 2407–8.

Initially both North and South Vietnam concentrated on internal consolidation. In the North, attacks on 'landlords' and 'rich peasants', together with anti-Catholic policies, sparked a revolt, which was firmly put down. 1956–7 brought a change of Party Secretary, some back-tracking, and a pause before the country proceeded to collectivisation.[45] Consolidation in the South was a good deal harder. But Diem was at first unexpectedly successful, purchasing, coopting, and outmanoeuvreing the religio-political sects in 1955 and staging a referendum that converted the state into a Republic under his presidency. Diem did attempt land reform, but a very limited one.[46] Basically, though, he relied on the rooting out of subversives. Some say this led to more political executions in the South than in the North. It reduced Communist Party membership from about 55,000 in 1954 to 5,000 in 1959, but it also alienated a wide spectrum of unattached opinion.

Hanoi had originally expected the Southern regime to collapse in a welter of faction fighting. In 1957 it turned down pleas from southern communists for an immediate insurrection, stressing the paramount need for the consolidation of the North and noting that neither the USSR nor China was yet ready to support moves that might risk a new confrontation. By 1959, however, it both feared the complete elimination of communist cadres if nothing were done and noted Diem's growing unpopularity. It therefore authorised a return to violence, to create a revolutionary base area in the Central Highlands, to assist the 'political struggle' elsewhere, and hopefully to encourage Diem's eventual overthrow by mass insurrections; that summer saw the start of the transfer of weapons south and of the creation of rudimentary supply routes for them. Late in 1960 local colouring was provided by the creation of an ostensibly non-communist National Liberation Front for South Vietnam (NLF), complemented by measures to ensure that its armed forces were wholly controlled by the North Vietnamese army.[47]

---

[45] William S. Turley, *The Second Indochina War* (paperback edn) p. 19; E.A. Moise, 'Land Reform and Land Reform Errors in North Vietnam', *Pacific Affairs*, il (1976) esp. p. 78; *Pentagon Papers*, i, p. 246; Philip B. Davidson, *Vietnam at War* (Novato, Ca., 1988) pp. 286–7.

[46] Landlords were allowed to keep as much as 100 hectares; and though rents were reduced, the state made possible their collection in many areas where they had lapsed during the anti-French insurgency.

[47] Ang, Chen Guan, *The Vietnam War from the Other Side. The Vietnamese Communists' Perspective* (2002) pp. 29–33, 41–4, 54–6; Turley, *Second Indochina War*, pp. 19–20, 24, 33; *The Pentagon Papers as published by the New York Times* (paperback – subsequently, *Pentagon Papers* [NYT]) pp. 76–7.

In considering Vietnam, Kennedy was much influenced by Moscow's proclaimed support for 'wars of national liberation' and strategy of overcoming capitalism by first detaching the Third World. As we have seen, he was prepared to pull back from earlier US policies and accept the neutralisation of Laos. But this made firm action elsewhere all the more important, both to impress Khrushchev (who had reactivated the question of Berlin) and to reassure pro-American Asians (whose concerns had been forcefully put to Vice-President Johnson during a rapid tour in May 1961).[48] Few people advised Kennedy against increasing US involvement. Of these the most notable was President de Gaulle, who urged Kennedy to take a tough line on Berlin at the Vienna Summit, but to keep clear of Indo-China: 'Once a nation has been aroused, no foreign power, however strong, can impose its will upon it'; 'you will sink step by step into a bottomless military and political quagmire, however much you spend in men and money.'[49] De Gaulle was no doubt thinking of French experience in Indo-China and Algeria, but Americans were apt to regard this as irrelevant, since they were both stronger than France and free from the taint of old-fashioned imperialism. William Bundy did see the danger 'that we would wind up like the French in 1954; white men can't win this kind of fight'; but he nevertheless believed early and forceful action had a 70:30 chance of success.[50] The military, which had opposed involvement in Laos, favoured sending troops to South Vietnam since they did not believe this would provoke major external intervention of the kind that had occurred in Korea.

Kennedy felt otherwise: open US troop commitments could upset the Laos ceasefire; he feared, too, that they might convert Vietnam 'into a white man's war, [which] we would lose as the French had lost a decade earlier'. There were also presentational problems, since, in contrast to Korea, there had been no overt aggression.[51] So in November 1961 Kennedy took a middle course, rejecting (for the time being) direct military participation, but increasing aid and providing South Vietnam with

[48] *Pentagon Papers*, ii, pp. 57–9.

[49] De Gaulle, *Memoirs of Hope* (1971) p. 256. Khrushchev too asked Kennedy 'what are the guarantees that the American troops would not get tied up in South Vietnam? I think that such a perspective is most real' (10 November 1961 – *FRUS* 1961–3, vi, p. 60); but his advice was at a discount in Washington, especially as he denied any external involvement in the assault on Diem.

[50] *Pentagon Papers* (NYT) p. 98.

[51] ibid. pp. 106, 108 (unsigned notes of 15 November 1961 NSC meeting); *Pentagon Papers*, ii, p. 117.

training, helicopter transport and 'combat advisers'. This was less than President Diem had asked for; perhaps for this reason, the USA did not insist on anything like the degree of control over his government that it had originally requested, and greatly watered down its demand for 'real administrative, political and social reform' and a sharing 'in the decision-making process in the political, economic and military fields'.[52]

Providing Diem with enhanced resources but still leaving him essentially in control was not a success. Indeed, it is remarkable how quickly his government's position declined. In 1959 he had seemed to have the communists on the run and to have gone far in recovering control over the countryside: in the province of Long An only 6 per cent of assessed land taxes had been collected in 1955 but 82 per cent in 1959. However, when the communists resumed the offensive, things rapidly went into reverse. Government forces increasingly withdrew into the safer areas; and the percentage of land tax collected in Long An (which may be taken as a proxy for other aspects of control) fell steadily to 21 per cent in 1964.[53]

Diem's 1962 recipe for stopping the rot was a 'strategic hamlets' programme modelled on British actions in Malaya. In Malaya, however, the British had had only to deal with the Chinese minority, not with the entire population; and though the compulsory relocation of the rural Chinese had been harsh, it did provide an immigrant community with the right to remain in Malaya, with land, and with amenities. Most of these inducements were not applicable to indigenous Vietnamese peasants. These were, if anything, more likely to feel indebted to the insurgents (whom it will be convenient to call Vietcong). Diem's land reforms had been very limited, while his restoration of order had enabled landlords to return to areas from which they had been driven by the Vietminh. By contrast the Vietcong reduced rent and redistributed landlords' lands, while carefully avoiding antagonising the peasants. In any case the strategic hamlets programme was, despite warnings, pushed through far too fast, with the result not only that amenities were lacking but also that their fortifications left much to be desired. Even so the hamlets posed problems for the Vietcong, but they would only work if they could be defended; given the political turmoil that set in mid-1963 this ceased to be the case.[54]

[52] ibid. pp. 120, 126.

[53] Jeffrey Race, *War Comes to Long An* (Berkeley, 1972) esp. pp. 113–16, 284.

[54] ibid. pp. 132–4 and pictures; Turley, *Second Indochina War*, pp. 49–50; Truong Nhu Tang, *A Vietcong Memoir* (New York, 1985) pp. 46–7.

This turmoil stemmed from collision between the Roman Catholic-dominated government and the Buddhists, who constituted the overwhelming majority of the population. In May 1963 the government chose to enforce a generally ignored ban on the display of religious flags. The army dispersed festival crowds in Hué, killing nine people, which sparked a Buddhist campaign for the punishment of those responsible, freedom to celebrate and an end of arrests. In June a monk alerted the press and burnt himself to death by way of protest, an action that had enormous impact on both national and American public opinion. As time went on Buddhist protest was aimed increasingly at the Diem regime and sought a neutralist and nationalist state. The USA urged tolerance on Diem, but his entourage saw the movement only as subversive. The last straw came in August when, shortly after Diem had promised the USA to be conciliatory, his brother Nhu sent troops into the pavilions and arrested 1,400 monks. Washington's response was to cable its ambassador that

Diem must be given the chance to rid himself of Nhu and his coterie and replace them with best military and political personalities available.

If . . . Diem remains obdurate and refuses, then we must face the possibility that Diem himself cannot be preserved.[55]

Diem's position had never been completely secure – a 1960 coup had nearly unseated him – and the Kennedy administration had always had at the back of its mind the possibility of switching support elsewhere if Diem proved a failure. In August 1963, after the pagoda raids, it began to listen to Vietnamese generals who were preparing another coup. Diem and Nhu, who had preserved some contacts with Hanoi, responded to US pressure by opening discussions on ditching the Americans and taking the National Liberation Front into a coalition government. It is unclear whether this was a serious initiative or simply an attempt to blackmail the USA.[56] In any case nothing had come of it by the time the presidential palace was attacked in early November. Diem unwisely rejected Ambassador Lodge's offer of personal protection, and he and Nhu were shot.

In countenancing a coup, the USA had deepened its commitment. Indeed, in August 1963 Lodge had been authorised to 'tell appropriate military commanders we will give them direct support in any interim

[55] *Pentagon Papers*, ii, pp. 226–8, 235.
[56] Ang, *Vietnam from the Other Side*, pp. 69–70; Stanley Karnow, *Vietnam. A History* (New York, 1983) pp. 291–2.

period of breakdown [of] central government mechanism'; following the coup Kennedy told Lodge, 'we . . . accepted the possibility that our position might encourage a change of government. We thus have a responsibility to help this new government . . . in every way we can.'[57] For its part, the North Vietnamese Central Committee saw Diem's murder as increasing the likelihood of direct American intervention, and decided to seek to win the war before the United States could move; it therefore began sending whole combat units (and not merely cadres) south.[58] Even before then Washington was convinced that Hanoi controlled the Southern insurgency and could call a halt if it wished. So in 1964 a number of low-key sabotage operations were launched against the North and plans made for major bombing, which, it was felt, would require a Congressional resolution of support. Against this background a warning was sent to Hanoi in June that, unless the insurgency in the South was halted, the USA 'would carry the war to the north'. The North Vietnamese premier rejected it,[59] and President Johnson took no immediate action, perhaps for domestic political reasons.

The 'Gulf of Tonkin' incident and Congressional resolution, 1964

The situation was transformed by a naval incident in early August. A US electronic intelligence destroyer, patrolling close to North Vietnam in the aftermath of a South Vietnamese commando raid, was attacked by Northern torpedo boats but emerged unscathed. Two days later radar and sonar indicated (probably mistakenly) another attack.[60] Johnson responded by bombing North Vietnamese naval bases in August 1964, and by securing a near-unanimous Congressional resolution that authorised the President not only to repel any further attacks on US forces but also 'to take all necessary steps, including the use of armed force, to assist any member or protocol state of the Southeast Asia Collective Defense Treaty requesting assistance in defense of its freedom'.[61] This was later to be

---

[57] *Pentagon Papers*, ii, p. 734; *FRUS 1961–3*, iv, p. 580.
[58] Ang, *Vietnam from the Other Side*, p. 75; Turley, *Second Indochina War*, pp. 44, 57–61.
[59] Ross, *In the Interests of Peace*, pp. 275–6; *Pentagon Papers* (NYT) p. 256.
[60] Ang, *Vietnam from the Other Side*, pp. 80–1.
[61] *Pentagon Papers* (NYT) pp. 257, 264–5.

known as the 'Gulf of Tonkin Resolution'. It resembled that passed during the 1954–5 offshore islands crisis and that launching the Eisenhower Doctrine for the Middle East in 1957. These could have had even more serious consequences, but no real trouble transpired, and neither Congressional nor public opinion was therefore upset. By contrast, Johnson was to act on the Gulf of Tonkin Resolution, treating it – controversially – as *carte blanche* for US military participation in the Vietnam War.

USA bombs North Vietnam and commits ground troops to South Vietnam 1965

Johnson wanted to contest the November 1964 presidential elections as the peace candidate, so he initially did little more than send a second (and equally unavailing) warning to Hanoi. But by July 1965 he had approved not only sustained bombing of North Vietnam but also the sending of 180,000 American troops to the South. At every crisis since 1954, the USA had increased its commitment to South Vietnam (as it would continue to do until 1968). So Johnson's decision lay well within the parameters of US policy. But he had crossed two major fire-breaks, the serious bombardment (though *not* the invasion) of North Vietnam, and American takeover of the war in the South. Volumes have been written to explain this, and to speculate on whether there was not an alternative that might have been adopted either by Johnson himself or by President Kennedy had he lived.[62]

One alternative would have been disengagement justified on the basis that the US had done all that could reasonably be asked of it, but that the South Vietnamese were too incompetent, corrupt, or unwilling seriously to fight for themselves. (This had been the Truman administration's justification of its 1940s disengagement from the Chinese civil war; it had not played well in US domestic politics.) Had the United States opted for this course, a face-saving exit might have been arranged through a new Geneva Conference, as favoured by the USSR (below, pp. 306–7), and a tripartite administration of the South on the Laotian model. North Vietnam

[62] Since Kennedy was *not* seriously contemplating disengagement at the time of his murder, we can only speculate as to whether his more genuinely consultative style, greater scepticism, and less unilateral approach to foreign policy would have led him to act differently from Johnson *in 1965* (Fredrik Logevall, *Choosing War. The Lost Chance for Peace and the Escalation of War in Vietnam* (Berkeley, 1999) pp. 69–73, 395–9; Lawrence Freedman, *Kennedy's Wars* (New York, 2000) Chap. 4).

would have accepted this,[63] but only as a way of taking over (or 'liberat-ing') the South. There were differences in Hanoi as to the best way of securing this outcome; but its commitment to reunification had been absolute ever since 1954, as had the belief that this would almost certainly require the application of 'violence'.

Johnson's major advisers, Defense Secretary McNamara, National Security Adviser McGeorge Bundy, Secretary of State Rusk, Chairman of the Joint Chiefs of Staff Maxwell Taylor, CIA Director McCone, were all against abandoning Vietnam. As McNamara wrote in March 1965, 'total US withdrawal' 'would simply mean a Communist take-over . . . Even talking about a US withdrawal would undermine any chances of keeping a non-Communist government in South Vietnam, and the rug would prob-ably be pulled before the negotiations had gone far.'[64] No doubt there were other voices and Johnson could have found alternative advisers. But he was himself fully committed, if at times rather apprehensive. As Vice-President he had in 1961 pushed for greater involvement to stem 'the decline of confidence in the United States', painting the alternative as to 'throw in the towel in the area and pull back our defenses to San Francisco'. On becoming President, he had declared, 'I am not going to lose Vietnam. I am not going to be the President who saw South-East Asia go the way China went.'[65]

In early 1964 this did not appear an immediate danger. That March McNamara had seen the despatch of a 'US Combat Unit to secure the Saigon Area' as counterproductive, and had held that 'the possible military advantages' of direct US assumption of military command 'would be far outweighed by its adverse psychological impact'.[66] By early 1965 such a hands-off policy no longer seemed viable. On 27 January McNamara and McGeorge Bundy told Johnson 'that our current policy can only lead to disastrous defeat', and that the only choices were the use of military force to compel a change of communist policy or 'negotiation, aimed at salvaging what little can be preserved'. They preferred the former, and Johnson agreed: 'we'll do what we have to do. I'm prepared to do that. We will move strongly.' Twelve days later, after further discouraging reports

[63] Logevall, *Choosing War*, p. 121
[64] *FRUS 1964–1968*, i, p. 158.
[65] *The Post-Imperial Age*, pp. 115–16; Lloyd C. Gardner, *Pay any Price. Lyndon Johnson and the Wars for Vietnam* (Chicago, 1995) p. 87.
[66] *FRUS 1964–1968*, i, p. 166.

on the military situation, he added, 'We face a choice of going forward or running. We have chosen the first alternative. All of us agree on this but there remains some difference as to how fast we should go forward.'[67]

The option of bombing North Vietnam had long been under consideration, so this was naturally the first step taken. Opportunity was provided in February with a Vietcong attack on a US special forces camp at Pleiku; and by March retaliatory raids had escalated into the continuous but controlled bombing of the North. But it soon became clear this would not turn things around. So from February to July 1965 the presidential circle debated the wisdom, nature and scale of a commitment of ground troops. The delay was due partly to Johnson's wish to condition Congress and so reduce the impact on his domestic Great Society programmes, but largely to his difficulty in screwing himself up to take so unpleasant a decision. However, the combination of major Vietcong victories and of the sixth governmental coup since the fall of Diem probably made active US intervention inevitable: the US commander, General Westmoreland, reported in June that 'The South Vietnamese armed forces [the ARVN] cannot stand up to this pressure without substantial US combat support on the ground', and asked for 180,000 men. By 21 July Johnson had decided:

Withdrawal would be a disaster . . . harsh bombing [of North Vietnam] . . . would not win and could easily bring a wider war, and standing pat with existing forces . . . was only slow defeat. Only doing what McNamara urged [committing over 175,000 troops] was left . . .[68]

On paper this decision had been reached after an impressive weighing of the options. Doubts were expressed both as to American staying power and as to whether 'an army of westerners can successfully fight orientals in an Asian jungle'. It was more usual to stress the importance of containing China and of proving US 'commitment'. This last had two aspects. 'If the Communist world finds out we will not pursue our commitments to the end, I don't know where they will stay their hand.' Equally:

In the eyes of the rest of Asia and of [other] key areas threatened by Communism . . . South Vietnam is . . . a test of US capacity to deal with 'wars of national liberation.' Within Asia there is evidence – for example,

---

[67] Logevall, *Choosing War*, pp. 317–18; Robert Dallek, *Flawed Giant. Lyndon Johnson and His Times 1961–1973* (New York, 1998) p. 248.
[68] Dallek, *Flawed Giant*, p. 275; Karnow, *Vietnam*, Chap. 9; *Pentagon Papers* (NYT) Chaps 6, 7.

from Japan – that US disengagement and acceptance of Communist domination would have a serious effect on confidence . . . More broadly any country threatened in the future by Communist subversion would have reason to doubt whether we would really see the thing through.

If South Vietnam were allowed to collapse, McNamara doubted the possibility of holding Thailand, and added 'Laos, Cambodia, Thailand, Burma, surely affect Malaysia. In 2–3 years communist domination would stop there, but ripple effect would be great [in] Japan, India. We would have to give up some bases. Ayub [Khan of Pakistan] would move closer to China. Greece, Turkey would move to neutralist positions.' And so on. In any case Johnson privately feared that failure in Vietnam would unleash a domestic right-wing backlash, comparable to that occasioned by the 'loss' of China in 1949, which would prove fatal to all he stood for in domestic politics.[69] So it can be argued that the real debates were those over the extent of intervention. The military would have liked a more rapid and intensive bombing of the North; Johnson preferred gradual escalation as less likely to upset US domestic opinion or to draw China into the war.[70] Westmoreland wanted US troops to play a major role in fighting the Vietcong; Maxwell Taylor and others felt they should be used only to hold enclaves, releasing ARVN forces to fight the Vietcong but not relieving them of the principal responsibility for the conduct of the war. Johnson eventually decided for Westmoreland.

It can be argued not only that the decision to escalate was mistaken, but also that the wrong strategy was adopted. Bombing North Vietnam had been advocated less on military than on psychological grounds – 'as a means of affecting the will of Hanoi to direct and support the VC', and for its impact on 'the minds of the South Vietnamese' who knew 'the United States could do much more if it would, and . . . are suspicious of our failure to use more of our obviously enormous power.'[71] More bombs were supposedly dropped on North Vietnam than on Germany in the Second World War, and the spectacle placed the USA in a bad light. Damage,

[69] *FRUS* 1964–1968, i, p. 13; *Pentagon Papers* (NYT) p. 326; G. McT. Kahin, *Intervention. How America Became Involved in Vietnam* (New York, 1986) pp. 360–1, 374 ff; Charles De Benedetti, in R.A. Divine (ed.) *Exploring the Johnson Years* (Austin, Texas, 1981) p. 31.
[70] Gradual escalation also increased US losses by allowing time for the installation of anti-aircraft missiles.
[71] *Pentagon Papers*, iii, p. 689.

and civilian casualties,[72] was naturally considerable; but no attempt was made to bomb the North 'back into the stone age'. Johnson chose targets (personally at first) with considerable restraint so as not to provoke Chinese intervention – to avoid which he quietly promised in 1965 not to destroy the vital Red River dams or attack the Chinese border. Even so there might have been scope for mining the North Vietnamese ports, as Nixon did in 1972. In the absence of such actions, and given that it was safeguarded by China from direct invasion, Hanoi was under no overwhelming pressure to discontinue its Southern interventions. Nor did the USA do all it could to prevent supplies and troops coming down from the North. The Ho Chi Minh trail in Laos was bombed repeatedly; but no major attempt was made to cut it on the ground until 1971. The USA also acquiesced in the despatch of supplies via Cambodia, and allowed the Vietcong to use Cambodian territory as a sanctuary. Lastly, within Vietnam itself the Americans tended to concentrate on conventional search-and-destroy operations against major enemy units, and to neglect local protection, reconstruction and the winning of 'hearts and minds'.[73] It was, indeed, not until may 1967 that US civil and military pacification programmes were brought together under a single director.

US intervention nevertheless staved off collapse in 1965; by 1966 US operations were apparently inflicting heavy casualties. Stable government followed, though more slowly and after much political infighting and a final Buddhist rebellion in 1966.[74]

The Tet Offensive (January 1968) and its consequences

In 1957 North Vietnam had rejected immediate resort to military action in the South. From 1959 Hanoi endorsed this as one component of a complex strategy: the balance of forces still precluded full scale revolution, so it was

---

[72] Nobody really knows their dimensions; the US put them in 1969 at 52,000 (Turley, *Second Indochina War*, p. 202), Karnow at 100,000 (*Vietnam*, p. 458). That Vietnam has not claimed higher totals is confirmation that (unlike the Second World War Allies) the USA was not practicing obliteration bombing.

[73] For a critique of this policy, see Race, *War Comes to Long An*, Chap. 5.

[74] General Thieu became President in 1965, was confirmed in office by imperfect (but not completely fraudulent) elections in 1967, and thereafter progressively consolidated his power.

necessary to 'guide and restrict within the South the solving of the contradiction between imperialism and the colonies within our country'; there
should, a January 1961 Politburo directive specified, be military struggle in
the mountains and jungles, a mixture of military and political in the low-
lands, and predominantly political in the towns.[75] The aftermath of Diem's
murder had brought direct involvement of North Vietnamese troop units
and a predominant emphasis on military action. US 'search and destroy'
counter-offensives in 1966 (and 1967) inflicted severe losses. China advised
prolonged guerrilla war, but the idea had little appeal in Hanoi. Premier
Pham Van Dong privately favoured disengagement and the proclamation of South Vietnam as a neutral state 'like Cambodia', but he was in a
minority.[76] Instead 1967 was devoted to planning for a surprise assault
that would bring 'decisive victory'.[77] The campaign began in January 1968
with an assault on Khe Sanh that Washington took to be an attempt to
repeat Dien Bien Phu; this diverted US attention and troops, but was inex-
plicably prolonged until April despite some 10,000 communist losses.
Meanwhile, during the agreed truce for the Tet festival, the communists
flung 70–80,000 troops against a hundred towns all over the country, with
audacious attacks on the US embassy, the Presidential Palace, and the
Saigon radio station. Surprise was complete – half the ARVN was on leave.
But the attacks failed to spark any sympathetic rising; and, now that they
had come out of hiding, communist forces were cut down in large numbers
by superior firepower. By March the USA reported 2,000 American, 4,000
ARVN and perhaps 50,000 insurgent deaths.[78] But the effort was continued with renewed attacks on cities in May and August, both (lacking
surprise) repulsed fairly easily.

In military terms the Tet Offensive was a disaster; as one of its planners
later wrote, 'we suffered heavy losses of manpower and material, especially
of cadres'. Thereafter, according to North Vietnamese sources, Saigon was
able to 'pacify' the greater part of the country.[79] Major communist attacks
accordingly declined sharply until 1972. As a disproportionate number of

[75] Ang, *Vietnam from the Other Side*, pp. 43–4, 56.
[76] January 1968 conversation with Jerszy Mikhalovsky – Anatoly Dobrynin, *In
Confidence. Moscow's Ambassador to America's Six Cold War Presidents (1962–1986)*
(New York, 1995) p. 170.
[77] Ang, *Vietnam from the Other Side*, pp. 112 ff.
[78] Karnow, *Vietnam*, p. 534.
[79] 9,200 out of 12,395 hamlets, 16m people out of 17.5m – Ang, *Vietnam from the
Other Side*, p. 134 Turley, *Second Indochina War*, p. 116.

the Tet casualties had been Southerners (since General Giap had sought to husband his Northern regulars), growing numbers of Northerners had to be sent to take their places. These were less familiar with the territory. Countermeasures, too, were now more effective in that, since 1967, Vietcong cadres were being deliberately sought out for arrest or elimination by counter-intelligence. This CIA-sponsored Operation Phoenix was morally dubious; and like much else in the South it was corrupt, with 70 per cent of those arrested supposedly able to buy back their freedom. But subsequent Vietcong testimony suggests that it was still distinctly damaging, though the claim that it accounted for 60,000 authentic agents cannot be tested.[80] After Tet, too, more emphasis was placed on 'rural construction', while in 1970 Thieu recognised the land redistribution effected by the Vietcong and embarked on a further programme that halved tenancy in the populous Mekong delta.[81]

There would, then, have been a case for *increasing* the US war effort after the Tet offensive. Instead Tet broke the American will to fight. This had been eroding for some time. Even in 1965 Johnson had worried about the question, 'Are we starting something that in two or three years we simply can't finish?'[82] Tet contradicted the official optimism about the course of the war, and public confidence in Johnson fell sharply. Tet also raised the question of despatching more troops. To do so would have meant mobilising the reserves. This was something Johnson had always been reluctant to contemplate; and it became clear that even Congressional hawks opposed significant troop increases. Then on 12 March Johnson almost lost the New Hampshire primary to the previously insignificant peace campaigner, Senator Eugene McCarthy. This convinced him that he needed 'a peace proposal'. The last straw came in late March, when the group of elder statesmen Johnson periodically consulted on foreign affairs reversed their previous stance and advised disengagement.[83] On 31 March Johnson finally decided to send only 13,500 more troops to Vietnam.

---

[80] Karnow, *Vietnam*, pp. 601–2.

[81] Turley, *Second Indochina War*, pp. 135–6. It is not clear how far these reforms benefited Thieu's government; but they left a land-owning peasantry that resisted later communist exactions and attempts at collectivisation (Nguyen Van Cahn, *Vietnam under Communism 1975–82* [Stanford, 1983] pp. 30–3, 38, 139).

[82] Kahin, *Intervention*, p. 383.

[83] In 1965 they had been all for committing US troops. Now the State Department briefed them, and later Johnson himself, that South Vietnam was in such a state that real progress might take five to ten years.

He also announced his intention not to seek re-election, discontinued the bombing of most (later all) of North Vietnam, and proffered unconditional peace negotiations – which, to his surprise, Hanoi promptly accepted.[84] Talks soon began in Paris. Although they made absolutely no progress, the US administration was to come under increasing pressure from an anti-war movement convinced that just one more concession would get them off the ground.

Nixon's plans to end the war 1968–9

The three main American presidential candidates in 1968 all held out hopes of ending involvement in Vietnam. Nixon looked partly to intimidating North Vietnam into negotiating, and partly to enlisting the good offices of the Soviet Union. Here, however, Nixon overestimated both Moscow's willingness and its ability to coerce Hanoi. Khrushchev had always seen Vietnam as a side-show, telling Ho Chi Minh in 1961 he was busy with preparations for his upcoming Party Congress 'and the solution of the German problem. When we . . . have more time . . . it will be possible to consider the issue of a trip to Vietnam.' In 1961–2 the USSR favoured a Laos-style Geneva Conference on South Vietnam, leading to the end of US involvement and neutralisation. But it noted that 'the Vietnamese friends have in practice undertaken measures aimed at the intensification of the armed struggle'. In the process Hanoi moved increasingly towards the Chinese side in the growing Sino-Soviet rift, thereby attracting Khrushchev's anger. On taking over, Brezhnev switched to endorsing the 'heroic liberation struggle', while Kosygin went to Hanoi in early 1965, promising the resumption of the aid Khrushchev had cut. Nevertheless Kosygin may still have been ready to promote restraint. The bombing of the North began during his Hanoi visit, and he later implied that had the USA first consulted him, the 'Soviet Union would at that time have been willing to do something about North Vietnamese intervention in the South'.[85] As it was, the Kremlin responded by denouncing the bombing, by helping to arrange protests against it in Western Europe, and by increasing its aid to North Vietnam. It also rushed in missiles, which were (in due course) to shoot down appreciable numbers of US bombers. But it continued to worry about growing US involvement, which (Brezhnev told

[84] Karnow, *Vietnam*, pp. 545–66; *Pentagon Papers* (NYT) pp. 607–23.
[85] Gaiduk, *Confronting Vietnam*, pp. 193, 196–201, 204, 262n, 264n.

the Hungarians) might change the current favourable military situation in the South. So Kosygin seems also to have talked in Hanoi and Beijing of de-escalation and of helping the USA 'find a way out' of Vietnam – to no effect. The Russians continued to worry about the possibility of major US escalation. So Kosygin jumped at the chance (which appeared to present itself when he was in London in February 1967) of arranging the discontinuance of US bombing against a secret promise by Hanoi not to send any more troops south. The ending of the bombing of North Vietnam in 1968, and the USA's obvious eagerness to disengage, probably stilled many of these fears. Soviet military aid to North Vietnam switched increasingly to the kind of equipment that would enable it to launch a major conventional offensive (as it did in 1972).[86] By contrast Egypt was to be deliberately starved in the early 1970s of the weapons it needed to attack Israel.

The Nixon administration, however, initially hoped the USSR could be brought to coerce Hanoi. Dobrynin was sounded out in April 1969, and in October Nixon sought to make the Soviet response a test case: 'If the Soviet Union found it possible to do something in Vietnam, and the Vietnam war ended, then we might do something dramatic to improve our relations . . . But until then . . . real progress will be very difficult.'[87] Given Hanoi's dependence on the USSR (*inter alia* for petroleum), Moscow could, in theory, have brought considerable pressure to bear (at the risk of driving Hanoi into Beijing's arms).[88] The USSR could deal very abruptly with its clients.[89] On this occasion it did not choose to; and unless subjected to intense pressure, Hanoi (like Israel) would go its own way. Nor, as things transpired, did Moscow have any reason to intervene. Nixon's threats notwithstanding, US–Soviet relations later improved dramatically,

---

[86] *Pentagon Papers* (NYT) esp. pp. 38–40, 151, 167, 189–90, 204; W.R. Smyser, *The Independent Vietnamese: Vietnamese Communism between Russia and China, 1956–1969* (Athens, Ohio, 1980) esp. pp. 73–4, 76–7, 88, 94; Douglas Pike, *Vietnam and the Soviet Union* (Boulder, 1987) esp. Chap. 5 and pp. 120–2, 139; Harold Wilson, *The Labour Government 1964–70: a personal record* (1971) Chap. 19; Karnow, *Vietnam*, pp. 495–6.

[87] Nixon, *Memoirs*, pp. 391, 399–400, 405–7; Kissinger, *Memoirs*, i, pp. 267–8.

[88] China could, presumably, have provided (inferior) substitutes for all Soviet military aid except, perhaps, missiles. Whether it would have greatly increased its aid to Hanoi at a time when it was seeking American support against Moscow is less certain.

[89] In 1967–9 the USSR successfully pressed Cuba to revert to the Soviet line by holding oil deliveries constant despite the 8% pa growth in Cuban demand and by imposing other economic sanctions (Tad Szulc, *Fidel: a Critical Portrait* (New York, 1986) pp. 678, 681, 684, 689).

with a summit conference being arranged for May 1972. That April North Vietnam staged a long-awaited offensive even larger than that of 1968, despite US warnings of its possible impact on the summit. The Soviet Union had provided the wherewithal. But equally it had no intention of allowing this to disrupt its own relations with Washington; a strong protest was made at the summit, but in such a way as to indicate that it was largely for the record.[90] In short, US–Soviet relations could not be 'linked' to events in Indo-China.

The other arm of Nixon's strategy was to threaten North Vietnam with terrible destruction unless it negotiated a compromise. But if there was ever a time for this approach, it had passed. There had been divisions within the North Vietnamese politburo in the early 1960s as to how far it was right to put the country at risk by open intervention in the South. Probably hardliners like Le Duan were firmly in control by 1965, but Johnson might just possibly have been able to bargain for Northern restraint by making sufficiently convincing threats of all-out air attack. In fact his bombing lost much of its impact through gradual escalation, and was so far limited that Hanoi may by 1969 have come to believe it could live with the worst the USA could do. Be this as it may, Nixon issued threats, telling Ho Chi Minh in July that, in default of a breakthrough by November, he would have recourse 'to measures of great consequence and force'. Many similar warnings were given, and 1 November was built up as a deadline. But to no purpose. Nixon's threats were not entirely empty since he had commissioned plans for intensive bombing ('Duck Hook'). Rather than further stir the cauldron of internal US unrest, however, he allowed his bluff to be called and confined himself to a firm speech for domestic consumption.[91]

Vietnamisation

But if US forces were to be cut, the South Vietnamese would have increasingly to take over the fighting (whereas since 1965 they had been regarded largely as auxiliaries to the better equipped and more effective Americans).

[90] Ilya Gaiduk, *The Soviet Union and the Vietnam War* (Chicago, 1996) pp. 238–41; Kissinger, *White House Years* (Boston, 1979) pp. 1226–7. In November 1971 China had also refused Hanoi's request that, failing major US concessions, it cancel President Nixon's forthcoming visit (Ang, *Ending the Vietnam War. The Vietnamese Communists' Perspective* (2004) p. 85).

[91] Nixon, *Memoirs*, pp. 393–411; Hersh, *The Price of Power*, pp. 120–34.

This policy of 'Vietnamisation' began early in 1969 while Nixon still hoped to bring North Vietnam to accept mutual troop withdrawal. When these hopes evaporated, only Vietnamisation remained. At one level it was quite effective. Troop cuts enabled the USA to reduce the draft, and the call-up machinery was also reformed. This did much to quieten US campuses; but the progressive reduction of American troops (from a peak of 543,000 in April 1969 to 157,000 by the end of 1971) opened up the possibility of their soon becoming militarily insignificant. An acute dilemma presented itself in early 1972 when a communist offensive seemed on the cards; but the compulsion to continue withdrawals was so strong that Nixon decided to halve US forces by May. However, if troops departed, air power could still be used – it cost relatively few US casualties and was much less sensitive politically than a conscript army. Still, as Nixon noted in 1972, 'all the air power in the world' would not save Saigon 'if the South Vietnamese aren't able to hold on the ground'. So Vietnamisation also demanded the further strengthening of the ARVN. Quantitatively this was easy; qualitatively the picture was more mixed. Some ARVN units were indeed good, and South Vietnamese forces sometimes did well; in other circumstances (especially when deployed away from their home bases) they simply collapsed. 'The real problem,' Nixon noted, 'is that the enemy is willing to sacrifice in order to win, while the South Vietnamese simply aren't willing to pay that much of a price in order to avoid losing.'[92] This must be qualified – ARVN deaths in battle (admittedly defending what was supposed to be their own country) were by late 1972 more than four times as high as the 46,000 the USA found unacceptable. But they pale before 'Vietcong' and North Vietnamese losses.[93]

The Lon Nol coup in Cambodia

A disastrous side-effect of Vietnamisation was the extension of the war in Cambodia. Cambodia had after 1954 been successfully governed by its former King, Prince Sihanouk, whose chief ambition had been to keep it out of trouble. In the 1960s this involved leaning verbally towards China, which he judged the predominant power in the region, condemning US

---

[92] Karnow, *Vietnam*, pp. 642–3; Nixon, *Memoirs*, p. 595; Peter Braestrup (ed.), *Vietnam as History: ten years after the Paris Peace Accords* (Washington, 1984), chronological table.
[93] See *The Post-Imperial World*, Chap. 6.

intervention, and not contesting the Vietcong presence in his country. By December 1967 Sihanouk was having doubts (the China of the 'Cultural Revolution' looked less impressive); so he suggested US 'hot pursuit' raids 'in uninhabited areas', which 'would be liberating us from the Vietcong'.[94] Johnson would not undertake them, but in early 1969 Nixon started bombing in border areas, seeking not only to destroy or dislodge the Vietcong headquarters (COSVN) but also to 'signal' his determination to Hanoi. Although Nixon told some leading Congressmen, he otherwise kept the operation secret from the American public; both Cambodia and North Vietnam also preferred to keep quiet about the bombing. North Vietnam did, however, begin to support the small communist resistance to Sihanouk, the Khmer Rouge.

As 1969 proceeded Sihanouk looked increasingly to the USA. But others were impatient: in March 1970, while Sihanouk was on holiday in France, he was formally deposed and a new regime constituted under General Lon Nol. Sihanouk proceeded to Beijing – where, in late April, China arranged a meeting, under his chairmanship, of North Vietnam, the Southern NLF, Pathet Lao and the Khmer Rouge, which provided legitimation for the continued 'Vietcong' use of Cambodia and for both North Vietnamese and Chinese support for the Sihanouk–Khmer Rouge coalition. There has been controversy as to how far the United States was responsible for Lon Nol's coup. He was probably acting independently, albeit in the belief that he was bound to get US support; both Nixon and Kissinger seem to have been taken by surprise.[95] Be that as it may, the effect was disastrous since it removed the constraints that had hitherto shielded Cambodia from full involvement in the Indo-Chinese struggle.

The North Vietnamese and Khmer Rouge were first off the mark, capturing or attacking several towns in April and cutting communications to the capital Phnom Penh. Official Washington was deeply divided as to whether to help Lon Nol militarily, but Nixon clearly felt something should be done: 'They are romping in there, and the only government in Cambodia in the last twenty-five years that had the guts to take a pro-Western and pro-American stand is ready to fall . . .' US action, however, was geared chiefly to the needs of its existing war in South Vietnam: Cambodian developments provided a tempting opportunity to take out the

[94] Karnow, *Vietnam*, p. 590.
[95] Karnow, *Vietnam*, pp. 603–7; Kissinger, *Memoirs*, i, pp. 457–70; Hersh, *The Price of Power* Chap. 15; Chang, Pao-Min. *Kampuchea between China and Vietnam* (Singapore, 1985) pp. 27–33.

Vietcong bases on the border, in particular COSVN. So on 30 April Nixon announced joint South Vietnamese and US attacks on the 'sanctuaries', justifying them chiefly in terms of protecting US forces in Vietnam and guaranteeing 'the continued success of our withdrawal and Vietnamization programs'. Then, to placate fears of getting bogged down in yet another Indo-Chinese war, he gave assurances that US troops would go no more than 21 miles into Cambodia and that they would leave by the end of June – which obviously limited their effectiveness. South Vietnamese forces penetrated further and stayed longer, but they too had to be withdrawn to cover for US troop withdrawals from Vietnam. Thereafter the only combat assistance provided to Lon Nol was from the air – at grave cost to Cambodian civilians.[96]

Although the 1970 incursion did little to save Lon Nol, it did relieve pressure on South Vietnam by capturing quite sizeable stocks of Vietcong weapons and equipment; however, it narrowly failed to intercept the bulk of COSVN personnel, who had begun to withdraw into the interior immediately after Sihanouk's deposition. So perhaps the USA's chief gain from the 1970 Cambodian developments was that they diverted enemy forces into fighting Lon Nol – 'If those [40,000] North Vietnamese weren't in Cambodia,' Nixon declared, 'they'd be over killing Americans' – and prevented Vietcong supplies using Cambodian ports.[97]

The 1971 South Vietnamese attempt to cut the Ho Chi Minh trail, and the 1972 North Vietnamese offensive

With these supplies cut off, the 'Ho Chi Minh' trail down through Laos became correspondingly more important. The trail had originally been a collection of jungle paths that took six months to travel and carried a considerable risk of malaria. From mid-1964 it was constantly upgraded, finishing as paved roads, supply depots, and even an oil pipeline.[98] The

---

[96] Precisely how grave became a matter of controversy; in the Appendix to *Years of Upheaval*, Kissinger defends himself against charges of indiscriminate bombing. The Cambodian civil war cost about half a million lives, but we cannot reliably apportion these as between bombing, fighting and Khmer Rouge atrocities.

[97] *Keesing's*, 24145; Truong, *Vietcong Memoir*, pp. 176 ff; Hersh, *The Price of Power*, p. 303.

[98] Karnow, *Vietnam*, pp. 331–4, 659–60, 663.

USA sought to block (or at least damage) the route by bombing. But it had not tried to cut it on the ground, since permanent blocking would have required large numbers of troops and since Johnson in any case did not want cross-border forays. Now Nixon decided to seize the staging-point of Tchepone in February 1971 and destroy as many trail facilities as possible before withdrawing – but to do so using only the ARVN, since (in the aftermath of Cambodia) Congress had forbidden the use of US troops in either Cambodia or Laos. The operation was badly planned and executed. Tchepone was ultimately captured, but by late March the ARVN had pulled out in disorderly retreat. The incursion did delay the communist build-up; but its chief effect was to confirm Hanoi's belief that it could beat the ARVN in conventional warfare.[99] The attempt was first made in June 1972, with the commitment of ten of North Vietnam's thirteen combat divisions. It almost succeeded – some cities were taken (provoking panic-stricken civilian flights), and guerrillas were able to return to 'pacified' regions when government troops withdrew to resist attacks elsewhere. But the communists, too, made mistakes and encountered logistic difficulties; they were battered by US air power, losing perhaps some 50,000 dead. Hanoi now decided the time had come to bargain seriously.[100]

Secret negotiations and the ceasefire agreement 1973; US inability to enforce it; The communist offensive of 1975 and the fall of Saigon

The Paris peace talks that started in 1968 achieved nothing but propaganda. They were supplemented in 1969 by secret North Vietnamese meetings with Kissinger (also in Paris). Initially these fared no better. As a precondition for a ceasefire and the return of US prisoners of war, the North Vietnamese demanded that the USA remove President Thieu and his regime. This Washington would not accept. The United States no longer pursued its pre-1968 goal of a unilateral suspension of Northern infiltration, but it still sought mutual US–North Vietnamese withdrawal. Hanoi objected on principle, since it regarded Vietnam as a single country and rejected the equation of US and North Vietnamese troops as being both aliens in the South. It also knew that, whatever the situation had been

---

[99] Kissinger, *Memoirs*, i, pp. 987–1010; Turley, *Second Indochina War*, pp. 141–3.
[100] US interdiction of its railways and mining of its ports may also have been a factor – Turley, *Second Indochina War*, pp. 143–9; Karnow, *Vietnam*, pp. 639–47.

in the mid-1960s, Saigon could now defeat the Southern insurgents if Northern forces withdrew. In May 1971 Kissinger made the major concession that a US withdrawal date might be fixed without a corresponding North Vietnamese one. But at their meeting in June Le Duc Tho still insisted that if the communists did not achieve their political goal of unifying and liberating the country, the fighting would not end.[101]

There was little progress till late 1972; then both sides wanted to settle before the November US elections, the communists probably fearing that a re-elected Nixon would be stronger and more obdurate, the Americans that the new Congress might bar even the use of air power in Indo-China. In October 1972, therefore, a deal was nearly reached on the basis of a ceasefire, the return of prisoners, a US – but *not* a North Vietnamese – troop withdrawal, and an interim arrangement in South Vietnam that (should it not lead to mutually agreed elections) would leave the government and the NLF to control whatever territory they occupied. At this point Thieu, who had not expected earlier negotiations to succeed and so had raised no objections, became seriously worried and demanded changes. To break the deadlock, and demonstrate his resolution, Nixon launched the 'Christmas bombing', which was suspended when Hanoi accepted his timetable for negotiations in early January. These soon proved successful. Thieu's acquiescence was then secured by the promise (which the 'Christmas bombing' made appear more credible) that the USA would 'respond with full force should the settlement be violated by North Vietnam', plus the carrot of further aid and the threat that if Saigon proved obdurate the USA would settle without it.[102]

The ceasefire was concluded in January 1973. The chief lever the USA had to enforce it was the possibility that it might resume bombing in the event of violations. Kissinger may not always have been confident of Saigon's prospects.[103] But in March–April 1973 he certainly urged air strikes in response to what he saw as continued Northern infiltration.

---

[101] Ang, *Ending the Vietnam War*, pp. 72–3.

[102] Nixon to Thieu, 5 and 17 January 1973. Nixon kept these letters secret, despite their bearing on Congressional moves to disengage completely from Saigon. Ford had apparently not read them when, in 1974, he reaffirmed to Thieu 'existing' US commitments. Thieu finally sent them to Washington in March 1975, with a mission invoking Nixon's pledges, but to no avail – Nguyen Tien Hung and Jerrold Schechter, *The Palace File* (New York, 1989 edn) esp. pp. 1, 3, 285–6, 309, 386, 392–5, 435.

[103] John Erlichman claims Kissinger said, on 23 January, 'if they're lucky they can hold out for a year and a half' (*Witness to Power. The Nixon Years* [paperback edn, 1982] p. 288).

Nixon was hesitant. Both then and later Kissinger blamed Watergate – 'If we didn't have this damn domestic situation, a week of bombing would put this Agreement into force.' But Nixon had already been reluctant to continue in early January, when he had noted that 'war-weariness has reached the point that Option Two [involving continued bombing] is just too much for us to carry on'.[104] So even without Watergate he would have found bombing very difficult to renew.

Nixon's threats might still have had value as a bluff; but Congress largely undercut them. Once it had recovered US prisoners of war, it felt free to bolt the door against further military involvement. The immediate occasion was Cambodia, where no ceasefire had been arranged since Hanoi claimed it could not control the Khmer Rouge. US air support for Lon Nol therefore continued. Amendments to delete all funds for this were attached in June to appropriations and other financial bills for the coming fiscal year. At first Nixon sought to resist; but he was being badly damaged by Watergate, and he eventually compromised on a measure that permitted continued bombing until 15 August, then cut off funds for all US military activity throughout Indo-China. The extension of bombing helped break a Khmer Rouge assault on Phnom Penh, but its real purpose was to buy time for discussions with China on Lon Nol's departure and the reconstitution of a neutralist coalition government under Sihanouk. Kissinger claims that Zhou Enlai's support for such an outcome evaporated when Congress halted the bombing.[105]

In South Vietnam Thieu ignored the fig-leaf provisions of the January 1973 agreement for a tripartite National Reconciliation Council, and sought, in fairly low-key fashion, to expand the territory under his control. Saigon claimed the takeover of 1,000 hamlets by mid-1974,[106] but it suffered economically from the withdrawal of US troops, from aid cutbacks, and (in 1974) from the oil price rise. By 1974 the country was in the grip of an inflation that did much to undermine army morale, and also led people to view the endemic official corruption with growing hostility. Meanwhile the Hanoi politburo held 'heated debate' over strategy in May–June 1973; this left open both violent but largely 'political' struggle to utilise the ceasefire agreement and more exclusively military action. In his instructions to the South, Le Duan explained that 'the revolution . . . can only

---

[104] Kissinger, *Memoirs*, ii, esp. pp. 318–26, 1237; Nixon, *Memoirs*, p. 743.
[105] Kissinger, *Memoirs*, ii, pp. 343, 349–55, 358–9, 362–9; T.M. Franck and E. Weisband, *Foreign Policy by Congress* (New York, 1979) Chap. 1.
[106] Turley, *Second Indochina War*, p. 164.

win victory by means of continuous revolution and by violence, by relying on the political and military strength of the people and by making use of new . . . advantages that will be brought about by the Paris Agreement.' The situation, he had told Zhou Enlai,

will be clear in three or four years' time. At any rate the government there must eventually be a democratic and nationalist one . . . [that] government can exist for ten or fifteen years. And then the name can be changed. So we are not in a hurry to turn South Vietnam into a socialist entity.[107]

The corresponding military plan was to build up supplies in 1974 (having spent the previous winter building roads to take mechanised forces and an oil pipeline to supply them), and for medium-sized battles in 1975, larger ones in 1976. Dates for the big push continued to be argued over, with Le Duan coming to favour a relatively early move. In July 1974 he warned that, following the US withdrawal, 'other countries' (presumably China and the USSR) 'are trying to gain influence in this area . . . even though they did not speak openly, all had secret strategies regarding the Southeast Asia region.' There was a need to act

before the situation could be reversed. A unified Vietnam with a population of 50 million would not be an easy target for any prospective invader or interventionist . . . We had to . . . win comprehensively before the Saigon administration could . . . reorganise and before any other country could intervene.

Accordingly in September–October the politburo decided on large-scale attacks in 1975, followed by a general offensive and insurrection in 1976. Communist troop strength in the South was supposedly increased (from 190,000) to 275,000 by March 1975.[108]

On paper the ARVN was the stronger force. But it was spread too thinly in an attempt to hold as much territory as possible; and though still probably the better equipped, it had been trained to fight American-style with prodigal use of ammunition and had difficulty to adjusting to reductions in its supply. Nor could its air force replicate the US air strikes that had done so much to stem the 1968 and 1972 offensives. But the primary mistakes were those of command. After the relatively minor town of

---

[107] Ang, *Ending the Vietnam War*, pp. 136–7, 147–8.
[108] ibid. pp. 148, 150, 152, 154–7; Chang, *Kampuchea*, p. 39.

Banmethuot fell on 11 March 1975, Thieu ordered the evacuation of the central highlands. In the process the troops, encumbered by dependents and panic-stricken civilians, disintegrated as a fighting force. A second communist offensive in the north first broke the ARVN around Hué, then isolated and shelled Danang, which was swamped by up to a million refugees and in no condition to face a siege. An attempt was made to withdraw the garrison by sea, but most troops deserted or were left behind. After taking Danang on 29 March, Hanoi decided to drive on Saigon before Southern morale recovered. Only once did it meet prolonged resistance; much of the ARVN command (like other high Southern officials) fled abroad. Saigon was taken on 29 April.[109] Phnom Penh, besieged since January, had already fallen to the Khmer Rouge. In Laos, after a symbolic Pathet Lao victory in May, rightist politicians fled and a gradual communist political takeover was complete by December.

Reasons for the US failure; The war's impact on the USA

In the 1960s the USA had increased its involvement in Indo-China to prove that communist insurgency could be resisted and to demonstrate the credibility of its guarantees to its allies. It had failed on both counts, not as a result of military defeat but because its will to fight had evaporated. There were many reasons for this. One was simply the length of the war. General Marshall had once doubted whether the USA could ever fight 'a seven years war'. The Korean War (with which the US involvement in Vietnam is most directly comparable) lasted less than three years, and by November 1952 the US electorate was clearly looking to see it ended. Arguably support for the USA's Vietnam involvement lasted nearly as long as that for the Korean War; it was not until mid-1967 that a majority came to see the Vietnam War as 'a mistake'. But from about that time, US administrations were operating against the background of a strident anti-war movement (which was joined by many former supporters of the war). This exposed official explanations – the phrase 'credibility gap' dates from the Johnson era – and brought out the indiscriminate destruction occasioned by American use of bombing, defoliation and fire power. It broadcast the unsavoury nature of the Saigon regime, and tended to romanticise the NLF

---

[109] A puppet Southern government was established; then in 1976 North and South Vietnam were formally united.

and deny (or excuse) Hanoi's actions beyond its borders. Its arguments came to sway many people inside as well as outside government.

Opposition to the war was, though, not a matter of argument only, but also of demonstrations – 'Hey, Hey, LBJ, How many kids did you kill today?' – and indeed, especially for substantial sections of educated youth, of a new mood and lifestyle. This had other sources besides Vietnam – notably the civil rights and black activist turmoil that had by 1967 degenerated into a 'long hot summer' of ghetto riots. By 1968–9 the United States seemed in a bad way – Nixon's inaugural noted that 'We are torn by division', and in March 1969 he said of the endemic campus disorders 'this is the way civilizations begin to die . . . None of us has the right to suppose it cannot happen here.'[110] So one constraint on US decision-makers was their reading of the likely domestic effects of their actions. The anti-war movement was not strong enough to induce them simply to pull out of Vietnam; but it did have a significant effect, especially in 1969–70, in deterring or limiting escalation. The desire to restore domestic calm was one important factor in encouraging the policy of 'Vietnamisation' and the withdrawal of US ground forces. Another was the fear that, if the administration did not so withdraw troops, Congress would simply cut off funds – as indeed it did in 1973 (once US prisoners of war had been recovered), thus removing any possibility that Hanoi would be constrained by fear of US air power to observe the ceasefire agreement.

The USA's Vietnam experience was undoubtedly traumatic. It led to some questioning of Cold War orthodoxies, and to a more widespread reluctance to risk further entanglements that would impose constraints on subsequent administrations' diplomatic freedom of manoeuvre. It also tarnished the United States' international image. All this had an appreciable effect on world politics, especially in the 1970s. It chastened the USA, but did not, in the last resort, turn it fundamentally from its former international course (as revulsion against the Afghan war was to do to Soviet foreign policy in the later 1980s).

Southeast Asia since 1975

Nor were the effects in Southeast Asia of the communist victories in Indo-China to be as far-reaching as many had feared. US involvement had been

---

[110] *Keesing's*, 23135; Stephen Ambrose, *Nixon: the triumph of a politician, 1962–1972* (New York, 1989) p. 263.

largely based on the 'domino theory', and not without reason. The 1959 Party Plenary Session in Hanoi that had decided on a return to arms in the South had located Vietnam's struggle as 'part of the world's revolution', and declared that victory would encourage similar liberation struggles in Asia, Africa and Latin America.[111] This perspective recurrs in Sino-Vietnamese discussions over the next decade, leading Stein Tønnesson to conclude that 'Hanoi and Beijing wanted dominoes to fall as much as Washington wished to keep them standing.'[112]

Vague aspirations apart, Hanoi was always clear that it must eventually dominate all of ex-French Indo-China, as, by the end of the 1970s, it did. The real question related to developments beyond that point. When in 1965 Ho Chi Minh talked of the need to build military roads in and through Laos, Mao added that 'Because we will fight large-scale battles in the future, it will be good if we also build roads to Thailand'. In March 1971 Zhou Enlai returned to this theme, telling North Vietnamese leaders that the

Thai government is very much afraid of the Thai Communist Party's armed forces. It knows that weapons . . . are transported [to them] via Vietnam and Laos. It also knows that China has a road that runs to the Sino-Lao border. Therefore it faces the threat of the war expanding all over South-East Asia. We hold that support to the peoples' revolutionary struggles cannot be sacrificed for the sake of relations between governments.

Le Duan's response was that Japan wanted 'to control the region. We want to smash the alliance between the US, Japan, and the regional bourgeois class'; accordingly he asked China to call a conference 'to oppose the Nixon Doctrine . . . weaken the US–Japan alliance and shake the Southeast Asian bourgeois class'.[113]

Aid to Thai or Burmese communist insurgents never approached the scale of that given to the Vietminh in 1950–4, but it was an important

---

[111] Ang, *Vietnam from the Other Side*, p. 30; Gaiduk, *Confronting Vietnam*, pp. 110–11.

[112] Odd Arne Westad, Chen Jian, Stein Tønnesson, Nguyen Vu Tung, James Hershberg, *77 Conversations between Chinese and Foreign Leaders on the Wars in Indochina, 1964–1977* (CWIHP Working Paper 22, 1998) p. 35; cf. Zhou Enlai's comments in 1966–7, ibid. pp. 93, 107.

[113] ibid. pp. 87, 179–80. There had also been discussion in 1967 of the prospects of revolution in Burma; conditions, Zhou said, had been good, and he did not know why development was so slow (p. 103).

consideration. Thai communists (CPT) had in 1952 established a base in jungle bordering Laos and China, while, following China's 1967 breach with the Burmese government, the Burmese communists transferred their headquarters to the Chinese border in 1968. Both also broadcast from China. Similarly the region's communist parties maintained liaison offices in Hanoi. But by the later 1970s the CPT derived most help from Khmer Rouge Cambodia ('Kampuchea') – in 1978 some 1,500 guerrillas, operating across that border with Khmer army support were supposedly responsible for half Thailand's civilian casualties, and had started carrying villagers off to their indoctrination camps.[114]

Thailand did indeed go through a distinctly disturbed period, especially after a 1976 coup had led many socialists to join forces with the CPT.[115] But the region as a whole had calmed down since the days of Sukarno and confrontation, when the initial commitment of US troops to South Vietnam had been made. The fall of Saigon led ASEAN members to seek to pull together by way of self-preservation. The communist states did not show such unity. Already in 1973 China was telling Kissinger of its fears of Hanoi dominating the region 'as an agent of the Soviet Union', and explaining its road-building into Laos as a means not of revolutionising Thailand but of checking a Vietnamese advance.[116] Following victory in 1975 Vietnam initiated curbs on 'comprador bourgeois' Chinese business-men that soon developed into a general assault on the ethnic Chinese – a pro-Chinese source says 270,000 were deported to China, while others were relocated to inhospitable 'new economic zones' in the interior.[117] Similarly the chief concern of the Khmer Rouge (apart from horrific domestic reconstruction) appears to have lain with Cambodia's traditional enemy, the Vietnamese. Vietnam fully reciprocated.

By July 1978 a Thai official could happily observe that 'the Communist Party of Thailand is having difficulty dealing with the Communist parties of the nearby countries. It is seeking support from all of them, but since these . . . are at serious odds with one another their material support for

---

[114] *Keesing's*, esp. 26311, 29819–20, 31583.
[115] By 1978 there were supposedly 9–14,000 full-time communist insurgents, plus part-time village militias of 10–15,000, operating in 46 of the 72 Thai provinces (*Keesing's*, 29819–20). But those in the south, who in fact proved the longest lasting, represented rather a spillover from the 1950s Malay insurgency.
[116] Ang, *Ending the Vietnam War*, p. 142; Kissinger, *Memoirs*, ii, pp. 58–9.
[117] Hoang Van Hoan, *A Drop in the Ocean. Hoang Van Hoan's Revolutionary Reminiscences* (Beijing, 1988) pp. 355–6.

the Thai communist insurgency has been reduced.' In fairly short order, incidents fell off as Khmer troops were first moved to the Vietnam border, then overrun. China and Vietnam came to blows, and both lightened ballast by disengaging from the Thai communists. Vietnam expelled their Hanoi mission, then (together with Laos) pushed many Thai communists back over the border, sometimes first warning the Thai military. The CPT split between pro-Chinese and pro-Vietnamese factions. In 1979 China closed down its radio station, and switched most of its support to Khmer Rouge forces now operating out of Thailand against Vietnam's puppet Cambodian government. 1979–82 saw Thai army sweeps against the thus debilitated communists, 1984 the claim that the CPT 'will never again be able to pose an armed threat to the country'.[118]

1978–9 was thus to set the regional pattern for over a decade. Vietnam (after signing a treaty with the USSR) overran Cambodia and installed a puppet government (a great improvement on the Khmer Rouge). China responded by casting its protection over Thailand, and by invading Vietnam to teach it a 'lesson'. The 'lesson' was militarily unimpressive. But China also embarked on a long-run policy of forcing Vietnam to maintain high readiness on its northern border and of channeling support to Khmer Rouge guerrillas operating out of Thailand, in the hope that 'Vietnam will be tied down and its plan to realise an "Indochina Federation" – a direct menace to Southeast Asia – will be delayed. The longer the delay, the greater will be the consumption of the national strength of Vietnam.'[119] This was a high-risk strategy, since fighting in Cambodia could easily have spilled over into Thailand; but (one or two episodes apart) Cambodia and Vietnam showed considerable restraint.

Meanwhile conditions within Vietnam deteriorated. Refugees had been leaving ever since the fall of Saigon. By 1979 they had become a flood,[120] the product of anti-communism, pressure on the ethnic Chinese, and, increasingly, a flight from poverty and hunger. By late 1986 things were serious enough for the Party Congress to be dominated by depressing

---

[118] The Burmese communists lasted longer, but in 1989 disintegrated along ethnic lines – *Keesing's*, 29819–20, 30287, 31583, 33281, 35004–5, 36869; Hoang Van Hoan, *A Drop in the Ocean*, pp. 357–8.

[119] Charles McGregor, *The Sino-Vietnamese Relationship and the Soviet Union* (Adelphi Paper 232, 1988) pp. 47–8, 52.

[120] In May–June 1979 over 100,000 'boat people' reached land (while another 35,000 may have drowned in the attempt). In the 1980s some 1.5m refugees were resettled: *Keesing's*, 30075–83, 36526.

economic reports and to lead to a major clear-out of the top leadership.[121] By now Vietnam was coming under increasing Soviet pressure to leave Cambodia – something China was insisting on before it would normalise relations with the USSR. The process of withdrawal, and still more of the negotiation of transitional arrangements to succeed the Vietnam-imposed regime, was prolonged. But a settlement was reached in 1991, and UN-supervised elections held in 1993. Another blow was inflicted on Vietnam by the economic difficulties of the USSR, which decided in 1991 to end its subsidy of some 2 billion roubles a year. This finally impelled Hanoi to make its peace with China.[122]

It also underlined the need, which Hanoi had already appreciated, of so conducting itself as to attract investment from the capitalist rim of Asia. This would be facilitated by an accommodation with the International Monetary Fund that the United States was in a position to block, and by the establishment of good relations with its Southeast Asian neighbours. Vietnam moved to secure both. It assisted US attempts to account for, and locate the corpses of, Americans 'missing in action' during the war; and in 1992 it met a key US demand by releasing the last of the South Vietnamese notables imprisoned in 're-education camps'.[123] In 1993 the US lifted its veto, Japan, France and other 'Friends' cleared Vietnam's IMF debt, and IMF, World Bank, and Asian Development lending resumed, providing the 'seal of approval' often required by (quantitatively more important) private investment. In time past Vietnam had condemned ASEAN as simply the imperialist Southeast Asia Treaty Organisation under another form, and demanded that its members should instead conclude bilateral treaties with (and so revolve around) Hanoi.[124] In 1992 (together with Laos) it acceded to ASEAN's 1976 Treaty of Amity and Cooperation, and secured observer status. 1995 brought full membership, and also full diplomatic relations with the United States.[125] Arguably the end of the Cold War and the dazzling economic attractions of the 'Rim of Asia' had achieved the accommodation into which the United States had so signally failed to force Vietnam in the 1960s.

---

[121] *Keesing's*, 35067–70, 35899–901.
[122] *The Independent*, 23 February 1991 p. 11; *Keesing's*, 38005, 38574, 38729, 1992 R86.
[123] Only 25 still remained, but 100,000 people had supposedly passed through them since 1973.
[124] M. Leifer, *Conflict and Regional Order in South-east Asia* (IISS Adelphi Paper no. 162, 1980) pp. 34–5.
[125] *Keesing's*, 38963, 39005, 1994 R88–9, 40643, 40650.

CHAPTER 7

Detente in Europe

De Gaulle: 'Europe from the Atlantic to the Urals'

In contrast to the bitter, if often clandestine, competition surveyed in the last chapter, once the Berlin crisis had faded away East–West relations in Europe moved slowly towards accommodation. The running was first made by de Gaulle. His full motives, and in particular the lengths to which he was prepared to push his differences with the USA, remain controversial. Over Berlin, Cuba and the 1960 summit he sided very firmly with the United States; despite talk in 1967–8 about omni-directional defence (*defense 'tous azimuts'*) he would probably always have done so in a crisis. After Cuba, however, he saw the United States as far stronger than the USSR and the threat from the latter as rapidly receding. In these circumstances he felt free to work to modify the international system, and probably enjoyed ruffling Anglo-Saxon susceptibilities while doing so. De Gaulle had always disliked French exclusion from the Yalta and Potsdam summit conferences in 1945; he was among those who saw Yalta as having divided Europe into two blocs, or (as he termed them) 'hegemonies'. French participation in the Western bloc might have been necessary at the time. But it threatened to destroy the independence and identity of the French nation-state, through NATO's supranational control of defence and through the way in which (de Gaulle believed) the international monetary system facilitated the takeover of European by US industry.

Most of de Gaulle's efforts were devoted to extracting France from such dependence (see pp. 489–93). But he was also anxious to transform the Soviet bloc – in two potentially conflicting ways. He sought to improve relations with the USSR itself, recalling the Franco-Russian alliance of the beginning of the century, and talking much of a Europe that extended from the Atlantic to the Urals (and not simply the Elbe). He also cultivated individual East (or, as he preferred to term them, Central) European states, encouraging them to imitate French national self-assertion and evolution away from rigid bloc subordination. In de Gaulle's eyes these two policies were complementary; he sought a general atmosphere of European entente, perhaps reinforced by external US guarantees, within which it would be possible to resolve the difficulties, chiefly over German reunification, that now seemed so daunting. But there was always a danger that French-style self-assertion on the part of some East European states might instead seem a threat to the socialist commonwealth, hence to the security of the Soviet Union and its partners.

Initially, at least, the Soviet Union took a relaxed attitude towards Gaullism, fully appreciating the trouble it was causing in NATO. Brezhnev's 1967 judgement was:

Have we not succeeded, at no risk to ourselves, in driving a breach through the imperialist camp? De Gaulle is our enemy and we are well aware of it . . . But look at our achievements! We have weakened the American position in the heart of Europe and this weakening will continue. De Gaulle . . . is aiming for mastery in Europe for himself and in opposition to us. But here we must be flexible. De Gaulle has virtually no chance of realizing his concept because the other West European countries are too powerful and they would never allow it.[1]

Accordingly the USSR was happy to welcome de Gaulle for a most successful visit in 1966 – he was shown the highly secret Baikonur cosmodrome and the launching of a satellite – and to conclude an imposing Joint Declaration. This looked to the development of trade and of scientific and cultural exchanges; it provided for a 'hot line' telecommunications link and for a permanent Franco-Soviet Commission; and it agreed 'that the problems of Europe should first of all be discussed within the limits of Europe' to secure the normalisation, and then the gradual development, 'of relations between all European countries on the basis of respect for the[ir] independence . . . and non-interference in their internal affairs'. Kosygin returned de Gaulle's visit in December and gained his acceptance of the idea of 'a general European conference to examine problems of security in

---

[1] Erwin Weit, *Eyewitness: The Autobiography of Gomulka's Interpreter* (1973) p. 140.

Europe and the establishment of general European cooperation',[2] a project that led in the 1970s to the Conference on Security and Cooperation in Europe (CSCE). There was also agreement on a joint Franco-Soviet standard for colour television, incompatible with that adopted by most of Western Europe. Otherwise it is hard to point to any very tangible consequences of the arrangements de Gaulle established;[3] they continued to operate, but the emphasis placed on them gradually diminished.

The East European aspect of de Gaulle's policy found expression in visits to Poland and Romania in 1967–8.[4] He recalled their historic links and inter-war alliances with France, and talked of the need for the nations of 'West, Centre and East' to practice 'the detente, entente, and co-operation' which alone will allow Europe to settle its own problems, notably the German problem, [and] to organize its security'. In Poland he emphasised the permanence of her new post-war frontiers, hailing Zabrze (formerly Hindenburg), where he was welcomed by a crowd of 1.5 million, as 'the most Polish of Polish towns'; he praised Romania for following a course in international relations exactly comparable with that of France, and suggested that the two countries 'together set the example for the union of our continent'.

De Gaulle was in fact going too fast for the countries he was visiting. Both stressed the need to recognise two German states, while de Gaulle talked of reunification; both, though more particularly Poland's Gomulka, insisted on the primary importance of their alliance with the USSR and other socialist countries. Later events in 1968 were to confirm the continuing reality of the two European blocs. De Gaulle had to leave Romania early, as the riots and strikes in Paris were getting out of hand; ultimately these were mastered, but they destroyed international confidence in the French currency. Since de Gaulle would not devalue, this became dependent on US and West German support, which restricted his diplomatic freedom of manoeuvre. Still more seriously, the Warsaw Pact showed – by invading Czechoslovakia in August to force the abandonment of its internal reform programme – that it did not share de Gaulle's vision of the dissolution of the blocs back into the sovereign states of which they were composed. Such factors led de Gaulle to moderate, though not abandon, his stance during his remaining time in office. His successors, while retaining

---

[2] *Keesing's*, 21543–4, 21879.

[3] It could be that Moscow restrained the French communists during the 1968 riots and strikes; but their moderation may reflect nothing more than a preference for securing pay rises rather than pushing to the limit and risking forcible repression.

[4] *Keesing's*, 22339 ff (Poland), 22805 ff (Romania).

the Gaullist legacy of a nuclear deterrent and armed forces not subject to any supranational command, edged slowly back into the main stream of the Western alliance.

West German Ostpolitik before 1969

Perhaps the chief consequence of the Gaullist opening towards Eastern Europe was the pressure it brought on West Germany to follow suit. 'We could not,' Brandt explains,[5] 'become the last of the Cold Warriors, the opponents of change and thus, perhaps, the world's leading trouble-makers (and whipping-boys).' Also the DDR was growing in stature. West German policy under the 'Hallstein Doctrine' had been to break off relations with any country (other than the USSR) that recognized East Germany. Were too many countries to do so, West Germany would itself become isolated: as early as 1965 Ulbricht's visit to Egypt had led (through a vicious spiral dragging in other grievances) to ten Arab states breaking off relations with Bonn.[6] In March 1966 Erhard's CDU–FDP government (a Christian Democrat-Free Democrat coalition) made overtures to Eastern Europe, offering to still any remaining fears of a West German attack by exchanging undertakings not to settle international disputes by force. But the pace was increased in December when the FDP was replaced, in the governing coalition, by the SPD (Social Democratic Party) which had always been more favourable to exploring openings to the East. The new Chancellor, Kiesinger, promptly declared an interest in improving cooperation with 'our Eastern neighbours . . . and even of opening diplomatic relations with them whenever the circumstances allow it'[7] – in other words of suspending the Hallstein Doctrine.

Romania took up the offer; and 1967 also saw a consular agreement with Czechoslovakia. But little further progress was made. One reason was opposition within the Warsaw Pact, notably from the DDR (which probably disliked the improvement of relations with West Germany in any event, and certainly did not wish to see itself isolated by a rush of its allies into Bonn's arms). The Soviet Union was also hostile. Its ambassador had in fact sought out the SPD leader, Willy Brandt, before he entered the Kiesinger government as Foreign Minister, but thereafter he kept his

[5] Willy Brandt, *People and Politics: The Years 1960–1975* (1978) p. 167.
[6] *Keesing's*, 20737 ff; relations were also broken with Tanzania after it recognised the DDR in 1964 – James Mayall, *Africa: the Cold War and After* (1971) p. 145.
[7] *Keesing's*, 21802.

distance. Indeed in 1967–8 the USSR even claimed the UN Charter gave it a right of intervention in West Germany to prevent the 'resumption of aggressive policies by a former enemy state'.[8] The claim reflected concern about the emergence of a (small) neo-Nazi National Democratic Party. But it also indicated a distaste for Bonn's new Eastern policy that is usually attributed to a feeling that West Germany was bypassing the USSR and seeking to deal direct with other East European states, thus weakening the Warsaw Pact. Brandt denies any such intention, but Soviet coolness was certainly a fact. When it became necessary to justify the 1968 invasion of Czechoslovakia, much play was made of its alleged penetration by West German revisionists.

There were real obstacles to proceeding further: Poland, for instance, was bound to insist on West German acceptance of its 1945 acquisition of Silesia and probably also of the existence of the DDR. But Kiesinger had made it clear he could not go so far, explaining that only a reunited Germany (i.e. one that had absorbed the DDR) could embark on such border negotiations with Poland. Meanwhile Bonn's official position remained that, since there had been no peace treaty, Germany's frontiers were in international law still those of 1937 – that is of the period before Hitler had gone on the rampage, but also before Poland moved to the Oder–Neisse line and expelled most of the local Silesian population. This view of the German question had been built into the Federal Republic's 1949 constitution: in enacting 'this Basic Law . . . for a transitional period' 'the German people in' what became West Germany

has also acted on behalf of those Germans to whom participation was denied.

The entire German people is called upon to achieve, by free self-determination, the unity and freedom of Germany. [Preamble]

Also, though the Basic Law had not been explicit on boundaries, it had referred, in the context of nationality, to 'the territory of the German *Reich*, as it existed on 31 December 1937' (Article 116). Departing from this mindset was not easy – Brandt records that he had himself 'hoped that it might be possible to modify the Oder–Neisse frontier, at least in places'.[9] Although politicians in Bonn could see this was becoming ever less likely, they were under some pressure from refugee organisations, and had little

---

[8] *Keesing's*, 23857; UN Charter, articles 53, 107.
[9] Brandt, *People and Politics*, p. 401.

to gain by renouncing the territories 'under Polish administration' unless they in turn received something clearly of benefit to the rest of Germany. Privately in an April 1968 *Foreign Affairs* article, and in his capacity as leader of the SPD, Brandt showed himself more flexible than his coalition partners. From late 1968 the USSR proved rather more forthcoming in official talks with him, in September 1969 proposing negotiations on mutual undertakings not to use force. Discussions through unofficial intermediaries probably went further, though how far subsequently became a matter of political dispute.

Brandt's Ostpolitik

In October 1969 Brandt became Chancellor after forming a coalition with the FDP. He says he hoped to facilitate reunion 'by easing the relationship between the two parts of Germany out of its present rigid state',

leaving open the door for the Germans – and the fact that this may take generations rather than years compels one to add the proviso: if they so desire – to . . . organize their coexistence otherwise than developments have so far enforced upon them.[10]

This Brezhnev recognised. Brandt, he told the rising East German politician Erich Honecker in 1970, was 'for the liquidation of the GDR.' 'He has to come to agreements with us. He hopes in this way to realize his goal . . . the social-democratization of the GDR.' But that would not happen. The West German–Soviet treaty currently under negotiation

will not solve all problems, but the conclusion of the treaty will be a success for us . . . The GDR will gain from this treaty. *Its international authority will be increased. Its frontiers, its existence will be confirmed for all the world to see, its inviolability.*

There is [not], there cannot be, and it should not come to a process of rapprochement between the FRG and the DDR.

On the contrary, the trench between . . . [them] will become deeper.[11]

---

[10] Brandt, *People and Politics*, pp. 237, 238. Bonn's 'letter on German unity' accompanying its 1970 treaty with the USSR looked to 'a state of peace in Europe in which the German people regains its unity in free self-determination'.

[11] Timothy Garton-Ash, *In Europe's Name. Germany and the Divided Continent* (paperback edn, 1994) esp. pp. 71, 77–8; Hannes Adomeit, *Imperial Overstretch: Germany in Soviet Policy from Stalin to Gorbachev* (Baden-Baden, 1998) pp. 118–19.

Brezhnev's and Brandt's long-term goals were, therefore, diametrically opposed. But their immediate desiderata were congruent. Brandt began by declaring an interest in opening diplomatic relations with Poland and establishing a *modus vivendi* with the DDR,[12] and he signed the Nuclear Non-Proliferation Treaty (thus laying to rest well-ventilated Warsaw Pact fears of a nuclear West Germany). Thereafter events moved fast. Negotiations started in December 1969, and in August 1970 Brandt visited Moscow to sign a treaty promising to regard 'as inviolable' existing frontiers including the Oder–Neisse line and that between the East and West Germany.[13] This opened the way to the conclusion with Poland in December 1970 of a treaty confirming the Oder–Neisse line and renouncing all future teritorial claims; it was accompanied by a Polish promise of rather more generous treatment for members of the remaining German minority wishing to travel or emigrate.[14] The treaty would have been striking in any event; it was made the more so by Brandt's kneeling in silence before the memorial to the Warsaw Ghetto, 'to ask pardon in the name of our people for a million-fold crime which was committed in the misused name of the Germans'.

Equally notable were Brandt's visit as Chancellor in March 1970 to Erfurt in East Germany and the return visit to Kassell of the DDR premier, Stoph. They were not so successful. In Erfurt Brandt's popularity proved embarassingly greater than Stoph's, while the Kassell visit was marred by the fighting of right and left-wing extremists, 1920s style, and the ominous chant:

> *Volksverräter*[15] *Hand in Hand,*
> *Willi Stoph und Willy Brandt!*

Nor were their talks initially productive. That autumn, though, negotiations started at a lower level. The following spring (1971) saw the replacement – partly through Soviet pressure – of Ulbricht as leader of the DDR's ruling party by the more flexible Honecker. Discussions were still difficult – much time was spent determining whether the term 'ties' (between West Berlin and West Germany) in the September 1971 Four Power Agreement

[12] *Keesing's*, 23618, 23701.

[13] *Keesing's*, 24144. Next year, on the conclusion of the Four Power Berlin Agreement, Brezhnev invited him again – to his Black Sea villa, a gesture of some warmth.

[14] *Keesing's*, 24346; C.C. Schweitzer *et al.* (eds) *Politics and Government in the Federal Republic of Germany, Basic Documents* (1984) p. 410.

[15] Betrayers of the Nation.

on Berlin should be rendered in German as *Bindungen* or *Verbindungen*. Probably after another intervention by Brezhnev, December 1971 saw the conclusion of a DDR–West German transit agreement governing access to West Berlin (in implementation of the Four Power Agreement), May 1972 a broader Traffic Treaty. Meanwhile, Honecker had indicated readiness for a more general settlement, which took the form in December of a 'Treaty on the Bases of Relations' between the two states.[16] This provided, 'without prejudice to . . . [their] differing concepts . . . on fundamental questions, including the national question', for the development of 'normal good-neighbourly relations . . . on the basis of equality of rights'; in 1973 both countries joined the United Nations, and in 1974 they established 'permanent representative missions' in each other's capitals.

In pushing these negotiations West Germany had been acting largely on its own initiative; in Kissinger's words, 'the new German government informed rather than consulted'. Kissinger was at first seriously concerned. The negotiations might give the USSR leverage over German and hence European policy. But the chief dangers were longer range; Brandt should not (Kissinger wrote in February 1970) initially have any serious difficulty in maintaining his basic pro-Western policy . . .

But assuming Brandt achieves a degree of normalization, he or his successor may discover that the hoped-for benefits fail to develop . . . [Kissinger himself thought Ostpolitik *more likely to lead to a permanent division of Germany than to promote ultimate reunion] Having already invested heavily in their Eastern policy, the Germans may at this point see themselves as facing agonizing choices . . . [and the 1950s] kind of debate about Germany's basic position [between East and West] could well recur in more divisive form, not only inflaming German domestic affairs but generating suspicions among Germany's Western associates as to its reliability as a partner.*[17]

Eventually Kissinger did reach, and press on the more sceptical Nixon, the view that Brandt had been right to open negotiations (since a continuation of earlier policies would only have isolated the Federal Republic). But in any case to have tried to prevent Brandt would have been explosive, and the United States really had no option but to go along with his initiative and try to put it to good account.

[16] *Keesing's*, 25621–2.
[17] Kissinger, *Memoirs*, i, pp. 408–11, 529–30.

As things turned out, its spillover effects were decidedly helpful. For most of the diplomatic questions of the day proved to be interlinked – Kissinger talks at one point of three-dimensional chess. From the West German point of view, the recognition of the Oder–Neisse line and of the DDR had been concessions, acceptable only if they led to a satisfactory settlement of the Berlin question. Yet Berlin was not part of the Federal Republic; so agreement would have to be reached between the Four occupying Powers, more especially between the Soviet Union and the United States. The USSR needed a success to secure West German ratification of the Ostpolitik treaties and agreement to attend a European Security Conference (a gathering the Warsaw Pact had been advocating since 1966). The USA thus gained a degree of leverage, which it was able to use in its bilateral dealings with the Soviet Union (notably over the ABM and SALT negotiations). It derived further benefit, after mid-1971, from its sudden ability to get on terms with its former arch-enemy China, and from the desire of the USSR (now China's principal opponent) to present itself to the USA as a far more valuable partner.

Kissinger claims that the breakthrough came in January 1971.[18] Negotiations over Berlin had already started, but were not making much progress. US–Soviet relations in 1970 were beset with many problems (crises in September over an apparent Syrian invasion of Jordan and the attempt to establish a Soviet SLBM base in Cuba, several lesser frictions, and a loss of momentum associated with the Moscow power struggle in which Brezhnev displaced Kosygin from the management of foreign policy). In December 1970 Brandt complained to Washington about the slow pace of the Berlin talks in terms that convinced the USA that something would have to be done. Next month Nixon secured Soviet acceptance of simultaneous negotiations (through the Kissinger–Dobrynin back-channel) on Berlin and on ABM/SALT with the aim of completion that summer. The Berlin talks, eased probably by West German and perhaps French initiatives of which Kissinger was unaware, more or less met this target. September 1971 saw a Four Power Agreement on Berlin that embodied minor Western concessions (a slight reduction of the Federal German presence in West Berlin and the opening there of a Soviet Consulate-General) and major Eastern ones (a *Soviet* guarantee that civilian access to Berlin would not be impeded, and acceptance of West German represen-

---

[18] ibid. pp. 800 ff.

tation internationally of West Berliners).[19] Naturally the USSR had at first tried for more, but the basic premiss of the 1970–2 Ostpolitik settlement was the recognition of facts, and if the Oder–Neisse line and East Germany were 'Eastern' facts, West Berlin was a 'Western' one.

It remained for West Germany to ratify the treaties it had signed. The incentives were considerable, as refusal would sink the Berlin Agreement and East–West detente, and would infuriate Germany's allies. So it is remarkable that Brandt's government encountered such difficulty. Indeed it almost collapsed as a result of parliamentary defections: in April 1972 a motion to overturn it failed only by two votes. There followed intensive negotiations, but the Opposition still abstained when the treaties were ratified in May, and the crisis led Brandt to the unprecedented step of forcing premature parliamentary elections. In November 1972 these gave the SPD its best ever result, which suggests that there was more support for Ostpolitik among the electorate than in the political class. In 1973 ratification of the 'Basic Treaty' with East Germany was rather easier.

Consequences of Ostpolitik

Ostpolitik's human consequences are clear. As Brandt proudly claims, it again became possible for West Berliners to telephone and visit the Eastern part of the city, and the number of West Germans visiting the DDR doubled between 1970 and 1975, as did that travelling overland to Berlin; East Germany, however, maintained its controls on emigration. Trade with Eastern Europe also trebled in these years (though it still accounted in 1981 for only 5 to 6 per cent of all West German trade).[20] These gains gave West Germany a real stake in detente and contributed to a certain modification of its international stance. The prospect of such a modification may have represented one of Ostpolitik's attractions to the USSR. Just as Brandt reasoned that only in an atmosphere of detente could any progress be made towards German reunification, so Brezhnev may, after the failure of so much ferocious bluster, have been inclined to try the effect of a little sunshine in inducing West Germany to doff its Cold War coat.

Certainly in the Adenauer era Bonn had always favoured a resolute policy, and it was usually doveish tendencies in the USA that had produced

---

[19] Brandt's intercession with Brezhnev was needed to gain agreement that West Berliners might travel in the East on a (specially endorsed) West German passport (Brandt, *People and Politics*, p. 391).

[20] Schweitzer, *Politics and Government in Germany*, pp. 413–14.

German–American friction. But when East–West relations started to deteriorate in the later 1970s, the boot was on the other foot – in 1977 Chancellor Schmidt urged in Washington more responsiveness to the 'good Brezhnev who is promoting detente and who needs our help'. Much of the friction between Bonn and Washington at this time stemmed from Schmidt's and Carter's mutual dislike. But President Carter also related it to policy, commenting in 1980 that West Germany 'opposes any sanctions against Iran or Soviets, are continuing business as usual with S[oviet] U[nion], refuse to commit publicly to Olympic boycott, and privately and in press are very critical of us'.[21]

Probably the Americans exaggerated. Schmidt may have been reluctant to jeopardise good relations in Europe because of US–Soviet quarrels over extra-European issues, thus raising the question of whether detente was divisible. But West Germany was in fact one of the few countries to follow the USA in boycotting the 1980 Moscow Olympic Games in protest over the Soviet invasion of Afghanistan. Schmidt had also taken very seriously the implications of the Soviet military build-up, being one of the leading promoters of the decision to deploy cruise and Pershing missiles to counter it.

This decision, however, was one of the factors that brought to a peak, in the early 1980s, the internal debate Kissinger had feared on where West Germany really stood. For leftist opposition to the missiles readily assumed a nationalist form – deployment was not in 'German interests' – and established contacts with a new autonomous Christian peace movement in East Germany. Such feelings, together with environmental concerns, contributed to the successful launching of a new (if small) 'Green' party that was then hostile to continued membership of NATO. Similar tendencies grew within the SPD, aided by several senior politicians including Brandt himself; and when the SPD–FDP coalition unravelled in 1982 (over economic issues), Schmidt was no longer able to check them. The parliamentary elections early next year were bitter, and were marked by US pressure to accept and Soviet to reject missile deployment. The CDU–FDP government was confirmed in office by a large majority, which ensured that deployment would go ahead.

Fortuitously 1983 was also the fifth centenary of the birth of Martin Luther; there were celebrations in both Germanies, but more especially

---

[21] Zbigniew Brzezinski, *Power and Principle: Memoirs of the National Security Adviser 1977–1981* (paperback, New York 1983) pp. 461–3.

in the East where he had actually lived. These focussed public attention on a common German heritage; and they must have been very welcome to Chancellor Kohl, one of whose chief concerns was to remind the world of what he saw as the continuing unnatural division of a single German nation. His views attracted lip-service from West Germany's allies, but no more: in 1984 the Italian Foreign Minister stated bluntly that, while 'We all agree that there should be good relations between the two Germanies ... Pan-Germanism has to be overcome. There are two German states, and two they shall remain.' This caused something of a flutter; but the Austrian chancellor, Kreisky, simply observed that 'Andreotti had the mishap to express somewhat more clearly what everybody is thinking.'[22] Until 1989 this remained the general view.

---

[22] Andreotti followed up by asking 'Who has ever asserted that Ostpolitik means reunification?' – Adomeit, *Imperial Overstretch*, p. 457.

CHAPTER 8

The United States, China and the World

US attitudes to China 1950–68

If one of the most hopeful symbols of the 1970s was Brandt's visit to Warsaw, another was Nixon's 1972 journey to China and reception by Chairman Mao, 'the week,' as he immodestly put it, 'that changed the world'.

Sino-American relations in the 1950s had been very bad, and at the rhetorical level the Americans and the Chinese were each other's worst enemies. From the Chinese perspective this was natural enough – the USA was the world's leading imperialist power (in the Marxist sense of the word) and its fleet preserved the Kuomintang regime on Taiwan. The Americans too had their reasons. Much bitterness had been generated by the Chinese intervention in Korea and ill-will towards the People's Republic ran deep: Eisenhower told Kennedy that the only development that would lead him to return to active politics after he had left office would be the prospect of Red China entering the UN.[1] But such hostility was not merely instinctive. For Dulles believed that 'the best way to get a separation between the Soviet Union and Communist China is to keep the pressure on Communist China and make its way difficult as long as it is in partnership with Soviet Russia'. In December 1953 he briefed a Western summit meeting on his hopes that 'pressure and strain would compel' Beijing 'to make more demands on the USSR which the latter would be unable to meet and the strain would consequently increase'. For, as NSC 166/1 had just put it with Eisenhower's approval,

---

[1] Arthur M. Schlesinger, *A Thousand Days: John F. Kennedy in the White House* (Boston, Mass., 1965) p. 423.

As the inevitable differences in interest, viewpoint, or timing . . . develop
between the Russians and the Chinese; as the Chinese tend to become
importunate in their demands for Russian assistance or support; or as the
role of the Chinese as viceregents for international communism in the
Far East becomes too independent and self reliant – there will be strong
temptation for the Russians to attempt to move in the direction of greater
disciplinary control over the Chinese Communists. If the time ever comes
when the Russians feel impelled to contest with the Chinese Communist
leaders for primacy in the domestic apparatus of control of the Chinese
regime, the alliance will be critically endangered. For . . . the Chinese
Communist leaders are Chinese as well as Communists.

This policy underlay the hard US line during the Chinese off-shore islands
crises (see pp. 215–17 and 246–7). By late 1958 intelligence reports were
leading Eisenhower to wonder whether 'the Soviets were not really becoming concerned about Communist China as a possible threat to them in the
future', while in 1958 Dulles felt that 'you could very well have a struggle
between . . . Mao Tse-tung and Khrushchev as to who would be the ideological leader of International Communism'.[2]

But if the USA anticipated trouble between China and the USSR, its
ideas as to how to turn this to its own advantage were less developed.[3]
Gromyko says that in mid-1959 he was sounded as to the possibility of
US-Soviet cooperation against the 'yellow peril', but refused to be drawn.
In the early 1960s the Sino-Soviet split came into the open (see pp. 554–6):
the Kennedy administration inclined towards the Soviet side. Even in 1961
briefing for the Vienna summit suggested that, by emphasising the Chinese
threat to both countries, Kennedy might gain Soviet agreement to help
restrain China within a 'stable viable world order'. Vienna, of course, produced no such meeting of minds. But after the resolution of the Cuba
missiles crisis, the idea returned. Kennedy feared a nuclear China 'would so
upset the world political scene [that] it would be intolerable.' In January
1963 he told the National Security Council that 'our primary purpose' in

---

[2] Richard H. Immerman (ed.), *John Foster Dulles and the Diplomacy of the Cold War*
(Princeton, NJ, 1990) pp. 60–3; John L. Gaddis, *The Long Peace: Inquiries into the*
History of the Cold War (New York, 1982) pp. 174–87.
[3] In 1955 Dulles hoped eventually for 'sufficient independence between Peiping and
Moscow as to create the beginnings of a balance of power relationship'. Given such
Sino-Soviet hostility and a gradual revival of Japanese power, the US would no longer
have to be quite so involved in the Far East.

seeking a Test Ban treaty with the USSR 'is to halt or delay the development of an atomic capability by the Chinese communists'. Although ambassador Dobrynin was deliberately unresponsive when the idea was raised, Harriman was directed to discuss with Khrushchev 'means of limiting or preventing Chinese nuclear development and his willingness either to take Soviet action or to accept US action' that might require 'use of military force'.[4] Khrushchev did not respond, but the issue was revived in 1964 as it became clear China was about to conduct its first nuclear test. In September the Johnson administration decided against unilateral US military action, but felt there were 'many possibilities for joint action with the Soviet Government if that Government is interested. Such possibilities include a warning to the Chinese against tests, a possible undertaking to give up underground testing and to hold the Chinese accountable if they test in any way, and even a possible agreement to cooperate in preventive military action.' Dobrynin was again sounded on US–Soviet cooperation, and again proved unforthcoming. Any such ideas were then ended by Khrushchev's dismissal – his successors' first thought was rather to improve Sino-Soviet relations.[5]

The Kennedy administration had been obsessed with the importance of guerrilla warfare in the Third World. Mao had both written on and practised such warfare (against the Japanese and the Chinese Nationalists), and China trumpeted these experiences as a model. The USA was determined to demonstrate otherwise. In Southeast Asia, Rusk claimed, 'the international community confronts a question that affects . . . every continent: shall this form of external aggression be allowed to succeed?' In Korea the 'international community [had] proved that overt aggression was unprofitable'; now it was necessary to show in Vietnam that 'semi-covert aggression across international boundaries cannot succeed'. Were this done, he later told the Senate, the militant Chinese approach would be

---

[4] There was also some contingency planning both of direct US action and of commando raids by the Chinese Nationalists.
[5] William Burr and Jeffrey Richelson, 'Whether to "Strangle the Baby in the Cradle". The United States and the Chinese Nuclear Programme, 1960–64', *International Security*, xxv (2000–1) esp. pp. 60–1, 67–73, 87–8, and supporting documents in their *The United States and the Chinese Nuclear Program, 1960–1964* (National Security Archive Electronic Briefing Book, 12 January 2001); Gordon Chang, 'JFK, China and the Bomb', *Journal of American History*, lxxiv (1987–8) esp. pp. 1289, 1296–1308; Arthur M. Schlesinger, *A Thousand Days: John F. Kennedy in the White House* (1965) pp. 771–2, 775–6.

discredited and the correctness of Soviet-style peaceful coexistence confirmed. Then, when Beijing stopped using force and abandoned its stategy for achieving revolution, 'we would welcome an era of good relations'.

Rusk himself seems initially to have favoured tying China with 'little threads' that might eventually draw her back into the community of nations; but the only overture made – feelers about food relief for her disastrous 1961 famine – was rebuffed.[6] Other ideas for reconciliation centred on a 'Two Chinas' policy, with UN membership for both China and Taiwan. This would actually have been anathema to Beijing, but it was not attempted since Kennedy adjudged it politically unacceptable in the USA. In the early 1950s the China lobby's resentment of Truman's 'betrayal' of Chiang Kai-shek had been one of the strongest forces in Congress; both Kennedy and Johnson were fearful of reviving it.

But though mutual hostility ran very high, there were no serious Chinese–American clashes in the 1960s despite US involvement in Vietnam. Nobody wanted to repeat the Korean experience. So in April 1965 (soon after the US had started bombing North, and had committed marines to South, Vietnam), China asked Pakistan to tell President Johnson that it would not take the initiative to provoke war, but would provide assistance to any country encountering 'aggression by the imperialists headed by the United States'; and should the US bomb or 'impose a war on China . . . it will have no boundaries'. China also promised Hanoi it would send troops in the event of a direct US invasion, and did in fact secretly despatch logistic and anti-aircraft forces (numbering, at their peak, 170,000 men).[7] Johnson, for his part, never invaded the North, and personally selected bombing targets to ensure that they did not trigger a Chinese intervention. US–Chinese war was thus avoided. But Mao took the possibility very seriously, rejecting a draft Five Year Plan as too consumer-oriented, and (after the Gulf of Tonkin incident) ordaining the massive 'Third Front' reorientation of strategic industry from China's exposed coastal and urban centres to the remote interior.[8]

[6] Warren I. Cohen, *Dean Rusk* (Totowa, NJ, 1980) pp. 164, 247, 287.

[7] CWIHP, *Bulletin*, vii (1995–6) pp. 236–7; Robert S. Ross and Jiang Changbin (eds) *Re-examining the Cold War. US–China Diplomacy, 1954–1973* (Cambridge, Mass., 2004) pp. 250, 256.

[8] Barry Naughton, 'The Third Front: Defence Industrialization in the Chinese Interior', *China Quarterly*, 115 (September 1988) esp. pp. 353–4, 365–6 – at its 1966–72 peak, the 'Third Front' accounted for 'at least two thirds of budgetary industrial investment'.

Sino-American rapprochement 1968–72

The end of the 1960s saw a startling transformation. On the American side this was partly due to Johnson's 1968 decision to begin winding down the Vietnam War (which led China to conclude that the USA was no longer an expanding power in Asia), but chiefly to the election that November of Richard Nixon. Nixon believed the USA to be overcommitted, and was anxious to recover freedom of manoeuvre by ending what he saw as unnecessary quarrels (whether with Gaullist France or with China). He also says he was encouraged by a number of Asian leaders to regard a new Sino-American relationship as a prerequisite for lasting peace in Asia after the end of the Vietnam War. He signalled this in an October 1967 *Foreign Affairs* article (that caught Mao's attention), and more plainly in an interview after his nomination next year as Republican presidential candidate.[9] In so doing, Nixon had one great advantage; as a former hardline conservative he was much less likely to encounter opposition at home from the right. Nixon had already spoken to the Romanian leader Ceausescu, who had close contact with China, about normalising relations with the People's Republic after the Vietnam War. Once elected he started putting out feelers through several channels, of which the most immediately effective was the French.

Chinese politics are more opaque. In 1966–7 China was absorbed in the internal power struggle of the 'Cultural Revolution', which spilled over into the rabbling of foreign embassies and other scenes that gave the rest of the world little reason to seek dealings with it. However, in response to the 1967 ultra-radical seizure of control over the Foreign Ministry, Mao moved gradually to reassert order and to tone down the rhetoric of external revolution. 1968 brought cause to question the relative danger from the United States and the Soviet Union. The former was apparently seeking to withdraw from Vietnam; but the USSR intervened in Czechoslovakia to displace a communist government not of its liking, and might well interfere in China, if not by direct invasion (though this could not be excluded) at least by supporting Chinese political factions ready to 'take the fortress from within'. Early in 1969 four leading marshals were asked to conduct a wide-ranging review of the international situation; they concluded in October that 'Soviet revisionism regards China as its major enemy. Its threat to China's security is bigger than that of US imperialism.' In this

---

[9] 'We must always seek opportunities to talk with' China; 'We must not only watch for changes. We must seek to make changes' – Kissinger, *Memoirs*, i, p. 164.

context they advised that China 'play the US card': when (in past Chinese history):

the states of Wei, Shu, and Wu confronted each other, the strategic principle of . . . [Shu] was to ally with . . . Wu in the east and attack the State of Wei in the north. We can learn from this lesson. We may also learn from Stalin, who signed a pact of mutual non-aggression with Hitler.[10]

Events on the ground reinforced this view. In March 1969 the Chinese Army seems to have ambushed a Soviet patrol on the disputed border island of Chenbao/Damansky. A fortnight later the Russians retaliated. Kosygin then sought border negotiations, but was allegedly treated with deliberate rudeness, the Beijing hotline operator declaring, 'You are a revisionist, and therefore I will not connect you.'[11] Soviet pressure followed in the form of border incidents (whose geographical location convinced Kissinger that the USSR, not as he had previously believed China, was the aggressor). The summer saw, on the one hand, a number of US gestures and messages of goodwill to China and, on the other, tough Soviet military speeches and manoeuvres.

Soviet diplomats also conducted soundings – that were presumably intended to leak – about the possibility of a preventive attack on Chinese nuclear installations. It is not clear whether this was just meant to intimidate, or whether (like Eisenhower's similarly diffuse talk in 1953 of escalation were no Korean armistice reached) it was a real threat. In August a middle-ranking Soviet diplomat told his US counterpart that, if the USSR destroyed China's nuclear installations, the blow 'would so weaken and discredit the "Mao clique" that dissident senior officers and Party cadres could gain ascendency in Peking.' 'What would the US do if Peking called for US assistance . . . ?' Would not 'the US . . . really welcome this move since Chinese nuclear weapons could threaten it too'?[12] The administration

---

[10] Ross and Jiang, *US–China Diplomacy*, pp. 308, 334–5.

[11] R.M. Nixon, *The Memoirs of Richard Nixon.* (1978) p. 568.

[12] William Burr (ed.) *The Sino-Soviet Border Conflict, 1969: US Reactions and Diplomatic Maneuvers* (12 June 2001 – National Security Archive Electronic Briefing Book) Doc. 10. See also: H.R. Haldeman with Joseph Di Mona, *The Ends of Power* (1978) pp. 89 ff (the most dramatic version); Thomas Powers, *The Man who Kept the Secrets. Richard Helms and the* CIA (paperback edn) pp. 267, 455; Zhou Enlai's account to Joseph Alsop, 'Thoughts out of China . . . Go versus No Go', *New York Times*, 11 March 1973, Magazine, pp. 31, 100–2; Barron, *KGB*, pp. 3–4, 179.

seems to have taken the possibility seriously, Nixon telling the National Security Council that it was not in US interests to let China be 'smashed', while lesser figures said the same in public in more elliptical language. On his way back from Ho Chi Minh's funeral in September Kosygin managed to arrange talks with Zhou, but they did not go well: the Chinese say Kosygin flaunted Soviet superiority, while they declared hostility would last for thousands of years. Tension remained high for the next month, with Victor Louis (a Soviet journalist with KGB connections) speculating in the *London Evening News* on the possibility of war or of anti-Mao forces in China appealing for Soviet 'fraternal help'.[13] In October China finally accepted border talks, but these made absolutely no progress. In December Kissinger thought the USSR would probably attack China by April, and had his staff draft plans for that contingency.[14]

Against this background several American messages reached Beijing; they were supplemented by mutual goodwill gestures, the US discontinuing naval patrols in the Taiwan straits, China releasing two American yachtsmen who had strayed into its waters. In December the US ambassador in Warsaw told his Chinese counterpart Nixon wanted 'serious talks', and Zhou reported enthusiastically to Mao that 'We have found the door; it is time to knock on it'. Ambassadorial contacts in Warsaw were openly resumed, and in February 1970 it was agreed to hold high-level talks in Beijing. Progress was then stalled by the US incursion into Cambodia in April (which China was bound to condemn). Nor were matters helped by a Chinese attempt to shoot down an offshore American spy plane, perhaps an attempt to sabotage moves towards accommodation with the USA. But by the autumn Mao was getting impatient. So he received the veteran American leftist, Edgar Snow, and discoursed on his readiness for discussions with Nixon. But Snow was not, as Mao believed, a CIA agent, so that 'trial balloon' went nowhere. More successful was the befriending, at a Japanese tournament in April 1971, of the US ping-pong team, and its invitation to Beijing. The White House picked up this signal, and Nixon may also have been reassured by US public enthusiasm for the visit. A further obstacle was removed when China dropped its insistence that, as a

[13] Kissinger, *Memoirs*, i, Chaps 6, 18; H.C. Hinton, *The Sino-Soviet Confrontation* (New York, 1976) pp. 16–21, 37; Clare Hollingworth, *Mao* (paperback edn, 1967) p. 227.
[14] Haldeman, *Ends of Power* p. 89 (citing his 10 December log); Kissinger, *Memoirs*, i, pp. 781–2.

precondition for a high-level meeting, the US should promise military withdrawal from Taiwan. So in July 1971 Nixon's Security Adviser, Henry Kissinger, was able secretly to visit Beijing, while purporting to be laid low with a stomach upset in Pakistan. The visit was a great success, Kissinger being much taken with Zhou's charm and intelligence, while the two found sufficient common geopolitical ground in their lengthy surveys of the international scene. Kissinger's return was followed by the immediate announcement of a prospective Nixon visit.

This seems to have brought internal Chinese resistance to a head. In part it was simply a power struggle. Mao always fell out with his number twos: one purpose of the Cultural Revolution had been to liquidate the overpowerful and pragmatic Liu Shaoqui, and the Army chief Lin Biao (who had succeeded Liu as Mao's heir) seems to have sensed that this was about to happen again. So in September 1971 he attempted to assassinate Mao and take over, then when the plot failed fled towards the Soviet Union, dying in a plane crash on the way. After the event he was accused of having been in touch with the USSR for some time, and of having been ready to seek (and pay for) Soviet military intervention in support of the coup. He is also said to have included in his secret listing of Mao's failings the move away from the 'sane socialists in the Soviet Union' towards the 'corrupt capitalists and imperialists' in Washington. There may be an element of exaggeration in all this.[15] But the episode occasioned substantial upheaval – Taiwan reported 37,000 arrests in the armed forces – and had the effect of consolidating the tilt towards the USA, approval of which Mao was always careful to signal by personally receiving Kissinger. In October Kissinger returned to negotiate a communiqué, which was surfaced as the 'Shanghai Communiqué'[16] in February 1972 when Nixon finally made his triumphant and much televised tour. It stressed the desirability of 'progress towards normalization of relations'. This did not imply immediate US recognition of the People's Republic, but in 1973 'liaison offices' were established in Beijing and Washington. The communiqué also brought US acceptance in principle that 'there is but one China and that Taiwan is a part of China', and an undertaking to reduce US forces on

[15] The charges are based on reconstituted captured documents – *Keesing's*, 25635–6, 30834–5; Hollingworth, *Mao*, Chap. 13. Philip Short, *Mao. A Life* (1999) pp. 589–99, 756n sees claims that Lin had opposed rapprochement with the US as *ex post facto* justifications on Mao's part.

[16] Text in Kissinger, *Memoirs*, i, pp. 1490–2.

Taiwan.[17] Finally the USA and China agreed to oppose efforts by 'any country' (i.e. the USSR) to establish 'hegemony' in the Asia-Pacific region. It was this that had brought the two together; 'The basic issue,' Mao had explained while the communiqué was being negotiated, 'is this':

No matter whether it is the United States or China, neither of us could fight simultaneously on two fronts. It is OK to say you will . . . in fact no country can do it. Of course, it will not do any good if you work it into the communiqué.[18]

China's new alignment and its consequences

Kissinger's original draft of the communiqué had, he says, been innocuous; it was immediately rejected, on Mao's instructions, as the sort of banality the Soviets would sign but never observe. Instead the communiqué – even after Kissinger had secured the excision of declarations like 'revolution has become the irresistible trend of history' – firmly stated the two countries' diametrically opposed views on a wide range of issues. This probably made it easier to explain within China, where the opening to the USA was justified strictly in terms of the optimum tactics to achieve a revolutionary outcome – even if to Nixon Mao described slogans, like 'the whole world should unite and defeat imperialism, revisionism, and all reactionaries, and establish socialism', as no more than 'a lot of big cannons'.[19]

But in moving towards the United States, China did *de facto* shift towards the maintenance of the international *status quo*. 'As long as the target is identical,' Mao told Kissinger in February 1973, 'we will not do anything to harm you, nor . . . you . . . us. We will cope with the same damned rotten egg.' Accordingly 'it is necessary to draw a parallel embracing the US, Japan, China, Pakistan, Iran, Turkey, and Europe.' Kissinger was so impressed that, on his return, he told Nixon that 'with the exception of the United Kingdom, *the PRC might well be closest to us in its global perceptions.*'[20]

---

[17] The US withdrew its last combat aircraft in 1975 (James Mann, *About Face. A History of America's Curious Relationship with China, from Nixon to Clinton* (paperback edn, 2000) p. 68.

[18] Ross and Jiang, *US–China Diplomacy*, p. 253.

[19] Kissinger, *Memoirs*, i, p. 1062; ii, p. 67.

[20] Ross and Jiang, *US–China Diplomacy*, pp. 357, 388.

In the developed world China's shift, and its subsequent internal evolution after Mao's death, gradually destroyed its appeal to the ultra-left (so strong in the later 1960s) as the mecca of revolution. Instead Beijing played host to rightist politicians and was prodigal with its advice:

The Soviet Union, Mao said, wanted world domination, and if their drive was ever to be stopped, the United States would have to stand up to them. That was why the US would have to remain strong in the Pacific basin . . . Would we do anything to challenge the Soviet–Cuban threat in Africa? When was the United States going to strengthen ties with its NATO allies? Were we going to continue helping our traditional friends in Asia?

Once Mao had argued within the communist world that Khrushchev's soft policy towards imperialism was more risky than firm confrontation; now he warned the West of the dangers of detente and appeasement: 'As for the Soviet Union, they bully the weak, and are afraid of the strong'.[21]

In the Third World, the shift in China's position was more uneven. In Africa (other than Rhodesia/Zimbabwe) and in West Asia China largely withdrew from the support of insurrectionary movements. In South–east Asia it was slower to discontinue support for subversion. 1971–3 saw a substantial increase in the supply of arms to Thai guerrillas. Later this did fall away, and China even moved to protect Thailand from Vietnam (below, p. 348); but it felt moral difficulty in disengaging, and seems to have permitted South-east Asian communist parties to broadcast from Chinese territory at least until 1980 – which earned it the continuing suspicion of some (not all) ASEAN countries.[22]

As for the Vietnam War, detente with China gave Nixon confidence that he could, as part of his tortuous disengagement, bomb Hanoi far more ferociously in 1972 than Johnson had ever dared. China also encouraged Hanoi to conclude a ceasefire with the United States and so secure the withdrawal of US troops, and even advised a period of consolidation after the 1973 ceasefire before resuming the attack on the Thieu regime. But it stepped up its economic aid, and (up till 1972) continued to offer help

---

[21] President Gerald Ford's account of an interview (after the fall of South Vietnam) – *A Time to Heal* (1979) p. 336; Kissinger, *Memoirs*, ii, p. 694.

[22] J.L.S. Girling, *Thailand. Society and Politics* (paperback edn, 1985) p. 269; A. James Gregor, *The China Connection. US Policy and the People's Republic of China* (Stanford, 1986) p. 191; Mahathir Mohamad (Prime Minister of Malaysia), in *Far Eastern Economic Review*, 30 October 1981, pp. 34–5.

with the construction of the Ho Chi Minh trail.[23] China also identified firmly with the Sihanouk–Khmer Rouge coalition opposing the Cambodian government. According to Kissinger it was in mid-1973 on the point of moving to secure a compromise settlement when Congress destroyed the US negotiating position by forcing an end to US bombing.[24] Be that as it may, China then reverted to a full endorsement of the Khmer Rouge, a position it maintained despite both the barbarity of their rule after they came to power in 1975 and their support for Thai guerrillas. But then the Khmer Rouge had what was by the later 1970s the cardinal virtue in Chinese eyes, that of being anti-Vietnamese.

In the more general power equation, reconciliation with the United States made China confident enough, in 1972, to reduce sharply its 'Third Front' programme, which, though originally started as a precaution against US attack, had recently shifted northwards to provide cover against the USSR.[25] Equally detente with China helped the US reduce its armed forces; to China's distress, American capacity was allowed to drop from a '2½' to a '1½ war' capability.[26] Meanwhile the USSR maintained up to a third of its army on the Chinese border, and people often suggested that, had it not felt the need to do so, its military preponderance within Europe would have been still greater. Perhaps. But it is equally possible that, without the requirement to keep troops in the east, the overall Soviet defence effort would have been that much (perhaps 10–15 per cent) smaller. In any case the build-up of Soviet forces in Asia had been a feature of the 1960s, and had long antedated Sino-American detente. Nor are the diplomatic consequences of the Chinese shift clear. The Nixon administration felt it derived considerable advantage from having better relations with both China and the Soviet Union than they had with each other – 'drinking your Mao Tai and having your Vodka too'. Certainly the USSR

[23] Ministry of Foreign Affairs, Socialist Republic of Vietnam, *The Truth about Vietnam–China Relations over the Last Thirty Years* (Hanoi, 1979) pp. 41–2, 46–9; Hoang Van Hoan, 'Distortion of Facts about Militant Friendship between Vietnam and China is Impermissible', *Beijing Review*, 7 December 1979, p. 19. The difference between the two accounts lies less in the realm of facts than in the attribution of motives. But the former does quote Haig to the effect that in October 1973 the Chinese advised Kissinger 'not to allow yourselves to be defeated in Vietnam'.

[24] Kissinger, *Memoirs*, ii, pp. 349–69.

[25] Naughton, 'The Third Front', p. 366.

[26] In response to Chinese criticism, Defense Secretary Brown 'pointed out that the other war plan had been designed for use against the People's Republic' – Jimmy Carter, *Keeping Faith: Memoirs of a President* (1982) pp. 192–3.

which had been stalling on a summit up to July 1971, in the hope of extracting further concessions, started pressing for one as soon as Nixon's invitation to Beijing was announced. For some time thereafter it sought to conciliate the USA to try to win it to the joint management of the Chinese problem. But the realisation that this would not work then reduced the value the Kremlin set on detente after 1974–5.[27]

Implications for Japan

What can be said is that the new Sino-American relationship smoothed both China's emergence as a major diplomatic player and Japan's adjustment to this. In the long run non-recognition of the largest country in the world was bound to seem increasingly artificial. In 1964 'With' (in de Gaulle's words) 'the weight of evidence and reason making itself felt more and more every day',[28] France had decided to recognise the People's Republic, becoming the 48th country to do so. The Cultural Revolution slowed the process down; but with the restoration of order it resumed, Canada, Italy, Ethiopia and Equatorial Guinea according recognition in 1970. The announcement that Nixon would visit China must have accelerated things; and in the autumn of 1971 (against US wishes) the United Nations unseated the Nationalist and admitted a Communist Chinese delegation. Japan had every reason to be upset. It had not been consulted before the secret Kissinger visit to China; it had dutifully played a leading role in managing the anti-Beijing group in the UN, and had attracted strong Chinese attacks (still in evidence at the time of Nixon's 1972 visit) on its supposedly reviving militarism and revisionism. Japan now feared the improvement of US–Chinese relations over its head, and moved rapidly to join in. In August 1972 the new Prime Minister, Tanaka, secured an invitation to Beijing, and in October the two countries issued a joint declaration and established diplomatic relations.

Historically much of Japanese culture had come from China, and the Japanese had felt (even in the 1930s, though its tangible manifestation had then been horribly skewed) a strong affinity with the Chinese. Since 1945 Japan had also established a special relationship with the United States, the provider of protection, the major market, and an important cultural model. The price of this relationship had been a breach with the People's

[27] Kissinger, *Memoirs*, i, pp. 759, 766; William G. Hyland, *Mortal Rivals. Superpower Relations from Nixon to Reagan* (New York, 1987) pp. 11, 60–6, 77.
[28] *Keesing's*, 19878.

Republic. Now the way was open for Japan to enjoy good relations with both countries at once. Indeed China's anxiety to contain the USSR led it in 1973 to commend the US–Japanese alliance it had once so warmly attacked, to lecture Kissinger on how best to manage it, and to stress the dangers for Japan's politics of forcing it to choose between China and the USA.[29] (China also made itself useful to Japan by supplying oil at the time of the 1973–4 Arab embargo.)

The Sino-Japanese-American triangle was further consolidated by the heavy-handedness of the other major East Asian power, the USSR. Tanaka had intended to conclude peace treaties with both China and the Soviet Union at much the same time. But in 1972–6 Soviet–Japanese negotiations always bogged down over Japan's demand for the restoration of four of the Kuril islands the USSR had occupied in 1945. Nor did talks about Japanese development of Siberian oilfields go well.[30] In addition Moscow became, as the Japanese put it, 'obsessed' with the clause China insisted in putting into any Sino-Japanese peace treaty to the effect that neither state 'should seek hegemony in the Asia-Pacific region . . . [and] each is opposed to efforts by any other country . . . to establish such hegemony'.[31] Though this was undoubtedly meant to annoy, as Japan pointed out it committed her to nothing, and the USSR was unwise to weigh in with heavy warnings. Japanese reluctance to sign the clause delayed the conclusion of a formal peace treaty with China until 1978. But in the absence of any Soviet counter-incentives, Japan then gave way (with US encouragement); the USSR retaliated by largely freezing relations.

China and Vietnam in the 1970s; The 1979 war

In the mid-1970s US–Chinese relations encountered difficulties over Taiwan (see p. 349), but in 1978 these were at least temporarily resolved, with full diplomatic relations established at the start of 1979. On China's side, the process was facilitated by its growing quarrel with Vietnam. Indeed the late 1978 Central Committee meeting that decided to accept US terms for the normalisation of relations also decided on military action to teach Vietnam a lesson.[32]

[29] Kissinger, *Memoirs*, ii, p. 293.
[30] G.L. Curtis, 'The Tyumen Oil Development Project and Japanese Foreign Policy Decision Making', in R.A. Scalapino (ed.) *The Foreign Policy of Modern Japan* (Berkeley, 1977) pp. 147–73; *Keesing's*, 25625, 27384, 27599.
[31] *Keesing's*, 29279–80.
[32] Carter, *Keeping Faith*, pp. 197–8; King C. Chen, *China's War with Vietnam* (Stanford, 1987) pp. 85–9.

The collapse of Sino-Vietnamese relations is, with hindsight, unsurprising. Kissinger says the North Vietnamese generally began negotiations by recounting 'the epic of Vietnam's struggle for independence through the centuries . . . The heroic saga of how the Vietnamese defeated all foreigners'; most of these foreigners, as Hanoi's History Museum made clear, were Chinese.[33] During the war with South Vietnam Hanoi naturally tried to keep on good terms with both its sources of aid, China and the USSR. But the USSR could give more, and the Vietnamese Politburo inclined increasingly towards it. By the end of the war friction with China was already evident: in 1974 China seized the Paracel Islands from South Vietnam and claimed the Spratlies (the area probably contains oil), while next year Hanoi scrambled to garrison the Spratlies and then claimed the Paracels.[34] More seriously, as the non-communist governments in Laos and Cambodia fell, Vietnam made sure of its pre-eminence in the one, China in the other. Further trouble stemmed from the position of the ethnic Chinese in Vietnam. Initially they were perhaps persecuted as capitalists (most had lived in the South), but by 1978 simply as Chinese. June 1977 is supposed to have seen an unsuccesful Vietnamese attempt at a coup in Cambodia; that autumn the Cambodian leader Pol Pot was welcomed in Beijing, while a counter visit by Vietnam's Le Duan proved fruitless. Border hostilities between Cambodia and Vietnam began in December; just as Cambodia looked to China for aid, so Vietnam turned to the Soviet Union. In June 1978 it joined the Soviet economic bloc, becoming a member of CMEA; so all Chinese economic aid to it was stopped. November saw a Soviet–Vietnamese Treaty of Friendship that, like the 1971 Soviet–Indian treaty, was the prelude to a military solution. In December–January Vietnam conquered Cambodia, installing a puppet government under Heng Samrin that was, at least in humanitarian terms, a vast improvement on that of Pol Pot.

China had decided not to send troops to Cambodia (which might draw it into a lengthy war of attrition), but nevertheless to teach Vietnam a 'lesson' (as it had done India in 1962). The new Chinese leader, Deng Xiaoping, discounted the likelihood of direct Soviet intervention, but thought it wise to secure the USA's moral support or at least tacit acquiescence. He therefore cleared up the remaining obstacles to normalising relations and invited himself to Washington, where in January 1979 he privately briefed Carter as to his intentions. Whether sincerely or *pro*

[33] Kissinger, *Memoirs,* i, p. 281; ii, p. 28.
[34] Chen, *China's War with Vietnam,* pp. 46–7.

forma, Carter voiced standard liberal objections; Deng thanked him politely, but added 'that it was highly desirable for China that its arrogant neighbors know that they could not disturb it and other countries in the area with impunity'.[35] In February China invaded northern Vietnam. Its army lacked recent fighting experience and was generally antiquated. So, though it was opposed mostly by Vietnam's second-best forces (the best being in Cambodia), the result was far from a walk-over. However in a month's heavy fighting China managed to flatten four provincial capitals and 320 villages and then retire, declaring a victory and carrying off some 150,000 buffaloes and 250,000 pigs.[36]

In April 1979 the Chinese ambassador to Thailand stated that, 'Supported by the Soviet Union, Vietnam is dreaming of dominating the whole of the South-East Asia region . . . [as] a component part of the global strategy of the Soviet Union to dominate the world', while in June Deng proclaimed that 'Any threat to Thailand is a threat to China'.[37] China was obviously operating a containment policy. Like any such policy it was open to charges of being unnecessary – perhaps Vietnam had no designs on Thailand – or counterproductive – in that it led Vietnam to turn over to the USSR the valuable ex-US base at Camranh Bay. But it was broadly welcomed by the USA, and for a time it seemed that China and the USA were establishing an unwritten alliance: two decades earlier China had angrily rejected Soviet proposals for a joint naval communications radio station; in 1979 it agreed to house, on a joint-operation basis, US electronic surveillance devices displaced from Iran by the Khomenei revolution. Then, in January 1980 in the immediate aftermath of the Soviet invasion of Afghanistan, Defense Secretary Brown undertook to sell military equipment, declaring that if Chinese or US interests were threatened, 'we can respond with complementary actions in the field of defence as well as diplomacy'. Next year the incoming Reagan administration was reportedly 'startled by the depth and breadth' of US–Chinese relations.[38]

[35] Carter, *Keeping Faith*, pp. 206–7.

[36] Chen puts Vietnamese dead at 30,000, Chinese at 26,000 (over half of America's Vietnam War dead) – *China's War with Vietnam*, Chap. 5; *Keesing's*, 29874.

[37] Girling, *Thailand*, pp. 246–7. Both China and America warned Vietnam during its June 1980 attack on Kampuchean refugee/guerrilla camps in Thailand – J.C. Hsiung and W. Chai (eds) *Asia and US Foreign Policy* (1981) p. 109.

[38] *Keesing's*, 30239, 30387, 31621; Hsiung and Chai, *Asia and US Foreign Policy*, p. 112; Mann, *About Face*, p. 98; Robert S. Ross, *Negotiating Cooperation. The United States and China. 1969–1989* (Stanford, CA., 1995) p. 150.

But thereafter they were gradually to cool, largely because of trouble over Taiwan.

China's relations with the USA and USSR in the 1980s

On his very first visit to China, Kissinger apparently promised both gradual disengagement from Taiwan and, during Nixon's second term, the establishment of formal diplomatic relations with Beijing.[39] But first Watergate and then, to China's growing annoyance, the challenge from the right to Ford in the 1976 primaries prevented the United States from delivering. Nor was President Carter initially in any hurry, preferring to give priority to his Panama treaty. But if delay was due chiefly to US politics, Taiwan did present real problems. For Washington wanted a Chinese promise to pursue reunification only by peaceful means, while Beijing pressed the USA not only to end all but informal contacts with Taiwan but also to discontinue arms sales. Both were disappointed, and in the 1978 negotiations these issues were fudged. Furthermore, in passing the necessary consequential legislation, the 1979 Taiwan Relations Act,[40] Congress stipulated that the US should continue to review Taiwan's defence needs and sell 'such defense articles . . . as may be necessary to enable Taiwan to maintain a sufficient self-defense capability.'

Trouble started in late 1980, with US proposals to sell Taiwan a new military aircraft, the FX. Then, when Reagan came into office, Beijing's reaction may have been sharpened by his earlier identification with Taiwan. Some writers argue that Beijing may also have been encouraged to step up pressure on the United States by the belief that, with the end of detente and advent of the 'Second Cold War', the US was now locked into confrontation with the USSR, and from a position of weakness. If so, it now needed China more than *vice versa*. Accordingly Beijing was not satisfied by the dropping of the FX project, but pushed in 1981–2 for the ending of *all* arms sales, threatening that otherwise 'relations will retrogress'.[41] Official Washington was deeply divided, with Secretary of State Haig the most alarmed by the prospect of thus again 'losing' China. This was one factor behind his 1983 resignation; his successor, Shultz, attached

[39] Ross and Jiang, *US–China Diplomacy*, p. 375.
[40] Text in Ross, *United States and China*, pp. 273 ff.
[41] ibid. pp. 187–93.

rather less importance to China's military contribution to the anti-Soviet coalition and more to that from the economic power of Japan and the 'Rim of Asia'. Meanwhile President Reagan insisted that arms sales continue. Deng seems to have accepted this during a May 1982 visit by Vice-President Bush, and in August a mutually face-saving statement was agreed to that effect.[42]

Against this background, China appeared to revert to an equi-distance between the USA and USSR: in his September 1982 report to the Party Congress, Chairman Hu Yaobang criticised US as well as Soviet 'hegemonists', and, under the slogan 'Adhering to an Independent Foreign Policy', declared that China belonged rather to the Third World.[43] Too much can be made of this. Sino-American friction continued into 1983, new issues including air services to Taiwan and US insistence that the island be allowed to retain its membership of the Asian Development Bank. But then China gave way; Taiwan issues were shelved for the time being, Prime Minister Zhao Zhiyang paid a very successful visit to Washington in December 1983, and in May 1984 Reagan was welcomed to China at the optimum time to boost his electoral fortunes. There ensued what one writer has called 'the Golden Years', with 'between 1983 and 1988 . . . a closer, more extensive relationship . . . than the two governments had before or have had since.'[44]

In the 1980s the USSR at last realised the stupidity of its China policy and started to correct it, notably in Brezhnev's 1982 Tashkent and Baku speeches. A variety of friendly contacts ensued, for instance at Brezhnev's funeral. But in 1982 China identified three major stumbling blocks to improved relations: Soviet troop concentrations on its borders; the maintenance of Soviet troops in Afghanistan; and Soviet support for the Vietnamese occupation of Cambodia. Accordingly the 'normalisation talks' then started made little real progress. After Gorbachev's advent to power, the USSR proposed both a nonaggression treaty and a summit –

[42] Text in ibid. pp. 270–2; Reagan secretly laid down that the promise not to *increase*, and 'to reduce gradually', US arms sales applied only so long as the existing favourable military balance between Taiwan and China continued (Mann, *About Face*, pp. 127–8).
[43] *Keesing's*, 31818.
[44] These paragraphs follow Ross, *United States and China*, Chaps 6, 7 and Mann, *About Face*, Chaps 6, 7. Both agree that while Haig's overvaluation of Chinese power invited pressure, Beijing respected the finality of Reagan's decisions; Ross argues that this was helped, too, by China's belief that the US was by 1983 clearly out-competing the USSR.

to no effect. So in a July 1986 speech at Vladivostok, Gorbachev hinted at both troop withdrawals and concessions on the border issue. Border talks resumed in 1987, reaching agreement in principle in August, but Gorbachev's calls for a summit were still not met. In April 1988 serious negotiations (between Afghanistan and Pakistan, mediated by their backers the USSR and USA) finally resulted in an unprecedented promise to withdraw all Soviet troops by February 1989. In December 1988 Vietnam was induced to announce some withdrawals – in April 1989 full withdrawal – from Cambodia. Gorbachev then obtained his long sought summit in Beijing in May 1989. As things turned out, it was largely overshadowed by China's domestic political crisis. But he announced further troop movements that would, by the end of 1990, reduce Soviet forces in the Far East to 120,000. And he secured the restoration of full Sino-Soviet party as well as state relations, though the Chinese were careful to balance this with a US naval visit.[45]

China in the 1980s; Tiananmen and the Western response

Mao's initial rapprochement with the USA had been a matter of strategy, not economics. He had not actually been able to manage without grain imports, but in principle he was (especially after the 1960 shock withdrawal of Soviet aid) a great believer in self-sufficiency. He was also, in domestic affairs, strongly socialist. Though he allowed periodic spells of order and consolidation, he was always concerned that they would lead, as in the USSR, to the emergence of a privileged 'new class' of officials and administrators. Hence the Cultural Revolution, and, in the closing years of his life, the support he seems to have given to his wife and the leftist 'Gang of Four'. A month after his death in September 1976 the Gang was arrested, after which power gradually fell into the hands of their former victim, the pragmatic Deng Xiaoping. Deng believed, above all, in modernising the economy to quadruple GNP between 1979 and 2000. China is primarily an agricultural country; and in 1979–84 Deng essentially wound up collective agriculture, restoring the land to the peasants, raising prices, and encouraging sales on the open market with dramatic results. Industrial reform was less drastic; but China went considerably further than the Soviet Union in facilitating entrepreneurship and reducing controls. Above

[45] *Keesing's*, 31818, 35064–6, 35840, 35970–2, 36377, 36448, 36588, 36641–2.

all Deng started to orient China towards the world market, by setting aside in 1979 four 'Special Economic Zones' where foreign capital (in practice mostly from Japan, Hong Kong and Taiwan) was welcomed and state controls drastically reduced, a process further extended in the 1980s. As a result the Chinese standard of living was reckoned by the World Bank to have doubled (albeit from a very low level) in 1977–87.[46]

There were, however, problems, notably corruption (for which the Hainan Special Economic Zone was particularly notorious) and inflation (unofficially said to be running at 20–30 per cent p.a. in the later 1980s). This was worrying, for inflation and corruption had contributed greatly to the collapse of the KMT in the later 1940s, and many hardliners did not wish to risk repeating the process. To appease them Deng sacrificed the Party Secretary Hu Yaobang in 1987, but did not really change course. In 1989 matters came to a head, with intellectuals demonstrating on ideological grounds for Western liberalism, and drawing support from a working class alienated from the regime by an inflation that was squeezing their real wages. Hu Yaobang's death touched off sympathy demonstrations by Beijing students, who took over Tienanmen Square, demanded Deng's retirement, and erected a Goddess of Democracy (modelled on the Statue of Liberty). All this coincided with Gorbachev's visit, and so took place under the eye of the world media. The current Party Secretary, Zhao Ziyang, was conciliatory. But hardliners in the army, Party and uneconomic state industry felt the country to be on the verge of chaos. So did Deng Xiaoping, who had once already imprisoned the 'Democracy Wall' activists of 1979, and who now backed the hardliners. On 4 June tanks cleared Tienanmen Square, leaving between 700 and 2,700 dead; this was followed up by arrests and executions throughout the country. Of the East European regimes similarly threatened later in the year, only that of Romania was prepared to use such force.[47] Zhao was soon dropped, and the authorities turned back to stressing socialism (and even Maoism) as the cement of order and Chinese unity.

All this shocked Western public opinion, hitherto confident that China was steadily liberalising; and it drew the attention of advocacy groups to continuing human rights abuses and suppression of minorities (especially in Tibet). The effect on governments was less durable. Loans from the

---

[46] *The Independent*, 8 July 1991, p. 21.
[47] Immanuel C.Y. Hsu, *The Rise of Modern China* (New York, 1990 edn) Chaps 37–8, 40; Mann, *About Face*, p. 399n.

World Bank ($2.3 billion had been scheduled for 1989–90) and the Asian Development Bank were suspended, as was a projected $5.6 billion package from Japan. Western weapons sales, which had begun in a small way in the 1970s and increased in the 1980s, were halted; and the 1979 American grant of 'Most Favoured Nation' tariff status, a prerequisite for significant exports to the USA, came to be targeted in Congress.

The ending of arms sales proved lasting; but in 1991 China mended fences with a now weakened USSR, and thereafter the sale of high-technology items proved a godsend to Russia's collapsing defence industries.[48] Economic pressures, however, proved unsustainable. Within a month of Tiananmen, Bush's National Security Adviser, Brent Scowcroft, had paid Beijing a secret visit to explain that the President hoped to preserve 'the long-term relationship' with China; 'further arrests and executions will inevitably lead to greater demands in the US to respond', but 'Efforts at national reconciliation . . . will find a cooperative US response'. The message was reinforced by a second Scowcroft visit in December 1989. The key to a settlement proved to be the prolonged negotiations over a democracy activist who had been accorded refuge in the US embassy. In June 1990 China let him emigrate; the July G-7 summit lifted restrictions on World Bank loans, and this cleared the way for the reactivation of the Japanese package.[49]

By 1992 the Chinese economy had recovered from the shocks and slow-down of 1989–90; overseas investment rushed in, with contracts for $111 billion being signed in 1993. Accordingly the Chinese government was much better placed to resist external pressure. So when the new Democratic US President, Clinton, signed an order linking the future renewal of China's Most Favoured Nation status to 'significant progress' on the release of political prisoners, easing conditions in Tibet, and ending the jamming of foreign broadcasts imposed after Tiananmen, China simply sat tight and highlighted the likely cost to US business of a diversion of Chinese purchases elsewhere – Premier Li Peng said, of an opportune visit by the German Chancellor and attendant businessmen, that 'Chancellor Kohl is sure to fly back with full cases'. Lobbied by American business, and also needing China's help to resolve the crisis over North Korea's nuclear programme (above, p. 53), Clinton reversed course in May 1994: 'We have

---

[48] However, China's 1992 purchase of advanced Sukhoi-27 aircraft backfired, leading the USA to sell Taiwan the F-16 planes it had always previously witheld (Mann, *About Face*, pp. 257, 264–8).

[49] Mann, *About Face*, esp. pp. 197, 206–8, 218–22, 240.

reached the end of the usefulness of that policy [of linking human rights and Most Favoured Nation status], and it is time to take a new path.'[50]

China, the US–Chinese relationship, and Taiwan since the 1990s

The Chinese government, then, remained very much master in its own house. It continued to believe absolute control essential for the preservation of 'order', and to see this as threatened, inter alia, by the strains of uneven development, both as between the ultra-dynamic (and mostly coastal) provinces and poor overpopulated agricultural hinterlands, and as between the old uneconomic state-owned industries and their lighter, newer, and more commercial private counterparts. Beijing also remained neuralgically alert to threats, not only from the handful of dissidents and advocates of democracy, but also from independent movements of any kind. In 1999, angered by a surprise demonstration mounted by the Falun Gong religious movement near official Beijing, and alarmed by the sect's appeal to some Party and army cadres, the government pulled in nearly 36,000 of its members.[51]

The other side of the coin is economic growth. GDP statistics are inevitably imprecise. But they suggest that, between 1978 and 2003, the economy grew nine-fold and real *per capita* GDP seven-fold, leading both to the emergence of an affluent and consumer-oriented middle class and to an impressive drop in the number of people living 'in poverty'.[52] Since China is a continental economy, the effects of this growth on the rest of the world have been muted – its overall trade in goods and services did not overtake that of the vastly smaller (if richer) Netherlands until the year 2000.[53] But thereafter Chinese growth emerged as a major factor in the world economy, sucking in imports of oil (China is, after the USA, the second largest importer) and producer goods (thus providing a welcome stimulus to the sluggish Japanese economy), and (with other East Asian countries)

[50] Mann, *About Face*, pp. 280, 284–5, 293, 296, 308, 332.
[51] Since then protests, arrests and imprisonments have continued, albeit more sporadically; in 1999 Falun Gong had claimed 70m members – *Keesing's*, 43060, 43263, 43313.
[52] National Bureau of Statistics of China, *China Statistical Yearbook 2004*, p. 56; China claims that, over the last 25 years, the numbers of those living on less than $81 pa (admittedly a very low threshold) have fallen from 250m to 26m (*The Independent*, 6 July 2005, p. 25).
[53] IMF, *Balance of Payments Statistics Yearbook*, 2004, Part 1, pp. 188, 666.

supplying cheap manufactures in quantities long sufficient to restrain inflation in the developed world.

Managing this process would seem to have been the Chinese government's chief concern, and it has kept a far lower profile in international affairs than that adopted in Mao's day – in the UN it has generally gone along with the USA, or at least (as over Kosovo in 1999) abstained rather than used its veto.[54] Both China and the United States have been in a position to assist each other, though they have chosen to do so only up to a point. Thus China can exercise restraint in its sales of missiles and nuclear or military technology, and is in a position to exert economic and perhaps political pressure on North Korea. Similarly US consent was needed for China to be able (in 2001) to join the World Trade Organisation; and the USA could exert influence over, or at least disengage from, Taiwan. Both the USA and China have chosen the path of engagement, and in some respects this has gone far. Academic contacts and diplomatic visits are frequent, much more so than those in the past between the USA and USSR. Above all, trade is important: China, like the rest of East Asia, has benefited enormously from access to the US market, and in 2004 supplied 10 per cent of US imports; the trade balance is massively in China's favour, and is funded partly by Chinese purchases of US government securities (totalling, in mid-2005, some $230 billion).[55] The result, therefore, is a significant degree of interdependence – though one that has generated a surge of popular US resentment and protectionism not unlike that directed in the late 1980s at Japan.

Overall, then, there is substantial contact and cooperation. But there are also elements reminiscent of the US–Soviet Cold War – concern, on the one side, over dissidents and human rights, on the other, resentment at foreign interference and attempts to prevent the penetration of disruptive ideas. China may have decided, at least for the present, not to challenge the United States' world pre-eminence, but it sometimes applies to this the opprobrious term 'hegemonism'; and when Chinese dignity is hurt, there can be outpourings of popular, if government-managed, xenophobia. One such was touched off by US bombing, during the 1999 Kosovo war, of the Chinese embassy in Belgrade, another by the 2001 collision,

---

[54] Kosovo's situation within Serbia had some analogies with the position of Tibet, and China was unhappy with the UN's decision to ratify its 'liberation' by NATO. China was also cool towards the US–British intervention in Iraq, but did not join the French–German–Russian front in diplomatic opposition to it.

[55] *The Economist*, 21 May 2005, pp. 85–6; 2 July, p. 13.

over international waters, between a US electronic intelligence plane and one of the Chinese fighters buzzing it.[56] The relationship has, therefore, proved remarkably volatile. For most of Clinton's first term it was strained, first by his campaign rhetoric and attempt to force China into concessions by threatening its 'Most Favoured Nation' status, then by his naval backing of Taiwan in 1995–6 (below, p. 357). But things had so improved by mid-1996 that China (overenthusiastically) directed contributions into Clinton's electoral campaign funds.[57] However, 1999 brought the Belgrade bombing and Chinese anti-American riots, on the one side, and, on the other, a scare about Chinese espionage. In 2000 candidate Bush described Chinese conduct as often 'alarming abroad and appalling at home'; and his Presidency began in 2001 with difficult negotiations over the release of the US intelligence plane (which had, after its collision, made a forced landing in China). But that October Presidents Bush and Jiang Zemin had a very amiable meeting, with China being thanked for its post-9/11 support in the 'war on terrorism', support that extended through and beyond the United States' defeat of the Taliban in Afghanistan.[58]

Probably the most disturbing aspects of the relationship are military. To judge by capabilities, the United States constitutes the chief, perhaps the only real, threat to China. Equally, if Chinese economic growth continues, it should in the foreseeable future become a continental power, on the same scale as the USA and its most plausible challenger in any renewed bipolar world. The Pentagon therefore monitors China's military build-up, amid suggestions that its real defence expenditure is well above the stated budget, on one estimate $60 billion p.a. rather than $25 billion. However, when Defense Secretary Rumsfeld voiced fears at an Asian Security Conference, China observed that in 2004–5 US defence spending had been $450 billion.[59]

What makes these concerns acute is Taiwan. Beijing holds that it is part of China and must eventually return, preferably by negotiating a long period of autonomy on the model of Hong Kong. But in Taiwan feelings of Chinese unity have been declining, attachment to a distinct local state

[56] Mann, *About Face*, pp. 277–8; *Keesing's*, 42955, 44101–2. Similar riots were directed against Japan in 2005, partly in response to school textbooks giving a euphemistic portrayal of the 1930s, but 'inspired mainly by Japan's bid for permanent membership of the UN Security Council' (*Economist*, 23 April 2005, pp. 65–6).

[57] Mann, *About Face*, pp. 341–52.

[58] *Economist*, 11 June 2005 pp. 60–1; *Keesing's*, 44400.

[59] *Economist*, 11 June 2005 pp. 60–1.

rising. In part this represents the passage of generations: the island was initially ruled by survivors from the KMT government of China defeated on the mainland in 1949; but in 1988 Chiang Kai-shek's son, Chiang Ching-Kuo, died and was succeeeded as President by a man of Taiwanese origin, Lee Teng-Hui. In part the change was the product of democratisation, which was bound to increase the importance of the islanders vis-à-vis the less numerous refugees from the mainland; Lee inaugurated genuine elections for the National Assembly in 1991, for the Presidency in 1996 (a development Beijing did not welcome). He also attempted to raise Taiwan's international profile in a variety of ways. Not all were opposed by Beijing (which agreed to Taiwan's joining APEC in 1991 and the World Trade Organisation in 2001 at the same time as itself), but many were. In June 1995 China responded to Lee's visit to his old university, Cornell,[60] by mounting military exercises in, and firing missiles into, the sea off Taiwan. Quiet US remonstrances were met, that autumn, by unofficial warnings that China would respond forcefully to any American intervention – 'You will not sacrifice Los Angeles to protect Taiwan'. This in turn drew a United States signal in the form of the despatch of an aircraft carrier through the Taiwan straits, for the first time since 1979. However, in the February–March 1996 run-up to Taiwan's elections, China mustered 150,000 troops for further exercises and fired missiles close to Taiwan's major ports. In response the US very publicly sent two carrier groups to the positions they would occupy if they really had to defend Taiwan.[61]

China's pressure proved counter-productive, Lee being comfortably re-elected. From Beijing's viewpoint worse was to follow. Before the 2000 Presidential elections it published a paper declaring that if Taiwan 'indefinitely' refused negotiations on reunion, China would be 'forced to take all possible drastic measures, including the use of military force', and warned the Taiwanese not to vote for a 'pro-independence' candidate. To no avail; a split in the ruling KMT party permitted the election of Chen Shui-bian, who had in the past spoken favourably of declaring Taiwan an independent state rather than the old 'Republic of China'. He did now promise not thus to declare independence unless China invaded; but he continued to explore changes and formulas designed to emphasise Taiwan's distinctive statehood. Not all subsequent developments have

---

[60] Supposedly a private occasion, but the first time since the 1970s that the US had permitted a visit by a high Taiwanese office holder.
[61] Mann, *About Face*, Chap. 17. In April 1996 mutual concern over China led to the strengthening of the US–Japanese Security Treaty.

been hostile – in early 2005 the first direct flights from Taiwan to the mainland were agreed. But there have been a string of Chinese warnings, notably a statement in 2004 that military action by 2008 could not be ruled out if President Chen persisted with his plans for constitutional reform, and, in March 2005, the passage of an 'Anti-Secession Law' formalising the warning of military action in the event of moves towards a Taiwanese declaration of independence.[62]

All this is reflected in regular military exercises,[63] and by armament. In July 2002 the Pentagon claimed that China was building up forces with the specific purpose of a surprise attack, and the Taiwanese Defence Ministry warned that it might lose local air/sea supremacy by 2010. In late 2002 there were perhaps 400 Chinese missiles targeted on Taiwan, a year later 496, and in September 2004 610; against this background the USA agreed that summer to sell Taiwan the Aegis 'advanced missile shield' and battle management system it had previously witheld as too much of an escalation.[64]

Behind the prospect of a Sino-Taiwanese war lurks that of US–Chinese catastrophe. The US could not easily permit a dictatorship to conquer a democracy, and in 2001 President Bush promised to do 'whatever it took to help Taiwan defend itself'.[65] This posture, in turn, has drawn at least unofficial warnings that China might respond to US military action in the Taiwan straits by nuclear attack on American cities.[66] The scenario does not at present appear very plausible,[67] and both US and Chinese statements aim probably chiefly at deterrence. But though many parts of the world seem more immediately dangerous, perhaps none has the same potentiality for escalation towards armageddon if things really go wrong.

---

[62] *Keesing's*, 43412, 43460, 45900, 46118, 46410, 46521.

[63] 2005 saw a joint Sino-Russian 'invasion' of the Shandong peninsula, clearly designed to send a message to the USA, and billed by the Chinese news agency as strengthening 'the capability of . . . jointly striking international terrorism, extremism and separatism'; Russian sources said it simulated intervention to assist a friendly ruler imperilled by either Islamic terror or popular revolt (on the Ukrainian model), but also that they had rejected suggestions that it be staged opposite Taiwan – *Daily Telegraph*, 19 August 2005, p. 16.

[64] *Keesing's*, 44101–2, 44898, 45088, 46063, 46204.

[65] *Keesing's*, 44101–2. Equally the USA has been at pains to discourage overt Taiwanese assertions of independence.

[66] *Financial Times*, 15 July 2005, p. 9.

[67] In late 2006 Sino-Taiwanese tension diminished as a result of political developments within Taiwan (President Chen's difficulties and the KMT's apparent revival).

CHAPTER 9

The rise and fall of detente in the 1960s and 1970s

Strained US–Soviet relations 1964–7;
The Glassboro Summit 1967;
The shift towards detente 1968

Nixon's 1972 visit to China had been impressive. But the climax of his travels that year was his journey to Moscow, which seemed to set the seal on a new relationship of detente between the superpowers. It had been a long time in coming. After the Cuban missiles crisis, the Soviet leadership decided on 'a temporary relaxation of international tensions'. By the same token Kennedy (despite a memorable Cold War speech when he visited the Berlin Wall) devoted much effort to trying to change attitudes – notably in his June 1963 address to the American University. This phase of detente yielded the Moscow–Washington hotline, the 1963 Test Ban Treaty, and US agreement *in principle* to sell wheat to the USSR.[1]

In 1963–4 both Kennedy and Khrushchev passed from the political scene. As far as the USA was concerned this made little difference. Johnson began by telling the UN that 'America wants to see the Cold War end', and soon arranged with Khrushchev a symbolic mutual reduction in the production of material for nuclear weapons. By 1969 he would say 'that his major mistake as President was in "trusting the Russians" too much' and that they created fewer difficulties for Presidents they feared.[2] But in his

---

[1] For the reality, see above p. 274n., below p. 366.
[2] Richard M. Nixon, *The Memoirs of Richard Nixon* (paperback edn, 1979) pp. 430–1.

memoirs he boasts of concluding 'more significant political agreements . . . than in the thirty' previous years of US–Soviet diplomatic relations. This may seem odd, since Johnson is chiefly remembered for expanding US anti-communist involvement in the Vietnam War until it surpassed (both in length and casualties) that in the Korean War. To Johnson the two policies were compatible: 'We were fighting in Vietnam to demonstrate that aggression should not, must not, succeed . . . On the other hand, we had to show that there was an alternative to confrontation . . . to create a climate in which nations of the East and West could begin cooperating to find solutions to their worst problems.' But not everybody saw it this way; indeed Johnson blames 'Resentment against nations supporting Hanoi' for Congressional refusal to remove the special tariff restrictions on East–West trade. The agreements he did achieve, while certainly an advance on what went before, now mostly appear rather minor.[3]

If Johnson wanted to continue the Kennedy–Khrushchev thaw, the new Soviet leaders were less sure: 'The Americans,' they told Nasser in 1967,

like to give the impression that their relations with us are continually improving, and that we and they consult together on everything. But this simply isn't true . . .

. . . The American aim is to isolate the Soviet Union from its friends and create an atmosphere of Soviet–American collusion, in the hope that this will damage the world communist movement and national liberation movements everywhere, and deepen the Sino-Soviet conflict by appearing to justify the Chinese claim that detente is simply another word for collusion, and weaken the fighting spirit of the Vietnamese. But in fact I can assure you that relations between us and the Americans are extremely tense.[4]

---

[3] Lyndon B. Johnson, *The Vantage Point* (1971) pp. 464–76. He cites: a cut back on the production of fissionable materials; a ban on nuclear weapons in space, and the 1968 Nuclear Non-Proliferation Treaty; a treaty providing for the return of astronauts/space vehicles landing accidentally in the wrong country; a consular convention, the renewal of a cultural agreement, the inauguration of a direct air service; and fisheries agreements. He could have added the discovery (in 1967–8) of a mutual interest in free maritime passage that led the USA and USSR (both great naval powers) to cooperate during the 1970s international negotiations on the Law of the Sea.
[4] Mohamed Heikal, *Sphinx and Commissar: The Rise and Fall of Soviet Influence in the Arab World* (1978) pp. 169–70.

Some of this was designed to reassure the Egyptians that they would not be sacrificed to achieve a superpower condominium. But there had been a definite, if low-key, shift away from a number of Khrushchev's foreign policies. Though the new leaders' chief concerns were probably domestic, they also abandoned overtures to West Germany, briefly sought to conciliate China, and in November 1964 hailed the 'courageous people of South Vietnam engaged in a heroic liberation struggle'. They showed little interest in Johnson's New Year proposals for an exchange of visits.[5]

Brezhnev did not expect early gains in Western Europe. His chief hopes related to the Middle East, where he would soon 'be in a position to deal' the Americans 'a decisive blow'. But his main East–West problems probably arose from the Vietnam War. The Soviet Union, he told the Hungarians in January 1965, wished

to re-establish close contact with the Korean and Vietnamese Communists who had been greatly neglected by Khrushchev. In . . . Vietnam, . . . the N[ational] L[iberation] F[ront] forces had already liberated almost 75 per cent of the countryside and units of the . . . North Vietnamese army had joined the guerrillas. But an American intervention might change this favourable situation.[6]

It did. American reprisal bombing of North Vietnam started during Kosygin's February visit there, and escalated into a sustained operation in March. The Kremlin responded by organising, and telling West European communist parties to organise, anti-American protests. It also, as time went on, profited enormously from spontaneous Western anti-war feeling. Indeed, by the end of the decade, revulsion against US involvement in Vietnam had probably done more than anything else to undermine both the favourable image the United States had previously enjoyed with European liberals and the confidence that American liberals placed in policies of containment.

In the mid-1960s, however, the Kremlin was probably more conscious of possible costs and dangers: it failed to end Sino-Soviet hostility, and the USSR had therefore to do at least as much as China for North Vietnam. This came quite expensive – the US put 1965–71 Soviet aid at $3.2 billion

[5]   R.W. Stevenson, *The Rise and Fall of Détente* (1985) pp. 127–8; William R. Smyser, *The Independent Vietnamese: Vietnamese Communism between Russia and China, 1956–1969* (Athens, Ohio, 1980) p. 77.
[6]   Erwin Weit, *Eyewitness: the autobiography of Gomulka's interpreter* (1973) p. 139; Janos Radvanyi, *Delusion and Reality* (South Bend, Indiana, 1978) pp. 38, 55.

(as against China's $1.2 billion) and it was later to rise further.[7] More alarming was the danger that the war would escalate. China allegedly urged on Shelepin (the hardest-line candidate for the Soviet leadership in 1965) the idea of 'putting military pressure on the Americans in Berlin and West Germany'; in 1966 the USSR accused the Chinese of seeking 'to originate a military conflict between the USSR and the United States . . . so that they may, as they say themselves, sit on the mountain and watch the fight of the tigers'. This Moscow could quite easily avoid. But it could not control the US response to the open despatch south of North Vietnamese regiments, and the worst case scenario certainly looked depressing:

High party officials were seriously concerned that the Americans . . . would call up reserves and launch an all-out attack against North Vietnam. Soviet Defense Ministry officials even predicted that American marines would execute amphibious landings deep in North Vietnamese territory as they did during the Korean War . . . [and] thought the United States might use tactical atomic weapons if the Chinese intervened militarily. The gloom deepened when reports reached Moscow . . . that the Chinese had offered to help Hanoi, if necessary, with an army of a half-million men on the condition that the DRV [North Vietnam] would launch simultaneous general attacks against South Vietnam and Laos. It was a great relief when Ho Chi Minh sidestepped that plan . . .[8]

To prevent such developments the Kremlin favoured negotiations, adopting 'a two-pronged policy . . . which corresponded generally with the two "faces" of the USSR's attitude towards the world. While supplying Hanoi with the necessary means for war against the United States and the Saigon regime, Moscow undertook behind-the-scenes efforts to convince the participants of the need for a negotiated settlement.'[9] But North Vietnam made its own decisions, playing the China card where necessary, and extracting increased Soviet aid in the process. The Russians appear to have found the whole process infuriating, and to have feared it could 'damage

---

[7]   King C. Chen, *China's War with Vietnam, 1979: issues, decisions, and implications* (Stanford, CA., 1987) pp. 24, 187; William S. Turley, *The Second Indo-China War: A Short Political and Military History, 1954–1975* (paperback edn, 1987) p. 168. Valuing the Chinese contribution is not easy since much was in the form of direct labour; the Chinese claim a total of $20bn over 1950–1978.

[8]   Radvanyi, *Delusion and Reality*, pp. 153, 167, 189–90, 235.

[9]   Ilya V. Gaiduk, *The Soviet Union and the Vietnam War* (Chicago, 1996) p. 248 and *passim*.

the Soviet revolutionary posture all over the world'. Some of their frustration over this (and over setbacks in Indonesia and Ghana) seems to have
been diverted on to President Johnson – 'He's more dangerous than
Dulles', Brezhnev told U Thant.[10]

However alarm and frustration did not lead to a complete break-down
of cooperation. Soviet and US policies in the Middle East were incompatible, and there are unanswered questions about the role of both countries
in connection with the 1967 Arab–Israeli war. But once war had started,
Kosygin for the first time ever activated the Moscow–Washington hotline;
the two countries undertook to work for a ceasefire, but did not initially
agree on its terms. When Israel strafed a US intelligence ship, the USA used
the hotline to explain to the Soviet Union (and get it to explain to Egypt)
that US overflights were solely to pick up the pieces. Finally, fearing that
Israel might stretch its victory over Syria to the seizure of Damascus,
Kosygin came on the line to say with some heat that, if Israel did not stop
within the next few hours, the USSR would take 'necessary actions, including military'. He managed to alarm the Americans, who responded by
directing their Sixth Fleet towards Syria to warn against such Soviet action,
but also by insisting that Israel stop.[11]

This was, of course, exactly how the hotline was meant to be used.
But coordinated crisis management implied only a very limited measure
of agreement. Later in June the USSR, against US wishes, secured an emergency meeting of the UN General Assembly to discuss the Middle East.
Johnson took advantage of Kosygin's attendance at this to arrange a summit. Their two days of talks at Glassboro, while quite amicable, produced
no results.[12]

The Soviet Politburo seems to have been divided, beforehand, over
the desirability of the Glassboro Summit. The Foreign Minister, Andrei
Gromyko, favoured such talks. Gromyko was still outside the Politburo.
But in January 1967 he had secured Politburo approval for a memorandum noting that 'Under certain conditions the Soviet–American dialogue,
suspended in 1963, can be resumed on even a far larger scale.' The
Vietnam War should not be an absolute bar to agreements 'on questions
of our interest'; but 'putting an end to the . . . conflict would undoubtedly

[10] Heikal, *Sphinx and Commissar*, pp. 154, 161, 164, 166–7, 172.
[11] ibid. pp. 176–7, 181–2; Johnson, *Vantage Point*, Chap. 13.
[12] Johnson later said Kosygin had advanced a helpful proposal on Vietnam but that
Moscow then dropped it (Nixon, *Memoirs*, p. 431); see also Gaiduk, *The Soviet Union
and the Vietnam War*, pp. 129–32.

have a positive impact on Soviet–American relations and open up new possibilities for solving certain international problems.'[13] Accordingly the Soviets were pleased by Johnson's March 1968 decision to suspend bombing over most of North Vietnam, by the May start of peace talks in Paris, and by the final signature of the Nuclear Non-Proliferation Treaty in July. They also changed their mind over ABMs and became anxious for negotiations (see pp. 57–8 above). A final catalyst was the Soviet decision to invade Czechoslovakia to stop what they saw as its dangerous reformist drift. Detente now seemed attractive as a way of limiting the resultant damage to the USSR's international image; and on 19 August (the day before the actual invasion) Johnson was invited to visit the USSR in early October to inaugurate talks.[14]

The invasion of Czechoslovakia forced Johnson to cancel; he also warned (in deliberately vague terms) that similar pressure on Romania could unleash 'the dogs of war' and gave Yugoslavia some security assurances.[15] But Brezhnev seemed pleased with Johnson's acquiescence in the invasion,[16] while in September Johnson declared that 'we hope – and we shall strive – to make this setback a very temporary one'. The Politburo that month approved another submission by Gromyko, to the effect that events in Czechoslovakia would not necessarily damage relations with the USA, and his conclusion that 'The Soviet–American dialogue of 1961–1963 was not . . . accidental; the reasons that gave rise to it are still in force today.' So when Johnson resumed his pursuit of a summit before the end of his administration, the Soviets seemed forthcoming; but President-elect Nixon poured cold water on the idea.[17]

[13] Anatoly Dobrynin, *In Confidence. Moscow's Ambassador to America's Six Cold War Presidents (1962–1986)* (New York, 1995) pp. 640–2 prints excerpts from the memorandum.

[14] Johnson, *Vantage Point*, p. 487. Johnson had been suggesting a summit since July – Kissinger, *Memoirs*, i, p. 50.

[15] Karen Dawisha, *The Kremlin and the Prague Spring* (Berkeley, 1984) p. 371.

[16] He told the semi-captive Czech leaders he had asked 'if the American government still fully recognizes the results of the Yalta and Potsdam conferences' (i.e. the division of Europe into Eastern and Western spheres), and that *before* the invasion he had 'received the reply: 'as far as Czechoslovakia and Rumania are concerned, it recognizes them without reservation; in the case of Yugoslavia, it would have to be discussed' – Zdenek Mlynar, *Night Frost in Prague: the end of humane socialism* (1980) p. 241. Dawisha knows of no specific evidence bearing on this claim (*The Kremlin and the Prague Spring*, pp. 292–3).

[17] Dobrynin, *In Confidence*, pp. 184–7, 643; Johnson, *Vantage Point*, pp. 489–90; Kissinger, *Memoirs*, i, p. 50.

The Moscow Summit of 1972

Once in office, Nixon sought an acceptable and face-saving disengagement from Vietnam, and he looked to Soviet mediation to achieve this. In theory Moscow's economic and military aid should have given it considerable leverage over Hanoi. In practice it would no more convert this into control of Hanoi's policy than would the United States later dictate to Israel in a similar situation. In October 1969 Nixon told the Soviet ambassador, Dobrynin, that this Soviet inaction precluded the possibility of any 'real progress',[18] though SALT talks did formally begin that November. In April 1970 Nixon nevertheless started making overtures for a summit, and discussion proceeded throughout the summer, but to no avail. Kissinger thinks Nixon hoped to upstage the anti-Vietnam War movement, but claims the USSR asked too high a price for the meeting (notably in terms of collusion against China) and so missed a promising opportunity of extracting ABM and other concessions.[19]

There followed an 'autumn of crises'. One was set off by King Hussein of Jordan's September 1970 crackdown on the Palestinian Liberation Organisation (PLO), which had been building a state-within-a-state inside his kingdom. To support him, the USA staged a naval build-up in the east Mediterranean. This in turn drew a polite expression of Soviet hope that there be no external intervention in the Jordanian civil war. There soon followed an invasion by Syrian tank units (albeit without their Soviet advisers), leading Hussein to appeal for US help. The United States persuaded Israel to ready itself for intervention if necessary, and ostentatiously continued its own preparations to provide air cover and reinforcements. Israeli mobilisation seems to have alarmed the Syrian military, and the tanks were first left unprotected against Jordanian air attacks and then withdawn.[20] The USSR and Egypt helped diplomatically. While all this was going on, the United States discovered that, despite the Soviet reaffirmation in August of the Khrushchev–Kennedy agreements over Cuba,

[18] Nixon, *Memoirs*, pp. 446–7.

[19] Kissinger, *Memoirs*, i, pp. 552–7; Dobrynin denies this, and claims there could in fact have been no summit as the question of whether the USSR should be represented by Brezhnev or Kosygin was not settled until 1971 (*In Confidence*, p. 207).

[20] Kissinger, *Memoirs*, i, Chap. 15; Nixon, *Memoirs*, pp. 482–5; S. Posner, *Israel Undercover* (Syracuse, NY, 1987) pp. 184–90; Mohamed Heikal, *The Road to Ramadan* (paperback edn, 1976) pp. 96–7; Barry M. Blechman and Stephen Kaplan, *Force without War: US armed forces as a political instrument* (Washington, 1978) pp. 260–86.

the USSR was in fact installing an SLBM base there. America waited until the Jordan crisis had subsided, then insisted forcefully but privately that it desist.[21]

This was not a very promising background against which to discuss a summit. But on his return to Washington at the end of the Jordan crisis Ambassador Dobrynin brought a softening of the Soviet position. He did, though, suggest that the summit await the next Party Congress in March 1971. When this came, it reflected Brezhnev's emergence as unchallenged leader and his takeover of foreign affairs from Kosygin. Nevertheless the Politburo decided that a summit meeting could 'wait', and endorsed Gromyko's idea of using Nixon's eagerness for one to speed up the current negotiations on Berlin. Privately Brezhnev told Dobrynin that 1972 was the most likely date.[22]

January 1971 had brought US–Soviet agreement to negotiate seriously on both SALT and Berlin; in May the USSR accepted US wishes for parallel negotiations on ABMs and on the limitation of strategic missile numbers. In June it became clear that the Berlin talks would succeed. But the Soviets made the mistake of holding out on US proposals for an autumn summit, only to discover that this enabled Nixon's China visit to come first. Eventually May 1972 was fixed on, with the expectation that a SALT treaty be worked out by then. Both the May 1971 breakthrough on ABMs and the mid-summer progress on Berlin were sweetened by the withdrawal of US export controls on machinery for the Kama River truck factory. More secretly, talks began to induce the American trades unions to relax their restrictions on the loading and shipping of grain to the USSR; they were given to understand 'that there would be no SALT agreement unless the grain deal was worked out'.[23]

The attractiveness of detente to the USSR must have been further enhanced by problems with its grain crop (which in 1972 came in at 27 million tons below its target of 195 million). 1972 saw both intensive negotiations with, and shrewd agricultural purchases (in all worth over $1 billion) from, the United States; it appears that Brezhnev set more store

[21] Kissinger, *Memoirs*, Chap. 16; Nixon, *Memoirs*, pp. 485–9; Raymond L. Garthoff, *Reflections on the Cuban Missile Crisis* (Washington, DC, 1987) pp. 94–6, 98–100.

[22] Raymond L. Garthoff, *Détente and Confrontation: American–Soviet Relations from Nixon to Reagan* (Washington, DC, 1985) p. 42; Dobrynin, *In Confidence*, pp. 216–18, 220.

[23] Kissinger, *Memoirs*, i, Chap. 20; Seymour H. Hersh, *The Price of Power: Kissinger in the Nixon White House* (1983) pp. 343–8.

by these than did some of his colleagues.[24] The Russians were also concerned at the difficulties the West German parliament was making about
ratifying the Ostpolitik treaties, and so sought the USA's good offices.

Nevertheless the summit was nearly wrecked by events in Vietnam,
where the North embarked on a major offensive in late March. Nixon was
determined that the US response should include heavy bombing of North
Vietnam. This did not prevent a visit by Kissinger to Moscow in April at
which he settled many of the outstanding summit issues. But Nixon would
have preferred him to concentrate on Vietnam and come home if he got no
satisfaction. Kissinger did arrange a meeting with the North Vietnamese
on 2 May, but it proved fruitless. Nixon decided to escalate the bombing;
and rather than risk the Soviets cancelling the summit by way of reprisal
(as in 1960), he considered calling it off himself. From this he was dis-
suaded by Treasury Secretary Connally, who was well-placed to know
how much Moscow wanted trade and credits. The onus was therefore put
on the USSR to cancel the summit. The Politburo seriously considered
doing so, but decided that this would be to give Hanoi a veto over Soviet
policy and that it would endanger West German ratification of the
Ostpolitik treaties.[25]

The May 1972 summit was a success. The final details of the ABM
treaty and the Interim Agreement on Strategic Arms Limitation were tied
up. There were at least two sessions on Vietnam, and Brezhnev undertook
to send Podgorny to Hanoi with the latest American proposals 'in the
interest of peace'. The hopes expressed for a trade agreement 'in the near
future' were realised by a July credit for Soviet grain purchases and an
October trade agreement, settling the USSR's wartime Lend-Lease debt,[26]
according her 'Most Favoured Nation' status[27] and credits, and looking to

---

[24] *Keesing's*, 25577–8; Garthoff, *Détente and Confrontation*, pp. 305–6; Kissinger, *Memoirs*, i, p. 1213.

[25] Garthoff, *Détente and Confrontation*, pp. 96–105; Nixon, *Memoirs*, pp. 586–607; Kissinger, *Memoirs*, i, Chaps 26–27; Hersh, *The Price of Power*, Chap. 36 – the last three being works of advocacy; Dobrynin, *In Confidence*, pp. 248–9, which notes that Kremlin sympathy had also been frayed by Hanoi's habit of acting without prior consultation.

[26] The USSR undertook to repay $722m for deliveries of *civilian* goods; the terms roughly followed those arranged with Britain in 1945.

[27] This status implies only that there be no special tariff discrimination against the country in question. But according it to a centrally planned economy is necessarily a concession, since the latter's planning system cannot provide comparable non-discriminatory access.

at least $1.5 billion worth of trade over the next three years. There was agreement, too, on the desirability of an early conference on European security (a long-standing Soviet wish) and on that of reciprocal military reductions in Central Europe. The opportunity was taken to sign several worthy, but minor, agreements on US–Soviet cooperation in technical fields. The whole was rounded off with a statement of the 'Basic Principles of Relations' between the two countries.[28] But only the future could show what all this would amount to in practice.

Nixon was aware of this. 'The pattern of US–Soviet summit diplomacy in the cold war era is well known', he told Congress on his return; 'One meeting after another produced a brief euphoric mood – the spirit of Geneva, the spirit of Camp David . . . but without producing progress on the really difficult issues.' Naturally he implied that this summit had been different, and claimed that there was now an 'opportunity to build a new structure of peace in the world'.

The 'Moscow detente', US views and Soviet foreign policy

Volumes have been written, first seeking to establish the characteristics of this new detente, later explaining why it soured. At the time it certainly seemed as if the international climate had been transformed. Ostpolitik had resolved the old Cold War disputes over Germany. The USA and China had buried the hatchet. The USA and the Soviet Union had apparently curbed their strategic arms race, and acquired (in the 'Basic Principles'[29] and through Kissinger's remarkable diplomacy) 'a solid framework for the development of better relations'. In January 1973 a Vietnam ceasefire was agreed. Some of these achievements ultimately proved more durable than others. But it is very natural that politicians should have taken credit for them all, and that public opinion (which was, of course, largely unaware of recent East–West crises) should have been delighted.

There was, too, a degree of personal rapport between the leaders of the day: the Russians took to Kissinger, and were anxious to have him over

[28] Garthoff, *Détente and Confrontation*, pp. 305–8; *Keesing's*, 25313–14, 25585–6.
[29] To which was added at the 1973 Washington Summit the 'Agreement on the Prevention of Nuclear War' (*Keesing's*, 25999). This promised consultation if relations, either between the signatories and third parties or simply between third parties, appeared 'to involve the risk of nuclear war'. Critics were to claim that the USSR had breached it by not giving advance warning of Egypt's 1973 attack on Israel.

for frequent negotiating visits. They also respected Nixon, though not his successors. They were good, if somewhat heavy-handed, hosts: arguably the high point of detente was Kissinger's May 1973 visit to the Kremlin dacha at Zavidovo and his excursions and boar-hunting with Brezhnev. The Americans, for their part, found ambassador Dobrynin congenial, and 'back-channel' negotiations with him were a welcome contrast to the vicious bureaucratic infighting of Nixonian Washington. Dobrynin's standing in Washington was such that Brzezinski was surprised to discover, at the 1979 Vienna Summit, that he was not in the Soviet inner circle. Both Nixon and Kissinger also responded to Brezhnev's personal charm. After his 1975 heart attack, however, Brezhnev became a less impressive, indeed by 1979 a rather pathetic, figure. Gromyko, by contrast, grew steadily in stature; but though his professionalism was always admired, he proceeded on the basis of well-informed attrition, not flexibility or creativity. Indeed Soviet leaders had little taste for the sweeping conceptual discussions and freewheeling strategic decisions, leaving the details to fall into place later, that appealed to Nixon, Kissinger, and, to an extent, Carter. Rather they usually preferred to concentrate on specific concrete issues, reserving major questions over direction for more collective decision within the Kremlin. The Americans were more impressed by the subtlety and sophistication of the Chinese leaders, and by their freedom from the Soviet negotiating habit of constantly seeking petty (and frequently counterproductive) advantages.[30] (But then the US–Chinese relationship did not, in the 1970s, go much beyond shared opposition to the Soviet threat, and could therefore be handled in very general terms.)

Although one should not underestimate personal factors, both the USA and the USSR naturally embraced detente in the belief that it would be in their own interests. Nixon was conscious, as he told Congress on his return from the Moscow summit, 'that Soviet ideology still proclaims hostility to some of America's most basic values. The Soviet leaders remain committed to that ideology.' But he preferred to operate on the basis of national interest, or, as Kissinger put it, 'geopolitics', concentrating on the USSR's *external* behaviour: 'The internal order of the USSR, as such, is not an object of our policy, although we do not hide our rejection of many of its features. Our relations with the USSR, as with other countries, are determined by its international behavior.' 'We will judge them by their

[30] Dobrynin, *In Confidence*, pp. 228–31; Henry Kissinger, *Diplomacy* (paperback edn, 1995) p. 727. The *American* negotiating vice was that of withdrawing, in response to domestic pressures, from positions already agreed with other countries.

actions as we expect to be judged by our own. Specific agreements, and the structure of peace they help to build, will come from a realistic accommodation of [our and their] opposing interests.'[31] Where such interests overlapped there was no problem. SALT I had been at the centre of the Moscow Summit; and, despite all the strains generated by rival strategic calculations and practices, there was enough common ground to secure further agreements/treaties at the 1974 Vladivostok and 1979 Vienna summits. Even where interests diverged, detente might be a helpful adjunct to crisis management – Brezhnev said after the 1973 Arab–Israeli war that without it 'the situation would look entirely different. If the current conflict would explode in an environment of general international tensions . . . the confrontation in the Middle East could become far more dangerous and be on a scale threatening the general peace.'[32] Still it was clear from the outset that both countries hoped detente would promote the type of international order they preferred. As it started to sour, increasing emphasis came to be placed on this theme, so that detente appeared more and more as cold war by other means.[33]

The key American concept here was 'linkage'. It was both a policy[34] – that only if the Soviet Union was accommodating in some respects should it be allowed what it wanted in others – and a statement of the fact that Congress was unlikely to 'support an expanding economic relationship while our basic relations with the Soviet Union are antagonistic'.[35] To succeed it demanded a degree of politeness: in the words of a British diplomat, the long-range objective was to enmesh the Soviets in 'a less competitive relationship, and we cannot get there by telling them to go to hell'.[36] But it involved chiefly the ability to *deliver* rewards for 'good' Soviet behaviour and the possession of so clear a capability to counter 'bad' behaviour that it was not attempted. It is Kissinger's basic contention

[31] *Keesing's* 25316–17; Nixon's 1970 and 1971 foreign policy reports (Kissinger, *Diplomacy*, p. 712). Equally Nixon's rapprochement with China reflected convergence in national interest, not ideology.

[32] D.K. Simes, 'The Death of Détente?' *International Security*, v (1980) p. 3.

[33] W.G. Hyland, *Soviet–American Relations: a new Cold War* (Rand, Santa Monica, Ca., 1981) illustrates this from Kissinger's changing definitions of detente (pp. 31–3) and touches on a similar Soviet process (pp. 38, 40).

[34] Firmly laid down by Nixon at the outset of his administration (Kissinger, *Memoirs*, i, pp. 135–6).

[35] President's Foreign Policy report, 1973 – Garthoff, *Détente and Confrontation*, p. 308.

[36] Kissinger, *Memoirs*, ii, p. 281.

(as well as excuse) that, in the mood of the 1970s and the aftermath of Watergate, Congress wilfully destroyed the United States' capacity either to reward or to punish. So 'not even Brezhnev will ever know how much he might have been prepared to pay in restraint for a genuine peace after 1972, had we maintained the right balance between firmness and conciliation'.[37] But the policy was also open to two other dangers. One was the belief that certain goals (like SALT or – for Europeans – detente in Europe) were so desirable that they should be pursued for their own sakes, regardless of Soviet behaviour elsewhere; this belief became attractive later in the 1970s, when the USSR began to act on the basis that detente was divisible and should not be affected by contretemps in the Third World. The converse was to allow conflict in one aspect of the US–Soviet relationship to spill back to poison other fields where agreements could still be reached. Once serious difficulties started to be encountered, the line between these two pitfalls would obviously become very hard to tread.

Kissinger is no doubt right that we shall never know what Brezhnev would have been prepared to pay. Nor will we ever know how great Kissinger's own expectations really were. Sometimes he spoke in high-flying terms:

The history of the post-war era has been a never-ending effort to maintain peace through crisis management. The structure of peace we envisage would instead be sustained by a growing realization on the part of all nations that they have a stake in stability, and that this stability is ensured by acting from a sense of justice and with moderation.[38]

But in briefing Nixon just before the 1972 summit he professed only moderate expectations: 'The prospect for a fundamental change in Soviet–American relationships is not bright.' SALT, economic ties, and the implementation of the *Ostpolitik* treaties would 'add to elements creating a more permanent Soviet interest in stable relationships'; but for both ideological and internal political reasons 'Soviet foreign policy will remain antagonistic', and it was likely 'that the USSR will press their challenge to Western interests with increasing vigor and in certain circumstances

[37] Kissinger, *Memoirs*, i, pp. 1143–4. Kissinger does not go into charges that the Congressional mood was fed, in part, by the inevitable revelation of the news (and other) manipulations essential to his own negotiating technique.

[38] August 1973 – Coral Bell, *The Diplomacy of Detente. The Kissinger Era* (1977) p. 32.

assume [greater] risks . . . [than] heretofore'. On the eve of the next summit he suggested that Brezhnev:

sees the US at once as rival, mortal threat, model, source of assistance and partner in physical survival . . . *he no doubt wants* to go down in history as the leader who brought peace and a better life to Russia. *This* requires conciliatory and cooperative policies toward us. *Yet, he* remains a convinced Communist who sees politics as a struggle with an ultimate winner; *he intends the Soviet Union to be that winner. His recurrent efforts to draw us into condominium-type arrangements . . . are intended both to safeguard peace and to undermine our alliances . . .*

Almost certainly, Brezhnev continues to defend his detente policies in Politburo debates in terms of a historic conflict with us as the main capitalist country and of the ultimate advantages that will accrue to the USSR in this conflict. Brezhnev's gamble is that as these policies gather momentum and longevity, their effects will not undermine the very system from which Brezhnev draws his power and legitimacy. Our goal on the other hand is to achieve precisely such effects over the long run . . .

The major, long term question is whether the Soviets can hold their own bloc together while waiting for the West to succumb to a long period of relaxation *and the temptations of economic competition. Certainly our chances are as good as Brezhnev's, given the history of dissent in Eastern Europe.*[39]

In short Kissinger suggested that the two sides were adopting similar tactics, but for opposite reasons, with the outcome in the lap of the gods.

Soviet calculations were set within the Khrushchevian framework of 'peaceful coexistence', the Foreign Ministry's interpretation of which had been spelt out at length in January 1967:

. . . On the whole, international tension does not suit the state interests of the Soviet Union and its friends. The construction of socialism and the development of the [domestic] economy call for the maintenance of peace. In the conditions of detente it is easier to consolidate and broaden the positions of the Soviet Union in the world.

Considering the experience of Vietnam and the Middle East, we should take timely measures to relax tension . . . where sharp conflicts . . . can combine to lead to an 'acute situation'. In this connotation we should,

[39] Kissinger, *Memoirs*, i, p. 203; ii, pp. 243–4 (non-italics represent Nixon's underlinings).

while supporting the Arab countries in their struggle against Israel's expansionist policy, flexibly dampen the extremist tendencies . . . of certain Arab states, e.g. Syria . . .

. . . If we consider relations between the Soviet Union and the United States in a broad perspective, rather than against . . . [current tensions over Vietnam] . . . in the present epoch of transition the question is . . . just how the transition of countries from capitalism to socialism will proceed: under the conditions of world peace or amidst a world war . . .

. . . We must resolutely . . . dissociate ourselves from adventurous schemes of the Chinese leaders, who have pinned their hopes on the inevitability of an armed confrontation between . . . the Soviet Union and the United States within 8 to 10 years. The opinion that the Americans are out for war anyway and, consequently, a war . . . is inevitable, would reflect precisely the position of the Chinese. The concentration of our main efforts on the domestic purposes is fully in line with Lenin's statement that the final victory of socialism over capitalism will be ensured by the creation of a new, much higher level of labor productivity.

. . . Under certain conditions the Soviet–American dialogue, suspended in 1963, can be resumed on even a far larger scale . . . [Gromyko cautiously invokes 'the possibility of coordinated Soviet–American actions aimed at maintaining peace and ensuring the solution of some major international issues'.] ['Needless to say, we should avoid a situation, where we have to fight on two fronts, that is against China and the United States. Maintaining Soviet–American relations at a certain level is one of the factors that will help us achieve this objective.']

We should not cut off the possibility of diplomatic maneuver for ourselves . . . In certain cases it is necessary to draw a more distinct line between the activity of the Comintern [sic] and that of the foreign ministry, the difference stressed by Lenin. In order to make our policy more flexible and effective in relation to the United States, the official foreign political statements and actions of the Soviet government should be . . . more clearly based on the interests of relations with other countries . . . the sociological and ideological aspects of the struggle between the two systems . . . should be conducted predominantly through the party, public organizations and the press.

. . . As to our objective of weakening US positions in Western Europe, we should consistently hold to the principle that European problems can have only 'European solutions'. We must tirelessly promote the idea that

*Europe itself can and must ensure its security and consolidate confidence
in the relations between Eastern and Western Europe.*[40]

*. . . The issues of the national liberation movement. The line of the . . .
[1961 CPSU Party Congress] for all-round support of this movement
meets our foreign policy interests in every way. [But] Considering the
shortage of our reserves, we should focus on economic cooperation with
the most progressive countries that have embarked on the road of non-
capitalist development, such as Egypt, Syria, Algeria, Mali, Guinea,
Burma, Congo [Brazzaville], Tanzania, and the countries of strategic
importance to us (Afghanistan, Turkey, Pakistan, and Iran) . . .*

*Disarmament . . . [Besides the traditional Soviet] struggle for universal
and comprehensive disarmament which is expected to take a long . . .
time, we must pay special attention to some limited measures, first of all,
to reaching an agreement [with the USA] on the nonproliferation of
nuclear weapons . . . to prevent any access of . . . [West Germany] and
other nonnuclear states to nuclear arms. [This achieved, Gromyko added
in 1968 that 'We should persist in . . . ensuring the most favorable
conditions for the construction of communism' within the USSR.
'This should particularly include measures aimed at curbing
the arms race etc.']*[41]

As befits someone not yet in the top leadership, Gromyko had here
touched most possible bases. His own, and the Foreign Ministry's, preferences centred on relations with the United States; agreements, and perhaps
even limited common action, were possible. These were, in the 1970s, to be
valued not only in their own right, but also as a symbol of the USSR's equality
with the United States[42] and status as a world power – 'Today,' Gromyko
told the 1971 Party Congress, 'there is no question of any significance
which can be decided without the Soviet Union or in opposition to it.'[43]

---

[40] In the previous paragraph, Gromyko had urged the 'struggle for the unity of socialist
countries', but only *en passant*. In 1968, after the intervention in Czechoslovakia, this
had become the 'main foreign objective': the situation required 'the integration of
socialist countries to be as broad and solid as that created in the West through a network of multilateral organizations connected with NATO or related to it (EEC . . .).'

[41] Dobrynin, *In Confidence*, pp. 640–2; the second paragraph is transposed from its
actual position later in the document.

[42] Brezhnev, Kissinger recalls, 'could not hear often enough my avowal that we were
proceeding on the basis of equality' (*Memoirs*, ii, p. 231).

[43] Richard Pipes, *US–Soviet Relations in the Era of Detente* (Boulder, Colorado, 1981)
p. 63.

Gromyko's 1967–8 memoranda had touched only vaguely on arms control. But the Moscow Summit centred on the ABM and SALT treaties; and Gromyko came to see further such US–Soviet treaties as crucial, telling his counterpart Vance in 1977 'that there were many keys to resolving numerous other world problems, but they were all locked in a box to which there were only two keys, and we could lay our hands on these many keys only by opening the [SALT II] box with these two . . . keys of keys.'[44] We should also note Gromyko's argument, even in 1967, that Soviet–American dialogue would serve to preclude a US–Chinese alignment. It did not; and a constant theme of the 1972–4 high detente period was what one of Kissinger's aides calls 'Brezhnev's obsession' – warnings against China's nuclear ambitions and the Chinese people *per se*, together with attempts to draw the USA into a nuclear condominium directed against them.[45] Constant US refusal must have dimmed the attractions of detente to the Kremlin.

Gromyko's 1967 memorandum invoked Lenin's claim that socialism's victory over capitalism would be ensured by its achievement of higher productivity. Khrushchev had really believed this, but the overtaking of the USA he had promised for the 1960s had not occurred. Hence, no doubt, Gromyko's concern that expenditure on the Third World should be carefully targeted, and his 1968 hope that curbs on the 'arms race' would benefit the domestic economy. This tapped into broader concerns. For one of the currents contributing to the 'Prague Spring' had been that of the Czech economic reformers. The political consequences of their experiments had proved unacceptable. This lesson was reinforced, in a different form, by 1970 developments in Poland, where an economically rational increase in prices triggered rioting serious enough to lead to the dropping of Party Secretary Gomulka. There is a school of thought that attributes detente largely to Brezhnev's reluctance to risk such economic reforms in the Soviet Union, and determination instead to seek economic growth by tapping Western grain and industrial technology, which would be much facilitated by an improvement in the international climate.

Gromyko's 1967–8 memoranda say relatively little about Europe. To retain Soviet post-war gains in the East ('consolidate the socialist

---

[44] Odd Arne Westad (ed.) *The Fall of Detente. Soviet–American Relations during the Carter Years* (Oslo, 1997) p. 34.

[45] William G. Hyland, *Mortal Rivals: superpower relations from Nixon to Reagan* (New York, 1987) pp. 63–8, 77–8; Kissinger, *Memoirs*, ii, pp. 233, 294–5, 1173–4; iii, pp. 280–1, 294; Dobrynin, *In Confidence*, pp. 314–15.

community') was the USSR's 'main foreign objective'. But for the 'weakening [of] US positions in Western Europe', he looked only to the consolidation of 'relations between Eastern and Western Europe' – presumably through the sort of detente soon to be effected by Brandt's Ostpolitik – and the promotion of 'the idea that Europe itself can and must ensure its own security' without transatlantic intervention. That Gromyko described this promotion as 'tireless' suggests that he had no very immediate expectations; and indeed Brezhnev himself supposedly said in 1968 of West European communist parties that they 'won't amount to anything for fifty years'.[46]

The Third World was another matter. The 'American government has set out to prevent communism from further spreading all over the world, which is of course impossible.' Rather 'the question is just how the transition of countries . . . from capitalism to socialism will proceed'; Gromyko contended, in the Khrushchevian tradition, that it could proceed best 'in the conditions of detente' (and, indeed, without 'acute situations' in Vietnam or the Middle East). The KGB head, Yuri Andropov, whose rise paralleled Gromyko's and who regularly joined him in foreign policy submissions to the Politburo, had said in 1965 that 'the future competition with the United States will take place not in Europe, and not in the Atlantic Ocean. It will take place in Africa, and in Latin America.' This competition was handled less through Foreign Ministry than through Party and KGB channels. Dobrynin's memoirs are accordingly full of complaints about the hawkish head of the (Party) Central Committee's International Department, Ponomarev. Above him, work with liberation movements

was coordinated by the . . . second man in the Politburo, Mikhail Suslov . . . He was convinced that all struggle in the Third World had an ideological basis: imperialism against communism and socialism. Under the slogan of solidarity, he and his zealous supporters in the party managed to involve the Politburo in many Third World adventures. The KGB supported him . . . because many of the party contacts in that area were handled through their agents.

Members of the Politburo lived in the certainty that a historical process was under way: the collapse of the old colonial empires and general weakening of the capitalist system. These were not of our making, declared Suslov [in 1978] with Brezhnev's support, because they were

---

[46] Mlynar, *Night Frost in Prague*, p. 241.

'historically inevitable'. For ideological reasons we should support this process wherever possible . . .[47]

Another area outwith the purview of the Soviet Foreign Ministry was the military. As Gorbachev put it, albeit with specific reference to his own experience a decade later, 'even a mention of' the growing military expenditure 'would mean instant dismissal. It was the General Secretary's turf.' 'All statistics concerning the military-industrial complex were top secret, inaccessible even to members of the Politburo.'[48] In this context military decisions were almost entirely divorced from consideration of their political (or economic) consequences. Dobrynin 'never heard any member of the Politburo discuss or even mention such political considerations' or see 'any Politburo or Foreign Ministry paper on the possible political opportunities or consequences of deploying our SS-20s. Military justifications were the only ones ever advanced.'[49] Here the essential view, as a former Deputy Defence minister later put it, was that 'to win a war, one has to have not less, but a little bit more weapons than the possible adversary';[50] so despite some Soviet talk of possible defence savings as a result of detente, the USSR's defence spending rose steadily throughout the 1970s, eventually alarming not only the United States but also West European governments and in 1979 prompting a NATO response in kind.

The Helsinki Final Act 1975

From detente the USSR sought, with a good deal of success, a final legitimation of its position in Eastern Europe. The way had, of course, been cleared by Brandt's Ostpolitik. The 1972 summit referred to the desirability of a European Security Conference and of mutual force reductions in Central Europe; in 1973 Brezhnev secured the convocation of conferences to discuss these themes in a way that greatly helped the USA with its political problems over the Mansfield amendment (above, pp. 64–5). In August

---

[47] Westad, *Fall of Detente*, p. 19; Dobrynin, *In Confidence*, pp. 403–4, 408.

[48] Mikhail Gorbachev, *Memoirs* (1996) pp. 121, 136; though Gorbachev was later encouraged by General Secretary Andropov to transcend his agricultural responsibilities, when he asked for access to the budget, Andropov told him it was 'off limits to you' (pp. 146–7).

[49] 'Except for Gromyko himself, even the very top Soviet diplomats including myself were completely ignorant of the Soviet military's expansion programs' – *In Confidence*, pp. 432, 475.

[50] Westad, *Fall of Detente*, p. 43.

1975 the heads of government of all European states, Canada and the USA signed the Helsinki Final Act; this accepted the territorial integrity of each participant and the right of each state to choose its own political system, and repudiated the changing of existing frontiers by force or economic coercion.[51] From the Soviet perspective, Helsinki endorsed the existing East European regimes, which were of course full participants. Indeed in December 1975 US ambassadors were briefed that, though 'There are almost no genuine friends of the Soviets left in Eastern Europe, except possibly Bulgaria', 'it must be our policy to strive for an evolution that makes the relationship between the East Europeans and the Soviet Union an organic one . . . We seek to influence the emergence of the Soviet imperial power by making the base more natural and organic so that it will not remain [dangerously] founded in power alone.'[52]

But the Final Act also contained other provisions that were, in the long run, to prove more important. One was the agreement, by way of 'Confidence [against surprise attack] Building Measures', that the rival alliances should give prior notice of significant troop movements and manoeuvres; immediate consequences were slight, but far-reaching effects are sometimes attributed to the expansion of this provision in 1986 (below, p. 416). The Final Act also contained, in 'Basket Three', human rights provisions. At the time Kissinger probably did not think them important; 'why,' he asked Gromyko, 'are we quibbling over these forms of words? No matter what goes into the final act, I don't believe that the Soviet Union will ever do anything it doesn't want to do.' The Basket was apparently queried by Kremlin heavyweights, but Gromyko's reassurance that 'We are masters in our own house' carried the day.[53] In the short run, Gromyko was right: when Soviet, and still more Czech, dissidents tried to invoke Helsinki's 'human rights' clauses, they were dealt with. But Helsinki had provided for follow-up meetings of the 'Conference on Security and

[51] *Keesing's*, 27301 ff. In deference to West Germany the possibility of change by 'peaceful means and by agreement' was left open.

[52] *Keesing's*, 27795 ff; there was, unsurprisingly, an outcry when this 'Sonnenfeldt Doctrine' leaked to the press. By 'organic' Sonnenfeldt meant that the East European states should develop sufficient autonomy and identity, but also sufficient ties of mutual interest with the USSR, to keep them content 'within the context of a strong Soviet geopolitical influence'. For Kissinger's explanation and down-playing of the episode, see his *Memoirs*, iii, pp. 863–6.

[53] Recollection of the Soviet interpreter, Sukhodrev (Westad, *Fall of Detente*, p. 17); Dobrynin, *In Confidence*, p. 345. The Final Act's text made it clear that the agreements were not binding in international law.

Cooperation in Europe' (CSCE). At these the United States repeatedly raised human rights issues, putting the communist regimes on the defensive; and it became an important goal of Gorbachev's early rule to extricate the Soviet Union from this position (below pp. 416–17).

US–Soviet competition in the Middle East

The Soviet Union sought to draw the USA into a joint management of the China and Middle East problems. It got no joy over China, but fared still worse with the Middle East where it gained nothing and lost the allegiance of the largest Arab state, Egypt. The Arab defeat in the 1967 war had made unlikely Brezhnev's original hope of driving out US influence; the USSR had then made the mistake of breaking off diplomatic relations with Israel, which disqualified it from acting as a mediator. In other respects things still went well. Nasser admittedly had to discontinue his (Soviet-funded) intervention in the Yemen civil war. But the British attempt to transfer power in Aden to conservative sheikhs collapsed; instead the People's Republic of South Yemen came to independence in November 1967, and soon gravitated into the Soviet orbit. In January 1968 Britain unexpectedly announced that in 1971 it would withdraw its troops from the Arab sheikh-doms bordering the Persian Gulf, which appeared to open up prospects for their overthrow (though in the event Oman was able to repress a South Yemen-supported insurgency). In 1969 coups brought apparently leftist military governments to Sudan and Somalia. The latter's leader, Siad Barre, as Ethiopia's enemy, inclined towards the USSR (which he accorded a naval base) and opted for scientific socialism – until in 1977 a similar figure, Mengistu Mariam, came to power in Ethiopia and the USSR shifted its support to the larger country.

Further north the 1967 defeat had made Egypt and Syria far more dependent than before on the USSR for the re-equipment and training of their armies. The Soviet Union did not find this an unmixed blessing: by 1970 Nasser was defenceless against Israeli air attacks; he therefore extracted from the USSR its most advanced surface-to-air missiles by declaring that, were they to be refused, his policy would be revealed as bankrupt and he would have to make way for a pro-American President. Unfortunately the missiles could only be operated by Soviet forces, which were thus drawn into the fighting. So it was probably a relief when Nasser decided to accept a US-sponsored ceasefire in order to get the missiles properly established. But if there were flies in the ointment, Russian influence in Egypt seemed to be progressing satisfactorily, the Soviet fleet gained facilities on Egypt's Red Sea and Mediterranean coasts, and its air force later acquired free use of Cairo West airport.[54]

This position unravelled remarkably quickly. In May 1971 Nasser's successor, Sadat, resolved a power struggle by purging the police and displacing a pro-Soviet grouping, some of whose members probably also worked for the KGB.[55] At the time Sadat was anxious to keep his lines to Moscow open, so he parallelled his consolidation of domestic power with the conclusion of a 15-year treaty of friendship and cooperation in which Egypt was described as 'having set itself the aim of reconstructing society along socialist lines'. But he put out several feelers to the USA, which was sending a series of messages to the effect that Washington and only Washington could deliver a settlement.[56] Sadat also got increasingly impatient with Soviet delays in supplying the weapons he would need to renew war with Israel, suspecting – probably accurately – that the Russians (who took a low view of Arab military prowess) were determined to prevent him doing so.[57]

For the Egyptians, the Moscow Summit represented the last straw. Sadat had repeatedly told the Russians they had done less for him than the USA had for Israel; now he urged them to talk firmly to Nixon. But the summit communiqué produced only the briefest and blandest of references to the Middle East. Sadat concluded that Moscow was not really interested; for a time he still kept up the pressure, then in July 1972 abruptly demanded the removal of the 21,000 Soviet military advisers. As he hoped, this did the trick. Marshal Grechko stressed the danger of losing the Egyptian alliance and argued successfully for providing all the arms the Arabs wanted: if they fought and won, the aid would be vindicated; if they lost they would have again to look to the USSR for rescue.[58]

---

[54] Heikal, *Road to Ramadan*, pp. 160, 165–6, 176–9; *Sphinx and Commissar*, p. 238.

[55] *Keesing's*, 24653–4; Heikal, *Road to Ramadan*, pp. 120 ff; Anwar el-Sadat, *In Search of Identity* (paperback edn) pp. 266–9; John Barron, *KGB Today: the Hidden Hand* (1984) pp. 51–3, 58–9; Christopher Andrew and Oleg Gordievsky, *KGB. The Inside Story of its Foreign Operations from Lenin to Gorbachev* (1990) pp. 415–16. To this setback there was added in July that of a communist coup in Sudan, which implicated the Russians, almost succeeded, but then collapsed.

[56] 'Remember that the key to a solution is here' – Heikal, *Road to Ramadan*, pp. 118–19, 174; *Sphinx and Commissar*, pp. 239–40.

[57] Ismail Fahmy, *Negotiating for Peace in the Middle East* (1983) Chap. 1; Heikal, *Road to Ramadan*, p. 163; *Sphinx and Commissar*, p. 238.

[58] Heikal, *Sphinx and Commissar*, Chaps 14–15; *Road to Ramadan*, pp. 166 ff; Kissinger, *Memoirs*, i, pp. 1151, 1246–8, 1296–7.

The way was thus cleared for Sadat's military option, but in 1973 Brezhnev made one final attempt to forestall it. At the close of his visit to Nixon's San Clemente home, he roused his hosts (as they were going to bed) for a heated discussion of the Middle East. The two countries should agree principles to govern a settlement;[59] otherwise, he implied (as he had done at Zavidovo), there might be 'a resumption of the war'. The Americans were annoyed at this attempt to bounce them into imposing a settlement, stuck to the view that peace could come only from talks between the parties, and held that if the superpowers promulgated such principles, the parties would simply refuse to talk.[60] Nor were Sadat's attempts at secret negotiation with Washington any more successful. So in October 1973 Egypt and Syria struck at Israel to force the world to take them seriously.

Taken by surprise, Israel began badly, but soon shattered the Syrian army, then turned on Egypt, crossing the Suez Canal and all but encircling the Egyptian Third Army. The early stages of the war had not been marked by superpower agreement, and both mounted large airlifts in support of their clients. But when satellite reconnaissance showed that Egypt faced major defeat, Kosygin persuaded Sadat to allow him to arrange a ceasefire. He then invited Kissinger to Moscow, and there (as the Egyptian military situation deteriorated) accepted his terms. A joint US–Soviet proposal at the UN speedily secured theoretical agreement on a ceasefire. But in practice Israel completed the Third Army's encirclement.

Sadat appealed with mounting desperation to the USSR, the UN, and the USA. Eventually Brezhnev requested that the USA join him 'without delay' in sending military contingents to enforce the ceasefire, warning that otherwise he would consider unilateral action; there were indications that some Soviet forces had been alerted. As in 1956 the USA rejected joint action, not wishing to legitimise a Soviet presence on the Canal, and fearing that attempts at joint enforcement on the part of two countries whose outlook on the area differed so widely could lead to quarrels. It responded instead by demonstrative military preparations, including an increase in

[59] Israeli withdrawal to the 1967 borders in exchange for non-belligerence and the opening of the Suez Canal, guaranteed apparently by the superpowers; final peace would depend on negotiations with the Palestinians. Dobrynin describes this as 'Brezhnev's favorite Mideast theme: employing joint US and Soviet diplomacy to impose a . . . peace on Arab terms, based on total Israeli withdrawal in return for security guarantees – which were not yet spelled out' (In Confidence, p. 283).

[60] Kissinger, Memoirs, ii, pp. 296–9; Nixon, Memoirs, pp. 884–6.

alert to DEFCON 3. It persuaded Sadat to withdraw his request for super-power intervention and substitute one for a UN force. It also insisted to Israel that the Third Army *must* be resupplied, while managing to arrange in exchange direct Israeli–Egyptian talks on disengagement. The net result was the establishment of a negotiating process that looked far more to Washington than to Moscow.[61]

Kissinger's comment is that 'detente had not prevented a crisis, as some' claimed

it should have – forgetting that detente defined not friendship but a strategy for a relationship between adversaries. After all, a principal purpose of our . . . Mideast policy was to reduce the . . . influence of the Soviet Union, just as the Soviets sought to reduce ours. But I believe detente mitigated the succession of crises that differences in ideology and geopolitical interest had made nearly inevitable; and I believe we enhanced the national interest in the process.[62]

The next few months were to see Kissinger flying around the Middle East, negotiating disengagement between the parties. Most of these negotiations were formally linked to an Arab–Israeli conference that met at Geneva for two days in December 1973 under joint US–Soviet chairmanship, then recessed. But by 1974 it was obvious that Moscow was being sidelined.

Washington certainly wished this, but so did the Arabs.[63] There were to be attempts to restore the Soviet relationship with Egypt, but they were dogged both by importunate pressure for the repayment of Egypt's arms purchase debts and by bad luck (Brezhnev's 1974–5 illness forced the cancellation of a planned summit with Sadat). Basically, though, Sadat was determined for both personal and political reasons to turn to the USA, and in March 1976 he abrogated the 1971 treaty and withdrew facilities from the Soviet fleet.

Egypt would thereafter put all its eggs into the American basket. The USA also enjoyed the friendship of the oil kingdoms, notably the

[61] Garthoff, *Détente and Confrontation*, pp. 371–85; Kissinger, *Memoirs*, ii, pp. 575–611 – their interpretations sometimes differ.

[62] *Memoirs*, ii, p. 600; for Brezhnev's rather similar comment, see above, p. 370.

[63] Sadat had told Kissinger at the outset that he was now looking to the USA. Assad of Syria also made it clear he did not want Gromyko involved in the disengagement talks – Gromyko's plane was kept circling over Damascus to demonstrate that he had no part in Syria's final offer to Israel, and next day he was left cooling his heels while the Syrian leaders, who had invited him to dinner, instead celebrated Israel's acceptance with Kissinger – Kissinger, *Memoirs*, ii, pp. 1101, 1104.

conservative and anti-communist Saudi Arabia, and (of course) of Israel. But if most major Middle Eastern powers were anti-Soviet, the Arab–Israeli dispute was deep enough to prevent them cooperating overtly (Egypt was generally ostracised after its 1979 peace treaty with Israel) and it provided the USSR with a way back into Middle Eastern politics. Even the 1974 and 1975 Israeli–Egyptian disengagement agreements had so alienated Libya that it abandoned its original hostility to godless Bolshevik Russia. When Sadat flew to Jerusalem in 1977, Syria reacted by mending fences with the USSR – which in return built it into a significant military power, thus enhancing its capability to dissuade other countries from following the Sadat line. 1980 saw a Soviet–Syrian friendship treaty and, reportedly, over $1 billion Libyan aid for Syrian arms purchases.[64]

US–Soviet trade and detente; The Jackson–Vanik amendment

If the Middle East constituted something of a disappointment for detente, so did US–Soviet trade. Not, admittedly, as severe a one as is sometimes suggested, for the Soviet Union was able to buy US grain. In 1972 it skilfully concealed the size of its purchases and thus got them cheap. This helped raise prices by a third, touched off bitter remarks about the 'Great Grain Robbery', and led in 1973–5 to some restrictions on US agricultural exports. But in October 1975 a five year orderly marketing deal was reached for guaranteed annual Soviet purchases of between 6 and 8 million tons of grain and sales to the USA of up to 10 million tons of oil a year. This worked smoothly, and (as pressure on US supplies slackened) Soviet grain purchases were allowed to rise steeply. US farmers benefited so much that, when Carter cut sales in 1980 to punish the USSR for invading Afghanistan, they persuaded the otherwise strongly anti-communist Reagan to reinstate them the next year.[65]

Non-agricultural trade was a different story. An agreement was reached in October 1972, and both trade and credits duly took off. (There is, indeed, controversy as to whether or not such imports of high-technology goods made a major contribution to the pace of the Soviet strategic build-up later in the decade.) But the concession to the USSR of 'most favoured nation' tariff status needed legislation, while credits could be

---

[64] *Keesing's*, 30703; see also *The Post-Imperial Age*, Chap. 13.
[65] *Keesing's*, 25577–8, 25953–4, 26169–70, 26851–2, 27641–2, 30882.

blocked by Congress. The Soviet decision of August 1972, supposedly taken at quite a low level, to impose a tax on emigrants had already aroused a furore. So in October the hostile Jackson–Vanik amendments were tabled in both houses of Congress, Jackson's being sponsored by no less than 72 senators. Initially the administration, rightly confident that the USSR could be quietly persuaded to withdraw the tax, did not take the amendments seriously enough. Only next spring did it become clear that the issue would not be allowed to die, and that it had linked together an alarmingly broad coalition – conservative opponents of detente, liberal critics of the allegedly amoral Nixon–Kissinger *realpolitik*, the Jewish lobby, and anti-communist and protectionist labor. In 1974 Ford determined to settle the issue, and the Soviets helped him by undertaking privately to let Jewish emigration go on rising (even though it was already high enough to cause friction with Egypt). But Jackson demanded assurances that, in both scale and publicity, went well beyond what the USSR would accept; and his ally Byrd managed to place an overall ceiling of $300 million on official US credits. By November 1974 Brezhnev was already saying at the Vladivostok summit that Congress 'had fouled up the progress we thought we were going to make with the expansion of trade'; and when the amended Trade Reform Act became law next January Moscow cancelled the 1972 agreement. Instead it turned increasingly towards Western Europe, deals with which probably served the same economic but not the same political purpose as those originally contemplated with the USA.[66]

Soviet restraint after the 1973 'oil shock' and the Portuguese revolution

Both sides insisted that the trade setback did not mean the end of detente, but it did reduce the incentives on offer for Soviet restraint at a time when the temptations to probe were increasing. Unfortunately, though we are conscious of the occasions when the USSR fished in troubled waters, we do not know whether there were occasions when it decided not to. Until the end of 1973 there had probably been little opportunity. But the then tripling of the price of oil administered an economic shock to Western

[66] Garthoff, *Détente and Confrontation*, pp. 309–10, 325–7, 356–7, 453–63; Gerald Ford, *A time to heal: the autobiography of Gerald R. Ford* (1979) pp. 216–17.

Europe that in turn highlighted major political weaknesses.[67] On top of this Portugal's authoritarian regime was overthrown in March 1974; for the next two years (but more especially between a failed rightist coup in March 1975 and an unsuccessful leftist/communist one that November) it seemed that communist-leaning officers in the army or security police might become dominant. All communists believe (in theory) in the capitalist order's ultimate collapse amid economic crisis; there is some evidence of debate in Moscow as to whether this had suddenly arrived, of exhortations to exploit it, and of impatience with the pusillanimous liberalism of the Italian communists. Certainly the USSR provided the Portuguese (and other) communists with financial aid (and presumably advice), as the West Germans did their Socialist competitors. But there is no evidence that they went much further. Perhaps they could not have done so in any case. Perhaps they were responsive to the warnings of Kissinger and Ford: the Soviet ambassador in Lisbon is reported to have told the pro-communist Prime Minister that the USSR had no interest in a confrontation with the USA over Portugal.[68]

Soviet intervention in Angola 1975–6 and its implications for detente

Africa was different. The USSR had adopted an 'African Strategy' in 1970. But little progress was made, and some disillusion set in, before the 1974 revolution brought to power in Portugal a new regime anxious to secure a rapid exit from empire. Guinea Bissau and Mozambique were turned over to their Marxist liberation movements. So presumably would East Timor have been had not Indonesia snapped it up, with the acquiescence of its anti-communist neighbours. But in Portugal's richest colony, Angola,

[67] For Italy, see pp. 440–1, 448. In Britain the Conservative government's 1974 defeat in an election called over a miners' strike led to a great increase in real, and a still greater one in perceived, trade union power; it also coincided with a dangerous economic crisis. In France power remained in strong right-of-centre hands, but electorally the country was very evenly divided between these and a left coalition in which the Communists were, until 1977, the largest party. General Franco, who had ruled Spain since the 1930s, was ageing, and it was not expected that the transition from his regime would be as smooth as it in fact proved after his death in 1975.

[68] Bell, *The Diplomacy of Détente*, Chap. 9 and pp. 204–5; Garthoff, *Détente and Confrontation*, pp. 485–7; Harry Gelman, *The Brezhnev Politburo and the Decline of Détente* (Ithaca, NY, 1984) pp. 163–4; *The Times*, 22 January 1974, p. 14; 24 June 1975, p. 1; 19 September 1975, pp. 1, 15; 30 October 1975, p. 5.

liberation movements had made almost no military progress, and were indeed split both along tribal lines and according to their outside patrons – China had aided UNITA and FLNA, the Soviet Union and Cuba the MPLA, the USA and the Congo (Zaire) the FLNA. In December 1974 the USSR decided to funnel heavy weapons to the MPLA through Congo Brazzaville. A power-sharing agreement of January 1975 disintegrated in March, and fighting began. The MPLA had the advantage of tribal support around the capital and of control of the oil-producing enclave of Cabinda. In April President Kaunda of Zambia lobbied the US to counteract the MPLA, which he represented as Moscow's tool. The Washington bureaucracy was reluctant, but in July Kissinger forced through a small covert programme[69] on the grounds that 'If the US does nothing when the Soviet-supported group gains dominance, I think all the [other Southern African] movements will draw the conclusion that they must accommodate to the Soviet Union and China.' The MPLA was soon hard pressed, especially after some 6,000 South African troops were committed in late October 1975 to bolster UNITA. So the Soviet Union turned to Cuba, which had in fact already sent troops to support the MPLA, and began a major airlift. By the end of November, Cuban artillery had shattered the FLNA and halted the South African advance.

December brought signs both of further escalation and of superpower compromise. The French President, Giscard d'Estaing, offered to mobilise contingents from Francophone Africa, and to contribute French helicopters to suppress the Cuban artillery, if the USA helped with transport. Equally the USSR seems to have taken note of US warnings that 'continuation of an interventionist policy must inevitably threaten other relationships', and on 10 December halted its airlift. Some exploratory discussions followed of a joint US–Soviet appeal for ceasefire and the withdrawal of external forces, probably in connection with the upcoming meeting of the Organisation of African Unity. Both tracks, however, were killed when the US administration sought another $28 million of covert funding. The request was leaked, along with negative evaluations from the bureaucracy; the resultant outcry led Congress on 19 December to ban all covert funding for Angola, lest the United States again be sucked into an unsavoury civil war in a not obviously essential area, as in Vietnam. But its decision both led South Africa to disengage, to avoid being left out on a limb, and

---

[69] Odd Arne Westad puts this at $50m ('Moscow and the Angola Crisis, 1974–1976: a new pattern of intervention', CWIHP *Bulletin* 8–9 (1996–7) p. 25), Kissinger at $20m (*Memoirs*, iii, p. 809).

gave the USSR and Cuba *carte blanche*; airlifts resumed, by April 1976 bringing the total of Cuban troops in Angola to 36,000. They rapidly extended MPLA rule over all the country except some UNITA territory in the far south-east, and then remained to protect it.[70]

The US administration was not prepared to break off the (then promising) SALT negotiations or to stop grain sales to the USSR by way of sanction, but it did see Angola as an alarming precedent. The trouble was not that a Marxist government had come to power – this had been acceptable in Mozambique – but that it had been put there by open Soviet/Cuban military intervention. 'Angola represents the first time that the Soviets have moved militarily at long distance to impose a regime of their choice . . . [and] that the United States has failed to respond to Soviet military moves outside the immediate Soviet orbit.' So, lacking other weapons, Kissinger resorted to rhetoric in an attempt to impress both on Moscow and on US liberals that Angola must not be repeated. 'It is intolerable,' he told Brezhnev in January 1975

that a country in the Western Hemisphere should launch a virtual invasion of Africa. Moreover the support of the Soviet Union to this Cuban force creates a precedent that the United States must resist. We have made it a cardinal principle of our relations that one great power must exercise restraint and not strive for unilateral advantage. If that principle is now abandoned, the prospect is for a chain of action and reaction with the potential for disastrous results.

Detente, he added in March, 'cannot survive a constant attempt to seek unilateral advantage'; it 'cannot, specifically, survive any more Angolas'.[71]

Moscow was unimpressed; indeed during Kissinger's January 1976 visit, Brezhnev declared publicly that if Kissinger wanted to discuss Angola

[70] Westad, 'Moscow and the Angolan Crisis', and Piero Gleijeses, 'Havana's Policy in Africa, 1959–76: New Evidence from Cuban Archives', CWIHP *Bulletin* 8–9 (1996–7) [at points the two articles disagree]; Piero Gleijeses, 'Truth or Credibility: Castro, Carter, and the Invasions of Shaba', *International History Review*, xviii (1996) p. 74; Kissinger, *Memoirs*, iii, Chap. 26 [which shows that many Congressmen approved US covert action in private, but reversed course when the question became public]; James P. Barber and John Barratt, *South Africa's Foreign Policy, the search for status and security 1945–1988* (Cambridge, 1990) pp. 186–96.
[71] Kissinger, *Memoirs*, iii, p. 855; Garthoff, *Détente and Confrontation*, pp. 524–5. Kissinger was invoking the 1972 'Basic Principles': 'Both sides recognize that efforts to obtain unilateral advantage at the expense of the other are incompatible' with the summit's objectives.

he should do so with his aide Sonnenfeldt – 'That will secure complete agreement.'[72] Brezhnev had complained bitterly to Kissinger in 1974 about the USSR's exclusion from the Middle Eastern disengagement agreements,[73] and may well have seen Egypt's shift from Soviet to US alignment as American acquisition of unilateral advantage. Again, though Angola may have been the first Russian 'military operation thousands of miles from Soviet territory', there had been many such American operations. The USSR had only recently acquired a major airlift and long distance naval capability, and now wanted to use it. Marshal Grechko, recently promoted to the Politboro, declared in 1974 that

At the present stage the historic function of the Soviet armed forces is not restricted merely to . . . defending our Motherland and other socialist countries . . . the Soviet state . . . supports the national liberation struggle, and resolutely resists imperialist aggression in whatever distant region of our planet it may appear.[74]

Moreover, Suslov contended, detente 'is based precisely' on a change in the world correlation of forces in favour of socialism.[75] If so, it was absurd for the USA to invoke it to try to restrict just such a further change. In February 1976 Brezhnev decided to be blunt, telling his Party Congress that

Our Party supports and will continue to support peoples fighting for their freedom . . .
  The Soviet Communists warmly acclaim the victory of the peoples of Guinea-Bissau and the Cape Verde Islands, Mozambique and Angola, which crowns many years of heroic struggle for independence. The CPSU has always sided with these peoples and rendered every possible support to these embattled patriots . . .
  Some bourgeois leaders affect surprise and raise a howl over the solidarity of . . . the Soviet people . . . with the struggle of other peoples

---

[72] This may have been only a press conference gaffe, but in Kissinger's view the phrase 'destroyed whatever sentiment was left in the United States for agreements with the Kremlin' (*Memoirs*, iii, p. 854).

[73] Kissinger, *Memoirs*, ii, p. 1022.

[74] Gelman, *The Brezhnev Politburo and the Decline of Detente*, p. 47.

[75] ibid. p. 161. Brezhnev said much the same to the 1976 Party Congress; and in 1975 an *Izvestia* commentator had observed that the 'purpose of detente was to make the process of international change as painless as possible' (Simes, 'The Death of Detente', pp. 9–10).

for freedom and progress. This is either outright naivety or more likely
a deliberate befuddling of minds. It could not be clearer, after all that
detente and peaceful coexistence have to do with interstate relations.
This means above all that disputes and conflicts between countries are
not to be settled by war . . . Detente does not in the least abolish . . .
the laws of the class struggle . . .

We make no secret of the fact that we see detente as the way to create
more favourable conditions for peaceful socialist and communist
construction . . .[76]

Further strains on detente: Shaba I and II and the Somali–Ethiopian war

This did not mean that the USSR was no longer interested in its relations
with the USA; it continued to value SALT negotiations. But it was moving
back towards Cold War practices – after a lull since 1972, its propaganda
forgeries of Western official documents increased again in late 1976.[77] The
incentives for restraint were by now very limited, while promising opportunities multiplied. 1977 brought an invasion, by former Katangese gendarmes (who had left the Congo after Tshombe's fall and fought first for
the Portuguese, then, adopting socialist rhetoric, for the MPLA) of their
home province, now renamed Shaba. The Congolese army proved ineffective, and Castro, while disclaiming advance knowledge of the invasion,
told the East Germans 'It will be a great event if Mobutu falls.' The new US
administration did not react: Carter said he did 'not intend to get militarily
involved, unless our own security is directly threatened'[78]. So Morocco
contributed 1,500 troops, who were flown in by France, and the invaders
withdrew. Next year they returned, again meeting little local resistance
and now capturing the city of Kolwezi and posing a significant threat to
the Mobutu regime. France and Belgium stabilised the situation by sending
in some 2,900 of their own troops – this time airlifted by the US. Later
Moroccan and Senegalese units were substituted, and Angola and the
Congo officially normalised relations. The 1978 Shaba invasion occasioned a proliferation of East–West accusations. Not all appear to have

[76] L.I. Brezhnev, *Report of the CPSU Central Committee* (Moscow, 1976) pp. 16, 19, 39.
[77] Garthoff, *Détente and Confrontation*, p. 317.
[78] CWIHP *Bulletin* 8–9 (1996–7) p. 20. *Europa*, iv (8 May 1977) p. iv – issued with *The Times*, 3 May 1977.

been well-founded; but had it succeeded, it would have greatly altered the configuration of Africa.[79]

The next flashpoint was the Horn of Africa. Here the pro-American Emperor of Ethiopia, Haile Selassie, had been toppled in 1974. There followed a period of confusion, from which the leftist Colonel Mengistu emerged (bloodily) the victor in 1977. The USSR had already concluded an arms deal with him the previous December, and both it and Cuba promptly welcomed his success. They also tried, but failed, to reconcile Ethiopia with their friend Somalia. Somalia turned out to be irredentist first and socialist only second; with Saudi assistance it made overtures to the USA, and may have derived more encouragement than was intended from the latter's agreement in principle to supply defensive weapons. Meanwhile the multinational Ethiopian state was falling to pieces. From June 1977 onwards Somalia attacked it, first under the guise of a 'West Somalia Liberation Front' and then openly. The invasion of the ethnically Somali Ogaden was initially successful, but faltered in front of the vital town of Harar. To the anger of America's friends (Saudi Arabia, Egypt, the Sudan and Iran), the Carter administration adopted the legally correct position that it would send Somalia no arms till it withdrew behind the international border; it also blocked the transfer to Somalia of Iranian Phantom jets that might have made all the difference. The USSR had already used troops from South Yemen to counter the Somali advance. November 1977 saw a massive Soviet and Cuban resupply of Ethiopia, January 1978 a Soviet-commanded counter-offensive (using 1,500 Soviet military advisers and 12,000 Cuban troops) that had by March driven the Somalis back over the border. The USSR followed up by helping Mengistu's regime reconquer the province of Eritrea, the bulk of which had been in secessionist hands. For good measure Cubans were used in June 1978 to determine the outcome of a power struggle in South Yemen.[80]

---

[79] Gleijeses, 'Castro, Carter, and the Invasions of Shaba', demonstrates that Cuba had opposed the invasion, lest the imperialists be afforded a pretext to attack Angola and end its training of South African, Namibian, and Zimbabwe guerrillas; but he believes Angola probably gave the invasion some assistance, and is open-minded about the USSR. Contemporary rumours of an East German 'assignment' to destabilise Zaire now seem unlikely.

[80] Ermias Abebe, 'The Horn, the Cold War, and Documents from the former East-Bloc: an Ethiopian View', and Paul Henze, 'Moscow, Mengistu, and the Horn: Difficult Choices for the Kremlin', CWIHP *Bulletin* 8–9 (1996–7) esp. pp. 43, 47; Garthoff, *Détente and Confrontation*, pp. 630–1; Steven R. David, *Third World Coups d'Etat and International Security* (Baltimore, 1987) pp. 87–92.

None of this encountered significant US opposition – Soviet action to support Ethiopia was acceptable in international law, and, though Arabs backed Somalia, most African states (and Israel) did not; the South Yemen episode was both obscure and soon over. The US official most alarmed by the strengthening of the Soviet position at the mouth of the Red Sea, and by the use of Cuban 'mercenaries' to effect it, was National Security Adviser Brzezinski. He would haved liked to signal concern by despatching a naval force to the area and hinting that over-forceful Soviet action might endanger Congressional ratification of SALT II, but he was overruled. Brzezinski came to believe that this US passivity emboldened the Soviets, against whose subsequent stances Americans then sometimes overreacted; accordingly 'SALT lies buried in the sands of the Ogaden'.[81]

Growing US criticism of detente in the mid-1970s

Detente was already in a bad way in 1976; indeed, President Ford, faced with a right-wing challenge for the Republican presidential nomination, stopped using the word. Angola suggested that the USSR remained expansionist. Sonnenfeldt's briefing on Eastern Europe (see p. 378) leaked, and was not well received. Concern was mounting both at the way in which Kissinger negotiated and at SALT's implications for US defences (see pp. 59–65). A further dimension was that of human rights. Soviet suppression of dissent, surprisingly tentative in the years after Khrushchev's fall, began to gather way in the early 1970s. This may have been partly because of detente – a Central Committee conference warned of 'the increasing danger of bourgeois ideology in direct connection with the broadening of contacts with the imperialist world'.[82] Such contacts, always important to dissidents, became more so with the suppression of *samizdat*, and they provided the West with a steady stream of information about Soviet brutalities. A further turn came with the Helsinki agreements; these included a 'human rights' basket, and dissident groups in the USSR and Eastern Europe sought to monitor its (non)application, a course that sooner or later led to their arrest.

The Nixon and Ford administrations took no official notice, believing overt interference likely to be counter-productive. Many critics viewed this

---

[81] Zbigniew Brzezinski, *Power and Principle: Memoirs of the National Security Adviser 1977–1981* (New York, 1983) pp. 178–89.

[82] Gelman, *The Brezhnev Politburo and the Decline of Detente*, p. 159.

as proof of Republican amorality, and saw no point in a detente that did not improve conditions in the USSR but only strengthened its oppressive leaders. In this they were encouraged by dissidents like Sakharov, who warned against pursuing detente on Soviet terms, endorsed the Jackson–Vanik amendment, and declared that Soviet leaders should be pressured into granting human rights as a price for detente. The issue spilt over into the 1976 presidential election. President Carter determined to give human rights a much higher priority. Accordingly his first months saw a string of criticisms of Soviet and Czech arrests and harassments, warnings that attempts to intimidate Sakharov would 'conflict with accepted international standards', the reception at the White House of the exiled Bukovsky, and a UN address affirming Carter's intention to press for human rights around the world.[83]

Soviet contempt for Carter

Carter's human rights campaign was by no means directed only against the USSR, but it was selective in that (for strategic reasons) it was not extended to either South Korea or China. Arguably the Soviets had no right to resent it, since they proclaimed that there can be no such thing as ideological coexistence. But resent it they certainly did: 'Suddenly, right there . . . in Brezhnev's office – to talk about human rights . . . Unheard of!'[84] In a generally harsh letter to Carter in February 1977, Brezhnev protested about 'correspondence with a renegade [Sakharov] who proclaimed himself an enemy of the Soviet state', and declared roundly that he would not 'allow interference in our internal affairs, whatever pseudo-humanitarian slogans are used to present it'. As Carter naively remarked a few months later, 'There has been a surprising, adverse reaction in the Soviet Union to our stand on human rights . . . apparently that's provided a greater obstacle to other friendly pursuits of common goals, like in SALT, than I had anticipated.'[85]

Carter's opening moves on SALT had been ill-received (see p. 67); as Arbatov later put it, they 'confirmed the impression in Moscow that

---

[83] Stevenson, *The Rise and Fall of Detente*, p. 162; Garthoff, *Détente and Confrontation*, pp. 568 ff.

[84] The recollection of interpreter Sukhodrev (Westad, *Fall of Detente*, p. 17).

[85] Brzezinski, *Power and Principle*, pp. 154–6; Garthoff, *Détente and Confrontation*, p. 568.

Carter was not serious'.[86] Furthermore, his human rights initiatives were perceived as aggressive, but the low profile he maintained during the Shaba and Ethiopia affairs suggested that he was not to be feared. In short Carter lost Soviet respect. In time, of course, he might have recovered it: SALT II was eventually steered through to a respectable deal, concluded at the June 1979 Vienna Summit, after which Brezhnev described Carter as 'quite a nice guy after all'. However, in August the Americans suddenly discovered a Soviet 'combat brigade' in Cuba, and a furore was set off when Senator Church revealed its presence and called for its withdrawal. Carter felt obliged to follow suit, and several senators made clear that its continued presence would jeopardise SALT's ratification. The Soviets regarded the whole issue as either bogus – the brigade had in fact been in Cuba since 1962 – or alternatively as a deliberate attack on detente. Gromyko and Andropov held that 'Any concessions on our part will lead to new brazen demands. Proceeding from this, we should react to any new claims of that kind by confirming our position, or just leave them unanswered.' In the absence of any face-saving Soviet adjustments, Carter had, in effect, to climb down in October.[87] The episode certainly did not add to the credibility of US warnings about Afghanistan.

Soviet invasion of Afghanistan 1979; Carter's reaction

In retrospect the Soviets' major Afghan mistake had been their over-enthusiastic response to the 1978 coup. Before then Afghanistan had been a non-aligned country in which the USSR, through aid and strategic road-building, had greater influence than any other power. President Daoud was engaged on building countervailing connections with China and the Islamic world when he was killed by a communist coup, of local origin. The USSR then assumed a tutelary position, mediating (unsuccessfully) between the rival Afghan communist factions *Parcham* and *Khalq*, and building up its general advisory presence. The result was disaster: the new rulers indulged in massive repression, justified to sceptical Soviet advisers as following Lenin's example; this and their modernising and non-Islamic reforms quickly led to rebellions. March 1979 brought a rising at Herat by locals, some Iranian Islamist guerrillas, and mutinous soldiers. It was, in fact, quickly put down, but it highlighted the regime's almost

[86] Garthoff, *Détente and Confrontation*, p. 566.
[87] ibid. Chap. 24; Dobrynin, *In Confidence*, pp. 426, 428–9.

total lack of support, and alarmed both the Kabul government and the Kremlin. The Politburo decided that 'we must not surrender Afghanistan', and that both aid and instruction to Kabul should therefore be stepped up. But the Soviet army should not be committed. 'Against whom,' asked Gromyko,

will it fight? Against the Afghan people first of all . . . Comrade Andropov correctly noted that . . . the situation in Afghanistan is not ripe for a revolution. And all that we have done in recent years . . . in terms of detente, arms reduction, and much more . . . would be thrown back. China, of course would be given a nice present. All the non-aligned countries will be against us . . .[88]

Moscow's advice was not very welcome – its ambassador came to be called 'the little czar'. Nor was it always taken: suggestions that the Afghan government be broadened to bring in not only members of the losing communist faction, *Parcham*, but also of the pre-1978 regime and even, perhaps, of some Islamic groups were vetoed by strongman Hafizullah Amin. In September 1979 President Taraki was called to Moscow, where Brezhnev promised yet more military aid if he would go easy on land reform and get rid of Amin. An attempt to do so by murder failed, and Amin in turn soon executed Taraki. Amin's chief wish was to secure acceptance by Moscow, which he was constantly asking to visit. But he also talked to the US charge in Kabul, perhaps hoping that the US might restrain Pakistani and Chinese assistance to the insurgency. These talks, Amin told a colleague in late December, had led nowhere. But they formed the basis of, or (some suggest) the pretext for, alarmist KGB reports that he was contemplating 'doing a Sadat on us'. Similarly contacts with the Muslim resistance were represented as signs of a possible rapprochement with Iran and establishment of an Islamic regime. Meanwhile the insurgency went from bad to worse, leading Amin to repeated appeals for the introduction of Soviet troops. By late November 1979 Andropov seems to have decided that Amin would have to go, preferably through poison or a Soviet-orchestrated coup. Defence Minister Ustinov agreed, but preferred to make sure through military intervention in overwhelming force. Gromyko, the third member of the Politburo commission on Afghanistan but politically less strong a figure, went along, perhaps reflecting that (as

---

[88] Westad, *Fall of Detente*, esp. pp. 291, 295–6, 301. Andropov's opposition to military intervention was, probably, still more important.

Dobrynin later put it) 'by the winter of 1979 detente was, for most purposes, already dead'.

Backed by Suslov, they urged intervention on Brezhnev in strong terms, citing 'Amin's behind-the-scenes activities which may mean his political reorientation to the West' and the resultant 'dangers to the southern borders of the Soviet Union and . . . possibility of American short-range missiles being deployed in Afghanistan'; they stressed the availability of *Parcham* leaders to head a new government; and they screened out contrary advice from the bureaucracy and the military. Brezhnev was amenable – in view of the disregard for his personal assurances to Taraki, he asked 'how should the world . . . believe what Brezhnev says, if his words do not count in Afghanistan?' Politburo assent duly followed. The Soviet invasion began on 25 December, and on the 27th the Presidential palace was stormed and Amin executed. Babrak Kamal was brought back from Moscow and installed as leader, and within a month 85,000 Soviet troops had moved in to consolidate the new regime.[89]

Past uses of Soviet military power in Angola and the Horn of Africa had quickly proved successful; and Brezhnev was confident (he told Dobrynin in January 1980) that 'It'll be over in three or four weeks'. It was not. Carter had warned at the Vienna Summit against intervention in Afghanistan, but received only standard rebuttals. There followed further (though deliberately low-key) US warnings (three in December). Then on the 28th, down the hotline, Carter demanded that the invasion be reversed: 'Unless you draw back . . . this will inevitably jeopardize the course of United States-Soviet relationships throughout the world'.[90] The USSR had been concerned only to consolidate a recent gain that now seemed likely to blow up in its face. But that was not how things were seen in Washington, particularly by Brzezinski:

Both Iran and Afghanistan are in turmoil, and Pakistan is both unstable internally and extremely apprehensive externally. If the Soviets succeed in Afghanistan [DELETION], and the age-long dream of Moscow to have direct access to the Indian Ocean will have been fulfilled.

[89] Westad, *Fall of Detente*, esp. pp. 127–36, 139, and 'Concerning the situation in "A": new Russian evidence on the Soviet intervention in Afghanistan', CWIHP *Bulletin* 8–9 (1996–7) esp. p. 159; Vasiliy Mitrokhin, *The KGB in Afghanistan*, CWIHP Working Paper no. 40 (2002) esp. pp. 83–7, 94, 97; David, *Third World Coups*, pp. 88–9, 97–9.
[90] Dobrynin, *In Confidence*, p. 439; Jimmy Carter, *Keeping Faith: Memoirs of a President* (1982) pp. 247 ff, 472.

> *. . . it could produce Soviet presence right down on the edge of the Arabian and Oman Gulfs.*[91]

Even the more doveish Secretary of State, Vance, felt 'The Soviets must recognize that they are going to have to pay a cost as long as their troops stay in Afghanistan'. So, in marked contrast to the 1968 Czech affair, the USA imposed sanctions. Many, admittedly, were trivial, and major ones, like the reduction of US grain sales, proved unsustainable. But Carter's own outlook had been transformed. The invasion 'has made a more dramatic change in my own opinion of what the Soviets' ultimate goals are than anything they've done in the previous time I've been in office'. 'We cannot be certain . . . if they seek colonial domination only in Afghanistan, or . . . other conquests as well. No President . . . can afford to gamble . . . upon wishful thinking about the present or the future intentions of the Soviet Union.' 'There is no doubt that the Soviets' move into Afghanistan, if done without adverse consequences, would have resulted in the temptation to move again and again' towards the control of warm water ports and oil supplies. Carter never formally abandoned detente. But in practice he had re-embraced containment, enunciating in January 1980 the 'Carter Doctrine' that any 'attempt by any outside force to gain control of the Persian Gulf region will be regarded as an assault on the vital interests of the United States' and 'repelled by any means necessary, including military force'.[92] The rest of 1980 was spent in trying to reassure Saudi Arabia, improve relations with Pakistan, and acquire the facilities around the Arabian Sea that would make possible the projection of a Rapid Deployment Force into the Gulf.

[91] 26 December 1979 report to Carter (Westad, *Fall of Detente*, p. 329). Both Taraki and Amin hoped to detach the Pushtuns and Baluchis from Pakistan and so reach the Indian Ocean; these were traditional Afghan aspirations, but now cast in a socialist and anti-imperialist mode. Amin's successor, Babrak Karmal, thought the time was not ripe; Moscow agreed – 'First it is necessary to conquer Afghanistan!' (Mitrokhin, *KGB in Afghanistan*, pp. 111–13).

[92] Garthoff, *Détente and Confrontation*, pp. 950, 954, 972–3. Washington now tended to link Afghanistan with recent events in Ethiopia/South Yemen, and to see the USSR as entrenching itself at both ends of an 'arc of crisis' around the valuable but volatile oil world, where the USA's long-time friend, the Shah of Iran, had collapsed in January 1979.

CHAPTER 10

Tension and the ending of the Cold War in the 1980s

East–West tension

By 1980 most of the components were in place for the United States' policy of the next few years. The USSR was perceived as internally repressive, externally expansionist, and engaged on a massive arms build-up. To meet this the USA had secured NATO agreement on a 3 per cent p.a. increase in real defence spending, and itself did likewise. There had also been agreement on the deployment in Europe of cruise and Pershing missiles to counter Soviet SS-20s. Meanwhile a 'new' strategic doctrine had been adopted in 1980; in fact a development of earlier reforms, it stressed options (as opposed to an all-or-nothing response) – including that of fighting a limited nuclear war. West European public opinion took some time to assimilate this; but later the combination of Carter's strategy and Reagan's cowboy image gave rise to visions of an America happy to fight a nuclear war *in Europe*.

Many West Europeans wondered whether they were not bound in too closely with superpower rivalries in other parts of the globe. This in itself was not new – Europe had shown little sympathy for US containment policy in the Chinese offshore islands crises, or for its application during the Vietnam War. Since then, too, a central European settlement had been reached; was it worth endangering this to contest a *fait accompli* in Afghanistan? The West German government agreed in condemning Soviet expansion there, but feared an American tendency to overreact – at one point Chancellor Schmidt said 'We will not permit ten years of detente and defense policy to be destroyed'. Similarly President Giscard d'Estaing of France declared that 'the balance of power in Europe is a separate problem'. In May/June 1980 both leaders travelled east to meet Brezhnev; later

Schmidt did his best to persuade Carter to dismiss Brzezinski (who was commonly seen as the initiator of the new hard line). West European trade with the USSR also increased sharply, thus undercutting US economic sanctions.[1] The Russians encouraged such moves by making token military withdrawals from East Germany and proposing INF talks.

The 1980s were clearly going to be a difficult period for East–West relations, but to begin with they saw more talk than action. For neither Vietnam's 1978 conquest of Cambodia (which had so alarmed China) nor the 1979 Soviet move into Afghanistan led to further expansion; very possibly neither had been directly intended to.[2] Perhaps too the containment inaugurated by Deng Xiaoping and Carter proved effective. Probably the most important factor was that there were no further vacuums like those produced by the Portuguese revolution and the collapse of the Haile Selassie and Daoud regimes in Ethiopia and Afghanistan. The Reagan administration, admittedly, worried deeply over the possibility of a new Cold War arena developing in Central America following the Nicaraguan revolution and adopted highly questionable tactics to prevent this.[3] But the USSR, far more cautious than it had been twenty years earlier, stayed largely on the sidelines. There were, therefore, no major East–West crises.

Instead the contest largely took the form of rival defence build-ups and of a publicity war (often justifying these build-ups by alarming portrayals of the other side's capabilities). All this was well advanced before President Reagan took office. His new defence increases, denunciations of the USSR – famously (in 1983) as an 'evil empire' – his past condemnations of detente, and the prominence of its hardline critics within his administration[4] were widely perceived as further stoking the 'New Cold War'. What remained long unrecognised was Reagan's originality.

[1] R.L. Garthoff, *Détente and Confrontation*, pp. 978–80; Zbigniew Brezinski, *Power and Principle: Memoirs of the Security Adviser, 1977–1981 (1983)* pp. 310, 462–3; Carl-Christof Schweitzer (ed.) *The Changing Western Analysis of the Soviet Threat* (1990) pp. 246–7; P. Short, *The Dragon and the Bear* (1982) p. 474.

[2] Though in retrospect Brezhnev listed the Afghan revolution, along with those of Ethiopia and Nicaragua and with the fall of the Shah, as 'new victories' for the 'revolutionary struggle of the peoples' – *Report of the Central Committee of the CPSU to the XXVI Congress of the Communist Party of the Soviet Union* (Moscow, 1981) p. 6.

[3] For a fuller discussion, see *The Post-Imperial Age*, pp. 415–21.

[4] Reagan himself wrote in his diary (in April 1983) that 'Some of the NSC staff are too hard line and don't think any approach should be made to the Soviets' – Ronald Reagan, *An American Life* (1990) pp. 569, 572.

Reagan's originality

Since the 'post-Cuba detente' the dominant perception had been of two broadly equal superpowers, locked into at least 'adversary-partnership', and hopefully better, by the 'Mutual Assured Destruction' (MAD) capabilities of their nuclear arsenals. True, vestigial aspirations remained, whether for the worldwide triumph of 'socialism' or the slow humanisation of Eastern Europe, but these were for the remote future: no early change in the existing world structure was either anticipated or desired.

In some ways Reagan harked back to Dulles's view that the Soviet system would suddenly implode. In 1975 he had described communism as 'a temporary aberration which will one day disappear . . . because it is contrary to human nature'. In 1982 he told the British Parliament that:

In an ironic sense Karl Marx was right. We are witnessing today a great revolutionary crisis . . . where the demands of the economic order are conflicting directly with those of the political order. But the crisis is happening not in the free, non-Marxist West, but in the home of Marxism-Leninism, the Soviet Union . . . The decay of the Soviet experiment should come as no surprise to us. Wherever the comparison has been made between free and closed societies – West Germany and East Germany, Austria and Czechoslovakia, Malaysia and Vietnam – it is the democratic societies that are prosperous . . . the Soviet Union is not immune from the reality of what is going on in the world . . . What I am describing now is a plan and a hope for the long term – the march of freedom and democracy which will leave Marxist-Leninism on the ash heap of history as it has left other tyrannies . . .

Reagan constantly stressed the weakness of a Soviet economy unable to bear the weight of its armaments. US rearmament was, therefore, not only necessary to redress previous neglect; it was also the vehicle for compelling the USSR to come to terms: 'We must,' he said in 1982, 'keep the heat on these people. What I want is to bring them to their knees so that they will disarm and let us disarm; but we have got to do it by keeping the heat on. We can do it. We have them on the ropes economically.' Again:

I don't underestimate the value of a sound [US] economy [and balanced budget] but I also don't underestimate the imperialist ambitions of the Soviet Union . . . I want more than anything to bring them into realistic arms reduction talks. To do this they must be convinced that the alternative is a build-up militarily by us. They have stretched their

*economy to the limit to maintain their arms program. They know they
cannot match us in an arms race if we are determined to catch up.*[5]

But if Reagan's espousal of ideological and economic pressure had
overtones of the 1940s and early 1950s, his attitude towards nuclear
weapons was quite different – they should go: 'I share your view of the
mutual assured destruction policy, it makes no sense whatever. Hopefully
a defense [against missiles] could result in real negotiations leading to the
total elimination of nuclear weapons.'[6] Reagan had launched the idea of
such a 'defense' in March 1983 in a speech challenging the scientists 'who
gave us nuclear weapons ... to give us the means of rendering these
nuclear weapons impotent and obsolete', and ordering a 'research and
development program aimed at an ultimate goal of eliminating the threat
posed by nuclear ballistic missiles.' This 'Strategic Defense Intiative' (SDI
– commonly dubbed 'Star Wars') is often viewed as another attempt to
force the Soviets either to give in or to embark on a ruinous attempt to
match superior US technology. To some extent, indeed, SDI had that effect.
But this seems to have been only the by-product of Reagan's intense concern over the millions of casualties nuclear war would entail; he always
promised that, if SDI could be made to work, it would be shared with the
USSR, though Moscow remained understandably sceptical.[7]

Acheson and (in his early years) Dulles had seen little use in talks with
the USSR until after a Soviet collapse. Reagan, however, believed that if
Moscow could be brought (or constrained) to the negotiating table, more
especially if he could himself sit down with his Soviet counterpart, meaningful agreements could be reached, first on arms reductions, then on a
wider complex of issues – 'I do want to let them see that there is a better
world if they'll show *by deed* they want to get along with the free world.'
In January 1984 Reagan publicly defined the desired dialogue as one
'that will serve to promote peace in the troubled regions of the world,
reduce the level of arms, and build a constructive working relationship.'

---

[5] Richard Reeves, *President Reagan. The Triumph of Imagination* (New York, 2005)
pp. 108–10; *Reagan. A Life in Letters*, Kiron K. Skinner, Annelise Anderson, Martin
Anderson (eds) (New York, 2003) p. 311. That most Labour MPs boycotted Reagan's
address to Parliament says much about the fears and attitudes then widely prevalent
among the West European Left.
[6] June 1983 – *Reagan. A Life in Letters*, p. 424.
[7] Reeves, *Reagan*, pp. 103, 142–6. Reagan had begun by calling for estimates of US
casualties (150m) in the event of a MAD exchange, and was the first president since
Eisenhower to sit through a war-game rehearsal.

He also suggested that progress in human rights 'can contribute to progress in other areas of the Soviet–American relationship'; and over time such progress joined the other desiderata to form a 'four-part [US] agenda'.[8]

1981–4: years of tension; 'Operation RYAN' and the November 1983 ABLE ARCHER exercise

This agenda was to structure US–Soviet negotiations in the later 1980s. Previously things were very different. NATO issued warnings against Soviet intervention in Poland, where the 'Solidarity' trade union had suddenly emerged as a de facto competitor with the government (see pp. 573–5). The warnings may have been heeded; certainly the USSR adopted the more subtle course of demanding that the Polish government itself suppress Solidarity, which it did in December 1981. This NATO naturally condemned; and the USA pushed for tough sanctions, short (however) of suspending its own grain sales to Russia. But little came of this apart from internal friction within the alliance, for the USA sought also to use the episode to force cancellation of the projected Soviet gas pipeline to Western Europe (which it did not wish to see become energy-dependent on the East). But it met with refusal. Even pro-American leaders like Thatcher resented US attempts to forbid European companies including American parts in equipment they made for the pipeline. Eventually Washington was forced to give way, but in return Western Europe agreed to a further tightening of controls on high-technology exports to the East.[9]

Talks on intermediate nuclear forces (INF) in Europe did open in Geneva in late 1981, with the US proposing what was widely seen as a deliberately unrealistic 'zero-zero' option (whereby, in return for NATO's non-deployment of cruise and Pershing missiles, the USSR would scrap its existing SS-20s). In 1982 the INF negotiations were complemented by 'Strategic Arms Reductions Talks' (START), but neither made any progress. While still recovering from an assassination attempt in 1981, Reagan had sent Brezhnev a handwritten letter appealing for 'meaningful and constructive dialogue'. Shortly after Brezhnev's death, Reagan concluded that 'this may be a particularly opportune time for external forces

---

[8] Reagan, *An American Life*, p. 572 (Diary, April 1983); Jack F. Matlock, *Reagan and Gorbachev. How the Cold War Ended* (New York, 2004) esp. pp. 61–2, 76, 84–5.
[9] *Keesing's*, 31458–9, 31965–8; Garthoff, *Détente and Confrontation*, pp. 1033–5.

to influence the policies of Brezhnev's successors', and invited the previously cold-shouldered ambassador Dobrynin for a long talk. During it he asked Moscow to permit the emigration of some Pentecostalists who had taken refuge in the US embassy. This was quietly done; and when, in July 1983, Reagan told Andropov that 'our predecessors have made better progress when they communicated privately and candidly', Andropov agreed.[10] However, any chances of favourable developments were stopped in their tracks when, in September, the USSR shot down a Korean airliner that had gone off course and strayed over military installations in the Soviet Far East. The Politburo was promptly told of the mistake, but decided 'to take the offensive, not defend ourselves' against criticism and to treat the episode as 'a deliberate [espionage] provocation by imperialist forces'.[11] The USA played (or overplayed) the disaster for publicity advantage. Soviet leaders reiterated their depressing warnings – Gromyko asserting that 'The world situation is now slipping towards a very dangerous precipice', while Andropov doubted 'whether Washington has any brakes at all'.[12]

Dobrynin claims that in 1981–3 Soviet leaders would readily have returned to dialogue on the basis of their understanding (which, of course, Reagan rejected) of detente. But once 'they came to the conclusion detente could not be recovered as long as Reagan remained in power, the inclination grew inside the Kremlin not to pacify him but to fight back'. Worse, Andropov felt 'Reagan is unpredictable. You should expect anything from him.' All post-Stalin leaders saw the USA as a long-term military threat; but 'with the probable exception of Andropov, they did not believe that an attack could take place unexpectedly at any moment, like Hitler's attack on the Soviet Union . . .' However, while 'still head of the KGB, Andropov did believe that the Reagan administration was actively preparing for war, and he was joined in this belief by [Defence Minister] Ustinov.' So in 1981 they persuaded the Politburo to launch 'the largest peacetime military

---

[10] Reeves, *Reagan*, pp. 53–5; Matlock, *Reagan and Gorbachev*, pp. 53–8; Reagan, *An American Life*, pp. 272–3, 302, 576–82.

[11] Dmitri Volkogonov, *The Rise and Fall of the Soviet Empire. Political Leaders from Lenin to Gorbachev* (paperback, 1999) pp. 362–9. The Soviet air command probably had taken the plane to be a spy, even though the fighter pilot reported seeing its navigation lights. Five years later a US warship shot down an Iranian airliner that it mistook for an attacking fighter; but the USA subsequently displayed more contrition than had the Politburo.

[12] *Keesing's*, 32513 ff; Christopher Andrew and Oleg Gordievsky, *KGB: The Inside Story of its Foreign Operations from Lenin to Gorbachev* (1990) p. 501.

intelligence operation in Soviet history . . . Operation RYAN, an acronym of the Russian words . . . Nuclear Missile Attack.'[13] Despite a steady flow (through the DDR) of NATO strategic plans, and the scepticism both of KGB officers in the field and of East German intelligence,[14] the KGB 'Centre' remained convinced of the danger and badgered its agents to monitor indicators (some highly implausible) that an attack was imminent.

The policy of deploying cruise and Pershing missiles had generated massive opposition in Western Europe (see p. 69), which the USSR naturally played up to – KGB residencies were told to popularise the slogan, 'Reagan means War'. In this context the key countries were Britain and West Germany. Both held elections in 1983, with pro-deployment governments facing anti-nuclear oppositions. The USSR interjected itself into the German 'missiles election' in a remarkably heavy-handed fashion, with Andropov expressing his preference for the SPD and Gromyko, during a visit to Bonn, denouncing the US administration as 'compulsive gamblers and adventurists who declare that they are ready to plunge mankind into a nuclear catastrophe for the sake of their ambitions'.[15] In March the West German and in June the British government secured comfortable re-election, and the way was clear for the missiles' deployment in November. By then the international scene had been further darkened, first by the shooting down of the Korean airliner, then in October by events in the Caribbean islet of Grenada, where the USA had taken advantage of murders within the communist leadership to invade and liberate it. There were fears in Moscow that this might be the prelude to greater things.

On 2 November KGB residencies were told the

threat of an outbreak of nuclear war is reaching an extremely dangerous point . . . The existing correlation of forces may be radically altered by deployment of new American medium-range missiles in Western Europe. In these circumstances, the task of not overlooking immediate

[13] Anatoly Dobrynin, *In Confidence. Moscow's Ambassador to America's Six Cold War Presidents (1962–1986)* (New York, 1995) pp. 477, 498, 503, 515, 522–3 – my italics.

[14] Markus Wolf with Anne McElvoy, *Man without a Face. The Autobiography of Communism's Greatest Spymaster* (1997) pp. 221–2, 317; Wolf indicates that Andropov's suspicions of the USA in fact dated back beyond Reagan to 1980.

[15] Later Vice-President Bush visited West Germany and spoke in Berlin as part of a tour 'to drum up support for American policy on missiles, and generally to remind the allies of the benefits of alliance membership' – Andrew and Gordievsky, *KGB*, p. 494; *The Annual Register. A Record of World Events, 1983*, pp. 136–7; *Keesing's*, 33346.

*preparations by the adversary for launching a surprise nuclear attack . . .
has acquired even greater . . . immediacy.*

Unfortunately from 2 to 11 November NATO was staging its annual
command and control exercise, ABLE ARCHER. No actual forces were
involved; but 'Soviet contingency plans for a surprise attack . . . envisaged
using training exercises as a cover for a real offensive. The Centre was
haunted by the fear that Western plans . . . might be . . . [their] mirror-
image'. On 5 November it told its residencies that, given the importance of
surprise, 'it can be assumed that the . . . time from the moment when the
preliminary decision for RYAN is taken, up to the order to deliver the
strike will be of very short duration, possibly 7–10 days.' On the 8th or
9th, the double agent Gordievsky recollects, Moscow cabled to report
(non-existent) alerts on US bases that might be preparations for a first
strike, though they might equally have more innocuous causes. Moscow
also placed at least some of its own forces on near-war alert. All this, of
course, was not generally known. But the USSR did respond to the deployment of cruise and Pershing missiles, *later* in November, by pulling out of
the arms limitation talks, the last remaining relics of superpower detente.[16]

In the event, the ABLE ARCHER crisis may have been a good thing.
For Gordievsky's accounts (passed on by the British, for whom he was
working) will have reinforced the realisation to which Reagan was already
coming that 'many Soviet officials' really did fear a US first strike: 'I feel,'
he had written in late November 1983, 'the Soviets are so . . . paranoid
about being attacked that without being in any way soft on them, we
ought to tell them no one here has any intention of doing anything like
that.'[17] Accordingly Reagan took a softer line in his January 1984 speech
(above pp. 400–1); and this approach was complemented by Mrs Thatcher's
visit to Hungary (chosen as a conduit to the Kremlin), her well-received
attendance at Andropov's funeral and interview with Chernenko, and her
subsequent invitation to Chernenko's most likely successor, Gorbachev.
On the Soviet side there was no change until after Andropov's death
in February 1984. But by that summer the feeling of KGB agents was
that Moscow was less uptight about RYAN (though the operation itself

---

[16] Andrew and Gordievsky, *KGB*, pp. 488–507, and *Comrade Kryuchkov's
Instructions. Top Secret Files on KGB Foreign Operations, 1975–1985* (paperback edn,
1993) pp. 4–6, 16–18, Chap. 4; Peter V. Pry, *War Scare. Russia and America on the
Nuclear Brink* (Westport, Con., 1999) Part 1, esp. pp. 38–41.
[17] Reagan, *An American Life*, pp. 588–9.

continued until December 1991). Also, Dobrynin says, once NATO's missile deployment had started, it 'was necessary to search for a compromise by resuming negotiations, and this applied [also] to nuclear weapons in space [SDI]. Otherwise we would miss the train. Moscow started a painful ressessment of its policy which lasted till mid-November' 1984, when Reagan's 'land-slide re-election' contributed 'in no small measure' to the decision to resume negotiations. In fact there had been contacts for some months, with Gromyko being symbolically received in the White House in September; and in January 1985 he and Secretary of State Shultz agreed that Geneva negotiations should resume in March on INF, START and, at Soviet insistence, 'preventing an arms race in space'.[18]

Reagan and Gorbachev

March 1985 also brought Chernenko's death. Reagan at once invited his successor, Gorbachev, to come and talk. Unlike Brezhnev, Andropov, and Chernenko, Gorbachev promptly agreed. The two leaders had similarities. For, like the 'Great Communicator', Gorbachev felt that a new rhetoric could transform both domestic and international society. Both men feared and disliked nuclear weapons (whereas leading contemporaries like Thatcher thought it was to these that Europe owed its long peace and security). Critics would see both Reagan's and Gorbachev's grasp of economics as vague and aspirational. But of course there were differences, not least in the crucial matter of luck. Reagan deserves credit for recognising, as his recent predecessors had not, that his was far the stronger superpower; but the contrast between the international relations of his first and of his second term shows how lucky he now was to deal with Gorbachev rather than a more stereotypical Kremlin figure like Grishin or Ligachev. Gorbachev, by contrast, was unlucky: by the time he took over, the boom in oil and gold prices that had sustained the USSR in the decade after 1973 had collapsed; in 1986 the explosion at Chernobyl, and resulting precautions in other nuclear plants, seriously constrained Soviet power supplies; and in 1988 Gorbachev's excellently received speech at, and bid for leadership in, the UN was at once undercut by an earthquake in Armenia that redirected attention to the USSR's inefficiencies and national strains.

---

[18] Dobrynin, *In Confidence*, pp. 557–61; George P. Shultz, *Turmoil and Triumph. My Years as Secretary of State* (New York, 1993) Chaps 25, 26.

The contrasts extend further. With his age, his well-publicised blunders,[19] his weak grasp of detail and laid-back work style (except, as was not widely realised, in relation to the few topics on which he chose to concentrate), and his amiable anecdotal manner, Reagan was an easy man to underestimate. Nor would his critics have been impressed had they known of his interest in apocalyptic biblical prophecies or the extent to which his schedule was shaped by his wife's astrological beliefs. But like Sir Isaiah Berlin's hedgehog, Reagan knew a few 'big' things – the USSR's weakness, both economic and ideological, and the will of the 'captive' nations of Eastern Europe to break with the systems imposed on them after 1945 if only the opportunity presented itself – whose time had come in the second half of the 1980s.[20] Reagan was also stubborn, and, as a former union official, a good negotiator.

Gorbachev was in many ways the opposite. Fluent, articulate, generally on top of his brief, and (at least in an international context) happy to argue rather than simply assert it, he represented a contrast to his predecessors that resonated well with foreigners throughout his time of office, with his compatriots for most of it. Unfortunately, when combined with a workaholic temperament and the centralised Soviet system that required Politburo approval for all manner of minor matters, this overloaded him,[21] and helps explain why he was readier to announce general propositions than to follow through on their implementation. Thus, following Azerbaijani killings of Armenians in 1988, Gorbachev told his colleagues they should have acted over the disputed territory of Nagorno-Karabakh three years ago, when the issue was first brought to Moscow's attention. Soon he was noting 'serious questions' in many other Union Republics, more especially the Baltics, and telling his colleagues 'they have to be

[19] During a 1982 tour, Reagan toasted his host as 'The President of Bolivia' when he was actually in Brazil.

[20] In 1987 Reagan challenged Gorbachev, as a test of his new policies and a move 'that would advance dramatically the cause of freedom and peace', to 'open this [Brandenburg] gate! . . . tear down this [Berlin] wall!' Gorbachev's response was that 'Whatever Ronald Reagan and other Western leaders can say on occasion, they cannot offer the slightest realistic proposition to resolve the pretended "German problem". That which has been formed by history it is better to leave to history . . . There are two German states equipped with different political and social systems' – Reeves, *Reagan*, pp. 400–1; Mikhail Gorbatchev, *Perestroika. Vues neuves sur notre pays et le monde* (Paris, 1987) p. 289.

[21] For illustrations, see Volkogonov, *Rise and Fall*, pp. 455–6 and Mikhail Gorbachev, *Memoirs* (1996) p. 409.

solved. Unless we do so, others will solve them in their own way, deciding against . . . the Union.' But then his attention shifted, and nothing was done until the Baltics had reached the point where the only alternatives were repression or secession, both of which Gorbachev found unacceptable.[22]

More fundamental, however, than overwork, or even Gorbachev's tendency to postpone hard decisions, was the fact that, though he knew what he did not want, he was less sure of what he did, or of how to get there. This was partly the product of his internal ambivalence – by 1986, his aide Chernyaev says, Gorbachev had

already formed an idea of 'new thinking.' But it was still contaminated by ideological and class mythology, and influenced by an outdated view of the situation even at that moment. And most important – it was hampered by old commitments to friends and allies as well as the duties of 'proletarian' and 'socialist' internationalism. The CPSU saw itself as the . . . guarantor of that internationalism and considered it as one of the main sources of our strength as a superpower. Hence the mixture of the new and the old, the imaginary and the real, the contradictions and inconsistencies in Gorbachev's views that I constantly encountered when reading my notes of his conversations.[23]

That, of course, was early 1986. But along with Gorbachev's historically far more important liberalisations and transformations of the Soviet system, signs remained of more traditional practices and attitudes,[24] most notably his turn in late 1990 to more authoritarian ministers (many of whom joined in the attempted coup next year) and his attempt, even after that coup, to protect the Communist Party from dissolution.

Gorbachev, then, was slower than some, though quicker than many, to break with the political culture and outlook in which he had grown up. But break he did, which meant that he increasingly came to see merit in some, at least, of the positions and values of his former Western opponents. To the extent that he did, deals and settlements were likely, even

---

[22] Anatoly Chernaev, *My Six Years with Gorbachev* (University Park, Pennsylvania, 2000) pp. 181 ff; Gorbachev, *Memoirs*, p. 333. Nor, as Gorbachev explains, was any decisive action taken over Nagorno-Karabakh, which was left to smoulder until it ignited war between post-independence Armenia and Azerbaijan.

[23] Chernyaev, *Six Years with Gorbachev*, pp. 51 ff.

[24] Many are chronicled in Volkogonov, *Rise and Fall*, pp. 453–4, 466–7, 469–71, 472–4, 479–81, 518, 520.

independently of Soviet weakness, to be on their terms, rather than on those the USSR had originally advocated.

Not, of course, that Gorbachev ever became a US Republican or a British Conservative. He remained, in his own eyes, a 'socialist', albeit an increasingly 'social-democratic' one, influenced, he says, particularly by the then Spanish Premier Felipe Gonzales. Arguably his visions of the future were cloudy and aspirational rather than concrete – certainly his 1990s conversations with his old university friend Zdenek Mlynar would suggest this. But he saw as a 'third dimension' of 'Perestroika' the changing of the conception of 'socialism' within the international communist movement. The Bolshevik–Menshevik split had deepened into a rift between Communists and Social Democrats, but the abandonment of the idea of violent revolution, and recognition of the priority of universal human values, the rule of law, and civil society opened up the possibility of overcoming it. The high point of this approach was the 'round table' of foreign Communist and Socialist Parties assembled in Moscow in 1987 to mark the seventieth anniversary of the October Revolution. Gorbachev records with pride the Finnish Communist Party secretary's declaration that his overturning of 'the old thinking' had 'removed all doubt that the CPSU could become the informal conductor of the international movement of the Left'. One wonders whether all the participants were ready to go so far. But the gathering seemed a success and there were calls for regular meetings in the future. Typically, though, this was, as Gorbachev admits, not properly followed up, despite much talk of the union of the different currents of the Left and even of 'concrete organisational measures' to establish cooperation between the CPSU and the West German SPD.[25]

Gorbachev thus looked, within the framework of 'our common European home', for communist-socialist cooperation, perhaps even a return to the post-Second World War coalitions; in this cooperation the CPSU (which continued to subsidise foreign Communist Parties) would certainly be a major player. But long before this vision could be realised, first communist Eastern Europe (in 1989) and then (in 1991) the USSR itself collapsed – a process hastened by two of Gorbachev's blind spots. One was economics – where he managed comprehensively to fall between two stools, doing enough to upset the USSR's system of central plans and controls, but always drawing back from attempts to substitute anything else. The other was an inability to appreciate the strength of nationalism, either in Eastern Europe, whose states, Gorbachev wrote in 1987, 'have

[25] Michail Gorbatschow, *Erinnerungen* (paper, 1996 edn) pp. 998–1002.

made their choice' and 'evolved towards socialism',[26] or within the USSR. Here, despite his recognition of some national grievances, he tended to go into denial, refusing to believe that people *could* wish to leave the USSR: in 1988 he told the Politburo that Ukrainian 'activists' were unable 'to make a spark', claimed that 'even the most refined among the intelligentsia have no problem' with Stalin's 1939 annexation of western Ukraine, and waxed lyrical about his personal reception in the intensely nationalist city of Lvov. It was, Chernyaev comments, 'wishful thinking, reality obscured by the comfortable old "internationalist" view.' Similarly in November 1990 Gorbachev was still maintaining, admittedly to a foreigner, that the Lithuanians realised their (recently elected) President's separatist policies

are leading to a dead end . . . They saw what nationalism did in Moldova, Azerbaijan, Armenia, Central Asia. People there . . . are realising more and more that nationalism and separatism will bring no good, that their venemous shoots have to be destroyed! You can scream about secession, but where do you go if you secede?[27]

Reality proved otherwise.

Gorbachev's policies 1985–8

In the spring of 1985, Gorbachev writes, the Soviet leadership concluded 'that the situation in the world was too dangerous to allow us to miss even the slightest chance for improvement and for more durable peace'.[28] This was certainly one of the factors underlying his subsequent moves to halt and reverse the nuclear arms race.

More controversial is the Cold War hawks' claim that the USSR was also moved by economic strains and the difficulties of competing with the US build-up. But the evidence for this is strong. On the eve of becoming General Secretary Gorbachev told his wife, 'We can't go on living like this.' That April he underlined the mess to his colleagues:

we annually lose about 30 per cent of our agricultural produce . . .
In Russia alone, two hundred million square meters of . . .
accommodation need urgent repair or have to be torn down . . .

---

[26] Gorbatchev, *Perestroika. Vues neuves*, p. 280.
[27] Chernyaev, *Six Years with Gorbachev*, pp. 191, 302.
[28] Mikhail Gorbachev, *Perestroika. New Thinking for Our Country and the World* (1988 edn) p. 225.

Plumbing and sewage facilities are strained to the limit. Over 300 cities don't have them at all. About half the streets in the Russian Republic still aren't paved.[29]

An arms race clearly would not help. Even Andropov had recognised problems, telling his East European allies that 'Probably the Soviet Union feels the burden of the arms race into which we are being pulled, more than anybody else', whereas 'It is not a big problem for Reagan to shift tens of billions of dollars of appropriations for social needs to the military-industrial complex.' Andropov had seen no 'other alternatives, except to respond to NATO's challenges'; Gorbachev attempted a different counter, his 'main target' being (in Dobrynin's words) 'to kill or neutralize Star Wars through diplomatic negotiations'.[30]

Gorbachev was not entirely consistent on defence spending – after the failed 1986 Reykjavik summit he stressed that it should not be touched.[31] Nor, despite numerous disillusioned outbursts about the USSR's Third World allies, could he bring himself to cut off their enormous subsidies until the Soviet economy imploded in 1990–1. Nevertheless, as time went on, the economic argument for pursuing disarmament was deployed more and more openly. Thus on the eve of the Reykjavik summit Gorbachev concluded a Politburo discussion by observing that 'if we won't budge from the positions we've held for a long time, we will lose in the end, because right now we're at the end of our tether'; even to get into an arms race would mean 'we can forget about all that we've said about our new policies.' Rather, Shevardnadze was to tell his Foreign Ministry officials,

the goal of diplomacy is to create a favorable environment for domestic development . . . to ensure that our state does not incur additional expenses for the maintenance of its defense capabilities . . . This means that we must search for ways to limit and reduce the military rivalry, to eliminate elements of confrontation . . . and attempt to reach a situation

---

[29] Gorbachev, *Memoirs*, p. 665; Chernyaev, *Six Years*, pp. 27–8.

[30] Andropov, 4 January 1983, in 'Did NATO Win the Cold War? Documentary Supplement to the article . . . by Vojtech Mastny' (National Security Archive Electronic Briefing Book no. 14, Document 19 p. 9); Dobrynin, *In Confidence*, pp. 564–5.

[31] Volkogonov, *Rise and Fall*, p. 494; even in 1989 Gorbachev sought, despite international agreements, to conceal his chemical weapons (Percy Cradock, *In Pursuit of British Interests. Reflections on Foreign Policy under Margaret Thatcher and John Major* (1997) pp. 100–1).

*where our interrelations with other states put the least possible burden
on our economy.*

By late 1988 Gorbachev's thinking had gone a step further, bringing
him to ask, 'Why do we need' an army of 6 million men? 'Our military
expenses are 2.5 times larger than those of the United States . . . without
reductions in the army and the military-industrial complex we won't be
able to deal with perestroika's tasks.'[32]

A third factor contributing towards the transformation of the USSR's
international posture was the wish to undercut Reagan by appealing to
Western public opinion. On Gorbachev's accession Yakovlev sent him, by
request, a memorandum arguing that Reagan's would-be summitry was
seeking 'to capture the initiative' by presenting the US as 'striving . . . to
improve the international climate'. Yakovlev recommended meeting
him to avoid creating the 'impression that it is Reagan solely, who pushes
the buttons of world development'; an alternative would be to 'use all possible factors of . . . political pressure on the United States, and first among
them . . . the interest of the Europeans in a relaxation of tensions', which
might be mobilised by proposing a general summit within the Helsinki
CSCE framework. Gorbachev chose a meeting with Reagan at Geneva; the
Politburo adjudged it a success – 'The willingness we showed for flexible
compromises . . . [has] placed the present American administration on the
defensive and landed a serious blow on the ideology and policy of their
"crusade".' Gorbachev was soon boasting that the White House Chief of
Staff had described him as an even more dangerous Soviet leader than
Andropov. Later in 1986, as US–Soviet relations seemed to be slipping
back, Gorbachev sought to jolt them out of the Cold War pattern by calling for a snap summit at which he intended to spring on Reagan a package
of radical proposals: 'The main goal of Reykjavik,' his aide Chernyaev
wrote, 'if I understand you correctly . . . is to sweep Reagan off his feet by
our bold, even "risky" approach to the central problem of world politics.
To get all we can out of an international situation currently favorable to us
for a major step toward disarmament.'[33]

---

[32] Chernyaev, *Six Years*, pp. 83, 84, 193–5 (Gorbachev); Jacques Levesque, *The
Enigma of 1980: the USSR and the Liberation of Eastern Europe* (Berkeley, CA., 1997)
p. 15n (Shevardnadze).
[33] Svetlana Savranskaya, 'Alexander Yakovlev and the Roots of the Soviet Reforms',
National Security Archive Electronic Briefing Book no. 168, Doc. 1; Volkogonov, *Rise
and Fall*, pp. 492–4; Chernaev, *Six Years*, pp. 81–2.

The initiative nearly, but not quite, succeeded. Gorbachev told the Politburo that 'After Reykjavik we have scored more points in our favour than we did after Geneva', adding angrily that the meeting 'showed that, in the representatives of the American administration, we are dealing with people who have no conscience, no morality'.[34] Two months later Yakovlev suggested following up by launching another initiative, one that would involve *Soviet* concession on the point that had blocked agreement in Iceland.[35] At Reykjavik, he wrote,

we have created an extremely important and effective beach-head *for our offensive against Reagan. Today* . . . we should expand it . . . *into* . . . *an offensive against the positions of the far right* . . . *of the active proponents of the arms race in general, while at the same time ensuring opportunities for cooperation in this sphere with* moderately conservative and liberal groups *in the US and Western Europe.*

. . . *Under the current correlation of forces, the USSR is confronting the USA not only in the international arena but also inside the US itself. Of course, we cannot elect a 'good' President for ourselves. However, we can protect ourselves from the worst. Today* . . . *[this] would mean: to increase pressure on Reagan and the circles standing behind him. Adding more flexibility and dynamism to the Soviet approach [by 'untying the [Reykjavik] package'] would strenthen such pressure.*

Yakovlev accordingly suggested proposing a 50 per cent cut in strategic weapons, INF missiles in Europe, and US 'forward-based' systems.

Will the US go for such decisions? . . . not under Reagan! *In these circumstance, our readiness for an agreement outside the [Reykjavik] 'package' would* . . .

. . . *uncover the true positions of the US, [and] become a powerful and long-term instrument of pressure on the Americans* . . .

. . . *[serve as] a stimulus to limit appropriations for SDI in the American Congress* . . . *The political and psychological effect of such a step would be very significant especially taking into account the US growing financial difficulties* . . .[36]

---

[34] 'In Reagan . . . we were fighting not only with the class enemy, but with one who is extremely primitive, has the looks of a troglodyte and exhibits mental incapacity' – Volkogonov, *Rise and Fall*, pp. 493–4.

[35] Soviet insistence on conditioning the nuclear cuts there agreed on the abandonment of Reagan's cherished SDI.

[36] Memorandum for Gorbachev, December 1986 – Savranskaya, 'Yakovlev and the Roots of Soviet Reforms', Doc. 3.

During 1987 the USSR did 'untie the package' and negotiate on nuclear matters without insisting on the abandonment of SDI. This led to an INF deal on Reagan's terms, and to Gorbachev's journey to Washington to sign the resultant treaty. In the process US–Soviet relations improved dramatically. But the Kremlin still sought to gain the high ground of international opinion by launching major initiatives involving the concession of previous Soviet positions. This culminated in Gorbachev's December 1988 speech to the United Nations endorsing liberal values, declaring that the USSR had released all political prisoners, and announcing unilateral cuts in the Soviet forces in Eastern Europe and their reconfiguration on a purely defensive basis. He was loudly applauded, and, on his return, proudly told the Politburo 'the unilateral reduction left a huge impression, and . . . created an entirely different background for perceptions of our policies and the Soviet Union as a whole', all of which alarmed US and Western conservatives; 'In the [KGB] classified information which we receive they speak directly: we cannot allow the Soviet Union to seize the initiative and lead the entire world.' Yakovlev elaborated: the Americans:

are very afraid of our European and Pacific policies. They would not like to [have to] jump on [a] departing train . . . They are used to being in the driver's seat . . .

. . . If we continue to advance in this direction . . . we will ultimately pull the rug from under the feet of the [US] military-industrial complex . . . the Americans will be forced to change their approaches radically.

The following month Moscow was visited by elder statesmen from the 'Trilateral Commission', anxious to discuss the international architecture of the new world. They wanted, Gorbachev told the Politburo, 'to channel the process in such a way as to limit as much as possible our influence on the world situation'; 'That is why we have to keep the initiative. This is our main advantage.'[37]

Arguably Gorbachev *had* gained the initiative in 1987–8, but only by making concessions that soon undermined the USSR's international standing. Gromyko was bemused, terming the new leadership 'the Martians' for their detachment from the real world, and observing that NATO must find it 'a mystery . . . why Gorbachev and his friends . . .

---

[37] 27–8 December 1988 – CWIHP *Bulletin* 12/13 (2001) esp. pp. 16–17, 24, 27. For the visit, during which Kissinger floated (with President Bush's unofficial blessing) the idea of a US–Soviet negotiation to agree the parameters and manage the evolution of Eastern Europe, see Michael Beschloss and Strobe Talbott, *At the Highest Levels. The Inside Story of the End of the Cold War* (Boston, 1993) pp. 13–17.

cannot comprehend how to use force and pressure for defending their state interests.'[38]

Gorbachev's popularity abroad soared, generating in West Germany by 1989 a degree of 'Gorby-mania' that significantly constrained Chancellor Kohl's defence policy.[39] But the really important constraint was that exercised on *Soviet* policy. For a reversion to old-style behaviour or repression risked blowing this achievement to smithereens. As Yakovlev said in 1989, when opposing Shevardnadze's plea for a resumption of air strikes in Afghanistan, 'We've made such painstaking efforts to gain international trust, we are beginning to score points because of the new thinking, and this action will dash it all.'[40] Shevardnadze had in fact internalised this argument, telling Secretary of State Baker in July 1989 that reversion to the use of force to deal with the USSR's domestic or East European problems 'would be the end of *perestroika*', 'a statement that he would repeat . . . in almost every one of their subsequent meetings'. Later it was to be the West that invoked the argument to head off a crack-down on the secessionist Baltic Republics: in January 1991 Baker explained that Germany, France and Britain had all told him this would affect their readiness to provide the economic aid the USSR increasingly needed; Congress, he added, would feel the same way:

Our ability to pursue the new relationship depends on your government upholding the principles of perestroika. I hope what we've seen [in Lithuania] doesn't represent a return to old thinking and past practices.[41]

Summitry and negotiation, 1985–8; 'Regional problems' – the Gulf, Afghanistan, Cambodia, Central America, Angola

On taking over in 1985, Gorbachev made several personnel changes, both to consolidate his power and to bring in new blood. Among these was

---

[38] CWIHP *Bulletin* 12/13 (2001) p. 10.

[39] Don Oberdorfer, *From the Cold War to a New Era. The United States and the Soviet Union, 1983–1991* (Baltimore, 1998) p. 294; Levesque, *The Enigma of 1989*, p. 26n; Margaret Thatcher, *The Downing Street Years* (1993) pp. 747, 786–7.

[40] Chernaev, *Six Years*, pp. 207–8.

[41] Oberdorfer, *From the Cold War to a New Era*, p. 360; Beschloss and Talbott, *At the Highest Levels*, p. 96; James A. Baker, *The Politics of Diplomacy. Revolution, War and Peace, 1989–1992* (New York, 1995) pp. 138–41, 239–40, 378–81.

the replacement of Foreign Minister Gromyko, who had opted for semi-retirement, not by his former deputy but by Gorbachev's long-time confidant Eduard Shevardnadze. Shevardnadze proved very different from 'Grim Grom': he began by telling his ambassadors that the diplomacy of exporting revolution was over and the time of constructive thinking had come – 'We must stop being perceived as Mr Nyet';[42] and he went on to establish personal friendships with his US counterparts (first Shultz, then Baker) that proved important in negotiations between 1987 and 1990.

Both superpowers wanted the November 1985 Geneva Summit to succeed, and settled beforehand that it should be presented as having opened the way to further meetings. Nor was this all spin. Reagan and Gorbachev struck up a degree of mutual rapport, through a combination of jokes and plain speaking (though this was *not* the case with their wives). Both leaders favoured substantial nuclear disarmament. But there was no agreement on the key issue, whether or not this should be conditioned on US abandonment of SDI. That was left for further negotiations in 1986, and these made no progress. Meanwhile Cold War frictions returned: the Krasnoyarsk radar station was in breach of the ABM treaty, and the US also questioned Soviet compliance with SALT II and itself threatened to 'break out' of the missile limits (above, pp. 67–8). A major espionage row erupted, with US arrest and Soviet counter-arrest. As this was being cleared up, Gorbachev suddenly invited Reagan to a summit in Reykjavik, intending to bounce him into a settlement. At Reykjavik Gorbachev and Reagan proved ready to agree the abolition of INF missiles in Europe, and on a 50 per cent cut in strategic missiles over five years and their complete abolition in ten. But Gorbachev conditioned this on limiting SDI research to the laboratory for ten years, while Reagan insisted on freedom, during that period, to test (though not deploy) in space. So the two parted, in a mixture of elation that they had come so far and anger at the obstinacy that had blocked agreement.

If Reykjavik failed, 1986 did bring two more positive developments. One, improbably, came from the explosion of a nuclear power station at Chernobyl. Initially Soviet politicians (including Gorbachev)[43] sought to hush it up, but the spread of radioactive material to Scandinavia made this impossible; and the episode reinforced Gorbachev's doubts about Soviet administrative culture and secrecy. More importantly the contamination brought home to leading Soviet officers the implications of nuclear war.

---

[42] *The Independent*, 6 September 1991, p. 9.
[43] Volkogonov, *Rise and Fall*, pp. 480–1.

General Yazov (Defence Minister 1987–91) later said he had believed the USSR could win such a war; but after Chernobyl he realised that even a conventional war could wreak devastation were nuclear power stations to be hit – which removed most of the attractions of the Warsaw Pact's preferred strategy, a massive invasion of Western Europe.[44] The second change came in September at the CSCE conference in Stockholm. Its predecessor in Madrid had been confrontational. Now, to build East–West confidence, it was agreed that observers from each military alliance should monitor all significant manoeuvres of the other. It is often contended that the contacts and 'engagement' this opened up between leading military figures did much to reassure them as to the intentions of their opposite numbers; actually suspicions remained quite widespread, but both Yazov and Chief of Staff Akhromeyev did play a helpful role in the East–West negotiations of the second half of the decade.

At Reykjavik Gorbachev had, in fact, been authorised to 'untie' the issues of SDI and of cuts in nuclear missiles, but had decided not to.[45] By March 1987 he had come round to making the concession, and over the course of the year an INF treaty was negotiated on the basis of Reagan's 'zero-zero' option in both Europe and Asia. This was signed that December at a Washington summit, and proved the key breakthrough. For though the Strategic Arms Reduction Treaty that was expected to follow at the May–June 1988 Moscow summit proved elusive (it was not concluded until 1991), negotiations rapidly broadened to other issues.

Gorbachev wanted to have the Soviet Union accepted by other European powers, which crystallised in 1987 into his slogan, 'Europe is our common home'. In itself this was not new – the Soviets had always contended that they were internal to Europe while the Americans were not, and the acceptance of Canada and the US as parties to the Helsinki 'Final Act' had represented a concession. But unlike his predecessors, Gorbachev came to the belief that the USSR could not really become part of Europe unless it mended its ways internally. In May 1986 he told his diplomats 'We are also changing course on humanitarian questions,' and instructed them not to put 'the words "human rights" into quotation marks . . . as

---

[44] Matlock, *Reagan and Gorbachev*, p. 12n. Gorbachev told his diplomats that while Chernobyl had, of course, been a tragedy, 'we must transform the wave of popular panic into an anti-war attitude, to the benefit of our policy-line . . . In effect, if peaceful nuclear energy is so risky, what about nuclear weapons!' (Mikhail Gorbatchev, *Avant-Mémoires* (Paris, 1993) p. 176.

[45] Gorbachev, *Memoirs*, p. 440.

pretended rights, just as if our revolution had nothing to do with them.' In December he allowed Sakharov back to Moscow from his forced residence in Gorky; this was followed in 1987–8 by the release of dissidents from prison, the much freer granting of permission to emigrate to Israel, and the ending of the jamming of the BBC and Voice of America (though not yet of *Deutsche Welle*). Already in 1986 Gorbachev had proposed the holding in 1991 of a human rights conference in Moscow, as a symbol of the USSR's new acceptability; this gave the Western powers a lever over his internal policies, something he had furiously rejected on his first visit to London. By December 1988 he had done enough to secure an Anglo-American promise to attend his conference.[46] This could, of course, always have been called off again (as might indeed have happened had his hardline policies of early 1991 continued); but in the meantime the internal transformation of the USSR did much to change Western attitudes and policies towards it.

In March 1987 Thatcher visited Moscow, and had with Gorbachev the robust arguments they both appreciated. On the utility of nuclear deterrence they remained far apart. But her criticisms of the USSR's policies in the Third World, its interventions in Eastern Europe, and its defence posture seem to have had some impact; Gorbachev told the Politburo, 'This is really something to ponder, comrades. We can't just brush it aside'; and, at least in his *Memoirs*, he conceded that Soviet 'policy toward developing countries had been highly ideological and that, to a certain extent, Mrs Thatcher had been right in her criticisms.'[47] Over the next three years Gorbachev's policies were to address these.

In the mid-1980s proxy conflicts in the Third World had been intense. The USSR wanted to extricate itself from an unpopular war in Afghanistan, but by victory; and it upped its military efforts accordingly. The USA responded by drastically increasing support for the insurgents, supplying both superior US missiles that had a devastating effect on Soviet helicopters and the products of its satellite and communications intelligence, in the hope that high Soviet casualties would lead to a withdrawal.[48]

[46] Gorbatchev, *Avant-Mémoires*, pp. 175 ff; Gail Sheehy, *Gorbachev: The Making of the Man who Shook the World* (1991) pp. 185, 242, 248–9, 284–5; *Keesing's*, 35471–2, 36413, 36440, 36490.

[47] Chernyaev, *Six Years*, pp. 101–4; Gorbachev, *Memoirs*, pp. 434–5; Thatcher, *Downing Street Years*, pp. 477–8, 481–3.

[48] Soviet supplies of military equipment etc. to Afghanistan from 1978 to 1991 have been estimated at $36–48bn, US, Saudi, and Chinese transfers to the guerrillas at $6–12bn (Steve Coll, *Ghost Wars. The Secret History of the CIA, Afghanistan, and Bin Laden,*

In Angola a 1984 disengagement agreement broke down, and in 1985 a Soviet-funded Cuban–MPLA drive on the headquarters of America's client UNITA led Congress to repeal its 1975 ban on covert US funding.[49] Vietnamese forces in Cambodia were being attacked, albeit not very effectively, by Chinese-supported and Western-countenanced guerrillas from Thailand. In Central America the USA was seeking to uphold an El Salvador regime threatened by rebels armed from Nicaragua, while itself trying to bring down the Soviet and Cuban supplied Nicaraguan government by arming and sustaining 'Contra' guerrillas. As Shultz put it in 1985, in what became known as the 'Reagan Doctrine':

For many years we have seen our adversaries act without restraint to back insurgencies around the globe to spread communist dictatorship . . . Today . . . the United States has shown the will and the strength to defend its interests, to resist the spread of Soviet influence, and to defend freedom . . .

How can we as a country say to a young Afghan, Nicaraguan, or Cambodian: 'Learn to live with oppression . . .' The forces of democracy around the world merit our standing with them . . .[50]

From 1987 onwards the superpowers started discussing these and other 'regional' conflicts, with mixed but sometimes very positive results. Early 1987 saw both countries commit forces, in the highly sensitive Persian Gulf, to the protection of Kuwaiti oil exports against Iranian attacks. Following a British initiative, the Permanent Members of the UN Security Council began to meet informally, leading in mid-1987 to a strong call for a ceasefire in the Iran–Iraq war.[51]

Over Afghanistan, the going was harder. Gorbachev had begun by warning Babrak Karmal that Soviet troops could not stay indefinitely and trying to persuade him to broaden his government by taking in some opposition figures. Making no progress, Gorbachev replaced Karmal in early 1986 by Mohammed Najibullah, but in November still felt that *'we've lost*

---

from the Soviet Invasion to September 10, 2001 (New York, 2004) p. 238). Soviet deaths in action are put at 14,453 (Radio Free Europe–Radio Liberty, *Daily Report* 29 December 1992), but there were also many thousands of incidental deaths.
[49] Shultz, *Turmoil and Triumph*, pp. 1114, 1118–19.
[50] ibid. pp. 525–6.
[51] *The Post-Imperial Age*, pp. 374–5; David Malone (ed.) *The UN Security Council. From the Cold War to the 21st Century* (2004) pp. 4–5; at the time, the passage of such a Chapter VII UN Resolution was seen as noteworthy.

time' and that on present policies things could stretch out indefinitely. By February 1987 the politburo had decided on a controlled departure, to facilitate which Gorbachev was ready to contemplate 'a deal with the Americans';[52] and first Shultz, then (at the Washington and Moscow summits) Reagan, were approached to this end. Success, however, was only limited. For though the Kremlin looked to a more inclusive Afghan government, it still insisted that this be based around Najibullah; and Shevardnadze, in particular, was sensitive to the potential dangers of Islamic extremism – a 'neutral, non-aligned Afghanistan is one thing, a reactionary fundamentalist Islamic regime is something else' – whereas their US backers still saw the *mujaheddin* simply as anti-communist freedom fighters. Moscow therefore hoped that, following the departure of Soviet troops, it would continue to arm and supply a (possibly reconstructed) Kabul government, while the USA and Pakistan cut off aid to its opponents. But Washington insisted that if Soviet aid continued, so would its own. So though an agreement was signed with international éclat in Geneva in April 1988 providing for the evacuation of Soviet forces within nine months, it was essentially a fudge. Proxy warfare continued (though now with much less news coverage).[53]

Soviet troop presence in Afghanistan had not only been anathema to Washington but had also constituted one of the 'obstacles' on whose removal Beijing insisted before it would improve relations with Moscow. Gorbachev had already made overtures to China in 1986, and he addressed another 'obstacle' by pressing his (heavily subsidised) ally Vietnam to withdraw from Cambodia.[54] Limited Vietnamese withdrawals in November 1987 touched off diffuse international negotiations. Here the USA was less central than it had been over Afghanistan; but that December Gorbachev mentioned Cambodia (along with the Persian Gulf and Central America) to Vice-President Bush as problems for which 'a suitable solution could be found', while in February 1988 Shultz listed Angola and Cambodia as ones on which 'we have agreed that there are opportunities for collaboration'. Progress was slow; but following setbacks in 1989, the US suggested attempts to reach a solution 'under the auspices of the UN Permanent Five' Security Council Members, and this led in 1991–3 to a

---

[52] Chernyaev, *Six Years*, pp. 41–2; CWIHP *Bulletin* 14–15 (2003–4) pp. 143, 146.
[53] Shultz, *Turmoil and Triumph*, pp. 987, 1086–94; Reeves, *Reagan*, pp. 443, 449, 464–5.
[54] Eduard Shevardnadze, *The Future Belongs to Freedom* (1991) p. 159; the remaining 'obstacle', Soviet troop deployments along the Chinese border, was more directly under Moscow's control.

Cambodian ceasefire, followed by a UN-supervised coalition government and elections.[55]

In Central America, where (Cuba apart) the USSR had never been very heavily involved, matters proved easier. Both the USA and the USSR endorsed the 1988 Esquipulas II agreement, worked out chiefly by Central American Presidents, whereby the USSR would end military aid to the Nicaraguan government and the USA to the Contras, while Nicaragua would hold free elections (which in 1990 the Sandinistas unexpectedly lost) and discontinue its aid to the El Salvador rebels. To tie this up in 1989, the new US Assistant Secretary for Inter-American Affairs went immediately after his Senate confirmation to meet Shevardnadze; he 'was the first, and no doubt will be the last' such Secretary 'to travel to Moscow on his first official trip.'[56]

The final 'regional conflict' featuring in the diplomacy of the time was that in Angola and Namibia. This was brought to a head by a Cuban–MPLA offensive, heavily funded by the USSR, against UNITA and South African positions in Angola. Its defeat in late 1987 was followed by a South African advance, halted in March 1988 by Cuban air superiority. This stand-off led to secret talks; and at meetings over Afghanistan and in connection with the Moscow summit Shultz pressed the USSR to join in reviving the unimplemented 1979 UN settlement of Namibia. With the US pressing South Africa and the USSR Cuba, a deal was signed in December 1988 providing for South African withdrawal to Namibia, UN-conducted Namibian independence elections and a phased Cuban withdrawal from Angola. But with the South Africans gone from Angola, late 1989 brought a further MPLA offensive, halted by emergency US arms supplies to UNITA. Meanwhile 'in every meeting with . . . Shevardnadze in 1989 and 1990', Baker urged joint US–USSR promotion of negotiations. In December 1990 Shevardnadze suddenly suggested that the two powers themselves devise a plan and try to sell it to their clients; this led in May 1991 to a settlement on the basis of full Cuban withdrawal and of UN-monitored Angolan elections.[57]

[55] CWIHP *Bulletin* 14–15 (2003–4) pp. 168, 170; Baker, *The Politics of Diplomacy*, p. 588; *Post-Imperial Age*, pp. 219–20.

[56] Soviet arms supplies to Nicaragua ended at the start of 1989, though Cuban ones continued, as did some Sandinista ones to the El Salvador rebels even after the change of Nicaraguan government – Shultz, *Turmoil and Triumph*, pp. 959 ff; Baker, *The Politics of Diplomacy*, pp. 59, 81; *Post-Imperial Age*, p. 417n.

[57] Shultz, *Turmoil and Triumph*, pp. 1123–9; Baker, *Politics of Diplomacy*, pp. 599–600; *Post-Imperial Age*, pp. 74–5.

The transformation of Eastern Europe, 1989[58]

The unprecedented agreements of the years following 1987 seemed to confirm that international relations were led and energised by the rapport between the superpowers. Gorbachev clearly felt this both could and should continue. He spelt out his vision in December 1989 during his first summit with President Bush:

the US and USSR are simply 'doomed' to dialogue, coordination and cooperation. There is no other choice.

But to do this we need to get rid of the view of one another as enemies . . .

All this means that we're proposing a Soviet–American condominium. [In this] We're talking about realities . . .

. . . I stress that a special responsibility rests on the Soviet Union and the United States at this historic moment.[59]

The vision had substance. But it was already eroding in parallel with the USSR's power-political position; for as what proved to be his last three years in office unfolded, Gorbachev increasingly found himself no longer initiating events but reacting to external developments. By the end, he had come close to a position of dependence.

East–West diplomacy in Gorbachev's early years had revolved around 'strategic' military questions and extra-European 'regional' conflicts. Westerners were anxious to foster forces for change in Eastern Europe – in a visit to Poland in 1988 (wearing green, the colour of hope), Thatcher urged the government to legalise Solidarity and Solidarity to join in round-table negotiations; however, expectations were generally not of the collapse of the East European system but, at best, of gradual evolution in ways that did not provoke renewed clamp-downs as in 1956, 1968, and 1981.

In the Kremlin there were worries, stimulated chiefly by the USSR's economic weakness: in October 1988 Shakhnazarov, the man chiefly responsible for policy towards Eastern Europe, asked Gorbachev to 'reflect on how we will react if one or several countries become bankrupt . . . Could the socialist countries come out of the pre-crisis situation without Western assistance? What price will they have to pay for this assistance?' Reflection did not go very far. In January 1989 Yakovlev called for reports

---

[58] See also below, Chap. 15.

[59] Chernyaev's notes (CWIHP *Bulletin* 12–13 (Fall 2001) pp. 233, 240.

on developments in Eastern Europe. But in March Gorbachev seemed fatalistic: Poland appeared to be 'crawling away from us . . . what can we do? Poland has a $56 billion debt. Can we take Poland on our balance sheet in our current economic situation? No. And if we cannot – then we have no influence.'[60]

Past Soviet influence had rested largely on the use of force, or more usually on the fear that force would be used if necessary. But already in 1981 the USSR, though very anxious that the Polish army should repress Solidarity, refused itself to commit troops whatever the outcome (below, pp. 575–6). In 1988–9 there was no high-level disposition to use force – all three of the reports Yakovlev had commissioned were clear that it would be disastrous for the USSR to do so. However, two also stressed the desirability of preserving 'a certain vagueness' on the subject 'so that we do not stimulate the anti-socialist forces . . . to "test" the fundamentals of socialism in a given country.' Of course such 'vagueness' could never be wholly dispelled, since leaders may change their minds in a crisis (as Khrushchev had done in 1956). But Gorbachev did his best, declaring (in 1988 at the UN) 'that force and the threat of force can no longer be . . . instruments of foreign policy . . . Freedom of choice is a universal principle to which there should be no exceptions.' In 1989 growing numbers of East Europeans became ready both to take him at his word and to make the greater gamble that their own governments would back down rather than use force to preserve their authority.[61]

Following a deal with Solidarity, the Polish elections in June were designed to leave the communists in control. But they polled so badly that their satellite parties began to break away; the outcome in August was a Solidarity-led government in which the Communists proved no more than junior partners. Gorbachev made no objections. The upset was such that the new Prime Minister fainted during his own installation ceremony, nor was the shock confined to Poland. Hungary, which no longer stopped its own citizens visiting Austria, accepted 500 million DM from West Germany to let East German holidaymakers do likewise; when notified, Shevardnadze did not object. But there ensued a flood of emigrants and would-be emigrants from East to West Germany. Another unsettling factor was the approach of the DDR's fiftieth anniversary in October. Anti-regime demonstrations mounted in the industrial south. Honecker may have been ready to repress them; but his colleagues were not, and he

[60] CWIHP *Bulletin* 12–13 (2001) pp. 10–11, 15, 52–72.
[61] ibid. pp. 29, 66, 70.

was replaced as leader by Egon Krenz, who at once flew to Moscow. While there, he told Gorbachev he would revise the arrangements governing foreign travel. The revision was handled so badly that, on the evening of 9 November, massive crowds of East Berliners assembled at the border believing it had already been opened; at 11.30 p.m. border guards, swamped and unbriefed, stood aside, and the crowds poured through amid huge emotional celebrations. The reaction next morning of Gorbachev's aide Chernyaev was:

The Berlin Wall has collapsed. This entire era in the history of the Socialist system is over . . . it has to do not only with 'socialism' but with the shift in the world balance of forces. This is the end of Yalta . . .[62]

Many East Europeans agreed; and by the end of 1989 the leaders of the other People's Democracies had been replaced in a domino effect – in Czechoslovakia by former dissidents, brought to power in a 'velvet revolution' of massive demonstrations followed by round-table talks, in Bulgaria by a communist rival, but with the aid of 'Ecoglasnost' demonstrations, and in Romania by what now appears to have been an army-backed coup. Only in Romania did the security forces resist, but there there was appreciable fighting. Such was the United States' new confidence in Gorbachev's intentions that it even suggested Soviet military intervention to ensure the revolution's success. The feeler drew a reiteration of the USSR's stand 'against interference in the domestic affairs of other states', and, in reference to the recent US invasion of Panama, the barbed addition that 'the American side may now consider that "the Brezhnev Doctrine" is now theirs as a gift.'[63]

German reunification 1989–90

The CDU had opposed Brandt's Ostpolitik, but on coming to power it continued both close contacts with and large loans to the East German government, even playing the DDR national anthem during Honecker's 1987 visit. Chancellor Kohl did reaffirm his belief in self-determination and German unity, but with no expectation that this would come any time soon. East Germany's troubles in 1989 changed things: in August Kohl

[62] CWIHP *Bulletin* 12–13 (2001) pp. 19–20, 136–8.
[63] CWIHP *Bulletin* 11 (1998) p. 191; the USA had invaded Panama on 20 December to arrest President Noriega for drug-running, so preventing him from murdering US servicemen stationed there and restoring democracy.

declared the German question 'back on the international agenda'; in September he told his party colleagues that the end of communism was coming and the 'idea of one Germany' closer than ever.[64] Eastern bankruptcy was soon to give him a lever. On a visit to Moscow, shortly after taking over from Honecker, the new leader, Krenz, told Gorbachev the DDR's foreign debt would soon stand at $26.5 billion, with an annual hard currency deficit of $12.1 billion. Gorbachev was 'Astonished . . . He had not imagined the situation to be so precarious.' Nor could he help much; as he said in another context, the USSR 'could do very little in economic terms. It was an absurdity to think that the Soviet Union could support 40 million Poles.' Accordingly the DDR sought substantial West German loans, and was told that if it wanted them it must 'declare publicly that the DDR is prepared to guarantee that opposition groups will be permitted and . . . that free elections will be held within a period to be announced'.[65] Two days later the situation was further transformed by the opening of the Wall.

On 28 November 1989, with prior notice to the USA but no other international consultation, Kohl launched a pre-emptive 'Ten Point Plan' for the two Germanies to move through inter-governmental cooperation (the endpoint wished by the DDR) to 'confederative structures' between the two states (after free elections in the East), and thence to their reunification. This touched off a wide-ranging debate, informed by the history of the previous century, about the future of Germany and its implications for the architecture of a new Europe. Until its substantial resolution in July 1990, this constituted the most salient international issue. As discussions proceeded, the tempo increased and timescales steadily shortened under pressure from the growing flood of migrants from the East – 'if we didn't want them to go to the D-Mark,' Kohl told his MPs, 'then the D-Mark would have to go to the [East German] people'. Soon afterwards, when Gorbachev asked about his timescale for reunification, Kohl replied that that 'could not be answered. At the end of December [1989] he had spoken of years, but in the meantime the people had voted with their feet.'[66]

---

[64] President Bush also spoke favourably of German reunion – Philip Zelikow and Condoleeza Rice, *Germany Unified and Europe Transformed* (Cambridge, Mass., 1997 edn) pp. 79–81.

[65] CWIHP *Bulletin* 12–13 (2001) pp. 144–5, 152–3.

[66] Horst Teltschik, *329 Tage. Innenansichten der Einigung* (Berlin, 1991) pp. 129, 139–40 (6 and 10 February 1990); on 3 December Kohl had spoken of East and West German federation 'in years, perhaps five', and scouted Kissinger's suggestion of

The debate was largely confined to the major Powers. For the United States feared that if too many players were involved, and particularly if (as the USSR sometimes wished) it was thrown into the pan-European CSCE forum where each state had a veto, it might drag on indefinitely. Also West Germans could be brusque with lesser allies, Foreign Minister Genscher at one point snapping at his Italian counterpart, 'You are not part of the game.'[67] Britain and France could not be so brushed aside, since both had sovereignty in West Berlin and other rights deriving from Potsdam. Like their Dutch and Italian counterparts, Thatcher and Mitterrand were alarmed by the prospective re-emergence of a power larger and economically more dynamic than either. At least initially both feared, on the basis of past history, that this might open up 'a Pandora's box of border changes right through central Europe.' Both also felt the disappearance, as opposed to the reform and democratisation, of East Germany would alarm Soviet traditionalists, and so end both Gorbachev's career and the emancipation of Eastern Europe. From November 1989 to January 1990 they often voiced such fears to each other, Mitterrand observing that 'at moments of great danger in the past France had always established special relations with Britain and he felt such a time had come again'.[68] But, as Mitterrand also recognised, there was little that either country could do. At times he spoke of a 'return to 1913', that is of a Franco-Russian-British alliance to contain Germany. However, that required Gorbachev's readiness to pull Franco-British chestnuts out of the fire by blocking reunion, and of this Mitterrand became less and less hopeful – 'Gorbachev tells me he'll be firm, and then gives up on everything' (February 1990); 'I'd enjoy' helping him resist 'if I thought he would. But why clash with Kohl if Gorbachev will only drop me three days later?' (May).[69] And on their fall-back positions, once Germany was clearly going to reunite, Thatcher and Mitterrand diverged sharply.

reunion in two as economically risky (ibid. p. 63; Zelikow and Rice, *Germany Unified*, p. 131).

[67] Zelikow and Rice, *Germany Unified*, p. 193. For the process of reunification, see also Kristina Spohr, 'German Unification: Between Official History, Academic Scholarship, and Political Memoirs', *Historical Journal*, xliii (2000) and Hannes Adomeit, *Imperial Overstretch: Germany in Soviet Policy from Stalin to Gorbachev* (Baden-Baden, 1998) pp. 438–558.

[68] Thatcher, *Downing Street Years*, pp. 796–8.

[69] Spohr, 'German Unification', p. 877; Zelikow and Rice, *Germany Unified*, pp. 205–6; Adomeit, *Imperial Overstretch*, pp. 459–60; Jacques Attali, *Chronique des Anrees 1988–91*, Verbatim iii (Paris, 1995).

Thatcher was fully in accord with Bush and Kohl that Germany must be firmly anchored in NATO; while not opposed in principle, Mitterrand was readier to oblige Gorbachev, as when he suggested in May placing Germany, like France, outside NATO's integrated command structure. Mitterrand looked rather to tie Germany into an upgraded EC. He therefore pushed at an accelerating pace for what eventually became the 1991 Maastricht Treaty (below pp. 507–8), enhancing the Community's 'federal' (i.e. supranational) elements and, in particular, paving the way for the replacement of the DM by a currency (in the event the euro) whose management would lie not with the Bundesbank but with Community institutions where French influence would be stronger. In general Kohl approved; but the DM was understandably popular in Germany, and Kohl had earlier been ambivalent about moves towards a common currency; he now abandoned such reservations. However, if both Mitterrand and Kohl saw the locking of Germany into a 'federal' EC framework as a safeguard, Thatcher did not; she felt the German Gulliver would not be tied down in Europe, but placed in a framework through which he would inevitably tend to dominate Europe, even *malgré lui*.[70] Mitterrand therefore found compensations for his inability to slow German reunion; Thatcher did not. But in the unification process itself neither was more than marginal.[71]

The key players were West Germany and the United States (whose positions were remarkably close) on the one hand, and the USSR on the other. Bonn and Washington were keen for self-determination to take its course. Both held that Germany must remain anchored in NATO; as NATO's Secretary-General, a former CDU politician, put it, were Germany not kept in alliance ' "the old Pandora's box of competition and rivalry in Europe could be reopened" '; a 'neutral or disaffected Germany would be tempted to float freely and bargain with both East and West. The EC and CSCE were all talk. Nothing could replace NATO as the only stable security structure.' Similarly Kohl told a highly receptive Bush that 'If the Europeans allowed the Americans to leave, it would be a . . . defeat on the scale of Wilson's failure to keep the United States engaged in Europe after World War I.' Europe needed not only a military but, above all, a political US presence; however 'There could be no NATO' to secure this 'without American troops in . . . Germany. The CSCE could not substitute for

---

[70] Thatcher, *Downing Street Years*, p. 791.

[71] After the two first 'Two plus Four' reunion negotiation meetings, no press questions were addressed to either the French or the British (Zelikow and Rice, *Germany Unified*, p. 367).

NATO. Were NATO dissolved, the security of the small European states like Norway or the Benelux countries would be endangered.' And not only of the smaller countries, Baker tried to persuade Shevardnadze: though 'that might be hard for you to believe . . . the risk comes not from the United States, which for a long time you've seen as your enemy, but . . . from a neutral Germany that becomes militaristic'; a Germany anchored in NATO, with a continued US presence, would be far safer.[72] Both Kohl and the Americans pushed hard for such a solution, seeing themselves in a position of strength. 'To hell with that,' Bush observed in February 1990 of Soviet objections to continued German NATO membership, 'We prevailed and they didn't. We can't let the Soviets snatch victory from the jaws of defeat.'[73] Both leaders were sensitive about the danger to Gorbachev's domestic position and anxious to let him down lightly. But in the last resort they saw his weakness as a reason to move fast, before there could be changes in the Kremlin. Foreign policy, Kohl used to say, was like mowing grass for hay – you had to gather what you had cut in case of a thunderstorm; if German unity did not come now, there would not be another opportunity in his lifetime.[74]

Moscow's strength lay in its military presence in East Germany. But it found itself driven back from one position to another. A pre-emptive offer of unification on the basis of German neutrality would have proved hard to resist: as late as February 1990 a poll suggested that 58 per cent of West Germans favoured a reunited Germany outside both NATO and the Warsaw Pact, and the West and East German Social Democratic Parties jointly proposed this.[75] There were many reasons why the USSR played its cards badly. Initially it expected a reformed Communist Party to stabilise the DDR. By January 1990 this was out of the question; but the USSR still looked (not unreasonably, given the opinion polls) to an SDP victory in the East German elections, only to see the CDU triumph on 18 March. Also once Moscow had conceded in January that there should be some kind of reunion, it was bound to find it harder than Bonn or Washington to define the security outcome it desired. They could simply say the enlarged Germany should remain within its existing, functioning alliance; but the Warsaw Pact was already showing signs of collapse, and Gorbachev was, during 1990, in two minds as to whether to demand the preservation of

[72] Zelikow and Rice, *Germany Unified*, pp. 180–2, 256; Teltschik, *329 Tage*, p. 238.
[73] Zelikow and Rice, *Germany Unified*, p. 215.
[74] Zelikow and Rice, *Germany Unified*, p. 255; Teltschik, *329 Tage*, p. 239.
[75] Zelikow and Rice, *Germany Unified*, p. 203.

both NATO and the Pact until some new pan-European security architecture could be devised within the framework of the (hitherto purely consultative) CSCE, or to press for the rapid winding up of both alliances and their replacement by a new system. Nor indeed did Moscow ever proceed beyond talking of such a system to tabling definite proposals for one.

The USSR did, admittedly, have an alternative, the revival of Four Power preparation of a German peace treaty, no doubt incorporating some security restrictions, as envisaged at Potsdam. This had some appeal to France, but West Germany was determined not to risk the imposition of another external *diktat* reminiscent of 1919 and the USA backed it. The upshot was the so-called 'Two plus Four' arrangements: the two German states (both, as it proved, headed by the CDU) would negotiate the internal aspects of reunion; external aspects and implications would come to the four Potsdam Powers, but the USA (generally supported by Britain) managed to ensure that this would be for discussion and diplomatic good offices, not (as the USSR had hoped) for decision and imposition.

Furthermore, Soviet diplomacy suffered from a lack of focus. In part this simply reflected pressure of events – one official said 'I come to work every day to see what new disaster has befallen us'.[76] Not until January 1990 was a systematic review conducted of policy towards Germany, and not until May was the ambassador to West Germany brought back to coordinate things at the executive level. He found only what he later called a 'surrealistic jumble of ideas'.[77]

Part of the difficulty was that German policy was as much an internal as an external problem. Gorbachev was probably not that worried about a unified Germany *per se*: he told Baker in February there was 'nothing terrifying in the prospect'; it might worry Britain and France, but 'We are big countries and have our own weight.'[78] The trouble was, though, that it also worried Soviet traditionalists, the German experts in the Foreign Ministry, and the military. Ligachev, for instance, told a Central Committee Plenum in February:

The socialist commonwealth is falling apart, NATO is gaining strength . . .

It would be an unforgiveable . . . mistake not to see that a Germany with immense economic and military potential has begun to loom on the

[76] ibid. pp. 160–1.
[77] ibid. p. 260.
[78] ibid. pp. 182–4.

world horizon . . . the time has come to realize this new danger of our time . . .

As Shevardnadze explained to Baker, Soviet traditionalists once 'had their Wall, their Honecker, their security guarantees – what's it going to be now? They want to know.'[79] No doubt internal difficulties were sometimes highlighted to strengthen the Soviet negotiating position; but they seem to have been genuine – Gorbachev's final decision to settle followed closely his successful surmounting of a difficult Party Congress in July.

Well before that, however, he had undermined the credibility of Soviet positions by his requests for financial aid: an 8 January he asked Kohl for food (securing a promise of $100 million worth on the 24th; in May the West Germans were informed that the USSR needed an immediate loan of 1.5 to 2 billion DM, with a further 10–15 billion DM to follow soon, and Shevardnadze did not demur when told that this could come only as part of an overall settlement; Gorbachev followed up by asking the USA for $20 billion. Surprisingly, when Gorbachev agreed to settle during Kohl's July visit, questions of money were not raised. But they returned in September, when the USSR put in for 36 billion DM as a condition for implementing that agreement; haggling ensued until a deal was struck on the basis of 15 billion DM, two days after which the final reunion treaty was signed.[80]

On 9 December 1989 Gorbachev had promised 'no harm will come to the DDR. It is our strategic ally and a member of the Warsaw Treaty.'[81] During 1990 the state began to fall apart, with its secret police headquarters sacked and state enterprises and structures collapsing – West Berlin was asked to take over garbage collection in the rest of the city. Such developments prompted a high-level Kremlin reassessment, at which the options presented ranged from military intervention[82] to the adoption of Kohl as Moscow's preferred German partner. In February Gorbachev told Kohl reunification was for the Germans themselves to decide – though the USSR continued to hope for a slower and more confederal outcome than the simple adhesion to the Federal Republic that the newly elected East German government called for in April. But the chief Soviet effort now switched to limiting the shift in the European power balance this would entail. Initially

[79] ibid. pp. 180, 192.
[80] ibid. pp. 258–9, 265, 351–2, 359, 417n; Teltschik, *329 Tage*, pp. 231–2.
[81] Zelikow and Rice, *Germany Unified*, p. 137.
[82] ibid. p. 425n.

it sought German neutralisation and demilitarisation, with a fall-back position that *if* Western Germany were to remain in NATO at least there should be no NATO presence in the former DDR. Before a summit in May–June, a cartoon depicted Bush as a waiter reciting the menu to Gorbachev: 'there's Germany in NATO sauce, Germany à la NATO, Germany avec Crème NATO, Germany NATO Flambé . . . what will you have?'; to which the reply was, 'Indigestion'. Actually Gorbachev accepted the formula that 'the matter of alliance membership is, in accordance with the Helsinki Final Act, a matter for the Germans to decide.'[83]

But this did not seem to alter the Soviet negotiating position; and as the two Germanies moved rapidly towards reunion – on 28 May Kohl and the DDR Premier de Maizière agreed on economic union (with the DM as the currency), on 2 July on full union before the end of the year – there was a danger that the USSR might just dig in, asserting its military presence and Four Power rights under Potsdam. Shevardnadze, never happy with this approach, attributed it in late June to 'our domestic situation'. He said it was 'not easy to convince our people today of what we're doing', and added that much would depend on the attitude NATO took at its forthcoming conference. The US response was a mixture of pressure – Shevardnadze was told that 'In the final analysis Germany will unify . . . and I hope you will not be isolated in opposition to German sovereignty' – and copious reassurance.[84] At the London NATO conference in early July, the US drove through a communiqué full of warm words 'for the countries of the East which were our adversaries in the Cold War', asserting that 'We will never in any circumstances be the first to use force', proposing a joint declaration with the Warsaw Pact 'that we are no longer adversaries', and promising to de-emphasise nuclear weapons, to move away from 'forward defence', and to enhance the political (as distinct from the military) side of the alliance.[85]

Though some scepticism might have been in order,[86] the NATO communiqué seems to have made a considerable impact in Moscow;[87] and following a successful Party Congress, Gorbachev struck a deal with Kohl during the latter's stage-managed visit to Moscow, to Gorbachev's home

---

[83] ibid. pp. 281, 290.
[84] ibid. pp. 286, 295–300.
[85] *Keesing's*, 37599–600; Zelikow and Rice, *Germany Unified*, pp. 303–24.
[86] Though NATO had never used force before 1990, it did so in 1999 (without UN sanction) to drive Serbian troops and administration out of Kosovo.
[87] Zelikow and Rice, *Germany Unified*, pp. 330–2, 336–7.

town of Stavropol, and to the Caucasus on 15–16 July. A reunified Germany might choose to stay in NATO, but would not, during the three to four years Soviet troops remained there, station in the former DDR any forces integrated into NATO's command structure. Germany would continue its renunciation of nuclear, chemical and biological weapons, and, as further reassurance, would *reduce* its armed forces (Kohl promised to 370,000, a lower figure than Gorbachev had expected). Kohl also undertook that, after incorporating the DDR and Berlin, the Federal Republic would expand no further, and would modify its constitution accordingly.[88] After last-minute financial haggling, this was cast in September into the form of a Four Power treaty with the two Germanies, with unification taking effect on 3 October.

The Treaty on Conventional Forces in Europe (November 1990); The USSR's weakness, troubles and collapse in 1991

The 'German question' had dominated the first half of 1990. In August attention was switched abruptly to the Middle East by Iraq's sudden seizure of Kuwait (*Post-Imperial Age*, pp. 375 ff). Such had been the transformation of international relations that the US and Soviet Foreign ministers staged a joint press conference to denounce this; and, despite the reluctance of officials who had worked closely with the Iraqi regime, the USSR joined in the UN votes requiring withdrawal. Meanwhile the process of winding up the Cold War in Europe continued with a CSCE conference in November. In a genuflection towards Soviet aspirations for a new security architecture, a 'Charter of Paris for a New Europe' provided for annual CSCE meetings at heads of government level, for a secretariat to organise them, for a Conflict Prevention Centre, and for an Office for Free Elections; only the last has ever amounted to much. The conference also provided a venue for NATO and the Warsaw Pact to conclude a treaty on Conventional Forces in Europe, providing for equal and inspected weapons ceilings for both sides west of the Urals, and incorporating a declaration that the signatories 'are no longer adversaries'. The treaty

[88] ibid. pp. 336–42; Adomeit, *Imperial Overstretch*, pp. 524–8. This further guaranteed Poland's Oder–Neisse border, which Kohl had (for electoral reasons) been disconcertingly slow to endorse in public – though he had done so from March onwards under pressure from both Genscher and Western and Polish leaders (Zelikow and Rice, *Germany Unified*, pp. 218–19, 222, 230).

represented the Warsaw Pact's swan-song, since the Hungarian Prime Minister (with Czech support) told the conference its members had decided to dissolve it by 1992; and November 1990 represents as good a date as any for the ending of the Cold War.[89]

Most European Cold War issues had thus been settled on Western terms. Elsewhere these changes reduced the appeal of the Soviet model – thus in March 1990 Mengistu of Ethiopia suddenly discovered that socialism had been a mistake. They also reduced Soviet ability to support former clients. In 1990 aid to Ethiopia was first scaled down and then stopped; aid to Vietnam was similarly cut.[90]

This growing weakness did not destroy the value the Bush administration set on cooperation with the USSR. Indeed, Secretary of State Baker enjoyed an excellent relationship with Shevardnadze until the latter's resignation in December 1990, and at least a correct one with his successor. When fighting actually started in Iraq in 1991 Moscow showed itself uncomfortable, but it never quite broke ranks. One restraining factor may have been a $4 billion credit obtained in October 1990 from Saudi Arabia through US good offices.[91] There seems also to have been some sort of tacit understanding that the USSR would not break with the Gulf War coalition, and that the US would not, at least overtly, press it over actions taken to bring the secessionist Baltic Republics to heel.

Most Western countries showed a marked reluctance to deal with Yeltsin and the other republics' leaders for fear of undercutting Gorbachev, with whom they now felt very comfortable. They were, however, divided on how far they should go towards bailing him out economically. Germany (anxious that nothing should upset the agreements for the withdrawal of Soviet forces from its territory) and France were favourable. Japan, in fact the only country in a position to make massive loans, came close to working out a deal extending $22 billion of credits and aid in return for at least private Soviet promises to return the four disputed islands off Hokkaido (*Post-Imperial Age*, pp. 170–2); but Gorbachev turned the idea down, and Japan adopted a correspondingly tough line on aid.[92] The USA and UK

---

[89] The Pact's military structures were dissolved in March 1991, its political ones in July – *Keesing's*, 37858, 37979, 1992 R160.

[90] *Keesing's*, 37310, 37368, 38053 (Ethiopia – Mengistu's regime collapsed in 1991); *The Independent*, 23 February 1991 p. 11 (Vietnam).

[91] Baker, *Politics of Diplomacy*, pp. 294–5.

[92] Adomeit, *Imperial Overstretch*, pp. 556–8; CWIHP *Bulletin* 10 (1998) pp. 194–5, 200–2.

took the line that aid would be useless unless Gorbachev introduced real economic reforms. As so often before he recoiled from this, and in July 1991 presented the Western G7 leaders with a fudged plan. In return they resolved to recommend the USSR for associate, not full, membership of the International Monetary Fund, a status that would enable it to receive guidance but not to borrow from the Fund. Another setback was Gorbachev's wish to join the G7.[93] Again he encountered some sympathy; but the final compromise decision was that, at least for 1991, he should meet the Western leaders, but only after the completion of their formal summit.

In these dealings, Gorbachev had shown a desire to join the leading Western institutions. But, by doing so from a position of economic weakness, he had assumed the role of a 'demandeur' and had made the USSR to some extent the subject of international diplomacy. In August hardliners sought to depose him and turn the clock back. Their failure prompted an internal upheaval, the banning of the Communist Party. In September 1991 Baker returned to Moscow, chiefly to offer support to both Gorbachev and Yeltsin, but also to 'lock in' gains by suggesting that Western assistance with the USSR's debt would be far more likely if all aid to foreign communist regimes were ended. 'Yes,' replied Gorbachev wryly, 'we spent eighty-two billion dollars on ideology'; Yeltsin and he agreed to withdraw troops from Cuba and to end all aid both to Cuba and to Najibullah in Afghanistan by the end of the year.[94]

For the time being the USSR had turned from being a world power to sorting out its own internal problems. In December 1991 the process went further, with the Republics ending the Soviet Union and assuming full sovereignty. For over a decade, against a background of low energy prices and both economic and political weakness, the largest, Russia, assumed a relatively low international profile – from which, in 2006, it was starting to emerge, on the basis of firmer (if less liberal) government, economic recovery on the back of high oil prices, and the prospect of using its position as an oil and gas supplier and its control over pipelines to exert influence abroad through 'energy diplomacy'.

---

[93] The seven economically largest capitalist countries, whose heads of government hold annual summits and whose finance ministers and central bankers meet more often and inconspicuously. Russia joined what then became the G8 in 1997, though Finance Ministers continued to meet without it.

[94] Baker, *Politics of Diplomacy*, pp. 528–9. Castro's regime survived, Najibullah's did not.

PART 3

Europe West and East, and the Sino–Soviet split

CHAPTER 11

Western Europe I:
The political order

The liberal political order

Though the Cold War assumed global dimensions, it began
(apart from the 1946 Iran crisis) in Europe; and it ended
with the transformation of Eastern Europe in and after 1989. So it is
appropriate, in chronicling it, to devote rather more space to Europe than
to any other continent. In fact Europe enjoyed remarkable stability from
1945–89, but within the framework of a division into communist and
capitalist halves. Chapters 14 and 15 will consider the USSR's attempts to
organise and transform its half of Europe. Here we discuss the more complicated, though less dramatic, evolution of Western Europe. Some of its
problems resembled those of its Eastern counterpart, notably the creation
of viable political systems and the establishment and maintenance of an
acceptable relationship with 'its' superpower. But it also needed to find
ways of preventing the recurrence of the national rivalries that had earlier
had such dreadful consequences, while still building on the sovereign states
that had been restored with Liberation and that were joined within a
decade by the ex-enemy countries of the Second World War. It proved
remarkably successful. Western Europe has not, in modern history, known
so long a period of peace, nor so great a measure of prosperity. Naturally
there were many causes. As these were mutually reinforcing, they cannot
be ranked in any definite order of importance; probably, indeed, a general
harmony could have been achieved even had one or two of them been
absent. One can say, though, that there has (so far) been no such unravelling as befell the European system of the later 1920s, a system that had
seemed, with the Locarno treaties, to have crossed 'the real dividing line
between the years of war and the years of peace'.

Very possibly the chief factor in Western Europe's post-1945 success has been the prevalence of an internal liberal political order. Certainly in no major state has such an order, once established, collapsed, as it did in Italy in 1922 and in Germany in 1933. (Rather the process ran the other way, with Portugal making a tortuous and Spain a surprisingly easy transition to liberal democracy in the 1970s.)[1] We have space for only the most cursory glance at domestic politics, but one influence after 1945 was a determination not to repeat past mistakes. This did not always work – despite constitutional reform, French politics soon returned to a Third Republican mould. But the Federal Republic did not go back to the ways of Weimar Germany, while in Austria the Socialists and the People's Party, instead of literally fighting like their inter-war predecessors, shared power in order to recover national sovereignty. We should also note that two great political forces, Catholicism and socialism, which had, in important countries, been ambivalent about the earlier liberal political order, now embraced it. In Italy and West Germany, indeed, the Christian Democrats had by the 1950s become the ruling party, while their counter-part the Popular Republican Movement (MRP) featured in virtually all French governments. The Socialists' evolution was less dramatic: the German SPD had already strongly supported the Weimar Republic, while the French party (the SFIO) had between the wars formed part of electoral alliances of the Left though only rarely of subsequent coalition governments. In Italy, where the Socialists had never really been incor-porated into the pre-fascist liberal order, they initially sided, during the Cold War, with the Communists against the system; and it was not until 1963 that the 'opening to the left' brought them into the governmental coalition.

The challenge of communism: the French and Italian Communist Parties

Mention of the Communists points up another challenge to the liberal order. It is, admittedly, arguable that, for at least the first two post-war decades, the perceived threat from 'international communism' was a stab-ilising factor, reminding those of other persuasions how much they had in common despite differences that had once seemed all-engrossing. Experience of Communist rule in East Germany also cut the Party's appeal

---

[1] John W. Young, *Cold War Europe 1945–89. A political history* (1991) Chap. 6.

in the rest of the country.[2] More generally, Western Communist Parties were upset by the developments of 1956, so much so that when the French leader heard that Khrushchev meant to rehabilitate Bukharin and Zinoviev, he rushed to Moscow to warn that, 'After the 20th Congress and the Hungarian events we lost almost half our Party. If you were formally to rehabilitate those who were tried in the open trials, we could lose the rest.'[3] Still the Communists were the largest party in France and the second largest in Italy; to begin with both behaved as arms of the Soviet Union, reversing their domestic policies in 1947 in accordance with Cominform dictates (see pp. 138–9). In neither country did they seem likely to gain power (though the US ambassador to Italy worried about the long-run implications of the Christian Democrats' decline from their 1948 electoral peak). But in both they contributed greatly to governmental instability; for, given their constant opposition plus that of the far Right,[4] it needed only a few extra critics to bring an administration down.

The French Communist Party (PCF) remained remarkably loyal to Moscow: a brief attempt to distance itself by such moves as abandoning its commitment to the 'dictatorship of the proletariat' in 1976 ended in 1980 with the party's endorsement of Soviet intervention in Afghanistan. Over the years its domestic support fell sharply. It dropped 1.5 million votes on the first ballot of the 1958 elections, and was trounced by the Gaullists on the second. In 1969 its candidate (though outvoting the Socialist) only managed third place in the presidential elections; it was clear that the Left could compete only if it came together. This was achieved in 1972 when the Communists, Socialists and Left Radicals settled on a 'Common Programme' of government and agreed to campaign together. In this alliance the Communists could hope for influence as the largest party. But the Socialist leader Mitterrand soon stated that his aim was to overtake the PCF and 'rebuild a great Socialist Party on the terrain occupied by the Communist Party itself and thus to show that of five million Communist voters three million can be brought to vote Socialist'.[5] By 1981 he had largely achieved this, helped by the PCF's return to the Soviet line and by its attacks on himself, which had the effect of convincing the electorate that he was not a Communist puppet. At the first ballot of the 1981

[2] It won only 15 seats in 1949, none in 1953, and was declared unconstitutional in 1956.
[3] R.W. Johnson, *Long March of the French Left* (1981) p. 51.
[4] In France Gaullists and then Poujadists, in Italy Monarchists and Fascists.
[5] D. MacShane, *Francois Mitterrand. A Political Odyssey* (1982) pp. 149–50.

presidential elections the Communist candidate polled only 15 per cent. The PCF then rallied to Mitterrand, pinning its hopes on securing ministries in a Socialist-led administration. Mitterrand went on to win both the presidency and an absolute Socialist majority in the National Assembly. Only then were four Communists taken into the government. They had little influence: Mitterrand surprised everybody with the firmly anti-Soviet tone of his foreign policy. Domestically too the Communists were squeezed, and their electoral decline continued.

The Italian Communist Party (PCI) was more lively than the French. It had followed Moscow into the Cold War, condemning Marshall Aid perhaps against the better judgement of its leader, Togliatti. But Togliatti used Khrushchev's acceptance of different roads to Socialism (and his revelations about Stalin) to float ideas of 'polycentrism', and of a distinctive 'Italian way' that would use parliamentary forms and involve collaboration with other political parties and the search for both peasant and middle-class support. The practical implications were still slight – the PCI accepted Soviet suppression of Hungary in 1956, and next year condemned Italian membership of the European Economic Community (EEC). The early 1960s brought further softening: in 1962 the PCI endorsed EEC membership; and it was cool towards Khrushchev's campaign against the Chinese Communist Party. Togliatti had no sympathy with the Chinese, but he held by the autonomy of individual Communist Parties. In 1964 he died in Yalta on his way to confront Khrushchev on the subject, and the PCI published his 'testament'. This stressed that all was not well even with the Soviet Union, and that Western Parties needed to liquidate 'old formulae which no longer correspond to present realities', make overtures to 'the religious masses', and think more about a peaceful transition to socialism.[6] In 1968 Togliatti's successors proclaimed the objective of a pluralist socialist democracy to be achieved through a union of all progressive forces, both secular and Catholic. They were shocked and frightened by the Warsaw Pact intervention, later that year, to suppress 'socialism with a human face' in Czechoslovakia. This much reduced their hostility to the NATO alliance that protected them from such action.

By the early 1970s the PCI was becoming alarmed by the possibility that the internal disturbances then multiplying in Italy would play into the hands of the Far Right, as in the early 1920s; it sought to enter the circle of accepted constitutional parties through a 'historic compromise' with the Christian Democrats (DC). This was brought nearer when, in 1974,

[6] *Keesing's*, 15020–1, 20032.

an old-fashioned Catholic and anti-Communist campaign flopped in a referendum on divorce. Later that year the Socialists pulled out of the government. The country seemed to be moving Left, a view confirmed by the 1975 regional elections when the PCI greatly narrowed the gap between itself and the DC. Against this background the PCI asked to enter the government as a party whose support would be needed to overcome political instability, domestic violence, and economic crisis. Its Secretary, Berlinguer, was free with assurances of devotion to democracy and liberalism, while declaring of NATO (though *not* in the Party newspaper), 'I feel safer on this side'. He acted as patron to the emergent, and ostentatiously liberal, Spanish Communist Party; and he repeated his unwelcome 'Eurocommunist' pronouncements at the 1976 Soviet Party Congress.[7]

By no means everybody believed them. The PCI still contained instinctively pro-Soviet elements. Its entry into the Cabinet might trigger defections from, or even a collapse of, the DC, hitherto the indispensable party of government. It could have had even wider consequences: one commentator observed that it was 'almost impossible to see right-wing Republican congressmen tolerating for long a situation in which American servicemen were stationed in Europe to protect Communist-dominated governments'.[8] There was a tradition of external intervention in Italian politics, which Kissinger was determined to continue. In 1975 he told US ambassadors that 'We cannot encourage dialogue with Communist parties within NATO nations . . . The extent such a party follows the Moscow line is unimportant . . . the impact of an Italian Communist Party that seemed to be governing effectively would be devastating – on France, and on NATO too'; indeed, the alliance, as now constituted, 'could not survive'. 1976 saw further elaborations, and also an agreement (soon revealed by Chancellor Schmidt) that if the PCI entered the government, the USA, UK, France and Germany would withold financial assistance. The policy was continued by the Carter administration: Brzezinski wrote that drift to the Left in Italy was 'potentially the gravest political problem we now have in Europe'.[9]

---

[7] *Keesing's*, 27694–6, 27736; Norman Kogan, *A Political History of Italy. The Postwar Years* (New York, 1983) p. 296.

[8] Coral Bell, *The Diplomacy of Detente: The Kissinger Era* (1977) p. 229.

[9] *Keesing's*, 27796–7, 27926; R.L. Garthoff, *Détente and Confrontation: American–Soviet Relations from Nixon to Reagan* (Washington, DC, 1985) p. 488; Zbigniew Brzezinski, *Power and Principle: Memoirs of the National Security Adviser 1977–1981* (New York, 1983) pp. 311–12.

Given the conflicting pressures, the DC adopted a step-by-step approach. After the 1976 elections a purely DC government was formed, but only after agreement on policy with the other moderate parties *including the Communists*, who all then abstained from voting against it. The 1977–8 winter saw a renewed crisis over demands, backed by some of the DC and most of the other parties, for the PCI's inclusion in a government of national emergency, an idea the USA publicly condemned. The leading Christian Democrat, Aldo Moro, eventually worked out a compromise whereby the government would remain DC, but accept the Communists into the ranks of its parliamentary majority. Left-wing terrorists then murdered him, thus removing the most influential proponent of dialogue with the PCI. This triggered demonstrations of national solidarity. But the Communist position of support for, but not full membership of, the system became uncomfortable, and they were in danger of losing votes to the Left. In 1979, when again refused entry into the government, they withdrew into opposition. New elections showed the PCI to have passed its peak; in 1980 the Socialists, who had for some time been squabbling with the Communists, stopped advocating their entry into government and themselves rejoined it. Despite a poor DC electoral performance in 1983–4, the 1980s were to see comparative political stability, based on broad moderate coalitions that excluded the Communists. They also witnessed a decline in terrorism and considerable economic growth, combined with the ballooning of budget deficits. Against this background the Communist vote fell gently to 27 per cent in the 1987 parliamentary elections. Two years later came the collapse of communism in Eastern Europe. After considerable discussion, the PCI was refounded in 1991 as the Democratic Party of the Left (PDS), with hardliners breaking away to form a rival splinter group. At the 1992 elections the PDS polled only 16.1 per cent.

The decline of communism rocked the structure that had been built over the previous four decades to contain it. For people no longer felt it necessary 'to hold their noses and vote' for the tarnished parties of the political establishment. In the 1992 elections the governing coalition only just secured a majority.[10] Later that year there followed a wave of arrests for corruption, exposing a structure where the established parties had routinely collected, and then shared, financial kick-backs from business. Distaste for this ended many distinguished political careers; and public opinion also turned against the 1980s system where elections seemed to

---

[10] Kogan, *History of Italy*, esp. Chap. 21; *Keesing's*, 37786, 38021.

decide nothing, since for reasons of political arithmetic the same parties, and almost the same people, were always in office. Propelled by referenda, such sentiments led to the adoption in 1993 of a largely first-past-the-post voting system intended to introduce genuine choice between rival and potentially stronger governments (on what was taken to be the British model). Fully majoritarian parties did not emerge, but the 1994 elections were contested between alliances of the Left (centred on the PDS) and Right (led by the media tycoon Berlusconi's new *Forza Italia*), with the (now renamed) DC squeezed and split in the middle. The change was such that people now talked of 'the Second Republic'. Berlusconi won, but his coalition soon splintered and the President refused him a dissolution. Therefore, 1995 saw a government largely of technocrats. But in 1996 a Left coalition (headed by Romano Prodi) defeated Berlusconi's 'Freedom Pole', and a succession of centre-left governments ensued; in 2001 the result was reversed, and Berlusconi managed to continue as Premier till he narrowly lost the 2006 election to Prodi. In the 1990s the 'Second Republic' did improve government finances enough to enable Italy to join the new 'euro' currency (below, p. 509). But in other respects there remains some doubt as to whether the new political configuration has been as successful as was hoped in generating strong government.

Military takeovers in Greece and Turkey

During the early Cold War the most obvious threat to the liberal system was from the Communists. But it was from the Right that takeovers had come between the wars. One such takeover did occur in Greece, when the army seized power in 1967 rather than risk the electoral victory of the Centre Union (a fairly moderate party, but one backed by the Communists and thought likely to purge rightist officers). However, military rule collapsed in 1974 after a rash adventure in Cyprus had brought Greece to the brink of war with Turkey. In Turkey, too, the army took over in 1960–1 and 1980–3, voluntarily restoring power to civilians under conditions meant to prevent a recurrence of the developments it disliked.[11] There have been no other such upsets. But it is again worth touching briefly on events in France and Italy, both of which went through turbulent periods.

---

[11] On the former occasion the rightist Menderes government's revival of appeals to religion and tough ways with opponents, in the second extremism and violence of both Left and Right.

Algerian settlers and the army overthrow the Fourth Republic; De Gaulle re-establishes Paris's control

The French Fourth Republic's constitution had been meant to turn over a new leaf and provide stronger government. That Republic had its successes, but public perception was rather of inflation, strikes, and international humiliation. This last went back to the defeat of 1940. Since then Britain had blocked the restoration of French control over Syria in 1945. France had lost its war in Vietnam in 1954. Repression had failed in Tunisia and Morocco, and they became independent in 1956. Revolt broke out in Algeria;[12] and in 1957–8 'the Anglo-Saxons' appeared to be intervening diplomatically, with the prospect of what the Minister for Algeria called a 'diplomatic Dien Bien Phu'. The army had had enough; as a 1958 broadcast put it, 'no more "strategic withdrawals"; no more "peace with honour"; no more "internal autonomy" . . . ; no more "representative negotiators"; no more "good offices" '.[13]

There appear to have been extremist plotters in Algiers since at least 1956, and the idea grew of using a settlers' rising to prompt a change of regime in Paris. The ex-Gaullist Minister of Defence and his aides started establishing contacts in order to turn the anticipated explosion to the General's advantage. This explosion was touched off by a political crisis that saw the failure of the hardliner Bidault's bid for the premiership and its replacement by that of Pflimlin, who was suspected of wanting negotiations with the Algerian resistance movement (the FLN). On 13 May 1958 a demonstration in the predominantly European city of Algiers developed into a takeover of government offices; the army commander, General Salan, went along with calls for a Committee of Public Safety, and on the 15th was induced to declare for de Gaulle. In response de Gaulle announced his readiness 'to assume the powers of the Republic'. From then on he played a double game, in touch with at least some of the rebels' moves while simultaneously negotiating with the existing political leaders a peaceful accession to power that would head them off. On 24 May paratroopers from Algiers seized Corsica, and there were known to be plans for an early descent on the mainland. Army leaders and the Paris police were sympathetic; despite a large pro-Republican demonstration in Paris,

---

[12] See *The Post-Imperial World*, Chap. 1.
[13] P.M. Williams and M. Harrison, *De Gaulle's Republic* (1961 edn) p. 61.

calls for strikes in support of the government failed outside the northern coalfield. What proved decisive was the determination of most leading politicians not to risk a confrontation in which any government opposing the insurgents would have to place itself in the hands of the (largely Communist) organised workers. 'It would', Mollet is quoted as saying, 'have been the [1936] war in Spain – without the republican army' – or, in de Gaulle's later words, a 'gamble, leading on to civil war in the presence of foreigners and soon their participation on different sides'. Negotiations were still not easy; but de Gaulle was induced to make enough concessions to secure his legal investiture as Prime Minister.[14]

There were fears that, in power, de Gaulle would be prisoner of the right-wing forces that had brought him there. When this was put to him, he is said to have replied, 'Prisoners escape'. Certainly he succeeded in so doing. He began by securing massive endorsement in a referendum for a new constitution, followed by parliamentary elections; and for the rest of his life he seems psychologically to have needed regular repetitions of such votes of confidence. He was also careful to promote most of the soldiers involved in the Algerian rising to positions where they would be less dangerous; he moved obliquely to disengage from *Algérie Française*, in September 1959 promising a choice between integration, association and independence. This led to the revival of earlier plots and to a plan for a coup in October, though it had to be dropped for lack of support. In January 1960 the army was ominously inactive when militants occupied the centre of Algiers for a week. In 1961 things were worse. De Gaulle's statement in April that France should disengage from Algeria prompted an army takeover there, organised by a network of colonels but attracting the support of retired generals like Salan and Challe (who had been in command in Algeria during the January 1960 affair). In response de Gaulle assumed emergency powers, and massive (and well-supported) preparations were made against any military move on the mainland. De Gaulle again broadcast, prompting demonstrations of loyalty from conscript servicemen in Algeria. Within three days General Challe decided to call things off to avoid bloodshed, and the revolt collapsed. He had in 1960 declared that 'if a defeated French army were to return home accompanied by half a million furiously angry Algerians, France would be under dictatorship before three months were up'. In 1962 such an exodus did occur,

---

[14] Philip Williams, *Wars, Plots and Scandals in Post-War France* (Cambridge, 1970) Chap. 7; Maurice Larkin, *France since the Popular Front* (1988) pp. 263–9; Charles de Gaulle, *Mémoires d'Espoir*, i, *Le Renouveau 1958–1962* (Paris, 1970) esp. p. 22.

but without the effects he had anticipated. As an Algerian senator had observed in 1959, de Gaulle 'has an enormous popular appeal ... The 13 May [1958 rising] succeeded because of a miracle, a conjuncture which brought Algiers, the army and the mainland together with the same aims at the same time. This conjuncture will not be repeated. A new 13 May will find no echo on the mainland.' Nevertheless the OAS terrorist resistance that mushroomed in Algeria in 1961 spilt over into France, with no less a figure than Bidault eventually assuming the leadership. During 1961–3 there were several plots against de Gaulle's life, one of which nearly succeeded. But such troubles died down as events in Algeria gradually receded into the past.[15]

Consolidation of French political stability under the Fifth Republic

Until Algeria had been resolved de Gaulle was widely regarded as indispensable. Thereafter he was expected to be much weaker. Instead he confounded the prophets by pushing through a further constitutional change – announcing (shortly after an attempt on his life) a referendum to make the Presidency directly elective, and threatening to resign if he did not get a good majority. His action was by normal criteria unconstitutional; and almost all the non-Gaullist deputies joined in censuring the government. Both de Gaulle and the idea of directly choosing a President were clearly popular, and 'the parties of the past' found they had put themselves in the wrong with the electorate: this not only voted for the referendum but also gave the Gaullists and their allies an unprecedented absolute majority in the parliamentary elections that followed. From then on, French administrations have (in marked contrast to experience since the 1870s) proved durable and have been able to count on parliamentary support. Some of the greater strength and decisiveness of Fifth Republican diplomacy must be attributable to these changes in the political system.

Initially, though, the system was still fragile. In May 1968 student demonstrations, caused chiefly by a recent university reform but reflecting also an international wave of leftist sentiment, touched off strikes and factory occupations (wages had been squeezed since 1967). By some accounts de Gaulle panicked and contemplated flight; and both Mitterrand and Mendès-France offered to form provisional governments in what would

[15] Larkin, *France since the Popular Front*, pp. 272–8; Williams, *Wars, Plots and Scandals*, Chap. 10; Williams and Harrison, *De Gaulle's Republic*, pp. 209, 227.

have been a mirror image of 1958. Prime Minister Pompidou kept his nerve, bought off the strikers with wage increases, and persuaded de Gaulle to dissolve parliament and campaign on an anti-communist law-and-order platform; the result was an electoral triumph. This did not resolve all problems. Strong government was re-established; but there was much nervousness as to what would replace first the elderly de Gaulle, then (in the early 1970s) his successor Pompidou, who proved to have cancer. As we have seen, Mitterrand joined forces with the Communists and made strong speeches: 'I have to say that anyone who does not accept a rupture with the established order, with capitalist society, cannot be a member of the Socialist Party.'[16] In the mid-1970s France was electorally very evenly divided, and the Right both played up and genuinely believed in the red peril. Perhaps for this reason, they did not lose power until it had become quite clear that Mitterrand controlled the Communists rather than *vice versa*. Then in 1981 *alternance* happened remarkably smoothly, and Mitterrand settled comfortably into the presidential system he had once opposed. So well entrenched, indeed, did the constitution prove that it could accommodate the return of a rightist majority in the 1986 parliamentary elections. Mitterrand appointed its leader, Chirac, Prime Minister and left government largely to him; then in 1988 he secured re-election as President, dissolved parliament and won his Socialists a working majority. Since then the system has continued to function under both Socialist and Gaullist Presidents, and also during two further periods of 'cohabitation' (when the President and Prime Minister were of opposing parties).

Threats from the right to the Italian political system; The troubles of the 1970s

Events in Italy were less dramatic. In the late 1950s, however, there were fears that the DC's hegemony might collapse if international detente had the effect of legitimising the communists,[17] and bitter controversy as to whether the DC should look for allies to the Left or the Right. In 1960 the Liberals pulled out of the government in protest against the idea of seeking Socialist support. This led to a long political crisis, with the Church and

---

[16] MacShane, *Mitterrand*, p. 141.

[17] Earlier, French opposition to Churchill's pressure for a summit had been based partly on the fear that it would legitimise, and so strengthen, the PCF (Pierre Hassner, 'Perceptions of the Soviet threat in the 1950s and 1980s: the case of France', in C-C. Schweitzer (ed.) *The Changing Western Analysis of the Soviet Threat* (1990) p. 176.

employers' and peasant proprietors' organisations seeking to block any opening to the Left. The Socialists asked too high a price; and the outcome was a DC government, headed by Tambroni, that could attract votes from no other party except the Fascists (MSI). That summer the MSI insisted on holding a congress in fiercely hostile Genoa; it touched off a wave of riots. Tambroni wanted to respond forcefully, but the disturbances were bad enough to enable his rivals to organise an alternative DC government of 'democratic restoration' that was opposed only by the Fascists and Communists.[18]

The experience ruled out any further possibility of a parliamentary evolution to the Right (which had been feared as leading imperceptibly to the return of the fascist 'regime'). But some people were tempted to achieve it by other means. The Carabinieri commander, General de Lorenzo, made unauthorised preparations to suppress disturbances and arrest a broad list of potential opponents; during a mid-1964 political crisis President Segni contemplated installing an emergency government of technicians, while perhaps readying the Carabinieri to put these preparations into effect in the event of trouble – which would have amounted to a 'Gaullist' coup. Any such development was forestalled by the hurried reassembly of a centre-left government.[19] But the temperature rose again at the end of the 1960s, with violent student demonstrations (which evolved over the 1970s into small-scale but murderous left-wing terrorism) and the labour disputes of the 1969 'hot autumn'. Ultra-rightists thought this propitious: Mussolini had gained power by utilising similar if more extensive threats to order and property. So they stoked things up through the so-called 'strategy of tension', beginning in 1969 with a Milan explosion that they represented as the work of an anarchist. 1970 saw an actual coup attempt by Prince Valerio Borghese; there were further plots in 1973–4 to kidnap the cabinet and to establish a Fascist Republic, in some of which the security service seems to have been compromised.[20] The Republic was probably

[18] Kogan, *History of Italy*, pp. 151–62; Elizabeth Wiskemann, *Italy since 1945* (1971) pp. 38–9; *Keesing's*, 17713–14.

[19] It should be remembered that the 1967 Greek coup took the form of an unauthorised activation of an official counter-insurgency plan – Richard Collin, *The De Lorenzo Gambit: the Italian Coup Manqué of 1964* (1976 – Sage Research Papers, Contemporary European Studies Series, no. 90–034).

[20] The far Right was encouraged by the Greek 'colonels' takeover, and probably received funds from them. *Keesing's*, 26410–12, 26821, 28494, 29057, 29224; Kogan, *History of Italy*, p. 287; Wiskemann, *Italy since 1945*, p. 88.

in no danger; but then failed coups generally look ridiculous in retrospect. The threat was taken seriously at the time, while rightist explosions (like leftist terrorism) continued for over a decade before they were gradually brought under control.

Post-war economic growth

We have discussed France and Italy. More generally we may note that earlier issues of strident nationalism and of Church versus state were in relative decline, while economic questions assumed greater prominence. These last may be politically easier to handle, at least while the economic cake is growing – as it has done to an unprecedented extent in all West European countries. Economic success does not cure all problems – during the Cold War Italy's growth rate exceeded Britain's, but Britain was usually politically the more stable country. However, economic setbacks – especially those accompanying the mid-1970s 'stagflation' – could cause serious difficulties.[21] So it is worth speculating as to why they were so few.

From today's perspective it looks as if economic growth is to be expected where governments provide a reasonably secure environment and a functioning infrastructure, but leave business exposed, and fairly free to respond, to market signals. Certainly Europe's 'economic miracle' has been more than matched by the capitalist countries of the west Pacific, which have operated broadly on this principle. But at the end of the 1920s the United States had been hit by the Slump despite the presence of such conditions; Europe then followed (with devastating political results in Germany), partly through contagion and partly through its own internal weaknesses. Happily there has been no post-war parallel in Western Europe; and states have generally sought to avoid the possibility by stimulating their economies when serious downturns threatened[22] and by fighting shy of 1930s beggar-thy-neighbour tariff and currency policies.

Beyond this, several interlocking factors have together constituted a strong 'virtuous circle'. They would include: the acceleration and diffusion of technological discoveries, a historically high investment ratio, cheap

---

[21] Including, in Britain, a 1974 election over 'who governs' the country (the government, with its incomes policy, or the National Union of Mineworkers), and an economy where successive cycles seemed to be becoming so much more extreme that one influential *Times* journalist proclaimed they would soon precipitate an authoritarian solution.
[22] Perhaps too readily, with the result that inflation was a distinctive feature of the period.

oil (from 1957 to 73 and again for over 15 years from the mid-1980s), rapidly rising trade bringing the benefits of specialisation and comparative advantage, the spreading of prosperity to Mediterranean countries through tourism, increasing managerial efficiency, and (except in Britain) the movement of workers out of agriculture into industry and services with higher productivity. In West Germany this last was supplemented first by people from the East and later by 'guest-workers' from Italy and subsequently Turkey. Many other areas have also thus replenished their labour force from abroad, even Sicily drawing on North African labour by the late 1980s – though elsewhere the decline of old industries and the resultant rise in unemployment has rendered this less necessary, and the attendant social problems have made it generally unwelcome. Beyond such generalities it is not easy to go, since states have differed considerably in their economic policies, nor have these always had the effects one would have anticipated.[23]

[23] D.H. Aldcroft, *The European Economy 1914–1980* (1980) Chap. 5.

CHAPTER 12

Western Europe II: France, Germany, Britain, and the USA

Marshall Aid 1947–52; European Payments Union, 1950

Immediately after the war, the overriding need was for economic recovery. In 1947 US Under-Secretary of State for Economic Affairs, William Clayton, could report that 'Millions of people in the cities are slowly starving', since farmers had insufficient incentive to supply food 'in normal quantities'. The present position 'represents an absolute minimum standard of living. If it should be lowered, there will be revolution'.[1] In fact the problem was more one of bottlenecks and transport difficulties; and though agriculture was generally down on pre-war levels, industrial production was up.[2] But further revival would have run into balance of payments crises had it not been for Marshall Aid, since (in the absence of German industrial and of East European agricultural products) Western Europe had a collective deficit of $7.4 billion, mostly with the USA. Marshall Aid (and then offshore military procurement) bridged the gap until exports could be expanded. Growth could thus continue, with the result that by 1951 per capita incomes were above pre-war levels in most countries (though not West Germany).[3] Marshall Aid had thus excluded the risk of 'economic, social and political deterioration of a very grave

---

[1] *FRUS* 1947, iii, p. 230.
[2] Except in the Netherlands (95%), France (92%), and the ex-enemy countries.
[3] D.H. Aldcroft, *The European Economy 1914–1980* (1980) pp. 148–57.

character' and enabled Western Europe to proceed in the 1950s to self-sustaining growth.[4]

What it did not do was to enable Washington to impose its views on how Western Europe should be organised. The State Department had wanted 'a European economic federation' on the Benelux model, but was divided as to how this could best be approached:

Balancing the dangers of appearing to force 'the American way' on Europe and the danger of failure if the major responsibility is left to Europe, Mr Bohlen suggested that the alternative is to place strong pressure on the European nations to plan by . . . making it clear that the only politically feasible basis on which the US would be willing to make aid available is substantial evidence of a developing overall plan for economic cooperation by the Europeans themselves, perhaps an economic federation to be worked out over 3 or 4 years.

Pressure was applied, sometimes rather bluntly,[5] but it did not work. In 1947 sixteen states formed a Committee of European Economic Cooperation to produce a response to Marshall's offer. Few wished it to become permanent; but the USA was able to persuade them, though only after concluding a package deal with France on German questions. So in April 1948 an Organisation for European Economic Cooperation (OEEC) came into existence. But Britain and France (with considerable support from smaller countries like Norway) were determined that it should not assume supranational dimensions; by 1949 Harriman was to remark that 'the British had prevailed in setting the pattern of an organization whose impotency was now becoming alarming'.[6]

However, by dint of earmarking $600 million of Marshall Aid, the USA did secure the establishment in 1950 of a 'European Payments Union' (EPU), in effect a clearing house for currency settlements between OEEC members (plus their colonies and the sterling area) that also provided conditional loans of the kind now associated with the International Monetary Fund (IMF). This saw Germany through its unexpectedly high 1950–1

---

[4] Later experience in Africa and elsewhere suggests that where underlying conditions are not right, the mere injection of money (even in amounts comparable to Marshall Aid) does not produce similar results.

[5] *FRUS* 1947, iii, pp. 232, 234–5, 317–18; Congressional support for European economic integration was expressed in the preamble of the Act authorising Marshall Aid.

[6] *FRUS* 1949, iv, p. 489.

deficit,[7] and (after interruptions due to the Korean war) edged its members towards ending quantitative trade restrictions.[8] By 1955 Europe was beginning to look to the return of convertibility; the process was slowed by the disruptions attending the Suez affair; but in December 1958 de Gaulle (who was determined to secure a hard currency) devalued the franc in a move that was synchronised with the adoption by major countries of external convertibility. This rendered the EPU superfluous, and it was wound up.[9] It is generally seen as having done an excellent job; but it did not fulfil US hopes (at the time of its creation) that it would lead to the establishment of a European central bank and common currency.

The Schuman Plan (1950) and the establishment of the ECSC; The EDC

Instead the creation of a significant European entity is usually traced to the 'Schuman Plan'. French policy towards Germany had since 1918 been a compound of cooperation and coercion, with the latter predominant. In 1945 France told the Americans that, 'With the aim of military security we prefer to increase French steel production . . . to the detriment of the Ruhr'.[10] There was, of course, international agreement that Germany's steel production should be curbed to prevent any revival of its military potential; and the Monnet Plan envisaged a great expansion of French steel output so that France could displace Germany as the heartland of continental industry. This did not work. French steel had to be smelted with German coke. But coke production was, up to 1950, well below pre-war levels – the French believed because of the incompetence with which Britain managed the Ruhr; also, to save imports, German steel plants had

---

[7] Fortunately German deficits coincided with sterling area surpluses and *vice versa*.

[8] By 1959 major countries had lifted over 90% of those on trade with other OEEC members. But France had scrapped the whole process in 1952–3 and 1957–8, while the restrictions that remained were, of course, the important ones. W.M. Scammell, *The International Economy since 1945* (Basingstoke, 1983 edn) p. 34; *Keesing's*, 16606, 16610.

[9] This left the OEEC with little to do. In 1960 it was reconstituted as the Organisation for Economic Cooperation and Development with more global interests; and in 1964 Japan was allowed to join as a symbol of its acceptance as an advanced industrial state. But the OECD has been extensively bypassed, and become largely a body for monitoring economic trends.

[10] A.S. Milward, *The Reconstruction of Western Europe 1945–51* (1984) p. 129.

to use not Swedish but inferior domestic ore that took twice as much coke to smelt. Against this background France fought hard to secure a lien on German coal production. A sliding-scale entitlement was agreed in 1947, followed in 1948 by the excision of the Saar's output from calculations of 'German' coal. Also, at the price of abandoning its insistence that a reconstituted West German state be only of a minimalist nature and subject to prolonged – Bidault spoke of permanent – occupation, France managed in 1948 to secure agreement on an international Ruhr Authority. However, as London noted, 'the Ruhr document is full of sound and fury but signifying practically nothing'; in 1949 France could no more than dent the dual pricing system whereby such German coal as was exported cost considerably more than coal for German domestic consumption.[11]

Repeated demonstrations that France could not prevent a reconstruction of Germany along US lines inspired an important change of tack. As civil service appreciations put it in the 1948–9 winter, there was 'only one solution: to abandon . . . our malthusian policy with respect to Western Germany and to establish a common ground of economic and political association with' it.

That is why the French government has come to the conviction that the guarantees it is seeking will only be capable of being validly secured in a kind of association of Germany in a larger framework, that of Europe . . . steel made in the Ruhr would no longer be German steel but a part of European steel. France would be associated on equal terms with Germany in the control of this steel cartel. In this way she would have her word to say, better than by international controls, in the question of [the capacity of] the German steel works.[12]

By late 1949 the time was propitious for trying out such an approach. For the USA was starting to soft-pedal its earlier policy of using Britain to bring about European integration. Acheson now felt France was the 'key':

France needs, in the interests of her own future, to take the initiative . . . if the character of West Germany is to be one permitting healthy development in Western Europe . . . France and France alone can take the decisive leadership in integrating Western Germany into Western Europe . . .

[11] ibid. esp. pp. 134–6, 154, 157, 378, 386–7.
[12] ibid. pp. 162–3.

Inability of the US and possibly of the UK and of other countries to join in actions involving some merger of sovereignty should not debar other countries from such progress.

So Acheson wrote to the French Foreign Minister, imploring him to take the lead.[13]

The upshot was the 'Schuman Plan', secretly prepared by the French technocrat Jean Monnet, bounced through the French cabinet, and released with a flourish in May 1950:

A united Europe was not achieved [after 1918]; and we had war. Europe will not be made all at once or according to a single general plan. It will be built through concrete achievements, which first create a de facto solidarity. The gathering together of the nations of Europe requires the elimination of the age-old opposition of France and Germany. The first concern in any action taken must be these two countries.

With this in view, the French government proposes to take action immediately on one limited but decisive point . . . to place Franco-German production of coal and steel under a common higher authority, within the framework of an organization open to the participation of the other countries of Europe.[14]

For Germany the offer, promising the end of discriminatory control by the Ruhr Authority and the lifting of restrictions on plant capacity, proved irresistible. Adenauer at once agreed in principle, later explaining that he had advanced similar proposals in 1923; and at one point in the subsequent negotiations he reminded German steel manufacturers that 'the political aim was in the foreground and economic aims were more or less subordinate'.[15] So 1951 brought agreement on a European Coal and Steel Community (ECSC) to consist of France, Germany, Italy, the Netherlands, Belgium and Luxembourg.

If this seemed a success for the 'European idea', a major setback followed. For, faced in late 1950 by strong US pressure for German rearmament, France proposed a 'European Defence Community' (EDC), partly to delay the unwelcome day, partly in hope that it would permit German mobilisation for Western defence while still precluding a national German army. Unfortunately it would also weaken the French army. The EDC

---

[13] October 1949 – *FRUS 1949*, iv, p. 470; iii, pp. 622–5.

[14] C. Tugendhat, *Making Sense of Europe* (Harmondsworth, 1986) p. 31.

[15] Milward, *Reconstruction of Western Europe*, p. 413.

soon became exposed to the criticisms of opposites (as going too far, or not far enough, in a European direction), but above all to residual fears of the revival of the *Wehrmacht* and of the old Germany. When the treaty was, after much foreign pressure, eventually put to the National Assembly in 1954, it was rejected, thus derailing the agreed restoration of sovereignty to West Germany. That things were eventually straightened out, this time in the context of NATO and its predecessor the Western European Union, was due chiefly to British and US diplomacy.

A European Common Market 1955–8

The next moves came in 1955 from Benelux, whose Foreign Ministers (with the backing of the ECSC Assembly) called for economic integration in a variety of sectors (including nuclear energy) and for a 'Common Market'. This resulted in a Foreign Ministers' conference at Messina, which endorsed these goals and established a committee to draw up plans under the guidance of the Belgian Foreign Minister Henri Spaak. The 'Spaak Report' called for the creation by stages of a European Common Market, modelled institutionally on the ECSC, and also for a European Atomic Community. Its efforts were reinforced by the lobbying of European federalists – notably the 'Action Committee for the United States of Europe', founded in October 1955 by Monnet (now retired after a rather unsuccessful term as first President of the ECSC High Authority) and containing an impressive international range of politicians and union leaders.[16] The French political situation had been altered by the decline of Gaullism and shift to the Socialists at the 1956 elections. But France still had serious reservations. It decided, however, to accept the Spaak Report as a basis for discussion while negotiating for a range of changes and safeguards, a process that lasted until March 1957.

In November 1956 key concessions were made by Adenauer in a meeting with Mollet: there should be harmonisation of social security (though this never really came about) so that France should not be competitively disadvantaged by its more generous arrangements, and France could continue to subsidise exports and tax imports until its balance of payments

[16] Monnet's immediate secretariat was funded by the Ford Foundation, as part of a complex of US support, run by the 'American Committee on United Europe', that also included some $4m of covert CIA spending between 1949 and 1960 – Richard J. Aldrich, *The Hidden Hand. Britain, America and Cold War Secret Intelligence* (2001) Chap. 16 (esp. pp. 343, 349, 365–6).

improved. Later it was agreed that after the Treaty had come into effect a Common Agricultural Policy (CAP) should be worked out. Finally French and Belgian colonies should be associated with, and receive development aid from, the EEC for five years, after which the arrangements should be renegotiated. On Euratom (European Atomic Energy Community) possible disputes over the military application of nuclear energy were shelved by a decision to exclude this for the time being. In 1957 the EEC and Euratom were created by the Treaties of Rome, to take effect in March 1958. The negotiations had succeeded as a result of commitment and a disposition to compromise. But they had also shown the strength of France's position, despite its apparently fragile economy. For the other large countries, Italy and Germany, both felt a political need that France did not share for European integration as an escape from the past. As (in the absence of the UK) such integration seemed impossible without it, France could bargain strongly to protect its economic interests.[17]

Euratom never amounted to much, and nuclear energy programmes remained essentially national (partly, in the French case, because of their military implications). But the EEC made unexpectedly rapid progress. This was helped by de Gaulle's firm devaluation of the franc, accompanied by the lifting of most quota restrictions on OEEC trade and a readiness to risk implementing the agreed initial tariff cuts in January 1959. There had been no certainty that French industry could face the resultant competition, but in fact it responded well – helped by a generally favourable trade environment.[18] A further stimulus came from the foundation of the rival European Free Trade Area (EFTA), of which more below; to avoid being overtaken, the EEC speeded up the removal of quota restrictions on internal trade (abolished by late 1961) and the construction of internal free trade and a common external tariff (completed by mid-1968).[19]

Adenauer and France

For many years the European concept's chief contribution to stabilisation was the framework it provided for the conduct of Franco-German

[17] F. Roy Willis, *France, Germany and the New Europe 1945–1967* (1968 edn) Chap. 9.
[18] Intra-EEC trade rose by 19% in 1959, 25% in 1960–1.
[19] Willis, *France, Germany and the New Europe* pp. 282–6; W.O. Henderson, *The Genesis of the Common Market* (1962) p. 164; Scammell, *International Economy since 1945*, pp. 137–8.

relations. We have seen that the Schuman Plan represented a new approach to an old problem, as did the ill-starred European Defence Community. The resolution (albeit by other means) of the German rearmament question encouraged Adenauer and Mendès-France to agree on the 'Europeanisation' of the Saar as an autonomous entity, but one within the French economic system.[20] However, the Saarlanders rejected this solution in a referendum, then voted in a new administration that in January 1956 demanded accession to Germany. Fortunately the French government did not want the Saar to wreck the discussions then in progress to create the EEC. So it agreed to the Saar's joining Germany in 1957, securing in exchange continued coal deliveries plus a German contribution to the canalisation of the Mosel to reduce the costs of shipping Ruhr coal to Lorraine.

Adenauer was obsessed with the need for Western unity in the face of godless Soviet communism, and the fear that this could not be preserved unless France and Germany were locked together in a European framework. In 1954, after the collapse of the EDC, *Der Spiegel* reports him as telling the Belgian and Luxembourg foreign ministers:

'When I am no longer there, I do not know what will happen to Germany if we have not yet succeeded in creating a united Europe . . .

'The French nationalists are just as ready as the German to repeat the old policies, in spite of past experience. They would rather a Germany with a national army than a united Europe – so long as they can pursue their own policy with the Russians. And the German nationalists think exactly the same way; they are ready to go with the Russians.'

Adenauer seemed completely possessed by the fear of a revival of a cynical, narrow German nationalism . . .

Again and again, he used the words 'when I am no longer there.'
'Make use of the time while I am still alive, because when I am no more it will be too late – my God, I do not know what my successors will do if

---

[20] To offset wartime destruction of French mines, the Saar had, from 1919–35, been detached from Germany and its mines placed under French control. In 1947 France (the local occupying power) transferred the territory to its own currency and customs zone; in the treaty establishing the ECSC France signed on the Saar's behalf. The Saar was accorded some political autonomy; but in its 1952 elections pro-German candidates were banned. Official policy, confirmed by the 1954 Adenauer–Mendès-France agreement, came to be that it should enjoy a special 'European' status but remain within the French economic zone. This the Saarlanders rejected in October 1955.

*they are left to themselves: if they are not obliged to follow along firmly
preordained lines, if they are not bound to a united Europe.'*

Adenauer continually returned to this theme. Thus in 1962 he descanted to
de Gaulle on the communist danger and continued:

*But if the French and German people were to be so strongly clamped
together that neither a French nor a German government could go with
the Soviet Union, then these two countries would accomplish a historic
task in building a firm European dam against communism.*[21]

In late 1955, when Britain again seemed to be contemplating security
concessions to the USSR to achieve German unification, Adenauer secretly
indicated his dissent.

*The bald reason was that Dr Adenauer had no confidence in the German
people. He was terrified that when he disappeared from the scene a future
German Government might do a deal with Russia at the German [sic]
expense. Consequently he felt that the integration of Western Germany
with the West was more important than the unification of Germany.
He wished us [the British] to know that he would bend all his energies
towards achieving this in the time which was left to him . . .*[22]

In January 1956 he gave his ministers a directive in connection with the
discusssions on the creation of the EEC: Soviet concessions would come
only through an integration that would both destroy Soviet hopes of winning over Western states one by one and enable the weight of a united
Europe to be thrown behind German reunification at the crucial moment;
'furthermore, a permanent ordering of our relations with France is possible
only on the basis of European integration. Should integration fail through
our hesitations or reluctance, the results would be incalculable.' Adenauer
was therefore ready to make the concessions France demanded, and to
override the hostility of his economics minister, Erhard, to the dirigiste and
inward-looking elements that resulted.[23]

[21] James L. Richardson, *Germany and the Atlantic Alliance* (Cambridge, Mass., 1966)
pp. 13–14; Konrad Adenauer, *Erinnerungen 1959–63* (Stuttgart, 1967) p. 166.
[22] Minute by Sir Ivone Kirkpatrick, 16 December 1955 – printed in J. Foschepoth (ed.)
Adenauer und die Deutsche Frage (Göttingen, 1986) pp. 289–90.
[23] Adenauer, *Erinnerungen 1955–9* pp. 253–4; Willis, *France, Germany and the New
Europe*, pp. 265 ff.

The decline of the Fourth Republic presented a problem; during its final crisis in May 1958 Erhard declared that Germany would not extend credit within the EEC framework to an undemocratic Gaullist France. Adenauer also had his worries but decided to bury them. In September he visited de Gaulle at his country home in Colombey-les-deux-Eglises. There may be an element of hindsight in the two leaders' later accounts – de Gaulle in particular would have us believe a detailed deal was struck to cover the range of European, German, and NATO questions; but the meeting was clearly a great success.[24] De Gaulle then almost spoilt things by leaking his proposals for a Franco-British-American NATO directorate, to which Germany would be clearly inferior (see p. 489). Adenauer was not pleased. Macmillan hoped this would induce him to help establish an industrial free trade area between the EEC and neighbouring states. But at a second meeting with de Gaulle in November 1958, Adenauer agreed to the termination of the negotiations, 'which sought to drown the Community of the Six at the outset, by plunging them into a vast free trade area including England, and, soon, the whole West'.

This meeting was held while Adenauer was still soliciting British diplomatic intervention over Berlin. But the Berlin crisis soon provided a further reason for preferring France to Britain. Adenauer, who had not been consulted in advance, deplored Macmillan's February 1959 visit to Moscow: he assumed it had been undertaken for purely electoral reasons, and asked the British ambassador if he realised what it would mean were the Federal Republic lost to the West. This made all the more welcome de Gaulle's declaratory position that the West should simply refuse to negotiate under Soviet pressure. So in March 1959, when Erhard gave a talk favouring a European free trade zone, Adenauer dashed off a rebuke: 'It is quite impossible for you to make a speech that insults France and approves of Britain's behaviour just at the moment when Britain is injuring us most severely . . . and we are absolutely dependent on French help. Such performances are in glaring contradiction with the lines of my policy which are well-known to you.'[25] Adenauer had never liked Erhard, and was already manoeuvring to block his succession to the chancellorship. Now he had all the more reason to stay on in politics; he devoted his remaining time, until he was finally

---

[24] Adenauer, *Erinnerungen*, pp. 424 ff, 518; Charles de Gaulle, *Mémoires d'Espoir*, i, *Le Renouveau 1985–1962* (Paris, 1970) pp. 184 ff.

[25] Adenauer, *Erinnerungen*, pp. 469–70, 518–19; De Gaulle, *Mémoires*, p. 190; Alistair Horne, *Macmillan*, ii (1989) pp. 110–19.

pushed out of office in 1963, to the consolidation and institutionalisation of his relationship with de Gaulle.

This relationship was certainly close: by mid-1962 the two had had fifteen meetings and exchanged forty letters. De Gaulle was the dominant partner; not only did Adenauer's language (as recorded in his *Memoirs*) become increasingly 'Gaullist',[26] but, when necessary, de Gaulle could crack the whip; when Adenauer's government was making difficulties over agriculture in 1961, de Gaulle got his way by telegraphing to Adenauer that he would break up the EEC unless Germany changed course.[27] De Gaulle certainly found the relationship very convenient; for with German support he could usually dominate the EEC. But his attitude towards Germany was always ambivalent. On resuming power in 1958 he is said to have asked how much remained of his policy for dismembering Germany, and received the reply, 'Nothing'. Courtship of Adenauer was an adaptation to this. It was pursued with a degree of cynicism. In March 1959 he agreed with the British that 'one could not have a nuclear war' on the question of whether a Soviet or an East German sergeant 'signed the pass to go along the autobahn . . . to West Berlin'. German reunion, too, was impossible without war, though 'the "idea" of reunion should be kept alive in order to give some comfort to the German people', and there should be practical cooperation between the two German states: 'What Dulles had called *con*federation should be pressed'. But he had not told Adenauer this; 'It would depress him'[28] – and, no doubt, inhibit his tendency to look to France, not Britain.

De Gaulle's policy was also designed to forestall disillusion that might lead West Germans to an independent deal with the Soviet Union. In 1959–60 he said:

---

[26] Though some 'Gaullist' themes were already visible in his remarks to the French during the Suez crisis. US protection was unreliable since the USA would never start an atomic war; and as no West European country would ever again be of stature comparable to the USA and USSR, 'There remains to them only one way of playing a decisive role in the world; that is to unite to make Europe. England is not ripe for it but the affair of Suez will help her prepare her spirits for it. We have no time to waste: Europe will be your revenge' (Keith Kyle, *Suez* (1991) pp. 466–7).

[27] De Gaulle, *Mémoires*, pp. 193, 198.

[28] Harold Macmillan, *Memoirs*, iv, p. 637. Macmillan, who genuinely feared that Berlin could lead to war, always thought that de Gaulle, too, really hoped for a negotiated *modus vivendi* to prevent this but preferred that the odium attached to it should fall on the Anglo-Saxons. De Gaulle apparently told the Soviet ambassador in 1961 that he did not want German reunion (CWIHP *Bulletin* 3 (1993) p. 60).

The only thing that might make them desperate would be their abandonment by the West. Thus in the economic field it was very important that West Germany should be tied in with France. There must be no more economic 'Drang nach Osten'. It was for this reason that he had approved the Common Market, although he had no real liking for it.

'As regards Berlin, etc., his chief object is to support Adenauer, because – if he is let down – more dangerous sentiments may begin to develop in Germany.' Indeed, he told Macmillan in November 1961 that 'even if the present weak and incapable German Government accepted' the need for negotiations, he would still feel 'it his duty to be the protector of German interests . . . *plus royaliste que le roi*' so that 'the Germany of the future will know that France was true'. De Gaulle was by then looking with some apprehension towards the post-Adenauer era. Adenauer (he had told Sulzberger) would never deal with the Russians, but later things might change, as German industry was attracted by the Soviet market and a deal over Berlin plus a federation of the two Germanies was not inconceivable; hence the need to wall Germany in within a united Europe.[29]

De Gaulle's policy meshed well with that of Adenauer, who was keen to exclude any possibility of a *French* deal with Moscow; their work found its apparent culmination in the January 1963 Treaty of Franco-German friendship. This, according to Couve de Murville (then French foreign secretary), was meant to establish 'a sort of permanent concertation' or even interpenetration 'between everybody, heads of state and government, ministers and senior civil servants, in the areas covered . . . foreign affairs, defence, education and youth . . .' Unfortunately it coincided with de Gaulle's veto of Britain's application to join the EEC. Adenauer did not mind; but the West German parliament did, and ratified it only with an anti-Gaullist preamble looking to the integration of NATO members' armed forces, British accession to the EEC, and negotiations for the removal of trade barriers between the EEC and other members of GATT.[30] In October 1963 Adenauer was finally forced to retire, and his successor, Erhard, had very different views.

---

[29] Macmillan, *Memoirs*, v, pp. 110–11, 181, 426; C.L. Sulzberger, *The Last of the Giants* (1970) p. 45.
[30] Maurice Couve de Murville, *Une Politique Étrangére 1958–1969* (Paris, 1971) p. 256; RIIA, *Documents 1963*, pp. 54–5.

Franco-German relations since 1963

De Gaulle rapidly lost enthusiasm for the treaty; and though the stipulated regular meetings continued, they were the occasion for quarrels over the EEC,[31] NATO (from whose integrated command structure France withdrew in 1966), and France's new policy of entente with Eastern Europe. For if reconciliation and partnership with France was one of the goals of West German foreign policy, the other fixed point was good alliance relations with the United States (whose protection was in the last resort more important). In this context Erhard was an Atlanticist, though he continued to be sniped at by Adenauer and a group of German 'Gaullists'. In 1966 he fell (for more domestic reasons); the new Kiesinger–Brandt government sought a more even balance between Washington and Paris, and also launched its own East European policy. Germany was becoming increasingly self-confident, while de Gaulle's position was badly damaged by the 'events' of 1968 and the resultant weakness of the franc. That autumn Germany resisted international calls to revalue the mark so as to ease pressure on the franc, something Couve said would have been unimaginable a few years earlier. De Gaulle became worried by this German recovery, to the point of saying privately that an alliance with the USSR (or war) could prove necessary to contain it; as for Western Europe, he was in February 1969 apparently contemplating a loosening of the EEC and a political association between the four major West European powers, France, Germany, Britain and Italy. That December the new West German chancellor, Brandt, touched on this concern when advocating British membership of the EEC; next year President Pompidou told Nixon it had been fear of a revival of German nationalism (triggered by Brandt's Ostpolitik) that had caused him to lift the ban on British entry.

Even if the 1963 treaty had not realised all the hopes invested in it, it had, as Couve says, 'created habits by establishing procedures and demonstrated that France could keep up dialogue with Germany without intermediaries'.[32] These 'habits', too, were reinforced by a network of lower

---

[31] One of de Gaulle's worries about the supranational structure Hallstein proposed in 1965 was that in it Germany would 'acquire the preponderant weight that its economic capability would undoubtedly bring' – then use it to promote German reunification (*Mémoires*, p. 195).

[32] Couve de Murville, *Une Politique Étrangére*, pp. 276, 284, Chap. 7; C.L. Sulzberger, *An Age of Mediocrity. Memoirs and Diaries 1963–1972* (New York, 1973) pp. 507–10; Kissinger, *Memoirs*, i, pp. 110, 422; *Keesing's*, 23267, 24168. De Gaulle's February 1969 overtures developed into a major diplomatic fracas with Britain (the Soames affair), and the details are correspondingly disputed.

level Franco-German exchanges and associations that had been deliberately fostered since the 1950s and that did much to make cooperation seem
natural. At the summit the relationship has fluctuated. It was not especially
close in the early 1970s; when Britain joined the Community there seemed
some prospect of its developing into a triangle, but in 1974 Britain turned
instead to renegotiating the terms of its entry. France and Germany also
acquired new leaders, Giscard D'Estaing and Schmidt, both former
finance ministers and fluent English speakers; they proved personally
extremely close, meeting regularly and demonstratively and ringing each
other up frequently. They claimed a joint leadership, Giscard once remarking that France and Germany 'never forgot that they had in their charge to
a great extent the progress of Europe', and Schmidt explaining that 'Italy is
notorious for its lack of government. Britain is notorious for governments,
Labour and Conservative, that think the Atlantic is narrower than the
Channel. That leaves only the French and the Germans.' They had, in fact,
some divergent national interests even within the EC; but in the 1980s a
former British Commissioner observed that 'when they are at one they can
carry everything in the Community before them – except Mrs Thatcher
when she digs in . . . if Paris and Bonn are in agreement on something it is
well on its way to being accomplished. If they are not, no other combination has yet shown itself capable of achieving remotely similar results.'[33]
However (gestures apart), this combination could not really be carried into
the field of security, partly because French protection was no substitute for
American, partly because France cut herself off by withdrawing from the
main forums of NATO. This requires some qualification of the picture
painted above of Franco-German relations: as Schmidt put it to Vance,
'the United States was our most important ally but France was our
closest one'.[34]

Giscard lost office in 1981, Schmidt in 1982. Their successors were less
close. For one thing Mitterrand began by worrying about the advances
neutralist sentiment was making in the SPD, and adopting a strongly
pro-USA line during the general East–West tension of the early 1980s; for

---

[33] J.R. Frears, *France in the Giscard Presidency* (1981) p. 107; Tugendhat, *Making
Sense of Europe*, pp. 92, 104.
[34] Helmut Schmidt, *Men and Powers. A Political Retrospective* (1990) p. 205. Schmidt
was telling Vance not to play Bonn against Paris; but Bonn also always resisted French
attempts to make it choose between Paris and Washington. Questions of NATO strategy also generated a powerful Anglo-German partnership (above, pp. 35–6).

another Mitterrand and Kohl had no language in common. Later, however, they found common ground in relation to the construction of Europe. For Kohl placed greater emphasis than his predecessors on German reunification, and sought to balance it by stressing European integration: 'Our passionate advocacy of European unification', he had said in 1984, 'stems to a great extent from awareness that a peaceful settlement of the German question is only conceivable within a greater European frame-work'.[35] With the advent of German reunification, Kohl hoped that simultaneous progress with European integration would allay fears of an over-mighty Germany or one again tempted to look East away from its recent European partnerships. France sometimes seemed distinctly worried by such prospects. But talk of Franco-German tension repeatedly evaporated into demonstrative moves like Mitterrand and Kohl's joint appearance at an emergency European Parliament debate in November 1989 or the Franco-German call in April 1990 for immediate preparations for a conference on political unity. Also during the financial turbulence of 1992–3, the Bundesbank exerted itself far more to keep the franc in the European Exchange Rate Mechanism than it did to support any other currency;[36] and in 1994 Mitterrand secretly contributed some 10 million pounds to Kohl's election funds.[37]

After reunification Germany no longer had any direct need for external support, and it has perhaps been ready to stand up rather more for its own state interests. Such changes inevitably impacted on its relationship with France, and have often led commentators to forecast the end of the Franco-German axis: in 1999 the *Annual Register* felt this had 'all but collapsed', adding in 2000 that 'France was finding it difficult to adapt to a situation in which Germany was now the dominant partner.'[38] But then suddenly 'on the eve of a European summit' in 2002, 'President . . . Chirac and . . . Chancellor . . . Schröder met at the Conrad Hotel in Brussels and agreed a formula' protecting EU agricultural policy and spending until 2013 (a French interest) while limiting other EU spending (a German one), 'a

---

[35] Tugendhat, *Making Sense of Europe*, p. 99.

[36] Charles Grant, *Delors. Inside the house that Jacques built* (1994) pp. 222–3, 227–8, 262–4.

[37] 100 million francs, diverted from the state-owned oil company Elf-Aquitaine – *The Annual Register. A Record of World Events*, 2000, p. 53.

[38] *Annual Register*, 1999, p. 430; 2000, pp. 55–6, 398; a bone of contention in 2000 was Germany's wish, as the largest state in the EU, to have more votes on the EU Council than any other – interestingly it lost, France, Britain and Italy retaining parity.

deal which gave the French the assurances . . . they needed and removed a prime objection to' the EU's eastern enlargement. 'Much was made of UK Prime Minister . . . Blair's wounded reaction to this deal', but it sailed through the subsequent summit with only minor amendment.[39] In 2003 Germany and France were further drawn together by shared opposition to the US–UK intervention in Iraq, and by their common refusal to comply with the EU Stability and Growth Pact's limit on state deficit spending. The *Annual Register* was now talking of 'the renewal of the Franco-German axis', with a new treaty on cooperation signed on the fortieth anniversary of the 1963 De Gaulle–Adenauer one; 'Chirac pictured the two countries as the "driving force" in the promotion of the "European project",' and even himself 'symbolically represented Germany' at an EU summit when Schröder had hurriedly to leave for a Bundestag vote.[40] Relations continued good until 2005, when Chirac encountered massive domestic setbacks and Schröder lost office altogether. At present it remains to be seen how Chancellor Merkel will interact with the new French leadership elected in 2007. Past experience suggests both downs and ups, but with the capacity (during the latter) to collaborate more closely than with any other countries. There is also a French feeling that such collaboration, even bilateral integration, is the best way to influence a potentially stronger Germany,[41] a feeling likely to grow more urgent should Germany fully emerge from the socioeconomic stasis that set in in the early to mid 1990s. (In all this, there are parallels with the Anglo-American 'special relationship', though here, of course, the disparity of power is vastly greater.)

Britain and European integration 1945–59

If the development of the European Communities helped the reintegration and revival of West Germany, it played a role in Britain's diplomatic decline. At bottom, of course, decline stemmed from relative economic weakness and loss of empire; but the decision to stand aloof from the early stages of Western European economic integration imposed appreciable

---

[39] *Annual Register*, 2002, p. 416.
[40] ibid., 2003, pp. 52–3.
[41] cf. the 2001 call by French Socialists, concerned at the then deteriorating relationship, for a core group to take Europe forward, 'beginning with a "strengthened union of two"' – *Annual Register*, 2001, pp. 435–6.

costs. Bevin had initially been attracted by a European Customs Union, not least because of the possibility it held out that the European states and their colonies 'would form a bloc which, both in population and in production capacity, could stand on an equality with the Western hemisphere and Soviet blocs'. So in September 1947 Britain both joined in a European 'Customs Union Study Group' and established its own cabinet committee to look into the idea. But the Study Group moved only very slowly, largely because it came to feel that tariffs were not the real problem and that a gradual lifting of trade restrictions under the aegis of the OEEC was more promising. This was consonant with the ideas of the British Treasury, which did not like customs unions (whether European or Commonwealth) and which saw the exercise as a diversion from the immediate need to earn hard currency.[42]

Over the course of 1948, Bevin seems gradually to have come over to the Treasury viewpoint. At first he had sought, in his call for a Western Union, a British-led Europe that could (once it had recovered) 'be independent both of the United States and of the Soviet Union'.[43] As the Cold War deepened, his interests shifted towards closer involvement with the United States on the basis of NATO and other security cooperation. In January 1949 an interdepartmental conference agreed to look chiefly to

the Atlantic Pact. We hope to secure a special relationship with the USA and Canada within this, for in the last resort we cannot rely upon the European countries . . . we must in practice establish the position that US will defend us, whatever happens to the Europeans.

. . . Our policy should be to assist Europe to recover as far as we can . . . But the concept must be one of limited liability . . . [not extending] beyond the point at which the assistance leaves us too weak to be a worth-while ally for USA if Europe collapses – i.e. beyond the point where our own viability was impaired . . . Nor can we embark upon measures of 'co-operation' which surrender our sovereignty and which lead us down paths along which there is no return.

In February 1949 the Cabinet confirmed that its plans should be coordinated with those of other OEEC members, but only 'so long as' British

---

[42] British trade with Europe then resulted in an appreciable loss of dollars.
[43] cf. e.g. CAB 129/23, C.P. (48) 6 [4 January 1948], and the 'Confidential Annex' to the Cabinet Conclusions of 5 March.

'economic recovery was not thereby prejudiced'. In October it accepted that 'We must remain, as we have always been in the past, different in character from other European nations and fundamentally incapable of wholehearted integration with them.'[44]

This was less negative than it sounds – Britain did much to organise West European response to the offer of Marshall Aid, and contributed both to functional cooperation within the OEEC and to the establishment of the European Payments Union (which in combining Western Europe, its colonies and the sterling area had much in common with Bevin's 1947–8 vision). But it resisted federalist and supranational proposals. In 1948–9 this led to a contest with France as to whether the 1948 Brussels treaty should lead on to a real European parliament. Bevin had in 1949 to concede a Consultative Assembly attached to the new 'Council of Europe', but he ensured that it should remain 'as little embarrassing as possible'; with the important exception of the 1950 European Convention on Human Rights,[45] it has never amounted to much. In 1950, as we have seen, France was more insistent; come what may, it would secure a supranational High Authority over coal and steel. Schuman does not seem to have sought to exclude Britain, were it to accept this. But he was quite prepared to go forward without it.

This is often seen as the point where Britain 'missed the bus' – experience of the ECSC clearly accustomed its members to working together. But staying outside the ECSC imposed no obvious economic costs; and the next 'European' venture, the Defence Community, never got off the ground. The general British view, often expounded by Churchill, was that the UK was strategically placed at the intersection of three circles, the United States, the Commonwealth, and continental Europe: for both sentimental and power-political reasons, the first two were the more important. Accordingly Britain rejected an invitation to join in the elaboration of the EEC, even though France appeared flexible on policy and anxious for

[44] John W. Young, *Britain, France and the Unity of Europe 1945–51* (Leicester, 1984) esp. pp. 68–9 and Chap. 13; Milward, *The Reconstruction of Western Europe 1945–51* (1984) Chap. 7; Bullock, *Bevin*, esp. pp. 517–20, 733–4; Sir Richard Clarke (ed. Sir Alec Cairncross) *Anglo-American Economic Collaboration in War and Peace 1942–9* (Oxford, 1982) pp. 208–9; Cabinet Conclusions, 24 February 1949, p. 81.
[45] Several states (including in 1998 Britain) have incorporated this into their domestic legislation; some others allow their nationals to take them to the European Court of Justice, and so *de facto* expose themselves to a degree of external judicial review.

British collaboration. The decision was influenced (as Macmillan later put it) by two considerations, both mistaken: 'We thought they would not succeed [a view shared, at least in some moods, by Spaak][46] – or if they did that we could work out a satisfactory association'.[47] In the course of 1956 Macmillan persuaded his colleagues at least to consider association; and by July he was able to propose that the OEEC study plans for a free trade area between the EEC Six and other member states. Elaborating these plans took time, partly because of the need to square the Commonwealth and partly because of Suez; the Six were not disposed to wait the outcome, or to contemplate further negotiations until the Rome Treaties had been ratified. What Britain ideally sought (though it was increasingly prepared to make concessions) was that the EEC should be surrounded by an area with which there should be free trade in *industrial* products; this would square the circle, permitting Britain to continue to allow Commonwealth goods free access and subsidise its own farmers (an important political interest whose vulnerability to competition was much exaggerated). France had other ideas, and negotiations were slow. They were further interrupted by the French May 1958 political crisis; but in October it was agreed to push them forward with a view to conclusion before the first EEC tariff cuts took effect in January. By then de Gaulle had privately made his hostility clear to Macmillan, provoking the anguished plea, 'The Common Market is the [Napoleonic] continental blockade. England will not accept it. I beg you to give it up. Or we shall enter a war that will doubtless only be economic to start with, but that may later extend itself by degrees to other areas.' Macmillan had always looked, not without some encouragement, to Germany to overcome French opposition; after the uproar engendered by de Gaulle's proposals for a Three Power NATO directorate, he was still hopeful in November. But on the 14th, while a meeting was in progress, Paris announced that 'it is not possible to create a Free Trade Area as wished by the British'; despite Benelux attempts to mediate, this brought matters to an end.[48]

[46] cf. his gloomy prognostications of February 1956 and his appeal to Britain 'to take the lead in the creation of a united Europe' – Macmillan, *Memoirs*, iv, p. 76.
[47] *Memoirs*, vi, p. 15; S. Burgess and G. Edwards, 'The Six plus One: British policy-making and the question of European economic integration, 1955', *International Affairs*, xliv (1988) pp. 101–2.
[48] Macmillan, *Memoirs*, iv, Chaps 3, 14; Horne, *Macmillan*, i, pp. 349–51, 362–3, 385–6; ii, pp. 31–4; de Gaulle, *Mémoires*, p. 199; *Keesing's*, 15098, 15394–5, 17613–14.

Britain's applications for EEC membership, vetoed by de Gaulle in 1963 and 1967, successful in 1973; Wilson and Thatcher renegotiate terms; Developments since 1984

The seven excluded countries[49] responded by adopting a Swedish plan for a European Free Trade Area of their own (with effect from 1960). After British and Swedish concessions on agriculture, this was easily negotiated. EFTA members' economies were, for geographical reasons, not really complementary. But the organisation worked smoothly, and it eventually secured the industrial free trade area with the EC that Britain had been seeking before 1958: 1972 agreements freed most industrial goods from tariffs in 1977, all such goods plus some processed foodstuffs in 1983.[50] Macmillan, however, hardly gave EFTA a fair trial. For in July 1960, depressed by the collapse of the Four Power summit, he asked:

Shall we be caught between a hostile (or less and less friendly) America and a boastful powerful 'Empire of Charlemagne' – now under French but later bound to come under German control? Is this the real reason for 'joining' the Common Market (if we are acceptable) and for abandoning a) the Seven b) British agriculture c) the Commonwealth? It's a grim choice.

Eventually he decided to make it. For, as he told ministers in 1961, 'If we stand aloof, we shall find ourselves in a position of growing weakness. Europe under France could well wield more power than the UK both with the Americans and some Commonwealth countries.'[51] The process of reaching a final decision, sounding out (unhappy) Commonwealth partners, and convincing colleagues and party took until August 1961.

Macmillan had asked Kennedy to prepare the ground for Britain's application by talking to de Gaulle. After his visit to Paris (on the eve of the Vienna Summit), Kennedy told Macmillan 'The general has no wish whatever to see the United Kingdom join the Common Market'. During a visit in November 1961 de Gaulle made this plain in person. Macmillan

---

[49] Sweden, Norway, Denmark, the UK, Austria, Switzerland, Portugal.

[50] *Annual Register*, 1983, p. 352.

[51] Horne, *Macmillan*, ii, p. 256; *The Times*, 1 January 1992, p. 5. Macmillan also looked to US investment to rejuvenate the economy, and knew this was less likely if Britain remained outside the EEC.

countered by forecasting a dangerous and unpredictable response were Britain rebuffed; it might, for instance, junk its expensive troop commitments to European defence 'if the Europeans did not want her in Europe'. De Gaulle was unmoved: one of the things he had found most attractive about the EEC in 1958, his biographer judges,[52] was the concern it occasioned across the Channel: 'if his British neighbours were so very much alarmed by it, it must be of benefit to the Continent'. Now he explained that if Britain came in with its Commonwealth connections, the USA would want to join too. 'In short, if Europe let the rest of the world in, it would lose itself; Europe would have been drowned in the Atlantic'.[53]

Serious negotiation could not begin until the Six had resolved their own deep differences over agriculture in January 1962. Even then talks went slowly, partly because the British wished to tie up every detail and to minimise the impact of entry on the Commonwealth. The original hope that most points would be settled by the summer holidays proved unfounded; and in December Macmillan thought the crunch would come in February 1963. These delays must have reinforced the French contention that Britain would not easily be assimilated. More importantly, de Gaulle's domestic position strengthened enormously during 1962 with the ending of the Algerian war and his remarkable referendum and electoral victories, and he may have felt freer to act as a result. That summer Adenauer seconded his suspicions – 'England could not bear it that France was the leading power [in the EEC]. It was the old English game with the continent, divide and rule' – and advised him to 'negotiate toughly'. A meeting between Macmillan and de Gaulle in June had not gone too badly. For Macmillan made concessions on both Commonwealth preferences and the need for an EEC common agricultural policy, though de Gaulle expressed some doubt as to whether he would be politically able to deliver them. When Macmillan returned in December, claiming that he had done so (though privately expecting a 'great battle' with the General), the result was a disaster. The details of their conversations at Rambouillet are controversial (below, p. 94). De Gaulle's primary concerns seem to have been those of power: at present 'France could say "no" even against the Germans; she could stop [EEC] policies with which she disagreed . . . Once Britain and all the rest joined the organisation things would be different.' More generally, contrary to the pattern of much recent history, Britain was now the supplicant, and de Gaulle wanted to take advantage of this:

[52] Jean Lacouture, *De Gaulle: The Ruler 1945–1970* (1991) p. 213.
[53] *The Times*, 1 January 1992, p. 5; *The Independent*, 2 January 1992, p. 6.

'I want her naked'.[54] In January 1963 he put an end to the formal negotiations on EEC entry, a decision Adenauer tacitly endorsed by concluding the Franco-German treaty.

In 1967 de Gaulle vetoed another British application to join the EEC. In 1969 de Gaulle's successor was induced to allow serious negotiations by the promise that the Six would in the mean time press on with European construction and in particular the completion of the CAP. British accession in 1973 was expected to lead to something of a Bonn–Paris–London triangle within the Community. But in Opposition the Labour party had reverted to its initial hostility to EC membership. Wilson's strategy for containing this, when he returned to office, was to demand renegotiation of British entry terms, declare the result a success and then get it legitimated by a domestic referendum. In his own terms he succeeded, though Labour's hostility to membership re-emerged even stronger after it fell from power in 1979. But the episode strained the patience of other EC members, and returned Britain to the role of *demandeur*. Nor did it really tackle the issue of Community taxation: as a result partly of its pattern of imports, partly of the way the CAP had developed, Britain found itself the only net contributor to Community funds apart from Germany. The sums involved were not huge, but they were burdensome to pay over the exchanges and, given the UK's comparative poverty, clearly unjust. Since there had already been one 'renegotiation', there was little disposition to reopen the question; and when Thatcher did so in 1979 she was apparently subjected to sexist bullying by the Schmidt–Giscard axis. That proved a mistake, and led to much thumping of the table before a settlement was reached with the 1984 Fontainebleau compromise.[55]

This brought Britain temporarily to the centre of the Community, where it played a major role in the creation of a true internal market. But Thatcher soon found herself at odds with both the federalist and the social trends that then set in (see pp. 504, 507–8, 511), a development that

[54] Without her American guardians and her Commonwealth cousins – Lacouture, *De Gaulle*, pp. 347–60; Horne, *Macmillan*, ii, pp. 256–8, 326–9, 428 ff; Macmillan, *Memoirs*, vi, Chaps 1, 5, 11; Adenauer, *Erinnerungen 1959–63*, pp. 160, 165, 178.

[55] This still left the net British contribution disproportionately high, but reduced and capped it by providing a 66% rebate (Tugendhat, *Making Sense of Europe*, pp. 120–5; *The Economist*, 28 July 1990, p. 42). Threats to reopen the question were often used to pressurise Britain in EC/EU negotiations; but there was no substantial change until 2005, when Blair had to concede modifications during negotiation of the first budget of the expanded 25-member EU.

contributed to her domestic political downfall in 1990. Her successor, Major, managed to patch things up, letting the Maastricht treaty go forward in 1991, but securing a semi-detached position (including an opt-out from the Social Chapter). However, his government was almost destroyed by 'Black Wednesday' in 1992, when financial speculation forced sterling out of the European Exchange Rate Mechanism (ERM); this fed a surge of hostility to the EU in the Conservative party (historically the more 'European' of the two), and parliamentary ratification of Maastricht proved difficult and politically damaging to secure. Thereafter Britain stayed aloof from moves to create a 'single currency'. Labour's advent to power in 1997 brought some changes (like adhesion to the Social Chapter). But the UK joined neither the euro nor the Schengen area within which border controls have been abolished;[56] and Blair's government, like its predecessors, remained hesitant about federalist extensions to EU powers, and therefore often at odds with Franco-German visions of 'Europe'.[57] On the other hand, the European Commission and Court of Justice's growing activism, in the early 2000s, in promoting free economic competition and restraining dirigiste state protectionism within the EU, together – at least in the short term – with the Union's eastwards extensions, have brought it, in many ways, closer than ever before to the preferred British vision of 'Europe'.

NATO

If the Community had emerged as an increasingly important element in the politics and horizons of Europeans, in 1991 it still had no military component. For Western Europe that aspect of security came from the Atlantic alliance, which, while directed against the threat from the East, simultaneously provided reassurance against the wrong kind of German revival; as its first Secretary-General undiplomatically put it, NATO existed to keep the Americans in, the Russians out, and the Germans down. NATO turned out to have been more securely based than its Warsaw Pact counterpart; but it might have disintegrated either because the people in one or more

---

[56] Without continued British border controls there would clearly have been an influx of non-EU immigrants (who congregated very visibly near Calais in hopes of smuggling themselves through the Channel Tunnel); also, unlike continental countries, Britain (still) rejects a system of national identity cards.

[57] Opinion polls strongly suggested that the UK would reject the proposed European Constitution in a referendum. However, a major crisis was at least temporarily avoided in 2005 by its prior rejection by French and Dutch voters.

countries would stand it no longer, or as a result of the mutual suspicions of governments.[58] Unsurprisingly both the French and the Italian Communist Parties opposed NATO (though the latter eventually came round to accepting it). In Germany the SPD, though well disposed towards the West, saw Adenauer's foreign policy as sealing their country's division and campaigned against military alignment, conscription, and (most strongly) in 1958 against the 'Atomic Death' stationing of nuclear weapons on German territory. In 1959–60 the party changed course; for twenty years it stood firmly behind military integration with the West; and it was an SPD-led government that procured the 1979 NATO agreement on the deployment of cruise and Pershing missiles. This was meant to re-assure West Europeans that they would remain linked to the US strategic deterrent; but as East–West relations froze after the Soviet invasion of Afghanistan, many came to see it as preparation for fighting a nuclear war on German soil. The SPD veered sharply towards a policy of disengage-ment and the dissolution of blocs; Schmidt managed, with increasing difficulty, to contain this trend, but after he lost the chancellorship in 1982 his policy was ditched (with the support of his predecessor, Brandt). Practically, however, the SPD's change had little effect, since the new CDU–FDP government continued with the previous policy and was sus-tained by the 1983 election.

In Britain, too, the Labour party, though it had done much to create the American alliance in the first place, twice came to query it. In 1960, a year of rising East–West tension with the failure of the Paris Summit, a number of moves (like the decision to base US Polaris submarines in Scotland) emphasised British involvement with the US deterrent and consequent exposure to Soviet attack. At the same time attempts to modernise Britain's own nuclear forces were much in the news. The result was the sudden upsurge of the Campaign for Nuclear Disarmament (CND). Meanwhile the Labour party was reeling from a third electoral defeat and rejecting its leader's attempts to steer it towards a different domestic policy. In this context the 1960 Party Conference resolved in favour of scrapping British and expelling US nuclear weapons; in other respects the

---

[58] War between Greece and Turkey, though not between any other NATO members, has certainly been thinkable on a number of occasions: in 1974 the Greek military regime (then *in extremis*) is said to have been stopped by the USA from launching what would then have been a suicidal attack; and in 1996 confrontation over the disputed Imia/Kardak islets was diffused by the direct intervention of President Clinton (*Annual Register*, 1996, pp. 90–1, 96).

insurgents were less successful, and in 1961 the leadership managed to reverse Conference's decision on American weapons. Thereafter the issue gradually died down, aided by Labour's electoral recovery and its desire to present itself as 'the natural party of government'. Twenty years later Labour's loss of office and violent swing to the Left coincided with decisions to deploy US cruise missiles and to replace British Polaris with Trident submarines. CND revived from the dead; this time Labour's attachment to it ran deeper, with the adoption of two unilateralist leaders (Foot and Kinnock) in succession and of a fully unilateralist programme. As in Germany, the 1983 and 1987 elections decided otherwise. No country, therefore, has yet broken with NATO as a result of popular disillusion.[59]

There have, however, been some near misses. Iceland let it be understood that it might leave if the 'Cod War' with Britain (see *The Post-Imperialist Age*, pp. 476–7) was not settled to its satisfaction. After the 1974 revolution Portugal adopted a leftist and Third World stance; but it did not seek to expel the crucial US bases from the Azores, for fear that this would bring the islands to declare independence with the USA's blessing; in late 1979, elections brought into office a government anxious to mend its fences with NATO. Turkey's 1974 intervention in Cyprus led the US Congress to impose an arms embargo, so Turkey closed US bases in retaliation; the quarrel, however, was not of Turkey's seeking, and the bases were reopened in 1978–80 after Congress first rescinded the embargo and then voted to restore military aid. In 1981 Greece elected a government (under Papandreou) with considerable sympathy for the Soviet point of view and a mandate for the closing of US bases.[60] In office, it was checked partly by the loss of dollars this would entail, partly by fear of the consequences if Turkey continued to receive US military aid while Greece did not. So negotiations over the bases were very leisurely; a settlement was reached in 1990 after Papandreou's fall. The 1980s also saw difficulties with Spain: defence agreements with the USA in the 1950s had helped restore international respectability to the Franco regime, but had not endeared the Atlantic connection to his opponents. In 1986 the Socialist government nevertheless brought Spain into NATO by referendum, to strengthen both its European credentials and its claims to recover

[59] However, de Gaulle did take France out of NATO's supranational military structures, if not out of the 1949 North Atlantic Treaty itself (below, p. 492).
[60] The USA was widely blamed for not having distanced itself from the 1967–74 Greek military regime, and for not protecting Cyprus from Turkey.

Gibraltar; to balance this, it pressed the US to abandon its great air base near Madrid; in late 1988 Washington at last gave way, though only after Spain had undertaken not to inquire too closely into the presence of nuclear weapons in other US facilities.

Mostly, though, disputes within NATO, while sometimes intense, were during the Cold War deliberately conducted in low key, and revolved around questions of strategy often incapable of resolution as long as peace held. There was little disposition to push things to extremes, and a general preference for accepting assurances in which one only half-believed, rather than so rocking the boat as to destroy entirely the alliance's credibility and utility. Nor did the alliance disintegrate with the disappearance of the Soviet threat, for the continued engagement in NATO of both Germany and the United States was generally seen as essential for European security. But new problems arose: how should NATO respond to the obvious East European eagerness to join; how should it handle troubles and crises outside its immediate area; and how should it relate to the European Union?

When discussing German reunification, the USSR had shown itself unhappy with the idea of NATO's extension to former Warsaw Pact territory; and there is a conflict of evidence as to whether the USSR was or was not given informal assurances at the November–December Paris CSCE conference that NATO would come no further east. Unfortunately, from the Russian perspective, no sooner had East European states broken with the Warsaw Pact than they, and more especially Poland, Hungary and Czechoslovakia, started pressing to join NATO; as the Polish Defence Minister put it in 1993, 'NATO should be the foundation of European security and for that reason we should like to be a member'. The initial US response was to persuade NATO, in October 1993, to offer East European and ex-Soviet states, including Russia, a 'Partnership for Peace'. This provided for consultation and joint military exercises with NATO, and enabled its members to join NATO in mounting possible peace-keeping operations. By the end of 1994 22 states, including Russia, had signed up, by late 1995 27; and it was further supplemented by a 'Mediterranean Dialogue' with North African states and a 'Euro-Atlantic Council'. US Secretary of State Warren Christopher expressed the hope that the 'Partnership for Peace' would encourage 'useful habits of cooperation'. But, as one account observed, 'it would not give the East Europeans what they wanted most, namely a Western promise to guarantee their security'. So the problem remained.

Attempts were made to conciliate Russia by concluding special arrangements for political consultation in 1994, upgraded in 1997 to a

'Permanent Joint Council' with copious liaison at NATO headquarters in Brussels. Assurances were also given that NATO had no plans to station nuclear weapons or 'substantial' numbers of troops on the territory of new members. But Russia still felt sore, President Yeltsin saying in 1997 that NATO expansion represented the most serious dispute since the Cuban missiles crisis, Foreign Minister Primakov calling it 'the biggest mistake in Europe since the end of World War II'. Nevertheless invitations were finally issued to Hungary, the Czech Republic and Poland in 1997, and in April 1999 they duly joined NATO. Neither Hungary nor the Czech Republic bordered on Russia, and Poland did so only with the Russian enclave of Kaliningrad. But NATO reserved the right to consider new members, and further adhesions might have been expected to be more controversial. In fact President Putin (who at first enjoyed excellent personal relations with George W. Bush and warmly supported the 'War on Terror') proved surprisingly relaxed when he was told in late 2001 that enlargement would definitely proceed (and compensated by a new NATO–Russia decision-making Council). In 2002 invitations were issued not only to Slovenia, Slovakia, Bulgaria and Romania, but also to Lithuania, Latvia and Estonia, all former Republics of the USSR.[61] They joined without incident in March 2004.[62] Even so, the problems of extension have not gone away. For in Ukraine's late 2004 presidential elections 'orange revolution' popular protests (aided by some Western technical assistance) overturned the rigged return of a pro-Russian candidate strongly backed by Putin, and installed Viktor Yuschenko, who promised to reorient Ukraine and seek both EU and NATO membership. Though the prospect of such a transformation was necessarily distant, the episode alarmed the Kremlin (and definitely ended the by now already strained Putin–Bush honeymoon). By 2007 Putin was strongly denouncing NATO's eastern expansion.

Throughout the Cold War, NATO (to use Gilbert and Sullivan's language) 'Did nothing in paticular, And did it very well', projecting deterrence to the East and reassurance to the West without firing a shot. This happy condition did not last. The neighbouring state of Yugoslavia

[61] Albania, Croatia and Macedonia were seen as not yet ripe for membership. Romania and Bulgaria had been supported by Greece and Turkey, which they linked geographically with the rest of NATO; and Romania had made airfields etc. available for US use against the Taliban in Afghanistan.

[62] *Annual Register*, 1993, pp. 440–1; 1994, p. 458; 1995, pp. 433–4; 1996, pp. 132, 428–9; 1997, pp. 139, 438–9; 1999, pp. 405–6; 2000, pp. 377–8; 2001, p. 415; 2002, pp. 394–6; 2004, p. 370.

collapsed in 1991, with Bosnia succombing to civil war in 1992 (below, pp. 599–600). The United Nations duly deployed 'peace-keeping' forces; in 1993 it decided to buttress these with a 'no-fly' zone over Bosnia, and turned to NATO to enforce this. Enforcement was actually very lax, but in February 1994 four Serb aircraft were destroyed in NATO's first ever use of force. 1994–5 then saw occasional NATO air strikes in defence of UN-appointed 'safe havens', though not the protection of Srebenica (which Serbs captured in July 1995, massacring the male population). That summer UN forces were moved out of harm's way; in late July the UN Secretary-General waived the right of his local representative to veto air strikes, and in August–September 1995 NATO flew over 300 sorties. The operation's dimensions reflected NATO rather than UN decisions, and as it progressed its aims may have expanded from simply protecting Sarajevo to, in the NATO Secretary-General's words, bringing 'the Bosnian Serbs to the negotiating table'.[63] Together with offensives by the armies of Croatia and of Bosnia's Muslim–Croat coalition, the air strikes did bring the parties to Dayton, Ohio, where they accepted a settlement largely devised by the USA; December 1995 then saw the deployment of an overwhelming NATO-led UN force to impose this locally.

That UN resolutions in mid-1995 had been vague, leaving much latitude to NATO decisions, had been due to a wish not to trigger a veto by Russia. When Western revulsion was next kindled by Serbia's 1998 repression in Kosovo, it was clear Russia would not permit UN intervention. To bypass this, the USA (with strong Franco-British support) acted instead through NATO, which first sought to impose a settlement, then, when Serbia predictably rejected this, bombed it until it withdrew its army and administration from Kosovo; the UN occupation forces that replaced them, though (as in Bosnia) again containing a Russian component, were again NATO-led. Logistically they were supported by NATO troops in Macedonia; this proved fortunate, since these were able, when Albanian–Slav tensions there came close to boiling over in 2001, to exercise a calming influence until the UN transformed them into the peace-keeping force China had earlier vetoed.[64] 2001 also saw the first ever invocation (in solidarity with the United States after 9/11) of NATO's fundamental article whereby an attack on one member must be treated as

---

[63] *Keesing's*, 40606–7, 40688–91; Mats Berdal, in David M. Malone (ed.) *The UN Security Council. From the Cold War to the 21st Century* (Boulder, Colorado, 2004) pp. 461–2.

[64] *Annual Register*, 1999, p. 405; 2001, p. 414; Malone, *Security Council*, p. 14n.

an attack on all. But this was for show only; the USA bypassed the alliance when toppling the Taliban regime in Afghanistan, and, later, Saddam Hussein in Iraq. Both wars, of course, were 'out of area', and operations of this kind would never have come within NATO's purview before the end of the Cold War. However, most of NATO's recent planning had centred on the capability to mount 'out of area' missions; and in 2003 NATO took direct control of the UN's 'International Assistance Force' in Kabul, an operation much expanded in 2006.[65]

As a result of the European Defence Community debacle (pp. 190–1, 207–18), the EEC/EC steered clear of military matters. So throughout the Cold War, security for almost all countries in Western Europe came from NATO.[66] NATO remains the provider of collective security for its members, and several 'new members' were said to view it 'in unreconstructed Cold War terms, as a guarantee of collective self-defence, perhaps against a resurgent Russia'.[67] But in the 1990s this, which had been the alliance's central mission, came largely to be taken for granted. Instead NATO turned to planning, and occasionally mounting, what would previously have been seen as 'out of area' operations. However, the EU developed aspirations to do likewise, and so became at least a potential competitor. The 1991 Maastricht treaty had included a genuflection towards the establishment of a 'common foreign and security policy' as one of the 'pillars' of the EU; its 1997 Amsterdam successor envisaged future peace-keeping operations mounted by the 'Western European Union' (WEU); and in 1999 the EU decided to absorb the WEU.[68]

Any credible EU defence pillar would require the cooperation of Britain and France, the two countries still able to mount military operations

---

[65] *Annual Register*, 2003, p. 419. NATO's 2006 operations there were much hampered by widespread reluctance to contribute troops or allow those contributed to be sent to the more disturbed districts; this left most of the fighting to British, Canadian, Dutch, and (operating independently) US soldiers.

[66] Finland (and Austria) relied on not offending the USSR; Sweden and Switzerland, both neutral, mounted major defence efforts of their own. Gaullist France left NATO's command structure, though continuing *de facto* to cooperate with it, and maintained an independent nuclear deterrent; so did Britain, though its nuclear forces had both NATO and national targets. Lastly Greek and Turkish forces were directed as much against each other as against the Warsaw Pact.

[67] *Annual Register*, 2002, pp. 395–6.

[68] John Pinder, *The Building of the European Union* (Oxford, 1998 edn) pp. 241–6; *Annual Register*, 2000, p. 379 – the WEU military alliance had been established to cover West German rearmament (above, p. 218), but had never acquired any real functions.

outside Europe. From 1998 they did so cooperate, but their aims often differed. President Chirac often spoke of creating a purely European defence capability; on the fortieth anniversary of their 1963 treaty France and Germany called for a full EU defence union with a mutual security guarantee, and they were joined in April 2003 by Belgium and Luxembourg. Such a Union would tend to freeze out the US-dominated NATO, and was described by an American ambassador as 'one of the greatest dangers to the transatlantic relationship'. Britain (with Italian and Dutch support) was very sensitive to such dangers. But it also wanted to enhance the defence capabilities of the European states (significantly reduced, by the late 1990s, as a result of 'peace dividend' post-Cold War cuts), for fear that otherwise the USA might either ignore or disengage from an alliance to which it seemed the sole contributor. These divergencies within Franco-British collaboration led Lady Thatcher to observe in 2001 that 'The public could be forgiven for thinking there are two plans: one for strengthening NATO, and one for creating a rival organisation to it.'

Essentially this remained true in 2006. But in the interim, practical EU–NATO compromises were worked out: a small EU Military Staff was created in 2001, but EU operations were to draw on NATO 'assets', and in 2003 it was agreed there should be a NATO presence within the EU Staff as well as vice versa. Using such facilities, the EU took charge of the police in Bosnia in 2003, and of the (by then much reduced) military force there in late 2004. 2003 also saw the EU (at France's urging) take over from NATO the peace-keeping mission in Macedonia, and mount a French-led stabilisation operation in the Congo (albeit of a kind France could well have undertaken on its own). NATO therefore faces a degree of competition, but very much at the lower end of its register. A European Rapid Reaction Force of 60,000 was projected in 2003; however, until this is achieved, it will be impossible to say whether the EU's comparatively recent interest in defence matters has served to strengthen or to displace NATO.[69]

The US–UK 'special relationship'

For both Britain and France questions relating to the US alliance have assumed particular importance. Indeed the 'special relationship' was an important component of Britain's post-war claims still to be a Great

[69] *Annual Register*, 2000, p. 379; 2001, pp. 417–19; 2003, pp. 422–3; 2004, pp. 371–4.

Power: 'It was clear,' reported the British ambassador (Sir Oliver Franks) after talks in 1949, 'that the Americans decided to regard us once more as their principal partner in foreign affairs, and not just as a member of the European queue.' From a British perspective, such a relationship offered the prospect of making 'use of American power for purposes which we regard as good', or (in Bevin's words) exerting 'sufficient control over the policy of the well-intentioned but inexperienced colossus on whose co-operation our safety depends . . . It can only be done by influencing the United States Government and people, not by opposing or discouraging them.'[70]

There has been much debate as to how special this 'special relationship' really was. No cut and dried answer is possible, since it varied from time to time, person to person and issue to issue. Thus during Truman's administration the two governments did *not* see eye to eye on Mossadegh's Iran, but the great US oil companies instinctively took Anglo-Iranian's side. Dulles dropped his predecessor's policy and had the CIA join the British in covert action to topple Mossadegh. But he (and the CIA) initially so inclined towards the Egyptians in their disputes with Britain as to prompt Eden's outburst, 'they want to replace us in Egypt . . . they want to run the world'. When national interests diverged there could be much asperity. But the relationship rested on similar (though not identical) world views, and had a strong core of perceived mutual self-interest. The more obvious benefits came to Britain, as the weaker partner; Americans sometimes found embarrassing the way in which the British stressed the relationship, Eisenhower once remarking that Churchill was 'just a little Peter Pan' who would not adjust to Britain's changed position in the world. But US resources were not unlimited; the United States has generally found it desirable to work with partners (or 'proxies'), and for two decades after 1945 no other friendly country matched the British range of international positions or involvements. Indeed subsequent critics have claimed that, partly through delusions of grandeur, the British functioned as US mercenaries, and also risked Soviet retaliation by accepting so many US nuclear facilities as to become, in effect, an unsinkable American aircraft carrier.

Institutionally the relationship gave rise in 1946–8 to 'the complex package of agreements' between the USA and the Commonwealth (UK, Canada, Australia, New Zealand) 'often referred to as the "UKUSA

[70] Kenneth O. Morgan, *Labour in Power 1945–51* (Oxford, 1984) p. 385; David Reynolds, 'Rethinking Anglo-American Relations', *International Affairs*, lxv (1989) pp. 96–7.

treaty" that sealed a vast Western alliance',[71] and later to the arrangements made from 1957 for nuclear US–UK cooperation. But its essence lay rather in the habit of mutual consultation and the access this gave each country to the decision-making processes of the other: the legacy, in part, of being (in Churchill's words) 'mixed up together' in the combined planning of the Second World War, but one reinforced by a range of personal friendships and collaboration that spread well beyond the official sphere. Acheson recalls that, when Secretary of State (1949–53), he invited Franks to talk

regularly, and in complete personal confidence, about any international problems we saw arising. Neither would report or quote the other unless he got the other's consent . . . We met alone, usually at . . . at the end of the day . . . No one was informed even of the fact of the meeting.

Later, comparing the relations between our governments during our time with those under our successors, we concluded that whereas we thought of those relations and their management as part of domestic affairs, they had regarded them as foreign affairs.

A similar picture was given in late 1962. Acheson then fluttered the dovecots by pronouncing that, with the loss of its empire, Britain's 'attempt to play a separate power role – that is, a role apart from Europe, a role based on a "special relationship" with the United States . . . this role is about to be played out'. In reply, though perhaps also to soothe hurt British feelings, the White House instructed the State Department to tell the press that

US–UK relations are not based only on a power calculus, but also on a deep community of purpose and long practice of close cooperation. Examples are legion: nuclear affairs, Sino-Indian crisis, in which Sandys and Harriman missions would have been ineffective without each other, Berlin, and also Cuba, where . . . President and Prime Minister were in

---

[71] Aldrich, *The Hidden Hand*, Chap. 11. Of the 1980s a Foreign Office mandarin writes that, though Britain drew much more from the shared intelligence 'than we put in . . . in certain areas we provided an irreplaceable contribution and in general the Americans sought a second opinion from another world-wide operator whose skill and discretion could be relied on . . . We were in constant contact at all levels . . . and on such trips I felt less than at any other time that sense of inequality that customarily descends on British government representatives' in Washington ([Sir] Percy Cradock, *In Pursuit of British Interests. Reflections on Foreign Policy under Margaret Thatcher and John Major* (1997) p. 41).

daily intimate consultation to a degree not publicly known.[72] *'Special relationship' may not be a perfect phrase, but sneers at Anglo-American reality would be equally foolish.*[73]

Since it is so intangible, attempts to chart the rise and decline of the 'special relationship' can only be imprecise. That said, it would seem that in 1945 neither the Truman administration nor the Congress was particularly inclined to continue it. From 1946 onwards, though, the administration came increasingly to see the USSR as an adversary, and to back (or shore up) Britain against it. Certainly this did not extend to all policy areas: the USA cut off the wartime collaboration on the atom bomb, and Britain went it alone – Bevin observing that, to save future Foreign Secretaries from being talked at by their US counterparts as he had just been by Byrnes, Britain needed a bomb with 'the bloody Union Jack flying on top of it' 'whatever it costs'.[74] But NATO developed out of secret US–UK–Canadian talks, and many other Cold War developments followed this pattern.

In his early years President Eisenhower felt Britain was trying to push things too far; he noted that Churchill:

has fixed in his mind a certain international relationship he is trying to establish . . . This is that Britain and the British Commonwealth are not to be treated just as other nations would be treated by the United States . . . On the contrary, he . . . intends that those countries shall enjoy a

---

[72] Macmillan did indeed phone Kennedy frequently during the crisis, and held a grouchy cabinet to public support of the US position. Ambassador Ormsby-Gore persuaded Kennedy to locate the blockade far closer to Cuba than the US Navy would have liked, so as to give Khrushchev more time to back off (though it is not clear that the Navy did in fact comply) – Graham T. Allison, *Essence of Decision: explaining the Cuban Missile Crisis* (Boston, 1971) pp. 129–32; and he was trusted with early thoughts on the missiles in Turkey that he did not believe 'the president would repeat . . . to any member of his administration except his brother Bobby'. But the British input was essentially marginal. On the 22nd Macmillan asked Ormsby-Gore what 'the President is really trying to do', adding that 'Since it seemed impossible to stop his action, I did not make the effort, although in the course of the day I was in a mind to do so' – but also that, if things looked like escalating into war, he would try 'by calling a conference of my own, or something of the kind, to stop it' – The *Independent*, 2 January 1993, p. 7; *The Times*, 1 January 1993, pp. 1, 6.

[73] Reynolds, 'Rethinking Anglo-American Relations', p. 109; Acheson, *Present at the Creation*, p. 323; Stephen E. Ambrose, *Eisenhower: the President* (1984) p. 146.

[74] *The Times*, 30 September 1982, p. 10.

relationship which will recognize the special place of partnership they occupied with us during World War II . . .

In those days he had the enjoyable feeling that he and our President were sitting on some rather Olympian platform . . . and directing world affairs from that point of vantage . . .

In the present international complexities, any hope of establishing such a relationship is completely fatuous.[75]

This was, of course, far from the end of close Anglo-American cooperation – Eden's 1954 triumphant settlement of the Italo-Yugoslav dispute over Trieste (that had led to Italian threats to leave NATO) was underpinned by quiet US aid to Yugoslavia.[76] At the 1954 Geneva Conference on Indo-China, however, Eden did not let himself be unduly deflected by Dulles's wishes; and in 1956 Britain and France went it alone in their invasion of Egypt. US action in blocking this was bitterly received by much of the Conservative Party, but the episode had the improbable effect of tightening Anglo-American relations. Drawing on their wartime friendship, Eisenhower and Macmillan met in Bermuda in March 1957 determined to put Suez behind them. They there arranged for American IRBM's to be deployed in the UK; and in October 1957 Eisenhower promised to seek repeal of the 1946 McMahon Act ban on the exchange of nuclear information. Thereafter Macmillan enjoyed excellent relations with the Eisenhower administration, and showed considerable skill in continuing these with its successor – helped by the remarkable personal popularity of the British ambassador, David Ormsby-Gore, with both President and Bobby Kennedy.

It was perhaps unfortunate that a major symbol of the post-1957 relationship was nuclear cooperation, since this was bound to appear exclusive. The McMahon Act amendment permitting exchanges of nuclear information restricted them to countries that had 'made substantial progress in the development of atomic weapons', a condition then met only by the UK.[77] In 1960 Britain afforded basing facilities to US Polaris submarines; and Eisenhower offered Macmillan cheap access to US strategic delivery systems then under development. Of these Macmillan unwisely chose the air-launched rocket 'Skybolt', since it fitted with the existing

---

[75] David Carlton, *Britain and the Suez Crisis* (Oxford, 1988) pp. 5–6.

[76] Blanche Cook, *The Declassified Eisenhower* (Garden City, NY, 1981) pp. 193–4.

[77] Horne says this had been agreed between Eisenhower and Macmillan (*Macmillan*, ii, p. 109), Ullman that it was insisted on by Congress ('The Covert French Connection', *Foreign Policy*, 1989, p. 6).

British bomber force. Development proved difficult, and in December 1962 McNamara made clear his intention to cancel it. He was no doubt acting chiefly on cost and technical grounds, but he thought small nuclear forces only served to invite Soviet pre-emptive strikes, and probably did not regret the prospect of the British force being squeezed out of existence. Macmillan, however, saw this as a devastating blow, and (at his Nassau meeting with Kennedy) pulled out all the stops and persuaded him to allow Britain to switch to Polaris. (The rockets were offered also to France; but as she could not then manufacture warheads to fit them, this was a deliberately empty gesture.) Implementation of the Nassau agreement proved remarkably smooth, and the life of the national British deterrent was thus prolonged at minimum cost.[78] By the late 1970s, when it became time to consider a replacement, US opinion had shifted to the Gaullist view that the uncertainties inherent in there being more than one centre of nuclear decision would tend to deter an aggressor. The Carter and Reagan administrations were both happy to let Britain replace Polaris with the current submarine-launched missiles, Trident, on the same terms. The controversy attending the decision to take up this option was all internal to the UK.

But if the 1960s saw the preservation of the British deterrent with US assistance, they also brought a sharp decline in the importance of the special relationship. In part this was for personal reasons – President Johnson was offended by the lack of British support for his Vietnam War. It reflected, too, Britain's decision to withdraw from East of Suez. The British Defence Secretary had been told in 1964 that the USA wanted the UK 'not to maintain huge bases but to keep a foothold in Hong Kong, Malaya, the Persian Gulf, to enable us [Britain] to do things for the alliance which they can't do . . . they think that our forces are much more useful to the alliance outside Europe than in Germany'. In 1967, despite pleas to the Foreign Secretary of 'Be British, George, be British – how can you betray us?'[79] the government decided to pull out of Malaysia and – more worryingly from the US point of view – the Gulf. Actually the vacuum there was to be filled, for a time, by America's friend the Shah of Iran. As the recession of its power left Britain less and less to offer, so such relationships with regional powers became ever more important to the USA; they too could be

---

[78] Supposedly Britain also secured a secret discount in 1966 in return for the 50-year lease, for a US base, of the Indian ocean island of Diego Garcia (*Daily Telegraph*, 12 May 2006, pp. 16–17).

[79] Reynolds, 'A "special relationship"? America, Britain and the international order since the Second World War', *International Affairs*, lxii (1985–6) pp. 14–15.

'special', notably that with Israel (which had always possessed great political clout and an excellent intelligence service, to which was added from the mid-1960s rapidly growing military connections). The 1970s also brought better US relations with France (the only Western ally besides Britain with significant out-of-area capabilities), and indeed at least an adversary-partnership with the Soviet Union.[80]

Of course, the attitudes underlying the British 'special relationship' did not simply vanish. Nixon prided himself on having forecast Heath's election in 1970, and often sought to re-establish the old relationship with personal telephone calls and bilateral joint working parties. Heath, however, seemed scarred by de Gaulle's judgement that Britain was not 'European' enough to be allowed to enter the EEC, and determined to forestall any further complaints on this score. He:

not only accepted that Britain's future lay with Europe, he preferred it that way. And so paradoxically . . . when the other European leaders strove to improve their relations with us . . . Heath went in the opposite direction. His relations with us were always correct, but they rarely rose above a basic reserve that prevented – in the name of Europe – the close coordination with us that was his for the asking.

Despite this, Kissinger says, as National Security Adviser, he kept the Foreign Office 'better informed and more closely engaged than I did the State Department' – which was, admittedly, not difficult. Some previous patterns continued: 'most of the actual drafting' of the 1973 US–Soviet Agreement on the Prevention of Nuclear War was done by a Foreign Office team invited to Washington to advise on the negotiations.[81] However, this did not prevent the 1973 Arab–Israeli war and oil shock from severely straining US relations with Britain, as with other West European countries, until Heath's fall brought improvement next year.

By the mid-1970s the leaders of the major Western countries (barring of course the USA) had, for most diplomatic purposes, become a group of equals, meeting each other (from 1975) at annual summit conferences.

---

[80] Though basically very different, this shared features with the 'special relationship'; thus until Reagan's inauguration Ambassador Dobrynin had privileged and inconspicuous access to key foreign policy-makers not unlike that earlier enjoyed by Sir Oliver Franks.

[81] For Kissinger's views on the 'special relationship' see e.g. his *Memoirs*, i, pp. 89 ff, 421, 610, 964; ii, pp. 140–3, 191–2, 278, 281–6, 920–1, and 'The Special Relationship', *The Listener*, 13 May 1982, p. 16.

Accordingly the USA's choice of partners was coming to depend chiefly on the policy areas in question and on the personal preferences of policy-makers. Thus it offered Britain support over Rhodesia (as a second, except briefly in 1976 when Kissinger personally took command of the negotiations); and the US and British ambassadors worked closely together in urging the appeasement of the Iranian revolution in 1978–9 – with National Security Adviser Brzezinski dissenting. Brzezinski did not share Kissinger's partiality for the UK; rather he admired France and 'consulted more frequently with my French colleagues than with either the British or the Germans'.[82] He was, however:

amazed how quickly Callaghan succeeded in establishing himself as Carter's favorite, writing him friendly little notes, calling, talking like a genial older uncle, and lecturing Carter in a pleasant manner on the intricacies of inter-allied politics. Callaghan literally coopted Carter in the course of a few relatively brief personal encounters.[83]

This pattern continued in the 1980s. Thatcher made great play of supporting American leadership (and in 1986 allowed the use of British-based US planes to bomb Ghadaffi, at some political risk and in sharp contrast to the rest of Europe). She had herself profited greatly, during the 1982 Falklands war, from logistic support accorded by Defense Secretary Weinberger (a strong Anglophile, unlike UN ambassador Jeane Kirkpatrick, who doubted the wisdom of risking US relations with Latin America to satisfy what she saw as British pride). Thatcher got on remarkably well with President Reagan, thereby reviving international perceptions of the 'special relationship', and acquiring a degree of diplomatic leverage (reinforced by her early position as Gorbachev's preferred Western interlocutor) that she used, after the failure of the 1986 Reykjavik Summit, to help steer negotiations back to the more promising field of 'Intermediate Range' missiles (IRM).[84]

The next US administration sought to differentiate itself from its predecessor, in part by looking more towards the West Germans whom President Bush described, in a 1989 speech, as America's 'partners in

---

[82] He was suspicious of the revival of German power, and got on badly with Schmidt.
[83] *Power and Principle*, pp. 291, 313.
[84] For comments on Anglo-American relations from the Foreign Policy Adviser to the Prime Minister and chairman of the UK Joint Intelligence Committee, see Cradock, *In Pursuit of British Interests*, esp. Chaps 6–10, 19.

leadership'.[85] In 1989–90 this greatly eased reunification, a process that seemed yet further to reinforce German economic pre-eminence in Europe. Over the Gulf crisis, though, Germany proved a broken reed: its constitution then prevented it from sending troops outside the NATO area; and, since it was habituated to consume, not provide, security, it made heavy weather even of sending planes to reassure Turkey. Britain and France were more attuned to geopolitics, and both made useful military contributions. John Major drew on the position this gave Britain to call for UN-mandated 'safe havens' for Kurdish refugees in northern Iraq; the idea was 'not at first well received' in Washington, but the USA soon came round and both countries sent troops.[86]

Major's relations with President Bush became so close that he appeared to assist Bush's re-election campaign. This may have annoyed the victor, Clinton. Certainly Clinton's first years saw friction with Britain and France over Bosnia, with Britain over Northern Ireland as a result of his decision to permit Sinn Fein fund-raising in the USA. However, in 1995 these strains were buried during a visit in which Clinton addressed parliament, reaffirming the strength of the 'special relationship', announcing that the US Navy would name a ship after Sir Winston Churchill, and declaring support for the Northern Irish approach just endorsed by the British and Irish premiers. Clinton then successfully visited both parts of Ireland, and thereafter the USA assumed a supportive role in the Northern Irish 'peace process'. After 1997 ideological affinity between 'New Labour' and the Democrats yet further warmed official Anglo-American relations.[87] These might have been expected to cool again with the succession of the Republican George W. Bush in 2001, but the cycle was interrupted by the 9/11 Al-Qaida attacks on New York and Washington. Most leaders rushed to sympathise with the USA and initially supported its 'War on Terror', but none more so than Blair. The removal of the Taliban regime from Afghanistan, though almost entirely orchestrated by the USA, was initiated by a joint Anglo-American rocket strike. More importantly, the UK joined Bush in concentrating troops on Iraq's border, in seeking unambiguous UN authorisation of the use of force (if Iraq did not immediately

[85] Philip Zelikow and Condoleeza Rice, *Germany Unified. Europe Transformed* (Cambridge, Mass., 1997 edn) p. 31.
[86] *Annual Register*, 1991, p. 7. With aerial protection, the 'safe havens' developed into *de facto* autonomy for the Kurdish area of Iraq.
[87] During the 1999 Israeli elections both political parties gave Barak's Labor Party campaigning help and advice.

extend full assistance in locating its 'Weapons of Mass Destruction'), and then in 2003 invading and toppling Saddam Hussein. The UK shared in the subsequent occupation of Iraq, albeit under overall US policy control, taking primary responsibility for the Basra area. The contrast between such British support and the Franco-German role in blocking the desired UN resolution and opposing the invasion earned the UK, for a time, remarkable popularity within the United States. It remains to be seen how relations will be affected by the growing disillusionment in both countries with the Iraq war, and at a non-governmental level in Britain also with other aspects of US conduct of the 'War on Terror'.

De Gaulle and the Anglo-Saxons, 1958–68

Franco-American relations have been more uneven. Fourth Republican governments were predominantly Atlanticist, though their domestic weakness, procrastination on German rearmament, and entanglement in colonial wars prompted a mixture of US concern and exasperation. From 1958 de Gaulle sought to transform France from a courtesy to a real Great Power. For this he needed nuclear weapons. The Fourth Republic already had a nuclear programme, and de Gaulle pressed forward in pursuit of a purely national deterrent.[88] He also, in September 1958, sought to define France's status by proposing a new Franco-British-American body responsible for 'taking joint decisions on all political matters affecting world security, and . . . [for] drawing up, and if necessary putting into action, strategic plans, especially those involving the use of nuclear weapons'.[89] This, French diplomats usually confirmed, implied a French veto on the use of *any* US weapons, not just of those based in France.

Opinion differs as to whether this proposal was serious, or just advanced to provide a pretext for the gradual disengagement of French forces from supranational NATO command that began in 1959. Though no US president would ever promise more than prior *consultation*, some effort was made to devise diplomatic arrangements that would satisfy French aspirations without grating on the susceptibilities of countries like

[88] In so doing, he put an end to the recently concluded arrangements for joint French, German and Italian nuclear development (Beatrice Heuser, *Nato, Britain, France and the FRG. Nuclear Strategies and Nuclear Forces for Europe 1948–2000* (Basingstoke, 1997) pp. 125–6, 149–51).
[89] The text was leaked but never officially published – Brian Crozier, *De Gaulle. The Statesman* (1973) p. 525.

Italy and West Germany. 1958–9 saw more discussion than action, but in December 1959 Eisenhower agreed, to the State Department's annoyance, that there should be regular, if 'clandestine', Three Power discussions in London on 'matters of common interest, outside and transcending NATO'. By March 1960, however, he was telling Macmillan of his 'amazement' that de Gaulle seemed 'unable to fathom the methods by which our three governments could easily keep in close touch on main issues. I explained to him how you and ourselves used both normal diplomatic exchanges, personal communications, and, in acute cases, ad hoc committees to keep together.' It is unclear how far French difficulties in plugging into the Anglo-American relationship were cultural. There were language barriers;[90] but France may also have been uneasy with informal arrangements and preferred structure for its own sake. Eisenhower briefed Kennedy about de Gaulle's 'obsession' with a 'triumvirate of the United States, France, and Great Britain . . . organized on a joint staff concept' (which, Eisenhower thought, 'would break up NATO immediately'). Macmillan felt de Gaulle attached 'more importance to the *fact* of the Tripartite talks than to . . . [their] substance', a view consistent with the very limited French contribution to those discussions that were arranged at the official level.[91]

Still Macmillan was increasingly anxious to satisfy France, provided this was not 'at the cost of our arrangements with the Americans', in the hopes of reciprocal concessions over British trade relations with the EEC: 'The future of British trade in Europe is far more important than whether a few French fighters are or are not to be put under the command of SACEUR'. In May 1960 he proposed frequent meetings of the three Foreign Ministers under cover of the various international gatherings they would have attended anyway. Eisenhower was agreeable both to this and to military discussions in Washington on questions outside the NATO area, but insisted on maintaining existing NATO arrangements for Europe. De Gaulle initially pressed for a summit to take matters further; but he then cooled, possibly offended by policy differences (which he was far quicker than Britain to voice in public) over the Congo and by US reluctance to see France as speaking for the whole of continental Western

[90] Kennedy's attempts at telephone calls broke down for this reason (Sorenson, *Kennedy*, p. 561); and though Macmillan spoke excellent and Dulles passable French, there have been suggestions that important points were sometimes missed.
[91] Ambrose, *Eisenhower*, p. 615; John Newhouse, *De Gaulle and the Anglo-Saxons* (1970) pp. 88–9; Horne, *Macmillan*, ii, p. 295; Macmillan, *Memoirs*, v, pp. 106, 246.

Europe.[92] So further developments were left to the next US President, Kennedy.

With his eye on Britain's European relations, Macmillan sought to persuade Kennedy to take Tripartism further and to offer France help in developing nuclear weapons. Kennedy was delighted to intercede with de Gaulle for a British move into 'Europe' (though the attempt was probably counter-productive), happy with Tripartism, but unwilling 'to assist France's efforts to create a nuclear weapons capability . . . If we were to help France . . . this could not but have a major effect on German attitudes.' The subjects were discussed during Kennedy's June 1961 visit to Paris, but to little effect.[93] De Gaulle was by now placing more emphasis on the Fouchet proposals for the coordination (inevitably under French leadership) of EEC defence and foreign policies; the Tripartite Foreign Ministers' meetings became increasingly acrimonious, and were not continued into 1962. Macmillan, though, was becoming really anxious about the progress of Britain's EEC application, and considered offering France nuclear aid if Britain was admitted. He discussed the idea with colleagues before meeting de Gaulle at Champs in June 1962, but found no way of overcoming Washington's objections to passing on US technology. So at Champs and (in December) Rambouillet, he probably did no more than speculate about a possible 'European' (i.e. Anglo-French) deterrent and promise such nuclear cooperation as did not involve US technology, though the French ambassador was convinced that a definite offer was made of collaboration in exchange for EEC entry.[94] In late December, when a French EEC veto seemed likely, Macmillan did ask the USA to allow Britain to offer France Polaris warheads in exchange for entry. Kennedy refused – though next summer he was to offer France nuclear

[92] ibid. pp. 112–14, 245–6; Crozier, De Gaulle, pp. 536–41. Chaban-Delmas was later to explain that France represented Europe just as Britain represented the Commonwealth, and that it therefore had as much right to be admitted to US counsels.
[93] Macmillan, Memoirs, v, p. 325; Horne, Macmillan, ii, pp. 295, 301; Arthur M. Schlesinger, A Thousand Days: John F. Kennedy in the White House (1965) pp. 319–23; Crozier, De Gaulle, p. 543.
[94] Some say that, at Rambouillet, Macmillan promised to replace Skybolt through nuclear collaboration with France, and that when instead he later arranged the exclusive purchase of American Polaris missiles, this proved to de Gaulle that Britain was not really European and precipitated his EEC veto. But de Gaulle subsequently confirmed that he had been told at Rambouillet of the British intention to seek Polaris; he also made it plain before Nassau that he had turned Macmillan down over the EEC (Horne, Macmillan, ii, pp. 430 ff, 673; Lacouture, De Gaulle, pp. 355–7).

data and underground test facilities in a vain attempt to get de Gaulle to accede to the treaty banning atmospheric testing.[95]

De Gaulle's EEC veto went down extremely badly in both Washington and London; his relations with the Anglo-Saxons deteriorated rapidly. The post-Cuba detente gave his foreign policy more scope. He had unhesitatingly backed the USA during the missiles crisis, and over Berlin had advocated a firm Western front. But he had told Kennedy that, while France would do nothing to disrupt NATO during the Berlin crisis, it would seek a different organisation for the future. De Gaulle was never attracted by the various US schemes designed to head off this trouble: a French SACEUR, a multilateral nuclear force where all participating countries would possess vetoes, or even the commitment of some Polaris submarines to NATO to be controlled by a 'tri-partite' authority.[96] Now his public pronouncements about NATO became increasingly hostile; in early 1966 he declared that, though France would continue to accept the obligations of the original 1949 treaty to 'fight on the side' of any member subject to 'unprovoked aggression', it would withdraw from the subsequent supranational military arrangements and resume sovereign control over all armed forces on its territory. Accordingly 1966–7 saw the departure of foreign forces and support facilities from France, and the relocation of NATO headquarters to Brussels. In many ways the alliance worked more smoothly without France. But the loss of logistic depth, and uncertainty as to what French forces would do in the event of war, could have had serious military consequences. The French action was seen as rather cynical sabotage: President Johnson said it raised 'grave questions regarding the whole relationship between the responsibilities and the benefits of the alliance'; for, in protecting West Germany, NATO would inevitably protect France even though France had ceased to contribute much to it.[97]

Nor were de Gaulle's other policies widely appreciated. With hindsight one might judge that they usually incorporated a real insight and voiced feelings quite widely held in Europe, but that no other country would countenance the extremes to which they were carried. Thus de Gaulle's fears that the USA would not put itself at risk, now that the USSR had nuclear weapons too, were not unreasonable – US Secretary of State Herter had once suggested as much – and de Gaulle's view that even small national deterrents contributed to stability by increasing a potential

[95] Horne, *Macmillan*, ii, pp. 326–9, 440–5; Schlesinger, *Thousand Days*, pp. 780–1.
[96] ibid. pp. 320, 322; *New York Times*, 9 April 1990, p. A9.
[97] *Keesing's*, 21604 ff, 22123 ff; Don Cook, *Charles De Gaulle* (1984) p. 383.

aggressor's uncertainty as to the likely response was later adopted by official London and Washington. But successive US presidents resented his questioning of America's determination to honour its obligations, while most Europeans thought it counter-productive. De Gaulle's denunciation of the 1963 Test Ban Treaty was widely seen as unhelpful; the final progression, the 1967 declaration that France must be able to defend itself against attacks 'from all points of the compass', appeared gratuitously offensive.

There was, too, much to be said for de Gaulle's attempts to open up Eastern Europe diplomatically (see pp. 323, 324), and they were ultimately adopted and developed by West Germany. But his constant lumping together of the US and Soviet hegemonies was more debatable, especially after the 1968 Soviet intervention in Prague. Similarly de Gaulle had warned the USA privately against getting involved in Vietnam, but his 1966 visit to Cambodia, and his denunciations of the US war apparatus, were not appreciated. Recognition of Communist China in 1964, and dissociation from Israel in 1967–8, can be seen as in advance of their time, but then seemed more like disengagement from the West. De Gaulle's 1964 tour of Latin America looked like an attempt to woo it away from its Yankee affiliations, and his 1967 cry in Montreal of 'Vive le Québec libre' (and possibly deeper involvement with Québequois, and Biafran, separatism) appear simply mischievous. For the most part, though, these were words only. In economic matters de Gaulle proceeded to deeds. Here too he was voicing widely felt fears of a takeover of Europe by technologically superior US multinationals, financed (in effect) by the United States' ability, in virtue of the dollar's reserve status, simply to print internationally acceptable money. He was also correct in observing that the system rested on US ability to keep gold at an artificially low price.[98] But there was less enthusiasm for his call for a new gold exchange system that would benefit chiefly South Africa, the USSR – and France. De Gaulle's conversion, between 1965 and 1968, of large quantities of French dollars into gold, while well calculated to squeeze the USA, was seen also as risking the collapse of the international monetary system with incalculable consequences. To the Cold War was added the Franco-US 'Gold War'.

US–French relations since 1969

Although it was not easy to accommodate Gaullist France within the Western alliance, the US–French rift was to be healed far more easily than

---

[98] For a fuller discussion, see *The Post-Imperial Age*, pp. 489–91.

the contemporary Sino-Soviet one. The process may be said to have begun with the weakening of the franc by the 1968 'events'. Thereafter France needed foreign help, especially as de Gaulle refused to devalue. In 1969 Nixon became president. He was personally well disposed towards de Gaulle, and anxious to end what he saw as the unnecessary and constraining quarrel with France (as also that with China). His visit to de Gaulle went well. Then de Gaulle was succeeded by Pompidou, a more cautious man who valued his predecessor's achievements but worried about Germany and sought to edge back towards Atlanticism. US–French relations were mostly smooth, if unremarkable, though they were nearly marred when Pompidou and his wife were jostled and sworn at by demonstrators in Chicago. In 1971 the USA was able to use France's position in Europe to negotiate with Pompidou the package of currency realignments that became known as the Smithsonian agreement, instead of seeking a general monetary summit that would probably have collapsed into mutual acrimony. More friction developed, however, from Pompidou's view that 'while it would be absurd to conceive of a Europe constructed in opposition to' the USA, 'the very closeness of these links requires that Europe affirm its individual personality with regard to the United States'.[99] During 1973–4, with Pompidou enfeebled by terminal illness, this requirement was strongly pushed by the prickly French Foreign Minister Jobert. Kissinger had, perhaps unwisely, launched an attempt to rethink the Atlantic relationship in the very year the European Community had expanded from six to nine members and had to adjust its own functioning accordingly. The result was stiffness and misunderstanding, subsequently exacerbated by the combination of European refusal to back the USA during the 1973 Arab–Israeli war and a most uncollective scramble for oil by its individual countries. Not until things had settled down again, and governments changed in France, Germany and Britain, did transatlantic relations return to a more even keel; then 1975 saw the institution (at French initiative) of annual gatherings of the leaders of major Western countries (including Japan) that, though very far from the Three Power directorate de Gaulle had been seeking, do go some way towards providing a loose framework for discussion and coordination, without however denting US pre-eminence in any but the economic field.

Nixon and Kissinger always regarded doctrinaire opposition to the French nuclear deterrent as unwise; it had certainly created considerable anti-American feeling. Accordingly they held out hopes of collaboration as

[99] Kissinger, *Memoirs*, i, pp. 958–62; ii, p. 132.

a carrot to improve relations, and in 1973 are supposed to have offered it to still French fears (after the Nixon–Brezhnev summit) of a US–Soviet condominium.[100] Setting up the collaboration proved difficult, as both countries required secrecy for domestic reasons; the transfer of information proved patchy – France was given advice on miniaturising warheads, but not on silencing submarines. As intended, the exercise seems to have tightened links, especially those running through military and presidential channels bypassing the two countries' diplomatic services. It may have encouraged Giscard to offer Kissinger help in Angola in 1975 (above, p. 386), and to oblige the USA by keeping French troops in Djibouti. Under Mitterrand, it is claimed, cooperation grew to the point where arrangements were worked out for the placing of French forces under SACEUR's command in time of war, and for integrating French nuclear targeting, like British, into SACEUR's plans.[101] Certainly, though France still adhered to the Gaullist posture of sovereign national defence, it surprised the world, in the early 1980s, by the depth of its suspicion of the Soviet arms build-up and by its support for (though not participation in) the deployment of cruise missiles to counter it. French public opinion, too, was, for a time, far more pro-American than British or West German.[102]

A decade later relations with the USA were still good. Despite close contacts with, and oil interests in, Iraq, when Saddam Hussein invaded Kuwait in 1990 France readily sent forces to help defend Saudi Arabia. As the coalition prepared to liberate Kuwait, French diplomacy appeared to 'wobble' and seek a compromise; but when land operations actually began, French troops played an important role; and the subsequent meeting between Presidents Mitterrand and Bush 'marked the highest point in Franco-American relations for many years'.[103] Thereafter France appeared to move away from two aspects of the Gaullist legacy, becoming active in the Security Council of the United Nations the General had so much despised, and edging ever closer to NATO. After 1995, indeed, France offered to re-enter the supranational command structure de Gaulle had left

---

[100] This paragraph is derived from Ullman, 'The Covert French Connection', *Foreign Policy*, lxxv (1989). His narrative is consistent with some points in the public record, but given its subject matter it inevitably rests on unattributable interviews.

[101] Both countries have two sets of targets, those assigned by NATO, and those they would attack if they were to fight alone.

[102] For the evolution of French attitudes, see Pierre Hassner, 'Perceptions of the Soviet threat in the 1950s and 1980s: the case of France', in Carl-Christoph Schweitzer (ed.) *The Changing Western Analysis of the Soviet Threat* (1990).

[103] *Annual Register*, 1991, p. 99.

– but only if the United States relinquished the Mediterranean command to be held by rotation among the European NATO members most closely involved. This President Clinton, in 1997, definitively refused to do.[104]

This rebuff may have been one factor in altering France's international posture – certainly France returned, in and after 1998, to its attempts to build an EU military capability independent of the US-dominated NATO (above, pp. 479–80). Another factor was simply the 1995 change of Presidents, from a Mitterrand who had for some time been weakened by cancer to the Gaullist Chirac; in 1996 Chirac embarked on a round of foreign visits, and highlighted differences with the USA to indicate 'a return of France to a tradition of solo activism on the world stage'. That said, both Chirac and his Socialist Prime Minister Jospin faced down criticism to support the United States first over Kosovo in 1998–9, then, following 9/11, in the 2001 toppling of the Taliban in Afghanistan. Chirac's Afghan stance, moreover, seems to have enjoyed majority popular support.[105]

The most salient disagreement was over Iraq. By 1998 France felt (as did much of continental Europe, and indeed many of Iraq's neighbours) that it was time to come to terms with Saddam; in so doing France was motivated partly by the belief that continuing sanctions hurt the Iraqi people more than the regime, partly (its critics maintained) by the wish to reactivate past connections with Baghdad and benefit from the resultant reconstruction contracts.[106] Given the prospect of a US veto, France could not induce the United Nations to lift these sanctions; but it could condemn the half-hearted US–British air strikes in retaliation for Iraq's 1998 extrusion of the UN weapons inspectors, and it withdrew from the enforcement of the 'no-fly zone' over southern Iraq. The rift became more serious when, in 2002–3, the US–UK sought unambiguous UN authorisation for an invasion of Iraq in the likely event of Saddam's continuing to impede weapons inspection. For Chirac war would be 'the worst of all possible solutions'; to oppose it he combined with Russia and with Germany (which happened then to be on the Security Council), and also made it clear that, come what may, he would cast France's veto. Accordingly the US–UK proceeded without further UN authority, and rapidly overran Iraq.[107]

[104] France actually wanted the USA to relinquish two of the four senior NATO commands, but always stressed the Mediterranean command in Naples – *Keesings*, 40882, 41298–9, 41521, 41756.

[105] *Annual Register*, 1996, p. 50; 1999, p. 63; 2001, p. 70.

[106] It seems too that Saddam rewarded individual foreign supporters by manipulating oil deliveries under the UN 'oil for food' programme.

[107] *Annual Register*, 1998, pp. 53, 234; 1999, p. 63; 2002, p. 58; 2003, p. 53.

At one level this brought the dispute to an end. France refused to involve itself in the ill-fated occupation of the country, but did not stand in the way of a UN resolution regulating the post-war position. US verbal hostility to France, and all things French, ran high, leading the House of Representatives café to substitute 'Freedom' potatoes for 'French fries'. But little came of such insults, or of talk of popular boycotts. Nor did Franco-American cooperation cease – in 2004 France was a major contributor to the US-led UN force that sought to stabilise Haiti immediately after President Aristide's overthrow.[108]

At another level, though, the rift ran deeper, reflecting different visions of the world that were, on the French side, to some extent reminiscent of de Gaulle. While not hostile to the United States, France resents what it sees as a tendency to US 'unilateralism' and would prefer a more balanced international system than has obtained since the USSR's collapse. In the special case of the UN Security Council, France, through its veto, can itself supply some of this balance. In some other contexts this can be provided through European cooperation. One example is civilian aircraft construction, for decades a virtual US monopoly; by 2001 the collaborative European Airbus project appeared to have overtaken America's Boeing (though in 2006 their positions reversed). More importantly the 'euro' has emerged as the world's second currency. France had pushed its creation more in the context of its German than of its US policy; but from the 1960s onwards Paris had been conscious of the advantages the US derives from the dollar's 'reserve currency' position, and it has been quick to promote the euro as an alternative store of value, one which may be particularly attractive to countries, or regions, that are irritated with Washington.

Lastly there is competition at the level of images. France promotes itself, and the EU, as guardians of a gentler, more state-rooted, and more 'social' approach than the free-market capitalism of 'Anglo-Saxon' globalisation. To its detractors such rhetoric can appear as merely a cover for self-interested mercantilism, and 'old Europe's' concomitant dirigisme and over-regulation a recipe for unemployment and economic stagnation. In this debate, US criticism is strident, but probably of less importance than disputes *within* the EU over its future direction, disputes that cannot of course be reduced simply to a Franco-British contest but that it sometimes suits the protagonists to present as such.

[108] *Keesing's*, 45841–2.

CHAPTER 13

Western Europe III: The European Union

De Gaulle and the 'Luxembourg compromise' 1966

The negotiations that established the EEC had not always been easy. But the real problems came later over the Community's decision-making processes and over agriculture, two topics on which France had strong views. For enthusiasts, economic cooperation had been the way to political union, a slow route but the only possible one since the failure of the European Defence Community had shown that the high road was not available. As Monnet's Action Committee had explained in 1958:

Tomorrow's political unity will depend on making the economic union effective in the everyday activities of industry, agriculture and government. Little by little the work of the communities will be felt, and the already distinguishable bonds of common interest will be strengthened. Then, the everyday realities themselves will make it possible to form the political union which is the goal of our Community, and to establish the United States of Europe.

In 1960 it became clear that de Gaulle thought otherwise:

What are the pillars on which [Europe] can be built? In truth, they are the States . . . the only entities with the right to give orders and the power to be obeyed. To fancy one can build something effective in action, and acceptable to the peoples, outside or above the States, is a chimera.

The machinery of the European Communities was for fair weather only: 'So long as nothing serious happens, they work without any commotion, but as soon as a crisis occurs . . . it becomes apparent that a high authority like that has no authority over the different national affairs.'

In 1961–2 de Gaulle sought to reorient the conduct of business around regular meetings of heads of government and Foreign Ministers (aided by a political secretariat) that would also harmonise foreign and defence policies. Italy and Germany were prepared to accept this, Belgium and the Netherlands would not.[1] The real showdown came in 1965, when the EEC Commission unveiled a plan that would complete the Common Agricultural Policy, but strengthen the powers of the Commission and the European Parliament as against the Council of [Foreign] Ministers of the member states; the latter would also in some circumstances reach decisions by majority voting. The Commission thought France would accept for the sake of the agricultural benefits; but deadlock was reached in July, and France responded by boycotting all but routine EEC workings – the policy of the 'empty chair'. In January 1966 the French position was accepted in practice, if not in so many words, by the 'Luxembourg compromise'. The Commission would in future work much more closely with representatives of the member states and with the Council of Ministers; and the Council would, when faced with important matters, seek unanimity – 'The French delegation considers that, when very important issues are at stake, discussion must be continued until unanimous agreement is reached'.[2] Countries tended to treat this as a licence to hold up business until they were satisfied, indeed to veto one item until they were reassured about another. Decisions continued to be made, but slowly and collegially; and the key body came to be not the Commission but the Council of Ministers.

The Common Agricultural Policy

De Gaulle's other requirement, a Common Agricultural Policy (CAP), went less smoothly. Almost all developed countries protect their farmers; so it is not surprising that the EEC did so too, especially as a fifth of its working population (more in France and Italy) was still engaged in agriculture in 1958. But the Netherlands and France were also anxious to profit by their competitive advantage in farming, and saw this as quid pro

[1] The scheme was known as the Fouchet plan – Jean Lacouture, *De Gaulle: The Ruler* (1991) pp. 347–50; F. Roy Willis, *France, Germany and the New Europe 1945–67* (1968 edn) pp. 293–7.
[2] *Keesing's*, 21591–5; France subsequently forced the retirement of the Commission's President, Walter Hallstein.

quo for the opening of their markets to industrial imports: 'We have,' de Gaulle once remarked, 'already done a lot for Germany: ECSC, Euratom, EEC. It is really up to her to do something for us.'[3] In any case his farmers were demanding remunerative outlets for the surpluses earlier modernisation had called into being; he pressed his colleagues accordingly. What resulted was conceptually simple. The Community sought self-sufficiency in temperate agricultural products. It set prices at which key commodities should trade throughout the Community;[4] variable duties prevented cheaper imports, while, as a safety net, the Community stood ready to buy and store surplus production, or subsidise its sale abroad.

The system painfully negotiated in the 1960s soon got out of hand. The price explosion that began in 1972 with the advent of Soviet grain purchases (see p. 366), and the attendant fears of a world shortage of food, made the goal of maximising Community production look attractive. Since prices were set by a Council of Ministers *of Agriculture*, they were naturally high – especially as German farmers were both high cost and politically powerful, with the result that the country that (as the largest contributor to the Community budget) had the chief interest in keeping prices down often took the lead in raising them. High prices called forth high production, which then had to be taken off the market and stored in 'grain mountains' and 'wine lakes', or dumped abroad with the aid of further subsidies. But the Common Agricultural Policy did not equate to a true internal market. Indeed this started to unravel before its construction was quite finished. For in 1969 France devalued and Germany revalued its currency. Since agricultural prices were now fixed in terms of a notional 'European unit of account', the French should have raised prices payable in francs and the Germans lowered those in marks; but both were allowed to keep their old prices and to impose countervailing border taxes to stop these being undermined by trade at the new exchange rates. Much the same happened when the Dutch and German currencies floated upwards in 1971–2. As floating became general in the 1970s this developed into a system of politically determined national 'green currencies', differential payments, and border controls. (It used to pay to land French grain in Hamburg, then instantly reload and export it with the 'German' subsidy.)[5]

---

[3] Willis, *France, Germany and the New Europe*, p. 287.

[4] Choice of key products depends on political pressure. Thus in 1970 Italy insisted on a Community regime for wine; but there is none for poultry.

[5] *Keesing's*, 23522–3, 23682, 24972, 25250; Dick Leonard, *Pocket Guide to the European Community* (1988) p. 95; *Daily Telegraph*, 19 July 1990, p. 14.

By 1984 agriculture accounted for 70 per cent of the EC budget, and funding (from the proceeds of the common external tariff, supplemented since 1970 by a 1 per cent Value Added Tax [VAT]) was insufficient. In this context Mitterrand negotiated the 1984 Fontainebleau package deal whereby British consent for raising VAT to 1.4 per cent was gained by placing the UK contributions rebate (above, p. 472) on a continuing basis. Measures, like the 1984 imposition of milk production quotas, were also taken to control farm spending; but it still rose by a third between 1984 and 1988, prompting the introduction of incentives to 'set-aside' arable land as fallow, and (from 1992) some shift of agricultural support away from pure production (which rewards the largest and richest farms) to environmentally friendly practices.[6] 1993 also saw important reforms in the system of 'green currencies', though the rules governing the translation of exchange rate changes into actual farm prices continued both complex and subject to political interference until the coming of the euro in 1999.[7]

However, a new problem had arisen, international trade. Agriculture had not really featured in earlier multilateral tariff negotiations under the GATT; but in the 1980s it was placed on the agenda of the Uraguay round by a combination of the USA and of the 'Cairns Group' of fourteen major agricultural exporters. In 1990 this alliance sought to tie the round's other agreements to cuts of 75 per cent in the EC's farm support and 90 per cent in its – internationally more disruptive – export subsidies. This stalled negotiations until 1992–3, when a US threat to impose punitive tariffs on $1 billion worth of EC exports induced a deal – despite riotous protests in France and a French threat to veto it.[8]

There followed a period of relative calm. But agriculture returned to the political forefront in the new millenium. Germany had been pressing for reductions in EU expenditure, and had supported Commission proposals for CAP reform. But later in 2002 President Chirac and Chancellor Schröder unexpectedly struck a deal that they then pushed through the European Council (of heads of government) against

[6] C. Tugendhat, *Making Sense of Europe* (Harmondsworth, 1986) p. 48; John Pinder, *The Building of the European Union* (Oxford, 1998 edn) pp. 102–3, 110–11, 185, 194–5.

[7] Alan Swinbank, *Understanding the Implications of Green Currency Revaluation* (paper for the Tenth European Agrimonetary Conference, March 1997); *International Herald Tribune*, 7 January 1999.

[8] For GATT negotiations and the 'Uraguay Round', see *The Post-Imperial Age*, pp. 502–3.

Dutch–British opposition: measures should be worked out to reduce the link between agricultural production and farm income support; but overall expenditure would be protected until 2013. Chirac later used this entrenched position in two contexts, the British rebate and the Doha world trade negotiations (the successor to the Uraguay round).

The rebate had become vulnerable, partly by reason of the UK's growing prosperity, but chiefly because money was needed to support the EU's 2004 extension to Eastern Europe and the 2007–13 budget had to be agreed in 2005. Initially the British Prime Minister, Blair, sought to condition any change in the rebate on reform of the CAP that dictated a pattern of EU expenditure disadvantageous to the UK. Chirac flatly refused to reopen the 2002 agricultural settlement, and after much bad feeling Blair gave way.[9] Over Doha France proved slightly more flexible. The 'round' was meant to secure the opening of developed countries' agricultural markets and the ending of their subsidised agricultural exports with, in return, an acceptance by developing countries of freer trade, more especially in services. Negotiations were for the EU to conduct as a single unit, and in October 2005 Trade Commissioner Mandelson offered significant cuts in agricultural tariffs, though with no change in export subsidies until 2013. Despite complaints that he had exceeded his negotiating mandate, and a threat by Chirac to veto a Doha settlement rather than accept more changes to the CAP, Mandelson's offer held. But trouble exploded in 2006 when he suggested that, to clinch a settlement, it might be further expanded: in May the French agriculture minister declared, with Austrian support, that he would prefer Doha's failure to 'negotiations that would raise questions about the CAP . . . and its future'; in June, after briefing representatives of member states, Mandelson again announced readiness to 'significantly improve' the EU offer, prompting the French trade minister to declare flatly that there was 'no margin of manoeuvre in that direction'; 'We will,' her agricultural colleague added, 'stick strictly to our offer of October 2005.' In the event, the occasion did not arise, since the USA (to the relief also of farm lobbies in Japan and India) proved equally inflexible, and negotiations were suspended in July.[10]

---

[9] *Keesing's*, 46703, 46996.

[10] The EU also stressed it was already by far the world's largest agricultural importer – *Finfacts*, Ireland, 18 October 2005; *The Economist*, 3 November 2005 ('Charlemagne'); AFP/*EUbusiness*, 29 May 2006; *Le Monde* and the *Financial Times (Germany)*, 30 June 2006; *International Herald Tribune*, 21 October 2005, 29 June 2006.

The 'Single European Act' 1985; Schengen; Airline deregulation; The draft Directive on services, 2004–6

In the Community's[11] first decade it had achieved the removal of tariff barriers on manufactured goods and the legal framework for the free movement of labour, though *not* its third desideratum, the free movement of capital.[12] To this was added a Common Agricultural Policy that had, by the early 1980s, degenerated into a fraud-ridden[13] bureaucratic mess whose cost precluded any very considerable development of other policies. Important fields of economic activity, like financial services and air transport, were kept outside the Community's purview. Frontiers remained a reality, as illustrated by massive tailbacks of lorries when Italian customs officials went on strike; indeed it was not until 1988 that the seventy different national forms were replaced by a standardised border declaration for goods. There were, of course, some supranational elements, and many instances of intergovernmental harmonisation and cooperation, but in the early 1980s the Community remained very much a *Europe des patries*, and was widely derided for its 'Euro-sclerosis'. In 1983, at Stuttgart, the European Council decided, in response to these 'challenges', 'to take broad action to ensure the relaunch of the European Community'. Little progress was made until after the 1984–5 resolution of the linked problems of raising the EC's VAT levy (to meet mounting CAP costs), settling the UK's rebate, and agreeing the accession of Spain and Portugal (and a concomitant increase in Mediterranean spending). But by 1985 there was a general anxiety to move forward that a new European Commission, under the able and ambitious French politician Jacques Delors, was determined to use. As to desirable advances, there was no shortage of ideas: the Stuttgart Council had enumerated some fifteen multi-purpose headings; Italy pressed strongly for political union; the 1984 Fontainebleau Council had set up the Dooge committee on institutional reform; Delors talked of 'two great dreams', an area without frontiers and monetary union; more mundanely

---

[11] The EEC, ECSC, and Euratom merged in 1967 into a single body, styled first the European Communities and later the European Community (EC).

[12] This finally came in 1990–3, in connection with the 'Single European Market' (Pinder, *Building the European Union*, p. 162).

[13] Sometimes picturesquely so – in three areas of Germany, the European Parliament found, 80% of all cattle were officially slaughtered more than once (*Keesing's*, 36493, 37209).

Thatcher sought the removal of non-tariff barriers to the free trade within the Community that had been only notionally achieved by the abolition of tariffs. The Dooge committee had urged an 'Inter-Governmental Conference' to draft a new treaty conferring further powers and competences on the Community, and this was agreed over British, Danish and Greek opposition.

The upshot was the 'Single European Act' of December 1985, an omnibus measure aspiring towards 'the convergence of economic and monetary policy', greater spending on disadvantaged regions and on research and technological development, safeguarding the environment, advancing social policy, increasing the powers of the European Parliament, and attempting 'jointly to formulate and implement a European foreign policy'. Its most immediately important component was that committing the EC to removing all internal barriers to trade in goods – in the rhetoric, to creating 'Single Market' – by the end of 1992. This would involve harmonisation of a mass of national standards and regulations, to achieve which the Single European Act abandoned the Luxembourg compromise and provided instead that, on most (though not all) issues connected with the Single Market, decisions should be reached by a 'qualified majority'.[14] Thatcher accepted this as the price of obtaining the Single Market; but inevitably, though to her disgust, the practice of 'qualified majority' voting spilled over into other areas.[15]

Securing the mass of harmonisation regulations represented a major hurdle, but a more or less free flow of goods across national borders came into effect on 1 January 1993. This 'Single Market' achievement fostered several others. 1985 had seen Benelux, France and Germany sign up to the independent Schengen initiative to end border passport controls. Implementation was slow. But in 1995 these countries, plus Spain and Portugal, returned a large area of Western Europe to the passport-free conditions obtained before 1914; in 1997 they were joined by Italy and Austria, in 2001 by Greece and Scandinavia (including the non-EU states of Norway and Iceland). Britain and Ireland have continued to opt out, chiefly for reasons of immigration control,[16] but the 1997 Amsterdam

---

[14] Effectively this meant it would take the opposition of two large countries plus one small one to block a proposed law.

[15] *Keesing's*, 32404, 34107–8; Margaret Thatcher, *The Downing Street Years* (1993) pp. 549–67.

[16] The besieging of the French portal to the Channel Tunnel certainly suggests that there would otherwise have been a convergence on the UK of immigrants/asylum-seekers.

Treaty added 'Schengen' to the *acquis* that all new EU members must accept – 2007 is the current target for implementation by most of the states joining in 2004. The move has implications beyond those visible at borders; for implementation required EU inspection to ensure adequate arrangements for border control, police cooperation and the like, and also the common policies for the issue (and waiver) of 'Schengen' visas for non-European Economic Area nationals.

Movement within the EU was also transformed by the emergence of airline competition. By the 1980s there was an extensive network of charter flights to holiday destinations, but international scheduled services remained, under the IATA regime,[17] in the hands of national airlines that were often protected and if necessary subsidised in the interests of national prestige. Private individuals lobbied (and litigated) to secure a change, and an EC liberalisation process was eventually instituted. Initially airlines might fly between two EC member states if either gave permission – and British consent made possible the start-up of the fledgeling Irish Ryanair, despite Ireland's opposition (aimed at protecting its national airline). After 1997 any EU-based airline might, with minor exceptions, fly anywhere in the Community. Modelling themselves on 'no-frills' US domestic airlines, Ryanair and its British counterpart easyJet took advantage of this, offering cut-price fares, and customer numbers ballooned – from 3.9 million in 1998 to 21.4 million in 2003 for Ryanair; from 3.1 million to 20.3 million for easyJet. A host of imitators (no fewer than 60 in 2004) followed (albeit with mixed success), national airlines responded by cutting prices, and European travel was correspondingly transformed.[18]

All this was accompanied by the advent (for most of the EU) of a common currency, the euro, in 1999–2002, and by a plethora of directives and European Court of Justice judgments tending to break down national barriers to intra-community trade – the cartel-like disposition of manufacturers and distributors to keep British car prices above their continental counterparts was gradually chipped away at the turn of the millenium. But one should not go overboard in chronicling this trend; the European market remains segmented. In part this results simply from national differences in taste: the UK drinks more Australian than French wine; and one of the factors leading the multinational 'C&A' to sell its British shops was the adoption of a centralised European buying system that produced a range of clothes it described as not meeting 'UK customers'

<hr>

[17] *The Post-Imperial Age*, p. 480.
[18] *Wikipedia* articles on Ryanair and easyJet.

needs'.[19] Moreover states still follow different taxation policies: one of the features of Schengen (Luxembourg) itself is how much cheaper petrol is there than in the adjoining countries; and British and Swedish alcohol taxes far exceed the European average, which leads to both smuggling and residual border controls.[20]

But, above all, the EU has concentrated on liberalising trade in goods rather than services. Yet – in a 'developed' 'post-industrial' world – services now account for some 70 per cent of its economy, but only 20 per cent of its internal trade – while German goods compete, very effectively, in British markets, British insurance products have been largely excluded from German. To remedy this the Commission, in 2004, proposed an ambitious directive on services, that would have reserved their regulation not to the country in which they were sold ('country of destination') but to that from which they were supplied ('country of origin'). The proposal came at an unfortunate time, with unemployment high and protectionist concerns about 'globalisation' widespread. 'Critics . . . charge that the [draft] Directive is a sign that "Anglo-Saxon" style economics are running rampant over the EU, and . . . warn that the directive will lead inevitably to "social dumping" – companies and jobs relocating to the low-cost and less regulated economies of [new members in] eastern Europe.' Such fears, expressed in shorthand grumbling about the 'Polish plumber', featured in the debate surrounding France's 2005 referendum rejection of the proposed European Constitution; and mass trades union and other protests were mounted, especially in France, Belgium, Sweden and Denmark.

In February 2006 the Directive was presented to the European Parliament, and drastically modified: the 'country of origin' provision was struck out (though with no clear vision of what should replace it), a range of politically sensitive public services were excluded, as were temporary employment agencies, telecommunications and audiovisual services and provisions impinging on national lotteries; and states could continue to control foreign-provided services for reasons of 'public policy'. Ministers accepted the changes, and a draft directive revised along these lines will be resubmitted.[21]

---

[19] BBC News, 15 June 2000.

[20] Travellers may freely bring in from elsewhere in the EU (large) purchases for personal consumption, but not for resale; and the Schengen passport-free regime permits 'random' searches for alcohol and drugs.

[21] *Wikipedia*; *Keesing's*, 47114; Lieven Tack in *Le Taurillon/thenewfederalist.eu*, 24 June 2006.

Clearly the EU is not the 'single market' of a unified state. Equally it is far more coherent than, say, the North American Free Trade Area of Canada, the USA, and Mexico (with its now highly defended internal borders, migration controls, and economic unilateralisms). As so often in international affairs, one's image depends on one's expectations and choice of comparators.

The advent of a common currency, the 'euro'

The Community would in any case have sought a single currency as a symbol of unity, and a further stimulus was given in 1969 by the strains placed on the CAP by changes in the parities of the franc and the mark (above, p. 500). A plan was indeed adopted in 1971, but the currency instability of the era[22] proved too strong. 1972 saw an arrangement (the 'snake in the tunnel') whereby participant currencies were to fluctuate within much narrower limits than those permitted under the Smithsonian agreement: Britain, Italy and others left fairly soon; France left in January 1974, went back in March, then finally pulled out in 1976, leaving the snake in effect only a DM bloc. Disquiet with the effects of floating currencies produced a new effort to secure, as from 1979, a 'zone of monetary stability' in the form of a 'European Monetary System' (EMS). Here, as under Bretton Woods, participant currencies could fluctuate (against a notional 'European Currency Unit' or ecu) only within narrow limits. But agreed realignments were permitted – and proved common.[23]

After 1987, however, they ceased, which emboldened people to push for further convergence and ultimately a single currency managed by a European central bank. This had been foreshadowed in the Single European Act, but it raised major issues of sovereignty – Thatcher claimed it would only work if there were a European government rather than twelve national states: 'That being not on the cards, I see no point in having anyone study a European central bank.' But despite Kohl's initial coolness, the project was widely taken up, with a bankers' committee chaired by Delors recommending, in April 1989, a three-stage transition to a single currency. German reunification provided a further stimulus: Mitterrand saw a common currency under European control as one way of off-setting Germany's increased power, while Kohl, a convinced European

[22] *Post-Imperial Age*, pp. 491–7.
[23] Leonard, *Guide to the European Community*, p. 86; C.P. Kindleberger, *A Financial History of Western Europe* (1985 edn) pp. 456–62.

federalist, agreed, believing it would reassure Germany's neighbours (above, p. 426). Intense discussion followed as to details, rules, and dates; and in October 1990 a timetable was worked out at a meeting of Christian Democrat leaders and unexpectedly sprung on Thatcher at a European Council. She dissociated Britain from it; the absoluteness of her refusal 'to abolish the pound sterling, the greatest expression of sovereignty',[24] set off a chain of events that led to her political downfall next month.[25]

There were in fact difficult negotiations before a final draft could be adopted in the Maastricht Treaty of December 1991. This provided for general surveillance of the project by Finance Ministers, and for the establishment in 1994 of a shadow European Central Bank. It allowed British and Danish opt-outs, laid down the criteria to be met by states wishing to adopt the desired common currency,[26] and provided that the European Council could decide, by late 1998, whether a majority of participating states had met these criteria. Should no such decision be reached, the final transition to a common currency would, for qualifying countries only, begin in 1999.[27]

One might have expected all this to be blown out of the water by the currency turmoil of 1992–3, which forced widespread devaluations, and would have claimed the franc but for massive Bundesbank support and the decision to widen to 15 per cent the margins of currency fluctuation permissible within the European Exchange Rate Mechanism (ERM).[28] But by 1994 the storm had subsided, and the shadow Central Bank duly came

---

[24] She also held that transfer of financial control from paliament to unelected European bodies would be undemocratic, declared that the predominant voice in any European Central Bank would be that of Germany, and stated the economic case against a single currency – 'the differences come out . . . in unemployment or vast movements of people' or major financial transfers to poorer regions (*Parl. Deb.* 6th series 178 (30 October 1990) 869–90). Critics see unemployment in depressed (and house-price inflation in booming) areas as the most likely outcome, since EU funds for financial transfers are very limited, and linguistic and other barriers to labour mobility much greater than in the USA.

[25] Charles Grant, *Delors. Inside the House that Jacques Built* (1994) Chap. 7; Thatcher, *Downing Street Years*, Chap. 25.

[26] A budget deficit below 3% of GDP, a debt ratio below 60%, inflation rates not more than 1.5% and interest rates not more than 2% above the average of the best performing countries, and a currency that had for two years remained within the 2.5% fluctuation margins of the European Exchange Rate Mechanism.

[27] *Keesing's*, 38658, 42076–7; Grant, *Delors*, pp. 181–5.

[28] Grant, *Delors*, pp. 222–3, 227–8, 262–3, 269.

into being, at Germany's insistence in Frankfurt. More important was the surprisingly poor fiscal performance of most continental states, which had the side-effect of extending participation in the new common currency well beyond what either Germany or France really wished. The German government was ready to abandon the much-loved DM, but did not want the new currency to be weakened (and interest rates driven up) by what it saw as feckless Mediterranean deficit budgets. In what Italians sometimes described as 'economic apartheid', it had pressed for tough Maastricht conditions for participation. France too had become attached to the *franc fort*; it also looked to derive influence from being part of a restricted group pioneering integration in a complex of European concentric circles. But too few countries met the Maastricht criteria for there to be any possibility of an early currency launch, and meanwhile Mediterranean countries, determined (partly for reasons of status) not to be left out, made major efforts to cut their deficits. In 1996 a Franco-German summit had reaffirmed commitment to launching in 1999, with Chirac claiming that 'the French and the Germans will be at the same rendez-vous at the same time and under the same conditions', but (he soon publicly suggested) without the Italians. However, when states' 1997 performance came to be considered, only Finland, Luxembourg and the UK would have met a strict reading of the Maastricht terms; and both France and Germany had had to employ statistical devices to keep their budget deficits from exceeding the requisite 3 per cent of GDP. This led all concerned to take a broad view; and though both Belgium's and Italy's debt was double the desired 60 per cent, it was held to be falling towards this level 'at a satisfactory pace'. Only Greece was rejected; and in 2000 it too was allowed to join in, on the basis of figures that now seem to have been cooked.[29]

One more issue remained – who should head the projected new European Central Bank? It had been assumed that the Dutch head of the shadow bank, Wim Duisenberg, would do so for eight years. But Chirac wanted a Frenchman, and threatened to veto Duisenberg. This did not go down well. But the final May 1998 decision for a 1999 launch provided that, though Duisenberg would be appointed, he would step down after the actual 2002 introduction of the new 'euro' currency notes 'to make way for a Frenchman'.[30] That settled, things went remarkably smoothly. In January 1999 the euro came into being, with national currencies valued

---

[29] *Keesing's*, 41285, 42076–7, 42152–3, 42289–90, 46227.
[30] *Keesing's*, 42290; the handover in fact occurred in 2003.

in relation to it – an arrangment not challenged on the exchanges. For two years it remained only a currency of account; then from 1 January 2002 euro notes and coins were introduced, with the old currencies being rapidly phased out. Britain, Denmark and Sweden have opted out (the two latter after referenda). But there is an expectation (though, as the Swedish case shows, not a requirement) that all new EU members will adopt the euro as soon as their finances meet the requisite criteria, and most are eager to do so.

One problem soon became apparent. In late 2002 Portugal was issued with an 'excessive deficit procedure warning' that would have led to fines had it not, painfully, reduced its budget deficit below 3 per cent. In January 2003 the procedure was invoked against Germany, and a less formal warning given to France. Both simply refused to comply; and though they were challenged by the Commission, proceedings against them eventually had to be dropped.[31] Economically little harm will have been done, since the deficits were not great and could be defended on Keynesian grounds. But it will now be harder to curb member states' deficits, and this could impact on the euro's international value and/or on its interest rates. That, however, is for the future; and in other respects too the cumulative effects of the adoption of the euro, whether positive or negative, will take years to work through.

It is, though, already apparent that the euro, based on an economy not much smaller than that of the USA, is the world's second most important currency, and as such a more credible competitor to the dollar than there has been for a long time. Business is indeed gravitating towards it, but since over 50 per cent of international trade is invoiced in dollars the process has a long way to go.[32] Change could be accelerated by a weakening of the dollar (perhaps in response to the US current account deficit) or conceivably by political displeasure with the USA – producers have talked of no longer invoicing oil in dollars but in euros or in terms of a basket of currencies, though so far only Saddam Hussein and Iran seem to have done it. Even so the international repercussions would probably be limited, since

[31] *Keesing's*, 45106–7, 45207, 45718, 46830.
[32] Between the first quarter of 1999 and that of 2006, the euro's share of allocated foreign exchange reserves grew from 18% to 25%, the dollar's shrank from 71% to 66%. In 1998 48% of bonds were denominated in dollars, 20% in ecus/euros, while in 2005 the figures were 44% and about 30% – IMF Statistics Department, *Currency Composition of Official Exchange Reserves (COFER)*; Deutsche Bank Research, *The Euro: Well established as a reserve currency* (8 September 2005) p. 4.

it would take a big shift to affect US behaviour. But some day the United States might find itself exposed to external financial pressures of the sort that so affected the USSR/Russia in the 1980s and 1990s, pressures from which it was immune throughout the twentieth century.

Debates over the EU's architecture; Difficulties over the adoption of the Maastricht and Nice Treaties and of the draft EU Constitution

The Single European Act had derived partly from aspirations towards political unification – indeed Italy initially blocked it as not going far enough, though it desisted in return for the lifting of Danish and Greek 'reservations' imposed for the opposite reason. The Act greatly expanded the volume of EC legislation – in the first half of 1988, Delors claimed, more had been enacted than in the whole of the 1974–84 decade, and in '10 years, 80 per cent of economic legislation, perhaps even tax and social, will come from the EC.' Delors sought to harness this tide to convert the EC from a primarily state-based confederation into a supranational federation. One part of his project was the push for a single currency; the second was even more directly political. 'My objective,' he declared in 1990:

is that before the end of the millenium [Europe] should have a true federation. [The Commission should become] a political executive which can define essential common interests . . . responsible before the European Parliament and before the nation-states represented how you will, by the European Council or by a second chamber of national parliaments.

Thatcher's 'No! No! No!' became famous; but suspicion was much more widespread, the Spanish minister for Europe observing of the Commission's 1991 proposals that its 'chief concern seems to have been to give themselves more power', a view later echoed by Mitterrand's adviser on Europe.[33]

The upshot was a prolonged period of institutional discussion. Should the EU develop as a tree, with uniform branches springing from the same root, or as a classical temple with its various functions constituting distinct 'pillars', each with their own decision-making rules? Should it give priority to 'broadening' (by accepting new members) or 'deepening' (by enhancing

---

[33] Grant, *Delors*, pp. 88, 135, 137, 189.

the development of its institutions and competences)? Should it adopt a model of 'concentric circles' with some or most of the existing members at the 'core' and East European aspirants at the periphery, or perhaps one of 'variable geometry' whereby groups of states might launch new initiatives within the Community framework without having to secure the consent of all member states (including Britain, widely perceived, at least until its 1997 elections, as the odd one out)?

In this debate national positions were not clear-cut: they might change over time (and elections); moreover, as has been observed, every state wants of the EC/EU what it wants but also something incompatible with this. Broadly, though, Britain would have preferred to avoid further institutional reform and instead concentrate on 'broadening' the EU by incorporating new members, on expanding international trade through the Uraguay and Doha GATT/WTO rounds, and on removing Europe's still considerable internal barriers to trade. Kohl deplored the view 'that the future of Europe lies in a super free trade area', and said he wished instead to submerge German in European sovereignty.[34] Germany's supra-nationalism has perhaps waned over time, but it still favours a federal European constitution somewhat along its own model. It has also sought tax harmonisation, or at least a uniform withholding tax on investment income to counter its citizens' propensity to avoid tax by moving funds to Luxembourg; Luxembourg (otherwise strongly federalist) objects, as does Britain which fears such measures would drive bond trading from London to Zurich or New York. France worried deeply about, indeed at one point threatened to veto, both Uraguay and Doha; and in 2006 it produced a diffuse list of companies it would defend, as 'strategic', from takeover, whether from without or within the EU.[35] It had reservations, too, about 'broadening' the EU, believing (correctly) that this would reduce its influence in Brussels.[36] But it did believe in 'deepening', by pressing forward (albeit chiefly on an intergovernmental rather than supra-national basis) in several directions: introduction of the euro, Schengen, development of a 'Common Foreign and Security Policy' and a defence capability distinct from NATO, and tax harmonisation and extension of European social

[34] Arthur Cockfield, *The European Union. Creating the Single Market* (Chichester, 1994) p. 136; Chris Patten, *Not Quite the Diplomat. Home Truths about World Affairs* (2006 edn) p. 27.

[35] ibid. p. 26; *Keesing's*, 47064.

[36] The influx of new members contributed towards the supersession of French by English as the EU's chief working language.

policy not only for their own sake but also to protect French (and German) businesses from 'social dumping' competition from EU members with lower corporate taxes and less union or worker-friendly labour law. To effect this France often favoured a system of 'variable geometry' that would enable it to bypass British opposition, and also leave it, with Germany, at the heart of a system of concentric circles.

Unsurprisingly all countries had to make concessions, and the upshot was a sequence of treaties – Maastricht, 1991, Amsterdam, 1997, Nice, 2001 – that extended EU subject areas and competences, albeit far less than federalists would have wished, and effected the voting and other changes required by increases in the number of EU members. Nice also prescribed the convening of a 'Convention' to draft a 'Constitution', under the chairmanship of the former French president Giscard d'Estaing. Giscard compared the undertaking to the 1787 Philadelphia convention that had transformed the United States from a confederation with only the weakest of central authorities to a federation with a President and a much strengthened Congress. His own proposals did not go so far; but they also differed from their US counterpart in their prolixity (350 articles) and 'often . . . impenetrable language'. It is, therefore, not surprising that they have been very differently interpreted; and since they have not yet (2007) been put into effect, there is no firm basis for judging between these interpretations.[37]

The treaties, and still more the constitution, did, however, indicate the existence (in a number of countries) of a gap between the European enterprise, largely a matter of governments and elites,[38] and grass-roots sentiment. To take legal effect, EU treaties must be ratified by all member states. In June 1992 Maastricht was, against the advice of most of the Danish establishment, rejected in a referendum that had been much influenced by reports of a Commission plan to accompany EU enlargement by further centralision of power in Brussels. To restore momentum, Mitterrand decided France should ratify not through parliamentary action but by referendum. This was unwise – the 1972 referendum on EC expansion had been closer than anticipated. Delors' forecast that by 1998 Brussels would be producing 80 per cent of all economic legislation was

[37] *Annual Register*, 2002, pp. 421–2; *Keesings*, 46072; Patten, *Not Quite the Diplomat*, pp. 130–1.
[38] Unlike in the United States, where national political parties emerged in the 1790s, elections to the European parliament are still contested, in all countries, on the basis of the local party system – and often of protest votes relating to it.

recalled, amid fears that it would cut back the CAP and expose French commerce and workers to destructive foreign competition; and Mitterrand had to struggle to secure a 51 per cent yes vote.[39] In Britain all this impacted on Conservative euro-scepticism, which was further boosted in September by the markets' ejection of the pound from the ERM. In Parliament Labour opposed ratification for opportunistic reasons, and it passed in July 1993 only after a struggle that did much to weaken the Conservative party's former European commitment. Meanwhile the Danish electorate had been induced to change its mind, partly by minor changes in the Maastricht terms, but chiefly by the possibility that otherwise the country might have to leave the EU.

The 1997 Amsterdam treaty was better received. But to everybody's surprise hitherto *communautaire* Ireland rejected the Nice treaty in a 2001 referendum that was partly protest vote, partly the result of fears that Nice might reduce small countries' influence within the EU and also compromise Ireland's international neutralism. The decision was admittedly reversed in a second referendum.[40] But in 2000 Denmark, and in 2003 Sweden, voted against adopting the euro, in the belief that this might make it more difficult to maintain their generous social welfare systems.

It should therefore have been clear that an EU Constitution would not be easy to sell; and indeed it was agreed that should it be rejected by no more than five states, it should be modified and resubmitted, not dropped. Danish rejection was likely; and when British public opinion forced Blair to promise a referendum, rather than simple parliamentary ratification, a crisis seemed probable. However, Chirac, anxious to point up the contrast with his *bête noire* Blair, forgot Mitterrand's narrow escape, and himself called a French referendum. In a campaign that had little to do with the Constitution's actual text, 'Right-wing opponents . . . claimed it would erode French sovereignty and facilitate the admission of Muslim Turkey to the EU, whilst those on the left argued that it enshrined "Anglo-Saxon" economic liberalism and would . . . undermine the French social market model.' In May 2005 the referendum was lost by 55 per cent to 45 per cent. The Netherlands then confirmed this verdict, by an even larger majority, in a vote

seen as a protest against EU enlargement and the speed of European integration, which was widely perceived as threatening the country's sovereignty and its national identity, especially through the possibility of

[39] Grant, *Delors*, pp. 213–15, 221–5.
[40] *Annual Register*, 2001, pp. 82, 435; 2002, p. 49.

increased immigration. Growing anti-Muslim sentiment . . . had fuelled
hostility to Turkey's proposed EU accession . . . [and there was]
resentment at being the EU's largest net per capita contributor
and anger at the inflated cost of living, which was blamed on the
introduction of the euro.[41]

For the time being, these votes (by founder members of the EEC) killed the draft Constitution. The sky did not fall in – the EU continued to work smoothly on the basis of its previous *acquis*, and has in fact taken decisions more rapidly after its 2004 expansion than before. But most governments regretted the Constitution's rejection, and wished to salvage as much of it as possible. Chancellor Merkel accordingly presented the June 2007 European Council with a draft 'Reform Treaty', preserving, she said, the 'substance of the Constitution', but with sufficient symbolical changes to enable France (and perhaps also the UK and the Netherlands) to ratify it without risking another referendum. With the help of the new French president, Sarkozy, general approval was secured, the intention being that a final text should be agreed in December 2007 and come into operation in 2009.

The Community's external influence, economic and diplomatic

One impulse to union has always been the belief that the whole would be greater than the sum of its parts, that Europe will be better able to influence the outside world as a unit than as a collection of separate states. Some people have, indeed, described the EU as a potential, or even an actual, superpower. Support for this claim might perhaps most naturally be sought in the economic sphere, since the EU started as the European *Economic* Community. As we have seen, the EU now deploys the world's second currency; but this development is too recent for its external impact yet to be very evident. In the field of trade, however, the Commission (negotiating on behalf of the EC/EU as a whole) has been a major player in successive tariff 'rounds' from the 1960s onwards – though its very prominence exposes it to external pressures to modify its agricultural policy that a smaller unit, like Switzerland or Norway, may escape. The size of the EU's internal market also confers on it a degree of extra-territorial power, since foreign concerns can only access it if they comply with EU regulations. A striking, if unusual, instance was the Commission's 2001 veto of

[41] *Keesing's*, 46067, 46634, 46695.

the merger of two large US companies, GE and Honeywell; this was, of course, imposed only to preserve competition in the European market, but it had the effect also of blocking the merger of their more important US interests.[42] Moreover, if producers seek to sell to Europe, their products must comply with EU technical standards; and the Commission would like to facilitate and capture trade by inducing outside countries to adopt these.[43] In such ways, Brussels' influence can extend surprisingly widely, albeit in respect of what are mostly fairly trivial matters.

The EU has also surrounded itself with a cats cradle of special economic relationships hinging on preferential tariff-free access to its market, accompanied by development aid but also protective EU controls on agricultural and other 'sensitive' imports. These stemmed from the EEC's initial arrangements to accommodate French and Belgian colonies, extended (under the 1975 Lomé Convention) to African, Caribbean and Pacific (but *not* Asian) Commonwealth countries; ad hoc arrangements with Greece, Turkey, Tunisia and Morocco led on to deals with other countries, and in 1995 the Barcelona 'Euro-Mediterranean' Process was launched, aiming at a free trade area by 2010; similarly from 1989–91 onwards more or less far-reaching agreements have been concluded with East European and ex-Soviet states.[44]

Such market access policies, like those the United States has adopted towards the Caribbean, Central and South America, tend to reinforce regionalism along axes largely reflecting past political or economic dependence. They do not, however, provide for the free movement of labour. Yet the contrast between EU wealth and the poverty of most of the countries thus looking towards it exerts a magnetic pull. Accordingly, from the 1990s onwards, there has been a mounting flow of would-be illegal immigrants (often aided by high-priced people smugglers) prepared to try desperate ways of reaching the EU – and to heightened Italian and Spanish naval patrolling (with EU assistance) to prevent them doing so.

The EC and EU have aspired also to more conventional diplomatic influence on the world scene. The 1973 oil crisis provided a stimulus. To

---

[42] It was, though, only the second all-American merger the Commission had blocked since 1990 – Commission Press Release, 3 July 2001.

[43] A 2004 Commission Staff Working Paper (SEC (2004) 1072) expressed hopes of extending EU standards to, or agreeing international rulers for industrial products (to which these would contribute) with, the 'countries participating in the . . . Association Process, the Mediterranean, Russia, Ukraine, China and the Gulf Co-operation Council'.

[44] Pinder, *Building of the European Union*, Chap. 9; Patten, *Not Quite the Diplomat*, pp. 158–9, 189, 192–6.

Kissinger's dismay, EC member states did not adopt a common front to the oil producers, but drove up prices by each scrambling competitively to secure supplies. On the rebound, however, the 1973 EC summit responded to Arab oil offers by issuing a pro-Palestinian communiqué, leading eventually to a 'European–Arab dialogue' but at too low a level to have any effect.[45] Thereafter Foreign Ministers began general discussions, at first deliberately outside but soon within the EC context. In 1982 the EC responded to Argentina's seizure of the Falkland Islands by banning all imports from, and financial aid to, it; even though Italy and Ireland soon opted out, this 'display of European solidarity, with France as its most stalwart champion, was as valuable politically as it was materially to the British cause.' But this was very much an isolated development;[46] and when the possibility arose of German reunification, West Germany handled the matter by itself, in triangular Great Power dealings with the USA and USSR (above, pp. 424–31). There followed Iraq's seizure of Kuwait; again the EC was on the sidelines, and while Britain and France contributed to the US-led UN force that expelled Iraq, Belgium declined to sell Britain ammunition.[47]

So when Yugoslavia was shaken in June 1991 by Slovene and Croat declarations of independence, the EC was glad to encounter a problem it thought it could handle. A 'troika' of its Foreign Ministers descended on Belgrade, arranged a ceasefire, and returned elatedly proclaiming that 'this is the hour of Europe, not of America'.[48] By August fighting had broken out in Croatia; EC observers and good offices were ignored, and when, by the end of the year, the parties were ready for a ceasefire, it was to the UN, and to a UN peace-keeping force, that they turned. If this was, from the EC's perspective, ignominious, worse was to follow. For Germany insisted that, with or without the EC, it would recognise Croat and Slovenian independence by Christmas. This unilaterally reversed past EC policy, but could be defended as a recognition of the *de facto* situation. Though EC Foreign Ministers had qualms about its likely consequences elsewhere, they proceeded to make matters worse by inviting other Yugoslav republics to apply (within a week) for independence. Their provisions for

---

[45] *Post-Imperial Age*, pp. 351–3.
[46] *Annual Register*, 1982, p. 9. EC sanctions on South Africa may also have been of some consequence; but they were clearly less influential than pressures from the USA, the Commonwealth, and from individual banks, nor did they prevent *increases* in South African sales to Germany (*Post-Imperial Age*, pp. 79–82).
[47] Grant, *Delors*, pp. 144–5, 185–6.
[48] *ibid.* p. 192; below, Chap. 15.

minority and other rights would then be vetted by a French jurist; this might have posed problems for Croatia, but Germany's prompt recognition of Croatia (and Slovenia) cut the process short. Macedonia proceeded peacefully to independence in 1992; but EU recognition was stalled by Greek hostility, and it was to the UN that Macedonia turned for a stabilising peace-keeping force. Bosnia was another matter. It might in any case have been destabilised by Croatia's secession from Yugoslavia; but the EC made trouble certain by first soliciting an application for independence, then (in April 1992) recognising this following a referendum the Bosnian Serbs had boycotted. Civil war ensued. Mediation by an EC and a UN commissioner nearly succeeded in 1993. But fighting actually ended, in 1995, only after NATO air strikes and the diplomatic involvement of the US, whose importance was illustrated by the peace conference venue, an air base in Dayton, Ohio. Later, too, the EU was completely bypassed, in favour of NATO, in the 1999 forcible coercion of Serbia over Kosovo, though Finland's President (acting for both the EU and the UN) played a significant role in negotiating Serbia's final withdrawal.

In 1997 the Amsterdam treaty sought to raise the profile of EU foreign policy by creating a High Representative to act as the voice of the Council of Foreign Ministers alongside a Commissioner for External Affairs who would oversee EU aid and other relevant Community programmes. Much diplomatic travel followed – one year the Commissioner supposedly boarded over 180 aeroplanes – and there were worthwhile low-key achievements. More visibly, the EU is (with Russia, the UN and the USA) a member of the 'Quartet' promoting the 'road-map' route to Israeli–Palestinian peace: 'European foreign ministers discussed Palestine and Israel virtually every month', and the EU provided appreciable sums to consolidate the Palestinian Authority; but, as events in 2006 made clear, the EU has little influence on the ground. Moreover member states continue to run, and usually to attach more importance to, their own foreign policies; and, in the view of the EU's 1999–2004 Commissioner for External Affairs:

there is no European policy on a big issue unless France, Germany, and Britain are on side. Unless they work together, nothing else will work . . .

That was most evident over Iraq [in 2002–3] . . . The subject was scarcely debated in the Council: as the arguments hotted up elsewhere – at the UN . . . , on the telephone lines between London, Paris and Berlin – we pretended in Brussels that there was nothing amiss.[49]

---

[49] Patten, Not Quite the Diplomat, esp. pp. 162, 196.

The Community's external influence – the attraction of new members

Whatever the EC's and EU's failings when viewed from inside, they have exerted an attraction so powerful that few neighbouring states in a position to join have held aloof. The UK applied in both 1961 and 1967, in the belief that it needed access to a large trading bloc and that the EC was the only one available, and also that its international influence would wither if it long remained excluded; and if Britain joined, it seemed logical to the governments of countries with close economic links to the UK that they should join too. De Gaulle vetoed Britain's accession; but his successor, Pompidou accepted it on condition that construction of the CAP should first be completed; so in 1972 the EC agreed that Britain, Ireland, Denmark and Norway should join. Irish membership was a great success; it facilitated the diversification of Irish trade (and from 1979 the Irish currency) away from the UK; Ireland also benefited both from the CAP and from significant EC/EU 'structural' spending to overcome its relative poverty. Adding to this good education and a low tax regime for business, Ireland became the 'Celtic tiger', in a process that, in the new millenium, several East European states believed EU membership would enable them to replicate. The Norwegian electorate, however, decided, by referendum, that the price of EC membership was too high – the CAP would inhibit the subsidy of small-scale agriculture, while a 'Common Fisheries Policy' would remove control of that resource from Norwegian hands.[50] Since then Norway has boomed, albeit largely as a result of the development of offshore oil and gas; in 1994 another referendum again rejected EU membership.

The 1980s EC enlargement was very different, in that it represented a deliberate attempt to reward and consolidate countries that had recently emerged from dictatorship. After the uncomfortably strong showing of the crypto-communists in the 1958 Greek elections, Prime Minister

---

[50] In 1972 the world was moving from a regime of 3 to one of 200-mile national fishing limits, which would have harmed the six existing EC members, but benefited the four applicant states. So the former unilaterally added to the EC *acquis* that most of the new fisheries should be controlled, and catch quotas within them awarded, by Brussels. While catches have been sustained in nationally managed waters, EU ones are in danger of being fished out. This may explain why Iceland has shown no interest in EU membership, and was one factor behind the departure from the EC in 1985 of the near-independent Danish colony of Greenland.

Karamanlis had approached the EEC, seeing it as an anchor to the West complementary to Greece's increasingly strained relationships with the US and NATO. In 1961 this led the EEC to conclude its first association agreement, holding out the prospect of full Greek membership in the comfortably remote year of 1984. The agreement was frozen after the colonels' 1967 coup. But on Karamanlis' return to power, with the US and NATO still more unpopular, he renewed his pursuit of EC membership. The Commission saw the state of Greco-Turkish relations as an obstacle, and suggested, on economic grounds, a pre-membership transition period. But after Karamanlis had exploded against such humiliating terms, the Council of Ministers decided on negotiations for immediate entry; and in 1979 Karamanlis could tell his parliament that 'by joining the mighty European family as an equal member [in 1981] . . . Greece will be no longer obliged to seek protection from this or the other superpower.'[51] Greece's admission to the EC had been the more readily agreed since it was relatively small, but it set an important precedent in that Greece was not a *West* European state.

Spain and Portugal had also applied for membership in 1975 as they emerged from lengthy dictatorships. Again it was felt their admission would help consolidate democracy. On the other hand, the scale of Spain's wine and olive oil production, and of its fishing fleet, led to protectionist fears; and in the early 1980s the Community was, until the 1984 Fontainebleau agreement, chiefly concerned with its own internal affairs. Also Britain insisted that Spain could not join until it had lifted its long-standing closure of its land border with Gibraltar.[52] All this made for lengthy negotiations, further complicated at the end by Greece's threat to veto the enlargement unless it received substantial EC development funding. Agreement was, however, finally reached in 1985, with Spain and Portugal joining next January.

[51] R.J. Crampton, *The Balkans since the Second World War* (2002) pp. 210, 218, 224–5; *Annual Register*, 1976, pp. 169, 337–8; 1979, p. 170.
[52] This Spain grudgingly did in 1985. In return Britain accepted talks at which Spain might raise the issue of sovereignty. Since Britain still pledged 'to honour the wishes of the people of Gibraltar', that issue made little progress. In 2001–2 joint sovereignty was discussed, though in Spain's view only as a transitional state; but the Gibraltar government secured a 99% referendum vote against it – *Annual Register*, 1982, p. 173; 1984, p. 45; 1985, pp. 161–2; 2002, p. 84. In 2006, following negotiations in which Gibraltar as well as Britain participated, Spain lifted its restrictions on air and sea links with Gibraltar – but still opposes its application for membership of the football association UEFA.

The next round of expansion was partly the result of the end of the Cold War. Despite its geographical position, Austria had been confined to EFTA by fears that the USSR would regard EC membership as incompatible with the neutrality on which its independence had been conditioned. But in 1989 it felt able to apply for membership, and other applications seemed in the offing. Delors feared such numerical growth might make the EC unmanageable, and floated the idea of a European Economic Area that would enable EFTA states to participate in the 'Single Market's removal of non-tariff barriers. But it proved hard to give them a significant voice in the framing of the multifarious regulations this required.[53] As this became clear, most EFTA governments concluded that, if they had to accept so many of the EC's regulations anyway, they might as well become full members: Sweden applied in 1990, Finland, Switzerland and Norway in 1992. All were eminently fitted for membership, and most were likely to become net contributors to Community funds. So it was hard for those worried about these applications to do more than postpone their consideration until after the Maastricht reforms were fully in place. In 1995 Austria, Sweden and Finland duly joined.[54]

Other would-be members still pressed. Turkey's application dated from 1987, Malta's and Cyprus's from 1990. Attention, however, centred on the ex-communist states who saw 'joining Europe' as the natural completion of their transformation, and argued (with President Havel of Czechoslovakia) that it was 'in the West's own interest to seek the integration of eastern and central Europe into the family of European democracy because otherwise it risks creating a zone of hopelessness, instability and chaos, which could threaten Western Europe every bit as much as the Warsaw Pact tank divisions of old.' Such pleas carried weight, especially with Britain and countries north and east of the Rhine. But Delors feared that a plethora of new members would paralyse EU decision-making, while Mitterrand did not 'want the Community to become a vague free trade area, as certain . . . countries wanted from the very beginning';[55] 'deepening' should therefore take precedence over 'broadening'. In any case East European poverty would make the region expensive to subsidise

---

[53] When agreement was reached in 1991, the European Court of Justice struck it down, and the deal had to be renegotiated, giving non-EU states even less input – Grant, *Delors*, pp. 128, 212.

[54] Norway's voters had again rejected membership, while Switzerland's had, narrowly, voted even against EEA entry. Neither, of course, has been impoverished as a result.

[55] *Keesing's*, 38115; *Financial Times*, 13 September 1991, p. 1.

(as Greece, Spain, Portugal and Ireland had been supported), while the applicants would require massive internal reorientation to achieve Western free market economies. Meanwhile vulnerable EC interests like steel and agriculture did their best to restrict competition from the products Eastern Europe was best placed to export.

In the short term the EC/EU could compromise between these approaches by concluding association agreements. The idea was first mooted in 1990, and, in relation to Poland, Czechoslovakia and Hungary (the most developed, and pressing, East European states), accelerated in 1991 when the coup in the USSR seemed, if only briefly, likely to reinstate the Cold War. By 1993 seven such agreements had been signed, by 1996 ten, providing for the EU to remove industrial tariffs (save in 'sensitive' areas) in five years, the associates in ten.[56] More importantly, though, the 1993 Copenhagen Council agreed in principle to admit East European states, provided they had functioning legal and democratic institutions, respected human rights, and possessed market economies capable of assuming the burdens of EU membership. Arguments continued within the EU; but with the 1997 Amsterdam Treaty out of the way, it was decided to open actual entry negotiations with Hungary, Poland, the Czech Republic, Estonia, Slovenia and Cyprus, and to prepare for similar negotions with several other countries (though *not* Turkey). 'Negotiations' is perhaps a misnomer, since the EU always insists on acceptance of its entire legal *acquis*,[57] subject only to temporary 'derogations' from their immediate application (whether by new or existing EU members). But in 2004 ten states joined the EU,[58] adding 20 per cent to its population but only 5 per cent to its GDP, with Romania and Bulgaria to follow in 2007.

The goal of EU membership had kept East European governments remarkably constant in policies of economic adaptation, despite the social and political costs, much as the lesser goal of joining the euro zone had stimulated the EU's Mediterranean members to reduce their debts and deficits. There may also have been wider effects. In order to join the EC, Spain lifted its blockade of Gibraltar; similar calculations may have helped discourage the revisionist aspirations sometimes detectable in post-communist Hungary and have contributed to the 1996 deal whereby

[56] Pinder, *Building of the European Union*, pp. 236–7; *Annual Register*, 1991, p. 397; 1993, p. 411.

[57] 80,000 pages by 2004 – *Annual Register*, 2004, p. 391.

[58] Estonia, Latvia, Lithuania, Poland, Hungary, the Czech Republic, Slovakia, Slovenia, Malta and Cyprus – *Annual Register*, 1993, p. 411; 1997, pp. 403–4; 2004, p. 391.

it confirmed its border with Romania, which in turn undertook to improve the treatment of its Hungarian minority. But EU influence is not unlimited. As the (Greek) Republic of Cyprus approached EU membership, the island, partitioned *de facto* in 1974, came closer than ever before to accepting a UN reunification plan: indeed the 'Turkish Republic of Northern Cyprus', hitherto regarded as the chief obstacle, saw this as a price worth paying to secure the benefits stemming from entry; but the plan's provisions for northern autonomy proved unacceptable to the south.[59] Nor has the lure of talks on accession yet induced Serbia to extradite to the International Criminal Court locally popular Serb leaders in the Bosnian civil war.

Nevertheless, Eastern Europe's transformation leads many to see the EU as 'an outstanding agent and sustainer of regime change', with the conditional offer of membership 'the most potent instrument in European foreign policy'. This offer is currently in play with respect both to the Balkans and to Turkey. By 2007 most of the Balkans will already have joined, but not Albania or the majority of ex-Yugoslavia, the areas with the most troubled recent histories. Patten claims that here 'delivering on the promises we have made – to Croatia, Bosnia, Albania, Serbia[,] and Montenegro, Macedonia and Kosovo, that if they reform, if they meet our standards, they will be welcome to join . . . could ultimately make the difference between war and peace in that region', the alternative being (in Crampton's words) reversion to 'the closed societies', 'dirigiste economies', and 'destructive ethnic nationalism' of the past.[60] Some also hope that promises of early EU membership may secure Serbia's acceptance of the Kosovo independence that now (2006) seems inevitable. There are, however, difficulties: Kosovo, Bosnia, Macedonia, and Albania have shown few signs of developing a normal economy, while the first three still require stabilisation by an external military force; and within the EU there are obvious signs of expansion fatigue, apparent, inter alia, in the 2005 Dutch and French referenda.

Even more important, though, is the antipathy these showed to the inclusion of Turkey. Since the days of Mustafa Kemal, Turkey has proclaimed itself 'European'. It followed Greece to conclude an association agreement with the EEC in 1963, with the Commission's President declaring roundly that 'Turkey is part of Europe'. This, however, was just rhetoric; Turkey's 1987 application was put on one side, with further

---

[59] *Annual Register*, 2003, pp. 89–91; 2004, pp. 74–5.
[60] Patten, *Not Quite the Diplomat*, p. 144, Crampton, *The Balkans*, pp. 343–4.

postponement ten years later. Events conspired to bring it forward: after 1999 improving relations transformed Greece from an obstacle to an advocate of Turkish membership. Then '9/11' heightened, in some quarters, perceptions of Turkey as a secular and democratic state that could serve as a bridge between Europe and the Middle East and a role model to the Moslem world, whereas rejection would convey the message, both to that world and to Moslem minorities within Europe, that 'Turkey is not welcome within our club because it is Islamic'.[61] Others, however, including Giscard d'Estaing, felt precisely that – Turkey was not of 'Europe', and its inclusion would prove fatal to EU cohesion. Such sentiments were reinforced by concerns over past Moslem immigrants and fears that Turkey's accession would much increase their numbers; this played a considerable role in the 2005 Dutch and French referenda votes. Not that these are the only difficulties: Turkey would be both the most populous and the poorest EU member; its laws and military culture may be secular, but are still not always liberal; a serious, and harshly repressed, Kurdish insurrection is not entirely resolved. On the other hand, Turkey has already addressed some of these problems, while the need to qualify for EU membership may, as in Eastern Europe, provide a powerful incentive to resolve others. In late 2005 the EU decided, after considerable debate, to open negotiations with a view to Turkish accession in 2015, but with the clear caveat that they may not succeed. Meanwhile European criticism, and perhaps also rising Islamic sentiment, has reduced *Turkey's* enthusiasm for EU membership; and its reluctance to recognise, even indirectly, the Republic of Cyprus, has not got talks off to a good start.

[61] Patten, *Not Quite the Diplomat*, pp. 147–9. In 2002 the USA pressed the EU to give Turkey membership quickly so as to avoid apparent confirmation of a 'clash of civilisations' with the Moslem world (*Annual Register*, 2002, p. 416).

CHAPTER 14

Splits in the communist world

The Western half of the developed world has enjoyed considerable success. This has rested on the consolidation or creation of political systems incorporating its general values, on its economies' ability to grow and to overcome without really serious damage those strains and shocks they have been subjected to, and on the ability of the United States to avoid fundamental rifts with its allies. The Communist world failed in each of these respects. For first Yugoslavia and then China broke with the Soviet Union. Despite a promising start, the economies of the USSR and of a number of East European countries slowed down in the 1970s, then stopped (or otherwise ran into major difficulties) in the 1980s; and their shortcomings in comparison with those of the West were driven home by the penetration of Western TV and radio and by the increasing openness of East European society. In most of Eastern Europe, too, communism was imposed, not indigenous; there was always a danger that it would simply collapse if the USSR did not maintain it, by force if necessary. Admittedly there was also the possibility that communist governments would eventually acquire national roots, and come to be accepted by their subjects as inevitable since there was apparently no way in which they could be changed. We can now see that this seldom happened, and that they lost further ground with the economic strains of the 1980s. Attempts at reform proved destabilising. The Soviet Union, itself in grave economic trouble, lost the will to intervene. The upshot was the collapse of communist regimes first in East Europe, then in the USSR itself.

East European Communist Parties and the USSR in the immediate post-war period

In the 1930s almost all communists had accepted that the interests of foreign parties were identical with those of the USSR since these parties could not prosper without the support of the 'socialist motherland'. They also believed that there were 'objectively correct' doctrines and policies, and that the Communist Party of the Soviet Union (CPSU) – and more especially its leader, Stalin – was an infallible guide to these. As a result they followed the current Moscow line with remarkable discipline, opposing first Germany (until the Nazi–Soviet pact), then from 1939 to 1941 the anti-German war effort that they were to back strongly as soon as Germany invaded the USSR. Stalin naturally hoped that these attitudes would continue after victory, as for the most part they did. But since, with the takeover of Eastern Europe, there would now be other 'communist' states besides the Soviet Union,[1] a new pattern of relationships would have to be worked out. For this there was no clear model. Marxist *theory* stressed ideological not nationalist alignments. But between the wars communist and USSR patriotism had been fused through the doctrine of 'socialism in one country'. Similar developments could potentially occur in other countries. And indeed *some* communists showed solicitude for the national interests of the countries they had returned to rule, at least where these did not clash with those of the USSR. 'Thus the Polish and East German communists were soon making discrepant statements about . . . the Oder-Neisse frontier, the Polish and Czechoslovak ones about their states' respective border claims in the Teschen . . . and Glatz . . . districts, the Czechoslovak and Hungarian ones about the treatment of the Magyar ethnic minority in Slovakia,' etc.[2] Nor is this surprising; even foreign occupiers, like the US Army in Germany, came to identify with the interests of 'their' areas.

At the same time the state structure of Eastern Europe was perceived to be fluid. This view was not exclusively communist; the area's inter-war history had been disappointing, and in 1943 Britain had toyed with ideas of an Eastern, or at least Danubian, Federation. Stalin did not like them.

---

[1] Outer Mongolia had had a Soviet-supported regime since 1922 and had formally become independent in 1942; but it had been too small and dependent to pose problems.

[2] Joseph Rothschild, *Return to Diversity. A Political History of East Central Europe since World War II* (New York, 1989) p. 125.

But he allowed the canvassing, after the war, both of various Balkan federations and of a more ambitious extension of the Soviet Union, merging 'the Ukraine with Hungary and Rumania, and Byelorussia with Poland and Czechoslovakia, while the Balkan states were to be joined with Russia'.[3] Interestingly, in 1945 Kardelj, a prominent member of the Yugoslav leadership that broke with Moscow three years later, told the Soviet ambassador

he would like the Soviet Union to regard them, not as representatives of another country, capable of solving questions independently, but as representatives of one of the future Soviet Republics, and the C[ommunist] P[arty of] Y[ugoslavia] as a part of the CPSU . . . For this reason they would like us to . . . give them advice which would direct the internal and external policy of Yugoslavia along the right path.[4]

Tito's break with Stalin

In the early post-war years Yugoslavia was to cast itself as Moscow's leading ally. Tito had emerged from the war in full control, whereas in all other East European countries except Albania the communists were to take two to three years to consolidate their power. Tito loved power, and the perquisites and palaces that went with it, and looked to extend his rule; as early as 1943 he had written, 'In our opinion, and also in that of . . . [Comintern], we should be in the centre for the Balkan countries, both in the military and in the political sense'. He had been instrumental in founding and backing the Albanian Communist Party; after the war he extended the Yugoslav presence there through the Soviet-style despatch of advisers

[3] Milovan Djilas, *Conversations with Stalin* (1969) p. 137. In November 1941 Maisky had sketched a scheme for a Balkan federation centred on Yugoslavia, a federation of Poland, Czechoslovakia and Hungary, and another of the Baltic states, all to lean economically and militarily on Russia (*FRUS 1941*, i, pp. 337–8). In 1948 Gottwald suggested to Stalin that Czechoslovakia accede to the Soviet Union (*Khrushchev Remembers*, iii, p. 131); and an SED leader told Wolfgang Leonhard it was quite possible, though not inevitable, that in due course all the People's Democracies would join 'as new Union Republics' (*Child of the Revolution* (1957) p. 403). As late as 1972 Zhivkov agreed with Brezhnev to create conditions for Bulgaria to do so, something he continued to hope for until the advent of Gorbachev (*Keesing's*, 37745).
[4] S. Clissold (ed.) *Yugoslavia and the Soviet Union 1939–1973* (1975) pp. 166–7; Ivo Banac, *With Stalin against Tito. Cominformist Splits in Yugoslav Communism* (Ithaca, NY, 1988) p. 17.

and formation of joint-stock companies; in 1946, Enver Hoxha claims, Tito dangled before him the carrot of the transfer of the primarily Albanian-inhabited province of Kosovo when Albania federated with Yugoslavia.[5] Yugoslavia had also been discussing federation with Bulgaria since 1944, in the hope that Bulgaria would first cede its sector of Macedonia (an object of dispute since the beginning of the century), then become a seventh republic within Yugoslavia. It took the lead in helping the communist insurgency in Greece, partly out of what Djilas was later to describe as 'revolutionary idealism', partly with the aim of securing Greek Macedonia in return.[6] Lastly Yugoslavia had territorial claims on Italy and Austria.

We do not know how Stalin really viewed all this. Occasional sharp words were exchanged, notably in May 1945 when the USSR took Tito's nationalist speech over Trieste[7] as an 'unfriendly attack' and threatened to reply in public. But Yugoslavia mostly seemed to be in high favour, if possibly seen as a little too impetuous. Tito had been accorded a triumphal tour of the USSR in April 1945. Next year Stalin singled him out for distinction, declaring that 'Tito must look after himself. I won't live long, and Europe needs him.' Stalin also cited him as a model when rebuking the Poles for their mild treatment of political offenders: 'Tito is a tower of strength . . . he wiped them all out.'[8] When in September 1947 Stalin decided to revive the Communist International, under the name of Cominform, and to realign the policy of the French and Italian parties, the Yugoslavs were cast in a star role as their accusers.[9] This is not to say that there were no frictions – Stalin resented Yugoslav criticism of the Red Army's

---

[5] Clissold, *Yugoslavia and the Soviet Union*, pp. 46, 105; Nora Beloff, *Tito's Flawed Legacy. Yugoslavia and the West: 1939–84* (1985) p. 192 – cf. also Djilas, *Conversations with Stalin*, p. 112.

[6] Clissold, *Yugoslavia and the Soviet Union*, pp. 46–8; Milovan Djilas, *Rise and Fall* (1985) pp. 277–8. From 1946–8 Yugoslavia arranged for the supply of untraceable Wehrmacht weapons, provided food, clothing and medical assistance, and gave (bad) military advice; almost half the insurgent fighting forces, too, were Slav Macedonians (Banac, *With Stalin against Tito*, pp. 35–6).

[7] 'We do not wish to be petty cash used in bribes; we do not wish to be involved in a policy of spheres of interest'; 'We will not be dependent on anyone ever again'.

[8] Djilas, *Rise and Fall*, p. 105, *Tito. The Story from Inside* (1981) p. 39; Beloff, *Tito's flawed legacy*, p. 142.

[9] This may have led Tito to think Stalin had put caution aside and was now fully endorsing his own uninhibited sponsorship of revolutionary takeover – Geoffrey Swain, 'The Cominform: Tito's International?', *Historical Journal*, xxxv (1992) pp. 641–63.

propensity to loot and rape. The Yugoslavs, too, saw the Soviet approach to commerce as hard-nosed and exploitative. But in 1947 Stalin tried to mend this by backing away from joint companies; 'Clearly, this isn't a good form of collaboration with a friendly ally like Yugoslavia . . . Such companies are appropriate for satellites.'[10] When relations worsened both issues were paraded; but they probably reflected rather than caused the breach.

Two matters were more serious, Yugoslav expansionism, and the Soviet propensity to recruit agents and intervene directly in the working of Yugoslav government. In retrospect Djilas felt that conflict with the USSR was bound to come some time, but that it was touched off by events in Albania. Yugoslav encroachment had divided the Albanian party, and driven its director of economic affairs to suicide in protest. It also seemed to be encountering increasing opposition from the Soviet Mission in Tirana. Then in late 1947 Tito sent two divisions into Albania, ostensibly to protect it from Greece, but chiefly to pre-empt any Soviet inclination to shoulder Yugoslavia aside and 'grab' the country.

Stalin had not been consulted; he summoned Djilas to Moscow in January 1948 for an explanation, then jovially told him (on arrival) to go ahead and swallow Albania. Djilas, however, suspected a trap, and relations continued strained. Later in the month Tito was himself invited to come and clear up 'complications', but prudently sent his deputy Kardelj instead. Though the Yugoslavs may not have realised it, Stalin was on edge over Czechoslovakia, being determined to complete the communist takeover and apprehensive about possible Western intervention (see p. 153); this may have reinforced his natural disposition not to tolerate independent initiatives by his satellites. On 10 February (the Czech crisis came to a head on the 20th) the Soviet leadership staged a session in which the Yugoslav leaders were attacked, and their Bulgarian counterparts humiliated, for taking initiatives (in their relations with each other, Albania and Romania) without first consulting Moscow.[11] They were also not invited to the customary dinner that evening at Stalin's *dacha*. Next day Kardelj was intimidated into signing a treaty pledging Yugoslavia to consult before

---

[10] Djilas, *Rise and Fall*, p. 97. Only three such companies were established; but after the rift Yugoslavia denounced them to the UN as exploitative.

[11] Dimitrov had exposed himself by advocating a customs union with Romania and an eventual Balkan federation, but the Yugoslavs felt Stalin's abuse of the Bulgarians was really directed at them. Embarassingly the Bulgarians and Yugoslavs could both show that Molotov *had* been informed of some of the initiatives of which Stalin complained.

taking any initiative in international affairs. Nevertheless Stalin's attitude may not have been entirely negative, since he enjoined the rapid consummation of a Yugoslav–Bulgarian–Albanian federation. But in the context of Stalin's other behaviour, Tito saw this as a Trojan horse, designed to dilute his own control of Yugoslavia.[12]

The other cause of the rift was the USSR's attempt, in Yugoslavia as elsewhere, to recruit agents at all levels – by means ranging from sexual entrapment to appeals to socialist loyalty – and to give orders directly, bypassing the formal Yugoslav leadership. As early as 1945 one such recruitment had led Tito to exclaim, 'A spy network is something we will not tolerate! We've got to let them know right away.' But the process did not stop, Soviet penetration being particularly obtrusive in the army. By 1947–8 the Yugoslavs seem to have countered by subjecting Soviet officials and advisers to police surveillance. In March 1948 the USSR suddenly withdrew its advisers, and an exchange of accusations ensued. Moscow was clearly taking the initiative, and its tone was undignified (dredging up incidents from the distant past and throwing in touching complaints about the undemocratic nature of the Yugoslav party and its supervision by the secret police). Belgrade continued to protest its loyalty, but it insisted it was 'improper' for Soviet agents:

to recruit in our country, which is moving towards socialism, our citizens for their intelligence service . . .

. . . such recruiting is not done for the purpose of a struggle against some capitalist country, and we must inevitably come to the conclusion that this recruiting is destroying our internal unity, that it . . . leads to the compromising of leading people and becomes a channel for the collection of false information . . .

We cannot allow the Soviet Intelligence Service to spread its net in our country. We have our state security and intelligence service . . .

To Stalin this accusation seemed to be 'made solely for the purpose of justifying the . . . [Yugoslav police] in placing the Soviet workers in Yugoslavia under surveillance'. Similarly when Tito and Kardelj complained that the Soviet ambassador had no right to pry into Yugoslav party business, Stalin replied that this was to equate him with 'an ordinary bourgeois ambassador'; did they not understand 'that the Soviet ambassador,

---

[12] Djilas, *Rise and Fall*, p. 145, *Conversations with Stalin*, pp. 104–6, 111–14, 132–43; Clissold, *Yugoslavia and the Soviet Union*, pp. 51, 106; Beloff, *Tito's flawed legacy*, p. 144; Rothschild, *Return to Diversity*, p. 130; Banac, *With Stalin against Tito*, pp. 39 ff.

a responsible communist, who represents a friendly power which liberated Yugoslavia from the German occupation, has not only the right but the duty . . . to discuss with the communists of Yugoslavia all questions which may interest them?'[13]

By May, not having secured a Yugoslav surrender, the USSR referred the decision to Cominform. Though protesting 'that we are resolutely building socialism and that we remain loyal to the Soviet Union, loyal to the doctrine of Marx, Engels, Lenin, and Stalin', the Yugoslavs declined to attend; and on 28 June 1948 – tactlessly the historic Serbian national day – Cominform announced their excommunication; they had:

taken the path of seceding from the united socialist front against imperialism, have taken the path of betraying the cause of international solidarity of the working people, and have taken up a position of nationalism . . .

The Information Bureau considers that, in view of all this, the Central Committee of the Communist Party of Yugoslavia has placed itself and the Yugoslavia Party outside the family of the fraternal Communist Parties, outside the united Communist front and consequently outside the ranks of the Information Bureau.

It then appealed to 'healthy elements' within the Yugoslav party to 'compel their present leaders to recognize' and rectify their mistakes, or 'to replace them' with 'a new internationalist leadership'.[14]

Khrushchev says Stalin expected an easy victory – 'I will shake my little finger – and there will be no more Tito'. But Tito had his country well in hand. With most of his subjects, indeed, external abuse probably made him more popular; and few will have been influenced by Soviet propaganda stories of a miraculous image of Lenin that had wept tears over his apostasy.[15] His chief problems were with the army (perhaps as a result of recent Soviet training) and the party (which had been raised in a climate of uncritical enthusiasm for the USSR). He was careful to associate the party with replies to Soviet letters, convening central committee plenums and even a Party Congress in a way he had never done before – *but* against the background of the arrest of two leading pro-Soviet politicians. By good

---

[13] Djilas, *Rise and Fall*, p. 83; Beloff, *Tito's flawed legacy*, p. 144; Clissold, *Yugoslavia and the Soviet Union*, pp. 170 ff.

[14] RIIA, *Documents on International Affairs 1947–8*, pp. 396–7.

[15] *Khrushchev Remembers*, i, p. 544 (the 'Secret Speech'); D.L. Larson, *United States Foreign Policy Toward Yugoslavia, 1943–1963* (Washington, DC, 1979) p. 195.

luck, too, the now pro-Soviet former army commander was shot by a border patrol while escaping to Romania, perhaps with the intention of creating a government-in-exile. Police surveillance of the party, already intimidating in 1947, was stepped up. In the summer of 1948 there was a sweep of pro-Cominform suspects, who were despatched to a deliberately unpleasant island concentration camp. Probably the chief danger Tito faced was assassination – apparently Soviet agents in his bodyguard planned to shoot the top leadership while it was playing billiards. More conventional pressure came from a Soviet and East European trade embargo. Together with drought and the effects of agricultural collectivisation, this made conditions extremely difficult for several years – indeed there was a small peasants' revolt in Bosnia in 1949.[16]

Stalin's pressure led Yugoslavia to turn towards the West. The process took time, since its leaders were at first determined to disprove Soviet charges by demonstrating the purity of their socialism (farm collectivisation was stepped up after the breach with Moscow) and their continued foreign policy alignment with the East (there was no interference in 1948 with the airlift of Czech arms via Yugoslavia to Israel). But Tito clearly hoped for Western support should it prove necessary; 'The Americans are not fools,' he remarked in mid-1948, 'They won't let the Russians reach the Adriatic'; and he made overtures to the effect that Yugoslavia was ready to discontinue its aid to the Greek insurgents.[17] The first tangible assistance came from Britain in the form of a £30 million trade agreement in December 1948. In May 1949 Yugoslavia promised to abandon the insurgents and close its Greek border, and it sought a $250 million loan from the USA. The administration thought this too much to ask of a strongly anti-communist Congress, but it moved gingerly to provide aid in dribs and drabs: $150 million by August 1951 (plus about another $60 million from Britain and West Germany). This was matched by more open diplomatic support; the USA and Britain warned in September 1949 that a Soviet attack on Yugoslavia could have serious consequences, and shortly afterwards secured Yugoslavia's election to the UN Security Council in preference to the Soviet candidate, Czechoslovakia. In 1950 the Yugoslav leadership began to worry about its military equipment. That autumn it at last criticised the Northern invasion of South Korea; and in January 1951 Attlee was sounded out over arms and found sympathetic. The USA was

---

[16] Djilas, *Tito*, pp. 71–2, 79–90, *Rise and Fall*, pp. 227, 235–6.
[17] Djilas, *Tito*, p. 125; *FRUS 1948*, iv, pp. 1084–5.

then approached; its Chief of Staff visited Belgrade, and by the end of the year some $60 million of military supplies had come through. The trend continued in the early 1950s, with Tito visiting London and the Yugoslav secret service obliging the CIA. It culminated in the 1954 Balkan mutual defence Pact between Yugoslavia, Greece and Turkey (the two latter being NATO members).[18]

All this led Yugoslavia to distance itself ideologically from the USSR, which (Tito declared) had 'long since diverged from socialist development into state capitalism and an unprecedented bureaucratic system'.[19] To distinguish itself, Yugoslavia experimented from 1950 with workers' self-management: 'The factories belonging to the workers', Tito exclaimed, 'something that has never been achieved'. In practice it was not achieved, and the system eventually proved economically disastrous.[20] But it helped Yugoslavia claim to be pioneering an original form of socialism, and enhanced its standing with the European left. In 1953 self-management was complemented by de-collectivisation, though this was no more than a belated reaction to agricultural disaster. By now the swelling criticism of centralised bureaucracy and political monopoly was beginning to worry Tito; it was carrying the ideologue Djilas towards the conclusion that the governing elite under 'socialism' constituted a 'New Class'. Stalin's death in March 1953 stilled Tito's fears of a Soviet invasion and provided an occasion to call a halt. In June Tito ordered a Central Committee Plenum on ideology. In 1954 he turned on Djilas, who was dropped from the leadership and forced into (temporary) self-criticism, in a move probably intended to open the door to a reconciliation with the USSR.

On breaking with Belgrade, Stalin had hoped to secure Tito's collapse without overt recourse to force. By 1949 this seemed unlikely. So pressure was increased by troop concentrations on the borders, which prompted Tito to proclaim in August that Yugoslavia would defend itself (presumably by reverting to the guerrilla tactics of 1941–4). Incidents mounted to nearly 4,000 over 1949–51, with 40 Yugoslavs killed. It has been claimed,

[18] Dean Acheson, *Present at the Creation: my years in the State Department* (1970) pp. 332–3; Larson, *US Policy Toward Yugoslavia*, pp. 201, 205, 210, 212, 240–1, 255; Djilas, *Rise and Fall*, pp. 257, 273–4; John Ranelagh, *The Agency: The Rise and Decline of the CIA* (1986) pp. 255, 302.

[19] Clissold, *Yugoslavia and the Soviet Union*, p. 246.

[20] It had sufficient substance to add to inflationary wage pressures and prevent the closure of uneconomic plants; but it did not motivate the workforce, and central planning remained in being.

by a defecting Hungarian general, that plans were drawn for an invasion (probably in 1951), but abandoned when the Korean War suggested that a US response could not be ruled out. Moscow would then seem to have turned to other means. Planning to poison Tito was apparently well advanced in 1952–3, but was cancelled by Beria after Stalin's death. Beria indeed made secret overtures to Belgrade, and bawled out the author of a study that took the traditional Stalinist line on Yugoslavia.[21] His fall limited any rapprochement to the restoration of diplomatic relations.

Soviet–Yugoslav relations 1953–74

The question of how much further to go proved controversial. Molotov, in particular, had participated in the original rift, and in 1955 still defended it. He did not mind improving interstate relations, but thought it unwise to chase after Yugoslavia to restore party-to-party relations. (As we have seen – pp. 220–1, 232 – Molotov favoured a policy of keeping tightly what the USSR already held, rather than risking it in pursuit of wider gains.) Khrushchev took the more adventurous line, at any rate once he no longer needed support against Malenkov. He had a committee examine Yugoslavia and conclude that it was still a socialist state, cleared with other Communist parties the goal of restoring party-to-party relations, and invited himself to Belgrade. His visit in May 1955 was only a limited success, since Yugoslavia would not go beyond interstate relations. But he did not give up. His efforts are chronicled at great length in the memoirs of the Yugoslav ambassador, Micunovic, who was sent in 1956 with a brief neither to quarrel with the Russians nor to 'give in to them on matters of major political importance'.[22]

Many forces pulled the Yugoslavs back towards 'the camp', notably their communism and a nostalgia, probably felt most strongly in police and army circles, for past relationships. Also Yugoslavia had, in 1954–5, struck out as a founder-member of the third world 'non-aligned' movement,

---

[21] Clissold, *Yugoslavia and the Soviet Union*, pp. 247, 252; M. Charlton, *The Eagle and the Small Birds: crisis in the Soviet Empire: from Yalts to Solidarity* (1984) p. 78; *The Independent*, 12 June 1993, p. 15; Vladislav Zubok, *Soviet Intelligence and the Cold War: the 'Small' Committee of Information* (CWIHP Working Paper no. 4, 1992) pp. 16–17.

[22] S. Bialer, 'Ich wählte die Warheit', *Hinter dem Eisernen Vorhang*, x (October 1956) pp. 23–4, 27–8; *Khrushchev Remembers*, i, Chap. 12; V. Micunovic, *Moscow Diary* (1980) p. 13.

whose stance – especially as evidenced at their 1961 Belgrade summit – was much closer to the Soviet vision of anti-imperialist change through competition and 'peaceful coexistence' than to Western interests; in particular, until the mid-1970s, Yugoslavia served as a useful bridge between Egypt and the USSR, and is praised accordingly in Khrushchev's memoirs.[23] On the other hand, the Yugoslav economy could not easily dispense with what had become a significant level of Western aid; and in the 1960s it deepened this dependence by permitting the migration of *gastarbeiter* to Western Europe, thus easing its unemployment and securing valuable income from remittances. There were, too, occasional reminders that Yugoslav sovereignty had been more obviously threatened from the East than from the West. In any case Tito was probably too attached to his uncommitted position – 'Without an independent foreign policy there is no true independence'[24] – to opt irrevocably for either East or West. On the Soviet side, even Khrushchev was remarkably touchy, and some of the recurrent Soviet–Yugoslav flare-ups seem to have been over quite minor points. Nor did Khrushchev have a free hand: Molotov's opposition continued until the final 'Anti-Party Group' showdown of 1957; and by 1958 Yugoslav–Soviet relations had got caught up in the growing Sino-Soviet rift.

The result was something of a see-saw. Relations improved in 1955–6, with Tito consulted on the management of Eastern Europe and approving the 1956 Soviet invasion of Hungary. In 1957 there was first renewed friction, then mutual visits by Defence Ministers and Yugoslav recognition of East Germany, and finally further trouble over the version of recent history presented in the Yugoslav party's draft programme. Coolness deepened in 1958, as China attacked Yugoslavia and the USSR thought it politic to join in. By 1962 the Sino-Soviet rift was past healing, so good relations were restored and Tito fêted when he demonstratively visited Moscow after the Cuban missile crisis. Relations continued warm for most of the 1960s, Tito apparently sympathising in 1964 with Khrushchev's plans for a general anti-Chinese gathering of world Communist Parties and later adopting positions on Vietnam and the Middle East that were close to Brezhnev's. In 1968, however, the Czech crisis came as a rude shock; this time Tito condemned the Soviet intervention, conferred with Ceausescu of

---

[23] These themes are (perhaps slightly over) developed in Beloff, *Tito's flawed legacy*, Chap. 5.
[24] Djilas, *Rise and Fall*, pp. 319–20.

Romania (who also seemed threatened), and mobilised his own armed forces.[25] In due course, however, things mended. 1971 saw Sino-Yugoslav rapprochement, and, perhaps to limit the spread of Chinese influence, Brezhnev again visited Belgrade. Thereafter there were occasional frictions, but no serious rifts.

By 1970, however, Yugoslavia's importance was much reduced. After 1945, Tito had aspired to be Stalin's leading ally; and the way in which the USSR first quarreled and then sought reconciliation with him had, as we shall see, an important influence on the rest of Eastern Europe. Tito had played a major role, too, in supporting the communists in the Greek civil war; his need for Western assistance led him to disengage in 1949, and accelerated their defeat. Yugoslavia's Western orientation also facilitated the settlement in 1954 of its border dispute with Italy. Although its relations with the USSR then improved, the fact that Yugoslavia stayed outside the Warsaw Pact saved Italy from the pressures borne by Norway, West Germany and Turkey as militarily front-line states.

Yugoslavia continued to play a conspicuous role on the international stage, partly as a leading member of the 'non-aligned' movement, partly as a stalking-horse in the Sino-Soviet dispute. But from the 1960s its salience diminished. The cause of 'non-alignment' became no longer remarkable, or coherent, enough to secure international prominence. Yugoslavia's position as a communist state with an independent foreign policy seemed less unusual – indeed by the end of the 1960s Romania had overshadowed it. Also the USSR came, in its European policy, increasingly to seek the consolidation, recognition, and legitimation of existing alignments. It was, admittedly, still tempted to dabble: there was talk of links with Croatian separatists and of a 'Revolutionary Communist Party of Yugoslavia in Exile' in 1970, and in 1974 some Montenegrins founded a secret pro-Soviet party with encouragement from Kiev.[26] But serious action along these lines would have been fatal to detente. The usual view, from both East and West, was probably of support for Tito and fear of the consequences should he – or more probably his successors – fail to keep his heterogeneous country together. For a struggle, whether over the succession or between the various national groups, could have led to appeals for external assistance and so drawn in rival outside Powers.

---

[25] Clissold, *Yugoslavia and the Soviet Union*, pp. 77–82.
[26] ibid. pp. 86, 93, 111, 112.

'Tito-ism' and East European purges

In the 1940s many East Europeans were attracted to the idea of building states that, though both 'socialist' and aligned with the USSR, did not slavishly follow its example or obey its orders. As Leonhard makes clear, several East German and Czech communists privately sympathised with Yugoslavia. At a higher level, the Polish party secretary Gomulka had, in 1947, opposed agricultural collectivisation and appeared unenthusiastic about the foundation of Cominform. In 1948 he declared that Polish communism had suffered politically between the wars as a result of its ambivalent attitude towards Poland's national independence; he may even have sought to negotiate with Tito a face-saving exit from his confrontation with Stalin. Worse still, the Bulgarian leader Dimitrov had, while passing through Belgrade, secretly urged the Yugoslavs to 'hold firm'. Stalin did not propose to risk the further spread of 'Tito-ism', and laid down that 'the attitude towards the Soviet Union is now the test of devotion to the cause of proletarian internationalism'.[27] He insisted on purges, had his police chief for Eastern Europe (General Belkin) help arrange them, and contributed Soviet interrogators. Implementation, however, differed from country to country. In Albania Hoxha moved rapidly after the Cominform denunciation of Tito to break off economic relations (with Soviet compensation) and expel Yugoslav advisers. His pro-Yugoslav rival Xoxe was arrested in October 1948 and executed next June. Hoxha probably saw Tito's defection as a golden opportunity and required no prompting to take it. In Bulgaria Dimitrov denounced the Yugoslavs, but in fairly moderate terms. He may have been protected by the reputation he had established before the war in Comintern; but he conveniently died when visiting the USSR in July 1949. Party Secretary Kostov, who had clashed with the USSR in defence of Bulgaria's economic interests, was arrested in March, tried and executed in December 1949 – though at his trial he repudiated his confession of having worked for the pre-war Bulgarian police, the Trotskyists, the West, and Tito. In Hungary the tough Interior Minister, Rajk, was moved sideways in August 1948, arrested next June, and executed in the autumn. This puzzled the Yugoslavs, since they had had little to do with him;[28] but he was induced (by appeals to party loyalty

---

[27] Leonhard, *Child of the Revolution*, Chap. 9; Nicholas Bethell, *Gomulka* (paperback edn) pp. 138–43; Djilas, *Rise and Fall*, p. 199; Clissold, *Yugoslavia and the Soviet Union*, p. 55; Alan Bullock, *Ernest Bevin*, vol. 3 (1983) p. 599.

[28] Djilas, *Rise and Fall*, pp. 252–3.

and the promise of a new life in the USSR) to admit to working for Horthy–Himmler–Dulles–Tito. The Czech secretary, Slansky, then declared 'We need a Czechoslovak Rajk' and set about finding one. But the security services kept changing their minds as to quite what conspiracy they wanted to unmask, and in 1951 turned on Slansky himself. In 1952 he was tried and executed – for Zionism as well as Tito-ism. In Poland the process was milder. Gomulka was expelled from the Politburo in 1948; in 1949 several of his associates were arrested, and he was dropped from the party. There seems to have been Soviet pressure to do more, but he was not arrested until 1951, and even then treated gently. His associates were less fortunate; but they too were imprisoned not executed – presumably because the Polish leader, Bierut, was more restrained than his counterparts elsewhere in Eastern Europe.[29]

These cases were only the tip of the iceberg. Matters were perhaps worst in Hungary, where 2,000 communists were executed, 150,000 imprisoned, and 350,000 expelled from the party, and Czechoslovakia, where 136,000 were imprisoned or executed.[30] *Some* purges were unsurprising as Communist Parties that had recruited everybody they could during the period of forceful takeover were reduced to the more disciplined Stalinist model. Tito's defection, and the deepening Cold War, made matters worse. Not only was overt hankering for national routes to socialism suppressed, but the process also removed from the leadership men who had (like Gomulka or Rajk) lived in their countries before or during the war. They were replaced by exiles trained in the USSR in the 1930s and brought home in the wake of the Red Army, who might be expected to be more docile. Romania provides something of an exception. The purge of local communists began in 1948, before Tito's defection, with the imprisonment of the Justice Minister (and founder-member of the party) Patrascanu. Power was thus securely in the hands of the three 'Muscovites', Bodnaras, Luca and Ana Pauker. But in 1952 the party secretary, Georghiu-Dej, an ethnic Romanian who had spent 1933–44 in local prisons, coalesced with Bodnaras to ditch Luca and Pauker and inaugurate a second purge of the party. Tito was duly denounced and Stalin praised, but the net effect was to make the regime rather more

---

[29] Rothschild, *Return to Diversity*, p. 121, Chap. 4; Christopher Andrew and Oleg Gordievsky, *KGB* (1990) pp. 336 ff; François Fejtö, *A History of the People's Democracies* (1971) Introduction; Bethell, *Gomulka*, Chaps 10–12.
[30] Fejtö, *History of the People's Democracies*, p. 8; Rothschild, *Return to Diversity*, p. 137.

indigenous.[31] Perhaps the fact that Luca and Pauker were Jewish helped keep Stalin happy; anti-semitism certainly played a major role in the Slansky trial in Czechoslovakia later that year. But it was not really extended to either Poland or Hungary, where much of the leadership was Jewish, though it might have been had Stalin lived longer.

Changes in Soviet policy 1953–6

Stalin's death was soon followed by a disorganised workers' rising in East Germany (see pp. 206–7). With hindsight we can see that this pinpointed two major weaknesses in the structure of communist Eastern Europe. One source of the explosion was the squeeze on workers' living standards (as a result of rearmament and of Ulbricht's insistence on the construction of socialism). The other was the wavering in the regime's determination, the result partly of its leaders' rivalries and partly of a shift in Soviet policies (linked, probably, in this case to Beria's machinations). Order was restored by Soviet tanks; Ulbricht was always to see the timely application of force as the most reliable prophylactic, and to commend it accordingly to his colleagues in other countries.

In East Germany the Kremlin was now prepared to back Ulbricht. Elsewhere in Eastern Europe its approach, from 1953 to 1956, was more ambiguous. This was partly a function of Soviet politics; thus Nagy's installation in 1953 as Hungarian premier, and his dismissal in 1955, seem linked to Malenkov's fortunes. Still the USSR appears in this period to have been attempting a controlled relaxation and a distancing of itself from the day-to-day running of East European countries. At a secret 1955 Central Committee Plenum, Khrushchev and Kaganovich (in the course of attacking Molotov) criticised the proconsular intervention in Polish affairs of ambassadors Lebedev (1945–51) and Popov (1953–4).[32] Nevertheless they kept on, as Polish Defence Minister, the Soviet Marshal Rokossovsky, a Pole by origin but a man whose heart was very much in the Soviet Union. In economic matters the USSR was more forthcoming, selling almost all its

---

[31] ibid. pp. 113, 138, 231, 233.

[32] Bialer, 'Ich wählte die Warheit', pp. 28–9. To the end, however, Soviet ambassadors continued to be personally chosen by the Politburo, largely from high Party officials, and to go 'directly to the top . . . ignoring the foreign ministries' of the countries to which they were accredited (Eduard Shevardnadze, *The Future Belongs to Freedom* (1991) p. 113).

'joint' companies back to their host countries over the period 1953–6, but it continued to collect coal from Poland at negligible prices.[33] The chief tension, however, lay between the position, accepted as part of the process of wooing Tito, that 'the ways of socialist development vary in different countries', and the instinctive Soviet feeling that their allies should do as they did in domestic as well as foreign policy.

Revolutionary ferment in Poland 1953–6; Gomulka comes to power

Such interference proved destabilising in Poland (and, more seriously, in Hungary). In 1953 the Polish leadership embarked, probably quite readily, on a 'New Course' parallel to the slow thaw in the USSR. In 1954 a former leading secret policeman, Swiatlo, started telling all on Radio Free Europe. The revelations damaged Bierut's prestige and prompted an outburst of criticism within the party that left the leadership, as Ochab later put it, 'in complete isolation'; it also led to the sub-division of the security services (as in the USSR) and to Gomulka's release from prison, though not his rehabilitation. By his own confession, Khrushchev continued to needle Bierut. Bierut attended the Soviet Twentieth Party Congress, and the 'Secret Speech' came as a further shock to him. Indeed he died a fortnight later, probably from a heart attack, though Warsaw gossip said he committed suicide when Khrushchev told him to go home and dismantle Stalinism.[34] His successor, Ochab, opened the jails (pardoning 28,000 people by June), and accepted the resignation of the Politburo member responsible for security, Berman. Censorship collapsed, and a muck-raking journalism ensued. Then in late June riots broke out in Poznan. They originated in a minor pay grievance in an enormous local factory. Workers demonstrated, then, when ignored, boiled over into looting, the demolition of a radio-jamming station, and attacks on the police. The army restored order, shooting 53 people.

The Poznan riots seem to have set alarm bells ringing in Moscow, but not in Warsaw. For though initially Polish leaders condemned the riots as of foreign provocation, they changed their tone to stress the limited and

---

[33] M.C. Kaser (ed.) *The Economic History of Eastern Europe 1919–1975*, ii (Oxford, 1986) pp. 253–4; *Khrushchev Remembers*, ii, pp. 208–9.

[34] ibid. p. 197; Erwin Weit, *Eyewitness: the autobiography of Gomulka's interpreter* (1973) p. 37.

justified nature of the original grievances.[35] In July Ochab told his Central Committee that he meant to press ahead with reform, and managed to exclude from its deliberations a Soviet delegation headed by Bulganin and Zhukov. Bulganin, however, denounced those who 'on the pretext of democratization are undermining the power of the people' and declared that 'We must not permit a weakening in the international links of the socialist camp through an appeal to national determinism'. Most Polish leaders were unmoved; they readmitted Gomulka to the party and placed some of his former associates in influential jobs. Other signs of the times were the pilgrimage in late August of nearly a million Catholics to the shrine of Czestochowa and the emergence in Warsaw factories of workers' councils assisted by intellectuals and students. Outside Warsaw, however, local party secretaries often soft-pedalled reform and kept more control. The hardline minority of the leadership, known as the Natolin group, conducted a rearguard action and fed alarming reports to Moscow.

Gomulka seemed the key to the situation. The Russians tried to come to terms with him by inviting him (in vain) to holiday in the Crimea. Ochab negotiated, hoping to coopt him into some high office short of the Party Secretaryship (for which Gomulka held out). In early October Ochab decided, perhaps on Chinese advice, to give way, and called a central committee meeting for the 19th. The Natolin group planned a preemptive coup, but the plot was blown. So the top Soviet leadership, accompanied by the Pact commander and eleven generals, invited itself to Warsaw, and Soviet troops started to move on the city. In extremely tense talks it was made clear that they would be resisted (ferociously, if the city's performance during the war was anything to go by). Soviet troops were pulled back, but the talks ended without agreement. Gomulka was then elected First Secretary, and supported, over the next few days, by massive rallies throughout Poland.

Khrushchev's initial reaction was angry: 'there's only one way out – by putting an end to what is [going on] in Poland'. But on 21 October the Soviet Praesidium decided to hold off from intervention for the time being; and Khrushchev soon concluded that 'Finding a reason for an armed conflict now would be very easy, but finding a way to put an end to such a conflict later on would be very hard.' Gomulka had insisted that the Polish party alone should choose its leaders, but he also assured the Russians that he would continue their ally: 'Poland needs the friendship of the Soviet

[35] Z.A. Pelczynski, in R.F. Leslie (ed.) *The History of Poland since 1863* (Cambridge, 1983 edn) pp. 346–51; Bethell, *Gomulka*, pp. 202–4.

Union more than the Soviet Union needs the friendship of Poland.'
Eventually Khrushchev decided to accept Gomulka on these terms. Events
in Hungary were to show that the USSR could have done much worse;
and it was soon ready to buttress his position by providing credits and by
cancelling all outstanding Polish debts in compensation for past inequit-
able Soviet trade practices.[36]

Gomulka took control of the situation with a range of national and
popular measures. The Defence Minister, Marshal Rokossovsky, was
sent back to the USSR for which he had worked in October. The Catholic
primate, Cardinal Wyszcynski, was freed from detention. Collective farms
were dismantled and land restored to the peasants. Foreign travel was
permitted, though in practice limited by the absence of hard currency; the
censorship and police were so remodelled that, for a decade, Poland was
the freest country in Eastern Europe. But Gomulka was not about to scrap
the communist rule he had done so much to institute after 1944. His initial
speech as Secretary had declared that:

*At the head of the democratization process stands our Party, and our
Party alone . . . We must give a decisive rebuff to all voices . . . that aim
at weakening our friendship with the Soviet Union . . . We shall not allow
harm to come to the vital interests of the Polish state and of the building
of socialism in Poland.*

And he insisted that Soviet troops would have to stay in Poland as long as
NATO bases remained in West Germany.

Above all, Gomulka confronted the hurdle of parliamentary elections
in January 1957. In Poland (as elsewhere in Eastern Europe) the ruling
party was flanked by the relics of non-communist former parties, and
reforms of October 1956 had provided that there be more candidates than
seats; so there could have been trouble had the electorate taken the opportunity to vote systematically against communist candidates (as it was to do
in 1989). Gomulka therefore employed both the stick –

*What is at stake in the elections is not whether . . . our Party will go on
keeping power. A revolutionary party of the working class . . . will never
surrender power to reaction and the restorers of capitalism in Poland . . .*

---

[36] Mark Kramer, 'The Soviet Union and the 1956 Crisis in Hungary and Poland:
Reassessments and New Findings', *Journal of Contemporary History*, xxxiii (1998)
pp. 169–75; Fejtö, *History of the People's Democracies*, pp. 64–73; Bethell, *Gomulka*, pp. 206–12; *Khrushchev Remembers*, ii, pp. 198–205; Leslie, *History of Poland*,
pp. 321, 358.

What is at stake is whether we shall be able to go on widening the democratisation of our life or whether we shall be forced to restrict it

– and an implicit warning of possible Soviet intervention (as in Hungary) – 'Crossing off our Party's candidates means crossing out the independence of our country, crossing Poland off the map of European states'. He also turned the elections into a personal vote of confidence; he was rewarded with massive support. In due course Gomulka's rule was to deteriorate and his image to sour; for the time being he had secured great improvements in Poland's autonomy and condition, while reconciling its people to the constraints still imposed by its geopolitical situation.[37]

The Hungarian rising 1956; Soviet intervention and installation of Kadar; Repression 1956–61

Hungary provides an unhappy contrast. 'Stalinist' repression under Rakosi had been perhaps the worst in Eastern Europe. After Stalin's death the Kremlin moved rapidly to effect a change, summoning Rakosi to Moscow and dressing him down severely. Perhaps because of the fall of Beria (in this context a liberal), Rakosi managed to limit the damage to a separation of the party secretaryship (which he kept) from the premiership, which went to the reformist Imre Nagy. Nagy followed a policy of pushing light industry and consumer goods, slowing collectivisation, winding down the prison camps, and general liberalisation. Rakosi sought to check it, and the two were at loggerheads until 1955. The USSR then dropped Malenkov as Chairman of its own Council of Ministers, and, in a 'friendly intervention' that Voroshilov descibed as 'a model for our relations with all the People's Democracies',[38] replaced Nagy as Hungarian Premier. Rakosi also managed to extrude him from the party.

The experience may have radicalised Nagy, who wrote a long defence of his position including reflections of a rather Tito-ist bent.[39] It also upset much of the communist intelligentsia, whose eyes had been opened to

[37] Bethell, *Gomulka*, pp. 223–34; Z.A. Pelczynski, 'Poland 1957', in D.E. Butler (ed.) *Elections Abroad* (1959) esp. pp. 159–60, 165.

[38] Kramer, 'The Soviet Union and the 1956 Crisis', p. 175.

[39] Thus, 'the five basic principles [of Bandung, including respect for the sovereignty and equality of all countries] cannot be limited to the capitalist system or the battle between the two systems, but must extend to the relations between the countries within the democratic and socialist camps' – *On Communism. In Defence of the New Course* (1957) p. 22.

Rakosi's earlier doings by contact with prisoners released in 1954. Writers, in particular, came to constitute a liberal and nationalist pressure group through clubs like the Petöfi Circle, which in 1956 progressively broke from official party supervision. After Khrushchev's Secret Speech Rakosi tried to preempt trouble by blaming other people for Rajk's execution and announcing his rehabilitation. This failed to calm things. In June Rajk's widow asked the Petöfi Circle to campaign for the punishment of those responsible for his death, and soon there were calls for Rakosi's resignation. He countered by expelling critics from the party and closing the Circle down. In July the Kremlin at last decided that Rakosi had become a liability, so Mikoyan and Suslov visited Budapest and forced his resignation – despite his warnings that this might bring down the whole political system. But his replacement, Gerö, had been too closely associated with Rakosi to convince the Hungarians that things had really changed.[40]

By mid-1956 the Kremlin was seriously worried. In late June Khrushchev had warned that counter-revolution was possible, notably in Poland (though Ochab denied this).[41] In July Khrushchev was stressing, for Yugoslavia's benefit, that 'If the situation in Hungary gets still worse, we here have decided to use all means at our disposal to bring the crisis to an end . . . the Soviet Union could not at any price allow a "breach in the front" in Eastern Europe'. But he bent his chief efforts to securing Yugoslav endorsement of Gerö (Tito's antipathy having been a factor in undermining Rakosi's position).[42] Pressures continued to mount within Hungary: in September a writers' conference demanded 'complete freedom for literature'; and the Petöfi Circle resumed meeting and sparked off imitators in other towns. The regime did little to prevent this, and on 6 October accorded Rajk a state funeral, which drew a huge procession, headed by Nagy. To the Yugoslav ambassador in Moscow it seemed that 'The initiative is slipping out of the hands of the authorities and into the hands of the people'.[43] But Gerö spent 14–23 October on a visit to

---

[40] Fejtö, *History of the People's Democracies*, pp. 23–6, 53–4, 61, 74–5; Rothschild, *Return to Diversity*, pp. 154–7.

[41] Z.A.B. Zeman, *The Making and Breaking of Communist Europe* (Oxford, 1991) p. 273.

[42] Tito was particularly set against Chervenkov (who resigned the Bulgarian party secretaryship in April 1956) and Rakosi; but though this may have influenced the Kremlin against them, they were not simply sacrificed to secure Tito's goodwill since both survived the 1955 reconciliation with Tito for some considerable time.

[43] Micunovic, *Moscow Diary*, pp. 87–8, 121.

Yugoslavia; by the time he returned things were out of control. Stimulated, no doubt, by Gomulka's advent to power in Poland, the Petöfi Circle called for Nagy's promotion and for extensive reform (albeit within the system). Students went much further, demanding multi-party elections and the withdrawal of Soviet troops, and arranging a major demonstration for 23 October. This was first banned, then authorised. It swelled into a nationalist movement (destroying the Stalin monument, displaying a Hungarian flag with the communist insignia removed, and occupying the radio building) that proved beyond the capacity of the police to disperse. That evening Gerö responded with the dual tactic of making Nagy Prime Minister and of appealing to Soviet troops to restore order.

Khrushchev authorised a move into Budapest. But since the Hungarian army would not help and left Soviet tanks unprotected, this proved a complete failure, serving only to touch off a general strike in Budapest. Mikoyan and Suslov flew in, accepted Nagy's view that military intervention had been a mistake, and dismissed Gerö. He was replaced as Party Secretary by Kadar, who had been imprisoned during the Rakosi purge and stood to attract sympathy accordingly. Nagy, however, was generally seen as the overall leader. Unlike Gomulka, he failed to control the situation. The Budapest strike spread, provincial towns were taken over by workers' councils, and there were attacks on the secret police, which disintegrated. Nagy responded with successive concessions, endorsing the national uprising, announcing a return to the 1945 pattern of multi-party coalition government, and promising free elections. He also secured a ceasefire, and sought the withdrawal of Soviet troops, which Mikoyan and Suslov apparently promised on 30 October.

By now it looked as if, failing external intervention, communism was doomed in Hungary. Other countries were worried, Czechoslovakia and Romania warning of the possible effect on their own Hungarian minorities, while Tito and Gomulka remonstrated with Nagy over the restoration of multi-party government. Ulbricht had long regarded the entire policy as crazy – he had told a leading Hungarian, 'Just keep on going the way you are. First you depose Rakosi, then you institute reforms, and the end result is collapse.'[44] The USSR had, as we have seen, come close to using force in

[44] Fejtö, *History of the People's Democracies*, pp. 76–9; Janos Radvanyi, *Hungary and the Superpowers: the 1956 Revolution and Realpolitik* (Stanford, CA, 1972) pp. 6–13; Zeman, *Making and Breaking*, p. 276; Carola Stern, *Ulbricht* (1965) p. 160.

Poland, and had warned that it would do so if necessary in Hungary.[45] On 23 October only Mikoyan opposed the idea in the Praesidium, and hardliners continued to criticise his activities in Budapest. Even so, on 30 October the Praesidium felt it would be best to work through the Hungarian government (as was attempted more successfully in Poland), and hoped that the declaration they then issued on relations 'between the USSR and Other Socialist Countries' (above, p. 229) would succeed in 'extracting us from an onerous position' and 'putting an end to the bloodshed'.

It did not; reports came in of the capture of party headquarters and the lynching of secret policemen. Khrushchev regretted the 30 October decision almost at once. Next day he recalled the Praesidium. It decided overwhelmingly in favour of intervention; and the Chinese, who had earlier advised against this, now withdrew their objections in the face of the probable collapse of communism in Hungary. Marshal Konev was ordered to make preparations, while Soviet leaders proceeded to brief their East European allies, including Gomulka and Tito.

Meanwhile the Soviet troops pulling out of Budapest regrouped around the airport, and others began moving into Hungary from Romania. Nagy warned the Soviet ambassador that, if these movements did not stop, Hungary would pull out of the Warsaw Pact. On 1 November he announced that it had done so, and appealed to the UN and the Great Powers to protect Hungary's neutrality (though he privately offered to rescind this if the USSR foreswore military intervention).[46] Meanwhile the party leader, Kadar, had gone to Moscow to persuade the Praesidium that a peaceful solution might still be possible; finding it set on intervention, he reversed course on 4 November, announcing the formation of a rival government and appealing to the USSR to crush the forces of reaction. The Red Army broke into Budapest, and in a week had extinguished armed resistance throughout the country. There followed a general strike, orchestrated by the Budapest Central Workers' Council. Initially Kadar was prepared to negotiate. But in early December, under Soviet pressure, he restored the old secret police, and in February sealed the borders and ended the exodus

[45] Mikoyan and Suslov had accompanied their dismissal of Rakosi with the message that, should unexpected events follow, the USSR would not hesitate to come to the Party's aid (Csaba Bekes, *The 1956 Hungarian Revolution and World Politics* (CWIHP Working Paper 16, 1996, p. 5).
[46] ibid. pp. 10–11; Vojtech Mastny and Malcolm Byrne (eds) *A Cardboard Castle? An Inside History of the Warsaw Pact, 1955–1991* (Budapest, 2005) pp. 8, 83.

of refugees. This was accompanied by 100,000 arrests, 26,000 trials, and 300 executions (including that of Nagy in 1958). By 1960 Kadar felt secure enough to begin amnesties, close the internment camps, and in 1961 to announce that only active opponents would now be repressed: 'Those who are not against us are with us'.[47]

Sino–Soviet relations to 1957

The year 1956 is the first in which we are aware of the exertion of Chinese influence in Eastern Europe. It was soon to become more visible, with Zhou En-lai touring Hungary and Poland in January 1957 and Mao himself attending the Moscow conference of Communist Parties in November. Admittedly the Chinese were, at least overtly, strongly supportive of the CPSU, stressing its position as 'head' and 'leader' of the socialist camp. But the Chinese Party's stature was evident in the care taken to settle with it the terms of the declaration of ruling Communist Parties, which was then presented as a joint Soviet–Chinese draft.[48] Over the next three years the two parties' 'monolithic unity' collapsed, with important repercussions for both the socialist and the wider world.

Many hold that, to understand this breach, we need to go back to the origins of the Chinese party. For (unlike those of their European counterparts) these were strongly tinged with nationalism; they also proved Soviet advice could be disastrous. Lenin had proclaimed his readiness to give up Russia's special rights in China, and some Chinese intellectuals were attracted to communism by this marked departure from standard Western behaviour. Others were disillusioned by the 1919 Paris Peace Conference's refusal to return to China the former German concession in Shandong. This sparked major student protests, and drew people towards direct action to rebuild China independently of Western liberalism. The Chinese Communist Party [CCP] was founded in 1921 and soon steered by Comintern agents into alliance with the nationalist Kuomintang [KMT], which then looked towards Russia. By 1926 much of the KMT was worried by the extent of communist penetration and began to clamp down. Stalin

---

[47] Csaba Bekes, 'New Findings on the 1956 Hungarian Revolution', *Cold War International History Project Bulletin*, 2 (1992) pp. 2–3, and *The 1956 Hungarian Revolution*, esp. pp. 9–14; F.A. Vali, *Rift and Revolt in Hungary* (Cambridge, Mass., 1961) pp. 438–41; Paul Ignotus, *Hungary* (1972) pp. 254, 263–4.

[48] John Gittings, *Survey of the Sino-Soviet Dispute* (1968) pp. 70, 73–8; Micunovic, *Moscow Diary*, pp. 319 ff.

encouraged the communists to stay within the KMT the better to manipulate it – it was 'to be utilized to the end, squeezed out like a lemon, and then thrown away'. Two could play at this game; and in 1927 the communists were hopelessly handicapped by Stalin's mistaken orders – first to allow Chiang Kai-shek's army into Shanghai, after which it promptly turned on them, then to stage takeovers and risings in central China, which were duly suppressed, and finally to establish a 'Canton commune', which lasted three days. Meanwhile the attempts of Mao Zedong and Gao Gang to establish rural resistance movements of a more traditional Chinese kind were cold-shouldered since 'a purely peasant uprising without the leadership and help of the working class cannot achieve conclusive victories'. Successive disasters drove the party leadership to Mao's territory, but did not bring it to accept his tactics. Eventually Mao was, with Comintern assistance, first down-graded and then placed under house arrest in 1934. That year also brought crushing defeats, partly as a result of the orthodox communists' dislike of guerrilla warfare, and the Red Armies were forced into the devastating flight of the Long March. Mao then turned on their directors for military ineptitude, and managed to resume control. What remained of the communists found refuge in Yenan; and KMT pressure was relaxed in response to the need for all Chinese to unite against mounting Japanese aggression. Mao used his time well, emerging from the 1937–45 war far stronger than he had been at its start. Nevertheless Stalin discouraged him from attacking the KMT; in February 1948 he confessed to the Yugoslavs that he had urged the CCP to reach:

a modus vivendi with Chiang Kai-shek. They agreed with us in word, but in deed they did it their own way when they got home: they mustered their forces and struck. It has been shown that they were right and we were not.[49]

Of course Stalin may simply have been mistaken – until well into 1947 most people thought the KMT the stronger force. But the suspicion has been voiced that Stalin did not want the communists to succeed, whether because he feared that a communist China could become a rival to the USSR or simply because he felt that Moscow would be better served by a KMT regime kept weak and pliable by pressure from a sizeable communist minority. Certainly the USSR had been actively pushing its interests in the Chinese borderlands. For despite having in 1924 recognised Outer

---

[49] Djilas, *Conversations with Stalin*, p. 141. For a fuller discussion of the Chinese civil war, see *The Post-Imperial Age*, Chap. 5 and above pp. 157–60.

Mongolia as an integral part of China, Stalin had developed it into a 'sovereign' but satellite state. From 1934 he had also intervened on occasion to distance Sinkiang from the rest of China. In 1945, as his price for entering the war against Japan, Stalin had stipulated for the recovery of the Port Arthur naval base lost to Japan in 1905, and of control over the railway through Manchuria; and he extracted from the KMT a treaty confirming both this and the independence of Outer Mongolia. If the CCP came to power in China all might be reopened. Indeed when proclaiming the People's Republic in 1949, Mao was to declare that 'Ours will no longer be a nation subject to insult and humiliation. We have stood up.'[50]

Whatever Stalin's motivation, Soviet conduct during the Chinese civil war was distinctly ambiguous. In Manchuria the communists were allowed to capture a plentiful supply of Japanese weapons; one of their armies was reformed and equipped after being driven out into North Korea; North Korean 'volunteer' units were allowed to join in Manchurian fighting; and Soviet logistic and engineering support contributed substantially to the victories of 1948. But there were rumours that Stalin sought to mediate between the CCP and KMT in both December 1947 and July 1948; and it was later to be claimed that even in 1949 'there were some well-meaning friends . . . who said that we should be content with separate regimes in North and South China and should not provoke the intervention of . . . American imperialism'. Meanwhile Moscow was still concluding agreements with the KMT government to extend its mining concessions in Sinkiang.[51]

Once China and the USSR had quarrelled all this was to be recalled in anger. At the time it had little impact on Mao's decision to side with Russia in the Cold War. He had, admittedly, been saying in 1945 that America was 'the only country fully able to participate' in China's economic recovery, and seeking an invitation to Washington. But even if this was sincere, he had since changed his mind, and by 1948–9 feared US military intervention to salvage the KMT or (on the analogy of imperialist intervention during the Russian civil war) to upset his new regime. A recent Chinese judgement is that it was this perception of 'the possibility of military intervention from imperialist countries that decided the necessity of China allying itself with socialist countries'.[52] Already in 1948 Mao was

[50] D. Wilson, Mao. The People's Emperor (1979) p. 259.
[51] Gittings, Survey, pp. 13–14.
[52] Quoted by Chen, Jiang, The Sino-Soviet Alliance and China's Entry into the Korean War (CWIHP Working Paper 1, June 1992 p. 3).

anxious to visit Moscow. And though Stalin initially put him off, 1949 saw successful mutual visits by senior Soviet and Chinese politicians – in preparation for one of which, and to show that he was not Titoist, Mao praised the USSR as the undisputed leader of international progressive forces and insisted that 'all Chinese without exception must lean either to the side of imperialism or the side of socialism. Sitting on the fence will not do, nor is there a third road'.

Eventually the stage was set for Mao to visit Moscow in December 1949 to clear up all outstanding questions and, if possible, secure a defence treaty. He was warmly received. But subsequent negotiations were not easy, partly because of the two sides' differing negotiating tactics and partly because Stalin was upset by a report he received on the currency of anti-Soviet attitudes in the Chinese Party. Eventually China had to reaffirm Mongolia's independence and accept 'joint stock' companies on the usual Soviet model for the exploitation of Sinkiang. The USSR was to give up the rights it had acquired in 1945 in Manchuria, though not immediately, and to lend China the trivial sum of $300 million. The two countries also concluded a trade, and far more importantly a defence, treaty: Soviet fighters were sent to China to provide cover against the KMT air force; and the impression was certainly given that the USSR would protect China against US attack.[53] (For the half-decade after the outbreak of the Korean War such a contingency did not appear unlikely, and China had every reason to value this Soviet pledge.)

Mao was to say that Stalin did not really begin to trust him until after China's intervention in the Korean War. But he himself cannot have been pleased by Stalin's caution in providing air cover for this (above, pp. 180, 181n), and Khrushchev was to contend that 'tenseness in relations continued right up to the time of Stalin's death'. Indeed the Soviet ambassador sent back reports of anti-Russian attitudes in the Chinese leadership, derived from the Manchurian boss Gao Gang. Stalin's response was to turn these over to Mao; and they may have been a factor in a political struggle that culminated in Gao Gang's defeat and suicide in 1954. Later that year Khrushchev visited Beijing 'to remove causes of tension', with mixed results. The 'joint stock' companies were wound up, and the USSR arranged to give up its naval base in Port Arthur (though it was too mean

---

[53] ibid. pp. 6–18; Gittings, *Survey*, pp. 14–17, 43–5; Immanuael Hsu, *The Rise of Modern China* (New York, 1983 edn) pp. 674–5. The USSR had already started (in October 1949) to deliver planes and help establish a Chinese air force.

to present China with the guns that had defended this). Mao also sought in vain to recover Outer Mongolia. On the surface the visit was a success. But there were a number of sources of friction (including the indigestibility of the green tea liberally pressed on the Soviet delegation). Khrushchev claims that, on his return, he told his colleagues that 'Conflict with China is inevitable'; and next year he spoke to Adenauer of China as one of his greatest problems: 'Just think of it. Red China now has more than 600 million people, with every year another twelve million. All people who can live on a handful of rice. What will become of it?'[54]

These, however, were only premonitions. Relations between the two great Communist Powers at the 1954 Geneva Conference on Indo-China had been excellent. The Chinese economy was oriented towards the Soviet model. And Mao appeared to be happy discussing Marxist philosophy with the Soviet ambassador Yudin. In retrospect the Chinese were to say that major disagreements started with Khrushchev's condemnation of Stalin without prior consultation (in the 1956 Secret Speech), while the Russians saw the Chinese policy later that year of letting 'a hundred flowers bloom, a hundred schools of thought contend' as providing the seed-bed for chauvinist anti-Soviet sentiments. Also as we have seen China was beginning to make its presence felt in Eastern Europe. Still in 1957 it was careful not to rock the boat but rather to insist on Soviet primacy within the communist movement. The USSR reciprocated, promising 'to provide China with a sample of an atomic bomb and technical data concerning its manufacture', and then concerting with it the declaration presented to the November meeting of Communist Parties in Moscow. However, the Yugoslav ambassador suspected that all was not well, and he was quite right. Mao had in private told the Russians that 'there existed no such thing as brotherly relations among all the parties because [Soviet leaders] merely paid lip service and never meant it; as a result, the relations between parties can be described as between father and son or between cats and mice'.[55]

---

[54] Gittings, *Survey*, p. 57; *Khrushchev Remembers*, i, p. 429; ii, pp. 243–50; J. Guillermaz, *The Chinese Communist Party in Power 1949–1976* (Boulder, Colorado, 1976) pp. 99–105; Konrad Adenauer, *Erinnerungen*, ii (Stuttgart, 1966) pp. 527–8. In due course the Chinese were to stress the racial implications of this exchange with Adenauer; but they themselves invoked anti-European sentiment against Russia.

[55] Mao had also deputed Deng Xiaoping to raise five controversial issues privately – 'The Emerging Disputes between Beijing and Moscow: Ten Newly Available Chinese Documents, 1956–1958', CWIHP *Bulletin* 6–7 (1995–6) pp. 155–6.

Khrushchev's 1958 and 1959 visits to Beijing; Polemics, Soviet sanctions, and 'relative reconciliation', 1960–61; Mao's 1962 decision to 'compete with [Soviet] revisionism for leadership'; Open breach in 1963

In 1958 a relatively minor naval issue touched off an explosion. Encouraged by Soviet advisers, China asked for help in building nuclear submarines. The response was a proposal for a jointly owned fleet,[56] and wireless station to communicate with it. This revived all China's memories of past humiliations and foreign extra-territorial rights; 'you made me so enraged,' Mao told the Soviet ambassador, 'that I could not sleep at all last night':

You never trust the Chinese! . . . only . . . the Russians! The Russians are first-class [people] whereas the Chinese are among the inferior . . . Therefore you came up with the joint ownership and operation proposition. Well, if [you] want joint ownership and operation . . . have them all – let us turn into joint operation our army, navy, air force, industry, agriculture, culture, education . . . With a few atom bombs, you think you are in a position to control us through asking for the right of rent and lease.[57]

Khrushchev rushed to Beijing to mitigate the damage. He managed to get the issue dropped – but not before some extremely unpleasant 'informal' conversations besides Mao's swimming pool during which Deng Xiaoping accused the Russians of 'Great Nation' and 'Great Party' chauvinism, while Mao repeated his shocking views on the acceptability of war, given the numerical supremacy of the socialist countries (and more especially China).[58]

A month later, without proper consultation, Mao started shelling KMT-held Quemoy and Matsu to demonstrate his ability to take independent

[56] This would have given the USSR safer access to the Pacific than was obtainable from a Vladivostok ringed by US allies.

[57] 'Ten Chinese Documents, 1956–1958', pp. 155, 158, 162–3n.

[58] Vladislav Zubok, ' "Look what Chaos in the Beautiful Socialist Camp!" Deng Xiaoping and the Sino-Soviet Split, 1956–1963', CWIHP *Bulletin* 10 (1998) p. 156, and 'The Mao–Khrushchev Conversations, 31 July–3 August 1958 and 2 October 1959', ibid. 12–13 (2003) pp. 244–6, 250–62; *Khrushchev Remembers*, ii, pp. 255–7, 260–1; iii, pp. 147–50.

action and to complicate Khrushchev's attempts to improve relations with the United States (see p. 246). This did not, of itself, bring on a breach; though it took some time to do so, the USSR went beyond Chinese requests and publicly declared that it could not stand idly by were the USA to attack the Chinese mainland. But the episode, and particularly Mao's decision not to press on to seize the islands, left the Kremlin puzzled. Nor did the Chinese endear themselves by refusing to send to Moscow for inspection a state-of-the-art US missile that had landed, unexploded, on their territory; as Khrushchev later put it, 'The Chinese were following a Russian saying, "Friendship is fine, but let's keep our money separately".'[59] Over time he brooded on such matters, and on the multitude of other frictions; and when, in mid-1959, the time came to send China the sample atom bomb that had been promised in 1957, he decided not to: the Soviets should not be 'docile slaves' committed to past agreements even though the Chinese violated the spirit of the alliance.[60] This will have come as a considerable blow to Mao, since, for all his descriptions of atomic weapons as 'paper tigers', he was determined to get them.

In October 1959 Khrushchev returned to Beijing to celebrate the People's Republic's tenth anniversary. He did so with a Foreign Ministry brief listing many (though not all) the sources of friction over the last decade, and in a truculent mood. For their part, the Chinese, nettled by the fact that he had gone first to the USA, staged a deliberately cool reception with no cheering crowds. Khrushchev behaved badly, privately (but in a probably bugged room) rhyming his hosts' names with Russian obscenities. In the official talks the chief bone of contention was India. The USSR was wooing it as part of a strategy (which Mao disliked) of winning over 'bourgeois' Third World leaders from their Western orientations. China was not only suppressing an Indian(and CIA)-supported Tibetan revolt, but had also had a minor collision with Indian troops over their disputed border. China appealed for Soviet endorsement, but Moscow distanced itself, calling on both sides to withdraw and reach a negotiated settlement. Beijing took this as public criticism, something quite different from

[59] Vladislav Zubok and Constantine Pleshakov, *Inside the Kremlin's Cold War. From Stalin to Khrushchev* (Cambridge, Mass., 1996) pp. 225–7; *Khrushchev Remembers*, ii, p. 270; iii, pp. 151–2.
[60] Zubok and Pleshakov, *Inside the Kremlin's Cold War*, p. 228; admittedly the Praesidium had long been disinclined to send the weapon (Mark Kramer, 'The USSR Foreign Ministry's Appraisal of Sino-Soviet Relations on the eve of the Split, September 1959', CWIHP *Bulletin* 6–7 (1995–6) p. 175).

previous private exchanges of dissenting opinions, and condemned it as 'time-serving'. When Khrushchev's talks in Beijing reached the issue they degenerated into furious and circular argument. Khrushchev believed Mao had set up Marshal Chen Yi to attack him, and saw in Chen's use of the term 'time-serving' an imputation of the major Marxist sin of 'opportunism':

If you consider us time-servers, comrade Chen Yi, then do not offer me your hand. I will not acept it.
    Chen Yi: Neither will I. I . . . am not afraid of your fury.
    N.S. Khrushchev: You should not spit at me from the height of your Marshal title. You do not have enough spit. We can not be intimidated. What a pretty situation we have: on the one side, you use the formula '[the socialist camp] headed by the Soviet Union,' on the other . . . you do not let me say a word.[61]

Neither Moscow nor Beijing were pleased; indeed on both sides most transcripts of the talks were suppressed. But Suslov briefed the Soviet Praesidium on policy disagreements, attributing them largely to Mao's megalomania, reminiscent 'of the atmosphere . . . in our country during the last years of . . . J.V. Stalin.'[62] In February 1960 Khrushchev also retailed his complaints about Mao to Warsaw Pact leaders, and China decided to hit back. On Lenin's birthday in April, it published three articles, 'Long live Leninism', attacking revisionism, albeit ostensibly of the Yugoslav variety. Khrushchev responded in June at the Bucharest conference of the Romanian party, and the dispute was in the open. Beijing still desired Sino-Soviet unity, for both ideological and strategic reasons, but, typically, Mao thought this could best be achieved by 'struggling' against Khrushchev: the Chinese and Soviet parties 'should be united. There's no question about it. The problem is how solidarity is to be reached . . . Our guideline is to insist on struggle, but within the limits of no split. To struggle is to achieve agreement, not split.'[63]

Khrushchev ratcheted up the pressure by abruptly withdrawing Soviet aid technicians (and, often, their blueprints), a considerable blow since

[61] CWIHP *Bulletin* 6–7 (1995–6) pp. 170–9; 12–13 (2001) esp. pp. 247, 265–70; Zubok and Pleshakov, *Inside the Kremlin's Cold War*, p. 230.
[62] CWIHP *Bulletin* 8–9 (1996–7) pp. 244, 248.
[63] Dong, Wang, *The Quarrelling Brothers. New Chinese Archives and a Reappraisal of the Sino-Soviet Split, 1959–62* (CWIHP Working Paper 49, February 2006) pp. 31–2, 37–9.

the Chinese economy was reeling after Mao's ill-judged 'Great Leap Forward'.[64] However, mediation, in particular by Ho Chi Minh, brought the USSR and China to agree on the desirability of a reconciliation. This was achieved at a prickly conference of 81 Communist Parties that met in Moscow in November 1960: China conceded that this should endorse the 20th CPSU Party Congress (where Khrushchev had attacked Stalin in his 'Secret Speech'), provided the USSR dropped the idea of condemning factionalism. The conference also emphasised the national liberation struggle of colonial peoples against imperialism – on which, in the abstract, both countries could agree. President Liu Shaoqi then paid a state visit to the USSR; and in early 1961 some Soviet aid, and assistance to China to build MIG-21 jets, was resumed.[65]

This 'relative reconciliation', as Mao termed it, did not survive the 1961 Soviet 22nd Party Congress, at which the Chinese party (like others) was fraternally represented. One bone of contention was Albania, which had in 1960–1 broken with the – in Hodza's view – revisionist USSR after an internal power struggle, forced the closure of the Soviet naval base there, and turned to China for economic aid. Chinese leaders saw the consequent Soviet sanctions as largely directed against themselves, an attempt to 'kill the chicken to frighten the monkeys'. But when Zhou protested, Khrushchev replied that 'We used to be in great need of your support. But . . . now we're in a much better position, and we'll walk our own way.' Zhou then flew home, after laying a wreath on Stalin's tomb 'to the memory of a great Marxist-Leninist'.[66] This was, perhaps, even more provocative than he intended, since Khrushchev was to make the public condemnation of Stalin (the 1956 speech had been meant only for Party circles) the centrepiece of the second half of the Congress, culminating in his removal of Stalin's body from Lenin's tomb.

Matters only got worse in 1962. Questions as to the Sino-Soviet border had cropped up before; but the 1962 flight to the USSR of 60,000 Chinese Moslem Kazakhs intensified China's fears of Soviet influence in its weakly held west. October 1962 then saw China's launch of a brief border war with India – and the USSR's readiness to sell the latter arms. Soviet moves towards a nuclear test ban treaty with the USA came as a further blow,

---

[64] Such withdrawals were part of the communist 'operational code': Soviet technicians had been pulled out of Yugoslavia in 1948, and China would, in its turn, do likewise when it dropped Albania.

[65] ibid. esp. pp. 46, 51, 56–7.

[66] ibid. pp. 58, 60–1; *Khrushchev Remembers*, i, p. 435; ii, pp. 266–70.

being perceived (accurately enough) as 'colluding with the enemy to sell out [China] on the issue of nuclear proliferation'.[67]

So whereas in 1960 the official line had been that, unlike Tito, Khrushchev was only 'half-revisionist' and possibly capable of reform, by late 1962 this hope had been abandoned: 'Some say "brothers are still brothers", but this brother is a bad one, a revisionist elder brother.' That did *not* mean any warming towards the USA: 'the most important thing is still to oppose imperialism headed by the United States. It is under the premise of opposing the United States that we expose revisionism.' A corollary of this was the momentous decision, in December 1962, that China should now 'compete with revisionism for leadership in the international struggle'.[68] An opportunity arose in 1963, when the USSR sought further Sino-Soviet talks. The CCP preempted these by publishing a 25-point 'Proposal for the General Line of the International Communist Movement', with the sonorous conclusion that:

If a party is not a proletarian revolutionary party but a bourgeois reformist party;

If it is not a Marxist-Leninist party but a revisionist party; . . . If it is not an internationalist party but a nationalist party; . . . such a party is incapable of leading the proletariat and the masses in revolutionary struggle, absolutely incapable of . . . fulfilling the great historical mission of the proletariat . . .

Unsurprisingly the talks got nowhere, and were suspended shortly after the publication of the CPSU's 'Open Letter' of riposte.[69]

The conduct, nature and effects of the Sino–Soviet dispute

The Sino–Soviet rift, previously still disguised as attacks on the Yugoslav or Albanian parties, was now explicit. The dispute was to prove impervious to political changes within the two countries. When it began, Mao's domestic position had been damaged by the Great Leap Forward and more pragmatic forces were in the ascendant. In 1962 he began to reassert himself, and in late 1965 launched what was to become the 'Cultural

[67] Dong, *Quarrelling Brothers*, pp. 62–5.

[68] ibid. pp. 43, 65, 67, 70.

[69] RIIA, *Documents on International Affairs 1963*, pp. 231 ff (Chinese letter, 14 June 1963), 250 ff (Soviet reply, 16 July).

Revolution' – to prevent Liu Shaoqi and other pragmatists from taking China away from socialism down the 'revisionist' trail supposedly blazed by Khrushchev. Unsurprisingly the feud with the Soviet Union was continued, the road to the Soviet embassy being renamed 'Anti-revisionist Lane'. However, 1969, when internal tumult in China was subsiding, brought not reconciliation with the USSR but the beginnings of the opening to the USA (see pp. 338–41). This opening was personally blessed by Mao, but chiefly conducted by Zhou Enlai, who became heir-apparent after the 1971 defeat and death of Lin Biao. Mao never tolerated his prospective heirs for long, and from 1974 Zhou and his protégé Deng Xiaoping were under attack by the radical 'Gang of Four'; but this in no way damaged relations with the United States. Mao then died in 1976, and by the end of the 1970s Deng had achieved pre-eminence (using criticism of Mao as a political weapon, much as Khrushchev had used de-Stalinisation). In 1979 he visited the USA, attacked Vietnam, and took advocacy of the containment of Soviet influence to a very high pitch. In the 1980s he gradually modified this posture; in 1989 Deng at length allowed Gorbachev a summit meeting in Beijing, healing the Sino-Soviet rift, though not breaking with the USA.

On the Soviet side, the rift began under Khrushchev. Indeed, after Khrushchev's fall, he was accused of reducing the ideological dispute to the level of a personal feud between himself and Mao. Such signals brought a Chinese delegation to Moscow in November 1964. But it had no great expectations, and returned home in a huff after Marshal Malinovski suggested that China should ditch Mao as the USSR had Khrushchev.[70] Polemics resumed in 1965, and China refused to attend the 1966 Soviet Party Congress. In response Moscow built up its troops on the Chinese border; and in the early 1970s Brezhnev angled for US support in dealing with China. For most of his rule he thus let Sino-Soviet relations go from bad to worse. But he eventually started to change his tune, calling for improvement in a major speech in 1982. Relations warmed gradually under both Andropov and Chernenko, though it may be that no leader but Gorbachev would have made all the concessions that China required as the price of reconciliation. Of course it is unlikely that the Sino-Soviet rift never figured in domestic politics: both Liu Shaoqi and Lin Biao were to be accused of looking to the Soviet Union. But in both communist giants the policy to be adopted towards the other seems to have been surprisingly

[70] Zubok, 'The Mao–Khrushchev Conversations' pp. 249–50; *Sunday Times*, 7 February 1988, p. 1; Mohamed Heikal, *Sphinx and Commissar: The Rise and Fall of Soviet Influence in the Arab World* (1978) p. 139.

uncontroversial, which suggests that their 'Cold War' commanded in its day a consensus comparable with that generated by US–Soviet rivalry.

The dispute was initially conducted in terms of ideology, sometimes indeed at quite a high theoretical level. Perhaps one should not take this too seriously. Chinese leaders may temperamentally have favoured a hard line, whether against US imperialism in the 1950s or Soviet 'social imperialism' in the 1970s. But their earlier revolutionary rhetoric did not stop them turning to the USA, clearly a status quo power. Also, though it suited them to denounce Khrushchev's doctrine of peaceful coexistence and his cultivation of non-socialist Third World leaders, they had themselves embraced peaceful coexistence at the 1955 Bandung conference, and had urged Moscow, in terms remarkably close to Khrushchev's own thinking, to arm Nasser and non-communist Arab nationalism since their victory over the colonialists 'would be in the interest of the socialist camp'.[71] Even in the 1960s the major country that China drew closest to was Ayub Khan's Pakistan; this was neither socialist nor revolutionary, but it was anti-Indian and therefore welcome (on the principle that the enemy of my enemy is my friend). Ideology, then, was as much a convenient weapon in the Sino-Soviet dispute as a deep-seated conviction.

Other issues soon arose, notably over borders. One school of thought sees border incidents as consequential on the souring of Sino-Soviet relations, and notes that similar (though far worse) Soviet–Japanese fighting had occurred in the same areas in 1937–9 (when relations between the two countries were bad) but ended when they improved. It is also true that the issues in dispute between the USSR and China on the ground were relatively minor, and no longer impeded improving relations after Gorbachev had made in 1986–7 a concession Khrushchev had offered in 1964.[72] But

---

[71] ibid. pp. 58–9; come the Sino-Soviet quarrel, China showed Cairo the text to disprove Soviet charges that it wished to confine aid to communists.

[72] Khrushchev says that, to forestall serious border skirmishes, the USSR proposed boundary talks. These were held in 1964; it was agreed they should proceed from the existing frontier line, but accepting (as China demanded) the international *thalweg* principle whereby the border runs down the middle of rivers (rather than, as Moscow had previously contended, down the Chinese shore leaving all islands to the USSR). However, talks broke down over Khabarovsk, where this would have brought China 'literally up to the walls', impacting on Soviet communications and, it is believed, nuclear installations. They resumed only in 1987, following Gorbachev's conciliatory 1986 speech. In all 35,000 square kilometres were in dispute. Most of the line was settled in principle in 1991, with a supplementary 1995 agreement on 55 more difficult kilometres in the east, actual demarcation being completed in 1997. But some knotty

for long periods border negotiations were stalled by Chinese insistence that, even if the current border were to be taken as a point of departure, Moscow should first accept that the treaties establishing it had been imperialist and 'unequal'. So no doubt they had; but for the Soviets to accept this would, as the Chinese were well aware, have had embarrassing implications for several of their other borders, and conceivably have opened the door to much wider Chinese claims. In any case the USSR did not concede territory easily – witness the four diminutive islands in dispute between it and Japan (whose claims Mao endorsed in 1964). Equally China's border claims have precipitated hostilities not only with the USSR but also (on a larger scale) with India and Vietnam. Indeed of the countries large enough to stand up to China, only Pakistan has adjusted its borders amicably – almost certainly because it sought Chinese support in its more important dispute with India over Kashmir. Perhaps border troubles were initially only a manifestation of a prior deterioration of relations, but they soon assumed a dynamic of their own. The Soviet defence build up of the later 1960s, followed by the 1969 fighting over Chen-pao island, raised Sino-Soviet friction to a new plane in which war was by no means inconceivable, and provided an added reason for China's turn towards the United States.

In the 1960s the Soviet Union was not the only superpower to have trouble with a major ally: the decade also witnessed de Gaulle's revolt against the US 'hegemony'. Of course several of the issues in contention differed between the two alliances: France had no borders with the USA; Western beliefs did not provide the same scope as Marxist-Leninism for polemics as to their correct interpretation; nor, equally, did the socialist camp possess a monetary structure capable of being contested along the lines of France's 'Gold War' with the USA. But both sides shared the problem of nuclear weapons. The USA's initial instinct had been to disregard Britain's wartime share in their development and keep them to itself. Admittedly Eisenhower changed course. But in the 1960s US doctrine was again hostile to other national deterrents. Although special factors preserved US assistance to Britain, it was – at considerable political cost – witheld from France. At first the USSR had seemed readier than the USA to

problems remained until 2004, when Presidents Putin and Hu Jintao struck a deal assigning most of the disputed islands to China but leaving Khabarovsk's 'economic outlets' in Russian hands – *Khrushchev Remembers*, ii, p. 288; *1991 Sino-Soviet Border Agreement* (Wikipedia), with map; *Eurasia Daily Monitor*, 2, no. 102 (Jamestown Foundation), 25 May 2005, article by Sergei Blagov.

share nuclear technology; but in 1959 it abruptly changed its mind, partly because China was more resistant even than France, and certainly than most NATO countries, to the idea of integrated military structures that would necessarily be dominated by the presiding superpower. China proceeded to build its own bomb, as Britain had done after 1946 and France from 1958.

Given the levity with which Mao appeared to treat nuclear war, this was worrying. President Kennedy seems always to have hoped the Soviet Union would be so concerned that it would join the USA in putting a stop to it. By 1963 the deterioration of Sino-Soviet relations was plain enough for the Americans to think it worth broaching the question during negotiations for the Test Ban Treaty. Later Chinese hints notwithstanding, this was to go too far: 'Khrushchev and Gromyko,' Harriman reported, 'have shown no interest and in fact brushed the subject off on several occasions.'[73] Khrushchev's fall ended any hope there may have been of Soviet connivance in US action against Chinese nuclear plants; but, as we have seen (pp. 339–40), there are grounds for believing that in 1969 Brezhnev was at least considering the idea of a Soviet strike with US acquiescence.

Be that as it may, the Sino-Soviet rift proved more serious than de Gaulle's dissent. This was partly because it lasted longer, partly because China loomed larger in the communist world than France in the Western alliance. Also, whereas other countries were little moved by French attacks on American hegemony, a number of Communist Parties sought to turn the Sino-Soviet split to their own advantage. We have already seen that it precipitated a break with Moscow on the part of Albania, a country that could not easily be disciplined since it did not border on Warsaw Pact territory. Khrushchev's pressure to secure a general condemnation of China prompted the Italian party to publish Togliatti's 'Testament' and thus accelerated its drift into revisionist 'eurocommunist' unorthodoxy. Romania, too, managed in 1963–4 to establish itself as a mediator between Moscow and Beijing, reassuring Moscow through its own domestic conservatism, but declaring eirenically that 'no party must label the fraternal party with which it differs anti-Marxist and anti-Leninist', and pronouncing for 'a qualitatively new system of relations' based on 'the principles of independence and national sovereignty' and of 'non-interference'.[74] Later in the 1960s this was broadened into a diplomacy

---

[73] Zubok, '"Chaos in the Socialist Camp!" Deng Xiaoping and the Sino-Soviet Rift', p. 159; see also pp. 335–6.
[74] Fejtö, *History of the People's Democracies*, pp. 109–10, 183.

that departed from the Soviet line not only over China but also over Israel, and that sought to set itself up as a bridge between East and West.

Meanwhile both the Soviet Union and China were competing for the support of Communist Parties throughout the world. This had its ridiculous side – the tiny New Zealand party did not deserve the attentions China bestowed on it. But then China was not directly very successful. In the end the only ruling party to choose the Chinese side was the Khmer Rouge (1975–9), with North Korea balancing between its two great neighbours. Cuba's advocacy of romantic insurrection inclined it towards China, but in 1968 the USSR so restricted its oil and other deliveries that by 1970 Castro had returned to the Soviet fold.[75] As the Cuban example suggests, the competition was unequal, since the USSR had so much more to give both economically and militarily; even parties like that of Mozambique that had won power through Chinese-style rural guerrilla war tended to align with the USSR. Such considerations weighed less with non-ruling parties, and here China had more success – especially with those of Asia.

As Soviet propaganda stressed, the most important effect was probably the 'splitting' of many communist movements, largely over the issue of whether a peaceful and constitutional evolution to socialism was possible (as the USSR claimed) or whether socialism could come only through violent struggle. In Latin America the outcome was 'the withdrawal of the more militant members from the pro-Moscow parties . . . a swing to the right . . . of the more orthodox Communist parties in favour of legality, and . . . [their] abandonment of the armed struggle',[76] which (given the disturbed state of the continent) may have been a factor of some importance. In Western Europe a similar stress on organisation and order distanced the orthodox parties from the surge of *Marxisant* revolutionary sympathies so evident in and after 1968. Some sought to put this to good account by turning to a liberal 'eurocommunism'; some (notably the PCF) fell between two stools. Many of the leftist groups (*groupuscules*, the French derisorily called them) saw themselves as 'Maoist', but they never followed Beijing's direction in the disciplined way in which Communist Parties had clung to the Moscow line down to the 1950s; and once China had turned to the right after Mao's death, it lost any particular claim on their allegiances.

---

[75] Tad Szulc, *Fidel. A Critical Portrait* (New York, 1986) pp. 671–5, 681–5, 689.
[76] Richard Gott, *Rural Guerrillas in Latin America* (Harmondsworth, 1973 edn) p. 44.

CHAPTER 15

Eastern Europe since 1957

In 1957 the break-up of 'international communism' lay in the future. But Khrushchev had still to find a way of managing Eastern Europe which would, without counterproductive repression, keep in power communist governments that (unlike Tito's) saw themselves as part of the 'camp' led from Moscow. 1956 seemed to have established ground rules: the USSR would allow local parties some internal autonomy, accept leaders like Gomulka whom it would not itself have chosen, and allow them to adapt the Soviet model (by, for instance, de-collectivising agriculture), provided they stayed within the Warsaw Pact and the Soviet alliance system; but if, like Hungary, they tried to go neutral, the USSR would intervene. Khrushchev recognised that keeping troops abroad was expensive and liable to irritate the local population. So he himself proposed partial withdrawal from Poland and Hungary, and in 1958 he eventually accepted Romania's desire for all Soviet troops to leave its soil. East Germany he says he regarded as a special case, where the Red Army would have to remain in force at least until the state was internationally recognised.[1] From 1958–62 he pressed hard for such recognition, using the vulnerability of West Berlin as a lever, but did not achieve it. He did, however, put an end to the outflow of the East German population, by building the Berlin wall; this enabled the regime to consolidate, and to secure general recognition a decade later.

[1] *Khrushchev Remembers*, ii, pp. 219–30.

Failure to gain economic integration through CMEA; East European trade with the USSR; Hungarian economic reforms

Khrushchev also sought, but did not secure, economic integration. For in copying Stalinist Russia, the East European countries had created their own centrally planned systems, all oriented towards industrial self-sufficiency. In 1961, partly to counter the EEC, the USSR moved to revivify the moribund 'Council for Mutual Economic Assistance' (CMEA or 'Comecon'). It proposed 'Fundamental Principles of Socialist Division of Labour', aimed at coordinating individual countries' plans so as to permit some specialisation and cooperation in economic production. East Germany and Czechoslovakia approved, since their developed industries stood to benefit. Romania did not; it felt it was being invited to give up industry and concentrate on agriculture. Nor did it relish the suggestion that it sell its oil within Eastern Europe rather than for hard currency on the world market. So, with some Polish and Bulgarian support, it took its stand on national sovereignty, and sniped at CMEA for the rest of Khrushchev's time in office.[2] It made its point. For in 1963 CMEA agreed to shelve plans for supranational integration and to concentrate instead on agreed, and generally bilateral, deals.[3] These were not wholly ineffective; Hungary, for instance, came to forego car manufacture and concentrate on buses, while Bulgaria specialised in forklift trucks. But CMEA as a whole never moved much beyond the facilitation of interstate barter. This was partly because (despite some Hungarian pressure) it never established a currency genuinely transferable between its members. The integration of centrally planned systems must always be harder than that of market economies, since it depends more on high-profile supranational intervention, and less can be left to the piecemeal operation of the 'invisible hand'.

Eastern Europe was, therefore, not as economically integrated as the EEC. But it was oriented towards the Soviet Union, which offered a large and undemanding market for manufactured goods and which became the

[2] 'The idea of a single planning body for all Comecon countries has the most serious . . . implications. The sovereignty of the Socialist State requires that it should hold in its hand all the levers for managing economic and social life.'

[3] *Keesing's*, 18896–7, 19911, 20365; R. Medvedev, *Khrushchev* (Oxford, 1982) p. 242; François Fejtö, *A History of the People's Democracies* (1971) pp. 107–9; M.C. Kaser (ed.) *The Economic History of Eastern Europe 1919–1975*, ii (Oxford, 1986) pp. 236–43.

major supplier of oil and gas. Initially the USSR still used its political power to drive hard bargains (which led to the 1965 suicide of the chairman of the East German planning commission); in 1968 Czechoslovakia was unable to transmute its favourable balance on Soviet trade into hard currency with which to buy from the West.[4] After the 1973 oil price rise Eastern Europe derived real benefits from Soviet supplies at below world market rates. But they were not sufficient to compensate in the public mind for the overall costs of an economic system that was manifestly falling behind Western Europe, and that was widely perceived to be doing so precisely because it was communist.

With hindsight, it is clear that economic failure undermined East European systems that had anyway never put down much in the way of roots. At the time it was hoped problems could be overcome by 'economic reforms' that would strengthen rather than endanger these systems; the 1960s saw a rash of such reforms. They seemed most successful in Hungary, whose experiments (Shevardnadze says)[5] some Russians saw as a model for their own economy, but others 'derailed'. By the 1970s Hungary had permitted a measure of individual economic enterprise, and introduced into the still heavily preponderant state sector some proxy for market forces. The result was the plentiful availability of goods and the emergence of a degree of affluence. Eventually this prosperity proved delusive: it was based on foreign borrowing, and on widespread 'moonlighting' by individual workers to supplement the exiguous earnings from their official, but undemanding, employments. For the time being, though, it was appreciated; and Kadar's policy of 'he who is not against us is with us' provided considerable scope for the unpolitical, while never endangering ultimate Party control. So he achieved some popularity, it being felt he had gained as much for Hungary as was feasible without again provoking Soviet intervention.

The Prague Spring

Czechoslovakia was less fortunate. Its leaders had maintained a hard line throughout the 1950s, but then ran into trouble on several fronts. The economy went into deep recession: there were food shortages, and in 1962

---

[4] *Keesing's* 21156; Galia Golan, *The Czechoslovak Reform Movement* (Cambridge, 1971) pp. 281–2.

[5] Kaser, *Economic History of Eastern Europe*, pp. 160 ff; Eduard Shevardnadze, *The Future Belongs to Freedom* (1991) p. 114.

the current five-year plan had to be scrapped. This gave scope to a group of economic reformers who advocated moving towards supply and demand; one of their leaders, Ota Sik, who became a Deputy Premier in 1968, was later to say that, though he had naturally kept quiet about it, he had also believed political pluralism would have to accompany economic. In 1961 Khrushchev had renewed his support for de-Stalinisation, and pressed for a re-examination of the 1949–54 Czech trials. This encouraged jurists to seek the establishment of a genuine rule of law to preclude any further repetitions. Rehabilitations also entailed the dropping of the charge that the Slovak, Slansky, had been guilty of 'bourgeois nationalism'. Slovaks used this to press for more autonomy. For some time the Party Secretary, Novotny, managed to live with, even to derive advantage from, this ferment. But in 1967 he seems to have decided that it had gone far enough. An economic reform was introduced, but its practical implementation blocked. Writers were warned to respect the party's doctrinal primacy; as elsewhere in Eastern Europe, the 1967 Middle Eastern war prompted an anti-Zionist campaign that spilt over into anti-semitism. This was denounced at a writers' congress, and Novotny moved towards repression. The Slovak Party Secretary, Dubcek, then took up the intellectuals' cause, especially after Novotny had unwisely attacked him as a 'bourgeois nationalist'. Novotny had fused together all the currents of discontent, and his position looked shaky. In December 1967 Brezhnev visited Prague, intending to 'save' Novotny, but decided this was impossible and went home, telling the Czechs to 'Do as you wish'. There followed a central committee meeting that recessed without agreement over Christmas. As a last throw, Novotny sought a coup d'état, but it failed. When the central committee resumed in January, it replaced Novotny by Dubcek as Party Secretary.[6]

In April the party propounded a new 'Action Programme'. This envisaged the party's retaining its 'Leading Role ... A Guarantee of Socialist Progress', but repudiated the past 'monopolistic concentration of power in the hands of party organs'; instead it would work in partnership with the (previously puppet) parties of the National Front, permit the emergence of voluntary organisations, devolve economic powers to Parliament and to

[6] Fejtö, *History of the People's Democracies*, pp. 115–18; Joseph Rothschild, *Return to Diversity: A Political History of East Central Europe since World War II* (New York, 1989) pp. 167–9; Zdenek Mlynar, *Night Frost in Prague: the end of humane socialism* (1980) pp. 68–71; Golan, *The Czechoslovak Reform Movement, passim*; Jaromir Navratil (ed.) *The Prague Spring 1968* (Budapest, 1998) pp. 24–5.

the enterprises themselves, and guarantee freedom of speech. Dubcek himself remained Marxist even after the 1989 revolution, when this was no longer politically wise; in 1968 he would not permit the re-establishment of the Social Democrats, maintaining that in Czechoslovakia there was no route to socialism other than 'the marxist programme of socialist development which our party upholds. Nor is there any other force, loyal to the revolutionary traditions, which would be a guarantee of the socialist process of democratisation.'[7] Most reformers did in fact come from within the Party, and opinion polls suggested that this commanded 70 per cent support. But the reform movement fed on itself, particularly after censorship was tacitly dropped in March. Mlynar (in 1968 himself a leading politician) describes the Prague Spring as 'snowballing' into a 'nationwide democratic and humanitarian movement'; and he believes Dubcek 'did not perceive the . . . potential political consequences of the radical democratic criticisms he had more or less set free in February and March', or 'that a mechanism had been introduced capable of forcing change on the system . . . a kind of public lobby backed by a free press and the free expression of opinions outside the power structure'.[8]

To most reformers, the chief need was to lock in their gains by working within the party to transform its *apparat*. It would, the radical 'Two Thousand Words' manifesto declared in June, be 'foolish' to attempt 'a democratic revival . . . without the communists'; the party

is preparing for its congress, where it will elect its new Central Committee. Let us demand that it be a better committee than the present one. Today the communist party says it is going to rest its position of leadership on the confidence of the public, and not on force. Let us believe them, but only as long as we can believe in the people they are now sending as delegates to the party's district and regional conferences.[9]

This 'Extraordinary Party Congress' had been decided on in May; delegates were chosen in June and July, and four-fifths were reformers. They were to meet in September, and approve new statutes that would have shattered the traditional model whereby Communist Parties were controlled from the top downwards: elections should be by secret ballot,

---

[7] Navratil, *Prague Spring*, pp. 92–5; R.J. Crampton, *Eastern Europe in the Twentieth Century* (1994) p. 333.

[8] Mlynar, *Night Frost*, pp. 101–3, 117, 169.

[9] Navratil, *Prague Spring*, pp. 179–80.

and dissent (though not the operation of minority factions) was to be permitted.[10]

Hardliners, both at home and abroad, were appalled. Poland and the DDR had expressed concerns to the Soviet leaders as early as January; criticisms were conveyed privately to the Czechs in February, and in March Czech leaders were summoned to Dresden for what proved to be a Warsaw Pact discussion of their domestic developments. Gomulka talked flatly of the parallels with Hungary in 1956, Ulbricht of rampant Western influence. Soviet leaders were calmer; but Kosygin stressed that the Czech media were 'in the hands of the enemy' and that the leadership must 'find a resolution', while Brezhnev felt that though 'the situation can be changed . . . the counter-revolution can still be dealt a blow . . . one needs the desire, the willpower and also the courage . . . to implement the necessary actions.' The Soviet Politburo hoped 'that you will be able, under the leadership of Dubcek, to . . . stop these very dangerous developments. We are ready to give you moral, political and democratic support.' Brezhnev's aide, Aleksandrov-Agentov, recalls that that spring 'Ulbricht and Gomulka, who were worried about the security of their own countries if Czechoslovakia broke away from the alliance', called urgently for military intervention. In the Kremlin there were both hawks and doves, with Brezhnev long undecided. He feared it would lead to bloodshed, but equally said that 'If we lose Czechoslovakia, I will step down from the post of general secretary.'[11]

By May 1968 the USSR had drawn up an invasion plan.[12] But it would have much preferred Dubcek himself to take action, and constantly pressed him to align with 'healthy forces' in the party and purge the counter-revolutionaries. The pressure was reinforced by massive military movements around Czechoslovakia's borders and, in June, by Warsaw Pact manoeuvres on Czech soil (after which the Soviet troops were ominously slow to withdraw). This pressure in fact stimulated Czech national, reformist, and anti-Soviet sentiment, making more difficult any clampdown Dubcek may have contemplated. As to whether he did intend one, there is a conflict of evidence. Brezhnev certainly felt it had been promised: thus he claimed (on 17 July) that, when telephoned about the 'Two

[10] Crampton, *Eastern Europe*, p. 322; Fejtö, *History of the People's Democracies*, pp. 150, 154; Robert Rhodes James (ed.) *The Czechoslovak Crisis 1968* (1969) p. 20; Golan, *The Czechoslovak Reform Movement*, pp. 300–1, 303, 305, 308.
[11] Navratil, *Prague Spring*, pp. 64–72, 102.
[12] Crampton, *Eastern Europe*, p. 334.

Thousand Words', Dubcek promised that 'very strong countermeasures would be adopted. Unfortunately this did not happen'; and on 13 August he told Dubcek directly 'that by dragging your feet in the fulfillment of these obligations, you're committing outright deceit and are blatantly sabotaging the decisions we jointly reached.' Dubcek later denied that he had made any such promises, and said that in their discussions the Soviets heard only what they wanted to. This may often have been so. But Dubcek did claim to have 'gone over to the offensive' after the subsidence of the March–April 'wave of euphoria'; 'We are intent on eliminating the right-wingers in the eyes of the public.'[13] By mid-1968 Dubcek was, very understandably, wilting under the enormous pressure: Kadar recollected Dubcek and Cernik in July as 'crying and constantly repeating that they could now see that all doors were closed to them'; and when bullied by Brezhnev on the telephone in August, Dubcek three times suggested that he was 'running out of steam' and thinking of quitting. In this context he may well have bought time by promising to dismiss leading liberals and rein back the media, but then have continuously postponed action.[14]

Matters appeared to improve with talks in late July between Czech and Soviet leaders at Cierna nad Tisou on the border and a meeting of East European Communist Parties at Bratislava. However, during the latter, Vasil Bilak surreptitiously passed the Soviets a letter asking for their intervention, signed by five senior Czech party officials. These later told the Soviet ambassador that, as troops moved in, they would secure a Praesidium vote of no confidence in Dubcek, take over the government, and issue a formal appeal for Soviet assistance. This would have to happen soon, since the Czechoslovak party congress would vote the hardliners out when it met in September. So, after a three-day session the Soviet Politburo decided, on 17 August, 'that Dubcek is not going to fulfill any of his commitments, that he has gone over completely to the . . . Right', and that the USSR should 'provide military assistance to the healthy forces'.[15]

---

[13] To the French communist Waldeck Rochet, 19 July 1968 (Navratil, *Prague Spring*, p. 262).

[14] Dubcek's handwritten notes after the Cierna nad Tisou talks support Brezhnev's insistence that he then gave specific promises, and suggest that the hardliner Vasil Bilak was told of them; Bilak's later recollections here also support Brezhnev's claims (Navratil, *Prague Spring*, pp. 254, 303, 347, 352, 353, 355, 367–9, 428).

[15] Navratil, *Prague Spring*, pp. 309, 324–5, 397–9.

Soviet, Polish, East German, and Hungarian troops moved in on the night of 20 August, but the Czech hardliners failed to muster their promised majority. Instead the Praesidium roundly condemned the invasion; sympathisers managed to broadcast its communiqué, then to convene an emergency meeting of the '14th Party Congress'. So though the invasion secured control of the country and arrested its former leaders within a day, the political situation was so confused that the anticipated hardline government could not be formed, and President Svoboda insisted on a resolution through compromise negotiations in Moscow. These extended from 23 to 26 August, and were not easy – at almost the last moment Dubcek burst out that the invasion 'jeopardizes our friendship and creates objective conditions for the growth of anti-Soviet sentiment'. But his colleagues' advice, and fear of the openly threatened consequences for Czechoslovakia should he not concurr, led him finally to sign a secret protocol repudiating the '14th Party Congress' and undertaking to dismiss 'those persons whose activities were not in keeping with . . . ensuring the leading role of the working class and the communist party'. He was, therefore, able to return to Prague as Party Secretary; and he still hoped 'to salvage at least part of the process of renewal and democratisation'.[16] But the USSR kept urging the removal of reformers, and the Slovak leader, Husak, completed his shift from reformer to hardliner. The final showdown came in March 1969; Czech ice hockey victories over the USSR were celebrated by enormous anti-Soviet crowds, with *agents provocateurs* improving the occasion by smashing Aeroflot and other Russian premises. The USSR's Defence Minister, Marshal Grechko, then descended on Prague and ordered Dubcek's replacement by Husak.[17]

Husak's 'normalisation' clamp-down was far less drastic than that Kadar had imposed after 1956. But, perhaps as a result, Husak never created the feeling Kadar later generated in Hungary that conditions were again improving. What remained was stasis. The Prague Spring was rolled back. Communist control was not threatened. Most people were sullenly acquiescent. A few, mainly philosophers, writers, and former politicians, bravely protested despite persecution and exile (but not physical elimination). They included a dissident playwright, Vaclav Havel, who helped launch the human rights manifesto 'Charter [19]77', was arrested in 1978, and was repeatedly in and out of prison until May 1989.

[16] ibid. pp. 314–15, 437–42, 478, 483.
[17] ibid. pp. 441–2.

The Brezhnev Doctrine and the Helsinki Final Act (1975)

The 1968 intervention destroyed both long-standing Czech affection for Russia and the popularity the Prague Spring had brought to the Czech Communist Party. It shocked many Western communists, notably the Italians. It also alarmed the Chinese, whose fears that they too might be subjected to intervention under the 'Brezhnev Doctrine'[18] impelled them to bury their quarrel with the USA. But it had surprisingly little direct effect on East–West relations, and it seemed to establish clear ground rules for the division of Europe. During the August 1968 Moscow negotiations with Dubcek, Brezhnev had uttered a number of home truths. On the one hand, 'the Communist movement in Western Europe . . . won't amount to anything for fifty years'. On the other, the USSR's sacrifices during the Second World War had gained it security. The guarantee of that security was the post-war division of Europe, and in particular the fact that Czechoslovakia was linked to the Soviet Union 'forever'. 'For us the results of the Second World War are inviolable, and we will defend them even at the cost of risking a new war.' Nor indeed would there be any such risk, since President Johnson had confirmed that he accepted the results of Yalta and Potsdam.[19]

Over the next few years Brezhnev proceeded to consolidate this vision. After 1968 little more was heard of Gaullist hopes of the dissolution of the Soviet and US 'hegemonies' over Europe. By 1969 the West Germans had recognised that Ostpolitik could not bypass the USSR but would have to be conducted through it. Brezhnev then proved forthcoming, engineering the removal of Ulbricht as East German party secretary in 1971 so as to secure DDR acceptance of the new policies.[20] In return for confirming the status quo in West Berlin, Brezhnev secured full international legitimation and UN membership for East Germany. Building on this, and on detente

---

[18] The generic term given by the West to official Soviet explanations that when socialism was threatened, 'it becomes not only a problem of the people concerned, but a common problem and concern of all socialist countries', justifying (in extreme cases) 'military assistance to the fraternal country'. For 'The sovereignty of each socialist country cannot be opposed to the interests of the world of socialism': *Keesing's* 23027; Rhodes James, *The Czechoslovak Crisis*, p. 446.

[19] Mlynar, *Night Frost*, pp. 239–41.

[20] Martin McCauley, *Marxism-Leninism in the German Democratic Republic* (1979) pp. 174–5.

generally, he gained recognition in the 1975 Helsinki 'Final Act' of the Conference on Security and Cooperation in Europe (CSCE) that 'The participating states regard as inviolable all one another's frontiers as well as the frontiers of all states in Europe'. This, to the Soviets, meant the long-delayed acceptance by the West of the new order in Eastern Europe created at the end of the war.

The United States does seem to have seen it as unchallengeable, if unattractive. In December 1975, in what became known as the 'Sonnenfeldt Doctrine', Kissinger's aide briefed US ambassadors:

it must be our policy to strive for an evolution that makes the [present 'unnatural'] relationship between Eastern Europeans and the Soviet Union an organic one . . .

our policy must be a policy of responding to the clearly visible aspirations of Eastern Europe for a more autonomous existence within the context of a strong Soviet geopolitical influence.

This has worked in Poland. The Poles have been able to overcome their romantic political inclinations which led to their disasters in the past. They have been skilful in developing a policy that is satisfying their needs for a national identity without arousing Soviet reactions. It is a long process.

A similar process is now going on in Hungary. Janos Kadar's performance has been remarkable in finding ways which are acceptable to the Soviet Union, which develop Hungarian roots and the natural aspirations of the people . . . To a considerable degree he has been able to do this because the Soviets have four divisions in Hungary and, therefore, have not been overly concerned . . .

We seek to influence the emergence of the Soviet imperial power by making the base more natural and organic so that it will not remain founded in sheer power alone . . . there is no alternative open to us other than influencing the way Soviet power is used.[21]

It was not good domestic politics to say such things; instead the West came to focus more sharply on human rights in Eastern Europe. The Helsinki 'Final Act' had also contained a human rights 'basket' that had encouraged Soviet and East European activists. A crack-down resulted; at subsequent CSCE conferences (held to monitor implementation of the 'Final Act'), Western delegations sought to probe this in ways the USSR saw as subversive and inimical to detente. But that Eastern Europe would

[21] *Keesing's,* 27302, 27795–6.

for the foreseeable future remain both 'communist' and aligned with the USSR was scarcely doubted.[22] Few Western politicians hoped for more than its internal softening and the establishment of non-antagonistic relationships between the two halves of Europe. The chief exception was Helmut Kohl, West German Chancellor from 1982, who made it his business constantly to remind the world that the partition of Germany was cruel and unnatural, and therefore unacceptable. Even he never suggested that it could, under existing circumstances, be reversed.

Poland 1970–81

No sooner had the situation in Czechoslovakia been 'normalised' in 1968–9 than trouble arose in Poland. For in 1970 sudden price increases sparked rioting in cities like Gdansk. Order was restored by force (those killed being later regarded as the precursors of 'Solidarity'). But the episode prompted Gomulka's forced retirement, and his replacement as First Secretary by Gierek. The USSR welcomed the change, and gave the new government economic aid. All went fairly well until 1976, when Gierek introduced new price increases, then, in the face of massive demonstrations, dropped them to avoid a repetition of the 1970 bloodshed. An important development was the formation by intellectuals (many of whom had become deeply alienated by various clamp-downs in the later 1960s) of a 'Committee for the Defence of Workers' (KOR) to help those punished for their part in the demonstrations. A further dimension was added when the Archbishop of Krakow became Pope John Paul II in 1978 and made a triumphant return visit next year. Poland had always been strongly Catholic, and religious enthusiasm had further increased as an expression of popular attitudes towards the communist regime. Meanwhile the economy was kept afloat only by massive borrowing – Poland's hard currency debt went from $7.4 billion in 1975 to over $21 billion in 1980.

---

[22] Indeed the once notable Romanian breach with the USSR gradually healed. Romania had felt threatened after 1968 and responded by raising its international profile and welcoming visitors like President Nixon. In 1971 the USSR accused it of organising a Balkan bloc under Chinese and US patronage, and staged intimidatory manoeuvres. But Romania later ran into economic difficulties, partly because its distinctive pro-Israeli stance had not endeared it to Arab oil producers; accordingly it became increasingly dependent on Soviet energy exports. Its repressive regime seemed no threat to 'socialism'; and though it retained contacts with the West, Brezhnev is said to have hoped to use them to acquire Western technology. In 1976 he and Ceausescu exchanged reconciliatory visits: *Keesing's*, 24934, 25209, 26887–8, 27786, 28163–4.

July 1980 saw another attempt to increase prices. Poland was already in ferment; the increases touched off widespread strikes, increasingly orchestrated by unofficial 'workers' committees' that elbowed aside the puppet official trade unions. In mid-August the Lenin shipyard in Gdansk was occupied by its workers, who demanded not only the rolling back of price increases but also the establishment of freely elected independent unions, and managed to get these demands broadcast. A week later 150,000 people were on strike around Gdansk, panic buying had led to food shortages, and the Church was calling for restraint to avoid bloodshed. Its advice was eventually taken. Negotiations ensued; on 31 August the government concluded an agreement with the Gdansk strike leader, Lech Walesa, that provided not only for wage increases but also for the right to establish independent unions, for the revision of censorship, the broadcasting of Catholic services, and the review of sentences passed on civil rights activists over the previous decade. In September Walesa went on to found an independent trade union, Solidarity, with the support both of KOR intellectuals and of the Church. The authorities were initially reluctant to register it, but gave way after a threatened strike. A further struggle followed in 1981 over the recognition of 'Rural Solidarity'. In March this led to the beating up of Solidarity activists by police thugs at Bydgocscz; Solidarity demanded an investigation, and threatened a general strike; finally a compromise was struck that allowed Rural Solidarity to organise.[23]

That a communist regime should allow such autonomy to the workers, or such a political role to the Church, was unprecedented. But Solidarity sought to avoid trouble by incorporating (in an annex to its statutes) a recognition of the leading role of the Communist Party, thus hopefully making it impossible for the USSR to claim, under the Brezhnev Doctrine, that socialism was endangered. In practice the party's leading role could not easily be reconciled with the free operation of a massive trades union of very different outlook, and there was much friction, especially as the economy deteriorated and shortages increased. Despite restraining counsels from Walesa, Solidarity's September 1981 Congress rejected government proposals for economic reform and demanded round-table negotiation of an 'anti-crisis' agreement that would incorporate revision of the economic system and the democratisation of many public institutions. In effect Solidarity was seeking a position of co-determination with the

---

[23] *Keesing's*, 30565 ff, 30717 ff; Crampton, *Eastern Europe*, p. 372.

communist authorities. The Congress also sent a 'Message to Working-Class People in Eastern Europe', offering to help them establish their own independent unions – which Brezhnev termed a 'summons to counter-revolution'.[24]

Soviet concern over Polish developments in fact dated right back to August 1980, when a Politburo commission had been established to monitor them. Of its four members, two, Andropov, and Ustinov, had in 1979 pressed for intervention in Afghanistan; now they were more cautious, accepting Gromyko's view that 'we cannot afford to lose Poland', but concluding from Gomulka's 1970 experience that forcible repression might damage the Polish party. Gierek also distrusted force, but he stepped down in September 1980, to be succeeded as Party Secretary by Kania. Kania talked of seizing 'the counter-revolution by its throat', and for many months proved able to convince Brezhnev that, unlike Dubcek, he would in fact do so – once proper preparations had been made.[25]

East Germany saw no reason to wait. By September 1980 a Central Committee study had compared current events in Poland with those of 1968 in Czechoslovakia, concluding that 'In both their essence and their goals . . . there is a striking congruity.' Thereafter Honecker lobbied constantly for intervention, telling Brezhnev on 26 November that 'any delay in acting . . . would mean . . . the death of socialist Poland'; his views were endorsed by Husak of Czechoslovakia, Zhivkov of Bulgaria, and, in 1981, also by Fidel Castro.[26] Such intervention came very close in December 1980, when the USSR unveiled plans to move fifteen Soviet, two Czech and one East German division to the neighbourhoods of major cities to force the Polish government to take action.[27]

Warsaw Pact leaders then met in Moscow to consider the situation. But Kania put on a remarkable performance, stressing the preparations that had been under way since October for 'introducing a state of war' and arresting 'the most active supporters of the counter-revolution', but

[24] ibid. pp. 373–4; *Keesing's*, 31218–19, 31389, 32018; Mark Kramer (ed.) *Soviet Deliberations during the Polish Crisis, 1980–1* (CWIHP Special Working Paper no. 1) (April 1999) p. 24.

[25] Vojtech Mastny, *The Soviet Non-Invasion of Poland in 1980/81, and the End of the Cold War* (CWIHP Working Paper no. 33) pp. 8–9, 23.

[26] CWIHP *Bulletin* 5 (1995) pp. 121, 124, 127.

[27] 18 divisions were apparently thought too few to act alone, let alone *against* Polish army opposition; but a further 12 were held in reserve. Both the Czechs and the East Germans planned on the basis that there would be bloodshed – Mastny, *Soviet Non-Invasion of Poland*, pp. 11–13; CWIHP *Bulletin* 5, p. 120.

also warning that 'if there were an [external] intervention there would be a national uprising. Even if angels invaded Poland, they would be treated as bloodthirsty vampires and the socialist ideas would be swimming in blood.' Honecker, Husak and Zhivkov were unimpressed. But Brezhnev gave Kania the benefit of the doubt: 'OK, we will not go in, although if complications occur we would. But without you we won't go in.'[28]

In February 1981 the hawkish Polish Defence Minister, General Jaruzelski, also assumed the premiership, and promptly rehearsed the mass arrest of Solidarity leaders. The real thing was intended to come off in March, with 'very discreet . . . external support' from Warsaw Pact military manoeuvres. But Kania and Jaruzelski were so struck by the strength, and popularity, of Solidarity's response to the Bydgoszcz incident that they told the Soviets that 'As far as the introduction of troops is concerned . . . this was absolutely impossible, and so was the introduction of martial law.'[29]

Brezhnev accepted this; instead 'all necessary measures must be taken to ensure that our Polish friends act on their own', to which end, though not 'pestering them without need . . . we should keep them constantly under pressure'. Over the course of the summer, he lost confidence in Kania's, though not in Jaruzelski's, willingness to act. By August he was consulting Honecker as to whether Kania could 'master the situation'; and in October Kania was induced to yield place to Jaruzelski, who now added the Party Secretaryship to all his other offices. Even so, Jaruzelski would not strike till he was quite ready, and until the momentum behind Solidarity showed some signs of slackening. As the moment approached, he became increasingly nervous, bombarding Moscow with requests for economic aid, and for promises of military assistance if 'the Polish forces do not manage to break the resistance by Solidarity'.

In fact no assistance was needed – Jaruzelski's crack-down on 13 December achieved complete surprise and, in the short term, success. But the Soviet Politburo had proved extraordinarily reluctant to give Jaruzelski the assurances he had sought, even though he had warned that, failing 'political, economic, and military support by the USSR, then our country might be lost'.[30] One view is that it did not see Jaruzelski as the last resort, but suspected him of looking for excuses not to strike; if so, there were ideas of replacing him by a more determined, and yet harder line, figure.

[28] Mastny, *Non-Invasion*, pp. 14–15; CWIHP *Bulletin 5*, p. 127.
[29] Mastny, *Non-Invasion*, pp. 20–2.
[30] ibid. pp. 23–5, 28, 30.

In any case, Gorbachev (then already a significant Politburo figure) recollected in 1992, 'the Soviet leadership believed that under no circumstances must Poland be allowed to leave the Warsaw Pact.'[31]

However, this seems hard to square with the politburo's proceedings on 10 December 1981. Andropov then explained that 'We can't risk such a step' as the introduction of troops; 'even if Poland falls under the control of "Solidarity", that's the way it will be.' For 'if the capitalist countries pounce on the Soviet Union . . . [with] a variety of economic and political sanctions, that will be very burdensome for us. We must be concerned above all with our own country.' Andropov's views were echoed by the other members of the Politburo commission on Poland: Gromyko declared explicitly that 'There cannot be any introduction of troops into Poland'; Ustinov and Suslov cited earlier Polish warnings against so doing. Suslov also worried about undercutting past Soviet diplomacy and propaganda:

We've done a good deal of work for peace, and it is now impossible for us to change our position. World public opinion would not permit us to do so. We have carried out via the UN such momentous diplomatic actions to consolidate peace. What a great effect we have had from the visit of L.I. Brezhnev to . . . [West Germany] and from many other peaceful actions . . . This has enabled all peace-loving countries to understand that the Soviet Union . . . consistently upholds a policy of peace. That is why it is impossible for us to change the position we have adopted vis-à-vis Poland . . . Let the Polish comrades themselves determine what actions they must pursue. It would be inappropriate for us to push them toward more decisive actions.[32]

Not mentioned, but perhaps underlying some of this caution, were the repercussions of the USSR's 1979 intervention, largely at Andropov's and Ustinov's behest, in Afghanistan. Be that as it may, the reasons cited for leaving the decision to the local communist government – fear of encountering a national rising, of the impact of Western economic sanctions, and of throwing away the achievements of the USSR's foreign policy drive towards the non-communist world – all applied with greater force when similar threats to communist rule arose throughout Eastern Europe in 1989.

[31] Mark Kramer, 'Poland, 1980–81. Soviet Policy during the Polish Crisis', CWIHP *Bulletin*, 5 (1995) pp. 122–3, 126n.
[32] ibid. pp. 136–7; Gorbachev was not present at the meeting.

A general crisis of communism in Eastern Europe, 1989? The Soviet attitude

Though Jaruzelski's December 1981 repression bought communist rule in Poland a respite, eight years later it was gone; and it was collapsing, too, in most of the rest of Eastern Europe. There had always been fears that the collapse of any one communist state could bring down more, and the crises of 1953, 1956, 1968 and 1980–1 had all prompted strikes or disturbances in other countries than those chiefly involved. But in no case had communist rule collapsed. In 1989 the Polish and (more gradually) the Hungarian parties relinquished power, setting off a chain reaction.

Perhaps we need look no further. But one could see other developments converging to promote a general crisis of communism. One factor common to all Warsaw Pact members except Czechoslovakia was high hard currency debt. Servicing this led to the squeezing of living standards and corresponding discontent, in Poland and Hungary also to attempts to co-opt the opposition so as to gain popular acceptance of the necessary measures, and in East Germany (though only after Honecker's fall) to simple dependence on West German aid despite the political strings attached. It may be, too, that people had always been aware of higher living standards in the West – a Polish saying ran that only fools need a free press. But images and information were now more readily available than ever before, from Western radio and tapes, from West German, Austrian, and (along the Adriatic) Italian television, and, indeed, from the *post-glasnost* Soviet and Hungarian media.

Alongside this went a collapse in communist belief. Several retired Polish leaders from the Stalin era told their young interviewer in the 1980s that of course she could not understand their Leninist faith; one who had lost it was at pains to explain that 'communists' like himself had had 'absolute faith in the party . . . uncritical at every stage, no matter what the party . . . [was] saying', and to contrast 'one of our party members after years of party rule' with the still pristine 'communist from [El] Salvador', who 'loathes opportunism and strives with total dedication to realize his *idée fixe*.'[33] By the later 1980s the East European, and Soviet, parties had become, ideologically, broad churches, still retaining authoritarian Leninists but also people who had essentially become social democrats, plus many who were simply government-oriented politicians

---

[33] Teresa Toranskaya, *Oni. Stalin's Polish Puppets* (1987) esp. pp. 43 (Ochab), 128–9 (Staszewski).

and administrators, as ready to operate within liberal capitalism as Marxist socialism.

Finally there were the changes in the Soviet Union. These do not constitute a sufficient explanation for the passing of communism in Eastern Europe, for this occurred also in Yugoslavia and Albania which had long left the Soviet sphere. But within it, Moscow mattered. By 1987 Gorbachev had clearly embarked on *perestroika*, *glasnost*, and even some anodyne economic reform. In March 1989 he conducted partially free elections. The joke ran that to save socialism, Czech tanks would have to move on Moscow; and it was not easy to maintain that what was done in the USSR was unacceptable in Eastern Europe. All this was peculiarly upsetting in Czechoslovakia and in East Germany, which eventually came to censor Soviet publications, observing that 'If my neighbour decides to change the wall-paper, that doesn't mean that I have to do the same.'[34]

Gorbachev says that at his first meeting with Warsaw Pact leaders in 1985, he implied that the Brezhnev Doctrine was a thing of the past. But as long as this was not publicly stated, the Doctrine could still serve as a deterrent, and some even of those opposed to implementing it argued for keeping 'a certain vagueness' on the subject 'so that we do not stimulate the anti-socialist forces to try to "test" the fundamentals of socialism in a given country'. Gorbachev, however, had done his best to dispel such vagueness by making non-intervention a central theme of his December 1988 address to the United Nations; and when occasions actually arose in 1989, there was no disposition in Moscow to change course.[35] Nor indeed, did Gorbachev often use the USSR's prestige and leverage even to press Warsaw Pact leaders to copy his own reforms; 'We had,' an aide publicly explained, 'given our allies so much bad advice in the past that we now hesitate to give them good advice.'[36]

By 1988 events were starting to move quite fast in Poland and Hungary. In October Gorbachev's aide Shakhnazarov urged a general discussion of potential developments in Eastern Europe; and in January

---

[34] Mikhail Gorbachev, *Memoirs* (1996) p. 484.

[35] ibid. p. 465; CWIHP *Bulletin* 12/13 (2001) pp. 66, 29, 192.

[36] Gorbachev had, in 1987, criticised Ceaucescu during a visit to Romania, and had summoned Zhivkov to Moscow to tell him his recent reforms would make Bulgaria a 'mini-Japan' or West Germany, whereas all solutions must be based on socialism (Jacques Levesque, *The Enigma of 1989. The USSR and the Liberation of Eastern Europe* (Berkeley, CA, 1997) pp. 58, 69; R.J. Crampton, *The Balkans since the Second World War* (2002) pp. 179–80). But leaders of the major East European states were treated more circumspectly.

1989, further stimulated by Kissinger's attempt to secure his support for a new European political architecture (above, p. 413), Gorbachev called for studies and contingency plans. Three of these have been published, though not, alas, that from the KGB; all decried direct military intervention, but made no other very concrete recommendations; and all were reasonably optimistic about future Soviet–East European relations even in the event of Poland or Hungary's transition to a largely bourgeois democracy.[37] It is not clear that the reports had any impact; and Shakhnazarov recalls that, given the Soviet elections in march, the crisis surrounding the suppression of nationalist demonstrations in Georgia in April, and the meeting of the new Congress of People's Deputies in May, 'The attention of all of the leadership switched to internal problems, and so Eastern Europe was [put] on the backburner.' That May a Solidarity negotiator asked Jaruzelski, 'What are the limits to the changes the Soviets are willing to accept in Poland?' He replied, 'I do not know myself. Let us find them together.'[38]

Gorbachev's instincts were in fact fairly traditional: in March 1989 he still regarded 1956 in Hungary and 1968 in Czechoslovakia as 'counter-revolutions', and told the Hungarian Secretary, Karoly Grosz, 'we clearly have to draw boundaries'; while 'Democracy is much needed', 'the limit is the safekeeping of socialism and assurance of stability'. Interpreting this limit was left largely to the East European parties – in July 1989 Shevardnadze privately told the Hungarians to 'Do what you think is best to preserve the positions of the Party'. Gorbachev remained surprisingly optimistic of essential success. Even after the formation in August of a Solidarity-led government in Poland, he continued to treat the Polish party like a ruling one, inviting it to the December 1989 Warsaw Pact conference of Party and state leaders, and adjuring its Secretary not to 'forget that our socialist ideas have a future'; the latter's bleak response was, 'The ideas do, but we don't . . .'[39]

Poland 1982–9

Jaruzelski's 1981 imposition of martial law seemed so successful that he soon felt able to relax; in November 1982 he negotiated with the Pope,

---

[37] Vladislav Zubok, 'New Evidence on the "Soviet Factor" in the Peaceful Revolutions of 1989', CWIHP *Bulletin* 12/13 (2001) pp. 15–17; Jacques Levesque, 'Soviet Approaches to Eastern Europe at the Beginning of 1989', ibid. pp. 50, 52–71.
[38] CWIHP *Bulletin* 12/13, pp. 10, 51.
[39] CWIHP *Bulletin* 12/13, p. 78; Levesque, *The Enigma of 1989*, pp. 127, 139.

agreeing to release Walesa in exchange for a papal visit in 1983 that would imply acceptance of the new order. Martial law was lifted shortly after this visit, though repression (both official and unofficial) continued in lower key. An informal dialogue was established with the Church (which was itself in touch with Walesa and other activists); Solidarity preserved a restricted and clandestine existence; a certain normality had returned. What Jaruzelski could not do was restore the economy. In 1986 Poland defaulted on $1.4 billion of debt payments to the West; in 1987 debt reconstruction was agreed, but one partially dependent on accepting an IMF recovery programme. In November 1987 economic (and some political) reforms were put to a referendum, but, following a Solidarity boycott call, narrowly failed to secure sufficient votes. In February 1988 food prices were nevertheless raised by 40 per cent; demonstrations and strikes followed; the regime rode out the first wave, but after a second in August it accepted the Church's advice to talk to Walesa. Following promises that Solidarity would be invited to round-table discussions, Walesa successfully appealed for a return to work. From then on his popularity and public standing, long in the doldrums, rose sharply. In fact obstacles on both sides stopped the round table convening. But in November, during a high-profile visit first to the government then to Solidarity, Thatcher suggested that Western economic aid could be forthcoming, but only on the basis of political reforms and 'real dialogue with representatives of all sections of society, including Solidarity.'[40]

In January 1989 Jaruzelski took the issue of negotiations with and the relegalisation of Solidarity to his Central Committee. His intention was still to buttress the regime by associating opposition elements with it, a policy that dated back to his establishment of a Consultative Council in 1986. But most delegates seem to have thought it a step too far, and he could carry his proposals only by threatening resignation. The 'Party apparatus,' he later wrote, 'sensed that power was at risk of slipping away. It was not mistaken: we, the architects of the "Round Table", were the ones who . . . were fooling themselves. We were sincerely convinced that we would win the June elections.' And with reason; for in the talks, Solidarity (in return for full legalisation) offered assistance in securing foreign loans, and agreed a new constitution with a strong President – Jaruzelski – a freely elected Senate, and a predominant lower chamber (the Seym) where (for the first elections only) the government parties were guaranteed 65 per cent of the seats, other parties 35 per cent. Moscow was

[40] *Keesings*, 35649–52, 36297–302; Levesque, *Enigma*, p. 111n.

delighted, *Kommunist* writing in May 1989 that the Polish party (PUWP) had succeeded in 'reestablishing its leadership in society and reinforcing its leading role in the state' in a system based 'on a parliamentary socialist democracy and on a civil society'; its 'experience carries significance not only for Poland but also for the other countries.'[41]

Come polling day, however, Solidarity candidates won all but one seat in the Senate and all the non-government seats in the *Seym*, while only five government candidates secured the 50 per cent vote needed to gain election on the first ballot. The remainder were, admittedly, returned a fortnight later, on a low turn-out; but the damage had been done. Even Jaruzelski's election as President could not be assumed, though it was achieved in July with the aid of some Solidarity abstentions (encouraged by President Bush during a flying visit). Then when Jaruzelski proposed the re-election of the previous communist Prime Minister, the PUWP's former allies rebelled. This opened the door to all kinds of combinations since, with Solidarity's deputies, they would have commanded a *Seym* majority. There were now low-key growls from Moscow about the dangers of a 'destabilization of the situation in Poland, which would inevitably have serious consequences for . . . Europe as a whole.' But once Walesa indicated readiness to include communist ministers, these disappeared. Offered two posts, the PUWP managed to stand out for four, and secured Gorbachev's blessing for the outcome. With Defence, the Interior, and Transport, the PUWP still seemed strongly placed, and may have hoped for support from the President. But Jaruzelski behaved as a non-political head of state, and Solidarity dominated the government. Cut off from its former leading role, and then demoralised by shock waves from Honecker's fall and East Germany's abandonment of the Berlin Wall, the PUWP began to disintegrate in December 1989, split and dissolved itself in January 1990. Meanwhile the state had, on 29 December, resumed the name, and flag, of the inter-war 'Republic of Poland', and had embarked on a 'big bang' economic reform to bring about transition to capitalism.[42]

Hungary 1987–90

Hungary's evolution was less eventful. Its regime seemed solid and opposition slight. But its economy was faltering by 1985–6, and its net debt was the highest per capita in Eastern Europe. In 1987 the hitherto orthodox

[41] Levesque, *Enigma*, pp. 110, 114–16.
[42] Levesque, *Enigma*, pp. 123–6, 208; Crampton, *Eastern Europe*, p. 392.

Karoly Grosz became Prime Minister to devise an austerity programme. This was adopted, but only after sparking a debate in which intellectuals urged the need for more general reform. They were joined, from within the party, by Imre Pozsgay, who called for a new constitution and cultivated the new intellectual activists. The now elderly Kadar was uneasy; he felt Gorbachev's policies 'would bring a catastrophe upon the USSR', and believed that he alone had the necessary experience to ensure that the Hungarian reforms would not run out of control. In 1988 he seems to have looked to Gromyko and Ligachev for backing, whereas Grosz hoped for Gorbachev's support. Gorbachev did not intervene directly, but his coolness towards Kadar was palpable; in May Grosz was able to take over, in alliance with Pozsgay and the economic reformer Nyers. Changes continued apace: in October a law permitted medium-sized private joint-stock companies; in November the government promised to allow competitive political parties, and these started to be formed even before the requisite legislation was passed.

Pozsgay still warned that two subjects remained taboo – the rehabilitation of Imre Nagy and withdrawal from the Warsaw Pact – but his inhibitions were soon eroded. Early in 1989 a party commission under his patronage declared that 1956 had been not a 'counter-revolution' but 'a popular uprising against oligarchical power'. The International Department of the CPSU prepared a rebuke, but Gorbachev forebade its despatch. March 1989 saw a massive opposition demonstration on the newly revived national day commemorating the 1848 revolution, June the formal reburial (attended by 250,000 people) of Nagy and other heroes of 1956. Meanwhile Grosz was feeling more and more unhappy. He saw himself as 'deserted' by Gorbachev, who had rejected his pleas both for political support in the internal Hungarian party debates and for a hard currency loan. He also contemplated a declaration of emergency to force through economic, and perhaps also block political, reforms, but felt (he later said) that:

Not only would we have been condemned by Western countries and subjected to sanctions, but, above all, such an action would have collided . . . with the whole thrust of Soviet foreign policy, and we would have been isolated in our own camp, as well. I therefore decided that the best I could do was to offer resistance, using political means, for as long as I could.[43]

---

[43] Levesque, *Enigma*, pp. 66–7, 129–30, 133.

At a June central committee meeting, Grosz effectively lost control; and the party began round-table talks with opposition politicians on a new system. In September these produced agreement, though only with part of the opposition, on the basis of free and direct Presidential and then parliamentary elections; Soviet sensitivities were still addressed by the retention of a reference to the 'socialist character of the system'. On this basis the 'Communist' Party reconstituted itself in October as the Hungarian Socialist Party (HSP), but in doing so it came unstuck: the reformers had hoped to secure 70 per cent of the old party's 700,000 members, but in the event got only 50,000 as compared to 100,000 for Grosz's unreconstructed hold-out party; and whereas the communists had apparently enjoyed 40 per cent public opinion poll support in the summer, by late November, after the opening of the Berlin wall, the HSP held only 16 per cent. Pozsgay was still expected to win the presidential elections; but the more radical groups, which had refused to sign off on the round-table accords, managed to force a constitutional referendum in late November, as a result of which the choice of president was transferred to parliament. When parliamentary elections finally came in March–April 1990 the HSP was pushed into fourth place. Victory went to the Hungarian Democratic Forum, whose leader was moved to claim that 'after decades of dictatorship the political reflexes of the Hungarian people have not changed' since his coalition had together 'achieved the same result as the Smallholders in 1945'.[44]

East Germany 1989–90

Long before this Hungary's evolution had helped set off an avelanche. In September 1989, having secured the promise of a West German loan,[45] it declared that it would no longer stop East Germans crossing its border with Austria. It was then full of DDR tourists, and by the end of the month 24,000 had crossed on their way to West Germany. Hungary was roundly denounced for this breach of Warsaw Pact obligations; and Czech guards began to stop East Germans going there. As a result would-be migrants swamped the West German embassy in Prague. It was eventually agreed

[44] Levesque, *Enigma*, esp. pp. 139, 208–9; *Keesing's*, 36164, 36468, 36746, 36960–1, 37048, 37380; The Observer, *Tearing down the Curtain: The People's Revolution in Eastern Europe* (1990) Chap. 3.

[45] 500m DM, plus compensation for any losses from DDR retaliation – CWIHP *Bulletin* 12/13, p. 133.

that they might leave too, but by train through East Germany; and there followed riots in Dresden as people tried to board these trains to the West. To prevent a repetition, the border with Czechoslovakia was then closed. Meanwhile East German intellectuals had illegally established a 'New Forum' to press for pluralist reforms, albeit without challenging the party's 'leading role'. Also there had for some time been small 'peace' movements and demonstrations, sponsored by the Lutheran church. In October they mushroomed, partly in consequence of developments abroad, partly as a protest against the manifestly rigged local government elections of the previous spring, and partly in response to the fortieth anniversary of the DDR.

In Poland and Hungary the regimes had attempted to co-opt dissidents; Honecker's line was that 'everything will collapse if we give an inch'. On 27 September he ordered the forcible maintenance of law and order. Demonstrations during the anniversary celebrations were roughly broken up, with over a thousand arrests. But the real crisis came with the – by now regular – Monday demonstration in Leipzig on 9 October. The regime's second man, Egon Krenz, had visited Beijing and been notably polite about the recent killing of demonstrators there, giving rise to fears that the DDR too would adopt the 'Chinese solution'. In fact Krenz is claimed to have concluded the opposite – 'Whatever may have happened at Tiananmen Square, nowhere should we act with military force against demonstrators. That would be the political and moral end for us.'[46] In the event, the huge Leipzig demonstration passed off peacefully, with Krenz, the Dresden Party Secretary Modrow, and the local mayor all claiming credit for restraining the local security forces.

There had for some time been contacts between Soviet and East German politicians unhappy with Honecker's immobilism. During his (reluctant) visit of 6–8 October to the DDR's anniversary celebrations, Gorbachev made a final, if diplomatically understated, effort to persuade Honecker to change; he later said it was like 'throwing peas against a brick wall.' He also concluded that Honecker's rule was both less efficient and more unpopular than he had previously realised; and though he would not directly force a change (as Brezhnev had done to dismiss Ulbricht), he left little doubt that he would welcome one. Indeed, the plotters briefed Gorbachev the day they finally struck; and he even told Brandt (who was visiting Moscow) slightly before the event that the SED Politburo would be effecting 'serious changes' to bring about 'a broad dialogue of the party

---

[46] Hannes Adomeit, *Imperial Overstretch: Germany in Soviet Policy from Stalin to Gorbachev* (Baden-Baden, 1998) pp. 360–2.

with society and the population'.[47] On 17 October Krenz ousted Honecker and took over. But things only got worse: the authorities counted 140,000 demonstrators over the week of 16–22 October, 540,000 next week, and 1,400,000 from 30 October to 4 November, the main demands being (at this stage) the recognition of opposition groups, free elections, and the right to travel. Also economists told the politburo that, without outside help, a 25–30 per cent cut in the standard of living would be needed to restore stability. Krenz took these figures with him on his 1 November visit to Gorbachev, revealing an annual hard currency deficit of $12 billion and overall debt of $26.5 billion: 'This meant that they had to take on new loans . . . Astonished, Comrade Gorbachev asked whether these numbers were exact. He had not imagined the situation to be so precarious.' Gorbachev made it clear that he could not help much. West Germany could, but only (Chancellor Kohl made clear on 7 November) if the SED relinquished 'absolute power', permitted opposition groups, and held free elections.[48]

The DDR held only one strong negotiating card, its control of the border; the economists had in fact suggested that the lifting of travel controls be placed on the table when a West German loan was sought, but Politburo sensitivities toned down the language in which this was done. In any case, the card soon evaporated through sheer administrative incompetence. At first Honecker's successors had talked only of providing, by the end of the year, that all citizens might apply first for passports, then for travel visas – a deliberately time-consuming process. On 7 November the politburo decided (for the time being) not to go even that far, and consulted the USSR on a measure dealing only with applications for permanent departure. However, the officials drafting the text expanded it to include those for temporary visits, and drew up a press statement to be released on 10 November if the Central Committee and the Council of Ministers approved. On 9 November several top leaders did so informally during a 'smoking break'; Krenz commended it to the Central Committee at the end of a long meeting, remarking gloomily that whatever the choice 'in this situation, we'll be making the wrong move'; he then short-circuited the Council of Ministers by directing the immediate release of the news. This was done that evening by an unbriefed spokesman, Gunter Schabowski, who misunderstood and floundered over the detail. The West

[47] ibid. pp. 378–9, 405–17.
[48] H-H. Hertl, 'The Fall of the Wall: the Unintended Self-Dissolution of East Germany's Ruling Regime', CWIHP *Bulletin* 12/13, pp. 135, 153.

German media interpreted him as saying that the borders had been opened, and Western television (which everybody in the East watched) broadcast to that effect. Huge crowds went to the Berlin Wall to see. The wholly unprepared border guards tried telling them to come back tomorrow, which did not go down well, then, at 11.39 p.m. simply decided on their own initiative to ease the pressure by opening the gates. The crowds poured through, and a wonderful – and well televised – party was had on and round the Wall by both East and West Berliners. Thereafter, failing a Soviet military intervention that was quite out of the question, there was no way the cork could be put back in the bottle.[49]

Gorbachev's aide Chernaev realised this (above, p. 423), but both the East German and the Soviet leadership continued hopeful. Krenz's close associate, Schabowski, later wrote that 'We hadn't a clue that the opening of the wall was the beginning of the end of the Republic. On the contrary, we expected a stabilization process'[50] – presumably as a result of the removal of the travel grievance and the belated opening (on 2 December) of round-table talks with the oppositionists of the New Forum. The latter would indeed have preferred the DDR's survival as an independent 'third way' state.[51] But by now the world had passed them by; the Leipzig demonstrations continued to grow, but switched their slogan from 'We are *the* people' to 'We are *one* people', accompanied by banners proclaiming 'Germany – united fatherland' and German black-red-gold flags without the DDR's emblem. Once Kohl had himself visited Dresden in mid-December and sensed the atmosphere, he saw no reason to prop up an unrepresentative East German government.[52]

This was, in any case, falling to pieces in December–January 1989–90: emigration soared; deprived of state subsidies, industrial concerns began to go bankrupt; there were revelations both of the scale of corruption and

[49] ibid. pp. 134–8, 152, and Docs 5–8.
[50] Philip Zelikow and Condoleeza Rice, *Germany Unified and Europe Transformed* (Cambridge, Mass., 1997 edn) p. 101. On 4 December Modrow found Gorbachev still 'thought that the path was now free for perestroika in the DDR'. 'I did not dissuade him . . . because I, at least in part, still believed in . . . democratization as a process that would strengthen socialism in the DDR' – though 'I [also] had the fear – he had no idea – that' it could have the opposite effect (Adomeit, *Imperial Overstretch*, p. 455).
[51] So would Brandt, who told Gorbachev on 17 October that the DDR's disappearance 'would be a spectacular defeat for Social Democracy since it considered the DDR as a great achievement of socialism' (Gorbachev's paraphrase to Krenz, CWIHP *Bulletin* 12/13, p. 145; also Adomeit, *Imperial Overstretch*, pp. 422–3).
[52] Adomeit, *Imperial Overstretch*, pp. 469, 471–3; CWIHP *Bulletin* 12/13, p. 140.

of Stasi attempts to destroy damaging evidence; and the government's decision in mid-January to maintain a 'reformed' Stasi provoked riots and mass occupations. Prime Minister Modrow, by now the country's effective leader, confessed to Kohl that parts of the governmental machine no longer obeyed his orders; and he soon brought forward to 18 March the elections he had planned for May. At the start of March opinion polls predicted a Social Democrat government, probably backed by the reformed successor party to the SED; this would have favoured only a loose German confederation and supported the USSR's insistence that Germany either opt for neutrality or continue the Warsaw Pact's presence in the East. The polls proved as unreliable as most East European polls of the era; for, following Kohl's promise to exchange ordinary people's DDR currency holdings into DM at an unrealistic one for one rate, his 'Alliance for Germany' won over 48 per cent of the vote on a platform of rapid reunification. Kohl still needed Soviet consent (above, pp. 425–31); but it is only a slight exaggeration to say that, over the inner-German arrangements for East Germany's adhesion (*anschluss*) to the Federal Republic, the CDU was negotiating with itself.[53]

Bulgaria, 1989 and after

In connection with the July 1989 Warsaw Pact meeting (held after Solidarity's electoral victory, but before the change of government in Poland) the DDR, Bulgaria, Romania, and Czechoslovakia all expressed opposition to the new accommodationist and Gorbachevian policies.[54] None of their leaders intended thus to put themselves at risk, but all had fallen by the end of the year. In the case of Zhivkov of Bulgaria, the USSR had probably been the chief destabilising factor. Fears of environmental disaster had been sparked by Chernobyl, though they were reinforced by chemical pollution from Romania; and 1988 saw the appearance of opposition groups like the 'Club for the support of *Glasnost* and *Perestroika*'. In mid-1989 persecution of Bulgaria's Turkish minority led to a highly embarrassing mass flight, and to Bulgaria's international ostracism. This upset senior party figures, who also felt threatened by Zhivkov's frequent

---

[53] Adomeit, *Imperial Overstretch*, pp. 468–9, 471–3; Levesque, *Enigma*, p. 222; Zelikow and Rice, *Germany Unified*, pp. 157–9, 228–30.

[54] Levesque, *Enigma*, pp. 120–1; Vojtech Mastny and Malcolm Byrne (eds) *A Cardboard Castle? An Inside History of the Warsaw Pact, 1955–1991* (Budapest, 2005) pp. 66–7.

personnel reshuffles. Then came both the example of Honecker's deposition and a 24 October letter from Foreign Minister Mladenov to the Central Committee; this claimed that Zhivkov meant 'to keep himself and his family in power at all costs', and that he had isolated 'Bulgaria from the rest of the world. We have even reached the point where we are estranged from the Soviet Union and . . . find ourselves . . . in the same pigs' trough as the rotten family regime of [Romania's] Ceausescu . . . Zhivkov has forced Bulgaria outside the currents of our age.' The letter was taken to Moscow under cover of a Comecon meeting, and plans for a coup formalised at a very high level;[55] on 9–10 November the Bulgarian Politburo forced Zhivkov out, and Mladenov took over.

Shortly thereafter a largely urban 'Union of Democratic Forces' (UDF) coalesced out of the various protest associations, in an environment of strikes and of both liberal and nationalist (anti-Turkish) demonstrations. The need for support against the latter (which appear to have been assisted by the Communist Party's rural machine) led the government to start round-table talks with the UDF in January 1990. During these Mladenov gave up the party leadership for the presidency, Lukanov became prime minister, and the party redesignated itself the Bulgarian Socialist Party (BSP). Drawing on its surviving *apparat* and mobilising an anti-urban vote in the countryside, it won elections in June 1990, thus apparently achieving the leading role within a pluralist system that had eluded the Hungarian, Polish, East German and Czech parties. This did not last. Mladenov was driven from office in July by revelations that he had, the previous December, favoured using tanks to curb demonstrations. Lukanov faced a catastrophic economic situation (only partly of his own making), and stepped down in November 1990 after massive street protests. A non-party government followed until a new constitution was agreed, and elections held, in 1991. Thereafter office oscillated between UDF and BSP until the former pulled ahead in 1997; the 2000 elections were won by the new 'Simeon II National Movement', headed by the former King, who had prospered in exile and could now draw both on royal and business prestige. The BSP recovered in 2005, to head a grand coalition whose Prime Minister declared 'our chief priority' to be the reforms required for Bulgaria to join the European Union.[56]

---

[55] On the Soviet side, Shevardnadze, Yakovlev and the Sofia embassy were apparently involved – Jordan Baev, '1989: Bulgarian Transition to Pluralist Democracy', CWIHP *Bulletin* 12/13, pp. 165–6, 169, 179n; Levesque, *Enigma*, pp. 171–2.

[56] R.J. Crampton, *The Balkans since the Second World War* (2002) pp. 180–1, Chap. 17; *Keesing's*, 46790.

Czechoslovakia 1989–90

In Czechoslovakia there had been numerous small demonstrations during the summer of 1989, some tolerated, some repressed. In the autumn, protest was probably stimulated by the Leipzig gatherings and Honecker's fall, and also, the security forces maintained, by assistance from Polish and Hungarian activists.[57] Then on 17 November 1989 a large and officially sanctioned demonstration in Prague was violently broken up, with rumours (apparently spread by the secret police) that one student had been killed.[58] On 19 November Vaclav Havel secured the coalescence of a plethora of dissident groups into a 'Civic Forum', as the 'mouthpiece of that part of the . . . public which is ever more critical towards the policies of the current Czechoslovak leadership and which was deeply shaken by the brutal repression of students who were peacefully demonstrating.' It demanded: the release of those then arrested and the sacking of the Prague Party Secretary and the Minister of the Interior; a committee of investigation with Civic Forum participation; and the retirement of six top political leaders (including the current Party Secretary Milos Jakes) who had been 'directly connected' with the 1968 Warsaw Pact intervention. This was a tall order, but not, as yet, a demand for the end of communist rule. Demonstrations spread with extraordinary rapidity; Prime Minister Adamec bestowed some status on the Civic Forum by meeting it on 21 November; on the 23rd it called for a dialogue on the basis that there could be 'no return to the previous totalitarian system of government' and that 'a free, democratic and prosperous Czechoslovakia . . . must return to Europe', and also for a general strike on the 27th to support these demands.[59]

It is claimed that Moscow sent Jakes a 'recommendation' against using force, but he was clearly drawn towards that solution. However, at an emergency Central Committee meeting on the 24th, Adamec argued that it would be only a palliative, and that after 'a certain period the situation

---

[57] Rothschild, *Return to Diversity* (1993 edn) p. 237; CWIHP *Bulletin* 12/13, pp. 198, 200, 204.

[58] The episode has generated claims and conspiracy theories to the effect that it was meant to discredit Jakes and secure his replacement by a more Gorbachevian leader. A Czech parliamentary commission initially believed the police action might have been pre-planned, but directed by two different commands with clashing instructions. However, it failed to find any conclusive evidence, and later reported that there had been no KGB involvement – *Keesing's*, 37737; Levesque, *Enigma*, p. 185n; *The Independent*, 15 May 1990, p. 8, 24 August, p. 11, 27 October, p. 11.

[59] CWIHP *Bulletin* 12/13, esp. pp. 189–90, 211.

could explode again'. Most 'of our people, including young people, have no reason to be against socialism', and to 'drive the young generation into the arms of the enemies of socialism would be an unforgiveable mistake.' Moreover 'the international support of the socialist countries can no longer be counted on . . . [while from] the capitalist countries, one must take into account the results of a political and economic boycott.' Were they instead to opt for 'a political solution', the many mistakes of the last twenty years would indeed have to be paid for; 'I am convinced, however, that we need not pay too high a price, if we can manage to mobilize the Party. No one else has such a numerous membership, such an experienced cadre of functionaries, and close connections with each collective.' To this end, Adamec proposed another meeting to determine strategy, and then the capture of the agenda from the demonstrations by advancing the party's own proposals for major reform.[60]

Adamec was so far successful that the party abandoned Jakes; but it did not immediately elect him Secretary, and he had instead to operate simply as Prime Minister. Whether for this reason or as a result of natural timidity, he was constantly appealing to Moscow for clear-cut support. Nor did he capture the initiative from the Civic Forum. On 3 December he offered it only five seats in a cabinet of twenty-one, and was turned down flat. He then left for a Warsaw Pact meeting, met Gorbachev and again failed to secure the kind of help he was seeking. On his return, he resigned as premier, to be replaced by a predominantly non-communist government. Husak then vacated the presidency (to which he had moved in 1987 on retiring as party leader); parliament chose Havel to succeed him. On New Year's day 1990, Havel amnestied 16,000 political prisoners, and on 2 January the secret police were dissolved. Other measures soon followed; and for over a decade the Czech agenda – that of Slovakia was, as we shall see, more complicated – was dominated by the ideas of the conservative monetarist Vaclav Klaus.[61]

Romania, 1989 and after

In Romania Ceausescu's rule had degenerated into a personal dictatorship (derided as 'socialism in one family') of an unpleasant and megalomaniac character. Ruthless priority was given to repaying foreign debt by

[60] Thomas Blanton (ed.) *The Revolutions of 1989: New Documents from Soviet/East European Archives Reveal why there was no Crackdown* (National Security Archive, Electronic Briefing Book no. 2) Document 7; Lesvesque, *Enigma*, p. 186.
[61] ibid. pp. 185–9; Crampton, *Eastern Europe*, pp. 297–9.

squeezing consumption. There had been strikes, but they had been firmly suppressed; and the Securitate cultivated an image of omnipresence and violence. In early December Ceausescu seemed unworried by developments at home, but he warned Gorbachev of the 'grave danger not just [to] socialism . . . but also [to] the very existence of the communist parties' in other East European states, and suggested (albeit in very general terms) that the USSR could 'help produce a better orientation'. When disturbances broke out in Romania on 15–17 December, Ceausescu ordered their violent repression, left for a foreign visit, and on his return described the protests as merely the work of a 'few groups of hooligan elements'. On 21 December he staged a traditional rally in Bucharest; but its chanting switched from the approved 'Ceausescu and the people' to 'Ceausescu is a dictator' (in Romanian the two rhyme). Then, hearing reports of crowds moving on party headquarters, Ceausescu panicked and made for a prepared mountain redoubt. On 22 December a 'National Salvation Front' (NSF), secretly formed some months earlier by reformists in the regime's upper echelons, stepped in to assume 'temporary control' of the anti-Ceausescu cause, against a background of confused shooting and street fighting. This was represented at the time as a last-ditch stand by the Securitate (aided by Arab terrorists) against the army which had come out for the revolution; but questions were later asked as to why 'Securitate' fire was never directed against the buildings occupied by the NSF and the television station, as to why no traces of the 'Arab terrorists' were ever found, and why so many senior Securitate figures were able to continue their careers under the new regime. Anyway on 25 December Nicolae and Elena Ceausescu were summarily tried and shot (on television), and the violence ceased.[62]

The new rulers suspended some of Ceausescu's most unpopular policies, released food stores he had earmarked for export, rehabilitated and cultivated the Church, and allowed a free press and political parties to emerge. It also let the small German minority emigrate, and improved conditions for the larger Hungarian one (though at a pace limited by the Romanian nationalist backlash this engendered). In January 1990 it decided to continue as a political party. Opposed chiefly by pre-communist parties with out-of-touch emigré leaders, it easily won the May elections. Despite some violence and official harrassment, these were viewed by

[62] Crampton, *The Balkans since the Second World War*, pp. 203–4, 325; Rothschild, *Return to Diversity* (1993 edn) pp. 247–8; CWIHP *Bulletin* 12/13, p. 220; *Annual Register*, 1990, p. 127.

international observers as acceptable. The opposition disagreed, and saw the NSF as a continuation of the Communist Party under another face. They occupied University Square in Bucharest from April to June, when police moves to clear it provoked attacks on official buildings akin to those of the previous December. The NSF responded by bringing in 10,000 miners, who beat up the demonstrators and smashed Opposition parties' offices; they were then thanked by President Iliescu.[63]

Part of the NSF's electoral appeal had lain in its cautious economic programme, which warned against a speedy transition to a market economy with its consequent high inflation and unemployment among the mammoth industrial plants Ceausescu had fostered. Even gentle moves in that direction prompted a second miners' descent on Bucharest in 1991. But in 1996 Iliescu was unexpectedly defeated in the second round of the presidential elections, with almost all the opposition parties coalescing behind his challenger.

For many Romanians these changes appeared to be a second . . . revolution . . . the first occasion since 1937 that a government . . . was changed through the ballot box . . . The opposition's victory was attributed . . . to the widespread feeling that Romania was lagging behind . . . in the transition to a successful market economy, and to dissatisfaction with the rampant corruption . . .[64]

Important changes were made among high officials; and the transition to electoral politics proved lasting. But in economic affairs little was effected until the IMF lost patience. 1999–2000 then saw the adoption of the more drastic reforms required to secure a renewal of IMF lending, and also both EU aid and the opening of negotiations for Romania's EU membership. The reforms' immediate effect was a further fall in living standards. President Constantinescu crashed in the 2000 elections, where the run-off was between Iliescu (who duly returned to office) and an inter-war-style ultra-nationalist. Fortunately the 1999–2000 reforms appeared to bear fruit in economic expansion; and though 2004 brought another swing in the electoral pendulum, the beneficiary was not (as had once been feared) the ultra-nationalists but the centre-right Mayor of Bucharest, Traian Basescu. In January 2007, early in his Presidency, Romania finally achieved its goal of EU membership, albeit subject to unusually close economic surveillance.[65] Politics, however, remained exciting: Basescu was

[63] Crampton, *Balkans*, pp. 326–7; *Annual Register*, 1990, pp. 128–9.
[64] *Annual Register*, 1990, p. 128; 1991, p. 162; 1996, pp. 108–10; *Keesing's*, 41376.
[65] Crampton, *Balkans*, Chap. 18.

soon suspended for exceeding his powers (he claimed in an assault on corruption), then reinstated following his victory in a referendum.

Eastern Europe's transition to EU membership; Slovakia

In December 1989 the Polish comrades told Gorbachev that though socialist ideas had a future, they themselves did not. Actually it was the other way round. Though only one top East European communist, Ionescu, survived in office for any length of time, discontent with the social costs of market-oriented economic reform later enabled several former communists to win elections. Thus in 1993 Solidarity splits and resentment at the hardships of the transition to a market economy propelled the ex-communist parties to victory at the Polish parliamentary elections. But though they had promised an end to 'dogmatic' privatisation, the leader of the main successor party, Aleksander Kwasniewski, declared that marketisation would continue and proffered an 'apology' for the communist period. The new government's chief policy goal remained integration within Europe, and concerns were expressed over the possible revival of 'the old concept of spheres of influence in Moscow.' Two years later Kwasniewski defeated Walesa in the presidential elections; but he was at pains to describe himself as a 'social democrat or even a social-liberal'.[66] Similarly in 1994 the Hungarian Socialist Party and its allies won an impressive two-thirds majority in parliament, chiefly on issues of competence and corruption, and on fears that the previous government had taken its concerns for Hungarian minorities abroad too far. But the new Prime Minister, Gyula Horn, and his government, 'came mainly from the reform wing of the old communist party', and pressed for the early admission of the East–Central European states into both NATO and the EU.[67] It has been said that the revolutionaries of 1989 produced no 'new ideas. They did not need to . . . They believed the west had shown them the solution to

[66] *Annual Register*, 1993, pp. 107–9; 1995, p. 105.
[67] ibid. 1994, pp. 120–3; 1995, p. 111. Not that politicians' pasts were forgotten. In 2006 the issue surfaced during the (lavishly staged) commemoration of Hungary's 1956 rising. The Prime Minister was already unpopular following his admission that he had 'lied' in recent elections about the state of the economy; critics and 1956 veterans now asked how a government led by a former communist youth leader, married to the granddaughter of a significant figure in the post-1956 crackdown, could properly celebrate the rebellion. Riots resulted – *The Times*, 23 October 2006 p. 31; 24 October p. 35.

their problems';[68] and this was as true of former communists as of other politicians.

A number of states balked at particularly difficult measures of economic transition. But perhaps in only one case was this of real importance. In Czechoslovakia there was from the outset constant friction over the federal relationship of the two parts of the country, even though they had voted for two wings of the same party. Moreover economic reform was likely to be more painful in Slovakia, with its large and obsolete heavy industry plants, than in the Czech lands. In 1992 trouble came to a head with the election in the latter of Klaus's Civic Democratic Party, but in the former of Meciar's 'Movement for a Democratic Slovakia'. Talks between the two failed, for when 'Klaus insisted on the continuation of economic shock therapy and a "strong federation" . . . Meciar made it clear that Slovakia would declare its sovereignty'. They therefore decided to go their separate ways, splitting the country (without further consulting a probably reluctant electorate) in the 'velvet divorce' (which took effect on 1 January 1993).[69]

Meciar had shown authoritarian tendencies even in 1992, and they later became steadily more pronounced, with (in 1995–6) a nasty scandal involving kidnapping and an apparent murder. Admittedly Slovakia had, in 1995, concluded a treaty settling its differences with Hungary. But the EU was sufficiently worried by Meciar's style of government to express concern publicly in both 1994 and 1995. In 1997 Poland, Hungary and the Czech Republic were invited to start EU membership talks (and to join NATO), but 'Slovakia was left behind because of its political problems.' All this changed after Meciar unexpectedly lost the September 1998 elections; by July 1999 the new 'cabinet had met all the political criteria the EU had recommended to the previous government as a condition of entry'; that December Slovakia was invited to open the talks that led to membership in 2004.[70] By then it had also attracted the World Bank's accolade 'as the world's top [economic] reformer and . . . one of the top twenty economies on the ease of doing business.'[71]

---

[68] Crampton, *Eastern Europe*, p. 415.

[69] *Annual Register*, 1992, p. 109.

[70] ibid. 1995, pp. 108–9; 1996, pp. 103–5; 1997, pp. 112–13; 1998, pp. 120–1; 1999, p. 119.

[71] ibid. 2004, pp. 87–8. Such reforms, and wage rates far lower than in Western Europe, made Slovakia particularly successful in attracting foreign car plants, and helped bring down unemployment. But this remained high, and may explain the 2004 change of government.

For over a decade, then, most of the former Eastern Europe was set on integrating into the West.[72] The process necessarily involved a period of dependence, since (as the *Annual Register* noted) 'the terms, pace and date were under the West's control'.[73] Now they have achieved EU membership, these countries may prove less malleable. One indication of this was given by Slovenia, in many ways the EU's model applicant. In 1992 it had removed all official recognition from 30,000 residents from other parts of Yugoslavia who had not registered as citizens after Slovenia's move to independence; this deprived 'the erased' of all residence, pensions and benefit rights. Under pressure from both its own Constitutional Court and the EU, the government moved to restore these to the 18,000 'erased' still remaining in the country. But in 2004 the electorate, admittedly on a low poll, voted overwhelmingly against this; a leading Slovenian journalist noted that 'because the negotiations with the EU are over people do not think that they are somehow monitored by the EU – and they believe they may speak whatever they want.'[74] This is no more than a straw in the wind. But a period of further adjustment must be expected while the new members decide how far the EU, when seen from inside, accords with their earlier external vision. As the largest new member, Poland's reaction will be particularly important.

The break-up of Yugoslavia

If in the 1990s most of Eastern Europe sought to imitate contemporary Western Europe, Yugoslavia seemed rather to be reverting to the Balkan patterns of the early part of the century. The 'south' ('Yugo') slav peoples then differed as a result of history, religion, and – though less markedly, save in the case of the Slovenes – language. It was, however, the proclaimed mission of Serbia before 1914 to unite them as Piedmont had

[72] Among the keenest, and most successful, were the three Baltic states, independent between the Wars but then part of the USSR. But of the other former Soviet union-republics now bordering on the EU, only Ukraine has shown serious interest in joining, and then only spasmodically. Things change; but there is at present some logic behind the EU's current eastern limits.

[73] 1995, p. 111.

[74] BBC News, 13 April 2004; *Annual Register*, 2004, p. 101. Slovenia's Interior Ministry resumed the issue of residence permits in 2005, but Amnesty International continued to be unhappy with its tempo (Kaitlin Dunn, 'Erased: Slovenia's troubled relationship with Croatia and its ex-Yugoslav minorities', and Amnesty's open letter of 28 November 2005 to the President of the EU Commission – both on the Internet).

united Italy in the *risorgimento*. This was achieved in 1918–19; but for most of its inter-war history the new state was torn by Serb–Croat rivalry. After its destruction by Germany in 1941, there ensued a complex of civil wars, with the Fascist regime imposed on Croatia seeking to expel, convert or exterminate all non-Roman Catholics, and the principal resistance movement in Serbia, the Chetniks, aspiring to the ethnic cleansing of Serb lands. There may have been a million deaths (the official figure was 1.7 million), and the inter-communal killings left a legacy of mutual fear and hatred that resurfaced almost half a century later.

The victorious communists' solution was a combination of exclusive party control and the gratification of national sentiment by the creation of Soviet-style republics for the Serbs, Croats, Slovenes, Macedonians and 'Bosnians', plus autonomous provinces within Serbia for Kosovo (with its large Albanian population) and the Vojvodina (with its Magyar minority). Initially the centre was firmly in control. But the 1960s saw a general devolution of power to the republican level and the curbing of the security apparatus. In Croatia this opened the way to pressure for the use in schools of the Croatian rather than the 'Serbo-Croat' language and for the elimination of Serb over-representation in the republic's economic and political life. The Serb minority was alarmed; and in 1971 Tito warned that 'in some villages . . . the Serbs are drilling and arming . . . Do we want to have 1941 again?' That December he forced the resignation of the Croatian leadership, declaring that it had been moving 'little by little towards a separatist line'; 'if we had not stopped that . . . perhaps in six months it would have come to shooting, to a civil war'.[75]

Surprisingly Tito did not reassert institutionalised central control. Rather the 1974 constitution provided for a collective 'presidency' consisting of a delegate from each republic *and autonomous province*, plus a weak and rotating federal executive, with the understanding that after Tito's death the formal office of president would rotate too. The system appeared to survive Tito's death in 1980. But the economy deteriorated and grievances mounted – with Serbia upset by the weight the richer Slovenia and Croatia enjoyed in economic decision-making, worried about the position of Serbs in Croatia, and alarmed by the situation in the province of Kosovo. As the original cradle of Serbia, this lay at the heart of Serbs' self-consciousness. But by the 1980s it had a large and growing Albanian majority, the product partly of differential birth rates, partly of Serb emigration that may have reflected economic forces[76] but that

---

[75] Dennison Rusinow, *The Yugoslav Experiment 1948–1974* (1977) Chaps 7, 8.

[76] It was said that the Serbs would do anything for Kosovo except live in it.

Serbs blamed on 'terror' and on discrimination by the province's Albanian leadership.

In 1986 a memorandum from the Serbian Academy of Sciences denounced the 'genocide' of Serbs in both Kosovo and Croatia, blamed Tito's 1974 constitution for partitioning Serbia into three by enhancing the status of Kosovo and Vojvodina, and asserted that Serbia was economically discriminated against. In 1987 the new leader of the Serbian communist party, Slobadan Milosevic, played the national card, promising Serbs in Kosovo's capital, Pristina, that 'nobody would ever beat them again'. He then pushed for constitutional reform, both to return Serbia to a unitary state and to enhance its (and his) position within Yugoslavia. Over the 1989–90 winter, riotous demonstrations staged by his 'Committee for the Protection of Kosovo Serbs and Montenegrins', managed to topple the governments in Kosovo, Vojvodina and Montenegro, thus giving Milosevic control of half the federal presidency; and at a monster rally in June 1989 to commemorate the anniversary of Serbia's central political myth, the fourteenth century defeat by the Ottomans at Kosovo Polje, he flamboyantly announced that 'After six centuries we are again engaged in battles and quarrels. They are not armed battles, but this cannot be excluded yet.'

All this went down badly in Slovenia and Croatia. In Slovenia friction between liberal investigative journalists and the Yugoslav army had led to fears of a military clamp-down; these were further heightened by Milosevic's behaviour in Kosovo, and by his projects for federal constituitional reform. In late 1989 the Slovene parliament asserted its right to veto the imposition of a state of emergency, and if necessary to leave Yugoslavia unilaterally. Meanwhile Croatian national sentiment was being galvanised by a torrent of Serbian media abuse, harking back to the Second World War era. This was rendered explosive by the move throughout Yugoslavia to permit the formation of independent parties, followed in 1990 by competitive elections. In Serbia these were won by Milosevic (against an anti-communist nationalist), but in both Slovenia and Croatia victory went, in April–May 1990, to opposition nationalists.

Both republics said they wanted to stay in 'Yugoslavia', but in a very loose confederation. In December 1990 a Slovene referendum called for independence unless such a confederation was agreed within six months. The omens were not good. Serbia and Slovenia had been imposing escalating mutual sanctions ever since Belgrade had ordered a cutting of industrial links in December 1989. In December 1990 Serbia helped itself to the equivalent of $1.4 billion from the Yugoslav National Bank. In May 1991 it blocked the accession of the Croat Vice-President to the office of President of Yugoslavia (which, by convention, it was his turn to hold by rotation) despite his warning that this would lead to immediate Croat moves to secession. The December 1989 Slovene referendum had set a time limit. On its expiry in late June 1990, Slovenia declared its independence, followed immediately by Croatia. The Yugoslav army countered by trying to seize control of Slovenia's borders and airport; but Slovenia had acquired arms and managed to fight back effectively. The EC then stepped in, seeking to use its economic power to promote a continued, but loose, Yugoslav state; a ceasefire was agreed, the Croat candidate was installed as President of Yugoslavia, and constitutional negotiations were resumed. But nothing came of them.[77]

Milosevic, as he said publicly on 3 July, had no objection to Slovenia's secession. Substantial military reinforcements would have been necessary to prevent this; but the Yugoslav presidency blocked these, and instead on 18 July 1990 ordered the army to pull out, redeploying chiefly to Croatia. Here the situation was far more volatile, since Croatia had a Serb minority, 12 per cent in numerical terms but occupying nearly a third of its territory. In the 1990 elections the victorious party had fought a strongly nationalist campaign. In office, President Tudjman excluded any possibility of 'a state within a state', and he did not come round to offering the Serb regions autonomy until July 1991. However local Serbs had, in the summer of 1990, already created no-go areas defended by barricades and unofficial police forces, and had proclaimed an 'autonomous region'. In 1991 Milosevic took the line that if Yugoslavia was divisible, so was Croatia (and later Bosnia). His long-run aim was probably a greater Serbia, incorporating all Serb areas plus some positions of strategic or economic importance. More immediately he assumed control of the already largely Serb Yugoslav army, and used its equipment (and locally recruited personnel) to make Serb residents impregnable in the areas of Croatia (and later Bosnia) that they had taken over. By August 1991 much of Croatia was in flames, with Serbs expanding their autonomous areas and, in November, taking Vukovar (in the east) after a bitter two-month siege; they also indulged in largely wanton shelling of coastal towns like Dubrovnik; the Croats retaliated by starving out isolated Yugoslav army barracks and taking their wepons.

At the time the UN's prestige stood very high. Given US backing, it could quite possibly have intervened effectively even from the air alone.[78]

---

[77] Crampton, *Balkans*, pp. 149–54, Chap. 14.

[78] Naval shelling, and the artillery bombardment of Dubrovnik, could certainly have been silenced; and the (rather incompetent) set-piece siege of Vukovar might well have been ended by sustained air strikes, backed by the prestige generated by the easy victory over a much larger Iraqi army in Kuwait.

But neither EC nor UN involvement went beyond the negotiation of ceasefires that were promptly disregarded. However, by late 1991 Serbia[79] had secured as much as it regarded as feasible, and indicated a readiness for a UN peace-keeping force. The fifteenth ceasefire, of January 1992, accordingly proved more lasting; Serbia insisted on its acceptance by the self-proclaimed autonomous regions, and the UN went ahead from April with the full deployment of a 10,000 strong 'Protection Force'. As Croatia had feared, its chief effect was to stabilise the country's existing partition; and the UN's inability to unblock the north–south highway led in January 1993 to a partially successful Croat offensive to do so.[80]

Bosnia, civil war (1992–5) and after

But if Croatia quietened down in 1992, a worse flare-up succeeded in Bosnia. In October 1991 its parliament had secretly debated sovereignty, prompting a Serb walk-out and warning that any secession from Yugoslavia would lead to war. Perhaps a crisis was inevitable; with Slovenia and Croatia's departure, 'Yugoslavia' would be dominated by Serbia, and neither the Bosnian Moslems nor Croats wished to remain in such a federation. But collapse was brought on by the EC's December 1991 invitation to the republics to get their applications for independence in quickly (above, p. 418). Having done the damage, the EC persuaded the Bosnians first to hold a referendum. So in March 1992 the Moslems and Croats voted overwhelmingly for independence; the Serbs abstained, their leader Radovan Karadzic declaring they would never accept it. Independence was nevertheless proclaimed. The EC then brokered an agreement to divide the country into ten provinces, of which all (bar the capital, Sarajevo) would, though containing important minorities from other groups, be designated as Serb, Moslem or Croat. But (Moslem) President Izetbegovic, an advocate of a unitary and non-racial state, reneged. Serb leaders then proclaimed the 'Serbian Republic of Bosnia-Hercegovina'.

---

[79] Officially the federation of Serbia and Montenegro continued to be known as Yugoslavia (or some variant thereof); but for practical purposes the federation was dominated by Serbia, and will be so called here. Montenegro joined in the initial bombardment of Dubrovnik etc., but from 1993 it sought increasingly to distance itself from Serbia, becoming independent in 2006.

[80] Crampton, *Balkans*, Chap. 14; *Keesing's*, 39279, 39471–2; the January 1993 fighting was ended by a May ceasefire brokered by Russia.

As forecast by UN representatives on the ground, fighting mounted rapidly. Each community fought for its own hand, the Moslems seeking to maintain control of the capital, Sarajevo, and as much of the rest of the country as they could, while demanding that Bosnia remain as a unified state. Serbs and Croats also sought to consolidate and extend their own areas, but with a view to later joining their ethnic parent states. Alignments depended on the locality – in early 1993 Moslems were fighting alongside Croats in Sarajevo, but against them in Mostar (where, on at least one occasion, they hired support from Serb artillery).[81] It is, perhaps, surprising that Croatia and Serbia did not simply agree to partition Bosnia between themselves, as President Tudjman kept advocating.[82] But Milosevic probably felt actual annexations would be too risky in the light of the international community's attachment to existing state borders and of the UN sanctions already imposed on Serbia. He therefore generally aimed at a settlement like that agreed for Croatia in 1992.

In March 1992 the EC had suggested the division of Bosnia into ethnic provinces, In early 1993 UN and EC mediators reworked this as the 'Vance–Owen' plan for ten cantons, plus a Moslem–Serb–Croat executive operating by consensus. Both the Bosnian Croats and President Izetbegovic were prepared to accept this. In April Serbia itself (following pressure from the Orthodox countries closest to it, Greece and Russia) advised the Bosnian Serbs to agree. But they now controlled 70 per cent of Bosnia, and would not make the territorial concessions required; the proposals were overwhelmingly defeated in a Bosnian Serb referendum. Later that year it was Izetbegovic who rejected a plan for a three-part division of Bosnia (with a weak central executive). Then in mid-1994 another international effort was made, this time on the basis of a 51:49 per cent division between a Moslem–Croat confederation and the Bosnian Serbs. Again these were pressed from all sides, including Serbia, to accept; and again they refused in a referendum.[83]

So the war continued, aimed chiefly at the acquisition of territory and, where necessary, its 'ethnic cleansing', by the deportation or killing of the unwanted groups or, more usually, by intimidating them into flight in a

---

[81] Crampton, *Balkans*, p. 258. There were also cases of Serb–Croat collaboration, and of fighting between the Moslem government and a dissident Moslem entrepreneur in Bihac.

[82] Laura Silber and Allan Little, *The Death of Yugoslavia* (1995) pp. 235, 324, 340.

[83] Crampton, *Balkans*, pp. 260–1; *Keesing's*, 39517, 40110–12, 40154, 1994 R104, 1995 R100.

process accompanied by deliberate rape and the destruction of buildings symbolising the 'other' (most famously of the Turkish bridge at Mostar). All sides were guilty; but the Bosnian Serbs (being militarily the strongest) had the most scope, and their crimes were the most widely reported. Since UN peace-keepers in Croatia had been based in Bosnia, UNPROFOR had been present from the outset. It delivered humanitarian aid (without which the besieged capital, Sarajevo, would not have survived), neutralised (or, in the case of the hills commanding Sarajevo, imposed arms limits on) some strategic territories, and negotiated innumerable local deals and disengagements. The UN also cast its prestige over half a dozen towns by declaring them 'safe areas'. Very occasionally, too, it staged limited coercive actions, in 1994 calling in NATO air strikes (the first shots the alliance had ever fired in anger). But essentially it saw its mission as 'peace-keeping, rather than 'peace-enforcing'.

More could certainly have been done. Following Serb air attacks, all Bosnia was made a 'no-fly' zone; this could readily have been enforced by NATO, but was not. Similarly UN sanctions[84] supposedly interdicted all fuel supplies and river traffic to Serbia; since Serbia was a land-locked state that – unlike Japan in 1941 – was in no military position to break such a blockade, this too could have been enforced; and without Serbian supplies the Bosnian (and Croatian) Serbs could not long have continued. But though the sanctions were sufficient to influence Milosevic's behaviour (and to generate massive smuggling from which leading political and criminal figures grew rich), they were not pushed to anything like Serbia's breaking point. One constraint was the fear of transforming Russia, which (like Greece) identified strongly with Orthodox Serbia, from a moderately helpful diplomatic partner to an outright supplier, or even (as in 1914) backer, of the Serbs. Another was the fear that drastic UN action would spread the conflict, whereas most major powers preferred to 'contain' it to Bosnia, while also trying to mitigate its effects there.[85] Lastly Britain and France, UNPROFOR's major contributors, feared that, if seriously threatened or attacked, the Bosnian Serbs would seize their troops on the ground as hostages – as indeed they did, though only briefly, in May–June 1995.

The USA was unhappy with such thinking. It saw the UN embargo on arms deliveries to the area as benefiting the Bosnian and Croatian Serbs, who had been well supplied from the Yugoslav army, against the Bosnian and Croat governments, which had to build up forces from scratch.

[84] S.C. Res. 787, 820.
[85] *Keesing's*, 39469, 39517.

Americans came to favour a policy of 'Lift [the embargo] and strike [the Bosnian Serbs]', though only from the air. But US influence was reduced, partly by the Clinton administration's early diplomatic introversion, partly by US reluctance (especially after its precipitate departure from Somalia)[86] to commit troops on the ground – 'we do deserts [like Iraq–Kuwait],' explained Chief of Staff Colin Powell, 'we don't do mountains'. In March 1994, however, the USA managed to broker a confederation between the Bosnian Moslems and Croats, which freed them both to concentrate on the Serbs. It seems too that the US had for some time been quietly supplying arms both to Croatia and to the Bosnian government, and in December 1994 it formally renounced the UN arms embargo. The 1994–5 winter saw a ceasefire, but in the spring of 1995 both the Croatian and the Bosnian governments appeared increasingly confident. That summer UN forces regrouped from a diffuse and vulnerable peace-keeping to a war-fighting posture. In July Bosnian Serbs seized the UN 'safe area' of Srebenica, then killed some 8,000 male prisoners of military age. This was not only a crime but a blunder; the UN's prestige was shattered, and it transferred control over miltary operations to NATO. In August a major Croatian offensive overran the Serb enclave of Krajina, 152,000 of whose inhabitants fled. Then on 28 August Serbs gratuitously shelled a Sarajevo market. This triggered serious NATO bombing of Bosnian Serb artillery and communications; without these, Serb forces wilted in the face of offensives by what were by now much strengthened Croatian and Bosnian armies.

Against this background negotiations started, a ceasefire was agreed in October, and in November the parties met on an air base in Dayton, Ohio, where settlements were worked out under heavy US pressure. A new UN Transitional Administration would preside over the return to Croatia of Eastern Slavonia (which it had lost in 1991–2). Bosnia would acquire a confederal central government; but it would be essentially split, on a 51:49 per cent basis, between the Moslem–Croat confederation and the 'Serb Republic', with special arrangements for the corridors linking the component parts of that Republic to each other and to Serbia proper. The whole was to be overseen by a proconsular 'High Representative', backed by a UN-authorised Implementation Force of, initially, 64,000. To provide reassurance to the Serbs (and to Russia itself), this contained a Russian

---

[86] In December 1992 the US sent troops into Somalia to enable the UN to deliver famine relief and sort out the anarchic clan warfare. In October 1993 18 US soldiers were killed, and President Clinton ordered the departure of all US forces within six months.

contingent; but it was NATO-led, with 20,000 US troops to boost its credibility. Its deployment in December 1995 ended a war that is thought to have cost 200,000 lives.[87]

Since then Bosnia has been quiet, and the tutelary foreign military presence steadily reduced – to 7,000 by 2004. But despite $5 billion in aid since 1995, and some economic recovery after 2000, unemployment then stood at 40 per cent. There had been significant successes: half the wartime refugees had returned to their former areas; and the much contested town of Brcko (commanding the corridor between Serbia and the Bosnian Serb heartland) has flourished since 1999 as a free-trade multi-ethnic local entity. A common currency had been adopted, and several other reforms forced through – but chiefly by successive High Representatives, who freely exercised their powers of dismissing both officials and elected politicians. There have been moves towards decolonisation; the High Representative announced that in 2007, though he would continue to function as EU Special Representative, he would close his office in Sarajevo, leaving Bosnia's elected representatives 'in charge'. Earlier in 2006, however, the Bosnian parliament had blocked a new, centralising, constitution drawn up under US and EU pressure; political alignments remain centred within the three ethnic groups; and in May 2006 the Serb Republic's president declared that Montenegro's recent referendum vote for independence (from its 'Yugoslav' federation with Serbia) constituted a possible model for his own polity.[88]

Kosovo 1998–9; Macedonia 2001

When in December 1991 the EU invited the Yugoslav republics to apply for recognition as independent states, it also received bids from the *de facto* autonomous Serb Krajina (within Croatia) and from an Albanian shadow government of Kosovo (within Serbia). Both were turned down. Until 1998 the international community was not prepared to interfere within what Milosevic had in July 1989 converted into the unitary republic of Serbia. Following that takeover, Albanian members of the former Kosovo assembly had proclaimed a 'Republic of Kosovo'. Kosovo Albanians then established a shadow state, supported by emigré donations; in 1992 they managed to hold elections, and Ibrahim Rugova

[87] Crampton, *Balkans*, Chap. 14.
[88] ibid. pp. 286–9; *Annual Register*, 2004, pp. 96–8; *Keesing's*, 47151, 47332–3; Bosnian Institute, *Bosnia Report*, new series 51–2 (April–June 2006).

became its president. He sought the diplomatic intervention of foreign powers, but restricted himself to non-violence and did not directly confront Belgrade. By 1997 he appeared to have achieved nothing; and in 1998 there appeared a 'Kosovo Liberation Army' (KLA), equipped with arms acquired during Albania's 1997 meltdown.[89] Whereas Rugova had merely appealed for external intervention, the KLA sought to compel it – by the nineteenth-century Balkan strategy of staging murders and insurrections in order to trigger repression on a scale the international community could not ignore. It succeeded. The killing of Serb policemen in February 1998 led to more extensive reprisals, then to insurrection, and, from May to September, to Serb repression on a scale that generated some 300,000 internal refugees. The United Nations started to take note in March. In September it requested an immediate ceasefire and negotiations, a demand reinforced by a NATO warning; and Milosevic was induced to limit his forces in Kosovo and permit the deployment of OSCE monitors.

In January 1999 45 Albanian corpses were found, with telephone intercepts linking their killing to Belgrade. Russia had made it clear that it would veto forceful UN intervention, but US, British and French leaders were determined not to replicate their early inaction over Bosnia. They therefore stepped outside formal international law, and, acting through NATO, summoned the parties to Paris. There, after lengthy negotiations (since the KLA was nearly as stubborn as Belgrade), they dictated terms: the KLA should disarm, but Kosovo's future should in three years' time be determined by a referendum (whose outcome was obvious). Serbia rejected this, NATO bombing began on 24 March, and Serbia countered with a probably pre-planned mass expulsion of Albanians from Kosovo. Militarily NATO's bombing was not a great success, since it was conducted from a safely high altitude and since Serbian forces in Kosovo were well camouflaged. So, as time progressed, the bombing spread increasingly to economically and politically important targets around Belgrade; and, despite US reluctance to incurr casualties, NATO began apparent preparations for a ground invasion. This alarmed both Russia and Milosevic; and following Russian (and Finnish) mediation, Milosevic pulled his forces out of Kosovo in early June.

---

[89] The collapse of widely patronised pyramid 'investment' ramps provoked a revolt against the dictatorial (if pro-Western) Albanian regime, during which crowds looted military stores. Order was re-established by a new government, a largely Italian UN force, and new elections – Crampton, *Balkans*, pp. 306–7.

They were replaced by a UN-blessed, but largely NATO, K-FOR; this had Russian participation,[90] but Russia was not accorded an occupation sector. Such a sector would have reassured the Kosovan Serbs, and might have led to the repartition of the province into an Albanian majority area and a small Serb district. As it was, the Serbs (where they did not leave) huddled into ghettoes that K-FOR has sought, not entirely successfully, to protect from harrassment. Meanwhile elections were held, and Rugova returned to office. But Kosovo was overseen by a UN Interim Adminis-tration, and the fiction was kept up that it was still a province of Serbia. Negotiations started in 2006 for a final settlement, which, the vast majority of Kosovans insist, can only be independence.[91]

There were fears that the troubles in Kosovo would spread to dest-abilise the whole region. In 2000 an attempt was made to replicate the KLA's strategy in the largely Albanian Presevo valley, within Serbia proper but bordering on Kosovo. It drew little foreign sympathy, and Serbia was allowed to increase its forces there. Then in 2001 KLA units from Kosovo began to operate in Macedonia, where a crisis had developed between the Slav majority and the large Albanian minority. Fear of ethnic troubles had lead to the (unusual) precautionary stationing in Macedonia of UN peace-keepers in 1992; but when, hoping for an investment bonanza, Macedonia recognised Taiwan, China vetoed their continuation beyond early 1999. Fortunately NATO forces were present, initially to handle Kosovan refugees and then as a logistic link with Kosovo. In 2001 they acted to head off conflict within Macedonia, and help with disarmament and polit-ical reforms to better incorporate its Albanian minority. The crisis was thus safely surmounted. But Macedonia remains potentially fragile; and major trouble there could conceivably draw in Bugaria and/or Greece.[92]

Ex-Yugoslavia and Albania

Yugoslavia has thus broken into six states, to which Kosovo will prob-ably soon be added. Their fortunes have been very different. Slovenia

---

[90] As K-FOR moved in, Russian tanks rushed from Bosnia to occupy Pristina's airfield. The local British commander would not oppose them, saying he had no wish to start World War III. But he arranged that they should be entirely dependent on British forces for food, a condition Russia could not remedy by air supply since Romania and Bulgaria barred overflights.

[91] Crampton, *Balkans*, pp. 241, 270–7.

[92] ibid. pp. 276, 297–8; Chris Patten, *Not Quite the Diplomat* (2006 edn) pp. 174–5.

encountered some difficulties with an Italy that still resented its loss of Istria and sought compensation for the 1945 refugees and expellees. But this was overcome in 1995, and Slovenia moved smoothly to EU and (in 2007) eurozone membership. The second richest Yugoslav republic had been Croatia. It was necessarily preoccupied with its internal ethnic problems until 1995, and even thereafter President Tudjman's nationalist regime did not appeal to the EU. He died in 1999, and the election of a social-democrat-led coalition in 2000 brought an early visit from the President of the EU Commission. But the conclusion of a 'Stabilisation and Association Agreement', the first step on the road to negotiations for EU membership, was stalled by Croatia's refusal, or inability, to send its 1995 war hero, General Gotovina, to The Hague for trial by the International Criminal Tribunal for the Former Yugoslavia. In 2003 President Tudjman's party recovered office, but under a reform leader who promised to steer Croatia towards Europe; in 2004 Gotovina was arrested, and the EU recognised Croatia as a candidate country. Economically Croatia is gaining, like Spain a generation earlier, from tourism and the diffusion of north european holiday homes along the coast. It should be well able to cope with the demands of EU membership; but this may be delayed by the widespread feeling that the Community has already expanded far enough.[93] Another country well placed to benefit from the tourist boom is Montenegro. It was internally divided, partly by region, on whether or not to leave the 'Yugoslav' federation with Serbia; but one of the motives for so doing was to clear the way for an approach to 'Europe' – to facilitate which it adopted the DM as the national currency. One obstacle, however, is widespread involvement in smuggling, in part the result of the 1990s UN sanctions imposed on it as a part of 'Yugoslavia'.[94]

In Serbia Milosevic had risen by exploiting nationalist feeling. By 1995 his support for Serbs outside the republic had proved disastrous, and in 1999 he lost Kosovo. The break-up of Yugoslavia and UN sanctions had also inflicted heavy economic blows. So it is not surprising that he became unpopular. The EU supported his opponents, both with money and by supplying oil to opposition areas. In September–October 2000 Milosevic's apparent fudging of votes in the presidential election led to massive demonstrations, encouraged also from outside the country, and eventually

---

[93] Crampton, *Balkans*, pp. 291–2; *Annual Register*, 2000, p. 121; 2003, pp. 115–17; 2004, p. 99.

[94] Patten also mentions Russian investors, not of 'the sort . . . who would get a seal of approval from Transparency International' – *Not Quite the Diplomat*, p. 172.

to occupation of the parliament buildings, proclamation of his rival as President, and Milosevic's retreat to his own compound. From there he was despatched to The Hague in June 2001; next day a donors' conference pledged $1.3 billion aid. Milosevic's deportation had, however, been very much the work of Serbia's dynamic but controversial Prime Minister, Zoran Djindjic, who was assassinated in 2003 (possibly by organised crime); and the despatch of other indicted war criminals to The Hague (on which both the US and the EU insist) remains a major stumbling block. In 2006 it seemed as if Serbia was at last about to apprehend Mladic, the Bosnian Serb commander at Srebenica. When it did not, the EU suspended talks on a Serbian 'Stabilisation and Association Agreement'.[95]

Serbia's economy, though, is presumably no less capable of adapting to EU membership than Bulgaria's. This is not obviously so for Bosnia, Kosovo and Macedonia. All three currently also have internal political problems that the EU would be reluctant to take on board. Such ethnic problems are less marked in Albania, but it has others. In Patten's words:

organised crime . . . is probably – apart from the need to escape from history – the greatest problem facing the whole region. The Balkan countries pretend to us that they are tackling it energetically; and we sometimes pretend that we believe them. We don't. The problem is particularly bad in Albania, where criminal gangs seem to have evolved naturally out of the old clan system.[96]

So, while 'joining Europe' remains the prevailing aspiration in ex-Yugoslavia and Albania, as elsewhere in Eastern Europe, problems abound on both sides. The alternative, however, is probably a growth of the peoples' disillusion 'with the European aspirations of their leaders', leading to a reversion to 'the closed societies and dirigiste economies' – and perhaps the ethnic violence – of the past.[97]

---

[95] Crampton, *Balkans*, pp. 280–3; Patten, *Not Quite the Diplomat*, pp. 171–2; Bosnian Institute, *Bosnia Report*, April–July 2006.

[96] *Not Quite the Diplomat*, p. 173, also p. 171.

[97] Crampton, *Balkans*, pp. 343–4.

PART 4

Conclusion

CHAPTER 16

Perspectives on the Cold War and its aftermath

It seems unexceptionable to conclude that the Cold War resulted from an admixture of ideology and geopolitics, both being necessary prerequisites. Had Stalin, after 1945, confined himself to the borders of the USSR (even as enlarged by the war) but continued to rule within them in his evil pre-war style, he would probably not have been perceived as a major threat; and it is most unlikely that the USA would have mobilised itself (through the 'long telegram', Truman Doctrine, Marshall Aid, and so on) to provide sustained, expensive, and burdensome leadership to a 'Free World' coalition – or that it would have been pressed to assume such a role.[1] It would, however, presumably have concluded with the Soviet Union, and the rest of the victorious alliance, the treaties of long-term guarantee against renewed German or Japanese aggression that it offered in 1945–6 – and, in contrast to 1920, probably have ratified them. The United States would still have disliked communism intensely, and there might have been an internal Red Scare reminiscent of the early 1920s. But Soviet ideology alone, had it been effectively confined to the USSR as in the inter-war period, would not have generated the Cold War as we know it. The war, however, had shattered the geopolitical constellation that had kept the Soviet Union and its purportedly universal ideology so constrained; Soviet and communist advance (the two being, in the Europe of the 1940s, initially indistinguishable) met United States containment. Here one can see the consequences of the 'power vacuum' in Central Europe created by the defeat of Germany. Although the USA was certainly averse (as it showed in two World Wars) to the dominance of the continent

---

[1] cf. Geir Lundestad, 'Empire by Invitation? The United States and Western Europe, 1945–1952', *Journal of Peace Research*, xxiii (1986) pp. 263–77.

by a Power it distrusted, had events in the later 1930s led instead to an Anglo-French coalition toppling the Fascist powers and restoring the imbalance of the 1920s, it would almost certainly have applauded. The world would then have continued safe for an 'isolationist' USA; and it is most unlikely that the United States' theoretical anti-imperialism would have brought serious conflict with the 'liberal' empires of Britain and France, any more than it had done earlier. Both ideological and geopolitical considerations, then, featured in the first phases of the Cold War.

As time went on, the USSR came, especially under Brezhnev, to seem an increasingly 'normal', even conservative, state, paying no more than lip service to 'communism' at home, and behaving like a restrained and cautious Great Power abroad. As far as Europe was concerned, this was probably true – Brezhnev may well have anticipated no change for the forseeable future; and even in the Middle East he was strongly attracted to a settlement to be jointly imposed by the two superpowers. However, Dobrynin says, 'his credo was based on the traditional "Marxist-Leninist class approach" to foreign policy, which cast even peaceful relations into a mould of confrontation', while the 'second man in the Politburo, Mikhail Suslov . . . was convinced that all struggle in the Third World had an ideological basis: imperialism against communism and socialism. Under the slogan of solidarity, he . . . managed to involve the Politburo in many Third World adventures.'[2] Brezhnev seems never to have wavered in his commitment to Soviet military build-up, and when, in his later years, opportunities occurred in the Third World, he took them and justified the process by a Khruschevian invocation of *competitive* 'peaceful coexistence' and the ineluctable advance of socialism. US anti-communists picked up these developments and used them to discredit detente (which they had already done much to damage by refusing the USSR 'most favoured nation' trade status, ostensibly on human rights grounds). So the stage was set for the 'Second Cold War' of the early 1980s. There then followed a quite unexpected denouement: Gorbachev decided to transform the Soviet Union and its international posture. This meant, in the first place, ending its antagonistic stance towards the United States (and the 'West' generally); then reducing defence expenditure and switching military doctrine from the offensive to the defensive; and finally accepting

[2] Soviet leaders 'often spoke the language of ideology even when conversing among themselves, falling into the language of the official newspapers' (Anatoly Dobrynin, *In Confidence. Moscow's Ambassador to America's Six Cold War Presidents (1962–86)* (New York, 1995) pp. 372, 403–4, 408, 474).

the collapse of communism in Eastern Europe, a remarkable exercise in self-abnegation to which the USSR could certainly not have been compelled. This collapse ended the adversary relationship of East and West (as was formally recognised in the 1990 Charter of Paris). In 1991, in combination with Gorbachev's internal reforms, it also destroyed Soviet communism, the unity of the USSR, and his own domestic position. In these transformations, ideological shifts within the Soviet Union played the primary role, though of course they had (in Soviet economic retardation) an important non-ideological cause, and they led to major geopolitical consequences.

It is possible to sketch other interpretations of the end of the Cold War. One would be the fairy story: the evil empire vanished, and everybody lived happily ever after. This vision was explicitly invoked by the Prague demonstrations that brought down communist rule in the 1989 'velvet revolution'.[3] It was widely shared at the time in both Eastern Europe and the Soviet Union. The West would extend massive aid, and so soon help to create in the rest of Europe prosperous free-market democracies. Alas, this was too simple. There was significant Western assistance,[4] but not on a Marshall Aid scale. Nor was the creation either of market economies or of stable and secure democracies easy, though the EU's 2004 expansion represented the judgement that both had been substantially achieved across most of Eastern Europe.

Another version of the fairy story was that the West's triumph reflected, at least in ideological terms, the 'end of history', leaving capitalism, liberalism and democracy supreme. But it soon became apparent that 'globalisation' had its critics, who rioted so destructively during the 1999 Seattle G7 summit and elsewhere that its 2001 Genoa sequel took place only in a wired-off area forcibly defended by 20,000 policemen. The demonstrators' specific counter-culture was, no doubt, a relatively small one; but fear of 'globalisation' spread much more widely, playing, for instance, a major role in French politics in 2005–7.

Far more important, however, was the rise of religious militancy, depicted in the 1990s by Samuel Huntington as a major (though by no means the only) factor in the *Clash of Civilizations* that he pessimistically anticipated. Many of its manifestations lay quite outside the Cold

---

[3] The Observer, *Tearing Down the Curtain: The People's Revolution in Eastern Europe* (1990) p. 111.

[4] Symbolically, the food stockpiled in West Berlin as insurance against a second blockade was sent east to help the USSR.

War context; but it had contributed to the unravelling of Soviet power both in Poland (where it was a major component of Solidarity) and in Afghanistan, where, after the 1978 coup, resistance to communism took a largely Islamic form, more especially among the *jihadi* fighters who flowed in from abroad to participate. On leaving Afghanistan, many of these either continued their struggle in other global hot-spots (like Kashmir, Chechnya and Bosnia) or attempted to convert their own homelands into true polities uncontaminated by religious backsliding, corruption and Western secularism. In the 1990s it was such manifestations of militant Islam that chiefly attracted attention, notably the decade-long Algerian civil war that followed the 1992 cancellation of elections that the Islamic Salvation Front was poised to win; military rule eventually prevailed (with logistic help from France) and restored elections, but not before terrible atrocities on both sides. Long before then, however, *jihadi* sights had been set on the United States. US aid had been welcome in the struggle against the USSR in Afghanistan; but it was natural to view the USA as another 'Satan', as, indeed, Ayatollah Khomeini of Iran had already termed it. For a wealthy Saudi associated with the Afghan resistance, Osama bin Laden, the tipping point came in 1990, when 'infidel' US troops were deployed on the sacred soil of the Arabian peninsula to drive Saddam Hussein out of Kuwait. Bin Laden converted what had originally been a network to recruit and support Arab *jihadis* in Afghanistan into one devoted, as he announced in 1998, to attacks on the Americans, who had declared war on 'Allah, His Prophet, and Muslims'.[5]

Initial plans were not very successful, but on 9/11 2001 hijacked airliners were flown into the World Trade Center and the Pentagon, killing about 3,000 people in the worst peacetime attack on the USA since Pearl Harbor. The US response, the 'War on Terror', was vigorous. President George W. Bush first overthrew the Taliban regime in Afghanistan that had accorded bin Laden protection and facilities, then, more controversially, Saddam Hussein. The hope was that the subsequent reform of Iraq would touch off a transformation of the Arab world on the basis of Western democracy, and so, since democracies do not fight each other,[6]

---

[5] Steve Coll, *Ghost Wars. The Secret History of the CIA, Afghanistan, and bin Laden, from the Soviet Invasion to September 10, 2001* (New York, 2004) pp. 204, 222–3, 380–1.

[6] Statistically this is so (though much depends on the definition of 'democracy' and/or of 'consolidated' or 'mature' democracy). Explanations vary; but 'democratic peace theory' had influenced the Clinton as well as the Bush administration.

usher in an era of real peace in the Middle East. The approach was strongly influenced by 'neo-conservative' ideas; it would (in 2006) seem to have backfired, weakening the international standing of the United States, and strengthening radical Islam (both Sunni and Shia) in and beyond the Middle East.

If, then, the outcome of the Cold War did not resolve all ideological contention, one might at least hope that it would calm many of the world's trouble spots, since local contests like those between Arabs and Israelis or Ethiopians and Somalis had so often been caught up into the transcendent East–West rivalry. To an extent this proved the case. In Indo-China it led to an end of hostilities, and at least a degree of power-sharing, in Cambodia; and Vietnam, Laos and Cambodia have since joined the regional association, ASEAN, that they once saw as crypto-imperialist. In southern Africa, US–Soviet collaboration delivered a South African withdrawal from, and settlement in, Namibia; and the ending of communism was one of the factors that emboldened De Klerk to risk negotiating the transition to majority rule in South Africa itself. But the settlement arranged for Angola fell apart, and despite the changed international constellation civil war continued for a further decade. In Central America, seen in the early 1980s as the Cold War's latest theatre of competition, Soviet disinterest later in the decade facilitated a succession of locally negotiated settlements; but it did not end the US–Cuban Cold War. More generally, the greater collaboration among the Permanent Members of the UN Security Council that began in 1986 eased the constraint of Cold War vetoes, and freed the UN to embark on a period of unprecedented activism that some hailed in the early 1990s as a 'new international order'; but in 1993–4 deplorable failures in Somalia and Rwanda showed that hopes had been pitched far too high. In some ways, indeed, the ending of the Cold War made matters worse. For although the break-up of the USSR was conducted remarkably smoothly and with considerable Russian restraint, it did occasion a number of post-imperial conflicts, notably Armenian–Azerbaijani war, civil war in Tadjikistan and struggles for independence in Chechnya (the two latter with Islamist participation).[7] It may be, too, that had the Cold War still persisted in 1996–7, France and Belgium would again have rescued Mobutu's tottering government in Zaire (as they had done before); in itself Mobutu's fall should have been

---

[7] The break-up of Yugoslavia, a function of the collapse of communism though not directly of the end of the Cold War, also brought wars of succession.

a blessing, but it proved the prelude to a 1998–2002 round of fighting, massacres and external interventions, with casualties, on some calculations, running well into the millions. Overall it seems that both the number of 'conflicts' worldwide, and the 'battle-deaths' they entailed, fell significantly in the 1990s.[8] But the ending of the Cold War left intact other cleavages like the Indo-Pakistani quarrel over Kashmir, or, as with the Arab–Israeli dispute, ameliorated but did not resolve them.

The resultant world contained many traditional elements – small states quite as much as great readily resorted to force. However, it was marked by an unfamiliar distribution of power. There have quite often been states like China or the Roman empire that had no real rivals in their own areas. Distance, though, has now shrunk; and no state has ever been so globally pre-eminent – militarily, economically, and in many dimensions of 'soft power' – as the USA in the decade after the USSR's collapse. But the implications for the international system were not obvious. With the Cold War ended and no threats apparent, the United States was tempted to turn inward: the feeling that President Bush had devoted too much attention to 'Athens, Greece' and not enough to 'Athens, Georgia' was one of the factors that cost him re-election; and of President Clinton's first Secretary of State, the jibe ran abroad that such-and-such a mishap 'could never have happened if Warren Christopher had been alive'. By 1995 Washington was showing increasing leadership, notably in bringing about the 'Dayton, Ohio' settlement of the Bosnian civil war, and in the subsequent 1999 driving of Serbian rule out of Kosovo. But other initiatives (like Clinton's attempts to broker a final Israeli–Palestinian settlement between Barak and Arafat) ran into the sands. President George W. Bush, in his turn, at

---

[8] Andrew Mack, *Human Security Report 2005* (www.humansecurityreport.org/info/) esp. pp. 8–9, Overview, and Parts 1, 5. Mack draws on several sources, but chiefly the highly respected Uppsala University-International Peace Research Institute, Oslo Uppsala/PRIO dataset (www.prio.no/cscw/cross/battledeaths), described in Lacina and Gleditsch, 'A New Dataset of Battle Deaths', *European Journal of Population*, 21 (2005). See also the revised 'Correlates of war' data, 1816–1997 (v.3.0) – http:cow2.la.psu.edu – described by Meredith Reid Sarkees, 'The Correlates of War Data on War: an update to 1997', *Conflict Management and Peace Research*, 18 (2000) pp. 123–44, and Vaughan Lowe, Adam Roberts, Jennifer Welsh, and Dominik Zaum (eds), *The UN Security Council and War* (Oxford, 2008), Appendix 7. 'Battle-deaths' unfortunately exclude massacres, and also the excess deaths from disease, malnourishment, displacement and economic breakdown attributable to conflicts (which account for the overwhelming majority of fatalities attributable to conflicts like the 1998–2002 Congo civil war).

first pulled back. However, shocked by the 9/11 attack, he pushed aside restraints to sort out what he saw as the Middle Eastern mess unilaterally, albeit buttressed by a supporting 'coalition of the willing'. By 2006 the attempt had gone badly wrong, and the USA seemed to be moving back towards disengagement and introspection. Global pre-eminence does not translate into world empire.

The Cold War had tended to funnel international politics into a bipolar mould, both in reality and, still more, in scholars' perceptions. Although its ending highlighted US strength (the magnitude of which had often been underestimated), by relaxing the previous East–West focus it also widened the agenda and so made international politics more multilateral. 'Balance of power' theory would postulate the emergence of a coalition to contain the United States, but of this there are only faint stirrings: a gathering centred on Chavez's Venezuela and Castro's Cuba; a precautionary Sino-Russian rapprochement; and ad hoc groupings to block the USA on particular issues, notably that of France, Germany and Russia in 2003 to deny it direct UN authorisation to invade Iraq. It would be surprising if things were to change much in the near future. Equally the international hierarchy will alter considerably in the medium term. There are pitfalls in projecting existing trends forward – 'X,' the jibe goes, 'is the country of the future, and always will be.' But the 'Brics', China, India, probably Brazil, and perhaps Russia despite its adverse demography, seem likely to join the USA, the EU, and an ageing Japan as the world's major economies. Naturally there are queries: will the EU prove sufficiently coherent to translate its size and wealth into power; is China less stable than it looks; and how will these states relate to the world around them, much of which is also developing fast? But, above all, may we look forward to a jostling but relatively amiable concert of these Powers (as in early nineteenth-century Europe), or to the mounting of a challenge by the rising Power, probably China, to the old US hegemon, a challenge that could potentially return the world to a bipolar rivalry more reminiscent of the Cold War?

Guide to further reading

(place of publication London, unless otherwise specified)

Since this book's first edition in 1994, there have been two major developments, the far greater availability of Soviet-bloc material (of which more below) and the advent of the Internet. Together with finding aids and search engines, the Internet makes it far easier to locate information, especially but not exclusively on more recent events; it has also facilitated the placing of material in the public domain in the form of document collections and 'electronic briefing books'. It has not replaced books and libraries; but it has certainly helped to spread and even up access to knowledge.

That said, much remains constant. Our sources still have a bias towards the United States: not only has the USA been the most important single actor in international affairs since 1945, but it has also led the way in the release and publication of historical documents. Scholars have tended to give it if anything disproportionate attention, partly for these reasons, partly (in some cases) from sheer insularity, and partly because, where space is short, it is easier to structure one's writing round an American, or a 'bipolar' USA–USSR, than around a multilateral, framework. There is also the case of national perspectives. Most scholars underplay the appreciable Canadian contribution to international diplomacy in the first two post-war decades; some Canadians err in the opposite direction; the result is a distinctive Canadian historiography. The same is true, to a lesser extent, in connection with Britain and France.

Post-war, like earlier, historiography has proceeded on the basis of a voluminous public record (of official documents and statements, parliamentary debates, press releases and comment, and the like). This is shaped and built on by memoirs, biographies, 'instant histories' (often by able and well-informed journalists), and comment and analysis by students of the contemporary scene. Coverage can be very rapid: German reunification in 1989–90 was recounted (from his diaries) by Chancellor Kohl's aide Horst Teltschik in *329 Tage: Innenansichten der Einigung* (Berlin, 1991), and by two senior officials, Philip Zelikow and Condoleeza Rice, who had worked for it on the US National Security Council, in *Germany Unified and Europe Transformed: a study in statecraft* (Cambridge, Mass., 1995). Such studies can now often rest on material retrieved or discovered from various governments, especially that of the USA, under 'Freedom of Information' legislation. But greater scholarly depth comes when the documents shaping and recording government deliberations and decisions become generally available. This takes much longer. The UK (whose archives are among the better organisaed and more accessible) operates a 30-year rule (with derogations), which means that the frontier of classic document-based history now lies in the 1970s, with what one might term cultivated territory not extending quite so far. This is broadly true also of the USA: my first edition wrote that 'study of the Truman and Eisenhower administrations is qualitatively different from that of their successors'; by now the frontier has advanced through the 1960s and into the Nixon era.

During the Cold War itself, the communist bloc lay at the opposite extreme, with archives closed and most memoirs uninformative – apart from Khrushchev's taped reminiscences, unofficially published in the West. With the collapse of communism, memoirs became much more informative, and there was an opening of the Moscow archives, but not an orderly one. Crucial material was transferred to the closed Presidential Archive, and access to other documents was influenced or constrained by contacts, politics, and shortage of official resources (though this last could sometimes be overcome by contributions of money or equipment). Nevertheless, archive-based research has extended to the end of the Khrushchev era, and in some cases beyond;[1] and in the 1990s there seemed to be something of a re-run of early Sino-Soviet frictions with archive-based Russian historians criticising Chinese narratives stemming either from reminiscences or from privileged and unattributable work among closed documents.[2]

---

[1] Ilya Gaiduk's *The Soviet Union and the Vietnam War* (Chicago, 1996) pp. xi–xvi explains how he benefited from what proved to be a temporary opening of many, though not all, of the relevant documents.

[2] Though Chinese archives remain far more firmly closed than Russian, Dong Wang recently consulted, in the Jiangsu Provincial Archives (Nanjing), both secret briefings and copies of numerous high-level documents sent from the centre (*The Quarreling Brothers: New Chinese Archives and a Reappraisal of the Sino-Soviet Split, 1959–1962*, Cold War International History Project Working Paper no. 49 [February 2006]). Also, there have been official publications of writings and correspondence by top Chinese leaders.

There was, too, another side to Moscow's unconventional practices, that of sporadic but sometimes remarkable disclosures. President Yeltsin accompanied his early official visits by turning over to his hosts material on Stalin's role in the Korean War and on the 1956 and 1968 Soviet interventions in Hungary and Czechoslovakia. Subsequently undertakings like the 'Carter–Brezhnev Project' secured the declassification of documents like the 1978–9 Soviet deliberations over Afghanistan that would certainly have been covered by a conventional 30-year rule. This process, indeed, has extended right up to the end of the Cold War with the publication of important Politburo papers and minutes from the Gorbachev era,[3] supplemented by, for instance, the diary notes and running comments of Gorbachev's aide Anatoly Chernyaev (in *My Six Years with Gorbachev* [College Park, Pennsylvania, 2000]). Moreover, many former Cold War figures, Russian as well as American, happily talked to interviewers and relived their experiences at the many historical conferences organised during the 1990s.[4]

There have, too, been major leaks. The originally mainstream, but increasingly disillusioned, General Dmitri Volkogonov made a number of disclosures in his historical writings; and in 1996, after his death, his extensive documentary collection was transferred to the Library of Congress. More dramatically, in 1992 a former KGB archivist, Vasili Mitrokhin, walked into the British embassy in a Baltic state and arranged to defect, bringing with him an extraordinary run of transcripts, which supplement the copious insights of the long-time Soviet–British double agent Oleg Gordievsky. We may therefore know as much about the KGB in the mid-1970s to mid-1980s as we do (from the leaked Congressional Church Committee inquiry) of the CIA in the 1960s and early 1970s. Lastly, regime change has made available a mass of material on Soviet relations with, and briefings of, East European leaders. Perhaps it is too much to say that 'We now know'. But we certainly know far more than we used to. Substantial cooperative histories are emerging on the basis of this new important material. Even so, for non-communists, the tone and focus of Cold War historiography has probably been less changed than was that of

---

[3] The Gorbachev Foundation Archive (in Moscow) also makes available 'the documents donated by the Gorbachev family and their closest associates . . . continuously updated through copying the most relevant documents, held in other collections, such as Russia's state archives, archives across the CIS states, presidential archives in various countries . . . etc.'

[4] Such interviews underlay the BBC's impressive 1995 television series, *Messengers from Moscow*.

inter-war history (previously centred on the captured German documents) by the early 1970s opening of the relevant British archives.

For documents always in the public domain, one convenient source is the series of *Documents on International Affairs* (nearly one volume for each year down to 1963) produced for the Royal Institute of International Affairs; they were accompanied by a companion series, *Survey of International Affairs*. Another annual commentary is provided by *The Annual Register of Public* [later of *World*] *Events*, now restyled *The Annual Register. A Record of World Events* (London, 1758–1995, thereafter Washington, DC). Much more material is contained in the well-indexed press digest *Keesing's Contemporary Archives* [from 1987 *Keesing's Record of World Events*] (until 1973, Keynsham, Bristol, then London, and now Washington, DC). Also valuable are the (London) International Institute for Strategic Studies' (IISS) annual *Strategic Survey* and its series of *Adelphi Papers* (short monographs on issues and developments of recent or current interest). The *World Today* (London) contains academic articles on recent events that emerge more rapidly than do their counterparts in heavyweight publications like *Foreign Affairs* (New York) and *International Affairs* (London); these in turn are less conventionally historical than *Diplomatic History* (Wilmington, Del.), *Cold War History* (Ilford, 2000–), or other scholarly journals.

Many countries have, like Britain and France, embarked on publishing their post-war documents. But by far the most extensive published collection of primary sources is the Department of State's *Foreign Relations of the United States* (*FRUS*) (Washington, DC). Publication has reached 1968, and is just starting on the 1969–76 Republican period. Even *FRUS* cannot include everything,[5] and the more recent sub-series are noticeably thinner than their predecessors. There is, too, a certain bias towards US State Department documents, which are not necessarily the most useful; of those bearing on the Middle East in 1956 it has been noted that the editor ' "did not have access to the full range of documentation on US intelligence operations and the diplomacy of the Suez crisis". Those interested in the CIA–MI6 plot to overthrow the Syrian government . . . will have to look elsewhere'; they also contain nothing on the US Treasury's crucial dealings with the IMF to pressurise Britain over Suez. Nevertheless, *FRUS* constitutes an enormous quarry, useful for the history of many countries

---

[5] For some documents, we are simply referred to *The Pentagon Papers: the Defense Department history of United States decisionmaking on Vietnam*, Senator Gravel edn, vols. 1–4 (Boston, 1971–2).

besides the USA. The trouble, for most people, is that *FRUS* is too large. This prompted Geoffrey Warner's review of 'twelve massive volumes of American diplomatic documents for 1945' – 'The United States and the Origins of the Cold War', *International Affairs*, xlvi (1970) – and its sequels: 'The Truman Doctrine and the Marshall Plan', ibid, l (1974); 'The Division of Germany 1946–1948', ibid, li (1975); 'The United States and the Rearmament of West Germany, 1950–54', ibid, lxi (1985); 'The United States and Vietnam 1945–1965', two articles in ibid, xlviii (1972) surveying the leaked *United States–Vietnam Relations 1945–67* based, as its common title *The Pentagon Papers* implies, on Defense Department documents, plus 'The United States and Vietnam: Two Episodes', ibid, lxv (1989) reviewing the *FRUS* coverage of the decision to extend aid to France in 1950 and the debate over US military intervention in April 1954; 'The United States and the Suez Crisis', ibid, lxvii (1991); and 'Eisenhower, Dulles and the Unity of Western Europe, 1955–1957', ibid, lxix (1993).

Supplementing *FRUS*, and often extending to a later date, are documents released under the Freedom of Information Act. Keeping track of them is not easy; but the 'National Security Archive' (at George Washington University, Washington DC) operates online subscription access (with a search engine) to over 61,000 declassified documents. Besides its holdings of 'primary documents central to US foreign and military policy since 1945', the Archive has acquired collections from other countries. It makes selections from its holdings available in a wide range of freely accessible 'Electronic Briefing Books', and has encouraged the publication of documentary collections like William Burr (ed.) *The Kissinger Transcripts. The Top Secret Talks with Beijing and Moscow* (New York, 1998). Also devoted to the assembly and diffusion of documents and historical studies based on them, but focussing primarily on those from the communist world, is the 'Cold War International History Project' (Woodrow Wilson Center, Washington DC – www.cwihp.si.edu). All issues of the CWIHP *Bulletin* are eclectic, printing a wide range of documents and articles or notes based on them, but most have had primary themes: thus Issue 4, 'Soviet Nuclear History'; 5, assorted 'Cold War Crises'; 6/7, 'The Cold War in Asia'; 8/9, '. . . the Cold War in the Third World and the Collapse of Detente in the 1970s'; 10, 'Leadership Transition [in the 1950s] in a Fractured Bloc'; 11, 'Cold War Flashpoints'; 12/13, 'The End of the Cold War, 1989'; 14/15, 'New Evidence on North Korea' and 'on the Soviet War in Afghanistan'. In addition the CWIHP has published over 50 downloadable 'Working Papers' by individual scholars, mostly – like nos. 23 (Vojtech Mastny, *The Soviet Non-Invasion of Poland in 1980–1 and the End of the Cold War)* and 26 (Vladimir Petchatnov, *'The Allies are pressing on you to break your will . . .' Foreign Policy Correspondence between Stalin and Molotov and other Politburo Members September 1945–December 1946)* – informative and of a very high standard.

This brings us to secondary sources. 'Of the making of books there is no end': new and valuable ones are continually emerging. Most of those I have used are cited in my footnotes, but both that choice and the suggestions that follow here should be seen only as indicative rather than in any way comprehensive or exclusive.

Writing on the origins of the Cold War has gone through many phases, classified by John L. Gaddis in 'The Emerging Post-Revisionist Synthesis on the Origins of the Cold War', *Diplomatic History*, vii (1983) as 'orthodox', 'revisionist' and 'post-revisionist' (though some scholars have resisted such classification, preferring to class themselves as 'honest eclectics'). Gaddis's own *The United States and the Origins of the Cold War, 1941–1947* (New York, 1972) had been broadly 'orthodox'. Such basically benign interpretations of US foreign policy were challenged, especially in the 1960s and 1970s, by writers (frequently of the New Left) who portrayed it as driven by the search for economic profit and expansion abroad (often under the impact of pressures inherent in the USA's own internal economic structure), and as using the fear of communism to effect repressive changes in US domestic society and politics. 'Revisionists' tended also to doubt whether Soviet communism was expansionist, to portray Stalin's actions as essentially fearful and defensive responses, and so to see the Cold War as, at best, an inevitable process of action and reaction, at worst as primarily the product of US initiatives. Moderate versions of this approach include Walter LaFeber, *America, Russia and the Cold War* (New York, 1967, with many later editions), extreme versions Joyce Kolko and Gabriel Kolko, *The Limits of Power: The World and United States Foreign Policy, 1945–54* (New York, 1972). As the domestic US scene calmed down, so did its polemic. In Gaddis's view, this led to a 'post-revisionist synthesis' that accepted the concept of an American 'empire', albeit (he thought) one that was both 'defensively' motivated and often welcomed abroad; it also conceded that US diplomacy has used economic instruments and pressures, that there had been some exaggeration of external dangers to achieve domestic political goals, and that Stalin had been an 'opportunist' with 'no ideological blue-print for world revolution'. Gaddis continued, however, to reject much 'revisionist' writing, and some critics termed 'post-revisionism' 'orthodoxy plus archives'. There was, then, no monolithic unity. But many of the most commonly used general accounts come from this period, like Daniel Yergin, *Shattered Peace: The Origins of the Cold War and the National Security State* (Boston, Mass., 1977) and Melvyn Leffler, *A Preponderance of Power. National Security, the Truman Administration and the Cold War* (Stanford, CA, 1992). Leffler here inclined towards an action–reaction interpretation of the Cold War, with both Washington and Moscow responding to the dictates of what theorists would call 'the international system', the dysfunctional 'legacy of World War II'. But he noted that 'the documents are still not available to determine the motives and objectives of Soviet foreign policy' or to assess whether 'the preponderance of power engineered' by the Truman administration served to 'promote revolution in the Soviet system or . . . [to] fuel the security dilemma, inducing Soviet counterthrusts and postponing adaptation', or 'both' (pp. 511, 515, 517).

The comment of two Russian historians, Vladislav Zubok and Constantine Pleshakov, on such accounts was that none had yet tried 'to look at the Cold War through the background and actions of both Stalin and his principal lieutenants and successors.' 'Each new revelation from . . . [communist archives] makes it . . . clear that the history of the Cold War must be reexamined'; so, using 'newly declassified materials', they sought to explore 'the psychology, motives and behavior' of major figures *Inside the Kremlin's Cold War. From Stalin to Khrushchev* (Cambridge, Mass., 1996), seeing in Khrushchev 'the last "true believer"' with 'a personal commitment to the revolutionary imperial paradigm'.[6] At much the same time, Vojtech Mastny observed (in *The Cold War and Soviet Insecurity. The Stalin Years* (New York, 1996) p. 193) that

The more that is known about Stalin, the less he looks like the shrewd calculator and hard-boiled realist, for which . . . he was respected even by his adversaries. He was given to illusions and wishful thinking to an extraordinary degree, repeatedly overestimating the extent of discord among his adversaries that might allow him to dictate his terms from a position of relative strength – something that his country never attained . . .

John Lewis Gaddis likewise concluded roundly that 'the "new" history is bringing us back to an old answer: . . . as long as Stalin was running the

---

[6] pp. xii, 274, 290. In their view, though this paradigm still influenced the 1970s Soviet involvements in Africa and Afghanistan, it had waned, leaving the second half of the Cold War increasingly routine, bureaucratic and traditionally power-political.

Soviet Union a cold war was unavoidable' (*We Now Know. Rethinking Cold War History* [up to the Cuban missiles crisis] (Oxford, 1997) p. 292).

Not everybody was happy with Gaddis's judgements,[7] but few would doubt that the next stage in Cold War historiography must be the integration of 'Eastern' and 'Western' materials and perspectives. Also the Cold War's beginning and end make it clear that, while of course we should not disregard geopolitical influences from the 'international system', we should pay more attention than before to ideology and its interrelationship with both perceptions of other countries and their leaders and the nature of the domestic societies people hoped to create;[8] in 'international relations' jargon, we should adopt a more 'constructionist' approach – and should do so with relation to a far broader canvass than that of the superpowers alone. (This broader canvass, and a balance between historiographical schools, is sought by Melvyn Leffler and David S. Painter (ed.), *Origins of the Cold War. An International History. Second Edition* (2005), which reprints a range of essays that first appeared between 1973 and 2001.)

'Revisionism' as such was an American phenomenon, but it is not only in connection with the US that the 'official' and/or traditional views of post-war developments can be challenged. Anne Deighton (ed.) *Britain and the First Cold War* (Basingstoke, 1990) not only presented the claim that British policy in the period was of far more importance than many US historians have recognised, but also demonstrates that in 1946 Britain (and especially the Foreign Office) gave up on cooperation with the USSR in Germany – and that thereafter it was chiefly concerned so to play things that the breakdown should appear to be the USSR's fault and redound to the advantage of the West. Of course the impact of this finding depends largely on what Stalin's German intentions really were.

---

[7] For dissents, see Melvyn Leffler, 'Inside Enemy Archives. The Cold War Reopened', *Foreign Affairs*, lxxv (July–August 1996), and Richard Ned Lebow, 'We Still Don't Know', *Diplomatic History*, 22 (Fall 1998). A more friendly reviewer, Ilya Gaiduk, writes in 'Stalin: Three Approaches to One Phenomenon', *Diplomatic History*, 23 (Winter 1999) p. 125, that though Mastny's and Zubok and Pleshakov's works 'replace a purely speculative approach to events with a more . . . concrete analysis', they demonstrate that 'the "new history" of the Cold War is still far from complete', and will remain so as long as access is denied 'to the materials from the Archive of the Russian President' and many other Russian documentary collections.

[8] Admittedly both 'orthodox' and 'revisionist' writers have stressed the emergence, under the Truman administration, of a remarkably broad coalition supporting Cold War policies, though they have differed in their evaluations of its origins and nature.

The 1945–55 handling of Germany has always been controversial. From a Western perspective, the greater part of the country was 'saved' from communism, rehabilitated, and erected into a successful state well integrated into a new and peaceful Europe. This story is told in, for instance, John Gimbel, *The American Occupation of Germany: Politics and the Military, 1945–49* (Stanford, CA, 1968), Avi Shlaim, *The United States and the Berlin Blockade, 1948–1949: A Study in Crisis Decision-Making* (Berkeley, CA, 1983), Michael J. Hogan, *The Marshall Plan: America, Britain and the Reconstruction of Western Europe, 1947–1952* (Cambridge, 1987), and, of course, in Hans-Peter Schwarz, *Adenauer: a German politician and statesman in a period of war, revolution and reconstruction* (2 vols, Providence, R.I., 1995). Social Democrats at the time saw some, at least, of these policies as needlessly sealing the division of Germany (at least until 1990). Revisionist historians returned to this perspective, and also demonstrated that, despite official rhetoric, the outcome was by no means necessarily unwelcome in London and Paris. In this tradition are Josef Foschepoth (ed.), *Adenauer und die deutsche Frage* (Göttingen, 1988) and Rolf Steininger, *Eine Chance zur Wiedervereinigung? Die Stalin-Note von 10 März 1952* (*Archiv fur Sozialgeschichte*, Beiheft 12, 1985 – abbreviated translation, *The German Question: the Stalin Note of 1952 and the Problem of Reunification* – New York, 1990).

Norman N. Naimark's *The Russians in Germany. A History of the Soviet Zone of Occupation, 1945–1949* (Cambridge, Mass., 1995), written on the basis of much but not all the Russian documentation,[9] is clear (pp. 9, 465–9) that 'from the outset . . . the Soviets thought of themselves as being in a struggle with the Western Allies for the future of Germany'. But there was no set policy; different factions probably looked to the easiest course, the 'Sovietization of the Eastern zone', to the ideal outcome 'the creation of a unified Germany run by the Socialist Unity Party', and to the most risky, 'the establishment of a demilitarized, "neutral" Germany in the center of Europe'. Stalin probably swithered opportunistically between the three, though he seems to have protected a controversial advocate of the first course. In the event this won out, partly as a result of developments on the ground and in international relations, but largely because it arose naturally out of the Soviet *modus operandi*; 'officers bolshevized the zone . . . because that was the only way they knew to organize society.' Whatever Stalin's hopes, both West and East Germany were

---

[9] Naimark had no access to the KGB, 'Presidential' and Defense Ministry archives in Moscow; this led him to omit discussion of the Berlin Blockade.

established in 1949 (as indeed he had forecast to the Yugoslavs in early 1948), and consolidation followed. Ruud van Dijk, *The 1952 Stalin Note Debate: Myth or Missed Opportunity for German Unification* (CWIHP Working Paper no. 14) would seem to have shown that Stalin's apparent offer of a united, neutral and democratic Germany was a propaganda move only. The rapid building of 'socialism' in the DDR was to continue till his death in 1953. But there now appears to be evidence (presented in Alexey Filitov, '"Germany will be a Bourgeois-Democratic Republic": the New Evidence in the Personal File of Georgiy Malenkov', *Cold War History*, vi [2006]) that both Beria and Malenkov saw East Germany as a serious liability that accelerated 'the remilitarization of West Germany, an open preparation for the new war', and therefore advocated Germany's reunification as a 'peaceful bourgeois-democratic state'. This would have faced opposition; but before anything could have come of them, such policies were discredited by the combination of the East German workers' rising and Beria's arrest in a Kremlin power struggle. Instead both Soviet and East German policy hardened. Hope M. Harrison, *Driving the Soviets up the Wall: Soviet–East German Relations, 1953–1961* (Princeton, NJ, 2003) recounts Ulbricht's pressure on Moscow for moves to buttress the DDR both domestically and internationally, which enjoyed partial success with the 1961 construction of the Berlin Wall. Hannes Adomeit, *Imperial Overstretch: Germany in Soviet Policy from Stalin to Gorbachev* (Baden-Baden, 1998) surveys the 'German question' over the whole course of the Cold War, though devoting most attention to the Gorbachev years.

Deighton's *Britain and the First Cold War* did not, of course, confine itself to the German question; it also contains John Kent's suggestion that Britain's efforts to redefine its Mediterranean position and global role 'were a prime cause of growing contention in 1945, and therefore an important element in the origins of the cold war'. Of course this brings us back to the question of Stalin's views on 'spheres of influence', and to his 1945–46 tactics (partially illuminated in his correspondence with Molotov, cited on p. 623). But it can also be argued that the origins of the Cold War should be approached through the investigation of a series of discrete issues. Judgements appropriate to one may not always fit another: there can be little doubt, for instance, that most Turks welcomed US support against Soviet pressure, but Greece, as its civil war shows, was more divided. Many works could be listed in connection with such case studies. Perhaps it is enough to refer the reader, as a starting-point, to R. Jervis and J. Snyder (eds), *Dominoes and Bandwagons: Strategic Beliefs and Great Power Competition in the Eurasian Rimland* (New York, 1991).

The Korean War, however, deserves more attention here in view of its remarkable impact on developments in a wide and disparate range of contexts. Background is provided in David Rees, *A Short History of Modern Korea* (Port Erin, Isle of Man, 1988), Dae-Sook Suh, *Kim Il Sung: the North Korean Leader* (New York, 1988), and Peter Lowe, *The Origins of the Korean War* (1986). The war's course and implications are described, from western sources, in Callum A. Macdonald, *Korea. The War before Vietnam* (Basingstoke, 1986) and Rosemary Foot, 'Making Known the Unknown War: Policy Analysis of the Korean Conflict in the Last Decade', *Diplomatic History*, xv (1991). Khrushchev's memoirs state firmly that Stalin authorised and equipped North Korea's 1950 invasion of the South, though (regrettably, in Khrushchev's view) he would not contribute Soviet troops. So it is surprising that 'revisionist' views became as widely accepted as they did in the 1980s. Soviet documents now fully confirm Khrushchev's account, shed light on the Chinese intervention in late 1950,[10] and on Stalin's refusal, in 1952, to permit an armistice. Their leading exponent is Kathryn Weathersby, whose writings include *'Should we fear this?' Stalin and the Danger of War with America* (CWIHP Working Paper no. 39). She and others have published material in the CWIHP *Bulletin*, 3 (Fall 1993), 5 (Spring 1995), 6/7 (Winter 1995–6), 8–9 (1996–7), 11 (1998), 14/15 (2002–3); James G. Hershberg's introduction to 'Russian Documents on the Korean War, 1950–53' in ibid. 14/15 summarises the current state of play. There is less certainty as to Stalin's motives: did he authorise invasion by his client Kim Il Sung to off-set China's prestige as the new centre of revolution, or because Mao's victory had led him to overestimate the revolutionary momentum and the change in the Asian power balance since Yalta? Similarly, was China's intervention an unwelcome (if necessary) diversion from its designs against Taiwan (for which see He Di, ' "The Last Campaign to Unify China": the CCP's unmaterialised Plan to Liberate Taiwan, 1949–50', *Chinese Historians*, v (1992)), or the product of Mao's romantic and fatalistic belief that he might as well have the inevitable showdown with the USA sooner rather than (a little) later? Chen, Jian, *China's Road to the Korean War: the Making of the Sino-American Confrontation* (New York, 1994), Zhang, Shu Guang, *Mao's Military Romanticism: China and the Korean War, 1950–1953* (Lawrence, Kansas,

---

[10] Sino-Soviet negotiations on Chinese intervention to rescue North Korea after its initial catastrophic defeat, and the question of whether Stalin sought to renege on his initial promise of air cover, provoked sharp exchanges between Russian and Chinese historians, but the issues between them now seem to have been sorted out.

1995), and Douglas J. Macdonald, 'Communist Bloc Expansion in the Early Cold War: Challenging Realism, Refuting Revisionism', *International Security*, xx (Winter 1995) bear on such questions.

One of the side-effects of the Korean War was the extension of US protection to Taiwan, and the USA's precipitation into a policy of massive rearmament and the geographical extension of 'containment' that had been advocated by the famous policy paper NSC-68.[11] J.L. Gaddis's survey of the shifting conceptions of the idea of containment, *Strategies of Containment* (New York, 1982 – 'Revised and updated edition', 2005) proved very influential, though I prefer his less schematic collection of studies, *The Long Peace: Inquiries into the History of the Cold War* (New York, 1987). Both works bear on the comparison between the policies of the Truman and Eisenhower administrations. In the 1980s the latter received enormous historical attention – mostly favourable. Stephen E. Ambrose, *Eisenhower: the President* (1984 – the second part of a two-volume biography) gives a useful overview, while Richard H. Immerman (ed.) *John Foster Dulles and the Diplomacy of the Cold War* (Princeton, NJ, 1990) examines a Secretary of State who (like Eisenhower) was more complex and thoughtful than he seemed. Later, historians also moved over into the 1960s. The Kennedy years we have always known quite well from Arthur M. Schlesinger's brilliant – if selective – *A Thousand Days: John F. Kennedy in the White House* (Boston, Mass., 1965), but the leading account of his foreign policies must now be Lawrence Freedman, *Kennedy's Wars: Berlin, Cuba, Laos, and Vietnam* (New York, 2000). For Johnson, we have Robert Dallek, *Flawed Giant. Lyndon Johnson and His Times 1961–1973* (New York, 1998).

Khrushchev was Eisenhower, Kennedy, and (briefly) Johnson's opposite number. Unlike most other Soviet leaders Khrushchev was deposed, and so had time to dictate, and smuggle to the West, bundles of recollections, which have been edited into three volumes of *Khrushchev Remembers* (Boston, Mass., 1971, 1974, and 1990). Inevitably there are episodes, notably his own involvement in Stalin's purges, that he does not dwell on; he is, too, only reminiscing without access to documents. But several of his claims have been confirmed by the materials that have since become available, and his accounts should be treated with respect. They are supplemented by Michael R. Beschloss, *The Crisis Years: Kennedy and Khrushchev, 1960–1963* (New York, 1991), and, above all, by William

[11] Thomas Etzold and John Lewis Gaddis (eds) *Containment: Documents on American Policy and Strategy, 1945–1950* (New York, 1978) pp. 385 ff.

Taubman's excellent biography, *Khrushchev. The Man and his Era* (New York, 2003).

Khrushchev's years were, 'not by accident', marked by major crises, the most serious (in an East–West context) being those over Berlin and the Cuban missiles. These can be followed from the general histories, Gaddis, *We Now Know*, and Zubok and Pleshakov, *Inside the Kremlin's Cold War*, from Beschloss, *The Crisis Years*, Taubman, *Khrushchev*, and from Freedman, *Kennedy's Wars* (cited on pp. 624, 625, 629). Supplementary sources on Berlin include Harrison, *Driving the Soviets up the Wall* (p. 627), and Vladislav Zubok, *Khrushchev and the Berlin Crisis (1958–62)* (CWIHP Working Paper no. 6). The outpourings on the Cuban missiles crisis are almost infinite: they include the document-based Aleksandr Fursenko, *'One Hell of a Gamble'. Khrushchev, Castro, Kennedy, and the Cuban Missiles Crisis 1958–1964* (1997); Laurence Chang and Peter Kornbluh (eds), *The Cuban Missile Crisis, 1962: A National Security Archive Documents Reader* (New York, 1992); James A. Nathan (ed.) *The Cuban Missile Crisis Revisited* (New York, 1992); and Robert A. Divine, 'The Continuing Cuban Missile Crisis Controversy', *Diplomatic History*, 18 (Fall 1994).

Eisenhower prided himself on crisis management (and was contemptuous of Kennedy's amateurish handling of the Bay of Pigs). But he looked largely to 'covert action' as the best way to effect change without crises. This is surveyed in John Prados, *Presidents' Secret Wars. CIA and Pentagon Covert Operations since World War II* (New York, 1986). Richard J. Aldrich's excellent *The Hidden Hand. Britain, America and Cold War Secret Intelligence* (2001) covers both covert action and the more routine pursuit of secret information, while John Ranelagh's, *The Agency* (1986) describes *The Rise and Decline of the CIA* up to the early 1980s. The story is taken forward, though in less detail, in Bob Woodward, *Veil: The Secret Wars of the CIA, 1981–1987* (New York, 1987) and in Robert M. Gates, *From the Shadows: The Ultimate Insider's Story of Five Presidents and How They Won the Cold War* (New York, 1996), while Steve Coll writes of *Ghost Wars. The Secret History of the CIA, Afghanistan, and bin Laden, from the Soviet Invasion to September 10, 2001* (New York, 2004). Soviet intelligence success was greatest at the start of the Cold War, when Molotov could expect to read the current Western negotiating documents and when Western atomic research was deeply penetrated. Yuri Modin's *My Five Cambridge Friends: Burgess, Maclean, Philby, Blunt and Cairncross – By their KGB Controller* (1994) describes some of the KGB's prize agents. Later the flow of information was largely (though never entirely) the other way. Christopher Andrew and the former KGB double agent Oleg Gordievsky have given us *KGB: The Inside Story of its Foreign Operations from Lenin to Gorbachev* (1991 edn), *Comrade Kryuchkov's Instructions: Top Secret Files on KGB Foreign Operations, 1975–1985* (Stanford, CA, 1993 edn), and *More Instructions from the Centre: Top Secret Files . . . 1975–1985* (1991), Andrew and the former KGB archivist Vasili Mitrokhin, *The Mitrokhin Archive*, i, *The KGB in Europe and the West* (1999), and ii, *The KGB and the World* (2006 edn). ('Operation RYAN' and Andropov's 1982 fears that a Western first strike was imminent are also described in Peter V. Pry, *War Scare. Russia and America on the Nuclear Brink* (Westport, Conn., 1999) Part 1.) The USSR secured much intelligence from its allies, notably the DDR, which found West Germany and thus NATO easy to penetrate; one account is Markus Wolf with Anne McElvoy, *Man without a face. Memoirs of a Spymaster* (1998).

Turning to more conventional armed forces, crude facts and figures as to spending and hardware are produced annually, for all countries, in the International Institute of Strategic Studies' (IISS) *The Military Balance*. But inevitably there are secrets: South Africa revealed, to the general surprise, that it had in the 1980s possessed nuclear weapons. Nor is it easy to translate into a common currency the defence efforts of very dissimilar countries; this occasioned a major and long-running debate on the true scale of Soviet defence spending. Fortunately the Third World War was never fought, so we can neither tell how appropriate preparations for it were, nor assess the voluminous literature compiled by people seeking to 'think [rationally] about the unthinkable' (much of which has been termed by its detractors 'nuclear theology' – very subtle, but unverifiable and quite possibly remote from reality). We cannot always even distinguish between declaratory and actual policy. A guide to the evolution of US nuclear doctrine is provided by A.L. Friedberg, 'The Evolution of US Strategic Doctrine, 1945–80' in S.P. Huntington (ed.) *The Strategic Imperative: New Policies for American Security* (Cambridge, Mass., 1982), by D.A. Rosenberg, 'The Origins of Overkill: Nuclear Weapons and American Security', *International Security*, vii (1963), and by Desmond Ball's instructive account of 'The Development of the SIOP, 1960–1983' (in Ball and Jeffrey Richelson (eds) *Strategic Nuclear Targeting* (Ithaca, NY, 1986), which also has material on Britain and France). The subject is further explored at the NATO and West European level in Beatrice Heuser, *NATO, Britain, France, and the FRG. Nuclear Strategies and Forces for Europe 1949–2000* (Basingstoke, 1997). A.H. Cordesman, *Deterrence in the 1980s: Part 1, American Forces and Extended Deterrence* (IISS

Adelphi Paper no. 175, 1982) provides both useful tables and a good expression of the fears that the US 'strategic' deterrent would soon become vulnerable. These fears came to impinge strongly on the Strategic Arms Limitation Talks and Treaties that lay at the heart of the 1970s US–Soviet detente, and that are well described in R.L. Garthoff, *Detente and Confrontation: American–Soviet Relations from Nixon to Reagan* (Washington, DC, 1985). Commentary on Soviet and East European defence policies is more difficult, since the Soviet Defence Ministry archives are unsurprisingly closed, the former East European members of the Warsaw Pact agreed, on its dissolution, to hold back their documents (though in 2006 Poland began to break ranks), and since much East German material was destroyed shortly before reunification. We do, however, have David Holloway's *The Soviet Union and the Arms Race* (New Haven, Conn., 1984 edn), whose focus is chiefly nuclear; and Beatrice Heuser has written on 'Victory in a Nuclear War? A Comparison of NATO and WTO War Aims and Nuclear Strategies', *Contemporary European History*, vii (1998), and on 'Warsaw Pact Military Doctrines in the 1970s and 1980s: Findings in the East German Archives', *Comparative Strategy*, xii (1993). Vojtech Mastny and Malcolm Byrne have produced the document-rich *A Cardboard Castle? An Inside History of the Warsaw Pact, 1955–1991* (Budapest, 2005), which is to be accompanied by a parallel history of NATO. Much of its material is political, since the Pact became a major vehicle for Soviet consultation with, and management of, Eastern Europe; but the book also includes some accounts of military plans, appreciations (especially of NATO manoeuvres) and exercises. One exercise, mounted in the aftermath of the 1961 building of the Berlin wall and based on an ominously current scenario, shocked its Polish participants by its cavalierly offensive nature; this leads Mastny and Byrne to conclude that earlier plans had been 'defensive', but Petr Lunak's 'Planning for Nuclear War: the Czechoslovak War Plan of 1964', CWIHP *Bulletin* 12/13 (2001) perhaps provides grounds for questioning this. Be that as it may, subsequent plans looked to the very rapid overrunning of much or all of Western Europe, often (not always) accompanied by nuclear first strikes. By the 1980s, however, concern was coming to be felt about NATO rearmament and 'high-tech' superiority; in 1986 Chernobyl came as a reminder of the devastation likely to be caused by nuclear strikes (or even damage to nuclear power stations in 'conventional' war); and from 1987 Gorbachev sought to recast Pact strategy into a defensive mode.

Of wars fought, as opposed to merely projected, one of the longest was the struggle (nearly continuous, save for the second half of the 1950s) by Ho Chi Minh and his successors for the liberation, control and unification of Vietnam. Direct US participation in this war in the 1960s and 1970s proved traumatic, and has generated a mountain of literature. Other aspects are less well covered; developments in the area after the fall of Saigon are often ignored. Stein Tønnesson, 'The Longest Wars: Indochina 1945–75', *Journal of Peace Research*, xxii (1985) has much to say on the origins of the conflict. R.E.M. Irving, *The First Indochina War: French and American Policy 1945–54* (1975) covers events up to the temporary settlement at the 1954 Geneva Conference. US interest in Indo-China is also explored in Geoffrey Warner's 1972 and 1989 *International Affairs* articles (cited on p. 622), and in Michael Schaller, 'Securing the Great Cresent: Occupied Japan and the Origins of Containment in Southeast Asia', *Journal of American History*, lxix (1982) and J.W. Dower, 'The Superdomino in Asia: Japan in and out of the Pentagon Papers', *Pentagon Papers* (Senator Gravel edn, vol. 5). (These last, by illustrating the perceived connection between the rehabilitation of a Western-oriented Japan and the keeping of Indo-China non-communist and open to Japanese trade, go far to undermine the distinction often drawn between an initial 'selective' and a post-NSC 68 universal containment policy.) Lawrence S. Kaplan, Denise Artaud, Mark R. Rubin (eds) *Dien Bien Phu and the Crisis of Franco-American Relations, 1954–5* (Wilmington, Del., 1990) describes the ending of the 'First' Vietnam War and the USA's move to become patron of the Diem regime in South Vietnam. The 'Second' War is covered in (among many other books): Stanley Karnow, *Vietnam: A History* (1994 edn); Jeffrey Race, *War Comes to Long An* (Berkeley, CA, 1972), a study of a single province; Ang, Chen Guan, *The Vietnam War from the Other Side. The Vietnamese Communists' Perspective* (2002) and *Ending the Vietnam War. The Vietnamese Communists' Perspective* (2004). Further insights are given in Odd Arne Westad, Chen Jian, Stein Tønnesson, Nguyen Vu Tong, and James Hershberg, *77 Conversations between Chinese and Foreign Leaders on the Wars in Vietnam* (CWIHP Working Paper 22). Debates and decisions in Washington can be followed in Freedman, *Kennedy's Wars*, Dallek's *Flawed Giant*, Nixon's and Kissinger's *Memoirs* (cited on pp. 629, 635), and in Fredrik Logevall, *Choosing War. The Lost Chance for Peace and the Escalation of War in Vietnam* (Berkeley, CA, 1999). International attention shifted away from Indo-China after Saigon's fall in 1975, but events did not therefore stand still. Some account of subsequent developments is given in: King C. Chen, *China's War with Vietnam, 1979* (Stanford, CA, 1987); Charles McGregor, *The Sino-Vietnamese Relationship and the Soviet Union* (IISS Adelphi

Paper no. 232, 1988); and James W. Morley and Masashi Nishihara (eds) *Vietnam joins the World* (Armonk, NY, 1997).

The Vietnam imbroglio was one of the factors that led Nixon to reverse the hostile US attitude towards China. This attitude had in fact been more sophisticated (at least at the highest level) than it had seemed in the 1950s, as is shown in Gaddis's *The Long Peace* (cited on p. 629). US–Chinese relations are followed in: Robert S. Ross and Jiang Changbin (eds), *Reexamining the Cold War. US–China Diplomacy, 1954–1973* (Cambridge, Mass., 2004), Robert S. Ross, *Negotiating Cooperation. The United States and China, 1969–1989* (Stanford, CA, 1995), and James Mann, *About Face. A History of America's Curious Relationship with China, from Nixon to Clinton* (2000 edn). For briefer reflections, see also Nancy Bernkopf Tucker, 'China and America: 1941–1991)', *Foreign Affairs*, lxx (1991). (Further works on China are cited in another context – below, pp. 636–7.)

Detente with China came to form one half of Nixon's foreign policy, detente with the Soviet Union the other. US–Soviet relations have attracted more attention. An overall view is given in R.W. Stevenson, *The Rise and Fall of Detente: Relaxations of Tension in US–Soviet Relations, 1953–84* (Basingstoke, 1985) while Brian White, *Britain, Detente and Changing East–West Relations* (1992) argues that the UK's contribution has been unduly overlooked. The rise and fall of the 1972 'Moscow' detente is recounted far more fully in Garthoff's massive *Detente and Confrontation* (cited on p. 622); a darker picture is painted by William G. Hyland, *Mortal Rivals: Understanding the Hidden Pattern of Soviet–American Relations* (New York, 1987). One feature of US–Soviet relations in the 1970s was that they were largely conducted through the Soviet ambassador in Washington (used, in Kissinger's time, as a 'back-channel' to bypass obstructive US bureaucracy, and enjoying privileged access to the Secretary of State until the advent of the Reagan administration). Though Anatoly Dobrynin was not in the top Soviet leadership, his position gave him insights and anecdotes that feature in his *In Confidence. Moscow's Ambassador to America's Six Cold War Presidents (1962–1986)* (New York, 1995). Even more durable was the Soviet Foreign minister, who produced discreet but sometimes informative *Memories. From Stalin to Gorbachev* (1989). The souring of relations in the later 1970s is explored in Odd Arne Westad (ed.) *The Fall of Detente: Soviet–American Relations during the Carter Years* (Oslo, 1997) and in CWIHP *Bulletin 8/9, '. . . the Cold War in the Third World and the Collapse of Detente'.* On the US side, assessments of the 'Moscow' detente meld with more general discussion of the Nixon, Kissinger and Carter foreign policies. One source is

R.M. Nixon, *The Memoirs of Richard Nixon* (1978); Nixon's presidency is covered more fully in Stephen E. Ambrose, *Nixon: The Triumph of a Politician, 1962–72* and *Nixon: Ruin and Recovery, 1973–1990* (New York 1989 and 1991). As time proceeds, greater emphasis will probably be laid on Nixon's personal foreign policy imput. At the moment this appears overshadowed by the *tour de force* of Henry Kissinger (National Security Adviser, then Secretary of State, 1969–77). Kissinger has reflected on the way statesmen 'have dealt with the problem of world order' in his important book *Diplomacy* (1994); this extends back through the nineteenth century (and beyond to Richelieu), but more than half is devoted to the period since 1939. Kissinger has also covered his own time in office in three enormous, and beautifully written, volumes, *White House Years* (1979), *Years of Upheaval* (1982), and *Years of Renewal* (1999). Even his enemies would admit that these cite and print copious quantities of documents. More are to be found in William Burr, *The Kissinger Transcripts* (cited on p. 622), which suggest that Kissinger aimed rather at a tacit alliance with China than at the equal relationships with both China and the USSR that his *Memoirs* depict. The best portrait of Kissinger is, perhaps, that of Walter Isaacson, *Kissinger. A Biography* (1992), but to this should now be added Robert Dallek, *Nixon and Kissinger. Partners in Power* (2007). Disputes over the Carter administration are less ferocious. But Carter, Vance, and Zbigniew Brzezinski have all written their memoirs, with Brzezinski's *Power and Principle: Memoirs of the National Security Adviser 1977–1981* (New York, 1983) perhaps the most useful. Elie Kedourie offers a devastating review of all three in 'Disastrous Years when US Foreign Policy Fumbled and Stumbled', *Encounter*, lxiii (November 1984). Detente, however, was not – especially in Europe – a matter for the United States alone. In the 1960s de Gaulle had spoken (possibly with prescience) of a 'Europe from the Atlantic to the Urals' and had launched overtures towards the East, for which see Jean Lacouture, *De Gaulle: The Ruler* (1991). West Germany followed with what developed into Willy Brandt's *Ostpolitik*. This is described in his *People and Politics: The Years 1960–1975* (1978), and, 'primarily from the perspective of . . . East Germany and the Soviet Union', in M.E. Sarotte, *Dealing with the Devil: East Germany, Detente, and Ostpolitik, 1969–1973* (Chapel Hill, NC, 2001); for a broader canvas, see also Timothy Garton Ash, *In Europe's Name: Germany and the divided continent* (1993).

The 1980s were a remarkable decade, beginning with talk of a 'Second Cold War' and concluding with the transformation of Eastern Europe and general declarations of amity. Early accounts include Don Oberdorfer,

The Turn: How the Cold War came to an End. The United States and the Soviet Union 1983–1990 (Baltimore, 1998 edn) and Michael R. Beschloss and Strobe Talbott, *At the Highest Levels. The Inside Story of the End of the Cold War* (1993). Ronald Reagan, *An American Life* (1990) quotes from his diaries and correspondence with Soviet leaders, while the publication of Kiron K. Skinner, Annelise Anderson, Martin Anderson (eds) *Reagan. A Life in Letters* (New York, 2003) further enhanced his reputation. Jack Matlock, who observed the 'turn' first from within the White House and then as US ambassador to Moscow, gives us his impressions (more favourable to the former) of *Reagan and Gorbachev. How the Cold War Ended* (New York, 2004). Reagan was very well served by his second Secretary of State, George P. Schultz, whose *Turmoil and Triumph. My Years as Secretary of State* (New York, 1993) is both solid and lengthy, as are the memoirs of Shultz's successor, James A. Baker, *The Politics of Diplomacy. Revolution, War and Peace, 1989–1992* (New York, 1995). It is clear, though, that the changes stemmed chiefly from developments within the USSR. Gorbachev has naturally attracted a mountain of studies. Perhaps the best are John Miller, *Mikhail Gorbachev and the end of Soviet Power* (1993) and Archie Brown, *The Gorbachev Factor* (Oxford, 1997); the focus of both is on domestic politics, but Brown has one chapter on foreign policy and one on the nationality crises that eventually broke up the Soviet Union. Gorbachev, his associates, and some of his opponents have produced memoirs. I have drawn extensively on Chernyaev's diary-based, *My Six Years with Gorbachev* (cited on p. 620). Mikhail Gorbachev's own *Memoirs* (1996) are less useful for foreign affairs than they might be, partly because they omit a good deal of material included in the German-language version, Michail Gorbatschow, *Erinnerungen* (Berlin, 1995). Further documents are printed in the CWIHP *Bulletin* 12/13 'The End of the Cold War'.

In 'Empire by Invitation? The United States and Western Europe, 1945–1952', *Journal of Peace Research*, xxiii (1986), Geir Lundestad argues that the USA was pressed to provide protection, aid, and leadership. Gaddis makes great play of this 'empire by consent', though he admits that the description better fits Washington's relations with Western Europe and Japan than those with some (not all) of the Third World. It is clear, however, that the Soviet alliance was both more fissiparous and less firmly based than the American. John Gittings produced an excellent *Survey of the Sino-Soviet Dispute: A Commentary and Extracts from Recent Polemics, 1963–1967* (1968), based on exchanges of public criticism. More document-based and political accounts of episodes, appreciations and encounters leading up to the rift are to be found in the CWIHP *Bulletin,* issues 6/7 (1955–6) through 12/13 (2001), in Dong, Wang, *The Quarrelling Brothers. New Chinese Archives and a Reappraisal of the Sino-Soviet Split, 1959–62* (CWIHP Working Paper no. 49), and in Odd Arne Westad (ed.) *Brothers in Arms: the Rise and Fall of the Sino-Soviet Alliance, 1945–1963* (Stanford, CA, 1998). More generally, Chen, Jian, writes on Mao's *China and the Cold War* (Chapel Hill, NC, 2001), Shao, Kuo-Kang, on *Zhou Enlai and the Foundations of Chinese Foreign Policy* (Basingstoke, 1996). Immanuel C.Y. Hsü gives us, in *The Rise of Modern China* (New York, 2000 edn), a substantial textbook history of China in and before the twentieth century, John Gittings a more interpretative account of *The Changing Face of China: from Mao to market* (Oxford, 2006). With Deng Xiaoping as paramount leader, China experienced economic (but not political) transformation; explosive growth followed, with, by the start of the new millenium, major impact on the world economy, and a quiet expansion of the international influence of what was coming to be seen as a potential superpower. Peter Nolan discussed *China's Rise, Russia's Fall: politics, economics, and planning in the transition from Stalinism* (Basingstoke, 1995) – admittedly at something of a temporary Russian low-point – and also wrote on *China and the Global Economy: national champions, industrial policy, and the big business revolution* (Basingstoke, 2001).

None of the USSR's other allies ever aspired to equality with it. Most remained loyal as long as their communist regimes lasted, but Yugoslavia (and later Albania) broke away. On the Tito–Stalin rift, see: Geoffrey Swain, 'The Cominform: Tito's International?' *Historical Journal,* xxxv (1992); S. Clissold (ed.) *Yugoslavia and the Soviet Union 1939–1973* (1975); Ivo Banac, *With Stalin against Tito: Cominformist Splits in Yugoslav Communism* (Ithaca, NY, 1988), which, as its title suggests, seeks to emancipate the story from the Titoist canon. More general surveys of East European developments are to be found in Joseph Rothschild, *Return to Diversity: A Political History of East Central Europe since World War II* (New York, 1991 edn), and in R.J. Crampton, *Eastern Europe in the Twentieth Century – and after* (1997 edn) and *The Balkans since the Second World War* (2002); both Crampton's books have very full bibliographies, that on the Balkans includes non-communist Greece but is particularly full on Yugoslavia and its tragic sequel, 'ex-Yugoslavia'. At various times the USSR sought to organise Eastern Europe into groupings, Cominform (which did not survive de-Stalinisation and Khrushchev's attempted reconciliation with Tito), the Council for Mutual Economic

Assistance (CMEA/Cominform – which never amounted to much), and, from 1955, the military-political Warsaw Pact, which was, by the later 1970s, working well; Mastny and Byrnes, *A Cardboard Castle?* (cited on p. 632) is an important source for both Soviet relations with and Soviet briefing/consultation of its East European allies. But for successive crises, see also: Mark Kramer, 'The Soviet Union and the 1956 Crises in Hungary and Poland: Reassessments and New Findings', *Journal of Contemporary History*, xxxiii (1998), and Csaba Bekes, Malcolm Byrne, Janos Rainer, *The 1956 Hungarian Revolution: a history in documents* (Budapest, 2002); Jaromir Navratil (ed.) *The Prague Spring 1968* (Budapest, 1998), and Zdenek Mlynar's memoir, *Night Frost in Prague: the end of humane Socialism* (1980); Vojtech Mastny, *The Soviet Non-Invasion of Poland in 1980–1 and the End of the Cold War* (CWIHP Working Paper no. 23); for the final communist collapse, Jacques Lesvesque, *The Enigma of 1989: the USSR and the Liberation of Eastern Europe* (Berkeley, CA, 1997), and the copious material and analysis in the CWIHP *Bulletin* 12/13 'The End of the Cold War'; and for German reunification, Kristina Spohr's review article, 'German Unification: Between Official History, Academic Scholarship, and Political Memoirs', *Historical Journal*, xliii (2000), Zelikow and Rice, *Germany Unified and Europe Transformed*, and Teltschik, *329 Tage* (both cited on pp. 618–19).

Western Europe is covered in John W. Young, *Cold War Europe 1945–89: A Political History* (1991) and Derek W. Urwin, *Western Europe since 1945* (1989 edn). Post-war developments are discussed in Beatrice Heuser and Robert O'Neill (eds) *Securing Peace in Europe, 1945–62. Thoughts for the Post-Cold War Era* (Basingstoke, 1992). Alfred Grosser, *The Western Alliance: European–American Relations since 1945* (1980) offers a broader overview of the Atlantic relationship. This is further discussed, as it affected Britain, in W. Roger Louis and Hedley Bull (eds) *The 'Special Relationship': Anglo-American Relations since 1945* (Oxford, 1986) and in C.J. Bartlett, *'The Special Relationship'. A Political History of Anglo-American Relations since 1945* (Harlow, 1992). Material on the more prickly relationship with France will be found in Jean Lacouture, *De Gaulle: The Ruler* (1991), in Richard Ullman, 'The Covert French Connection', *Foreign Policy*, lxxv (1989), and – indirectly – in Pierre Hassner, 'Perceptions of the Soviet Threat in the 1950s and the 1980s: the Case of France', in C.-C. Schweitzer (ed.), *The Changing Analysis of the Soviet Threat* (1990). A general view of Western European integration is given by D.W. Urwin, *The Community of Europe: A History of European Integration since 1945* (1991). There is a marked difference between the archive-based studies now appearing on the post-war decade and accounts of more recent developments. The densest study is A.S. Milward, *The Reconstruction of Western Europe, 1945–51* (1984); non-specialists may prefer John W. Young, *Britain, France and the Unity of Western Europe 1945–51* (Leicester, 1984). The actual foundation and early development of the EEC was well described, albeit from the public record, by F. Roy Willis, *France, Germany and the New Europe: 1945–1967* (Stanford, CA, 1968). Further insights are provided by Jean Monnet's *Memoirs* (1978), and by biographies of Adenauer and de Gaulle (cited on pp. 626 and 635). The subsequent Franco-German entente is considered in Haig Simonian, *The Privileged Partnership: Franco-German Relations in the European Community, 1969–1984* (Oxford, 1985). A picture of the EC's operation towards the end of that period is given by a former Commissioner in Christopher Tugendhat, *Making Sense of Europe* (Harmondsworth, 1986). The step change that began in the mid-1980s is described in Charles Grant, *Delors. Inside the House that Jacques Built* (Oxford, 1998); further insights on the start of the process can be found in Arthur Cockfield, *The European Union. Creating the Single Market* (Chichester, 1994); an updated summary of the EU's institutional evolution is given in John Pinder, *The Building of the European Union* (Oxford, 1998 edn), while the former Commissioner Chris Patten talks engagingly of the EU's recent East European expansion and of its essays in Mediterranean and foreign policy in *Not Quite the Diplomat. Home Truths about World Affairs* (2006 edn). Further insights into the EU's high-level decision-making can be gained from memoirs by and studies of national leaders, for instance Margaret Thatcher's *The Downing Street Years* (1993).

Finally, maps are almost indispensable: 'where you stand' often, though not always, 'depends on where you sit'. A good atlas should suffice, since topography does not change rapidly. Economic and population statistics do, and are in any case less trustworthy; but those presented in, for instance, the annual World Bank *Atlas* are both interesting and useful, provided they are taken with a pinch of salt.

Index